A HISTORY SHARED AND DIVIDED

A History Shared and Divided
East and West Germany since the 1970s

Edited by
Frank Bösch

Translated by Jennifer Walcoff Neuheiser

Published in 2018 by

Berghahn Books

www.berghahnbooks.com

English-language edition
© 2018, 2025 Berghahn Books
First paperback edition published in 2025

German-language edition
© 2015 Vandenhoeck & Ruprecht GmbH & Co. KG

Originally published by Vandenhoeck & Ruprecht GmbH & Co. KG as
Geteilte Geschichte: Ost- und Westdeutschland 1970–2000

The translation of this work was funded by Geisteswissenschaften International – Translation Funding for Humanities and Social Sciences from Germany, a joint initiative of the Fritz Thyssen Foundation, the German Federal Foreign Office, the collecting society VG WORT, and the Börsenverein des Deutschen Buchandels (German Publishers & Booksellers Association).

All rights reserved. Except for the quotation of short passages for the purposes of criticism and review, no part of this book may be reproduced in any form or by any means, electronic or mechanical, including photocopying, recording, or any information storage and retrieval system now known or to be invented, without written permission of the publisher.

Library of Congress Cataloging-in-Publication Data

A C.I.P. cataloging record is available from the Library of Congress

British Library Cataloguing in Publication Data

A catalogue record for this book is available from the British Library

ISBN 978-1-78533-925-7 hardback
ISBN 978-1-83695-056-1 paperback
ISBN 978-1-83695-199-5 epub
ISBN 978-1-78533-926-4 web pdf

https://doi.org/10.3167/9781785339257

CONTENTS

List of Illustrations	vii
Acknowledgments	ix
List of Abbreviations	x
Introduction. Divided and Connected: Perspectives on German History since the 1970s Frank Bösch	1
Chapter 1. Political Transformations in East and West Frank Bösch and Jens Gieseke	45
Chapter 2. Economic Crises, Structural Change, and International Entanglements Ralf Ahrens and André Steiner	102
Chapter 3. Entangled Ecologies: Outlines of a Green History of Two or More Germanys Frank Uekötter	147
Chapter 4. Social Security, Social Inequality, and the Welfare State in East and West Germany Winfried Süß	191
Chapter 5. Rationalization, Automation, and Digitalization: Transformations in Work Rüdiger Hachtmann	239
Chapter 6. The Individualization of Everyday Life: Consumption, Domestic Culture, and Family Structures Christopher Neumaier and Andreas Ludwig	293
Chapter 7. Paths to Digital Modernity: Computerization as Social Change Jürgen Danyel and Annette Schuhmann	348

Chapter 8. Educational Rivalries: The Transition from a
  German-German Contest to an International Competition   394
    Emmanuel Droit and Wilfried Rudloff

Chapter 9. Mobility and Migration in Divided Germany   447
    Maren Möhring

Chapter 10. Sports and Society in the Rivalry between
  East and West   501
    Jutta Braun

Chapter 11. Bridge over Troubled Water? Mass Media in
  Divided Germany   551
    Frank Bösch and Christoph Classen

Index   603

ILLUSTRATIONS

Figures

1.1. "In East and West: Swords into Ploughshares": Two Civil Rights Activists from the GDR (Peter Rösch and Roland Jahn), Who Had to Leave Their State, Protest against Nuclear Weapons of the NATO in Mutlangen, West Germany, in 1983 (source: Ullstein-Bilder)   67

4.1. Information Brochure for Citizens of the GDR about the Establishing of the Social Union, Presented during a Meeting of the Last GDR Parliament (Volkskammer), June 1990 (source: Ulstern Bild - AIDN - Bildarchiv)   213

6.1. *Left*, PUR-Chair, VEB Petrolchemisches Kombinat Schwedt, 1974; *Right*, Panton-Chair, Design by Verner Panton, Vitra AG, 1967 (photos: Südhoff, Dokumentationszentrum Alltagskultur der DDR; Werkbundarchiv/Museum der Dinge)   304

6.2. Overall Birth Rates in East and West Germany, 1960–2013 (source: Bundesinstitut für Bevölkerungsforschung [Federal Institution for Demographic Research])   315

9.1. Still from *Duvarlar-Mauern-Walls* (2000, dir. Can Candan)   475

11.1. Technical Coverage of Radio DDR I in West Germany, Medium Wave, Daytime, 1975 (BArch DM 3/14391)   567

Tables

5.1. Employment and Unemployment in Germany from 1970 to 2010   245

5.2. Labor Productivity in the Federal Republic of Germany per Employed Person and Hour of Work from 1970 to 2010   248

5.3a. Employment in the Federal Republic of Germany according to Economic Sectors from 1970 to 2010 — 266

5.3b. Gross Value Added in the Federal Republic of Germany according to Economic Sectors from 1970 to 2010 — 266

5.4. Employees in the GDR according to Economic Sectors from 1950 to 1989 — 267

5.5. Temporary Workers from 1970 to 2013 — 276

6.1. Household Possessions and Planned Acquisitions in the GDR, 1988 — 308

ACKNOWLEDGMENTS

Can and should we write a joint history of East and West Germany? The Center for Contemporary History in Potsdam (ZZF) has had a long tradition of researching and analyzing the history of Germany on both sides of the Berlin Wall, not only through a comparative lens, but also with an eye to entanglements. Nevertheless, a systematic overview for the period after 1970 was still lacking for a long time. Then, beginning in 2011, a group of Potsdam-based scholars of contemporary history began to develop a concept that would allow for an analysis of the fundamental transformations that had taken place since the 1970s and after the fall of the Berlin Wall in both East and West Germany. This process sparked an intense, productive debate between specialists of West German and East German history, and I am particularly grateful to all those who were involved. The collective book project sponsored by the ZZF that resulted from these discussions also benefited from the contributions of a number of external authors who were willing to join in our efforts to offer a German-German perspective. Although the intention was never to create a fully comprehensive handbook, this book nonetheless covers several important fields of inquiry in a systematic way. We are grateful to all those who participated in the discussion of those articles for their comments and suggestions. Our thanks also go out to Judith Koettniz, Jakob Mühle, Jakob Saß, and Beate Schiller for adapting and proofreading the endnotes and bibliographies in the English edition.

This translation has been made possible through the generous support of the Geisteswissenschaften International translation prize awarded by the Börsenverein des Deutschen Buchhandels (German Booksellers' Association). We would like to sincerely thank Jennifer Neuheiser for undertaking this translation, which was surely not an easy task. And, finally, we would like to thank Marion Berghahn and Chris Chappell at Berghahn Books, who quickly jumped on board to help make this translated edition happen.

Frank Bösch, Potsdam

ABBREVIATIONS

AfD	Alternative for Germany
ARD	Consortium of Public Broadcasters in Germany – First German Television Network
BGB	(West) German Civil Code
BStU	Stasi Records Agency
BKA	Federal Criminal Police Office
CAD	computer aided design
CAM	computer aided manufacturing
CDU	Christian Democratic Union of Germany
CIM	computer integrated manufacturing
COMECON	Council for Mutual Economic Assistance
CNC	computerized numerical control
CSSR	Czechoslovak Socialist Republic
CSU	Christian Social Union
DBD	Democratic Farmers' Party of Germany
DE-NIC	German Network Information Center, manager of the ".de" domain
DFB	German Soccer Federation
DGB	German Trade Union Federation
Die Linke	Left Party
DKP	German Communist Party
DOSB	German Olympic Sports Confederation
DSB	German Sports Federation
DTSB	East German National Olympic Committee
DVU	German People's Union
EC	European Community

ECSC	European Coal and Steel Community
EEC	European Economic Community
EFTA	European Free Trade Association
EOS	Erweiterte Oberschule (extended secondary school)
EPU	European Payments Union
FDGB	Free German Trade Union Federation
FDJ	Free German Youth
FDP	Free Democratic Party
FIFA	International Federation of Football
FRG	Federal Republic of Germany
GATT	General Agreement on Tariffs and Trades
GDP	Gross Domestic Product
GDR	German Democratic Republic
ICT	Digital Information and Computer Technology
IOC	International Olympic Committee
ISO	International Organization for Standardization
IT	information technology
JuLi	FDP's youth organization, Young Liberals
KOFAZ	Committee for Peace, Disarmament and Cooperation
LDPD	Liberal Democratic Party of Germany
MfS	Ministry for State Security / Stasi
MDR	Central German Broadcasting
NATO	North Atlantic Treaty Organization
NDPD	National-Democratic Party of Germany
OECD	Organization for Economic Cooperation and Development
OEEC	Organization for European Economic Cooperation
OSCE	Organization for Security and Cooperation in Europe
PDS	Party of Democratic Socialism
POS	Polytechnische Oberschule (polytechnical high school)
RAF	Red Army Faction
SEA	Single European Act
SBZ	Soviet Occupation Zone
SED	Socialist Unity Party of Germany
SGB	German Social Code

SPD	Social Democratic Party of Germany
Stasi	Ministry for State Security / State Security Service
STR	Scientific-Technical Revolution
VEB	Publicly Owned Operation
WDR	West German Broadcasting
UEFA	Union of European Football Associations
USSR	Union of Soviet Socialist Republics; Soviet Union
ZAIG	Central Evaluation and Information Group
ZDF	Second German Television

INTRODUCTION

Divided and Connected
Perspectives on German History since the 1970s

Frank Bösch

Over the last decade, the field of contemporary German history has changed considerably. It has been enriched by a broader thematic and methodological scope, as well as transnational perspectives that have propelled scholarship in new directions. Yet despite these shifts, historians still tend to approach the history of East and West Germany separately. Rather than peering over the Wall, scholars have contextualized developments in the Federal Republic of Germany (FRG) primarily with an eye toward Western industrialized nations or to the global South. For many historians of West Germany, the German Democratic Republic (GDR) was seen as a truly separate country whose history was the purview of research institutes in East Germany or Berlin. Even in the multifaceted theoretical debates surrounding a transnational, "shared," or "entangled" history, the idea of a German-German history was conspicuously absent.[1] Perhaps because the focus of these endeavors was to trace the "trans-state" history of a later reunited nation, a national narrative seemed to be out of place. Similarly, general overviews of contemporary German history have continued to approach the FRG or the GDR separately, even when they extend beyond reunification.[2] German-German perspectives have mostly been reserved for the bilateral relations and encounters between the two German states, ranging from Willy Brandt's *Ostpolitik* to Biermann's expatriation and Kohl's plans for reunification.[3]

By consciously adopting a German-German perspective, this book suggests a different approach to the history of contemporary Germany. Departing from the already well-researched diplomatic level, it offers a comparative look at changing social structures in East and West Germany, such as work, the economy, welfare, education, lifestyle, and politics, as well as the environment, sports, and media. It not only takes into account the separate histories or differences between the states, but also openly seeks to detect similarities and interactions between East and West. Embracing the double-edged meaning of a *geteilte Geschichte*, this book explores the "shared history" of Germany as well as its "divided" past, purposefully leaving open the question as to whether we can speak of an "entangled history."

At its core, this book analyzes how East and West Germany have changed since the 1970s. Up to now, the often rapid transformations that occurred in the last third of the twentieth century have been dealt with separately, either from the perspective of the specific problems associated with socialism or that of the structural shifts within Western industrialized societies brought about by globalization "after the boom."[4] With a comparative look on both sides of the Wall, this collection questions whether there was a prevalence of commonalities or whether system-based differences dominated the trajectories of each state.[5] Quite often, the significant changes that took place during these decades extended well beyond German borders, as with the economic crises of the 1970s, the general political paradigm shift, environmental and energy problems, consumption, sports, or the new role of electronic media and computers. Moreover, in terms of the GDR in particular, this book takes a critical look at whether the downfall of socialism can be explained through the prism of the challenges associated with the West. Flipping this perspective around, it also questions to what extent the FRG was influenced by the system rivalry with the GDR.

Additionally, the scope of this book consciously stretches beyond 1990 into the post-reunification era. On the one hand, it examines the extent to which East Germany adapted to the West while noting which differences remained in place. On the other hand, it discusses the changes in the West brought about through reunification. It also explores the idea that East Germany functioned as a laboratory for future developments in Germany as a whole, which has been put forth as a theory within the context of the "neoliberal reforms" in Eastern Europe.[6] Even in terms of the 1990s, a long-term perspective reveals that there was still very much a *geteilte Geschichte*, marked by the countless differences that persisted despite reunification and rapprochement between East and West.

In order to trace these parallel, interwoven, or separate developments, this book often adopts a comparative perspective, but it by no means intends to erase the differences between a market-oriented democracy and a socialist dictatorship with a planned economy.[7] It cannot be forgotten that these different forms of state pervaded all aspects of life. After all, systems of rule and power do not simply disappear when looking at social changes; to the contrary, it becomes all the more clear just how deeply such mechanisms were embedded within society.

A famous press photo of Renate Stecher (GDR) and Heide Rosendahl (FRG) crossing the relay finish line at the Munich Olympic Games in 1972 illustrates this idea of a *geteilte Geschichte* in many ways.[8] It represents the competition between the two systems as well as the social differences between East and West. Not only do the separate national emblems on the uniforms symbolize the race between the two countries, but also they allude to the different sport training systems and the doping accusations directed at the top GDR athletes.[9] Likewise, the photograph also visualizes overarching international and German-German developments, such as the major role of sports on the international stage in the struggle for prestige and recognition, which was undoubtedly a strong motive behind the FRG's concerted efforts to become the host country for the Olympic Games in 1972 and the World Soccer Championships in 1974.[10] Sports in the GDR also functioned as a means of communication across the Wall, for example in the guise of (supervised) teams traveling abroad or media reporting on events. The victory of the FRG's relay team in a neck-and-neck race with the GDR similarly underscores West Germany's intensive support of sports during this time as it sought to keep up with the world's leading athletic nations. Doping had also become widespread in the FRG after 1970, which made the Olympic Games in Munich a turning point for both German teams.[11] Additionally, as Stecher and Rosendahl crossed the finish line, they were both wearing shoes manufactured by Adidas, a West German company that dominated the global market in the 1970s; their similar hairstyles also reflected lifestyle trends that crossed the border between East and West. Behind the scenes at the time, their careers were also quite telling as both women attended sports colleges and pursued careers in sports after graduation. Indirectly, moreover, this snapshot finish underscores the great amount of public accolade enjoyed by high-performing female athletes on both sides of the Wall. When the photo later reappeared within the context of reunification, however, it spoke to the problems associated with bringing two national sports systems together, such as in the debates over the dismantling of East German training centers, doping, and broken careers. Ultimately, the East German Renate Stecher lost her job after reunification while the West German Heide Rosendahl enjoyed a successful career in sports education until her retirement.

Scholarship on Contemporary History and the Two German States

Shortly after reunification, a few scholars began calling for an integrated German-German history. Christoph Kleßmann in particular pleaded for an "asymmetrically intertwined parallel history" (*asymmetrisch verflochtene Parallelgeschichte*) that explored the tensions between division and entanglement, taking into account that the FRG was a stronger point of reference for the GDR than the GDR was for the FRG. As Kleßmann put it, "The Federal Republic could have easily existed without the GDR."[12] He also suggested that it was worth considering whether the development of the Federal Republic was also shaped by the existence of the GDR, especially given the major influence of anti-communism on many aspects of society.[13] Even West German consumption, sports, or gender roles took on a different political significance in a divided Germany. Kleßmann also proposed six phases and points of reference for such a discussion, including "the beginning of the block building," "the internal dynamics of both states," and "the cross-system problems faced by advanced industrial societies" since the 1970s.[14] Similarly, Konrad Jarausch has advocated a "plural sequential perspective."[15] Both Jarausch and Kleßmann cite the 1970s as a turning point. Others, including Thomas Lindenberger, have proposed that border regions should be approached as spaces created by political rule that foster a particular way of dealing with "others," bearing in mind that the process of demarcating boundaries also generates links.[16]

These approaches ensured much debate among German historians for a long time. In recent years, however, proponents of different schools of thought and methodologies have come to embrace the possibilities and the necessity of a cross-border perspective.[17] For the most part, these arguments differ from one another primarily in terms of how far they believe a comparative, or even an entangled, perspective can go without erasing the differences between the systems. Despite his general approval for this type of scholarship, Horst Möller has also cautioned that "a careful selection of those topics that can actually be compared for particular phases and that were at least relatively independent of the system is necessary."[18]

German-German perspectives have also become increasingly viable in recent years due to the changing regional, diachronic, and thematic trends within scholarship. Whereas Kleßmann and Jarausch were mostly interested in specifically German developments in the decades after World War II, it has now become more common to situate Germany within a European perspective—and less as the legacy of National Socialism than as the dawn of a unified Germany and Europe. In particular, the 1970s and 1980s now tend to be painted as the backdrop for present-day problems rather than a postwar history.[19] Instead of working from the rationale behind institutions emerging in the postwar period, these narratives look to their deterioration and renewal by following the trail from their formation to their later reproduction.[20] They are paving the way for a more nuanced joint German perspective that can shed more light on the historical context of cross-border, or specific West and East German, problems. After all, for at least half of the last fifty years of history, Germany has been a reunified nation. At the same time, there has been a move to sketch out continuities between the *Kaiserreich* (imperial era) and the 1970s for a variety of topics, bundled under the umbrella of modernity. In order to avoid constructing purely teleological narratives of the paths to liberalization or the postmodernity of the 1970s, however, it is also essential to look across the Wall to the GDR.

The last decade has seen an influx of new topics in historical scholarship that foster and even necessitate cross-border perspectives, such as energy and environmental history, the history of everyday life, the history of consumption, sports history, the history of medicine, or media history. Not least, moreover, global history has changed the way we look at Europe and Germany. From a German angle, the Federal Republic and the GDR may often have seemed to be two completely different worlds. But, from a European or even a global perspective, the ties between the two Germanys become all the more apparent. Correspondingly, some cultural history studies have recently been published in the United States that portray both East and West Germany as postfascist societies.[21]

In sum, although a joint German perspective has been relatively seldom employed, this book nonetheless draws upon an array of existing scholarship, not all of which can be explicitly mentioned here. One of the most important works on German-Germany history up to 1970 remains Christoph Kleßmann's two-volume study that came out prior to the fall of the Berlin Wall.[22] Since its publication, only a few general overviews have approached East and West Germany together. When such studies do include both states, the sections on the GDR more often than not tend to serve as a foil for the story of the FRG's success.[23] Furthermore, the joint chapters on both Germanys mostly concentrate on the political relationships within the framework of *Ostpolitik* and reunification.[24] Using such a comparative perspective, Mary Fulbrook, for example, describes both states as competing experiments and urges that the achievements of the GDR in social politics, women's rights, and family policies should be recognized.[25] A brief overview of German-German cultural history from the pen of Carsten Kretschmann also highlights Western transfers and niches within the GDR. He also highlights the shared cultural heritage of both countries that dated back to the eighteenth century and was successfully unified at an institutional level in 1990.[26]

Likewise, there are a number of histories of the GDR that range in scope from short introductions or accounts of everyday life to comprehensive handbooks on the SED (Sozialistische Einheitspartei Deutschlands / Socialist Unity Party of Germany).[27] In particular, they deal extensively with German-German relations during the 1970s and 1980s, and their chapters on consumption, media, or opposition to the regime refer to influences coming from the West. However, scholars of the GDR still disagree over the consequences of the rapprochement process between East and West Germany in the 1970s/80s. Some historians argue that the improved relations between the two countries stabilized and prolonged the SED regime, whose economy would have collapsed without support from the West, thereby paving the way for protests at an earlier stage. A more recent work has surmised that the Federal Republic continued to recognize the GDR, without paying attention to whether the East actually made the concessions that had been demanded of it.[28] Others have assessed the rapprochement between the two Germanys as a necessary precondition for reunification because it made the Wall more permeable. In particular, travel across the border and television from the West raised the expectations of GDR residents. Yet, these arguments are not mutually exclusive: entanglements such as those resulting from the so-called billion-mark loans from the FRG in 1983 simultaneously prolonged and weakened the rule of the SED.[29]

A more integrated German-German perspective has been put forth in essayist style by Peter Bender, who once worked in East Berlin as a WDR (Westdeutscher Rundfunk / West German Broadcasting) correspondent. He focuses primarily on the major political developments—that is, division, rapprochement, and reunification.[30] With an eye toward social history, Konrad Jarausch has interpreted German-German history as a process of recivilization and renormalization following the downfall of National Socialism, which was pushed forward in the West after 1945 and 1968, but not until 1989 in the East via civil rights advocates and their protests.[31] Additionally, a number of edited volumes on specific events or topics have been published that speak to interwoven phenomena beyond the realm of politics. Above all, the collection of case studies edited by Christoph Kleßmann under the banner of a "double postwar history of Germany" has opened the doors for a comparative approach.[32] A volume published by the Institut für Zeitgeschichte (Institute for Contemporary History) has also made reference to a "doubled Germany" and explored moments of German-German interaction as a springboard for examining the continuance of a culture of competition as well as new overarching problems within a longer time frame.[33] With a nod to Andreas Wirsching, this book suggests that "the opposition between the systems of democracy and dictatorship should not be overemphasized."[34] Contributions in more recent essay collections also deal with topics such as collective memory in both Germanys or microhistories of media and systems of infrastructure that crossed the border, such as transit routes.[35] Specialized studies have also analyzed economic relations and sports in the two states.[36]

Numerous social science publications have discussed the process of transformation that began in 1990. For the most part, these studies concentrate on the new federal states—that is, the old GDR—and the transfer of elites and institutions from West to East.[37] Additionally, they make use of statistics and polls to assess the persistence of a difference between East and West Germany that was still quite discernible even two decades after unification, especially in terms of wealth and political culture as well as structures of civil society and variances in the use of media.[38] In many of these books, East Germany is depicted as the "other" in the form of a "transitional society."[39]

As of late, calls to move beyond approaching the transformations in East Germany as a process of "delayed modernization" and adaptation to the West, for example, have grown louder. Scholars have pointed out that West Germany also changed during these decades, especially within the framework of unification and globalization. Heinrich Best and Everhard Holtmann, for instance, have pointed out a "doubled transformation in which problems related to unification and the challenges of the global economic and finance crises overlapped."[40] Likewise, the political scientist Timm Beichelt has urged that supposedly specific Central European problems should be approached from a pan-European perspective with respect to global challenges, suggesting that the term transformation be applied to all of Europe.[41]

On the other hand, it can be argued that some modern-day changes appeared earlier in the former East German states than in the old FRG, especially in areas such as childcare, family structure, secondary schooling, or shifts in mentalities and values. In some fields, reforms were initiated in eastern Germany in the 1990s that were just surfacing in the West, which meant that the East seemed to function as a laboratory for neoliberal experimentation, above all in terms of privatization and deregulation. Philipp Ther has argued, for instance, that calls for reforms coming out of East Germany also migrated rhetorically to the West in the second half of the 1990s, making the case for what he terms neoliberal "co-transformations."[42] The ambivalent nature of these changes is often coupled with the notion of freedom, as in the title of Padraic Kenney's book on the transformation of Eastern Europe, *The Burdens of Freedom*.[43] Andreas Wirsching has also alluded to the success as well as the downsides of liberalization by referring to "the price of freedom."[44] Yet the processes outlined here cannot be simply explained by looking at the constellations in East Germany after 1990; rather, they must be embedded within their proper historical context going back for decades on both sides of the Wall.

The increasing number of publications offering European and global overviews also deal with Eastern and Western Europe jointly, albeit in a more generalized way. They usually contrast the booming postwar decades in the West with the building of socialism into the 1970s, before comparing the period "after the boom" with the downfall of socialism in the two decades that followed.[45] In doing so, they have demarcated similar phases on both sides of the Wall, but they continue to build their arguments around the respective state systems.[46] Alongside these separate "rise and fall" narratives, some studies drawing on social science approaches have stepped toward a social history of Europe. Brief accounts such as Jeremy Black's *Europe since the 1970s* have drawn a line between East and West for some topics, such as economics, but deal with other aspects of society—including the environment, health, and education—from an overarching standpoint.[47] Given that these studies still work from a Western perspective, they have focused on overarching transformation processes that can be verified statistically, pointing—as Göran Therborn does—to a certain similarity in the erosion of a future-oriented sense of modernity at the beginning of the 1970s.[48] Hartmut Kaelble, in contrast, has highlighted the increasing divergence of the two states in the 1980s, citing the deteriorating economy in the East compared to the expansion of the welfare state and education in the West.[49] He also maintains that globalization drove Eastern and Western Europe further apart. Although some of their approaches and findings are questionable, these European overviews nonetheless offer a broader perspective that moves beyond German borders.

Studies on the cultural history of the Cold War, on the other hand, have analyzed direct links between Eastern and Western Europe. They have devoted a great deal of attention to the exchange of elites and elements of civil society, such as academics, dissidents, and youth groups. Likewise, media relations have been a major focus, especially in terms of the exchange of television programs and images.[50] In doing so, the gaze of scholarship has shifted to countries such as Hungary, Finland, or France because they were particularly open to contacts from the other side of the Iron Curtain. These examples underscore the extent to which some countries acted independently of the bloc during the Cold War. Undoubtedly, the interactions between East and West Germany must also be situated within the context of this broader rapprochement process.

The Promises and Pitfalls of a German-German History

The difficulty of grappling with two different political systems is not the only reason why existing scholarship has tended to separate the FRG and the GDR. Another important factor has been that Western historical narratives are generally linked tightly to the self-descriptions of contemporaries and corresponding observation techniques.[51] Public opinion polls, the media, and social science studies have provided the foundation for analyzing Western societies, but such avenues were virtually nonexistent in East Germany. We do not have any kind of media-based narrative of crisis for the GDR, nor do we have a comparable comprehensive and influential set of opinion polls that indicate a "value shift" or a fundamental ideological shift.[52] Correspondingly, sociological concepts such as "postmaterialism," "postmodernity," or "individualization" that emerged out of such observations have not been mapped onto the GDR. Thus, on many levels, a German-German perspective can foster a critical discussion of these concepts and ascriptions. Yet it also remains questionable whether it makes sense to use these kinds of concepts in the absence of corresponding self-descriptions and whether these notions are intimately linked to democracy, making them virtually incompatible with socialism and the GDR.

Additionally, the difference in access to archival material has contributed to a historiographic division between East and West Germany. Given that the majority of sources pertaining to the GDR are governmental records, many of which have been accessible for the period up to 1989 for a while now, the perceptions and practices of surveillance as well as the perspective of the SED have played a key role in narratives of East German history. Similar materials are not as prevalent for West Germany, especially since the files from the 1980s are just now becoming accessible. In the meantime, studies that work with alternative sources (ego-documents, oral history, etc.), and especially those that document everyday life, have demonstrated their potential for making comparisons between East and West easier while also allowing for overarching assessments that bridge across the Wall.

The rivalry between the two systems as well as détente and the acceptance of a "bipolar world" did in fact prompt a few comparative social science studies as early as the 1970s/80s.[53] Along the lines of a convergence theory, contemporaries detected a stronger rapprochement between the two systems in the postindustrial age. Alternatively, adopting a magnet theory approach, they observed how East Germany adjusted to follow the lead of the economically stronger West, at least in the early postwar years. They point out that this competition led to a permanent surveillance of the "other "on both sides of the Wall that extended to many different aspects of society. Yet the primary task of future scholarship should not be to determine whether these contemporary studies, which tended to overestimate the GDR, were accurate; rather, the more interesting question is what kind of impact these studies had. Did they lead to the approval or rejection of reforms, or did they foster appropriation in a modified way using different terminology?

A German-German history must become more than just a narrative that places existing interpretations of the Federal Republic and the GDR next to each other. Rather, it needs to take a lead from transnational history and examine reactions to general problems, cross-border relationships, and reciprocal perceptions. These three levels of interaction were often, but not always, mutually dependent. The cognizance of the other Germany at times culminated in action, at times in ignorance. Cross-border challenges, such as the oil crises in the 1970s, may have led to different reactions, but they nonetheless demonstrated the interdependence of the two states.

Of course, there are a number of potential pitfalls inherent in such a German-German perspective. The greatest danger surely lies in the risk of portraying East Germany as the "five new federal states" even prior to 1989, thereby neglecting the dictatorial power of the SED or fundamental differences between East and West. Careful reflections must also be made when choosing specific topics in order to determine whether they come from a more Western standpoint (such as environmental protection or migration) or rather an Eastern one (social equality).

Moreover, it must be taken into account that the differences between the German states were understandably large in some areas. This applies in particular to political history in a narrow sense, which can hardly be approached jointly. To an extent, however, such a classic political history has been pushed to the sidelines by a history of politics that relies more heavily on social perceptions and actions. Likewise, the economic differences between a statist planned economy and a more dynamic market economy were no less significant. That said, however, the economic exchanges between East and West grew over time, and a concealed structural change began to peek through in the GDR.[54] At the same, the limited ability of the social market economy to adapt flexibly to new problems also became clear as time went on. Furthermore, there were also quite apparent differences in terms of migration, which was virtually nonexistent in the GDR. But, as the contributions to this volume underscore, there were structural commonalities even in these areas, making it worthwhile to adopt a cross-border perspective.

The chapters in this book confirm Christoph Kleßmann's assertion that the respective perceptions of the other state were indeed asymmetrical; the GDR was more strongly oriented toward the FRG than the other way around. It must be added, however, that the people of the FRG and the GDR both looked westward: from West Germany to the United States, and from the GDR to West Germany. Impulses coming from the United States often came to the FRG first before wandering in translated form to the GDR. This doubled western gaze, however, also established a link between both states. Such twofold, mediated transfer processes can be found in a number of aspects of everyday life, ranging from the world of work to music culture and computer technology. Innovations from IBM, for example, migrated to Siemens before making their way to Robotron. Especially in terms of popular culture, there were also lines of direct exchange between the GDR and the United States, especially via Hollywood films from the 1970s onward.[55]

Some might question whether it is anachronistic to write a shared German history rather than a European or global history in this day and age because it risks generating a new national narrative. Others might suggest that the FRG and the GDR should be examined in relation to their neighboring states—as has been done elsewhere—especially given that France and Poland were both key players in German history. It also seems tempting to situate the GDR more strongly within the context of Western Europe. Such an approach might reveal that differences between the two Germanys did not necessarily always stem from the different political systems and the socialism of the GDR, but might also have emerged out of a specific West German culture in terms of issues such as women's work or childcare, major nonuniversity research centers, or centralization.[56] Many of these phenomena were not intrinsic to the GDR as they also appeared in France or Great Britain around the same time.

Despite the objections mentioned above and the trend toward focusing on a comprehensive history of Western Europe, there are four main points that speak in favor of a German-German perspective:

First, both Germanys had a common past that continued to shape society, economics, culture, and mentalities long after the Berlin Wall was built. As the division of the country lasted for only forty years, both states shared the common experience of National Socialism and World War II, as well as the Weimar Republic.[57] The memories of the Great Depression were just as present in minds of the population in the 1970s as those of

1968 in present-day society. Similarly, the continued existence of familial relationships across the Wall ensured for a divided but also at least sometimes shared family history. The official interpretations of the past were quite distinct in the East and the West, but a cross-border boom in history came at the end of the 1970s, bringing with it the restoration of old town centers, as well as the so-called "Prussian renaissance."[58]

Second, more so than other states, East and West Germany had a communicative connection. In particular, this was made possible through the cross-border (yet very asymmetrical) reception of radio and television in both Germanys, which Axel Schildt has pithily described as "two states, but one radio and TV nation."[59] Additionally, the significant increase in telephone calls and letters between East and West Germany in the 1970s and 1980s attests to growing communication networks between the two states that far exceeded those with the French or the Poles, thanks to the shared German language. Simultaneously, there was a rise in the interactions taking place within the realm of economics and church circles as well as the number of travelers to and from the GDR, such as journalists, athletes, and artists. According to the Federal Ministry for Intra-German Relations, five million GDR citizens visited West Germany in 1988; 1.2 million of them were under retirement age. In many ways, these experiences with the West more than likely fostered a renunciation of socialism as well as the wave of travel out of the GDR in 1989.[60] Beginning in the 1970s, even historians from the West increasingly sought out the archives in the GDR, where they often were able to make contacts—despite their isolation—that led to rather chilly official conversations in the decade that followed.[61]

Third, as a result of the intense rivalry between East and West Germany and the mutual insistence on drawing lines of demarcation, the two states were more closely tied to one another than to other neighboring countries. On the one hand, they were permanently engaged in refuting practices and concepts coming from the other side of the Wall; on the other hand, this rivalry spurred on domestic improvements in each state, be it in terms of social policy or education, sports, or dealing with the Nazi past.

Last, given the shared history of Germany since reunification in 1990, it also makes sense to look at the decades beforehand from a shared perspective, not with a focus on 1989, but rather with an eye to the difficulties involved in growing together as one Germany. Such an approach allows for a better understanding of why there are still significant differences between East and West even today. Both Germanys are the divided past of our unified German present.

It must be kept in mind, however, that many things were different in East and West, even if they shared the same name. A political party or trade union in the West was fundamentally different from a political party or trade union in the East. Likewise, the search for transfers and entanglements bears the risk of overinterpreting the relevance of individual contacts, interactions, or mutual observations—a danger that is inherent to transnational history in general. Moreover, the creation of a new teleological master narrative leading up to 1989 has to be avoided.[62] Not only do historians need to explain the downfall of the GDR, but also they have to account for its long-lasting stability, which made even West German experts think that reunification was not on the horizon in early 1989. And, finally, it cannot be assumed too rashly that a sense of national unity or a shared German identity in both states justifies a joint perspective in and of itself. Even within the GDR, a feeling of "we" evolved that did not necessarily correspond to the "socialist nation."[63] Too little attention has been paid up to now on how the concept of the "nation" developed within the context of divided Germany and how stronger supranational identities were built before and after unification.[64]

The 1970s as a Period of Transition: Approaches and Perspectives

The last third of the twentieth century is a particularly interesting period in contemporary history because it marks the formative phase of current challenges. The decades since the 1970s have brought societal progress as well as affluence to both East and West, but also new problems and crises of a quite fundamental nature. The ambivalence associated with these changes appeared in both German states, but it has mostly been discussed with respect to the Federal Republic. Although vocational training periods were extended and chances for upward mobility expanded in West Germany, the unemployment rate also climbed steadily. Income, personal wealth, and the welfare state grew, but so, too, did the gap between rich and poor. While the state began introducing new regulations in the 1970s, neoliberal concepts such as competition and self-reliance also gained a strong foothold. In addition, technological innovations such as computers, cable television, or nuclear power signaled the path to the future, but this technology also strengthened the fears of what was yet to come. Whereas politics and society feared the "limits of growth" and damage to the environment, mass consumption flourished during this time as discount supermarkets and shopping centers sprouted up around the country. The list of such ambivalent and long-lasting changes could go on and on. For instance, Germans became more cosmopolitan and international in their outlooks, and the number of migrants living permanently in Germany increased, but xenophobia also gained momentum over the long run. And, as one last example of this tension between advancement and crisis, emphatic demands for women's equality clashed with the problematic challenges of making family and career compatible in the West.

Without a doubt, a German-German history of the 1970s and 1980s evinces its own particular tensions. On the one hand, the division of Germany became more entrenched during this period. The international recognition of the GDR and its acceptance (for all intents and purposes) in the Federal Republic heralded a new era of self-confident independence for both states. The barriers along the border became more insurmountable as the commitment to reunification and the unity of the nation dwindled rapidly. For West Germany, at least, opinion polls clearly indicate this shift: in 1970, seventy percent of West Germans still believed that the Federal Republic and the GDR were part of one nation. By 1984, however, over half of those polled no longer believed this was the case.[65] On the other hand, the 1970s were the decade in which détente intensified the relationship between the two states at a political and economic level, as well as in the culture of everyday life. This exceeded the level of exchange of the 1950s, when there was still a great deal of traffic between East and West in Berlin before political, economic, and even cultural contacts dissipated as the border between the two Germanys was built up.[66] *Ostpolitik* under Willy Brandt and rapprochement within the context of the Helsinki Accords effectively amplified the interactions and expectations flowing across both sides of the Wall. The mounting independence of each state and the entanglements of the 1970s and 1980s belong together like the flip sides of the same coin. German-German phenomena, such as the often cited expatriation of the East German singer-songwriter Wolf Biermann in 1976, exemplify this tension between interaction and distance. This blend of independent development and new entanglements not only helps to explain why many East Germans came to see West Germany as an unattainable standard, prompting them to turn away from the SED, but also accounts for the persistence of a separate consciousness after the fall of the Berlin Wall.

In general, the 1970s are often portrayed as a period of crisis in historical scholarship. As Eric Hobsbawm has put it, "The history of the twenty years after 1973 is that of a world which lost its bearings and slid into instability and crises."[67] Scholars point to the collapse of "old" industries, the significant deceleration of the postwar boom in economic growth, and the rise of inflation, debt, and unemployment as indicators of the postboom era, although these trends actually began to appear a bit earlier.[68] Economically, the breakdown of the Bretton Woods system in 1973 also signaled the end of the postwar consensus. For the most part, these issues have been examined from a national perspective and tied to cross-border developments, but put down to accelerated globalization.⁶⁹ At the same time, historians have outlined a cultural shift that took place in the 1970s that was characterized by trends such as increasing individualization, secularization, and postmaterial values.⁷⁰ Above all, the dwindling faith in progress is cited as the major indicator that the era of modernity had come to an end. Göran Therborn has thus spoken of an "amazing concentration of social historical turns."⁷¹ Based on the corresponding contemporary diagnoses of the problems, step-by-step reforms were introduced in the late 1970s in many Western countries. These included the neoliberal trends that emerged in Great Britain and the United States, and then spread to other parts of Western Europe, arriving in a less aggressive form in the Federal Republic.⁷²

Yet it has seldom been discussed whether these crises narratives and terms such as the "end of modernity" or "high modernity" also apply for socialist countries. Ulrich Herbert's programmatic article on "high modernity," for instance, largely ignores socialism as it focuses on "processes of change in the West."⁷³ Stefan Plaggenborg, in contrast, argues that modernity can be used in reference to Soviet-style communism because it featured characteristics such as mechanization, scientification, disciplinary institutions, or secularization, even though modernization as such had failed in this context.⁷⁴ Moreover, it is still up for debate whether the term "modernity" aptly describes a phase of history extending into the 1970s. When approached analytically as a temporal category encompassing the experience of accelerated change, an openness to the future, and historicized self-portrayal, then "modernity" is by no means "over" in that it also aptly applies to the digital age.⁷⁵ Analyzing the fundamental assumptions that underlie "modernity" therefore promises to revise our understanding of the past as well as the present.

Most studies of the 1970s cite the oil crisis of 1973 as a decisive turning point because it accelerated other changes and symbolized them in a nutshell. Economically, the crisis stood for a financial downturn; culturally, it represented the abandonment of faith in the future and the belief in limitless growth; and, politically, it marked the displacement or extension of the East-West conflict and tensions between the northern and southern hemispheres. Furthermore, the oil crisis came to represent accelerated globalization because it underscored the mutual interdependence of the global market. Upon closer inspection, however, the oil crisis also marked a step-by-step and limited process of transformation. Energy costs, for instance, had already been on the rise and continued to fluctuate in the decades that followed. Simultaneously, "growth" remained a clear goal in politics and economics as well as among the majority of consumers.⁷⁶

Alongside this literature on crises, studies by American and UK scholars in particular have focused on the manifold breakthroughs and new beginnings that emerged in the 1970s, such as a new consumer culture, the expansion of education and a "knowledge-based society," computerization, or progress in equality for women and minorities.[77] In terms of the history of everyday life, however, this strong analytical focus on "crises" runs into problems. For many, the 1970s were associated with many positive cultural experiences and memories in the East as well as the West, especially given that available income and wealth were on the rise. This was coupled with improved housing, significant growth in terms of travel and consumption, and new experiences of individual freedom, especially in the West.[78] Correspondingly, future scholarship needs to take into account that the narratives of (public) crises often ran parallel to narratives of (private) satisfaction in the culture of everyday life.

For the most part, scholarship on the GDR in the 1970s and 1980s also emphasizes the growing economic problems, but it hardly connects them to the crisis discourse of the West. Likewise, most studies have stressed the state's inability to reform despite the fact that it was aware of these problems. In particular, they cite Erich Honecker's adherence to a course of "consumption socialism" that necessitated high subsidies for social welfare, housing, or food items.[79] Although this plan was supposed to ensure the loyalty of the population, it forced the government to borrow additional money from the West. Not surprisingly, given the fact that the Federal Republic remained an important point of reference, much of the scholarship on the GDR deals with the political and economic relations with the West, including cross-border communication or contacts made through the church or opposition groups.[80] Similarly, the Helsinki Accords have served as an ideal prism for cross-border perspectives because they opened the door for a discussion of human rights, and the so-called "third basket" fostered migration out of the GDR.[81] Scholarship investigating the sociology of the GDR has also used comparative statistics on the social and economic situations in both Germanys to underscore the superiority of West German society on all accounts.[82] Likewise, the impact of international transformations on the GDR has also been a popular topic for scholarly discussion. Recently, one study looked at the GDR's problems with its coffee supply coming from outside the Eastern bloc within a German-German context. It traces interactions with capitalist countries ranging from the private packages sent from the West filled with West German "Jacobs Krönung" coffee to the coffee crisis in 1977, when public outrage forced the SED to stop its attempts to increase the proportion of malt-based coffee substitutes in the ground coffee sold in the GDR; the government had begun changing the coffee "recipe" in light of the rising coffee prices on the global market.[83]

To what extent can the postboom era be approached as a *geteilte Geschichte* in which differences are tied to commonalities and interactions? First, the contributions in this book do not shy away from pointing out fundamental differences between East and West, as the authors are well aware that the SED sought to infiltrate all aspects of society ideologically. Yet, at the same time, they are keen to identify various relationships and contacts that linked the two Germanys together. For the most part, they show that changes that began to appear in the Federal Republic in the mid-1970s made their way to the GDR a few years later.

The international recession in the 1970s and the structural transformation processes affecting the economy in the West function as the main springboard for the analyses in this book. The consequences of these transformations often appeared more slowly and were less apparent in the planned economy, especially given that comparable economic data was not yet publicly available. But, as of the second half of the 1970s, the economic downtown was unmistakable in the socialist state. Thanks to the planned economy, it was not accompanied by visible phenomena such as high unemployment and inflation, but it did bring increasing debts, supply shortages, and slumping productivity.[84] Consequently, the faith in a better future considered to be characteristic of "high modernity" also disappeared under socialism in the 1970s, despite all the propaganda efforts to the contrary. The condensed five-year plans designed to adapt to the fluctuating global market were also evidence of this shortened sense of time. Peter Hübner, for example, has thus spoken of a "shift from a growth-oriented paradigm of progress to a security-oriented paradigm of consolidation" that also affected the GDR.[85] Although hardly any reforms were introduced in the East at the end of the 1970s, there was still a great awareness of the fact that the planned economy, even with the help of Western capital and technology, could not catch up.[86]

Furthermore, the oil crises in 1973 and 1979 resulted in significant consequences for the GDR, although this aspect has largely been neglected in scholarship up to now. Even in the socialist state, energy import prices spiked—albeit a few years later—especially after the Soviet Union began selling more natural gas and oil to the West and reduced its supply to the GDR. This exacerbated the shortage of foreign currency in the GDR, fueled rising prices at the beginning of the 1980s, and forced the GDR to rely even more heavily on its outdated coal mining industry.[87] In contrast to the Federal Republic, which had implemented energy saving measures in the 1980s, the GDR failed to reform. Simultaneously, the energy market actually stood for growing German-German entanglements as of the 1970s because the GDR increasingly supplied West Berlin, as well as the rest of the Federal Republic, with products processed in its refineries.[88] Likewise, the financial entanglements between East and West continued to grow substantially as a result of the global economic crisis. Accordingly, the GDR debts owed to nonsocialist countries climbed from DM 2 billion in 1970 to DM 40 billion in 1989.[89] The Federal Republic provided diverse loans in exchange for humanitarian concessions as well as more freedom to travel across the border, which in turn intensified these entanglements.[90] Other transfer payments also increased sharply in the 1970s, ranging from transit fees and bailouts for prisoners to wire transfers between churches and considerable private Deutsche Mark transfers.[91] These payments had more than far-reaching consequences. They not only fostered exchange at a personal level and altered the consumption potential in the GDR by enabling foreign currency transactions (such as at Exquisit, Delikat, and Intershop), but also this influx of money from the West helped to pay for the rebuilding and even construction of churches in the GDR beginning in the early 1980s.

As the contribution of Ralf Ahrens and André Steiner to this book illustrates, the long-term origins of the crises in East and West were certainly quite similar in that they stemmed from problems resulting from the ebbing of the sustainable economic boom of the postwar decades. Faced with staunch competition from East Asia, industrial sectors in both Germanys, such as the textile industry, collapsed as the energy sector grew. Naturally, there were also clear differences between East and West. East Germany, for example, still lacked something comparable to the booming West German automobile industry, despite its attempts at modernization.[92] Moreover, the short-term factors fueling the crises of the 1970s also varied, and the reactions to these problems differed even more so. These factors therefore further deepened the divide between the countries. Whereas the GDR restrengthened its centralized control over the planned economy, the FRG turned away from its Keynesian-inspired demand-based policies to monetary-oriented measures designed to reduce inflation and business-friendly "supply-side" economic policies. At the same time, Honecker's "consumer socialism" in particular necessitated economic interactions with the Federal Republic that ultimately made the GDR more dependent on the West and strengthened the longing for goods rather than appeasing such desires.

Especially in the world of work, the GDR came under intense pressure to reform, but at best it reacted only very slowly to international developments. Rüdiger Hachtmann's chapter analyzes the increasing significance of rationalization, automation, and flexible forms of work that came to the Federal Republic through globalization and augmented Fordist production models. Simultaneously, it points out how the modernization of production did not occur in the GDR, especially since the autarchism of the socialist conglomerates put the brakes on these processes. As with the contribution by Ralf Ahrens and André Steiner, this chapter also underscores that it would be misleading to think in terms of polar opposites and to categorize the West as a burgeoning service-based society and the East as a stagnating industrial society. Until 1970, Hachtmann argues, employment in the three main sectors developed quite similarly, and the service sector in the East continued to grow more strongly than most scholars have assumed. At the same time, he notes, the Federal Republic was also still quite industrial. Work became more important in the factory-centered GDR as the East Germans clearly worked more per capita and per year on average than West Germans.[93] There was, however, a tendency toward a decline in these numbers on both sides of the Wall.

In turn, leisure time, the family, and consumption increased in value. As the chapter by Christopher Neumaier and Andreas Ludwig illuminates, structural similarities appeared between East and West. A consumer society became firmly established, not only in West Germany, but also in the GDR; a certain diversification of lifestyles also took place on both sides of the wall, despite the often limited availability of consumer goods in the East. In the GDR, too, consumption went beyond necessity and was linked to status and self-realization. Additionally, the transition to self-service and supermarkets transformed consumption in both Germanys, while plastics, for example, came to symbolize modernity on both sides of the Wall. This chapter also exemplifies the related trend toward individualization by looking at the pluralization of different kinds of families in both countries. It must be noted, though, that divorce and domestic partnerships among unmarried couples sparked more controversy in the West than they did in the East.

Not only did Germans on both sides of the Wall use media in similar ways in their free time, but they also consumed similar content. As of the 1970s, it was generally tolerated to listen or watch Western radio or television channels (although it was never openly discussed). Viewing and listening to these broadcasts had become common practice for much of the GDR population and even among SED members. Yet, at the same time, the media also stands paradigmatically for the asymmetrical nature of the entanglements between East and West because West Germans received very little input from GDR media. As the chapter by Frank Bösch and Christoph Classen also stresses, media connections grew on other levels—for example, through the reports of West German correspondents based in East Berlin that made their way via Western media back to the

East or through the trade in Western programming or the adaptations of FRG programs on GDR channels that were designed to win back listeners and watchers. Based on these interactions, scholarship on television thus speaks of a "contrastive dialogue" in relation to the GDR.[94] The organization of journalism and the political content of the media, however, remained fundamentally different, especially in the print sector. On the newspaper market, in contrast, there was a tendency toward convergence that was linked to consumption and lifestyle changes.

Simultaneously, the FRG media called for a change in politics in East and West. The emergence of a camp of critical political journalists who raised fundamental political questions in relation to specific grievances nurtured the protest movements of the 1960s and 1970s and the general public interest in politics. Around 1980, a peace movement, as well as an environmental protection movement, emerged in the East along with an alternative milieu. Although they were much smaller than in the West, Western media made sure that these trends became visible in the East and could feed on Western input.[95] No less significant was the transformation in attitudes toward politics, as the contribution by Frank Bösch and Jens Gieseke illustrates. In East Germany, the general interest in politics also grew around 1970, especially over the course of Brandt's *Ostpolitik*, but then it waned in disappointment for a time. Bösch and Gieseke's chapter also explores the appearance of the much discussed "political disenchantment" in the West, as well as in the East, noting that an increased aversion to the SED could be detected in the GDR, even among party members.

Interestingly, environmental protection was taken up as an issue by both governments as early as 1970. This occurred within the context of an international trend in the West in which even the Republican Richard Nixon was involved. In both Germanys, however, the governments lost interest in the mid-1970s, increasingly turning to nuclear energy and coal power plants as they felt the effects of the oil crises. As the 1980s rolled around, the course of both states began to diverge on environmental issues. Whereas environmental protection was fostered in the FRG through numerous laws—primarily in response to pressure coming from civil society—the GDR turned into one of the largest pollution producers in Europe for its population and size, as Frank Uekötter's chapter points out. In a sense, East Germany proved to be more capitalist than the West, as the FRG had put more environmental restrictions on its industries. The fact that the GDR provided a depot for hazardous waste from the West in exchange for foreign currency further underscores this point. Frank Uekötter also notes how these dealings in waste likewise represent the environmental entanglements between East and West. Polluted rivers such as the Elba and the Werra did not stop at the border, nor did the soot from the smokestacks or the radioactivity unleashed by the Chernobyl disaster in 1986 (the latter of which the SED had tried to downplay to the dismay of many East Germans). At the very least, piecemeal solutions had to be found to deal with these situations, regardless of political borders and boundaries.[96]

A further challenge for both states in the 1970s proved to be the expansion of the welfare state. Both Germanys increased the scope of their welfare measures in an effort to bolster growth just as the economic crises took hold. Consequently, it has been argued that the sociopolitical developments in the two Germanys at this time were reactions to the structural economic changes that unfurled over the course of the third industrial revolution.[97] Likewise, some scholars have also claimed that Cold War competition spurred on the expansion of the welfare state in East and West.[98] Winfried Süß's chapter, however, presents a more nuanced perspective, noting that the GDR played less of a role in West German welfare politics in the 1970s and 1980s than in reverse. The SED state in fact sought to legitimize itself by expanding its welfare policies with an eye to the West. In both states, the welfare state quickly turned from a solution into a problem of its own, and both Germanys shied away from substantial restructuring.[99] The organization of welfare policies in the East and West differed, as did their emphases. However, pro-family policies played a larger role in both states, especially given the concerted efforts to increase sinking birth rates, that even met with short-term success in the GDR at the end of the 1970s. East and West also followed divergent paths when it came to social risks. Pensioners profited from the expansion of the welfare state in the West, for example, whereas they faced the threat of poverty in the highly work-oriented GDR. Simultaneously, unemployment generated a new kind of social inequality in the West, while GDR residents paid for job security by accepting less upward career mobility, a privilege that seemed to be reserved for SED officials. Another kind of social inequality also emerged in the GDR, and it was defined by personal access to Western products and currency.[100]

The world of work was also transformed in the 1970s by the introduction of computer technology. While the Federal Republic caught up with the United States at least incrementally, massive pressure was put on the microelectronics industry in the GDR to innovate. However, the East never managed to even get close to keeping up with the global market, despite investing billions in funding programs.[101] As Jürgen Danyel and Annette Schuhmann show, computers transformed the world of work in both German states, especially in government offices, security departments, and large factories. The impact of this computerization, however, was clearly more dynamic in the Federal Republic. Toward the end of the 1970s, they note, suspicions against computer-supported surveillance grew in the West; in the East where Stasi investigations relied on digital technology, however, fears about surveillance were not directed at computers per se. Their chapter revises the assumption that the population of the GDR had virtually no access to computers. They note that private computers primarily made their way to the East as personal gifts from the West, but many young people used computer technology in schools, factories, and youth clubs.

Sometimes the GDR was even the frontrunner, and it was the FRG's turn to play catch-up. For example, the duration of schooling and qualification processes had already grown significantly in the 1960s in the GDR, improving women's access to education in particular. The Federal Republic finally caught up in the 1970s, and then it actually went on to trump the GDR quantitatively.[102] Not only the Sputnik crisis but also the forecasting strength of comparative (OECD) statistics and forecasts became quite influential in this respect, as explained by Emmanuel Droit and Wilfried Rudloff. After both Germanys initially overcame the problem of an academic shortage, they found themselves faced with a "glut of academics" at the end of the 1970s, to which they reacted differently. Whereas the GDR limited the number of students, the Federal Republic slightly tightened access to the universities by introducing the numerus clausus, decreasing student loan amounts, and providing alternative career advice. In both states, the expansion of the educational system was supposed to improve opportunities for upward social mobility. However, it is quite telling that the chances for workers' children to move up the academic ladder ultimately remained limited in both systems.

Especially in terms of sports, the GDR clearly appeared to be in the lead. In the early 1970s, the large-scale efforts to promote competitive sports in the GDR began to bear fruit as the East overtook the FRG in the Olympic medal count. In response, the Federal Republic expanded its competitive sports programs, which Jutta Braun discusses in her contribution to this book. Simultaneously, the GDR neglected its mass sports programs, only slowly reacting to impulses from the West, but without sustainable results. In addition, the GDR adopted the use of Western advertising at the end of the 1980s, and officials in the East and West reached agreements in order to avoid any further boycotts of the Olympics.

All things considered, East and West seemed to have taken the most divergent paths when it came to migration and mobility. The Federal Republic not only made more of an effort to attract foreign workers, but also its many migrants were allowed to stay permanently despite deportation attempts. Nonetheless, Maren Möhring's contribution points out overarching similarities and links between East and West within this context. It was not Italy or Turkey that had the highest emigration rate in Europe initially, she notes, but rather the early GDR. The construction of the Wall put a stop to this emigration, but both Germanys increasingly sought to bring in unskilled foreign workers, who then settled on the margins of society in the East as well as the West.[103] The GDR was clearly more profit oriented when it came to migration, especially given that migrants to the East were only tolerated as long as they were economically useful and only granted limited rights; any transgressions (including pregnancy) resulted in deportation. Möhring also outlines similarities and connections in terms of mobility, noting that travel abroad was popular in both Germanys, although the East Germans were more limited in their travel destinations and usually only permitted to visit socialist states.[104]

This shared history could naturally be explored in many other areas. Chapters on architecture, the churches, and high or popular culture could further embellish this complicated picture of East and West Germany from the 1970s onward, a history that vacillated between new entanglements and the demarcation of boundaries.[105] A special chapter on gender has not been included because gender is a topic that touches on many aspects of society and played a major role in many of the transformations discussed in this book, including those affecting work, the family and lifestyles, education, and migration. After all, the high percentage of female employment in the GDR, which rose significantly in the 1970s—parallel to the expansion of childcare—is often cited today as one of the major differences and positive achievements of the GDR. Indeed, the contrast to the FRG in this context is unmistakable as the conservative sociopolitical model of the "male breadwinner" discriminated against women financially, socially, and legally. Abortion policies also differed markedly between East and West. At the same time, calls for reforms in gender politics were often put down in the Federal Republic with reference to the Eastern enemy, despite the fact that many neighboring countries to the West had already been offering full-time daycare for children.[106] The slight rise in women's employment in the Federal Republic in the 1980s mostly only applied to part-time work. Notwithstanding these differences, many chapters here also note the continued discrimination against women and the persistence of gender differences in West *and* East Germany. In both states, women only seldom climbed to the highest ranks of politics. Wage differences, the unequal distribution of housework, and clearly defined childcare roles also remained firmly entrenched in the GDR, despite other beneficial policies. Moreover, given that women in the GDR generally perceived themselves as having equal rights, a women's emancipation movement never really emerged in the East; in the West, however, the women's movement made sustainable inroads, especially in terms of issues such as sexism or male violence against women.[107]

In sum, it can be duly said that there were similar developments that often occurred in relation to each other, despite the well-known structural differences between East and West Germany. Both states had to develop crisis management policies that were designed to overcome present difficulties rather than to shape the future. The achievement of security was one of the main concerns behind such measures, which explains why both states refrained from making fundamental reforms during times of crisis, opting instead to cling to structures that they could hardly afford to finance.[108] As a result, not only the West, but also increasingly the GDR came under pressure to innovate. The term "innovation" steadily cropped up in the West in the 1970s. It became one of the main demands placed not only upon technology, but also the service and research sectors, as well as consumption, the media, and lifestyles—not to mention fashion, design, and music.[109] The GDR sought to copy these innovations or develop its own with a great outlay of capital, but it always lagged behind or failed entirely.[110] In doing so, the East German state was able to at least partially satisfy the desire for choice that was tied to growing desires to lead an individualized life. This transformation was propelled in both states by the media's increased penetration of society. Especially the full coverage offered by television generated cross-border communication and entertainment offerings related to almost all aspects of life.

Offset Transformations after 1990

Expectations were running high as the GDR joined the Federal Republic. However, in East Germany at least, this annexation proved to be fraught with myriad disappointments. The rapid transformation processes that engulfed the new federal states have often been described. The old Federal Republic, in contrast, has often been portrayed merely as a stagehand, financial backer, and liquidator for the transformation of East Germany, hardly changing itself over the course of reunification. At most, the fall of the Berlin Wall and reunification was transmitted through the media as a caesura of historical experience, but one that had only very little effect on daily life in the West.[111] Even after 1990, the relationship between East and West generally remained an asymmetrical one, especially since the East fixed its gaze more on the West than in reverse. Nonetheless, as different contributions to this book demonstrate, the West did not remain unaffected by the massive changes taking place in the East. For example, developments appeared in the new federal states that seemed to be specifically East German from a Western perspective until they crept over to the West a few years later. The pointed catchphrase referring to "East Germany as the avant-garde" only seems to partially fit in this context.[112] Rather, the notion of offset transformations seems to be more useful given the fact that many of these transformation processes emerged in the West back in the 1970s. Moreover, rather than moving closer together, the gap between East and West seemed to be growing larger again at the end of the 1990s. Consequently, we can still speak of a *geteilte Geschichte* after 1990 that was both shared and divided, shaped by differences as well as interactions and new commonalities.

When considering the massive migration movement unleashed at the end of the Cold War, 1990 was very much a caesura for all of Germany. In just the first four years after the fall of the Wall, 1.4 million people (approximately 8 percent of the population) left the former territory of East Germany for the old Federal German states, especially those in southern and northern Germany as opposed to the western portions of the country. Likewise, there was a rapid influx of "ethnic Germans" from Eastern Europe, as well as asylum seekers, although Germans judged "asylum cheaters" to be *the* main problem in 1991. As Maren Möhring explains, the marginalization of foreigners actually contributed to the process of German-German integration. At the same time, however, it also increasingly marginalized East Germans on the whole as more xenophobic, despite the fact that refugee centers also went up in flames in the West. Even today, the differences between East and West in terms of migration are still quite striking. There are far fewer foreigners in the East, but the biases against them are stronger than in the West. This phenomenon cannot be attributed simply to the GDR past, especially since right-wing populist parties are gaining strength across all of Western Europe. That said, however, the GDR's restrictive way of dealing with foreigners has had a lasting influence.[113]

Apart from the new right-wing populism that has emerged, the end of the Cold War brought a decline in political interest and commitment in the West as well as in the East. As of the end of the 1990s, democracy was valued much more negatively in the East than in the West, even among the youth.[114] But even this turn away from classic politics was part of an overarching international trend. In the West, however, the parties, unions, and associations could rely on an established support base despite their dwindling numbers. Meanwhile, these kinds of organizations could hardly even gain a foothold in the East, where protest movements and party preferences tended to be short-lived. As the chapter on the transformation of politics argues, this cannot be attributed solely to some kind of East German backwardness; rather, it was also part of a western European trend that also reached the Federal Republic a decade later.

The differences between East and West can certainly be explained to a great extent by the clearly weaker economic situation of the East, especially considering the high unemployment and the often traumatic career downgrades suffered by many after 1990. In contrast to other postsocialist countries, the restructuring process was quite successful in East Germany, admittedly thanks to the definite break with socialism as well as West German transfers. As Ralf Ahrens and André Steiner illustrate, however, numerous mistakes can also be detected in the deindustrialization of the East. The "Aufbau Ost" reconstruction program for the East, for example, generated a short-lived stimulus package for the West German economy until a longer phase of stagnation set in. After the collapse of socialism in the East, an unprecedented phase of privatization and dismissals took place that at least indirectly affected the West. Calls for privatization, cost reduction, and more flexibility had already been often voiced in the Federal Republic in the 1980s, but now they were finally being implemented, not only in conjunction with international trends, but also as part of privatization in the East.[115] Additionally, the East experienced the rapid advancement of "McJob" types of work, as Rüdiger Hachtmann refers to the increase in the number of tenuous, flexible, and poorly paid new jobs in the service sector. This kind of work can be seen in the call centers or private nursing facilities popping up all over that have become more commonplace throughout Germany since the 1990s. Concurrently, the state had to cough up the funds to pay for the social costs of this liberalization. Undoubtedly, the East was the forerunner in terms of work and especially women's employment, which only began to rise significantly in the West just a few years prior to reunification.

In order to avoid tax hikes, as Winfried Süß explains, reunification was paid for to a great extent out of social insurance funds. Consequently, reunification proved to be a challenge for unified Germany's welfare state. The increasing marketization of social welfare benefits—and pension provisions in particular—was one consequence of this. Others included the move away from traditional social security schemes in the West, especially given that the Hartz reforms, for example, also threatened the middle class's ability to uphold the status quo. At first, East and West aligned in terms of social status, although enormous differences could still be seen, particularly in wealth. In the 2000s, however, the differences began to increase again, as did the gap between rich and poor in the West.[116] Correspondingly, East Germans were more insistent in their demands for social equity and a stronger welfare state, which partly explains the enduring success of the SED successor party, the PDS (Partei des Demokratischen Sozialismus / Party of Democratic Socialism), at election time. These debates over social inequality also spilled over to the West, making it possible for the leftist party Die Linke, which had largely been formed out of the PDS, to firmly establish itself as a national party in Germany.

Even in the realm of sports, Jutta Braun identifies a "doubled transformation." Numerous competitive sports centers were closed down in former East Germany after 1990 to make way for recreational sports facilities. Debates over East German sports, and especially doping, however, have increasingly begun to make reference to doping practices in West Germany. Likewise, the dip in unified Germany's medal count sparked a conflict over sport promotion programs, which in turn prompted the adoption of approaches that had been used in the GDR. Simultaneously, however, there were also differences that persisted in the realm of sport. For example, although several competitive sports centers for Olympic disciplines survived in the East, recreational sports did not gain much of a foothold, even among the youth.[117] This trend toward individualized sports also extended to all of Germany and not just the East. Nowadays, more Germans belong to a fitness center than to a soccer association.[118]

The cultural and lifestyle differences between East and West can also be detected in terms of media use, as the chapter by Frank Bösch and Christoph Classen underscores. Although almost all East German media outlets were taken over by West German companies after reunification, it quickly became quite clear that there were lasting differences in terms of media use. Commercial television programming and local channels are more popular in the East than public broadcasters. The same applies to the national daily newspapers and other news magazines, such as the *Frankfurter Allgemeine Zeitung* or *Der Spiegel*, which are hardly bought in the East. Media with a regional identification (such as the former district press outlets, MDR [Central German Broadcasting] or illustrated magazines with an East German image) are clearly favored in the former GDR. These media not only strengthen a separate self-image of the East, but also the nostalgia for the old GDR or "Ostalgie" that has set in since the end of the 1990s. But here, too, the East Germans anticipated a trend that later reached the West in the move away from the national daily press and public broadcasting companies, which cannot be explained solely through the competition coming from the Internet.

Above all, however, the East was very clearly a trendsetter in the areas of family and education. The East proved to be the innovator when it came to providing more childcare facilities, the alignment of the school systems, or the introduction of the twelve-year *Abitur* (high school graduation exam) because the new federal states experimented with intermediary solutions when they began to adapt to Western models. As the chapter on education articulates, however, this process first took place within the competitive international context of the PISA (Programme for International Student Assessment) tests, which washed the taint of socialism off full-day and comprehensive schools, as well as off standardized testing.

At the beginning of the 1990s, many contemporary social scientists predicted that it would take a long time for East Germany to align with the West, and most estimates ranged between ten and fifteen years.[119] Most of these scholars never thought that a transformation would also take place in the West. Today, it has not only become quite clear that it has taken much longer for East and West to grow together, but also that life in the former FRG has also been transformed. The old Bonn Republic of the 1970s and 1980s now seems to be a "distant country," giving rise to a left-wing as well as a right-wing form of "Westalgie."[120] One major factor contributing to this accelerated experience of time is surely the rapid digitalization of almost all areas of life, which is why computer technology—as a new key topic in historical scholarship—is dealt with in a separate chapter of this book. With the advent of Internet-based digital communication, a world that was once populated by telephone boxes, singular television programs, and index card files has disappeared in both the East and the West.

A German-German perspective is just one of many possible approaches to the history of contemporary Germany, but it is particularly promising for the decades before and after 1990. The fact that all kinds of differences persist between East and West even twenty-five years after reunification speaks in favor of the need to account for the historical influence of divided Germany. At the same time, however, the rapid tempo of the reunification process can only be explained by looking at the myriad lines connecting East and West that were not stopped by the Wall in between.

Frank Bösch is professor of European history at the University of Potsdam and director of the Center for Contemporary History (ZZF) in Potsdam. He is the author of several books on modern German and European history, including *Die Adenauer-CDU* (2001), *Das konservative Milieu* (2002), and *Öffentliche Geheimnisse* (2009). His most recent book is *Mass Media and Historical Change: Germany in International Perspective, 1400–2000* (Berghahn Books, 2015).

NOTES

1. See Gunilla Budde, Sebastian Conrad, and Oliver Janz, eds., *Transnationale Geschichte: Themen, Tendenzen und Theorien* (Frankfurt a. M., 2010).
2. See Eckart Conze, *Die Suche nach Sicherheit: Eine Geschichte der Bundesrepublik Deutschland* (Berlin, 2009); Edgar Wolfrum, *Geglückte Demokratie: Geschichte der Bundesrepublik Deutschland von ihren Anfängen bis zur Gegenwart* (Munich, 2007); Manfred Görtemaker, *Geschichte der Bundesrepublik Deutschland: Von der Gründung bis zur Gegenwart* (Munich, 1999); Axel Schildt and Detlef Siegfried, *Deutsche Kulturgeschichte: Die Bundesrepublik—1945 bis zur Gegenwart* (Munich, 2009).
3. See Jan Schönfelder and Rainer Erices, *Willy Brandt in Erfurt: Das erste deutsch-deutsche Gipfeltreffen 1970* (Berlin, 2010); Karsten Rudolph, *Wirtschaftsdiplomatie im Kalten Krieg: Die Ostpolitik der westdeutschen Industrie* (Frankfurt a. M., 2004).
4. For the major point of reference for the debates over West Germany, see Anselm Doering-Manteuffel and Lutz Raphael, *Nach dem Boom: Perspektiven auf die Zeitgeschichte seit 1970* (Göttingen, 2010).
5. On the increasing number of shared problems in the 1970s, see Udo Wengst and Hermann Wentker, "Einleitung," in *Das doppelte Deutschland: 40 Jahre Systemkonkurrenz*, ed. Udo Wengst and Hermann Wentker (Berlin, 2008), 9.
6. Philipp Ther, *Die neue Ordnung auf dem alten Kontinent: Eine Geschichte des neoliberalen Europas* (Frankfurt a. M., 2014), 14.
7. Schroeder warns against this; see Klaus Schroeder, *Der SED-Staat: Geschichte und Strukturen der DDR 1949–1990* (Cologne, 2013), 902.
8. See the use of this image in *Tagesspiegel*, 11 August 2013 and 26 September 2013; *Die Welt*, 27 November 2009.
9. See image at the *Welt* website, retrieved 28 May 2018, https://www.welt.de/kultur/article5336579/Wie-die-DDR-die-BRD-sportlich-ueberholte.html.
10. Eva Gajek, *Imagepolitik im olympischen Wettstreit: Die Spiele von Rom 1960 und München 1972* (Göttingen, 2013); Uta Balbier, *Kalter Krieg auf der Aschenbahn: Deutsch-deutscher Sport 1950–72: Eine politische Geschichte* (Paderborn, 2007), 238.
11. Giselher Spitzer, "Doping in Deutschland von 1950 bis heute aus historisch-soziologischer Sicht im Kontext ethischer Legitimation," Bundesinstitut für Sportwissenschaft, 30 March 2013, 16; retrieved 12 July 2016, http://www.bisp.de/SharedDocs/Downloads/Aktuelles/Inhaltlicher_Bericht_HU.pdf?__blob=publicationFile&v=1.
12. Christoph Kleßmann, "Spaltung und Verflechtung—Ein Konzept zur integrierten Nachkriegsgeschichte 1945 bis 1990," in *Teilung und Integration: Die doppelte deutsche Nachkriegsgeschichte als wissenschaftliches und didaktisches Problem*, ed. Christoph Kleßmann and Peter Lautzas (Schwalbach, 2006), 22. For an older essay before he coined his much cited "parallel history" phrase: Christoph Kleßmann, "Verflechtung und Abgrenzung: Aspekte

der geteilten und zusammengehörigen deutschen Nachkriegsgeschichte," *Aus Politik und Zeitgeschichte* 29–30 (1993): 30–41.
13. See Martin Sabrow, "Historisierung der Zweistaatlichkeit," *Aus Politik und Zeitgeschichte* 3 (2007): 19–24.
14. Kleßmann, "Spaltung," 26–34.
15. See Konrad H. Jarausch, "'Die Teile als Ganzes erkennen': Zur Integration der beiden deutschen Nachkriegsgeschichten," *Zeithistorische Forschungen/ Studies in Contemporary History* 1 (2004): 10–30, 15; Konrad H. Jarausch and Michael Geyer, *Shattered Past: Reconstructing German Histories* (Princeton, 2003), 1–33.
16. Thomas Lindenberger, "'Zonenrand,' 'Sperrgebiet' und 'Westberlin'— Deutschland als Grenzregion des Kalten Kriegs," in *Teilung und Integration: Die doppelte deutsche Nachkriegsgeschichte als wissenschaftliches und didaktisches Problem*, ed. Christoph Kleßmann and Peter Lautzas (Schwalbach, 2006), 97–112.
17. See the contributions by Horst Möller, Andreas Wirsching, and Günther Heydemann in the special issue "Gemeinsame Nachkriegsgeschichte," *Aus Politik und Zeitgeschichte* 3 (2007); Dierk Hoffmann, Hermann Wentker, and Michael Schwartz, "Die DDR als Chance: Neue Perspektiven künftiger Forschung," in *Die DDR als Chance: neue Perspektiven auf ein altes Thema*, ed. Ulrich Mählert (Berlin, 2016), 23–70.
18. Horst Möller, "Demokratie und Diktatur," *Aus Politik und Zeitgeschichte* 3 (2007): 3–7.
19. As most recently argued with reference to Hans Günther Hockert's position: Thomas Raithel and Thomas Schlemmer, eds., *Die Anfänge der Gegenwart: Umbrüche in Westeuropa nach dem Boom* (Munich, 2014).
20. Klaus Naumann, "Die Historisierung der Bonner Republik: Zeitgeschichtsschreibung in zeitdiagnostischer Absicht," *Mittelweg 36*, no. 9 (2000): 63.
21. See Frank Biess, *Homecomings: Returning POWs and the Legacies of Defeat in Postwar Germany* (Princeton, 2006); Dagmar Herzog, *Sex after Fascism: Memory and Morality in Twentieth-Century Germany* (Princeton, 2005); Jeffrey Herf, *Divided Memory: The Nazi Past in the Two Germanys* (Cambridge, MA, 1997).
22. Christoph Kleßmann, *Zwei Staaten, eine Nation: Deutsche Geschichte 1955–1970* (Bonn, 1997); idem, *Die doppelte Staatsgründung: Deutsche Geschichte 1945–1955* (Göttingen, 1982).
23. Particularly the case in Hans-Ulrich Wehler, *Deutsche Gesellschaftsgeschichte*, vol. 5, *Bundesrepublik und DDR* (Munich, 2008), 88–108 and 338–61. In contrast, for a more balanced account, see Ulrich Herbert, *Geschichte Deutschlands im 20. Jahrhundert* (Munich, 2014).
24. For the strongest account of both Germanys and their (political) relations, albeit mostly within a political history context, see Peter Graf Kielmansegg, *Das geteilte Land: Deutsche Geschichte 1945–1990* (Munich, 2004).
25. Mary Fulbrook, *Interpretations of the Two Germanies, 1945–1990* (New York, 2000), 91–95.

26. Carsten Kretschmann, *Zwischen Spaltung und Gemeinsamkeit: Kultur im geteilten Deutschland* (Bonn, 2012), 170.
27. See, for example, Ulrich Mählert, *Kleine Geschichte der DDR* (Munich, 2009); Hans-Hermann Hertle and Stefan Wolle, *Damals in der DDR* (Munich, 2006); Schroeder, *Der SED-Staat*.
28. Margit Roth, *Innerdeutsche Bestandsaufnahme der Bundesrepublik 1969–1989: Neue Deutung* (Wiesbaden, 2014), 686f.
29. Matthias Judt, *Der Bereich Kommerzielle Koordinierung: Das DDR-Wirtschaftsimperium des Alexander Schalck-Golodkowski—Mythos und Realität* (Berlin, 2013).
30. Peter Bender, *Deutschlands Wiederkehr—Eine ungeteilte Nachkriegsgeschichte 1945–1990* (Stuttgart, 2007).
31. Konrad H. Jarausch, *After Hitler: Recivilizing the Germans 1945–1995* (New York, 2006).
32. With comparative articles and didactic concepts: Christoph Kleßmann and Peter Lautzas, eds. *Teilung und Integration: Die doppelte deutsche Nachkriegsgeschichte als wissenschaftliches und didaktisches Problem* (Schwalbach, 2006). For a more comprehensive perspective without a shared aspect, see Arnd Bauerkämper, Martin Sabrow, and Bernd Stöver, eds., *Doppelte Zeitgeschichte: Deutsch-deutsche Beziehungen 1945–1990* (Bonn, 1998).
33. Udo Wengst and Hermann Wentker, *Das doppelte Deutschland: 40 Jahre Systemkonkurrenz* (Berlin, 2008). For a similar study based more heavily on eyewitness testimonies: Andreas Apelt, Robert Grünbaum, and Jens Schöne, eds., *2 x Deutschland: Innerdeutsche Beziehungen 1972–1990* (Halle, 2013).
34. Andreas Wirsching, "Für eine pragmatische Zeitgeschichtsforschung," *Aus Politik und Zeitgeschichte* 3 (2007): 18.
35. Tobias Hochscherf, Christoph Laucht, and Andrew Plowman, eds., *Divided, but Not Disconnected: German Experiences of the Cold War* (New York, 2010); Detlef Brunner, Udo Grashoff, and Andreas Kötzing, eds., *Asymmetrisch verflochten? Neue Forschungen zur gesamtdeutschen Nachkriegsgeschichte* (Berlin, 2013).
36. See, for example, Jörg Roesler, *Momente deutsch-deutscher Wirtschafts- und Sozialgeschichte 1945 bis 1990: Eine Analyse auf gleicher Augenhöhe* (Leipzig, 2006); Balbier, *Kalter Krieg*.
37. See Heinrich Best and Everhard Holtmann, eds., *Aufbruch der entsicherten Gesellschaft: Deutschland nach der Wiedervereinigung* (Frankfurt a. M., 2012). For a historian's perspective, see Christoph Lorke and Thomas Großbölting, eds., *Deutschland seit 1990: Wege in die Vereinigungsgesellschaft* (Stuttgart, 2017).
38. For a more recent assessment of scholarship, see Manuela Glaab, Werner Weidenfeld, and Michael Weigl, eds., *Deutsche Kontraste 1990–2010. Politik—Wirtschaft—Gesellschaft—Kultur* (Frankfurt a. M., 2010); Peter Krause and Ilona Ostner, eds., *Leben in Ost- und Westdeutschland: Eine sozialwissenschaftliche Bilanz der deutschen Einheit 1990–2010* (Frankfurt a. M., 2010).

39. See also Raj Kollmorgen, *Ostdeutschland: Beobachtungen einer Übergangs- und Teilgesellschaft* (Wiesbaden, 2005).
40. Heinrich Best and Everhard Holtmann, "Der lange Wege der deutschen Einigung: Aufbruch mit vielen Unbekannten," in Best and Holtmann, *Aufbruch*, 11.
41. Timm Beichelt, "Verkannte Parallelen: Transformationsforschung und Europastudien," *Osteuropa* 63, no. 2–3 (2013), 277–94.
42. Ther, *Die neue Ordnung*, 97.
43. Padraic Kenney, *The Burdens of Freedom: Eastern Europe since 1989* (London, 2006).
44. Andreas Wirsching, *Der Preis der Freiheit: Geschichte Europas in unserer Zeit* (Munich, 2012).
45. See, for example, Mark Mazower, *Dark Continent: Europe's Twentieth Century* (New York, 1999); Harold James, *Europe Reborn: A History 1914–2001* (New York, 2003); Eric Hobsbawm, *The Age of Extremes: The Short Twentieth Century, 1914–1991* (London, 1994). Tony Judt traces connections between the East and the West most thoroughly, although he still analyzes the downfall of socialism in the COMECON states separately; see Tony Judt, *Postwar: Eastern Europe since 1945* (London, 2005).
46. Konrad H. Jarausch, *Out of Ashes: A New History of Europe in the Twentieth Century* (Princeton, 2015).
47. Jeremy Black, *Europe since the Seventies* (London, 2009).
48. See Göran Therborn, *European Modernity and Beyond: The Trajectory of European Societies 1945–2000* (London, 1995); Hartmut Kaelble, *Sozialgeschichte Europas: Die Bundesrepublik—1945 bis zur Gegenwart* (Munich, 2007).
49. Hartmut Kaelble, *Kalter Krieg und Wohlfahrtsstaat. Europa 1945–1989* (Munich, 2011), 240–41.
50. Tobias Hochscherf, Christoph Laucht, and Andrew Plowman, eds., *Divided, but Not Disconnected: German Experiences of the Cold War* (New York, 2015); Annette Vowinckel, Marcus M. Payk, and Thomas Lindenberger, eds., *Cold War Cultures: Perspectives on Eastern and Western European Societies* (Oxford, 2012).
51. Rüdiger Graf and Kim Christian Priemel, "Zeitgeschichte in der Welt der Sozialwissenschaften: Legitimität und Originalität einer Disziplin," *Vierteljahrshefte für Zeitgeschichte* 59, no. 4 (2011): 479–508.
52. For an assessment of this "Wertewandel" (value shift) in the West, see Bernhard Dietz, Christopher Neumaier, and Andreas Rödder, eds., *Gab es den Wertewandel? Neue Forschungen zum gesellschaftlich-kulturellen Wandel seit den 1960er Jahren* (Munich, 2014).
53. See Werner Weidenfeld and Hartmut Zimmermann, eds., *Deutschland-Handbuch: Eine doppelte Bilanz* (Bonn, 1989).
54. Annegret Groebel, *Strukturelle Entwicklungsmuster in Markt- und Planwirtschaften: Vergleich der sektoralen Erwerbstätigenstrukturen von BRD und DDR* (Heidelberg, 1997), 100; André Steiner, "Bundesrepublik und DDR in der Doppelkrise europäischer Industriegesellschaften. Zum sozialökonomischen

Wandel in den 1970er Jahren," *Zeithistorische Forschungen/Studies in Contemporary History* 3, no. 3 (2006): 347–48.
55. See, for example, Uta G. Poiger, *Jazz, Rock, and Rebels: Cold War Politics and American Culture in a Divided Germany* (Berkeley, 2000); Uta Andrea Balbier and Christiane Rösch, eds., *Umworbener Klassenfeind: Das Verhältnis der DDR zu den USA* (Berlin, 2006).
56. Kaelble, *Der historische Vergleich*, 127.
57. Jarausch, "'Die Teile als Ganzes erkennen.'"
58. Edgar Wolfrum, "Die Preußen-Renaissance: Geschichtspolitik im deutsch-deutschen Konflikt," in *Verwaltete Vergangenheit: Geschichtskultur und Herrschaftslegitimation in der DDR*, ed. Martin Sabrow (Leipzig, 1997), 145–66.
59. Axel Schildt, "Zwei Staaten—eine Hörfunk- und Fernsehnation: Überlegungen zur Bedeutung der elektronischen Massenmedien in der Geschichte der Kommunikation zwischen der Bundesrepublik und der DDR," in *Doppelte Zeitgeschichte*, ed. Arnd Bauerkämper, Martin Sabrow, and Bernd Stöver (Bonn, 1998), 58–71.
60. See Hanns Jürgen Küsters and Daniel Hofmann, eds., *Dokumente zur Deutschlandpolitik: Sonderedition aus den Akten des Bundeskanzleramtes 1989/90* (Munich, 1998), 40.
61. See Martin Sabrow, "Der Streit um die Verständigung: Die deutsch-deutschen Zeithistorikergespräche in den achtziger Jahren," in *Doppelte Zeitgeschichte*, ed. Arnd Bauerkämper, Martin Sabrow, and Bernd Stöver (Bonn, 1998), 113–30.
62. Wirsching, "Für eine pragmatische Zeitgeschichtsforschung," 13–18.
63. Jarausch, *Die Umkehr*, 286. It has also been argued that this sense of "we" first emerged with the nostalgic "Ostalgie" of the 1990s: Thomas Ahbe, "'Ostalgie' als eine Laien-Praxis in Ostdeutschland: Ursachen, psychische und politische Dimensionen," in *Die DDR in Deutschland: Ein Rückblick auf 50 Jahre*, ed. Heiner Timmermann (Berlin, 2001), 781–802.
64. Thomas Großbölting, "Geteilter Himmel: Wahrnehmungsgeschichte der Zweistaatlichkeit," *Aus Politik und Zeitgeschichte* 1–3 (2012): 21.
65. Bender, *Deutschlands Wiederkehr*, 204.
66. On the closely interwoven relationship between East and West Berlin in the beginning, see Michael Lemke, *Vor der Mauer: Berlin in der Ost-West-Konkurrenz 1948 bis 1961* (Cologne, 2011).
67. Hobsbawm, *Age*, 403.
68. Doering-Manteuffel and Raphael, *Nach dem Boom*.
69. Niall Ferguson et al., eds., *The Shock of the Global: The 1970s in Perspective* (Cambridge, MA, 2010).
70. See Thomas Raithel, Andreas Rödder, and Andreas Wirsching, eds., *Auf dem Weg in eine neue Moderne? Die Bundesrepublik Deutschland in den siebziger und achtziger Jahren* (Munich, 2009); Martin Geyer, "Rahmenbedingungen: Unsicherheit als Normalität," in *Geschichte der Sozialpolitik in Deutschland seit 1945*, ed. Martin Geyer (Baden-Baden, 2008), 6: 1–107.

71. Therborn, *European Modernity and Beyond*, 351; see also Hartmut Kaelble, *The 1970s in Europe: A Period of Disillusionment or Promise?* (London, 2010), 18.
72. See David Harvey, *A Brief History of Neoliberalism* (Oxford, 2005), 1.
73. See Ulrich Herbert, "Europe in High Modernity: Reflections on a Theory of the 20th Century," *Journal of Modern European History* 5, no. 1 (2007): 5–20. For a perspective that excludes the East, see also Thomas Großbölting, Massimiliano Livi, and Carlo Spagnolo, eds., *Jenseits der Moderne? Die siebziger Jahre als Gegenstand der deutschen und der italienischen Geschichtswissenschaft* (Berlin, 2014).
74. Stefan Plaggenborg, "Schweigen ist Gold. Die Modernetheorie und der Kommunismus," *Osteuropa* 63 (2013): 74.
75. Lutz Raphael, "Das Konzept der 'Moderne.' Neue Vergleichsperspektiven für die deutsch-italienische Zeitgeschichte?," in *Jenseits der Moderne? Die siebziger Jahre als Gegenstand der deutschen und der italienischen Geschichtswissenschaft*, ed. Thomas Großbölting, Massimiliano Livi, and Carlo Spagnolo (Berlin, 2014), 95–109.
76. See the essays in Frank Bösch and Rüdiger Graf, eds., "The Energy Crises of the 1970s: Anticipations and Reactions in the Industrialized World," special issue, *Historical Social Research* 39, no. 4 (2014), 1–292.
77. On these two interpretations, see Frank Bösch, "Zweierlei Krisendeutungen: Amerikanische und bundesdeutsche Perspektiven auf die 1970er Jahre," *Neue Politische Literatur* 58, no. 2 (2013): 217–30; Martin Geyer, "Auf der Suche nach der Gegenwart: Neue Arbeiten zur Geschichte der 1970er und 1980er Jahre," *Archiv für Sozialgeschichte* 50 (2010): 643–69. See also "The 1970s and 1980s as a Turning Point in European History?," *Journal of Modern European History* 9, no. 1 (2011): 8–26.
78. Frank Bösch, "Boom zwischen Krise und Globalisierung: Konsum und kultureller Wandel in der Bundesrepublik der 1970er und 1980er Jahre," *Geschichte und Gesellschaft* 42, no. 2 (2016): 354–76.
79. See Andreas Malycha, *Die SED in der Ära Honecker: Machtstrukturen, Entscheidungsmechanismen und Konfliktfelder in der Staatspartei 1971 bis 1989* (Munich, 2014), 177–256.
80. See, for example, Claudia Lepp and Kurt Nowak, eds., *Evangelische Kirche im geteilten Deutschland (1945–1989/90)* (Göttingen, 2001).
81. This is emphasized in Anja Hanisch, *Die DDR im KSZE-Prozess 1972–1985: Zwischen Ostabhängigkeit, Westabgrenzung und Ausreisebewegung* (Munich, 2012). For an international comparison, see Helmut Altrichter and Hermann Wentker, eds., *Der KSZE-Prozess: Vom Kalten Krieg zu einem neuen Europa 1975 bis 1990* (Munich, 2011).
82. Schroeder, *Der SED-Staat*, 853–74.
83. Monika Sigmund, *Genuss als Politikum: Kaffeekonsum in beiden deutschen Staaten* (Berlin, 2015).
84. André Steiner has already pointed to a "Growth Crisis of 1969/70." See An-

dré Steiner, *The Plan that Failed: An Economic History of the GDR* (New York, 2010), 132.
85. Peter Hübner, "Fortschrittskonkurrenz und Krisenkongruenz? Europäische Arbeitsgesellschaften und Sozialstaaten in den letzten Jahrzehnten des Kalten Krieges (1970–1989)," *Zeitgeschichte* 34 (2007): 144.
86. Ther, *Die neue Ordnung*, 72.
87. See André Steiner, "'Common Sense is Necessary': East German Reactions to the Oil Crises of the 1970s," *Historical Social Research* 39, no. 4 (2014): 231–50.
88. On these transactions with the West via the "KoKo," see Judt, *Der Bereich Kommerzielle Koordinierung*.
89. Werner Abelshauser, *Deutsche Wirtschaftsgeschichte: Von 1945 bis zur Gegenwart* (Bonn, 2011), 437.
90. Manfred Kittel, "Strauß' Milliardenkredit für die DDR: Leistung und Gegenleistung in den innerdeutschen Beziehungen," in *Das doppelte Deutschland: 40 Jahre Systemkonkurrenz*, ed. U. Wengst and H. Wentker (Berlin, 2008), 327.
91. Jan-Philipp Wölbern, *Der Häftlingsfreikauf aus der DDR 1962/63–1989: Zwischen Menschenhandel und humanitärer Aktion* (Göttingen, 2014).
92. Reinold Bauer, "Ölpreiskrisen und Industrieroboter: Die siebziger Jahre als Umbruchphase für die Automobilindustrie in beiden deutschen Staaten," in *Das Ende der Zuversicht? Die siebziger Jahre als Geschichte*, ed. Konrad H. Jarausch (Göttingen, 2008), 68–83.
93. Hans Mittelbach, *Entwicklungen und Umbrüche der Einkommens- und Vermögensverteilung in Ostdeutschland vor und nach der deutschen Vereinigung (1970–1994)* (Regensburg, 2005), 12.
94. Rüdiger Steinmetz and Reinhold Viehoff, eds., *Deutsches Fernsehen Ost: Eine Programmgeschichte des DDR-Fernsehens* (Berlin, 2008), 16.
95. For the most recent account, see Astrid Mignon Kirchhof, "Structural Strains und die Analyse der Umweltbewegung seit den 1960er Jahren: Ein Vergleich externer Mobilitätsbedingungen in Ost- und Westberlin," in *Theoretische Ansätze und Konzepte in der Forschung über soziale Bewegungen in der Geschichtswissenschaft*, ed. Jürgen Mittag and Helke Stadtland (Essen, 2014), 127–146.
96. Tobias Huff, "Ökonomische Modernisierung in der DDR und der Bundesrepublik Deutschland: Parallelen in der Entwicklung von Luftreinhaltung und Lärmschutz," in *Ökologische Modernisierung: Zur Geschichte und Gegenwart eines Konzepts in Umweltpolitik und Sozialwissenschaften*, ed. Martin Bemmann, Birgit Metzger, and Roderich von Detten (Frankfurt a. M., 2014), 287–313; idem, "Über die Umweltpolitik der DDR: Konzepte, Strukturen, Versagen," *Geschichte und Gesellschaft* 40, no. 4 (2014): 52–354.
97. Christoph Boyer, "Lange Entwicklungslinien europäischer Sozialpolitik im 20. Jahrhundert: Eine Annäherung," *Archiv für Sozialgeschichte* 49 (2009): 25–62.

98. Herbert Obinger and Carina Schmitt, "Guns and Butter? Regime Competition and the Welfare State during the Cold War," *World Politics* 63, no. 2 (2011): 246–70.
99. On West Germany, see Franz-Xaver Kaufmann, "Der Sozialstaat als Prozeß—für eine Sozialpolitik zweiter Ordnung," in *Verfassung: Theorie und Praxis des Sozialstaats*, ed. Franz Ruland, (Heidelberg, 1998): 307–22.
100. See Jens Gieseke, "Soziale Ungleichheit im Staatssozialismus: Eine Skizze," *Zeithistorische Forschungen/Studies in Contemporary History* 10, no. 2 (2013): 171–98.
101. Christine Pieper, "Informatik im 'dialektischen Viereck'—ein Vergleich zwischen deutsch-deutschen, amerikanischen und sowjetischen Interessen," in *Ungleiche Pfade? Innovationskulturen im deutsch-deutschen Vergleich*, ed. Uwe Fraunholz and Thomas Hänseroth (Münster, 2012), 68.
102. See Christoph Führ and Carl-Ludwig Furck, eds., *Handbuch der deutschen Bildungsgeschichte*, vol. 6, *1945 bis zur Gegenwart* (Munich, 1998).
103. On the East, for example, see Patrice Poutrus and Christian Th. Müller, eds., *Ankunft—Alltag—Ausreise: Migration und interkulturelle Begegnungen in der DDR-Gesellschaft* (Cologne, 2005).
104. For exact figures, see Rüdiger Hachtmann, *Tourismus-Geschichte* (Göttingen, 2007), 15–51.
105. See, for example, Poiger, *Jazz*.
106. Karen Hagemann, "Between Ideology and Economy: The 'Time Politics' of Child Care and Public Education in the Two Germanys," *Social Politics* 13, no. 2 (2006): 217–60; Karen Hagemann, Konrad H. Jarausch, and Cristina Allemann-Ghionda, eds., *Children, Families and States: Time Policies of Child Care, Preschool and Primary Education in Europe* (New York, 2011).
107. Ursula Schröter, "Abbruch eines Aufbruchs: Zur Frauenpolitik in der DDR," *Das Argument* 56, no. 3 (2014): 376.
108. At the moment, the term "Versicherheitlichung" (securitization) has only been used in reference to West Germany: Conze, *Die Suche nach Sicherheit*, 571.
109. Kendra Briken, "Gesellschaftliche (Be-)Deutung von Innovation," in *Kompendium Innovationsforschung*, ed. Birgit Blättel-Mink (Wiesbaden, 2006), 25, 28.
110. Manuel Schramm, *Wirtschaft und Wissenschaft in DDR und BRD: Die Kategorie Vertrauen in Innovationsprozessen* (Cologne, 2008).
111. Axel Schildt, "Politischer Aufbruch auch im Westen Deutschlands?" *Aus Politik und Zeitgeschichte* 24–26 (2014): 22–26; Martin Sabrow, "Zäsuren in der Zeitgeschichte," in *Zeitgeschichte: Konzepte und Methoden*, ed. Frank Bösch and Jürgen Danyel (Göttingen, 2012), 122.
112. Wolfgang Engler, *Die Ostdeutschen als Avantgarde* (Berlin, 2002).
113. See Jan C. Behrends, Thomas Lindenberger, and Patrice G. Poutrus, eds., *Fremde und Fremd-Sein in der DDR: Zu historischen Ursachen der Fremdenfeindlichkeit in Ostdeutschland* (Berlin, 2003).

114. Kerstin Völkl, "Überwiegt die Verdrossenheit oder die Unterstützung? Die Einstellungen der West- und Ostdeutschen zur Demokratie, zu politischen Institutionen und Politikern," in *Sind wir ein Volk?*, ed. J. Falter (Munich, 2006), 63–71; see also Kai Arzheimer, "Von 'Westalgie' und 'Zonenkindern': Die Rolle der jungen Generation im Prozess der Vereinigung," in *Sind wir ein Volk?*, ed. Jürgen Falter (Munich, 2006), 232.
115. See also Ther, *Die neue Ordnung*, 277–305. At the same time, Ther argues that, in terms of the metropolises, Warsaw reacted more effectively than Berlin.
116. Joachim Frick and Markus M. Grabka, "Die personelle Vermögensverteilung in Ost- und Westdeutschland nach dem Mauerfall," in *Leben in Ost- und Westdeutschland: Eine sozialwissenschaftliche Bilanz der deutschen Einheit 1990–2010*, ed. Peter Krause and Ilona Ostner (Frankfurt a. M., 2010), 509.
117. See the current statistics from the DOSB (German Olympic Sports Confederation). Retrieved from http://www.dosb.de/de/service/download-center/statistiken.
118. "Deutschland im Fitnesswahn," in *Die Welt*, 13 January 2013.
119. Peter Krause and Ilona Ostner, "Einleitung: Was zusammengehört. . . Eine sozialwissenschaftliche Bilanzierung des Vereinigungsprozesses," in *Leben in Ost- und Westdeutschland: Eine sozialwissenschaftliche Bilanz der deutschen Einheit 1990–2010*, ed. Peter Krause and Ilona Ostner (Frankfurt a. M., 2010), 16–18.
120. Ralph Bollmann, "Das ferne Land: Zur Historisierung der alten Bundesrepublik," *Merkur* 69, no. 5 (2015): 17–28.

BIBLIOGRAPHY

Abelshauser, Werner. *Deutsche Wirtschaftsgeschichte: Von 1945 bis zur Gegenwart*. Bonn: Bundeszentrale für politische Bildung, 2011.

Altrichter, Helmut, and Hermann Wentker, eds. *Der KSZE-Prozess: Vom Kalten Krieg zu einem neuen Europa 1975 bis 1990*. Munich: Oldenbourg, 2011.

Ahbe, Thomas. "'Ostalgie' als eine Laien-Praxis in Ostdeutschland: Ursachen, psychische und politische Dimensionen." In *Die DDR in Deutschland: Ein Rückblick auf 50 Jahre*, edited by Heiner Timmermann, 781–802. Berlin: Duncker & Humblot, 2001.

Apelt, Andreas, Robert Grünbaum, and Jens Schöne, eds. *2 x Deutschland: Innerdeutsche Beziehungen 1972–1990*. Halle: Mitteldeutscher Verlag, 2013.

Arzheimer, Kai. "Von 'Westalgie' und 'Zonenkindern': Die Rolle der jungen Generation im Prozess der Vereinigung." In *Sind wir ein Volk?*, edited by Jürgen W. Falter, 212–34. Munich: Beck, 2006.

Balbier, Uta A. *Kalter Krieg auf der Aschenbahn: Deutsch-deutscher Sport 1950–72. Eine politische Geschichte*. Paderborn: Schöningh, 2007.

Balbier, Uta A., and Christiane Rösch, eds. *Umworbener Klassenfeind. Das Verhältnis der DDR zu den USA.* Berlin: Links, 2006.

Bauer, Reinold. "Ölpreiskrisen und Industrieroboter: Die siebziger Jahre als Umbruchphase für die Automobilindustrie in beiden deutschen Staaten." In *Das Ende der Zuversicht? Die siebziger Jahre als Geschichte,* edited by Konrad H. Jarausch, 68–83. Göttingen: Vandenhoek & Ruprecht, 2008.

Bauerkämper, Arnd, Martin Sabrow, and Bernd Stöver, eds. *Doppelte Zeitgeschichte: Deutsch-deutsche Beziehungen 1945–1990.* Bonn: Dietz, 1998.

Beichelt, T. "Verkannte Parallelen: Transformationsforschung und Europastudien." *Osteuropa* 63 (2013): 277–94.

Behrends, Jan C., Thomas Lindenberger, and Patrick G. Poutrus, eds. *Fremde und Fremd-Sein in der DDR: Zu historischen Ursachen der Fremdenfeindlichkeit in Ostdeutschland.* Berlin: Metropol, 2003.

Best, Heinrich, and Everhard Holtmann, eds. *Aufbruch der entsicherten Gesellschaft: Deutschland nach der Wiedervereinigung.* Frankfurt a. M.: Campus, 2012.

Black, Jeremy. *Europe since the Seventies.* London: Reaktion Books, 2009.

Bollmann, Ralph. "Das ferne Land: Zur Historisierung der alten Bundesrepublik." *Merkur* 69 (2015): 17–28.

Bösch, Frank. "Boom zwischen Krise und Globalisierung: Konsum und kultureller Wandel in der Bundesrepublik der 1970er und 1980er Jahre." *Geschichte und Gesellschaft* 42 (2016): 354–76.

———. "Zweierlei Krisendeutungen: Amerikanische und bundesdeutsche Perspektiven auf die 1970er Jahre." *Neue Politische Literatur* 58 (2013): 217–30.

———, ed. *Geteilte Geschichte: Ost- und Westdeutschland 1970–2000.* Göttingen: Vandenhoeck & Ruprecht, 2015.

Bösch, Frank, and Rüdiger Graf, eds. "The Energy Crises of the 1970s: Anticipations and Reactions in the Industrialized World." Special issue, *Historical Social Research* 39 (2014): 1–292.

Boyer, Christoph. "Lange Entwicklungslinien europäischer Sozialpolitik im 20. Jahrhundert: Eine Annäherung." *Archiv für Sozialgeschichte* 49 (2009): 25–62.

Biess, Frank. *Homecomings: Returning POWs and the Legacies of Defeat in Postwar Germany.* Princeton: Princeton University Press, 2006.

Budde, Gunilla, Sebastian Conrad, and Oliver Janz, eds. *Transnationale Geschichte: Themen, Tendenzen und Theorien.* Frankfurt a. M.: Vandenhoeck & Ruprecht, 2010.

Briken, Kendra. "Gesellschaftliche (Be-)Deutung von Innovation." In *Kompendium Innovationsforschung,* edited by Birgit Blättel-Mink, 17–28. Wiesbaden: Springer, 2006.

Brunner, Detlev, Udo Grashoff, and Andreas Kötzing, eds. *Asymmetrisch verflochten? Neue Forschungen zur gesamtdeutschen Nachkriegsgeschichte.* Berlin: Links, 2013.

Conze, Eckart. *Die Suche nach Sicherheit: Eine Geschichte der Bundesrepublik Deutschland.* Berlin: Siedler, 2009.

Dietz, Bernhard, Christopher Neumaier, and Andreas Rödder, eds. *Gab es den Wertewandel? Neue Forschungen zum gesellschaftlich-kulturellen Wandel seit den 1960er Jahren.* Munich: Oldenbourg, 2014.

Doering-Manteuffel, Anselm, and Lutz Raphael, eds. *Nach dem Boom: Perspektiven auf die Zeitgeschichte seit 1970.* Göttingen: Vandenhoek & Ruprecht, 2010.

Engler, Wolfgang. *Die Ostdeutschen als Avantgarde.* Berlin: Aufbau, 2002.

Ferguson, Niall, Charles S. Maier, Eriz Manela, and Daniel J. Sargent, eds. *The Shock of the Global: The 1970s in Perspective.* Cambridge, MA: Harvard University Press, 2010.

Fulbrook, Mary. *Interpretations of the Two Germanies, 1945–1990.* New York: St. Martin's Press, 2000.

Führ, Christoph, and Carl-Ludwig Furck, eds. *Handbuch der deutschen Bildungsgeschichte.* Vol. 6, *1945 bis zur Gegenwart.* Munich: Beck, 1998.

Gajek, Eva. *Imagepolitik im olympischen Wettstreit: Die Spiele von Rom 1960 und München 1972.* Göttingen: Wallstein, 2013.

Geyer, Martin. "Rahmenbedingungen: Unsicherheit als Normalität." In *Geschichte der Sozialpolitik in Deutschland seit 1945*, edited by Martin Geyer, 6: 1–107. Baden-Baden: Nomos, 2008.

Gieseke, Jens. "Soziale Ungleichheit im Staatssozialismus: Eine Skizze." *Zeithistorische Forschungen/Studies in Contemporary History* 10 (2013): 171–98.

Glaab, Manuela, Werner Weidenfeld, and Michael Weigl, eds. *Deutsche Kontraste 1990–2010: Politik—Wirtschaft—Gesellschaft—Kultur.* Frankfurt a. M.: Campus, 2010.

Görtemaker, Manfred. *Geschichte der Bundesrepublik Deutschland: Von der Gründung bis zur Gegenwart,* Munich: C.H. Beck, 1999.

Graf, Rüdiger, and Kim Christian Priemel. "Zeitgeschichte in der Welt der Sozialwissenschaften: Legitimität und Originalität einer Disziplin." *Vierteljahrshefte für Zeitgeschichte* 59 (2011): 479–508.

Groebel, Annegret. *Strukturelle Entwicklungsmuster in Markt- und Planwirtschaften: Vergleich der sektoralen Erwerbstätigenstrukturen von BRD und DDR.* Heidelberg: Physica Verlag, 1997.

Großbölting, Thomas. "Geteilter Himmel: Wahrnehmungsgeschichte der Zweistaatlichkeit." *Aus Politik und Zeitgeschichte* 1–3 (2012): 15–22.

Großbölting, Thomas, Massimiliano Livi, and Carlo Spagnolo, eds. *Jenseits der Moderne? Die siebziger Jahre als Gegenstand der deutschen und der italienischen Geschichtswissenschaft.* Berlin: Duncker & Humblot, 2014.

Hachtmann, Rüdiger. *Tourismus-Geschichte.* Göttingen: Vandenhoek und Ruprecht, 2007.

Hagemann, Karen. "Between Ideology and Economy: The 'Time Politics' of Child Care and Public Education in the Two Germanys." *Social Politics* 13 (2006): 217–60.

Hagemann, Karen, Konrad H. Jarausch, and Cristina Allemann-Ghionda, eds. *Children, Families and States: Time Policies of Child Care, Preschool and Primary Education in Europe.* New York: Berghahn, 2011.

Hanisch, Anja. *Die DDR im KSZE-Prozess 1972–1985: Zwischen Ostabhängigkeit, Westabgrenzung und Ausreisebewegung.* Munich: Oldenbourg, 2012.
Harvey, David. *A Brief History of Neoliberalism.* Oxford: Oxford University Press, 2005.
Herbert, Ulrich. "Europe in High Modernity: Reflections on a Theory of the 20th Century." *Journal of Modern European History* 5 (2007): 5–20.
———. *Geschichte Deutschlands im 20. Jahrhundert.* Munich: Beck, 2014.
Herf, Jeffrey. *Divided Memory: The Nazi Past in the Two Germanys.* Cambridge, MA: Harvard University Press, 1997.
Hertle, Hans-Hermann, and Stefan Wolle. *Damals in der DDR.* Munich: Goldmann, 2006.
Herzog, Dagmar. *Sex after Fascism: Memory and Morality in Twentieth-Century Germany.* Princeton: Princeton University Press, 2005.
Hobsbawm, Eric. *The Age of Extremes: The Short Twentieth Century, 1914–1991.* London: Michael Joseph, 1994.
Hochscherf, Tobias, Christoph Laucht, and Andrew Plowman, eds. *Divided, but Not Disconnected: German Experiences of the Cold War.* New York: Berghahn, 2010.
Hoffmann, Dierk, Hermann Wentker, and Michael Schwartz. "Die DDR als Chance: Neue Perspektiven künftiger Forschung." In *Die DDR als Chance: neue Perspektiven auf ein altes Thema,* edited by Ulrich Mählert, 23–70. Berlin: Metropol, 2016,
Hübner, Peter. "Fortschrittskonkurrenz und Krisenkongruenz? Europäische Arbeitsgesellschaften und Sozialstaaten in den letzten Jahrzehnten des Kalten Krieges (1970–1989)." *Vierteljahreshefte für Zeitgeschichte* 34 (2007): 144–55.
Huff, Tobias. "Ökonomische Modernisierung in der DDR und der Bundesrepublik Deutschland: Parallelen in der Entwicklung von Luftreinhaltung und Lärmschutz." In *Ökologische Modernisierung: Zur Geschichte und Gegenwart eines Konzepts in Umweltpolitik und Sozialwissenschaften,* edited by Martin Bemmann, Birgit Metzger, and Roderich von Detten, 287–313. Frankfurt a. M.: Campus, 2014.
———. "Über die Umweltpolitik der DDR. Konzepte, Strukturen, Versagen." *Geschichte und Gesellschaft* 40 (2014): 523–54.
Jarausch, Konrad H. *After Hitler: Recivilizing the Germans 1945–1995.* New York: Oxford University Press, 2006.
———. "'Die Teile als Ganzes erkennen': Zur Integration der beiden deutschen Nachkriegsgeschichten." *Zeithistorische Forschungen/Studies in Contemporary History* 1 (2004): 10–30.
———. *Out of Ashes: A New History of Europe in the Twentieth Century.* Princeton: Princeton University Press, 2015.
Jarausch, Konrad H., and Michael Geyer. *Shattered Past: Reconstructing German Histories.* Princeton: Princeton University Press, 2003.
Judt, Matthias. *Der Bereich Kommerzielle Koordinierung: Das DDR-Wirtschafts-*

imperium des Alexander Schalck-Golodkowski—Mythos und Realität. Berlin: Links, 2013.

Judt, Tony. *Postwar: A History of Europe since 1945.* London: Heinemann, 2005.

Kaelble, Hartmut. *Kalter Krieg und Wohlfahrtsstaat: Europa 1945–1989.* Munich: Beck, 2011.

———. *The 1970s in Europe: A Period of Disillusionment or Promise?* London: German Historical Institute London, 2010.

Kaufmann, Franz-Xaver. "Der Sozialstaat als Prozeß—für eine Sozialpolitik zweiter Ordnung." In *Verfassung, Theorie und Praxis des Sozialstaats,* edited by Franz Ruland, 307–22. Heidelberg: Müller, 1998.

Kenney, Padraic. *Burdens of Freedom: Eastern Europe since 1989.* London: Fernwood, 2006.

Kielmansegg, Graf Peter. *Das geteilte Land: Deutsche Geschichte 1945–1990.* Munich: Bassermann, 2004.

Kirchof, Astrid Mignon. "Structural Strains und die Analyse der Umweltbewegung seit den 1960er Jahren: Ein Vergleich externer Mobilitätsbedingungen in Ost- und Westberlin." In *Theoretische Ansätze und Konzepte in der Forschung über soziale Bewegungen in der Geschichtswissenschaft,* edited by Jürgen Mittag and Helke Stadtland, 127–46. Essen: Klartext-Verlag, 2014.

Kittel, Manfred. "Strauß Milliardenkredit für die DDR: Leistung und Gegenleistung in den innerdeutschen Beziehungen." In *Das doppelte Deutschland: 40 Jahre Systemkonkurrenz,* edited by Udo Wengst and Hermann Wentker, 307–332. Berlin: Bundeszentrale für politische Bildung, 2008.

Kleßmann, Christoph. *Die doppelte Staatsgründung: Deutsche Geschichte 1945–1955.* Göttingen: Vandenhoeck & Ruprecht, 1982.

———. "Spaltung und Verflechtung—Ein Konzept zur integrierten Nachkriegsgeschichte 1945 bis 1990." In *Teilung und Integration: Die doppelte deutsche Nachkriegsgeschichte als wissenschaftliches und didaktisches Problem,* edited by Christoph Kleßmann and Peter Lautzas, 20–37. Schwalbach: Wochenschau-Verlag, 2006.

———. "Verflechtung und Abgrenzung: Aspekte der geteilten und zusammengehörigen deutschen Nachkriegsgeschichte." *Aus Politik und Zeitgeschichte* 29–30 (1993): 30–41.

———. *Zwei Staaten, eine Nation: Deutsche Geschichte 1955–1970.* 2nd ed. Bonn: Vandenhoeck & Ruprecht, 1997.

Kleßmann, Christoph, and Peter Lautzas, eds. *Teilung und Integration: Die doppelte deutsche Nachkriegsgeschichte als wissenschaftliches und didaktisches Problem.* Schwalbach: Wochenschau-Verlag, 2006.

Kollmorgen, Raj. *Ostdeutschland: Beobachtungen einer Übergangs- und Teilgesellschaft.* Wiesbaden: Verlag für Sozialwissenschaften, 2005.

Krause, Peter, and Ilona Ostner, eds. *Leben in Ost- und Westdeutschland: Eine sozialwissenschaftliche Bilanz der deutschen Einheit 1990–2010.* Frankfurt a. M.: Campus, 2010.

Kretschmann, Carsten. *Zwischen Spaltung und Gemeinsamkeit: Kultur im geteilten Deutschland*. Bonn: Bundeszentrale für politische Bildung, 2012.

Lemke, Michael. *Vor der Mauer: Berlin in der Ost-West-Konkurrenz 1948 bis 1961*. Cologne: Böhlau, 2011.

Lepp, Claudia, and Kurt Nowak, eds. *Evangelische Kirche im geteilten Deutschland (1945–1989/90)*. Göttingen: Vandenhoeck & Ruprecht, 2001.

Lindenberger, Thomas. "'Zonenrand,' 'Sperrgebiet' und 'Westberlin'—Deutschland als Grenzregion des Kalten Kriegs." In *Teilung und Integration: Die doppelte deutsche Nachkriegsgeschichte als wissenschaftliches und didaktisches Problem*, edited by Christoph Kleßmann and Peter Lautzas, 97–112, Schwalbach: Wochenschau-Verlag, 2006.

Lorke, Christoph, and Thomas Großbölting, eds. *Deutschland seit 1990: Wege in die Vereinigungsgesellschaft*. Stuttgart: Steiner, 2017.

Malycha, Andreas. *Die SED in der Ära Honecker: Machtstrukturen, Entscheidungsmechanismen und Konfliktfelder in der Staatspartei 1971 bis 1989*. Munich: De Gruyter Oldenbourg, 2014.

Mählert, Ulich. *Kleine Geschichte der DDR*. 6th ed. Munich: Beck, 2009.

Mazower, Mark. *Dark Continent: Europe's Twentieth Century*. 4th ed. New York: Knopf, 1999.

Mittelbach, Hans. *Entwicklungen und Umbrüche der Einkommens- und Vermögensverteilung in Ostdeutschland vor und nach der deutschen Vereinigung (1970–1994)*. Regensburg: Transfer Regensburg, 2005.

Möller, Horst. "Demokratie und Diktatur." *Aus Politik und Zeitgeschichte* 3 (2007): 3–7.

Naumann, Klaus. "Die Historisierung der Bonner Republik: Zeitgeschichtsschreibung in zeitdiagnostischer Absicht." *Mittelweg 36*, no. 9 (2000): 53–67.

Obinger, Herbert, and Carina Schmitt. "Guns and Butter? Regime Competition and the Welfare State during the Cold War." *World Politics* 63 (2011): 246–70.

Plaggenborg, Stefan. "Schweigen ist Gold: Die Modernetheorie und der Kommunismus." *Osteuropa* 63 (2013): 65–78.

Poiger, Uta G. *Jazz, Rock, and Rebels: Cold War Politics and American Culture in a Divided Germany*. Berkeley: University of California Press, 2000.

Poutrus, Patrice, and Christian Th. Müller, eds. *Ankunft—Alltag—Ausreise: Migration und interkulturelle Begegnungen in der DDR-Gesellschaft*. Cologne: Böhlau, 2005.

Raithel, Thomas, and Thomas Schlemmer, eds. *Die Anfänge der Gegenwart: Umbrüche in Westeuropa nach dem Boom*. Munich: Oldenbourg, 2014.

Raithel, Thomas, Andreas Rödder, and Andreas Wirsching, eds. *Auf dem Weg in eine neue Moderne? Die Bundesrepublik Deutschland in den siebziger und achtziger Jahren*. Munich: Oldenbourg, 2009.

Raphael, Lutz. "Das Konzept der 'Moderne.' Neue Vergleichsperspektiven für die deutsch-italienische Zeitgeschichte?" In *Jenseits der Moderne? Die siebziger Jahre als Gegenstand der deutschen und der italienischen Geschichtswissen-*

schaft, edited by Thomas Großbölting, Massimiliano Livi, and Carlo Spagnolo, 95–109. Berlin: Duncker & Humblot, 2014.

Roesler, Jörg. *Momente deutsch—deutscher Wirtschafts- und Sozialgeschichte 1945 bis 1990: Eine Analyse auf gleicher Augenhöhe*. Leipzig: Leipziger Universitäts Verlag, 2006.

Roth, Margit. *Innerdeutsche Bestandsaufnahme der Bundesrepublik 1969–1989: Neue Deutung*. Wiesbaden: Springer, 2014.

Sabrow, Martin. "Der Streit um die Verständigung: Die deutsch-deutschen Zeithistorikergespräche in den achtziger Jahren." In *Doppelte Zeitgeschichte*, edited by Arnd Bauerkämper, Martin Sabrow, and Bernd Stöver, 113–30. Bonn: Dietz, 1998.

———. "Historisierung der Zweistaatlichkeit." *Aus Politik und Zeitgeschichte* 3 (2007): 19–24.

Schildt, Axel. "Politischer Aufbruch auch im Westen Deutschlands?" *Aus Politik und Zeitgeschichte* 24–26 (2014): 22–26.

———. "Zwei Staaten—eine Hörfunk- und Fernsehnation: Überlegungen zur Bedeutung der elektronischen Massenmedien in der Geschichte der Kommunikation zwischen der Bundesrepublik und der DDR." In *Doppelte Zeitgeschichte*, edited by Arnd Bauerkämper, Martin Sabrow, and Bernd Stöver, 58–71. Bonn: Dietz, 1998.

Schildt, Axel, and Detlef Siegfried. *Deutsche Kulturgeschichte: Die Bundesrepublik von 1945 bis zur Gegenwart*. Munich: Carl Hanser Verlag, 2009.

Schönfelder, Jan, and Rainer Erices. *Willy Brandt in Erfurt. Das erste deutsch-deutsche Gipfeltreffen 1970*. Berlin: Links, 2010.

Schramm, Manuel. *Wirtschaft und Wissenschaft in DDR und BRD: Die Kategorie Vertrauen in Innovationsprozessen*. Cologne: Böhlau, 2008.

Schroeder, Klaus. *Der SED-Staat: Geschichte und Strukturen der DDR 1949–1990*. Cologne: Böhlau, 2013.

Schröter, Ursula. "Abbruch eines Aufbruchs. Zur Frauenpolitik in der DDR." *Das Argument* 56 (2014): 376–86.

Sigmund, Monika. *Genuss als Politikum. Kaffeekonsum in beiden deutschen Staaten*. Berlin: De Gruyter Oldenbourg, 2015.

Steiner, André. "Bundesrepublik und DDR in der Doppelkrise europäischer Industriegesellschaften: Zum sozialökonomischen Wandel in den 1970er Jahren." *Zeithistorische Forschungen/Studies in Contemporary History* 3 (2006): 342–62.

———. "'Common Sense is Necessary': East German Reactions to the Oil Crises of the 1970s." *Historical Social Research* 39 (2014): 231–50.

———. *The Plans That Failed: An Economic History of the GDR*. New York: Berghahn, 2010.

Steinmetz, Rüdiger, and Reinhold Viehoff, eds. *Deutsches Fernsehen Ost: Eine Programmgeschichte des DDR-Fernsehens*. Berlin: VBB, 2008.

Spitzer, Giselher. "Doping in Deutschland von 1950 bis heute aus historisch-soziologischer Sicht im Kontext ethischer Legitimation." Bundesinstitut für

Sportwissenschaft. 30 March 2013. Retreived 24 May 2018, http://www
.bisp.de/SharedDocs/Downloads/Aktuelles/Inhaltlicher_Bericht_HU.pdf?
__blob=publicationFile&v=1.
Therborn, Göran. *European Modernity and Beyond: The Trajectory of European Societies 1945–2000*. London: Sage, 1995.
Ther, Philipp. *Die neue Ordnung auf dem alten Kontinent: Eine Geschichte des neoliberalen Europas*. Frankfurt a. M.: Campus, 2014.
Vowinckel, Annette, Marcus M. Payk, and Thomas Lindenberger, eds. *Cold War Cultures: Perspectives on Eastern and Western European Societies*. Oxford: Berghahn, 2012.
Völkl, Kerstin. "Überwiegt die Verdrossenheit oder die Unterstützung? Die Einstellungen der West- und Ostdeutschen zur Demokratie, zu politischen Institutionen und Politikern." In *Sind wir ein Volk?*, edited by Jürgen W. Falter, 57–81, Munich: Beck 2006.
Wehler, Hans-Ulrich. *Deutsche Gesellschaftsgeschichte*. Vol. 5, *Bundesrepublik und DDR*. Munich: Beck, 2008.
Weidenfeld, Werner, and Hartmut Zimmermann, eds. *Deutschland-Handbuch: Eine doppelte Bilanz*. Bonn: Bundeszentrale für politische Bildung, 1989.
Wengst, Udo, and Hermann Wentker. "Einleitung." In *Das doppelte Deutschland: 40 Jahre Systemkonkurrenz*, edited by Udo Wengst and Hermann Wentker, 7–14. Berlin: Bundeszentrale für politische Bildung, 2008.
Wirsching, Andreas. *Der Preis der Freiheit: Geschichte Europas in unserer Zeit*. Munich: Beck, 2012.
———. "Für eine pragmatische Zeitgeschichtsforschung." *Aus Politik und Zeitgeschichte* 3 (2007): 13–18.
Wolfrum, Edgar. "Die Preußen-Renaissance: Geschichtspolitik im deutsch-deutschen Konflikt." In *Verwaltete Vergangenheit: Geschichtskultur und Herrschaftslegitimation in der DDR*, edited by Martin Sabrow, 145–66. Leipzig: Akademie Verlag, 1997.
———. *Geglückte Demokratie: Geschichte der Bundesrepublik Deutschland von ihren Anfängen bis zur Gegenwart*. Munich: Klett-Cotta, 2007.
Wölbern, Jan-Philipp. *Der Häftlingsfreikauf aus der DDR 1962/63–1989: Zwischen Menschenhandel und humanitärer Aktion*. Göttingen: Vandenhoek & Ruprecht, 2014.

CHAPTER 1

Political Transformations in East and West

Frank Bösch and Jens Gieseke

The political systems in East and West Germany were very different up to 1989. Consequently, it is not surprising that "politics" itself or even what was actually considered to be political varied across the border. Not only institutions and laws, but also the informal rules behind the game of politics were not the same. Political statements, especially those tinged with criticism or protest, were embedded within very distinct frameworks and bore specific implications. In the West, political debates were increasingly seen as indicative of a thriving democracy. In the East, however, prior to 1989 they were either carefully orchestrated from above or associated with risks for everyone involved because jobs, access to a university education, or even prison sentences could hang in the balance. Organizations such as political parties, unions, or solidarity groups may have borne similar names on either side of the Iron Curtain, but something completely different was often hiding behind them. Consequently, even terms such as "political culture" do not seem to apply in the same way in both contexts. The same also holds true for political communication, which functioned very differently in a democracy that guaranteed freedom of expression than in a society in which censorship and the media were mostly held under the thumb of the Politburo. Indeed, just how limited political maneuverability was in the German Democratic Republic—even compared to other socialist states—can be clearly seen in the case of its next-door neighbor Poland, where protests and a strong samizdat press managed to carve out a multivalent, albeit illegal, space for political discourse.

Given this backdrop, it comes as no surprise that the very nature of politics itself also changed in quite divergent ways in West and East Germany. The Federal Republic of Germany experienced a succession of shifts, beginning with a liberalization of political culture in the early 1960s. The more radical protests of the student movement followed on its heels, which in turn fed into a broader political mobilization of the population in the 1970s and early 1980s that manifested itself in civic movements, public demonstrations, and a spike in political party membership. However, this general transformation of social ideals and political goals, as well as the emergence of new topics alongside alternative forms of political participation and decision-making processes, generally took place within the existing institutional framework; of course, a few groups did indeed challenge the system as a whole and reject its premises. The situation in the GDR was different altogether because the incredibly static institutional order of the Communist regime first collapsed in the face of mass protests and the introduction of democracy at a much later point. Quite obviously, none of the political upheavals in the Federal Republic cut as deeply into the core of politics than this transformation in the East. Paradoxically, the Bonn Republic was actually utterly unprepared for this development when it came, despite all the talk about its constitutional and political commitment to reunification.

Given these fundamental distinctions, it seems rather senseless to compare the systems of government in both Germanys. However, it does make all the more sense to approach these political transformations from a social history perspective as part of a *geteilte Geschichte* of differences and interaction. A number of political phenomena lend themselves well to such a framework, including the growth of political discourses; the long-term dynamics of democratization, politicization, and depoliticization; and the political impact of overarching trends in late twentieth century industrial societies, such as educational expansion, reactions to economic crises, and environmental critiques of civilization. In the 1970s and 1980s, both Germanys experienced changes within these areas that manifested themselves in new forms of protest or waves of politicization. Examining these longer trajectories can also help explain the outbreak of protests around 1980 in the West and the seemingly sudden political eruption of 1989 in the East. Likewise, they help account for the mutual adaptations and differences in political culture that were also asymmetrically distributed.

With its broader approach to politics and what constitutes the political, this article consciously deviates from the focus on state (i.e., government) politics typical of the many studies that trace decision-making processes, analyze German-German politics, or investigate reunification as a political process. It defines "politics" as a communicative space—as an arena of social conflicts in which power and rules are negotiated.[1] Furthermore, by directing its gaze toward political culture, it outlines subjective political opinions and values that existed among the general population, which were well-documented by opinion polls in the West. As such an observation technique was rarely used in the East, reports on popular moods and microhistory studies help fill in the gaps.[2] The intent here is not to write a "political history with the politics left out" as many have cautioned against.[3] Rather, even if politics is narrowly defined as the establishment of collectively binding rules, its scope certainly extends beyond the level of legislation and state power to include broader public discourses and the legitimization of rule. Up until the very end, the Socialist Unity Party of Germany (SED) apparently saw "the people" as a homogeneous mass that shared the party's views. This identity had to be reinforced through the regular, choice-less "elections" or parades on holidays, and it shaped all political communication in the public sphere.[4] The regime rationalized the appearance of differences between the intended and actual attitudes of the populace by assigning the party propaganda machine the task of eliminating any such so-called ambiguities related to such obviously objective matters of fact.

Political Dialogues in the Age of International Communication

The political systems in East and West changed very little before the fall of the Berlin Wall. That said, however, the stronger political exchange between East and West Germany that took place at the government level beginning in 1970 cannot be overlooked. Merely the numerous official talks between government leaders attest to this intensified relationship, whether it be the meetings between Brandt and Stoph in Erfurt and Kassel in 1970 or Schmidt's GDR tour in 1981 and Honecker's visit to the FRG in 1987. These official German-German summits were accompanied by many other cross-border talks. As the West had hoped, economic relations between the two Germanys fostered a certain loosening of the political sphere in the GDR over time, although Stasi surveillance also increased accordingly. Especially the so-called billion-mark loans initiated by Franz Josef Strauß led to a few concessions on the side of the SED in 1983 that made it easier for families to be reunited, for pensioners to leave the GDR, and for travelers to cross the border.[5] Due to the wide reach of West German television, the GDR was also forced to consider popular opinion in both Germanys when it came to its foreign affairs policies.[6] The Basic Treaty of 1972 further intensified German-German interactions, primarily through the establishment of "permanent missions" (instead of embassies), and it set up the framework for later agreements and treaties.[7] All this was only made possible through the involvement of the respective alliance partners, and especially through the rapprochement between Bonn and Moscow. Undoubtedly, one of the most positive effects of these talks was the growing sense on both sides that they could count upon what had been agreed. Through this process, even SED emissaries such as Wolfgang Vogel, Hermann von Berg, or Alexander Schalck-Golodkowski became significant players. This political exchange also survived new Cold War confrontations sparked by incidents such as the NATO Double-Track Decision and the Soviet march into Afghanistan in 1979, as well as Helmut Kohl's election as chancellor—given the fact that his party had traditionally opposed *Ostpolitik*. Although this exchange was undoubtedly used by the GDR in its efforts to gain formal international recognition by other states, it definitely went beyond a merely symbolic level. Despite rather cool overtones at times, these talks nonetheless led to concrete agreements. Even the Social Democratic Party (SPD) continued its dialog with the SED after becoming the opposition party, which ultimately resulted in a joint paper in 1987 titled "Conflicting Ideologies and Common Security."[8]

Although the exchange via these dialogs increased, rapprochement was by no means a linear process. When the FRG denied Honecker's demands that it recognize GDR citizenship, accept East German embassies, agree to the Elbe as the official border between East and West Germany, and close down the registration office in Salzgitter, the GDR reacted indignantly by raising the minimum obligatory currency exchange amount for travelers to the West. In turn, Honecker also faced increased pressure from a "Moscow Faction" in the Politburo that had cautioned against rapprochement with the FRG.[9] Likewise, diplomatic talks were often plagued by quite frosty moments, such as when Helmet Kohl clearly made a plea for human rights and the right of self-determination in his toast on the occasion of Honecker's visit in 1987.[10] Nonetheless, the fundamental political trust on both sides remained intact, paving the way for the billion-mark loans as well as more official visits, which ultimately fostered political exchanges and transfers within society. Even Brandt's *Ostpolitik* raised political hopes and sparked an interest in politics among many in the GDR. But above all, this exchange carved out more space for the political opposition and those wishing to leave East Germany to express their opinions, even though the ever-expanding Stasi heightened its surveillance in return.

However, this increased political exchange cannot be attributed simply to the willingness of individual political actors to engage in such dialogs or to the economic crises that hit the GDR. Rather, rapprochement between the two Germanys was part of a number of growing cross-border political entanglements. Both German states increasingly sought international recognition as well as political, economic, and cultural relationships beyond their own borders, although it must be said that the GDR made more of an effort with less success.[11] At the beginning of the 1970s, for example, the FRG initiated diplomatic relations with neighboring communist countries, such as Poland, Hungary, and Romania, as well as China (1972), Finland (1973), and Cuba (1975). The number of international political talks, meetings, and events also climbed, and sometimes seemingly unpolitical major events such as the Olympic Games in Munich in 1972 became a space for political showmanship.[12]

The 1970s brought an increase in these types of encounters not only between East and West Germany, but also within the Cold War blocs and between the northern and southern hemispheres. In turn, this intensified the cooperation between the major Western industrialized countries who had come together to discuss current problems at venues such as the initial G6 global economic summit in 1975. The cooperative efforts within the framework of the European Economic Community (EEC) also gained momentum at the end of the 1970s, despite the fact that the first half of the 1970s had been marked by what has often been referred to as "eurosclerosis." As a result, the EEC expanded to the eastern, northern, and then the southern countries of Europe, and this cross-border cooperation was reinforced through the European Monetary System and the introduction of European elections in 1979. Similarly, cross-border contacts among the communist countries were also stepped up, even beyond the Soviet Union (USSR). The GDR, for instance, initiated talks with China as well as with the Western Eurocommunists who aimed at gaining independence from Moscow's leadership.[13] At the same time, China opened up to Western markets beginning in 1979. Both democracies and socialist states also sought to strengthen their contacts with developing countries.[14] The GDR was particularly keen to court the socialist states in Africa and Latin American, and then later the emerging countries in East Asia and major oil producers. An effort was even made to set up a state visit with the shah of Iran, who maintained friendly relations with the United States, but the overthrow of the shah in 1979 got in the way.[15] Furthermore, when the FRG cut its foreign aid to developing socialist countries such as Nicaragua, the GDR noticeably increased its solidarity contributions in return.[16] From the 1970s onward, moreover, the FRG's *Ostpolitik* and the "Westpolitik" of the GDR evolved within an international framework that was undoubtedly shaped by Cold War alliances.[17] Not surprisingly, the Organization for Security and Cooperation in Europe (OSCE) played a key role in these numerous cross-border talks. With the signing of the

Helsinki Accords, the East thus ensured the codification of the political status quo in Europe while the West was able to anchor its human rights agenda in international law.

Accordingly, the German-German political contacts made in the 1970s and 1980s can be seen as part of a growing process of cross-border political interaction and interdependence in which both German states vied for recognition. The so-called "change through trade" ("Wandel durch Handel") was therefore not specific to German-German history, but rather part of multivalent cross-border political entanglements. The long-term treaties that emerged out of these negotiations, such as the regulation of the natural gas supply from the USSR, helped to overcome tense political situations such as the one that occurred around 1980.[18] Many of these political talks ended—like German-German meetings—in disillusionment. Yet the network of cross-border relationships kept matters from escalating, and it created space for accommodation outside of the major conflict arenas. Simultaneously, this international integration relativized the importance of German-German talks because a large part of the diplomatic communication between the two Germanys ran through the respective bloc partners and neutral countries.

These talks also went hand-in-hand with an increasing social perception that the GDR and the FRG would remain separate states for the foreseeable future. Although the majority of FRG citizens saw the GDR in a mostly negative light, the 1970s saw an increase in the percentage of those in the FRG who were willing to acknowledge the East German state because of its (supposedly) more resolute anti-fascism and positive elements of its system, such as equality and education; there was also a widespread belief that a more open political sphere had been carved out in the GDR.[19] Yet, at the same time, over half of the people in the FRG indicated that they were not particularly interested in the GDR.

The focus on negotiations between states as a modus of the East-West conflict led to a disregard for nonstate actors that had far-reaching consequences. The reasons Egon Bahr cited for having disregarded the East German civil rights activists, for example, attest to this point: he claimed that he simply would not have been able to negotiate anything with Bärbel Bohley.[20] From this perspective, civil society actors "from below" seemed to interfere with the politics of negotiation. Politicians in Bonn therefore kept their distance from the Polish Solidarność movement as well as the East German civil rights activists until well into the revolution of 1989 and the accession process. Apart from a few individual politicians from the "established" parties, the Greens were the only ones who systematically went against the grain and maintained contacts with the East. Beginning in 1982, Petra Kelly, for example, visited the GDR several times a year in order to meet with civil rights activists, and she also corresponded with Honecker.[21] As most of these meetings were with prominent dissidents, however, the differing goals of the people's movement in the fall of 1989 came as quite a surprise even to politicians like Kelly.

Eventually, the GDR gained recognition at a price that Honecker thought was not too high considering the Soviet safety net. Accordingly, the GDR became involved in the Western discourse on human rights; it moved toward growing economic independence; and it came to terms with the Westernization of its society as a whole. The SED leadership was well aware of the risks associated with these moves. Consequently, it strengthened its periodic propaganda campaigns, cemented the institutions of SED rule, and grossly expanded its surveillance. It only began to moderate its confrontational tone slightly in the 1980s over the course of the billion-mark loans and the preparations for Honecker's trip to Bonn.

The reports on popular opinion prepared by the Stasi and secret Western investigations, however, continued to concur that the population of the GDR leaned toward those actors and political forms that promised more freedom and the opening of its borders. They thus enthusiastically approved of Willy Brandt's new *Ostpolitik,* but had little understanding for the NATO Double-Track Decision and the arms race of what has been referred to as the Second Cold War. For this reason, the majority of the GDR population was not opposed to the official international recognition of the GDR, but they saw their interests being championed in Bonn and not in East Berlin.[22]

German-German negotiations also left their mark on the loyal party milieu within East German society. This dialog, along with the general opening up to the West, often met with resistance within these circles, and collaboration with protagonists such as Franz-Josef Strauß, who engineered the so-called billion-mark loan, deeply demoralized this core of party support. As a result, a confrontation was brewing between those opposed to such measures and the more pragmatic circles of the GDR elite, which ultimately undermined the SED's ability to negotiate in the 1980s.

Politicization and Solidification

Scholarship has often pointed to a change in the Federal Republic in the 1970s/80s that liberalized its political culture. During this period, "authoritative" values sank while trust in the political system, as well as political interest itself, grew.[23] Konrad Jarausch has described this shift as a "recivilizing process" that took place after 1968, which he frames as a kind of "catch-up modernization" that also widened the political and cultural gap between East and West.[24] Comparative studies have pointed out that the Federal Republic of the 1980s was the most strongly politicized country in Europe, as measured according to opinion polls about political interest and rates of participation.[25] In the FRG, participation rates even topped the traditionally high rates in northern Europe and far surpassed those in France and southern Europe, although politicization was also on the march in these countries. Whereas only a student-based minority had taken to the streets in protest in 1968, millions of people joined in the protests in the 1980s. Nonetheless, around two-thirds of those up to twenty-four years of age still favored the alternative milieu.[26]

This politicization of society extended well beyond the universities and the left-wing alternative milieu in the West. As polls from the Federal Republic indicate, the general interest in politics had been rising strongly since 1965, reaching a zenith around 1983 after a small slump in 1973. The parallel climb in the popularity of daily newspapers, news magazines, and political shows on television also attest to this new kind of broad public interest in politics and critical debates. The market for political books also flourished, and not just those published by the political Left.[27] At the beginning of the 1970s, all the parties saw an increase in membership, as did the citizens' initiatives and protest groups. Voter turnout rates further underscored this shift, topping out at 91 percent for the Bundestag election in 1972 and remaining at a high level through the mid-1980s. Women in particular cast their ballots more often and began to show more political commitment. They also moved closer to the main political playing field, although they still only constituted less than 10 percent of the Bundestag.

The reasons for this shift were multifold. For one, the expansion of the educational system contributed to a rise in the number of high school graduates and students. Young people enjoyed more leisure time, as well as space, to engage in political discussions, which was coupled with more enthusiasm. Accordingly, more members of the middle class and women began to participate in the protest movements. Undoubtedly, media developments in the West also played a pivotal role. The growth of critical reporting in the press, on television, and at movie theaters in the 1960s was a socializing experience for many; a similar kind of critical reflection only appeared much later within the educational system.[28] This politicization was accompanied by a shift in attitudes and ideas that many contemporaries quickly described as a change in values. It was also linked to increasing criticism directed against existing norms and their often authoritarian character.[29] In particular, the United States functioned as both a role model and a bogeyman within this politicization process.

These basic politicization and depoliticization processes in the GDR featured a different dynamic, but they were nonetheless tightly in sync with the West. Yet there were no student riots akin to those in the West, for example, because demonstrated loyalty and conformity to the party regime were virtually indispensable for attaining high school diplomas and university degrees.[30] Furthermore, the seven universities in the GDR also lacked any kind of forum for a socially critical understanding of academics and politics.[31] As a result, the universities were by no means a hotbed of protest, not even in 1989.

According to the impressions of West Germans who visited the GDR, which were systematically assessed by Infratest, only a minority of 30 to 40 percent of GDR residents were interested in politics. This figure also included a gender gap of 10 to 20 percent between men and women.[32] Political interest reached a zenith of sorts in the early 1970s, when the largest percentage of the population basically seemed to be positively inclined toward the system and the approval rating peaked among the youth who were striving for upward mobility. However, this favorable attitude was coupled with expectations of further material improvements and political liberalization. At the same time, though, there was also strong interest in Bonn's new course of *Ostpolitik*, as well as the results of German-German negotiations that existed well beyond these circles.

Nonetheless, a decided downturn took place in these areas after 1974/75 in the GDR when Honecker swiftly tightened the political reins once again (for example, in the affair surrounding Plenzdorf's play *Die neue Leiden des jungen W.*). In terms of consumption and social policy, the mood shifted around 1976/77 as it became clear that Honecker's aspirations for the "main task" of "further improving the material and cultural standard of living of the people" in 1972 were nothing but illusions. The skeptical reactions to the Ninth Party Congress and the coffee supply crisis, as well as the general resentment against the upgrading of the Intershops, for instance, all pointed to a turn in the tide. In 1977, the Stasi spoke of an "increasing trend towards dissatisfaction." It reported that "some skeptical, pessimistic and negative opinions and even aggressive arguments" were circulating.[33] The high hopes that German-German negotiations would bring further benefits for GDR citizens in fact dissipated after the signing of the Basic Treaty and Brandt's resignation in 1974. At the same time, *Ostpolitik* had swept away ways of thinking about the two Germanys as part of one whole and dashed the prospects for policy revisions that would affect former refugees from Eastern territories.

According to the findings of the secret popular opinion assessments carried out on both sides of the Berlin Wall, this constellation remained relatively stable until about 1985. During this decade, the underlying discontent with the overall economic situation and the ongoing issues with the supply of goods, working hours, and wages increased slightly. As most citizens had the general impression that the state of affairs was quite static and immutable, they tried to keep their distance from the SED regime and stayed out of politics. At the same time, the SED spent a lot of energy trying to keep things this way. The West German polling institute Infratest, for example, estimated that a consistent 5 percent of the East German population avidly supported the regime. It categorized a further 16 to 18 percent as critical of the SED, but nonetheless still positively inclined on the whole. The majority of the population, according to Infratest, was conformist but latently dissatisfied (between 40 and 45 percent) or politically neutral (5 to 10 percent). Yet, about one in four GDR citizens described themselves as opponents of the system in private conversations.[34] As the initial postwar boom phase—driven by the enthusiastic desire to be part of the building of a new state—came to an end, the euphoric embrace of the new system and the desire to participate in politics also waned. Simultaneously, the tables had turned between East and West when it came to social mobility because improved educational opportunities in the FRG were making it easier for young West Germans from working-class families to climb the social ladder than their counterparts in the GDR.[35]

Supply failures and product shortages further heightened this discontent in the second half of the 1980s, as did the ignorant approach to information dissemination adopted by the media in the GDR as opposed to Gorbachev's *Glasnost* policies. Moreover, the wave of westward travel in 1986/87 just before Honecker's visit to Bonn dismantled many East Germans' biases against the West. By early 1989, a kind of elementary rage against the current state of affairs had built up even among those parts of the population that purportedly abstained from entering the political sphere. This marked a shift in the East German understanding of politics. At the beginning of the 1970s, a broad majority of the GDR population (regardless of the system they preferred) indicated in conversations with visitors from West Germany that they believed the GDR was a "more political" society than West Germany, which they judged to be fairly unpolitical. By the end of the 1980s, the situation was pretty much reversed.[36] Moreover, thanks in part to Gorbachev's more open policies, considerable portions of the SED party ranks entered into a phase of depoliticization or inner retreat from the principles of Communist politics.[37]

In the Federal Republic, the significance of politics increased in the 1970s because the general understanding of what was political changed. Whereas the SED more or less explicitly claimed that all aspects of society fell under the rubric of politics, many areas of life seemed to be apolitical for West Germans for a long time. By the end of the 1960s, however, this West German view of politics had begun expanding to include numerous elements of everyday life such as childcare, housing, the environment, and consumption. This shift in perception was shaped to a large extent by the rivalry between the systems, but also by the New Left, which defined the private as political and experimented with new lifestyles characterized by communal living arrangements, antiauthoritarian childcare initiatives, or alternative forms of work in self-managed enterprises.[38] Accordingly, what contemporaries judged to be political or rather a reflection of personal local interests fluctuated in both Germanys. Local initiatives to improve daycare facilities or preserve crumbling parts of a town were sometimes driven by personal interests, but at other times they invoked a community spirit that could easily become political. Moreover, any deviation from the SED party line in the GDR could turn into a political act that bore the risk of repercussions.

Generational shifts also contributed to the politicization process in East and West.[39] This was particularly true of the baby boomers of the late 1940s and 1950s, who grew up during the postwar economic upswing. In the West, for example, it was this generation that fueled the mass protests of the 1970s and 1980s. As they had come of age within a democracy, most baby boomers developed higher political expectations than their parents. In the East, some baby boomers joined the dissident groups that had begun to form a new oppositional movement in the wake of the Prague Spring. This generation no longer had any personal experience of the "great tales" of struggle and resistance within the communist movement and the early GDR. Yet, given that this generation was the main target group for the SED's social policies and consumption initiatives, it was the hardest hit when these efforts failed. From the 1970s onward, the baby boomer generation was also the most susceptible to the lure of Western capitalism. In the end, it was mostly the baby boomers who toppled the system, together with the younger 1960s generation.[40]

Traditional Political Organizations in Flux

In the Federal Republic, the politicization processes of the 1970s and 1980s are most commonly associated with the new social movements. Yet they also appeared to a similar degree within more traditional political organizations. The "old social movements" were less active in the early days of the FRG, but there were certainly mass protests in the 1950s, too.[41] When viewed from an international perspective, the level of organization of the West German unions and parties appeared to be mostly average, as was the number of strikes and the scope of the demonstrations. Traditionally, the long-standing resentments held against political parties by many citizens as well as a trust in the state accounted for this mediocrity. In the 1970s and 1980s, though, participation in political organizations and protests in the FRG had jumped to a higher level in international comparison.[42]

This shift even held true for the oldest party with the strongest membership figures, namely the SPD. The transformation of this party is often described as analogous to the chancellors it produced: whereas Brandt was seen as the embodiment of a visionary path of reform until 1973, Schmidt stood for pragmatic crisis management.[43] Given that the SPD had taken over the reins of the government for the first time, a retreat into executive authority might have been expected; but, instead, the party dynamically unfolded its wings. From the mid-1960s, its membership mushroomed by a third in just a decade, topping off at a million in the mid-1970s and staying at a high level—despite some losses—until reunification. Above all, young, well-educated people joined its ranks, effectively changing the profile of the party. The core of the party became more academic and inclined to debate, moving further left than the party elite. This constellation led to permanent rifts between the party base, the parliamentary faction, and the government. The Young Socialists in particular fueled conflicts over the Radicals Decree and the "Stamokap" (state monopoly capitalism) theory, which even led to the expulsion of the youth group's chairman, Klaus Uwe Benneter, from the party in 1977.[44] At the end of the 1970s, the peace and nuclear issues increasingly mobilized and polarized the Social Democrats. After losing control of the government in 1982, the stronger ties to the peace movement that had been made under the aegis of Willy Brandt had given the impression that the party was rather instable in terms of its foreign affairs agenda.[45]

A similar dynamic characterized the development of the trade unions in the FRG. Membership in the Deutsche Gewerkschaftsbund (DGB), the main umbrella organization of the German trade unions, rose from six million to almost eight million in the 1970s and 1980s, but its political clout increased even more. Since the early 1970s, it had quite successfully advocated for higher wages through strikes, similar to the unions in other Western European countries at the time. On average, West German wages increased by about twelve percent as a result. The trade unions continued their insistent campaigns after Kohl became chancellor, garnering broad support for their protests against planned social policy cuts.

What has often been overlooked, however, is that this politicization process in the 1970s also appeared within the middle classes. The CDU (Christian Democratic Union) was the party that grew the most strongly during this decade. It membership doubled to over 700,000, while the CSU (Christian Socialist Union) saw a 70 percent increase. This growth indicates that the 1970s were not simply a "red decade." There was also a corresponding conservative side to the political mobilization occurring among the youth at the time, although this was definitely more of a minority phenomenon within the university context.[46] Meanwhile, party members also began to take a more active role within party politics. At the 1968 CDU congress in Berlin, thirty thousand members took part in the discussion of the party's agenda. Moreover, in the decade that followed, the CDU entered into a five-year debate over its first party manifesto.[47] As in the SPD, this politicization sprouted debates and tensions within the party. Key issues, such as rights of participation, social security, or *Ostpolitik*, turned into hotly contested topics—for example, between the left and conservative wings or between the more liberal Young Union and the old guard. Simultaneously, the general public in the FRG began to wrestle with fundamental concepts such as freedom and security, political participation, and solidarity.[48] The SPD presented itself in 1972 as the "new middle," which the CDU countered in 1975 with its pithy "new social question" slogan that alluded to the poverty of families, single parents, and older individuals that had been neglected by the SPD with its focus on trade union workers. Indeed, a new "working group for semantics" was established in the CDU, which had otherwise traditionally shied away from theory per se. It was not until the CDU/CSU took over the government in 1982 that these debates over the party platform waned and the focus of the party leadership turned back toward the chancellor's office.

This dynamic expansion of the parties was also accompanied by a process of professionalization. Even the traditional middle-class parties began to train their own functionaries, who were charged with organizing politics at the local level. This professionalization was a reaction to the dissolution of the traditional social-moral milieu in the 1960s, which had been propped up by a stronger volunteer commitment to associations, municipal communities, and even the political parties. For example, the CDU began to employ local managers who took over the day-to-day running of the party, which used to be done on a volunteer basis by leaders of the local sports shooting associations or church congregations.

The politicization that occurred in the 1970s was linked to political polarization within West German society. Bitter conflicts not only erupted between the Right and the Left, but also within the individual political camps. While the SPD was divided over fundamental issues, similar splits plagued the radical Left Party and the newly established Green Party in which the fundamentalist "Fundis" pitted themselves against the more pragmatic "Realos." In the liberal FDP (Freie Demokratische Partei), leftists, national liberals, and economic liberals vied for control of the party, which ultimately led to the formation of splinter groups in 1969 and 1982. The FDP's youth organization, the Young Democrats, supported the leftist liberals in the 1970s, and it even detached itself from the main party in 1982; it was replaced by the newly established Young Liberals (JuLi). Even among the usually harmonious Christian Democrats, there were loud disagreements between the conservative and Christian-social wings of the party. The majority of West Germans disapproved of this political infighting as they favored political objectivity.[49] Most GDR citizens, who followed these political struggles via television coverage, were likewise unimpressed.

Party membership figures are well as the circulation of the party press outlets also increased in the GDR. But, this phenomenon primarily reflected an orchestrated identity between the party and the people as opposed to political mobilization from below. Given its role as the state party, the SED was fed by a constant influx of new members coming from the socialist service class. Rough estimates suggest that as of the early 1970s, these civil servants constituted about half of the party membership.[50] At the same time, the party apparatus made a concerted membership effort that included statistic manipulation as well as targeted recruitment with two main goals. On the one hand, it sought to achieve slight, but steady growth in waves corresponding with the party congresses in order to express the SED's "bonds with the masses" during the Honecker era. On the other hand, it carefully ensured the representation of social groups, and especially the "working class." Even in confidential internal statistics, around 38 percent of the party was supposed to be culled from this class.[51] In its officially published statistics, however, the SED lumped workers, functionaries, and salaried employees together, coming up with a figure of 80 percent for this group. Similar practices were applied for farmers, as well as university and vocational school graduates.

These kinds of machinations were also at work in the so-called transmission parties for Christians (CDU), farmers (DBD), tradesmen and freelancers (LDPD) as well as the somewhat diffuse National-Democratic Party of Germany (NDPD). Originally, the NDPD was supposed to be the party for converted National Socialists, but a considerable number of them actually belonged to the SED itself. Yet, many GDR residents somewhat obstinately joined such parties in order to avoid playing into the hands of the SED. Ultimately, the SED also orchestrated its supposed identification with the interests of the youth and the "working people," as well as others, through the more or less mandatory membership in organizations such as the FDJ (Freie Deutsche Jugend) youth league, the FDGB (Freie

Deutsche Gewerkschaftsbund)—which was the umbrella organization of the trade unions—or the Society for German-Soviet Friendship.

First and foremost, however, the growth in the membership figures for the GDR social organizations reflected a denial of change. It is therefore necessary to take a look at party life as well as informally expressed views in order to determine the degree of actual politicization among members. These kinds of sources reveal that in the 1980s, the attitudes of comrades hardly differed from those of noncomrades because a large portion of the party basis shared the general dissatisfaction that had pervaded East German society as a whole.[52] As of 1986, for example, the SED could no longer maintain its usual "upward curve." For the first time, its membership figures stagnated and a hardly detectable decline set in that proved to be quite significant in retrospect. The true status of the SED in terms of membership became quite apparent in the mass departure from the party that began in October 1989. Within a few months, the SED shrank to just a tenth of its former size.[53]

The same can also be said for the party press in that its political coverage was important first and foremost to those GDR residents whose professions required them to represent the party line or at least bear it in mind. Accordingly, most of the subscribers of *Neues Deutschland* were SED members, and its political pages were read with most interest by leading cadres, teachers, or party secretaries. The overwhelming majority of GDR residents, however, preferred newspapers that covered local news or topics related to culture and daily life.[54]

This coagulation of party life and the media was not irrelevant for the transformation of political life in the GDR that fed into its collapse in 1989. The internal commitment to the ideological core of the party's politics had waned even among its protagonists, leading to the crystallization of interest groups—often among party members—that increasingly followed their own agendas. Moreover, some markers indicate that as early as the late 1970s, top managers in the economic-technical sector had already adopted a primarily pragmatic approach to their jobs.[55] By the mid-1980s at the latest, some social scientists and journalists had also reevaluated the role of their professions under the banner of glasnost. Internally at least, they disavowed their propagandist role, promising to provide a realistic impression of what was happening in the republic.[56] Likewise, on the fringes of the official organizations, and especially within the Kulturbund (the Cultural Association of the GDR), space was carved out for seemingly "apolitical" activities, such as the cultivation of heritage, which effectively stripped these associations of their function as "transmission belts" of the party.[57] In the Gesellschaft für Natur und Umwelt (Society for Nature and the Environment) that was part of the Kulturbund and organized in local groups, for instance, the boundaries between oppositional, church-based, and state activists blurred over time. Grey areas such as these were experimental spaces for new forms of politics and issues that were swept into the limelight in the fall of 1989. Rather than concerning themselves with the big ideological questions of the day, these arenas fostered a pragmatic approach to issues that affected the local village or neighborhood, or problems such as air and water pollution. They were also forums for dialog and consensus-oriented communication as opposed to confrontation and power struggles.

Another "traditional" major organization that became politicized and polarized in the 1970s and 1980s was the Christian church(es). This came as a bit of a surprise in both Germanys. Whereas congregations in the GDR had been shrinking since the 1950s as a result of the state's repression of the churches, more and more people began to leave the churches in West Germany as well. The Catholic Church in particular came under public scrutiny.[58] Simultaneously, at the end of the 1960s, smaller political groups had already begun to attract more public attention, including the Protestant theologian Dorothee Sölle's "political evening prayers" and the young Christians who protested the Katholikentag in Essen in 1968[59] This resulted in a doubled political mobilization process in the early 1970s. On the one hand, conservative groups formed in opposition to the new left-liberal zeitgeist. The socioliberal reforms affecting the family and abortion rights prompted the churches to protest the government's policies with millions of pamphlets, countless critical public statements, and even protests on the streets.[60] The Catholic Church further reinforced its contra position in a pastoral letter concerning the federal elections in 1980 that also attacked the public debts that had been run up by the social-liberal coalition government. On the other hand, many Christians and some clergymen had become involved in the peace movement at the end of the 1970s. The Catholic congresses and the Protestant Church congresses, which were virtually insignificant in the 1970s because they were so small, underwent a revival, attracting massive crowds in turn. The Protestant Church Day in Hamburg (1981) and in Hannover (1983) in part resembled major peace demonstrations.[61]

In contrast, politicization was the last thing that the churches in the GDR wanted in the 1970s. Rather, they sought to leave the vehement confrontations of the 1950s behind them, which worked to some extent. The SED still maintained, for example, that the children of pastors should not be able to become teachers or hold other ideologically relevant positions. The Catholic Church reacted by focusing on its primary religious role, but the Protestant churches adopted a "church in socialism" approach as their modus vivendi, which corresponded to their long history as a loyal state church since the Reformation.

Notwithstanding, the churches came to play an essential role in laying the foundation for a democratic revolution in many respects. They were, in fact, the only major social organization that was tolerated outside the structures of democratic centralism. The SED made a concerted effort to undermine the relative independence of the churches by exercising subcutaneous influence through the secret police, but it was only partially successful. Young people in particular were attracted to the spiritual freedom afforded by churches in which the pastors and deacons permitted and fostered these kinds of spaces. It was here that the seeds were sown for the oppositional civil rights movement that unfurled in the 1980s. Likewise, the church synods and other assemblies proved to be a training ground for democratic processes, which meant that their members and officials were very much in demand in the fall of 1989. Furthermore, the churches functioned as a bridge to West Germany. The system of partner congregations created a functioning network at a basic level. The churches often had to intervene, for instance, when it came to tricky political and humanitarian missions, such as negotiating the release of political prisoners.

Ultimately, the government leaders and parliaments in both countries were also challenged by the structural transformation of the public sphere that had been taking place since the late 1960s. In the West, this changed the way in which the state responded to the demands of society. First, internal and public opinion polls had to be dealt with on a regular basis because these studies seemed to be representative of the will of the people. Although public opinion polls had been carried out on behalf of the party or the government since the late 1940s, they first began to circulate widely as political arguments in the public sphere a few decades later.[62] Second, the media took on a different role within society as its content and its journalists became more political. Once television had made its way into each household, each viewer was confronted with politics directly in a visual way, which effectively changed the world of political communication. Third, politicians had to respond more often to large protest organizations and events that shaped the contours of the political agenda.[63] And, last, experts challenged politicians in a much more public way, especially when the latter seemed to be inconsistent on complex issues such as nuclear power. Although politics had never taken place within the arcanum of power, the pressure to respond to political matters in the public sphere had become much greater than before.

However, this type of transformation did not occur in the GDR, especially because it was not possible for protesters or experts to freely express their opinions in the media, nor were the results of popular opinion polls made public. Rather, the occasional warning from experts or opinion surveys only cropped up at certain moments within the internal confines of the SED regime. Nonetheless, it can still be said that the SED had to become more responsive under Honecker. It was forced to react not only by the more direct West German television coverage of the GDR that had become possible after the accreditation of journalists in East Berlin in 1973, but also through Honecker's political agenda that sought to boost legitimacy and stability by improving standards of life in the East.

In contrast to Poland, Hungary, and even the Soviet Union itself, however, the SED leadership was not able to harness the chances afforded by this kind of responsiveness, nor appreciate its necessity.[64] It was apparently very much aware of the fragility of its rule, which meant that the risk of political transformation had to be avoided at all costs. Consequently, it sought to perfect its existing regime and ensure stability for its most important clientele by introducing "benefits" in terms of consumption and social policy.

The instruments of policy advising (which were by no means public) that had been created or reformed in the GDR in the 1960s, in particular the channels of expertise on the economy, were systematically dismantled or shoved into a corner where only acclamation was allowed. The same applied to the reports issued by the apparatus and the FDGB on popular opinion and the "implementation of resolutions" at the local level, as well as the economic reports coming from the planning bureaucracy.[65] From the very beginning, the Politburo's Institut für Meinungsforschung (Institute for Opinion Polling) that was established in 1963 as a corrective for a "scientifically exact picture" of "public opinion" was very restricted in its scope, and Honecker ordered its dissolution in 1979.[66] Other institutes weathered the changing of the tide, but lacked influence, such as the Zentralinstitut für Jugendforschung (Central Institute for Youth Studies).[67] Parallel to these institutes, the Stasi regularly analyzed the "reactions of the population," but even this channel was shut down as a source of information for Politburo members in 1972 after a report was issued regarding the enthusiastic response of the East Germans to the reelection of Willy Brandt.[68] All these institutes of political policy advising functioned according to the Communist rules of the game. Like the party leadership, they shared the conviction that the majority of the GDR population believed that it was in tune with the regime or at least thought that the party had the right to determine what was objectively necessary on the basis of its fundamental tenets. But even corrective instruments within this system were suppressed by Honecker and his closest allies.

Since the uncontrolled influences coming from the West and from within East German society were not shrinking, however, the SED was forced to react to them. In doing so, it recognized their presence within a subcutaneous "nonpublic" opinion discourse. In its surveillance and persecution practices, for example, the SED increasingly took into account anticipated negative resonance in the West, effectively applying Western standards. Like all socialist regimes, the SED also looked for alternative means of legitimizing its rule. Since nationalism, which had been dominant in Poland and other sibling socialist countries since 1957, apparently had little or even a negative effect in the GDR, the SED sought to cultivate instead a feeling of cultural belonging as well as a regional identity.[69] Although these efforts were somewhat successful, they could not really counter the regime's fundamental lack of legitimacy. This strategy first bore real fruit for the SED's successor party, the PDS, which campaigned as an "ostalgic" regional party after 1990.

In general, the faith in the two main ideologies of the Cold War began to fade at the end of the 1970s, making room for new visions and fears. Human rights, referred to as the "last utopia" by Samual Moyn, was one issue that began to fill this void, together with the corresponding calls for a stronger moral foundation for politics.[70] In the West, anti-Communist, Christian, and leftist groups shared this commitment to human rights. In Eastern Europe, like-minded groups sprouted up that profited from Western support, and they were able to help to chip away at the authority of the political elite and establish contacts between East and West.[71]

Demands for more transparency and the disclosure of personal transgressions by politicians were also associated with this more moralistic political culture. Increasing visual surveillance through cameras, investigative journalism, and higher expectations vis-à-vis democracy also contributed to this moralization of politics. At the same time, these measures resulted in an increasing number of scandals and resignations over issues such as campaign donations and suspicions of corruption (Lambsdorff), abuse of power (Barschel), or a tainted Nazi past (Filbinger). It remains to be seen whether a comparable "moralization" trend emerged in the GDR, either on its own accord as a product of East German political culture or through the adoption of West German standards. From the very beginnings of the SED, however, "privileges" had been a common topic of discussion in everyday life. This discourse ultimately culminated in the famous GDR youth television reportage *Elf 99* that aired on 24 November 1989 in which a camera team tried to film what the standard of living was like in the Politburo community in Wandlitz.[72]

New Protests in East and West

The most striking symbols of the politicization that occurred in the 1970s and 1980s in the West were the protests staged by the new social movements and their—apparent or real—counterparts in the East. The Western protest movements were often part of cross-border networks that spread from the West to the East. Environmental protests, for example, emerged in the United States and France at the beginning of the 1970s that funneled into joint actions along the Rhine in particular. Likewise, forms of protest that developed in the FRG spread abroad, such as the occupation of the construction site for the planned nuclear power plant in Wyhl in 1975.[73] Above all, it was the peace movement and the anti–nuclear power movement that accumulated an immense amount of support as well as influence over political decisions in West Germany, even when compared internationally.[74] These "new social movements" are referred to in the plethora of studies on this topic as a long-term "mobilizing collective actor" or as a network of social groups with a collective identity that either wanted to bring about or put a stop to a social change.[75] They can also be termed "communicative networks" because their main goals were to set the political agenda or influence the public, and due to their loose organizational natures, they were also permanently engaged in internal communication.[76]

Around 1980, corresponding protest movements also developed in the GDR that initially joined the pacifist bandwagon and later turned their attention to environmental issues. Although they were quite small, they were no less visible to the SED and the West, and they were well-linked to their Western counterparts. Initially, characteristic parallels can be detected between the movements in the FRG and the GDR. In contrast to the USSR, for example, the leading figures of dissidence (such as Robert Havemann, Wolf Biermann, or Rudolf Bahro) were reformist Marxist Communists with ties to the West German New Left as well as theorists of Western Marxism.[77] However, a programmatic shift also occurred in the East in the second half of the 1970s. Marxism and even the general social theory foundation of these movements were increasingly pushed aside by a muddled mix of programmatic interests such as the critique of militarization, calls for a basis democracy, ecological criticism directed against civilization, and, above all, an anti-totalitarian ethic of resistance against the pressure to conform and participate in the Communist regime. The idea was to counteract this coercion with "Living in Truth" à la Václav Havel. Additionally, these different political agendas shared a common critique against the alienation of modern industrial societies along with the mutual desire to find an "authentic" way of life. This affinity was personified, for example, by Petra Kelly and Bärbel Bohley, although their political fates reflected the limits of such an understanding of politics that distanced itself from the pursuit of power and compromises.[78]

Scholars still disagree as to whether the term "new social movements" can be used in reference to the much smaller counterculture of the GDR. Before the fall of the Wall, Hubertus Knabe argued that this term could be used for the GDR, citing the overwhelming sociocultural similarities.[79] Critics countered by noting that it was difficult to draw a line between "old" and "new" protest movements in East Germany; they also pointed out that protest took on an entirely different form and significance within a dictatorship.[80] Nonetheless, every protest in the GDR was—whether intentionally or not—also a protest against the prohibition against protesting, which meant that it questioned the system on two levels simultaneously. Even beyond such links, cross-system similarities can be detected between East and West Germany. For example, the protest groups were mostly local in their outlooks and loosely structured; they were formed temporarily, but had long-term moral goals that strove for social change without reflecting personal material interests. They were also more strongly rooted within the younger generation, enjoying more support from academics than workers and exhibiting a higher percentage of female involvement. Moreover, they often cultivated an alternative lifestyle on both sides of the Wall that differed in its habitus, which turned the movement itself into the message.

In the West, however, Communist groups remained rather small and often fluid groups. These "K-Gruppen" were hierarchically organized and dogmatic, and they pointedly rejected a leftist-alternative hippie lifestyle. At their peak in 1977, they had about twenty thousand members, but they disintegrated into smaller splinter groups following Mao's death and the RAF (Red Army Faction) terrorist attacks.[81] Even the German Communist Party (DKP) never surpassed 0.3 percent of the second ballot in the West German federal elections, despite massive financial support from the GDR. Yet the communists in the West received a disproportionate amount of public attention thanks to the Cold War and the RAF. In particular, the so-called Radicals Decree of 1972, which made constitutional loyalty a prerequisite for employment in the civil service and mandated checks on many university graduates, drew the question of membership in Communist organizations into the spotlight of public debate.

In general, however, the ideological spectrum of the West German social movements was much broader. Protests were often sparked by extreme events that mobilized support in East and West alike. The arms race, in conjunction with the NATO Double-Track Decision in 1979, as well as the introduction of instruction in warfare in GDR schools in the year prior, for example, blew wind into the sails of the peace movement. Likewise, on both sides of the Wall, the construction of nuclear power plants and nuclear accidents such as those at Three Mile Island in 1979 and Chernobyl in 1986 drew more people into social movements. The fears associated with these protests demonstrated that the general faith in a better future was waning in both Germanys. Beginning in the 1970s, moreover, many local groups and citizens' initiatives formed in the West that could be mobilized for major national protests thanks to their alternative press outlets and pamphlet circulations.

The oppositional protest movement in East and West Germany enjoyed the most support when it came to calls for peace as opposed to all other political issues. Accordingly, the peace movement functioned like an umbrella organization for different initiatives and strains of protest. It brought Christians, Social Democrats, leftist-alternatives, and Communists together for joint actions. Likewise, it created bridges between East and West, which is why some studies have highlighted its role in bringing about the end of the Cold War.[82] Furthermore, the broad base of support for the peace movement, with its millions of followers, demonstrated just how many people hoped for an end to the East-West confrontation and had committed themselves to the idea of "one world," which was also reflected in the anti–nuclear power protests and development aid projects. That said, however, the question of to what extent the GDR's Stasi influenced or even steered the West German peace movement has sparked intense discussions among scholars.[83] Without a doubt, the SED and the Stasi supported the Komitee für Frieden, Abrüstung und Zusammenarbeit (KOFAZ, Committee for Peace, Disarmament and Cooperation) and parts of the peace movement, including the initiators of the Krefelder Appell (Krefeld Appeal). Yet it is also quite clear that such a mass movement in all its plurality could not be controlled by a secret intelligence service, and certainly not one that would have then been agitating against rearmament and in favor of pacifism on behalf of the SED. Rather, it had in fact become quite apparent that the peace movement presented a true challenge to the militarism of the SED.

Regardless of these fantasies about the manipulative power of Communist fifth columns, the peace movement nonetheless aptly functions as a prism for exploring East-West entanglements. On the one hand, questions related to peace and the arms race hit a nerve among East Germans. Memories of the horrors of World War II were alive and well in the minds of the older generation while younger East Germans were skeptical about hefty measures of social discipline such as the military draft, and they were also on the lookout for an international political dialog. The SED could thus reckon with a certain amount of recognition as long as it did more than just invoke the idea of peace incessantly and actually worked to deescalate tense situations. This interest in peace also harbored potential for the opposition as it could expand its base of social support

Figure 1.1. "In East and West: Swords into Ploughshares": Two Civil Rights Activists from the GDR (Peter Rösch and Roland Jahn), Who Had to Leave Their State, Protest against Nuclear Weapons of the NATO in Mutlangen, West Germany, in 1983 (source: Ullstein-Bilder, used with permission)

through the strong resonance within church youth groups. For the first time in a long while, GDR citizens seemed to be willing to engage in collective action, demonstrated by the thousands of signatures collected in protest against rearmament within the Warsaw Pact states following the stationing of Pershing II missiles in West Germany.[84]

The environment, on the other hand, was not one of the top priorities of the organized protest movements in the GDR. Protests against pollution were important for the transformations of the 1980s because they unavoidably hit home with many people and had not been consistently criminalized by the East German authorities. The omnipresence of hefty air pollution, for instance, mobilized even "normal" GDR residents. Likewise, the detrimental effects of chemical manufacturing in the Halle-Bitterfeld region were so obvious that the first burgeoning alliances between local functionaries, scientists, and citizen activists were formed in response. This effectively resulted in the first cooperative efforts between church and state organizations, such as the Society for Nature and the Environment of the Kulturbund. All these actions took place locally, and they were not picked up by the GDR media. Yet this did not prevent the Stasi from keeping tabs on these activists. Regardless of these aspects, these developments significantly influenced the understanding of politics among the so-called "1989ers" at the local level, reappearing in the form of forums for dialog and round table discussions.[85]

In terms of the women's rights movement, however, the differences between East and West Germany were even greater. In the 1970s, political power still rested firmly in the hands of men in the FRG. At the most, only 7 percent of the seats in the Bundestag were occupied by women. Likewise, only one woman belonged to the cabinets of Brandt and Schmidt, as the minister for family affairs. The situation in the East was quite similar, despite the fact that the GDR claimed that it had achieved the epitome of equality given its high percentage of female employment. The pivotal positions of power, however, were all held by men. In the West, a variety of feminist groups emerged within the Left in the 1970s who protested women's exclusion within their own political camp. They were relatively successful in their endeavors, especially in a mid- to long-term perspective. Some of their achievements included the establishment of women's houses and female quotas, as well as increased awareness for sexual discrimination. Comparable groups or movements were barely existent within the GDR, only appearing within the context of the peace movement or occasionally under the auspices of the churches. The SED, however, even tried position itself as a role model at the official congresses of the international women's movement in the 1970s.[86]

Nonetheless, the GDR lacked a visible women's emancipation movement, perhaps because the majority of women perceived of themselves as equals. Yet, the high rate of female employment by no means protected women against a gendered wage gap, the unequal distribution of housework, and clearly demarcated gender roles.[87] All the efforts made to formulate a fundamental critique of gender relations, such as the foundation of an independent women's association in 1989 by a few reformist-socialist women's studies scholars, proved to be short-lived.[88] However, literary feminism did have a social impact, represented by works such as Maxie Wander's *Guten Morgen, Du Schöne* (Good Morning, Beautiful) and especially Christa Wolf's *Kassandra*. These works called for an individualistic search for women's identities and roles outside the boundaries of collectivism.[89]

On the whole, the protest movements did spark debates over the use of state and social violence in both East and West Germany. Indeed, violence had been a key issue discussed within leftist circles in West Germany ever since the protests of 1968.[90] In the 1970s, terrorism sharpened and complicated these debates as the West German state appeared to have failed and been too weak on the one hand, but also too extreme in its use of violence on the other. The doubled escalation of violence in 1977 as a result of terrorism, as well as the anti-nuclear power demonstrations such as the one in Brokdorf, prompted both sides to ponder the implications of this vortex of violence. While protesters and terrorists who were willing to resort to violence lost much of their support among the Left, the police made a stronger commitment to collective de-escalation in the 1980s. The excessive use of police force, such as in the case of the anti-nuclear protesters in Hamburg in 1986, was branded a scandal and declared to be illegal.[91] The explicit condemnation of violence on both sides also proved to be characteristic of the blossoming peace movement and green politics.

In the GDR, violence remained at the core of the official understanding of politics. As of the 1950s, the SED reigned in its capriciousness in this regard, creating a preventive state surveillance apparatus that was in a league of its own even within the Communist bloc.[92] Yet the Party did not completely give up on the idea of the state's unrestricted monopoly on violence. Bloodshed was still considered to be legitimate, but it tended to be kept better under wraps. The regime's support of West German and Arabic terrorism, as well as the assassinations of people who helped others flee the country, was all done secretly. However, it could not avoid the publicity surrounding shots fired at the Wall. But this battleground was far too vital for the SED to quit the field. The concessions made by the SED to civilize political conflicts led to the rather bizarre situation that demonstrators in the fall of 1989 feared a "Chinese solution" just as much as they were still outraged over the already more restrained use of police batons by the Volkspolizei ("people's police") given its claims to be on the side of the people. The opposition, on the other hand, had already deemed collective violence to be pointless in the second half of the 1950s and put such ideas on the shelf.

The transformation of politics in the 1970s and 1980s was not limited to explicit protests or formal political groups. Especially in the West, but also in some urban areas in the East, certain lifestyles expressed political distinctions. In particular, this could be seen in the leftist-alternative milieu that built its own world in old neighborhoods in university towns and large cities. Around 1980, it was estimated that the hard core of this like-minded community amounted to half a million activists plus a further 5.6 million sympathizers. The subjectification of politics and the elimination of its boundaries were hallmarks of this group. Rather than focusing on any particular political theory, personal experience of a leftist-alternative life characterized by empathy and self-discovery, as well as authenticity and camaraderie, was paramount.[93] Lifestyle and habitus thus drew lines of political demarcation. Similar to the social democratic and Catholic milieus of the late nineteenth century, West German university towns and large cities became home to a milieu with its own leftist-alternative infrastructure, shared living spaces, ecologically friendly shops, "red" bookstores, alternative childcare facilities, and a separate press. A colorful youth culture emerged out of this scene around 1980 that sometimes tried to consciously set itself apart from the rest of the milieu. This not only applied to the early punks who actually sought to defy the culture of the hippies, but also to the so-called poppers, who aimed to create a seemingly apolitical, consumption-based self-image that was in fact political in that it attempted to establish a separate identity.[94] Lifestyles thus took the place of older forms of expressing political convictions associated with social classes. Despite the formation of new groups, lifestyles stood for individualization because they offered more choice than the old milieus, although social background continued to play a major role in their profiles.[95]

With the establishment of the Green Party, the alternative milieu and the new social movements acquired a parliamentary foundation in the West, which served to politically anchor and institutionalize its interests. This move echoed developments in other Western countries, such as the British "Ecology Party" (1975) or the "écologistes" in France who gained over 10 percent of the vote in some major cities in the local elections in 1977. The German Green Party thus symbolized this transformation of politics on several levels. For one, it united different currents of political thought. Although the undogmatic Left from the alternative milieu was the largest group in the party, antiauthoritarian anthroposophists and ecologically minded conservatives with rather preindustrial ideas, as well as some communists, found themselves drawn to the Greens. One of the main bonds holding the party together was its critique of consumption.[96] Following the dissolution of many leftist groups at the end of the 1970s, the Green Party was like a political reservoir that was fed by the anti–nuclear power and peace movements in particular. Simultaneously, it was the indirect successor of the (Left-)Liberals who had attracted many motivated, well-read academics in larger cities and university towns. Even the CDU saw the Greens as a serious threat to its voter base.[97] The Greens were a symbol for the reformation of the rather rigid political system of the FRG. They also stood for an attempt to alter party politics and the way elections and parliamentary affairs were being conducted. This was reflected in the Green's ideas of grassroots democracy, the rotation of parliamentary representatives, dual leadership, and the depersonalization of politics.

Essentially, the Greens sought to build a new kind of bridge between the protest movements in the East and the West. In 1983, for example, figureheads Petra Kelly and Gert Bastian unrolled a large poster together with other parliamentarians on Alexanderplatz in Berlin that read, "Schwerter zu Pflugscharen" (swords to plowshares). When they were later invited to meet with Erich Honecker in the fall of the same year, Kelly also wore a t-shirt bearing this symbol.[98]

But, just how influential were these political groups? One can certainly say that they were successful when it came to setting the agenda. They also fostered an awareness of a looming crisis among the population that was not retrospective in nature, but rather looked toward the future in matters such as renewable energy sources, gender equality, or disarmament.[99] Likewise, they pushed the West German government to try to catch up with the environmental protection policies of forerunners such as the United States and Japan. That said, historians still disagree over the role of these groups in the peace movement. Some scholars suggest that the peace movement brought about disarmament, but the majority contend that Gorbachev and the economic crisis in the Communist bloc were the main factors.[100] However, it has often been overlooked that other actors such as the state, the schools, or the media also contributed significantly to reforms and shifts in attitudes.

Regardless of these debates, the question still remains as to just how closely all of this was related to the parallel development of an "alternative," antiauthoritarian milieu in the GDR that set itself apart not only from the state, but also from mainstream society. Waves of a youth subculture certainly spilled over from the West, which were easily recognizable by a common habitus on both sides of the Wall. Church-based peace and youth groups also worked with partners across the border, and even the punks maintained cross-border contacts. Likewise, the axis between West German Greens and East German opposition initiatives was one of the most stable elements of the 1980s. A kind of "biotope" marked by intensive exchange developed between East and West Berlin in particular, not least thanks to the many people within this scene who left the GDR for the West.[101]

Yet, the East German "alternative scene" faced different problems than its Western counterpart. In terms of "politics," the main difference was that this scene spawned fewer organized political activities, and it was marginalized in a much more fundamental way. A broad movement of citizens' initiatives was not an option; all the activities of such initiatives relied on the most rudimentary forms of organization within the private sphere. These circumstances made it necessary for this scene to maintain a fundamental distance from the established political realm. Consequently, this broad milieu developed a truly distinct political quality because it may have flirted with the literary subculture and the organized civil rights movement, but it did not really see itself as the opposition or resistance.[102] Aptly referred to as "anti-politics" in other Communist states, this constellation also carried over into post-unification society.[103]

In contrast, the political ideas of the antiauthoritarian students' movement, the New Left of the 1970s, and ultimately the green-alternative new social movements with their corresponding critique of democracy and "the system," hardly resonated within the GDR. Most GDR residents were put off by this Western brand of Marxism, in part because of its linguistic affinity with the SED. The older and middle-aged generations, at least, also saw a real provocation in such antiauthoritarian critiques of society or parenting and upbringing, as well as ideas about grassroots democracy. The SED establishment and large swaths of the population thus largely agreed, for example, that military service was still the best education for the younger generation and that young rowdies had to be put in their place.[104]

1989—Asymmetrical Aspects of a Democratic Revolution

In Central Europe, the paths leading to the sudden transformation of 1989 varied greatly in length from country to country. Especially in Poland, the Communist leadership had already begun to make some incremental changes in response to the myriad protests that had taken place, culminating in a "Round Table" in February 1989 as well as semifree elections in June 1989. These measures paved the way for the establishment of political competitors within the structures of the state. A "second" civil society, which included not only Solidarność and the heavy anchor of the Catholic Church, but also a lively youth and pop culture, was the motor behind this process.[105] In the GDR, however, it was the mass exodus that took place in the summer of 1989 that began to tear away at the foundation of the SED state. The sudden collapse of historic Communism as not only a form of rule, but also as a leitmotif, was without a doubt the most far-reaching "transformation of politics" for those in power. At the same time, it was a fundamental act of liberation for the majority of GDR citizens, most of whom had never before publicly questioned the Communist Party's monopoly on power. The path to this point had been paved by the corrosion of the old system of rule as well as the fusion of different actors and agendas—the exodus movement, the opposition, and the population at large—into a revolutionary subject.[106] The catalyst for this amalgamation was the call for the establishment of the New Forum on 10 September 1989 that was formulated by activists from the civil rights' opposition, but spread quickly throughout the republic in thousands of copies, acquiring tens of thousands of signatures on the way.

This call to action proved to be successful because it expressed a specific understanding of politics: avoiding a deeper analysis of the system, it explicitly attacked the rule of the party without formulating a political agenda per se. The New Forum was clearly presented as a "platform" that was supposed to feed into the formation of a republican public. It was supposed to be a place where a "democratic dialog" could be started in order to "listen to and evaluate opinions and arguments, and to distinguish between general and special interests." This combination of humility and radicalism corresponded with the group's express intention to become a legally registered political association (that is, as one among many) according to "Article 29 of the Constitution of the GDR," as well as to encourage "all citizens of the GDR who want to take part in the reshaping of our society" to join its ranks.[107] The rapid dissemination of this appeal from hand to hand throughout the republic alone illustrates that a new level of politics had been reached that tapped into the newly built intermediate sphere between party-state and society.

As in East Germany, the upheavals in the rest of Central Europe were also generally nonviolent and resolved through negotiations, despite some confrontations along the way.[108] This movement as a whole opted for "dialog" as opposed to a general strike or the defection of the military. Even the occupation of the Stasi offices took place in "security partnership" with the Volkspolizei. This strategy was not only adopted in light of a sober estimation of the strength of each side given the distribution of weapons, but also the strong commitment to civility within the pro-democracy movement.

On the other side of the fence, the SED leadership also opted for words instead of weapons. Despite expressing public solidarity with the Chinese Communist Party in the aftermath of the Tiananmen Square massacre in June 1989, Egon Krenz and fellow SED officials returned from Beijing having realized that the use of such violent tactics in the GDR would not only result in a pointless confrontation, but also catapult the country into isolation.[109] Apparently, this realization also motivated them to push Honecker out of the way since he still felt that violence could be used to stabilize the situation in the end if necessary.[110] The party leadership's decision to refrain from using violence was thus based on a political calculation rather than any kind of fundamental political-ethical aversion to the use of violence.[111] Sure enough, it was also the Communist party leaders who tried to turn around the economic crisis by strengthening ties with the West. Their tactical decisions were surely influenced by the negative experiences associated with the last two attempts to achieve stability through violence in Afghanistan (since 1979) and Poland (1981).

The revolution in the GDR, as well as in Eastern and Central Europe in general, quickly adopted a Western-style political and socioeconomic model, fixing its gaze on West Germany in particular. Not only did the fall of the Berlin Wall on 9 November clearly signal the way the wind was blowing, but also the fact that 75 percent of the votes in the elections for the Volkskammer (People's Chamber) in March 1990 went to parties planning for a joint future with their respective counterparts in Bonn.[112] The prospect of a fusion with West Germany proved to be decisive for the electoral victory of the Alliance for Germany, which had promised the shortest route to unification.

Thus, democratic notions prevailed in East Germany that can be pithily summed up by the notion of "no experiments" while resembling the longing for security and prosperity of the "Kanzlerdemokratie" (chancellor democracy) under Adenauer.[113] Whereas Helmut Kohl was often mocked in the West, for example, East Germans applauded him at his first appearance in Dresden as a political leader who appeared to guarantee this much sought-after sense of security.[114] This naturally affected Kohl's status in the West in turn: although Kohl seemed to have little chance of winning the next election, and he had almost lost his post as the head of the CDU in early 1989, his image in West Germany suddenly began to improve.[115]

That said, however, there were two big losers in the fall of 1989. Communism, for one, had been defeated as a political ideology, even in places where the Communist elite still held the majority of leadership positions, such as in the former Soviet Union/Russia or Romania. Second, the utopian idea of a "third way" leading to self-determination and "truly" democratic socialism had been swept away. Its demise came somewhat unexpectedly as most all of the actors who had paved the way for the revolution favored such an alternative. Their call to arms, titled "For our Country," which brought them together with the revived SED leadership, may have been signed by 1.1 million GDR citizens, but this represented only a minority.[116]

As the defeat of the utopian "third way" became manifest in the Volkskammer election in March, its protagonists reacted quite differently. Some, like Rainer Eppelmann, had already decided to switch to the path leading to Bonn; others, including Jens Reich, declared laconically that the movement had devolved back into a "small group," but one that had "achieved a lot."[117] Still others, such as Bärbel Bohley, turned away in disappointment. Ilko-Sascha Kowalczuk has thus rightly asserted that "from this perspective, 1989/90 was a revolution without a utopia"[118]—if the concrete, but also deceptive, notion of "flourishing landscapes" in the socialist market economy is ignored.

Did the revolution in East Germany ignite a transformation of politics in the Federal Republic? Even before the fall of 1989, it was readily apparent that Gorbachev's reform policies had shaken up the political sphere in the West. This time around, even the New Left in West Germany succumbed to the illusion of a new "socialism with a human face" in the Soviet Union itself.[119] This was coupled with the expectation, as Erhard Eppler put it in 1989 in his speech on 17 June, that the SED leadership would not be able to cling to its rigid stance against the "melting ice of the Cold War" forever, although he identified concrete prospects only for reform and dialog, not reunification.[120]

The upheavals that came in the weeks and months that followed thus took the political world of the Federal Republic mostly by surprise. The different political cultures became clearly manifest through this direct confrontation. Three major trends were associated with this process, the most visible of which was the renationalization of politics in the famous "We are one people" (*Wir sind ein Volk*) slogan. As the East German impulse to quickly discard the GDR as a separate state challenged the European order that had been established at Yalta, it awakened fears that the situation might escalate uncontrollably, unleashing a new form of aggressive nationalism. The conservatives in particular profited from this renationalization. They were able to soften its blow diplomatically by channeling this energy into the forum of European politics. At the same time, they successfully funneled what turned out to be a primarily economically driven impulse into a monetary union and unification treaty between East and West Germany.

Second, the pro-Western turn after 9 November presented a challenge to the alternative groups in the West. As they had identified themselves with the East German civil rights activists in 1989/90, they also suffered a defeat during the reunification process. Accordingly, they supported the ambitions of the central round table to get the ball rolling on a constitution for all of Germany. Many West German left-liberal constitutional law experts thus wore themselves out working on a draft constitution that was ultimately cursorily dismissed by the Volkskammer.[121] This was accompanied by acts of arrogance, such as the famous banana that appeared out of the pocket of the Green-Left politician Otto Schily when he commented on Helmut Kohl's victory in the Volkskammer elections.[122] After the SPD under the leadership of Oscar Lafontaine earned only 33 percent of the vote in the Bundestag elections in 1990—which did not come as a surprise—and the West German Greens did not even get the 5 percent needed to gain any seats, the West German democratic Left had to go through a strenuous "after socialism" rebuilding process in the FRG.¹²³ What remained was a rugged landscape of political-cultural differences engulfing more than just the left side of the political spectrum that would come to shape political life in Germany in the years to come.

Political Culture in Germany after Reunification

When it joined the Federal Republic, the GDR adopted the entire political system of West Germany. Yet the political cultures and practices on both sides of the former Wall remained quite distinct in the 1990s, and some of these differences still persist today. Not only the lasting influences of both systems, but also the economic crises in East Germany fed into this continued separation. Moreover, in an exercise in self-reflection, scholars of political culture have debated whether the developments in East Germany can best be assessed through the quantitative opinion poll research conducted in the West or, rather, participatory observations and qualitative descriptions.¹²⁴ In comparison to other postsocialist countries in Eastern Europe, the similarities between East and West Germany were actually quite pronounced, and democratization after communism was particularly successful in the former GDR.¹²⁵ Many things that are still considered to be specifically East German, for example, actually correspond to general trends in Western Europe as well. A transformation of political culture also occurred in the West in the mid-1980s, but it was overshadowed by the changes in East Germany and did not become as clearly visible until the 1990s.

In the years and decades after 1990, however, political culture in East and West Germany still differed in many respects. Whereas East Germans tended to be much more interested in politics after 1990 than West Germans, this trend later reversed itself.¹²⁶ As different studies quickly determined, the willingness to engage in demonstrations or to sign a letter of protest was much lower in principle in the East. That said, the actual number of East Germans who signed petitions and joined demonstrations proved to be similar to that of West Germans or even higher, as in 2003/04.¹²⁷ Above all, it was the protests of East Germans who were unemployed or on the brink of losing their jobs that boosted these figures. At the same time, a strong feeling of powerlessness continued to dominate public opinion, even after the transformation phase. In the mid-1990s, for example, more East Germans than West Germans believed that they had no political influence (80 to 64 percent). But, it must also be noted that these pessimistic numbers were much greater in both parts of Germany than in other industrial countries.¹²⁸ Similarly, most East Germans did not join political organizations such as the parties, unions, or NGOs. Their experiences in the GDR, but also the general impression that these groups were dominated by West Germans, undoubtedly played a role in this reticence to become involved. Whereas the CDU and the FDP could build upon the crumbling membership base of the bloc parties at least, the SPD and the Greens were hardly able to build up a base of support outside urban areas in the East. Those supporters who had been the backbone of the protest movement, most of whom were highly active in Bündnis 90, still lacked influence, despite the fact that the merger with the West German Greens had been touted as exemplary for having taken place "on equal footing."[129] Within the political landscape, they actually reverted to a role similar to the one that they had held before 1989 in the GDR as critics of the PDS and guardians of the critical reappraisal of the dictatorship. In conjunction with the West German political and journalistic establishment, they were at least able to adopt a strong historico-political position that produced a canonized narrative of perpetrators and victims in the GDR.

Yet, despite this seeming lack of political interest, the East Germans submitted a significantly higher number of petitions than the West Germans.[130] The strongly rooted tradition of making "submissions," which was a favored instrument for reporting local and individual grievances in the 1980s, undoubtedly contributed to this penchant for petitions as a form of political participation. In the 1990s, the number of petitions submitted yearly rose by almost twenty thousand. Voter participation among East Germans, however, lagged behind that of the West. The differences between East and West also remained pronounced in terms of voting behavior and party attachment. The parties in the West could still rely on their core constituencies in the 1990s, which largely remained loyal or at most vacillated within the same political camp in major elections (i.e., between CDU and FDP, or SPD and Grüne). East German voters, by contrast, were more strongly swayed by which party subjectively promised them the most benefits and therefore tended to switch between parties more often. Voting preferences at the municipal and state level also reflected a tendency that favored strong, integrative "fathers of the nation" who, in a certain respect, took up with the tradition of political dialog. Former GDR citizens with church ties were disproportionately more successful in winning over East German voters, as well as some experienced West German "center" politicians. The looseness of these political ties thus accounts for the great success of the CDU in East Germany in 1990 and 1994, as well as its electoral defeat in 1998.

The East and West German electorates also differed on a sociocultural level. Whereas the CDU/CSU was most popular among voters with ties to the church and mid to high incomes in the West, it enjoyed the most success initially among workers without a confessional background in the East, while the SPD tended to attract more salaried employees. Yet, in comparison to other postsocialist countries, the party system in East Germany proved to be quite stable, not least thanks to its close ties to the West.

The lasting success of the SED successor party, the PDS, remained the largest difference between East and West in terms of the history of the political parties. Initially, many experts had predicted that the PDS would gradually merge into the SPD. Initially, though, the PDS succeeded as the party of the (subjective) losers in the reunification process and the former socialist civil service class. It later survived as an East German regional party with manifold roots in local life.[131] When it came to organization, personnel, and financial matters, it was able to draw on the legacy of the SED. In the political arena, by contrast, it increasingly distanced itself from the SED, although it still cultivated the old ideological tenets and traditions within its milieu. It also intervened on behalf of those responsible for repression in the old East German state or adopted elements of the SED's anti-Americanism.

The rise of right-wing radicalism that did not shy away from violence with a broader base of support among the population was also quite noticeable in the early 1990s, especially in East Germany. This development was very much the result of the socioeconomic and cultural crisis that followed on the heels of reunification, which was further inflamed by media coverage on the "flood of asylum-seekers." That said, however, right-wing radical groups had already started to form in the 1980s. Unemployment and the discourse on Islamic migration had not only strengthened the right-wing radical skinhead scene, but also contributed to the success of populist right-wing republicans, who even gained seats in the European Parliament and a few state legislatures in the West (first Berlin, then Baden-Württemberg) in 1989. In the 1990s, the even more radical German People's Union (DVU) also managed to gain seats in some of the state legislatures in East and West Germany. The polarization of society, unemployment, and sagging party loyalty propelled the ascent of the Far Right.[132]

Right-wing extremism had also put down roots in the GDR. Racist and right-wing extremist stereotypes were alive and well under the surface in certain sectors of the GDR population. Although these ideas were repressed in public, they manifested themselves in exclusionary measures and physical violence aimed at foreigners. A small skinhead movement also germinated in the GDR in the 1980s that sprang onto the political stage at the end of the decade; in collaboration with the West German

Skins, for example, they sponsored a joint birthday celebration for Hitler in 1989.[133] The Stasi first began to keep closer long-term tabs on the skinheads after the attack on the Zionskirche (Church of Zion) in 1987, which prompted many neo-Nazis to dress more discreetly. Right-wing violence, however, often erupted at soccer matches in East Germany. But these attacks by right-wing radicals also sparked anti-fascist protest groups that were not necessarily associated with the SED.[134]

It must also be noted, though, that the rise of right-wing populism at the beginning of the 1990s was also a cross-European phenomenon, as was the increase in violence. The fading cohesive power of anti-Communism within Christian democratic circles paved the way for an exodus from these parties in many Western countries. Economic crises and increased immigration also gave a boost to right-wing populists in other countries, such as Austria, Switzerland, Italy, and France, as well as the Netherlands and Denmark. Given this international comparison, the question remains as to why this movement seemed to be contained at a regional level in Germany in particular and did not gain a foothold in former West Germany until the electoral success of the "Alternative for Germany" party (AfD) in 2015. There are three main reasons that can likely account for this. First, the success of right-wing populism is dependent on the economic situation, which remained relatively stable in West Germany, even during the crises of the 1990s and after 2008. Second, the Christian Democrats in particular ensured a quite rigid policy on foreigners and asylum-seekers, which helped curtail immigration with the help of new EU guidelines after 1993. And, last, through the process of coming to terms with the Nazi past, the majority of Germans have tended to trust the "center" and have been quite skeptical of right-wing populists. At the end of the 1990s, moreover, right-wing extremist violence ebbed in both parts of the country, attesting to the success of the established parties' efforts to marginalize the Far Right and right-wing populist parties.[135] This trend began to reverse, however, with the major influx of refugees in 2014 and the rise of the AfD (Alternativ für Deutschland).

Trust in the political establishment also eroded in the West, but not in connection with the fall of the Wall. As early as 1981, party identification began to dissipate and membership in the parties dropped gradually at first, but then accelerated.[136] The often-cited term *Politikverdrossenheit* (disenchantment with politics) was even named the word of the year in 1992. Beginning in the mid-1980s, the number of demonstrations also began to wane in the West, although they peaked again briefly in the early 1990s with the protests against the Persian Gulf War. The core issues that had once been espoused by the new social movements lost their relevance. Apart from the protests against the war in Iraq, the focus turned primarily toward the issue of how to deal with minorities, which evolved out of the debates on asylum seekers.[137] Social austerity measures introduced by Kohl's government, high unemployment, and deregulation also sparked protests headed by the "old social movements," such as the trade unions, and also the churches. Although unemployment rose past the four-million mark in 1997/98, this did not boost the potential for protest among those affected in either the East or the West. Attempts to symbolically invoke the spirit of the *Montagsdemos* (Monday demonstrations) in the East were particularly successful in 1998 and 2004, but their popularity was by no means constant.

The factors propelling this depoliticization process were myriad. Disappointment stemming from the inability to fully achieve political goals, the aging of the politically active postwar generation that had become caught up in family life, and the collapse of communism as a model and/or bogeyman surely counted among them.[138] The growing significance of consumption and the corresponding transformation of the media with the advent of a dual broadcasting system and later the Internet, which were accompanied by increased social differentiation, were no less relevant. Political media outlets had to make way for entertainment-based formats, especially on TV but also in magazines. Additionally, the widespread notion that the state should not interfere in economics, which had been circulating since the 1980s, also served to delegitimize the parliamentary system.[139] Moreover, the "German fear" that had propelled politicization also waned. The widespread pessimism that had been dominant around 1980 morphed into increasing optimism as the economic situation improved, accompanied by the generational and cultural shifts of the late 1980s.

The end of the Cold War also changed the political landscape in the West. It led to a crisis among communist groups who lost most of their financial support, as it had come from the East. The German Communist Party (DKP), for example, had received around a half billion German Marks form the SED in the 1980s alone.[140] Not only were they forced to rely solely on the support of their small membership bases, but also they crumbled in the face of internal public debates over the future of the party. In many countries, the fall of the Wall also shook up the traditional middle-class parties. The hitherto strong Christian democratic or conservative parties lost their fundamental anti-communist consensus, and the grip of their religious-moral bonds had already been weakening. In Italy, the Christian Democratic Party that had been governing for decades dissolved completely in the face of scandal. A similar fate befell the Christian democratic parties in the Netherlands, Austria, and Belgium, which effectively bolstered electoral support for right-wing populist parties. The crisis in the CDU following its electoral defeat and Helmut Kohl's resignation in 1998 therefore reflected an international trend, but it had been delayed in the West German case by the party's key role in the reunification process. As the party in government at the time, it was made responsible for the flailing socioeconomic situation, and especially the ongoing unemployment problem, but also for social austerity measures.

At the same time, Gerhard Schröder's election marked a new kind of pragmatism within the SPD in the wake of the demise of real existing socialism that also departed from the leftist JuSo (Young Socialist) tradition. As the so-called Schröder-Blair paper emphasized, the party distanced itself from neoliberalism as well as state intervention, which it had favored in the past.

Thus, to a certain extent, it can be said that the era of the Red-Green government was the capstone of the transformation of the 1970s. On the one hand, this government accomplished the goals of the protest movements, such as the nuclear phase-out, the reform of citizenship laws, and guarantees of equality for minorities. On the other hand, it also pushed through policies contrary to the peace movement, such as the deployment of German troops against Serbia. The Agenda 2010, which brought social austerity measures, poignantly underscored this shift within the Social Democratic and Green parties. Edgar Wolfrum thus referred to the Red-Green government as "the dawn of a new era" that adopted old policies while often boldly reshaping them. This paved the way for the Greens to develop into a "key party," at least in West Germany.[141] It was not until after the ardent new social movements lost ground that their political concerns met with a surprisingly broad, self-evident resonance within society.

In comparison to the 1970s, German society appeared to be increasingly apolitical from the late 1990s onward. Yet, reforms were introduced without much fanfare that had once been demanded only by highly politicized minorities. The majority of young people refused to serve in the military, for example, while recycling and energy-saving measures became widespread, and women began to take on an increasing number of leading positions in politics, finance, and university education. The emergence of an environmentally minded interventionist state cannot account for these changes alone. Rather, the protest movements had brought about a change of norms that even influenced supporters of the CDU and CSU. In 1994, for example, the CDU even adopted the idea of an "ecological market economy" in its party platform. Simultaneously, the traditional middle-class parties experienced a kind of rebirth that no one in post-unification Germany embodies as much as Angela Merkel—an East German woman following a pragmatic path to the political center that had first been paved for the SPD by Gerhard Schröder. It was thus an East German who helped to liberalize the rather West German leaning CDU/CSU and ensure that it could hold onto its majority. An internal party transition could hardly be any more entangled than that of the CDU.

As of yet, no term has been coined for this liberalization of German society around 2000. The longing for a new beginning was exemplified by the idea of the "Berlin Republic," but its short-lived popularity is quite telling. It has only occasionally popped up since then in the media, perhaps because it was really only reflective of the frenzied Internet and TV journalism scene in Berlin and not a general public phenomenon.[142] In the end, the idea of the Berlin Republic was more of a promise than a new national identity. Despite the boom that engulfed Berlin, the Federal Republic of Germany remained strongly federal in its political culture. Even in the new federal states, a special "East German" consciousness has continued to dominate alongside a strong attachment to one's "home state" within Germany.

The transformation of politics and what was considered to be political was therefore a conjoined history in more ways than one. Despite the many differences that existed before the fall of the Wall, ties existed between the protest movements and alternative cultures across the border. Moreover, at least on a subcutaneous level, social dissatisfaction and the distance to state institutions grew in East Germany. But, with the exception of DKP circles, the relationship between East and West remained quite one-sided as political culture in the FRG looked to the changes taking place in neighboring countries to the West, mostly ignoring the GDR.

Twenty-five years after reunification, the political cultures in East and West Germany have moved closer together, but the differences are still discernible. The acceptance of democracy is almost just as strong in the East, but its implementation has met with more criticism. Likewise, trust in the government and the parties is still weaker in the former GDR states, and only half of the East Germans feel "at home politically in the Federal Republic."[143] Yet, xenophobia is only marginally stronger in the East, and the convergence of notions of social justice has been getting stronger. In terms of political culture, the north-south difference is gaining ground alongside the east-west divide. The differing levels of success enjoyed by the Pegida demonstrations, the populist AfD (Alternative for Germany), and the Left Party in East and West, however, point to the continued existence of historical and socioeconomic differences across the old German-German border.

Frank Bösch is professor of European history at the University of Potsdam and director of the Center for Contemporary History (ZZF) in Potsdam. He is the author of several books on modern German and European history, including *Die Adenauer-CDU* (2001), *Das konservative Milieu* (2002), and *Öffentliche Geheimnisse* (2009). His most recent book is *Mass Media and Historical Change: Germany in International Perspective, 1400–2000* (Berghahn Books, 2015).

Jens Gieseke is head of the research department "Communism and Society" at the Center for Contemporary History (ZZF) in Potsdam. His publications include *Communist Parties Revisited* (with Rüdiger Bergien, eds., 2018), *The History of the Stasi* (2014), *The Silent Majority in Communist and Post-Communist Countries* (with Klaus Bachmann, eds., 2016), *Die Staatssicherheit und die Grünen* (with Andrea Bahr, 2016), *Staatssicherheit und Gesellschaft* (ed., 2007), and *Die hauptamtlichen Mitarbeiter der Staatssicherheit* (2000).

NOTES

1. For an overview, see Tobias Weidner, *Die Geschichte des Politischen in der Diskussion* (Göttingen, 2012); Frank Bösch and Norman Domeier, eds., *A Cultural History of Politics* (London, 2008).
2. Cf. Jens Gieseke, "Bevölkerungsstimmungen in der geschlossenen Gesellschaft: MfS-Berichte an die DDR-Führung in den 1960er- und 1970er-Jahren," *Zeithistorische Forschungen/Studies in Contemporary History* 5, no. 2 (2008): 236–57, http://www.zeithistorische-forschungen.de/2-2008/id percent3D4491.
3. Cf. Andreas Rödder, "Klios neue Kleider: Theoriedebatten um eine Kulturgeschichte der Politik in der Moderne," *Historische Zeitschrift* 283 (2006): 657–88.
4. Cf. Winfried Thaa, *Die Wiedergeburt des Politischen. Zivilgesellschaft und Legitimitätskonflikt in den Revolutionen von 1989* (Opladen, 1996), 54; See also "'Er hielt sich für den Größten.' Wie Erich Honecker die Deutsche Demokratische Republik in den Abgrund geführt hat," *Der Spiegel* 32 (3 August 1992): 25–27, quote p. 25. Cf. Martin Sabrow, "Der führende Repräsentant," *Zeithistorische Forschungen* 10, no. 1 (2013): 12; Hedwig Richter, "Mass Obedience: Practices and Functions of Elections in the German Democratic Republic," in *Voting for Hitler and Stalin: Elections under 20th Century Dictatorships*, ed. Ralph Jessen and Hedwig Richter (Frankfurt, 2011), 103–24.
5. Manfred Kittel, "Strauß' Milliardenkredit für die DDR. Leistung und Gegenleistung in den innerdeutschen Beziehungen," in *Das Doppelte Deutschland. 40 Jahre Systemkonkurrenz*, ed. Udo Wengst and Hermann Wentker (Berlin, 2008), 326.

6. Hermann Wentker, "Chance oder Risiko? Die Außen- und Deutschlandpolitik der DDR im deutsch-deutschen Kommunikationsraum," in *Außenpolitik im Medienzeitalter. Vom späten 19. Jahrhundert bis zur Gegenwart*, ed. Frank Bösch and Peter Hoeres (Göttingen, 2013), 208.
7. On the diplomatic aspects, which are not the central focus here, see Dierk Hoffmann, "Honecker in Bonn. Deutsch-deutsche Spitzentreffen 1947–1990," in *Das Doppelte Deutschland*, ed. Wengst and Wentker, 333–56; Martin Sabrow, "Der Pyrrhussieg. Erich Honeckers Besuch in der Bundesrepublik 1987," in *2 x Deutschland. Innerdeutsche Beziehungen 1972–1990*, ed. Andreas H. Apelt, Robert Grünbaum, and Jens Schöne (Halle, 2013), 201–37; Detlef Nakath, *Deutsch-deutsche Grundlagen. Zur Geschichte der politischen und wirtschaftlichen Beziehungen zwischen der DDR und der Bundesrepublik in den Jahren von 1969 bis 1982* (Schkeuditz, 2002).
8. The full text of the paper issued by the Grundwertekommission (Commission for Fundamental Values) of the SPD and the Akademie für Gesellschaftswissenschaften (Academy of Social Sciences) of the Central Committee of the SED can be found in Grundwertekommission der SPD (ed.), Der Streit der Ideologien und die gemeinsame Sicherheit, 3 August 1987, retrieved 28 May 2018, http://library.fes.de/library/netzquelle/ddr/politik/pdf/verfemte_4.pdf.
9. Heike Amos, *Die SED-Deutschlandpolitik 1961 bis 1989. Ziele, Aktivitäten und Konflikte* (Göttingen, 2015), 347–63.
10. Hans-Peter Schwarz, *Helmut Kohl. Eine politische Biographie* (Munich, 2012), 467–68; Hoffmann, *Honecker in Bonn*, 354–55.
11. Joachim Scholtyseck, *Die Außenpolitik der DDR* (Munich, 2003), 115–16.
12. Eva Maria Gajek, *Imagepolitik im olympischen Wettstreit. Die Spiele von Rom 1960 und Munich 1972* (Göttingen, 2013).
13. Hermann Wentker, *Außenpolitik in engen Grenzen. Die DDR im internationalen System* (Munich, 2007), 35.
14. For a cultural history interpretation of the symbolism attached to Honecker's visits to Africa, see Katharina Haß and Michael Pesek, "Kleiner Mann auf Reisen: Erich Honecker auf Staatsbesuch in Afrika," in *Die Ankunft des Anderen. Repräsentationen sozialer und politischer Ordnungen in Empfangszeremonien*, ed. Susann Baller (Frankfurt a. M., 2008), 106–34.
15. Verbal statement made by Honecker to the shah on 29 August 1978; reprinted in Harald Möller, *Geheime Waffenlieferungen der DDR im ersten Golfkrieg an Iran und Irak 1980–1988. Eine Dokumentation* (Berlin, 2002), 35–36.
16. From a more eyewitness perspective, see Erika Harzer and Willi Volks, eds., *Aufbruch nach Nicaragua: Deutsch-deutsche Solidarität im Systemwettstreit* (Berlin, 2010).
17. On the many efforts undertaken by the GDR with and without support from Moscow, see Ulrich Pfeil, ed., *Die DDR und der Westen. Transnationale Beziehungen 1949–1989* (Berlin, 2001).
18. Cf. Frank Bösch, "Energy Diplomacy: Germany, the Soviet Union and the Oil Crisis," *Historical Social Research* 39, no. 4 (2014): 165–85.

19. Manuela Glaab, "Geteilte Wahrnehmungswelten. Zur Präsenz der deutschen Nachbarn im Bewußtsein der Bevölkerung," in *Deutsche Vergangenheiten— eine gemeinsame Herausforderung. Der schwierige Umgang mit der doppelten Nachkriegsgeschichte,* ed. Christoph Kleßmann (Berlin, 1999), 206–20, here 212–13.
20. "Gauck muss 'Gegensatz zwischen Freiheit und Gerechtigkeit' auflösen: Egon Bahr über Joachim Gaucks voraussichtliche Wahl zum Bundespräsidenten" (Interview of Egon Bahr on Joachim Gauck's probable election as president of Germany), *Deutschlandfunk Kultur,* Deutschlandradio, 17 March 2012, retrieved 23 May 2018, http://www.deutschlandradiokultur.de/gauck-muss-gegensatz-zwischen-freiheit-und-gerechtigkeit.990.de.html?dram:article_id=154264.
21. Saskia Richter, *Die Aktivistin. Das Leben der Petra Kelly* (Munich, 2010), 164–72. Jens Gieseke and Andrea Bahr, *Die Staatssicherheit und die Grünen. Zwischen SED-Westpolitik und Ost-West-Basisbeziehungen* (Berlin 2016).
22. For a more detailed account, see Jens Gieseke, "Whom did the East Germans Trust in the Cold War?" in *Trust, but Verify: The Politics of Uncertainty and the Transformation of the Cold War Order, 1969–1991,* ed. Martin Klimke, Reinhild Kreis, and Christian Ostermann (Stanford, 2016), 143–66.
23. This interpretation was strongly put forth by scholarship on political culture published in the 1980s and 1980s; see, for example Oskar Niedermayer, ed. *Politische Kultur in Ost- und Westdeutschland* (Berlin, 1994).
24. Konrad H. Jarausch, *After Hitler: Recivilizing Germans, 1945–1995* (Oxford, 2006), 271.
25. Pierre Bréchon, "Politisierung, Institutionenvertrauen und Bürgersinn," in *Wertewandel in Deutschland und Frankreich. Nationale Unterschiede und europäische Gemeinsamkeiten,* ed. Renate Köcher and Joachim Schild (Opladen, 1998), 230.
26. Sven Reichardt, *Authentizität und Gemeinschaft. Linksalternatives Leben in den siebziger und frühen achtziger Jahren* (Berlin, 2014), 44–50.
27. Adelheid von Saldern, "Markt für Marx. Literaturbetrieb und Lesebewegungen in der Bundesrepublik in den Sechziger- und Siebzigerjahren," *Archiv für Sozialgeschichte* 44 (2004): 149–80.
28. See the chapter by Frank Bösch and Christoph Classen in this volume as well as Christina von Hodenberg, *Konsens und Krise. Eine Geschichte der westdeutschen Medienöffentlichkeit 1945–1973* (Göttingen, 2006).
29. Cf. Bernhard Dietz, Christopher Neumaier, and Andreas Rödder, eds., *Gab es den Wertewandel? Neue Forschungen zum gesellschaftlichkulturellen Wandel seit den 1960er Jahren* (Munich, 2014); see also the contribution by Christopher Neumaier and Andreas Ludwig in this book.
30. Heike Solga, "'Systemloyalität' als Bedingung sozialer Mobilität im Staatssozialismus, am Beispiel der DDR," *Berliner Journal für Soziologie* 4 (1994): 523–42.
31. See, for example, Hartmut Zwahr, *Die erfrorenen Flügel der Schwalbe. DDR und Prager Frühling. Tagebuch einer Krise* (Bonn, 2007); Wolfgang Bialas,

Vom unfreien Schweben zum freien Fall, Ostdeutsche Intellektuelle im gesellschaftlichen Umbruch (Frankfurt a. M., 1996).

32. The following statements are based on an analysis of the Infratest program on the attitudes and behaviors of the GDR population titled "Einstellungen und Verhaltensweisen der Bevölkerung in der DDR," which was commissioned by the government of the FRG and ran from 1968 to 1989; see Jens Gieseke, "Auf der Suche nach der schweigenden Mehrheit Ost: Die geheimen Infratest-Stellvertreterbefragungen und die DDR-Gesellschaft 1968–1989," *Zeithistorische Forschungen/Studies in Contemporary History* 12 (2015): 66–97. In addition, they draw on an analysis of the reports on public opinion compiled by the Ministry for State Security, see Gieseke, *Bevölkerungsstimmungen*.

33. For example, see Ministry for State Security (hereafter MfS), Zentrale Auswertungs- und Informationsgruppe (hereafter ZAIG), Hinweise auf Tendenzen der Unzufriedenheit in der Reaktion der Bevölkerung der DDR, 12 September 1977; BStU, ZA, ZAIG 4119, Bl. 1–8; cf. Mark Allinson, "1977: The GDR's Most Normal Year?," in *Power and Society in the GDR, 1961–1979*, ed. Mary Fulbrook and Alf Lüdtke (New York, 2009), 253–275.

34. Infratest: "Einstellungen und Verhaltensweisen der Bevölkerung in der DDR," Jahresberichte 1975 bis 1985, Infratest Archiv; cf. Gieseke, "Auf der Suche."

35. Heike Solga, *Auf dem Weg in eine klassenlose Gesellschaft? Klassenlagen und Mobilität zwischen Generationen in der DDR* (Berlin, 1995).

36. Gieseke, "Auf der Suche."

37. Cf. Jens Gieseke, "'Seit langem angestaute Unzufriedenheit breitester Bevölkerungskreise'—Das Volk in den Stimmungsberichten des MfS," in *Revolution und Vereinigung 1989/90. Als in Deutschland die Realität die Phantasie überholte*, ed. Klaus-Dietmar Henke (Munich, 2009), 130–48.

38. Reichardt, *Authentizität*, 319–498 and 724–40.

39. Annegret Schüle, Thomas Ahbe, and Rainer Gries, eds., *Die DDR aus generationengeschichtlicher Perspektive. Eine Inventur* (Leipzig, 2005).

40. Cf. Dorothee Wierling, *Geboren im Jahr Eins. Der Jahrgang 1949 in der DDR und seine historischen Erfahrungen* (Berlin, 2002).

41. Cf. Wolfgang Kraushaar, *Die Protest-Chronik 1949–1959. Eine illustrierte Geschichte von Bewegung, Widerstand und Utopie*, 4 vols. (Hamburg, 1996).

42. Dieter Rucht and Roland Roth, "Soziale Bewegungen und Protest—eine theoretische und empirische Bilanz," in *Die sozialen Bewegungen in Deutschland seit 1945. Ein Handbuch*, ed. Dieter Rucht and Roland Roth (Frankfurt a. M., 2008), 661.

43. See, for example, Bernd Faulenbach, *Das sozialdemokratische Jahrzehnt. Von der Reformeuphorie zur neuen Unübersichtlichkeit. Die SPD 1969–1982* (Bonn, 2011).

44. Ibid., 631–45.

45. Jan Hansen, "Making Sense of Détente. German Social Democrats and the Peace Movement in the Early 1980s," *Zeitgeschichte* 40, no. 2 (2013): 107–21.

46. On the "black decade," see Frank Bösch, "Die Krise als Chance: Die Neuformierung der Christdemokraten in den siebziger Jahren," in *Das Ende der Zuversicht? Die Strukturkrise der 1970er Jahre als zeithistorische Zäsur*, ed. Konrad H. Jarausch (Göttingen, 2008): 288–301; Massimiliano Livi, Daniel Schmidt, and Michael Sturm, eds., *Die 1970er Jahre als schwarzes Jahrzehnt. Politisierung und Mobilisierung zwischen christlicher Demokratie und extremer Rechter* (Frankfurt a. M., 2010).
47. For a more detailed account, see Frank Bösch, *Macht und Machtverlust. Die Geschichte der CDU* (Munich, 2002), 37–44, 99–120.
48. Wolfgang Bergsdorf, ed., *Wörter als Waffen. Sprache als Mittel der Politik* (Stuttgart, 1979); Thomas Mergel, *Propaganda nach Hitler. Eine Kulturgeschichte des Wahlkampfs in der Bundesrepublik 1949–1990* (Göttingen, 2010), 267.
49. Mergel, *Propaganda*, 296–302.
50. Jens Gieseke, "The Successive Dissolution of the 'Uncivil Society': Tracking SED Party Members in Opinion Polls and Secret Police Reports 1969–1989," in *Communist Parties Revisited*, ed. Rüdiger Bergien and Jens Gieseke (New York, 2018); Dietrich Staritz and Siegfried Suckut, "SED-Erbe und PDS-Erben," *Deutschland Archiv* (1991): 1038–51.
51. See the internal membership statistics of the Central Committee, Dept. party organs of the SED in Stiftung Archiv der Parteien und Massenorganisationen der DDR (SAPMO), Bundesarchiv (BArch), DY 30.
52. See Sabine Pannen, "Montag ist Parteiversammlung! Alltag und soziale Praxis des SED-Parteilebens," in *Aus einem Land vor unserer Zeit. Eine Lesereise durch die DDR-Geschichte*, ed. Marcus Böick, Anja Hertel, and Franziska Kuschel (Berlin, 2012), 15–24.
53. Suckut and Staritz, *SED-Erbe und PDS-Erben*; Gero Neugebauer and Richard Stöss, *Die PDS. Geschichte. Organisation. Wähler. Konkurrenten* (Opladen, 1996).
54. Burghard Ciesla and Dirk Külow, *Zwischen den Zeilen. Geschichte der Zeitung "Neues Deutschland"* (Berlin, 2009), 164–65; see Michael Meyen and Anke Fiedler, *Wer jung ist, liest die Junge Welt. Die Geschichte der auflagenstärksten DDR-Zeitung* (Berlin, 2013).
55. For example: MfS, Information über Vervielfältigung und Verbreitung die gesellschaftlichen Verhältnisse in der DDR diskriminierender Texte, 21 December 1978, 18; BStU, ZA, ZAIG 4131; "DDR: Leere Regale vor Weihnachten," *Der Spiegel* 51 (18 December 1978).
56. See, pars pro toto, for the journalism department at the Karl-Marx-Universität Leipzig and the local SED party organ *Berliner Zeitung*, ZAIG, Hinweise über beachtenswerte Reaktionen zur Medienpolitik der DDR, 13 January 1986; BStU, ZA, ZAIG 4202, Bl. 2–5.
57. Jan Palmowski, *Inventing a Socialist Nation: Heimat and the Politics of Everyday Life in the GDR, 1945–1990* (Cambridge, 2009).
58. Nicolai Hannig, *Die Religion der Öffentlichkeit. Kirche, Religion und Medien in der Bundesrepublik 1945–1980* (Göttingen, 2010).

59. Thomas Großbölting, *Der verlorene Himmel. Glaube in Deutschland seit 1945* (Göttingen, 2013), 137–47.
60. Jana Ebeling, "Religiöser Straßenprotest? Medien und Kirchen im Streit um den § 218 in den 1970er Jahren," in *Jenseits der Kirche. Die Öffnung religiöser Räume seit 1945*, ed. Frank Bösch and Lucian Hölscher (Göttingen, 2013), 253–84.
61. Siegfried Hermle, Claudia Lepp, and Harry Oelke, ed., *Umbrüche. Der deutsche Protestantismus und die sozialen Bewegungen in den 1960er und 70er Jahren* (Göttingen, 2007).
62. Anja Kruke, *Demoskopie in der Bundesrepublik Deutschland. Meinungsforschung, Parteien und Medien 1949–1990* (Düsseldorf, 2007).
63. Andreas Wirsching, *Abschied vom Provisorium. Die Geschichte der Bundesrepublik Deutschland 1982–1989/90* (Munich, 2006), 98–99.
64. On the function of channels of reporting in communist regimes, see Martin Dimitrov, "Understanding Communist Collapse and Resilience," in *Why Communism Did Not Collapse: Understanding Authoritarian Regime Resilience in Asia and Europe*, ed. Martin Dimitrov (Cambridge, 2013), 6–7.
65. Mark Allinson, *Politics and Popular Opinion in East Germany 1945–1968* (Manchester, 2000); Patrick Major, "'Mit Panzern kann man doch nicht für den Frieden sein.' Die Stimmung der DDR-Bevölkerung zum Bau der Berliner Mauer am 13. August 1961 im Spiegel der Parteiberichte der SED," *Jahrbuch für Historische Kommunismusforschung* (1995): 208–23.
66. Quoted in Heinz Niemann, *Meinungsforschung in der DDR. Die geheimen Berichte des Instituts für Meinungsforschung an das Politbüro der SED* (Cologne, 1993), 17.
67. On radio, see Brigitte Hausstein, "Die soziologische Hörer- und Zuschauerforschung in der DDR," *Info 7: Information und Dokumentation in Archiven, Mediotheken, Datenbanken* 23, no. 1 (2008): 67–73; Walter Friedrich, Peter Förster, and Kurt Starke, eds., *Das Zentralinstitut für Jugendforschung Leipzig 1966–1990. Geschichte, Methoden, Erkenntnisse* (Berlin, 1999).
68. See the online document collection: Daniela Münkel, ed., *Die DDR im Blick der Stasi. Die geheimen Berichte der SED-Führung 1953–1989*, retrieved 23 May 2018, http://www.ddr-im-blick.de. See Gieseke, "Bevölkerungsstimmungen."
69. Marcin Zaremba, *Im nationalen Gewande. Strategien kommunistischer Herrschaftslegitimation in Polen 1944–1980* (Osnabrück, 2011).
70. Samuel Moyn, *The Last Utopia: Human Rights in History* (Cambridge, 2010).
71. Sarah B. Snyder, *Human Rights Activism and the End of the Cold War: A Transnational History of the Helsinki Network* (Cambridge, 2011); Christian Peterson, *Globalizing Human Rights: Private Citizens, the Soviet Union, and the West* (New York, 2011).
72. Jürgen Danyel and Elke Kimmel, *Waldsiedlung Wandlitz: Eine Landschaft der Macht* (Berlin, 2016).
73. See Jens Ivo Engels, *Naturpolitik in der Bundesrepublik. Ideenwelt und politi-

sche Verhaltensstile in Naturschutz und Umweltbewegung 1950–1980 (Paderborn, 2006).
74. For a comparison, see Felix Kolb, *Protest and Opportunities: The Political Outcomes of Social Movements* (Frankfurt a. M., 2007), 205.
75. Joachim Raschke, "Zum Begriff der Sozialen Bewegung," in *Neue Soziale Bewegungen in der Bundesrepublik,* ed. Roland Roth and Dieter Ruch (Bonn, 1991), 32.
76. Frank Bösch, "Kommunikative Netzwerke. Zur globalen Formierung sozialer Bewegungen am Beispiel der Anti-Atomkraftproteste," in *Theoretische Ansätze und Konzepte der Forschung über soziale Bewegungen in der Geschichtswissenschaft,* ed. Jürgen Mittag and Helke Stadtland (Essen, 2014), 149–66.
77. On the legacy of the "other" 1968, see Ilko-Sascha Kowalczuk, "'1968'—ein ostdeutscher Erinnerungsort?" in *Annäherungen an Robert Havemann,* ed. B. Florath (Göttingen 2016), 351–406.
78. Bärbel Bohley, *Englisches Tagebuch 1988* (Berlin, 2011); Richter, *Die Aktivistin.*
79. Hubertus Knabe, "Neue soziale Bewegungen im Sozialismus. Zur Genesis alternativer politischer Orientierungen in der DDR," *Kölner Zeitschrift für Soziologie und Sozialpsychologie* 40, no. 3 (1988): 551–69.
80. See, for example, Gareth Dale, *Popular Protest in East Germany, 1945–1989* (New York, 2005), 112–13.
81. These figures are drawn from Reichardt, *Authentizität,* 11.
82. The influence of the peace movement on the USSR is emphasized in Matthew Evangelista, *Unarmed Forces: The Transnational Movement to End the Cold War* (Ithaca, 1999).
83. For a more balanced perspective, see Helge Heidemeyer, "Nato-Doppelbeschluss, westdeutsche Friedensbewegung und der Einfluss der DDR," in *Zweiter Kalter Krieg und Friedensbewegung. Der NATO-Doppelbeschluss in deutsch-deutscher und internationaler Perspektive,* ed. Philipp Gassert, Tim Geiger, and Hermann Wentker (Munich, 2011), 247–68. For a critique, see Holger Nehring and Benjamin Ziemann, "Do All Paths Lead to Moscow? The NATO Dual-Track Decision and the Peace Movement—A Critique," *Cold War History* 12, no. 1 (2012): 1–24.
84. See Gieseke, "Whom Did the East Germans Trust in the Cold War?"
85. Kerstin Engelhardt and Norbert Reichling, eds., *Eigensinn in der DDR-Provinz. Vier Lokalstudien zu Nonkonformität und Opposition* (Schwalbach/Ts., 2011).
86. Celia Donert, "Whose Utopia? Gender, Ideology and Human Rights at the 1975 World Congress of Women in East Berlin," in *The Breakthrough: Human Rights in the 1970s,* ed. Jan van Eckel and Samuel Moyn (Philadelphia, 2013), 68–87.
87. Ursula Schröter, "Abbruch eines Aufbruchs. Zur Frauenpolitik in der DDR," *Das Argument* 56, no. 3 (2014): 376.

88. Gislinde Schwarz and Christine Zenner, eds., *Wir wollen mehr als ein "Vaterland." DDR-Frauen im Aufbruch* (Reinbek, 1990).
89. Christa Wolf, *Voraussetzungen einer Erzählung: Kassandra. Frankfurter Poetik-Vorlesungen* (Neuwied, 1984).
90. Karrin Hanshew, *Terror and Democracy in West Germany* (Cambridge, 2012).
91. See Holger Nehring, "The Era of Non-Violence: 'Terrorism' and the Emergence of Conceptions of Non-Violent Statehood in Western Europe, 1967–1983," *European Review of History* 14, no. 3 (2007): 343–71.
92. Stephan Scheiper, *Innere Sicherheit. Politische Anti-Terror-Konzepte in der Bundesrepublik Deutschland während der 1970er Jahre* (Paderborn, 2010).
93. See Reichardt, *Authentizität*, 13.
94. For telling eyewitness accounts, see Jürgen Teipel, *Verschwende Deine Jugend* (Frankfurt a. M., 2001). For the best overview of these milieus, see Axel Schildt and Detlef Siegfried, *Deutsche Kulturgeschichte. Die Bundesrepublik von 1945 bis zur Gegenwart* (Munich, 2009).
95. On these links between different lifestyle ideas, see Michael Vester, *Soziale Milieus im gesellschaftlichen Strukturwandel. Zwischen Integration und Ausgrenzung* (Frankfurt a. M., 2001).
96. Silke Mende, *"Nicht rechts, nicht links, sondern vorn." Eine Geschichte der Gründungsgrünen* (Munich, 2011), 321 and 483–84; Joachim Raschke, *Die Zukunft der Grünen. So kann man nicht regieren* (Frankfurt a. M., 2001).
97. Kohl Fraktionsprotokoll CDU 24 April 1979, in ACDP VIII-001–1056/1. See also the sessions on 12 June 1979 and 10 September 1979.
98. See Richter, *Die Aktivistin*.
99. For a more nuanced perspective, see Roth and Rucht, *Soziale Bewegungen*, 658.
100. Lawrence S. Wittner, *The Struggle against the Bomb: A History of World Nuclear Disarmament Movement*, 3 vols. (Stanford, 1993–2003).
101. See Thomas Klein, *"Frieden und Gerechtigkeit!" Die Politisierung der Unabhängigen Friedensbewegung in Ost-Berlin während der 80er Jahre* (Cologne, 2007).
102. For one of the many literary monuments, see Adolf Endler, *Tarzan am Prenzlauer Berg* (Leipzig, 1994); see also the chapter titled "Zwischentöne," in Ilko-Sascha Kowalczuk, *Endspiel. Die Revolution von 1989 in der DDR* (Munich, 2009), 140–79.
103. Alexei Yurchak, *Everything Was Forever, Until It Was No More: The Last Soviet Generation* (Princeton, 2006).
104. See Thomas Lindenberger, "'Asoziale Lebensweise.' Herrschaftslegitimation, Sozialdisziplinierung und die Konstruktion eines 'negativen Milieus' in der SED-Diktatur," *Geschichte und Gesellschaft* 32, no. 2 (2005): 227–54.
105. Padraic Kenney, *A Carnival of Revolution: Central Europe 1989* (Princeton, 2003).
106. Detlef Pollack, "Der Zusammenbruch der DDR als Verkettung getrennter Handlungslinien," in *Weg in den Untergang. Der innere Zerfall der DDR*, ed.

Konrad H. Jarausch and Martin Sabrow (Göttingen, 1999), 41–81; Steven Pfaff, *Exit-Voice Dynamics and the Collapse of East Germany: The Crisis of Leninism and the Revolution of 1989* (Durham, 2006).
107. Printed in Bernd Lindner, *Die demokratische Revolution in der DDR 1989/90* (Bonn, 2010).
108. Philipp. Ther, "1989—eine verhandelte Revolution," Version: 1.0, *Docupedia-Zeitgeschichte*, 11 February 2010.
109. Bernd Schäfer, "Egon Krenz und die chinesische Lösung," in *1989 und die Rolle der Gewalt*, ed. Martin Sabrow (Göttingen, 2012), 153–72.
110. Martin Sabrow, "'1989' und die Rolle der Gewalt in Ostdeutschland," in *1989 und die Rolle der Gewalt*, ed. Martin Sabrow (Göttingen, 2012), 9–31.
111. Ehrhart Neubert, *Unsere Revolution. Die Geschichte der Jahre 1989/90* (Munich, 2008).
112. Kowalczuk, *Endspiel*, 530.
113. See this interpretation of West German history put forth by Eckart Conze, *Die Suche nach Sicherheit. Eine Geschichte der Bundesrepublik Deutschland von 1949 bis in die Gegenwart* (Munich, 2009).
114. Konrad H. Jarausch, *The Rush to German Unity* (Oxford 1994), 145.
115. Bösch, *Macht und Machtverlust*, 134–37.
116. Kowalczuk, *Endspiel*, 484.
117. Ibid., 530.
118. Ibid., 539.
119. Wolfgang Haug, *Gorbatschow. Versuch, über den Zusammenhang seiner Gedanken* (Hamburg, 1989).
120. Erhard Eppler, Rede zum 17. Juni im Deutschen Bundestag 1989 (Speech on 17 June in German Bundestag 1989), transcription in *Sozialdemokratischer Pressedienst* Z 9597 B (21 and 22 June 1989), retrieved 7 July 2016, http://library.fes.de/spdpd/1989/890621.pdf and http://library.fes.de/spdpd/1989/890622.pdf.
121. See Anja Schröter, "Eingaben im Umbruch. Ein politisches Partizipationselement im Verfassungsgebungsprozess der Arbeitsgruppe 'Neue Verfassung der DDR' des Zentralen Runden Tisches 1989/90." *Deutschland Archiv* 45, no. 1 (2012): 50–59.
122. See Kowalczuk, *Endspiel*, 541.
123. Joschka Fischer, *Die Linke nach dem Sozialismus* (Hamburg, 1993), 1.
124. Not surprisingly, the scholarly literature from the 1990s on the different political cultures is quite extensive; see, for example, Thomas Gensicke, *Die neuen Bundesbürger. Eine Transformation ohne Integration* (Opladen, 1998); Alexander Thumfart, *Die Politische Integration Ostdeutschlands* (Frankfurt a. M., 2002).
125. Günter Heydemann and Karel Vodicka, eds., *Vom Ostblock zur EU. Systemtransformationen 1990–2012 im Vergleich* (Göttingen, 2013).
126. Martin Kroh and Harald Schoen, "Politisches Engagement," in *Leben in Ost- und Westdeutschland. Eine sozialwissenschaftliche Bilanz der deutschen Ein-*

heit 1990–2010, ed. Peter Krause and Ilona Ostner (Frankfurt a. M., 2010), 545.
127. Manuela Glaab, "Politische Partizipation vs. Enthaltung," in *Deutsche Kontraste 1990–2010. Politik—Wirtschaft—Gesellschaft—Kultur*, ed. Manuela Glaab, Werner Weidenfeld, and Michael Weigl (Frankfurt a. M., 2010), 101–37, here 123; Steffen Schmidt and Anne Wilhelm, "Nicht-institutionalisierte politische Beteiligung und Protestverhalten," in *Bundeszentrale für politische Bildung Online*, 10 June 2011, retrieved 23 May 2018, http://www.bpb.de/geschichte/deutsche-einheit/lange-wege-der-deutschen-einheit/47408.
128. Kai Arzheimer, *Politikverdrossenheit. Bedeutung, Verwendung und empirische Relevanz eines politikwissenschaftlichen Begriffs* (Opladen, 2002), 277.
129. See the memoirs of the first co-leader of the party: Marianne Birthler, *Halbes Land, Ganzes Land, Ganzes Leben. Erinnerungen* (Berlin, 2014), 272–92.
130. Glaab, *Politische Partizipation*, 121.
131. Inka Jörs, *Postsozialistische Parteien. Polnische SLD und ostdeutsche PDS im Vergleich* (Wiesbaden, 2006).
132. Gideon Botsch, *Die extreme Rechte in der Bundesrepublik Deutschland 1949 bis heute* (Darmstadt, 2012).
133. See Gideon Botsch, "From Skinhead-Subculture to Radical Right Movement: The Development of a 'National Opposition' in East Germany," *Contemporary European History* 21, no. 4 (2012): 553–74; Jan C. Behrends, Thomas Lindenberger, and Patrice G. Poutrus, eds., *Fremde und Fremd-Sein in der DDR: Zu historischen Ursachen der Fremdenfeindlichkeit in Ostdeutschland* (Berlin, 2003).
134. See Jan Johannes, "Mit schwachem Schild und stumpfem Schwert—Staatssicherheit und rechtsextreme Skinheads in Potsdam 1983–1989," *Deutschland Archiv Online*, 20 September 2013, retrieved 23 May 2018, http://www.bpb.de/169248.
135. Roger Karapin, *Protest Politics in Germany: Movements on the Left and Right since the 1960s* (University Park, 2007), 226.
136. Kai Arzheimer, *Politikverdrossenheit*, 2.
137. Roth and Rucht, *Soziale Bewegungen*, 646–48.
138. Bernhard Gotto, "Enttäuschung als Politikressource. Zur Kohäsion der westdeutschen Friedensbewegung in den 1980er Jahren," *Vierteljahrshefte für Zeitgeschichte* 61, no. 1 (2014): 1–33.
139. Anselm Doering-Manteuffel, *Die Entmündigung des Staates und die Krise der Demokratie. Entwicklungslinien von 1980 bis zur Gegenwart* (Stuttgart, 2013), 14.
140. See the analysis conducted by an independent commission on behalf of the German Bundestag: Drucksache 12/7600, "Beschlußempfehlung und Bericht," Bonn 1994, S. 505: http://dipbt.bundestag.de/dip21/btd/12/076/1207600.pdf.
141. Edgar Wolfrum, *Rot-Grün an der Macht. Deutschland 1998–2005* (Munich, 2013), 15 and 709.

142. Axel Schildt, "'Berliner Republik'—harmlose Bezeichnung oder ideologischer Kampfbegriff? Zur deutschen Diskursgeschichte der 1990er Jahre," in *Teilungen überwinden. Europäische und internationale Politik im 19. und 20. Jahrhundert*, ed. Michaela Bachem-Rehm, Claudia Hiepel, and Henning Türk (Munich, 2014), 21–32.
143. See this study: Everhard Holtmann et al., *Deutschland 2014: Sind wir ein Volk? Kurzzusammenfassung der Ergebnisse*, Zentrum für Sozialforschung Halle e.V, and Martin-Luther-Universität Halle-Wittenberg, February 2015, retrieved 23 May 2018, http://www.beauftragte-neue-laender.de/BNL/Re daktion/DE/Downloads/Publikationen/deutschland-2014-kurzfassung.pdf.

BIBLIOGRAPHY

Allinson, Mark. "1977: The GDR's Most Normal Year?" In *Power and Society in the GDR, 1961–1979*, edited by Mary Fulbrook and Alf Lüdtke, 253–75. New York: Berghahn, 2009.

———. *Politics and Popular Opinion in East Germany 1945–1968*. Manchester: Manchester University Press, 2000.

Amos, Heike. *Die SED-Deutschlandpolitik 1961 bis 1989: Ziele, Aktivitäten und Konflikte*. Göttingen: Vandenhoeck & Ruprecht, 2015.

Arzheimer, Kai. *Politikverdrossenheit. Bedeutung, Verwendung und empirische Relevanz eines politikwissenschaftlichen Begriffs*. Opladen: VS Verlag für Sozialwissenschaften, 2002.

Ash, Timothy Garton. *In Europe's Name: Germany and the Divided Continent*. New York: Random House, 1993.

Behrends, Jan C., Thomas Lindenberger, and Patrice G. Poutrus, eds. *Fremde und Fremd-Sein in der DDR: Zu historischen Ursachen der Fremdenfeindlichkeit in Ostdeutschland*. Berlin: Metropol Verlag, 2003.

Benser, G., ed. *Dokumente zur Geschichte der SED*. Vol. 3, *1971–1986*. Berlin: Dietz-Verlag, 1986.

Bergsdorf, Wolfgang, ed. *Wörter als Waffen. Sprache als Mittel der Politik*. Stuttgart: Verlag Bonn aktuell, 1979.

Bialas, Wolfgang. *Vom unfreien Schweben zum freien Fall, Ostdeutsche Intellektuelle im gesellschaftlichen Umbruch*. Frankfurt a. M.: Fischer Verlag, 1996.

Birthler, Marianne. *Halbes Land, Ganzes Land, Ganzes Leben. Erinnerungen*. Berlin: Hanser Verlag, 2014.

Bohley, Bärbel. *Englisches Tagebuch 1988*. Berlin: Basis Druck, 2011.

Bösch, Frank. "Die Krise als Chance: Die Neuformierung der Christdemokraten in den siebziger Jahren." In *Das Ende der Zuversicht? Die Strukturkrise der 1970er Jahre als zeithistorische Zäsur*, edited by Konrad H. Jarausch, 288–301. Göttingen: Vandenhoeck & Ruprecht, 2008.

———. "Energy Diplomacy: Germany, the Soviet Union and the Oil Crisis," *Historical Social Research* 39, no. 4 (2014): 165–85.

———. "Kommunikative Netzwerke. Zur globalen Formierung sozialer Bewegungen am Beispiel der Anti-Atomkraftproteste." In *Theoretische Ansätze und Konzepte der Forschung über soziale Bewegungen in der Geschichtswissenschaft*, edited by Jürgen Mittag and Helke Stadtland, 149–66. Essen: Klartext Verlag, 2014.

———. *Macht und Machtverlust. Die Geschichte der CDU*. Munich: Deutsche Verlags-Anstalt, 2002.

Bösch, Frank, and Norman Domeier, eds. *A Cultural History of Politics*. London: Routledge, 2008.

Botsch, Gideon. "From Skinhead-Subculture to Radical Right Movement: The Development of a 'National Opposition' in East Germany." *Contemporary European History* 21, no. 4 (2012): 553–74.

Bréchon, Pierre. "Politisierung, Institutionenvertrauen und Bürgersinn." In *Wertewandel in Deutschland und Frankreich. Nationale Unterschiede und europäische Gemeinsamkeiten*, edited by Renate Köcher and Joachim Schild, 229–40. Opladen: Leske + Budrich, 1998.

Ciesla, Burghard, and Dirk Külow. *Zwischen den Zeilen. Geschichte der Zeitung "Neues Deutschland."* Berlin: Das Neue Berlin, 2009.

Conze, Eckart. *Die Suche nach Sicherheit. Eine Geschichte der Bundesrepublik Deutschland von 1949 bis in die Gegenwart*. Munich: Siedler Verlag, 2009.

Dale, Gareth. *Popular Protest in East Germany, 1945–1989*. New York: Routledge, 2005.

Danyel, Jürgen, and Elke Kimmel. *Waldsiedlung Wandlitz: Eine Landschaft der Macht*. Berlin: C.H. Links, 2016.

Decker, Frank. *Parteien unter Druck: Der neue Rechtspopulismus in den westlichen Demokratien*. Opladen: VS Verlag für Sozialwissenschaften, 2000.

Dietz, Bernhard, Christopher Neumaier, and Andreas Rödder, eds. *Gab es den Wertewandel? Neue Forschungen zum gesellschaftlich-kulturellen Wandel seit den 1960er Jahren*. Munich: Oldenbourg Verlag, 2014.

Dimitrov, Martin. "Understanding Communist Collapse and Resilience." In *Why Communism Did Not Collapse: Understanding Authoritarian Regime Resilience in Asia and Europe*, edited by Martin Dimitrov, 3–39. Cambridge: Cambridge University Press, 2013.

Doering-Manteuffel, Anselm. *Die Entmündigung des Staates und die Krise der Demokratie. Entwicklungslinien von 1980 bis zur Gegenwart*. Stuttgart: Verlag Stiftung Bundespräsident-Theodor-Heuss-Haus, 2013.

Donert, Celia. "Whose Utopia? Gender, Ideology and Human Rights at the 1975 World Congress of Women in East Berlin." In *The Breakthrough: Human Rights in the 1970s*, edited by Jan Eckel and Samuel Moyn, 68–87. Philadelphia: University of Pennsylvania Press, 2013.

Ebeling, Jana. "Religiöser Straßenprotest? Medien und Kirchen im Streit um den § 218 in den 1970er Jahren." In *Jenseits der Kirche. Die Öffnung religiöser Räume seit 1945*, edited by Frank Bösch and Lucian Hölscher, 253–84. Göttingen: Wallstein Verlag, 2013.

Endler, Adolf. *Tarzan am Prenzlauer Berg*. Leipzig: Reclam, 1994.
Engelhardt, Kerstin, and Norbert Reichling, eds. *Eigensinn in der DDR-Provinz. Vier Lokalstudien zu Nonkonformität und Opposition*. Schwalbach/Ts.: Wochenschau Verlag, 2011.
Engels, Jens I. *Naturpolitik in der Bundesrepublik. Ideenwelt und politische Verhaltensstile in Naturschutz und Umweltbewegung 1950–1980*. Paderborn: Schöningh, 2006.
"'Er hielt sich für den Größten.' Wie Erich Honecker die Deutsche Demokratische Republik in den Abgrund geführt hat." *Der Spiegel* 32 (3 August 1992): 25–27.
Evangelista, Matthew. *Unarmed Forces: The Transnational Movement to End the Cold War*. Ithaca: Cornell University Press, 1999.
Faulenbach, Bernd. *Das sozialdemokratische Jahrzehnt. Von der Reformeuphorie zur neuen Unübersichtlichkeit. Die SPD 1969–1982*. Bonn: Verlag J.H.W. Dietz Nachf., 2011.
Fischer, Joschka. *Die Linke nach dem Sozialismus*. Hamburg: Hoffmann und Campe, 1993.
Friedrich, Walter, Peter Förster, and Kurt Starke, eds. *Das Zentralinstitut für Jugendforschung Leipzig 1966–1990. Geschichte, Methoden, Erkenntnisse*. Berlin: Das Neue Berlin, 1999.
Gajek, Maria. *Imagepolitik im olympischen Wettstreit. Die Spiele von Rom 1960 und München 1972*. Göttingen: Wallstein Verlag, 2013.
Gensicke, Thomas. *Die neuen Bundesbürger. Eine Transformation ohne Integration*. Opladen: VS Verlag für Sozialwissenschaften, 1998.
Gieseke, Jens. "Auf der Suche nach der schweigenden Mehrheit Ost. Die geheimen Infratest-Stellvertreterbefragungen und die DDR-Gesellschaft 1968–1989." *Zeithistorische Forschungen/Studies in Contemporary History* 12 (2015): 66–97.
———. "Bevölkerungsstimmungen in der geschlossenen Gesellschaft. MfS-Berichte an die DDR-Führung in den 1960er- und 1970er-Jahren." *Zeithistorische Forschungen/Studies in Contemporary History* 5, no. 2 (2008): 236–57.
———. "'Seit langem angestaute Unzufriedenheit breitester Bevölkerungskreise'—Das Volk in den Stimmungsberichten des MfS." In *Revolution und Vereinigung 1989/90. Als in Deutschland die Realität die Phantasie überholte*, edited by Klaus-Dietmar Henke, 130–48. Munich: Deutscher Taschenbuch Verlag, 2009.
———. "The Successive Dissolution of the 'Uncivil Society': Tracking SED Party Members in Opinion Polls and Secret Police Reports 1969–1989." In *Communist Parties Revisited*, edited by Rüdiger Bergien and Jens Gieseke. New York: Berghahn, 2018.
———. "Whom Did the East Germans Trust in the Cold War?" In *Trust, but Verify: The Politics of Uncertainty and the Transformation of the Cold War Order, 1969–1991*, edited by Martin Klimke, Reinhild Kreis, and Christian Ostermann, 143–66. Stanford: Stanford University Press, 2016.
Gieseke, Jens, and Andrea Bahr. *Die Staatssicherheit und die Grünen. Zwischen SED-Westpolitik und Ost-West-Kontakten*. Berlin: Christoph Links Verlag, 2016.

Glaab, Manuela. "Geteilte Wahrnehmungswelten. Zur Präsenz der deutschen Nachbarn im Bewußtsein der Bevölkerung." In *Deutsche Vergangenheiten—eine gemeinsame Herausforderung. Der schwierige Umgang mit der doppelten Nachkriegsgeschichte*, edited by Christoph Kleßmann, 206–20. Berlin: Ch. Links-Verlag, 1999.

———. "Politische Partizipation vs. Enthaltung." In *Deutsche Kontraste 1990–2010. Politik—Wirtschaft—Gesellschaft—Kultur*, edited by Manuela Glaab, Werner Weidenfeld, and Michael Weigl, 101–37. Frankfurt a. M.: Campus Verlag, 2010.

Gotto, Bernhard. "Enttäuschung als Politikressource. Zur Kohäsion der westdeutschen Friedensbewegung in den 1980er Jahren." *Vierteljahrshefte für Zeitgeschichte* 61, no. 1 (2014): 1–33.

Großbölting, Thomas. *Der verlorene Himmel. Glaube in Deutschland seit 1945.* Göttingen: Vandenhoeck & Ruprecht, 2013.

Hannig, Nicolai. *Die Religion der Öffentlichkeit. Kirche, Religion und Medien in der Bundesrepublik 1945–1980.* Göttingen: Wallstein Verlag, 2010.

Hansen, Jan. "Making Sense of Détente: German Social Democrats and the Peace Movement in the early 1980s." *Zeitgeschichte* 40, no. 2 (2013): 107–121.

Hanshew, Karrin. *Terror and Democracy in West Germany.* Cambridge: Cambridge University Press, 2012.

Harzer, Erika, and Willi Volks, eds. *Aufbruch nach Nicaragua: Deutsch-deutsche Solidarität im Systemwettstreit.* Berlin: Ch. Links-Verlag, 2010.

Haß, Katharina, and Michael Pesek. "Kleiner Mann auf Reisen: Erich Honecker auf Staatsbesuch in Afrika." In *Die Ankunft des Anderen. Repräsentationen sozialer und politischer Ordnungen in Empfangszeremonien*, edited by S. Baller et al., 106–134. Frankfurt a. M.: Campus Verlag, 2008.

Haug, Wolfgang. *Gorbatschow. Versuch, über den Zusammenhang seiner Gedanken.* Hamburg: Argument Hamburg, 1989.

Hausstein, Brigitte. "Die soziologische Hörer- und Zuschauerforschung in der DDR." *Info 7: Information und Dokumentation in Archiven, Mediotheken, Datenbanken* 23, no. 1 (2008): 67–73.

Heidemeyer, Helge. "Nato-Doppelbeschluss, westdeutsche Friedensbewegung und der Einfluss der DDR." In *Zweiter Kalter Krieg und Friedensbewegung. Der NATO-Doppelbeschluss in deutsch-deutscher und internationaler Perspektive*, edited by Philipp Gassert, Tim Geiger, and Hermann Wentker, 247–268. Munich: Oldenbourg Wissenschaftsverlag, 2011.

Hermle, Siegfried, Claudia Lepp, and Harry Oelke, eds. *Umbrüche. Der deutsche Protestantismus und die sozialen Bewegungen in den 1960er und 70er Jahren.* Göttingen: Vandenhoeck & Ruprecht, 2007.

Heydemann, Günther, and Karel Vodicka, eds. *Vom Ostblock zur EU. Systemtransformationen 1990–2012 im Vergleich.* Göttingen: Vandenhoeck & Ruprecht, 2013.

Hodenberg, Christina von. *Konsens und Krise. Eine Geschichte der westdeutschen Medienöffentlichkeit 1945–1973.* Göttingen: Wallstein Verlag, 2006.

Hoffmann, Dierk. "Honecker in Bonn. Deutsch-deutsche Spitzentreffen 1947–1990." In *Das Doppelte Deutschland*, edited by Udo Wengst and Hermann Wentker, 333–356. Berlin: Ch. Links-Verlag, 2008.

Holtmann, Everhard et al. *Deutschland 2014: Sind wir ein Volk? Kurzzusammenfassung der Ergebnisse*. Zentrum für Sozialforschung Halle e.V, and Martin-Luther-Universität Halle-Wittenberg, 2015. Retrieved 23 May 2018, http://www.beauftragte-neue-laender.de/BNL/Redaktion/DE/Downloads/Publikationen/deutschland-2014-kurzfassung.pdf.

Jarausch, Konrad. *After Hitler: Recivilizing Germans, 1945–1995*. Oxford: Oxford University Press, 2006.

———. *The Rush to German Unity*. Oxford: Oxford University Press, 1994.

Johannes, J. "Mit schwachem Schild und stumpfem Schwert—Staatssicherheit und rechtsextreme Skinheads in Potsdam 1983–1989." *Deutschland Archiv Online*, 20 September 2013. Retrieved 23 May 2018, http://www.bpb.de/169248.

Jörs, Inka. *Postsozialistische Parteien. Polnische SLD und ostdeutsche PDS im Vergleich*. Wiesbaden: VS Verlag für Sozialwissenschaften, 2006.

Karapin, Roger. *Protest Politics in Germany: Movements on the Left and Right since the 1960s*. University Park: Pennsylvania State University Press, 2007.

Kenney, Padraic. *A Carnival of Revolution: Central Europe 1989*. Princeton: Princeton University Press, 2003.

Kittel, Manfred. "Strauß' Milliardenkredit für die DDR. Leistung und Gegenleistung in den innerdeutschen Beziehungen." In *Das Doppelte Deutschland. 40 Jahre Systemkonkurrenz*, edited by Udo Wengst and Hermann Wentker, 307–32. Berlin: Ch. Links-Verlag, 2008.

Klein, Thomas. *"Frieden und Gerechtigkeit!" Die Politisierung der Unabhängigen Friedensbewegung in Ost-Berlin während der 80er Jahre*. Cologne: Böhlau Verlag, 2007.

Knabe, Hubertus. "Neue soziale Bewegungen im Sozialismus. Zur Genesis alternativer politischer Orientierungen in der DDR." *Kölner Zeitschrift für Soziologie und Sozialpsychologie* 40, no. 3 (1988): 551–69.

Kolb, Felix. *Protest and Opportunities: The Political Outcomes of Social Movements*. Frankfurt a. M.: Campus Verlag, 2007.

Kowalcuk, Ilko-Sascha. *Endspiel. Die Revolution von 1989 in der DDR*. Munich: C.H. Beck Verlag, 2009.

Kraushaar, Wolfgang. *Die Protest-Chronik 1949–1959. Eine illustrierte Geschichte von Bewegung, Widerstand und Utopie*. 4 vols. Hamburg: Rogner & Bernhard bei Zweitausendeins, 1996.

Kroh, Martin, and Harald Schoen. "Politisches Engagement." In *Leben in Ost- und Westdeutschland. Eine sozialwissenschaftliche Bilanz der deutschen Einheit 1990–2010*, edited by Peter Krause and Ilona Ostner, 543–55. Frankfurt a. M.: Campus Verlag, 2010.

Kruke, Anja. *Demoskopie in der Bundesrepublik Deutschland. Meinungsforschung, Parteien und Medien 1949–1990*. Düsseldorf: Droste Verlag, 2007.

Lindenberger, Th. "'Asoziale Lebensweise.' Herrschaftslegitimation, Sozialdisziplinierung und die Konstruktion eines 'negativen Milieus' in der SED-Diktatur." *Geschichte und Gesellschaft* 32, no. 2 (2005): 227–54.

Lindner, Bernd. *Die demokratische Revolution in der DDR 1989/90*. Bonn: Bundeszentrale für politische Bildung, 2010.

Livi, Massimiliano, Daniel Schmidt, and Michael Sturm, eds. *Die 1970er Jahre als schwarzes Jahrzehnt. Politisierung und Mobilisierung zwischen christlicher Demokratie und extremer Rechter*. Frankfurt a. M.: Campus Verlag, 2010.

Major, Patrick. "'Mit Panzern kann man doch nicht für den Frieden sein.' Die Stimmung der DDR-Bevölkerung zum Bau der Berliner Mauer am 13. August 1961 im Spiegel der Parteiberichte der SED." *Jahrbuch für Historische Kommunismusforschung* (1995): 208–23.

Mende, Silke. *"Nicht rechts, nicht links, sondern vorn." Eine Geschichte der Gründungsgrünen*. Munich: Oldenbourg Verlag, 2011.

Mergel, Thomas. *Propaganda nach Hitler. Eine Kulturgeschichte des Wahlkampfs in der Bundesrepublik 1949–1990*. Göttingen: Wallstein Verlag, 2010.

Meyen, Michael, and Anke Fiedler. *Wer jung ist, liest die Junge Welt. Die Geschichte der auflagenstärksten DDR-Zeitung*. Berlin: Christoph Links Verlag, 2013.

Möller, Harald. *Geheime Waffenlieferungen der DDR im ersten Golfkrieg an Iran und Irak 1980–1988. Eine Dokumentation*. Berlin: Köster, 2002.

Moyn, Samuel. *The Last Utopia: Human Rights in History*. Cambridge, MA: Harvard University Press, 2010.

Münkel, Daniela, ed. *Die DDR im Blick der Stasi. Die geheimen Berichte der SED-Führung 1953–1989*. Retrieved 23 May 2018, http://www.ddr-im-blick.de.

Nakath, Detlef. *Deutsch-deutsche Grundlagen. Zur Geschichte der politischen und wirtschaftlichen Beziehungen zwischen der DDR und der Bundesrepublik in den Jahren von 1969 bis 1982*. Schkeuditz: Schkeuditzer Buchverlag, 2002.

Nehring, Holger. "The Era of Non-Violence: 'Terrorism' and the Emergence of Conceptions of Non-Violent Statehood in Western Europe, 1967–1983." *European Review of History* 14, no. 3 (2007): 343–71.

Nehring, Holger, and Benjamin Ziemann. "Do All Paths Lead to Moscow? The NATO Dual-Track Decision and the Peace Movement—A Critique." *Cold War History* 12, no. 1 (2012): 1–24.

Neubert, Erhart. *Unsere Revolution. Die Geschichte der Jahre 1989/90*. Munich: Piper, 2008.

Neugebauer, Gero, and Richard Stöss. *Die PDS. Geschichte. Organisation. Wähler. Konkurrenten*. Opladen: Leske & Budrich, 1996.

Niedermayer, Oskar, ed. *Politische Kultur in Ost- und Westdeutschland*. Berlin: Akademie Verlag, 1994.

Niemann, Heinz. *Meinungsforschung in der DDR. Die geheimen Berichte des Instituts für Meinungsforschung an das Politbüro der SED*. Cologne: Bund-Verlag, 1993.

Palmowski, Jan. *Inventing a Socialist Nation: Heimat and the Politics of Everyday Life in the GDR, 1945–1990*. Cambridge: Cambridge University Press, 2009.

Pannen, Sabine. "Montag ist Parteiversammlung! Alltag und soziale Praxis des SED-Parteilebens." In *Aus einem Land vor unserer Zeit. Eine Lesereise durch die DDR-Geschichte*, edited by Marcus Böick, Anja Hertel, and Franziska Kuschel, 15–24. Berlin: Metropol-Verlag, 2012.

Peterson, Christian. *Globalizing Human Rights: Private Citizens, the Soviet Union, and the West*. Routledge Studies on History and Globalization. New York: Routledge, 2011.

Pfaff, Steven. *Exit-Voice Dynamics and the Collapse of East Germany: The Crisis of Leninism and the Revolution of 1989*. Durham: Duke University Press, 2006.

Pfeil, Ulrich, ed. *Die DDR und der Westen. Transnationale Beziehungen 1949–1989*. Berlin: Ch. Links-Verlag, 2001.

Pollack, Detlef. "Der Zusammenbruch der DDR als Verkettung getrennter Handlungslinien." In *Weg in den Untergang. Der innere Zerfall der DDR*, edited by Konrad H. Jarausch and Martin Sabrow, 41–81. Göttingen: Vandenhoeck & Ruprecht, 1999.

Raschke, Joachim. "Zum Begriff der Sozialen Bewegung." In *Neue Soziale Bewegungen in der Bundesrepublik*, edited by Roland Roth and Dieter Rucht, 31–39. Bonn: Campus Verlag, 1991.

Reichardt, Sven. *Authentizität und Gemeinschaft. Linksalternatives Leben in den siebziger und frühen achtziger Jahren*. Berlin: Suhrkamp Verlag, 2014.

Richter, Hedwig. "Mass Obedience: Practices and Functions of Elections in the German Democratic Republic." In *Voting for Hitler and Stalin: Elections under 20th Century Dictatorships*, edited by Ralph Jessen and Hedwig Richter, 103–24, Frankfurt: Campus, 2011.

Richter, Saskia. *Die Aktivistin. Das Leben der Petra Kelly*. Munich: Deutsche Verlags-Anstalt, 2010.

Rödder, Andreas. "Klios neue Kleider: Theoriedebatten um eine Kulturgeschichte der Politik in der Moderne." *Historische Zeitschrift* 283 (2006): 657–88.

Roth, Roland, and Dieter Rucht . "Soziale Bewegungen und Protest—eine theoretische und empirische Bilanz." In *Die sozialen Bewegungen in Deutschland seit 1945. Ein Handbuch*, edited by Roland Roth and Dieter Rucht, 644–68. Frankfurt a. M.: Campus Verlag, 2008.

Sabrow, Martin. "'1989' und die Rolle der Gewalt in Ostdeutschland." In *1989 und die Rolle der Gewalt*, edited by Martin Sabrow, 153–172. Göttingen: Wallstein Verlag, 2012.

Sabrow, Martin. "Der führende Repräsentant." *Zeithistorische Forschungen* 10, no. 1 (2013): 61–88.

———. "Der Pyrrhussieg. Erich Honeckers Besuch in der Bundesrepublik 1987." In *2 x Deutschland. Innerdeutsche Beziehungen 1972–1990*, edited by Andreas H. Apelt, Robert Grünbaum, and Jens Schöne, 201–37. Halle: Mitteldeutscher Verlag, 2013.

———. "'1989' und die Rolle der Gewalt in Ostdeutschland." In *1989 und die Rolle der Gewalt*, edited by Martin Sabrow, 153–72. Göttingen: Wallstein Verlag, 2012.

Saldern, Adelheid von. "Markt für Marx. Literaturbetrieb und Lesebewegungen in der Bundesrepublik in den Sechziger- und Siebzigerjahren." *Archiv für Sozialgeschichte* 44 (2004): 149–80.

Schäfer, Bernd. "Egon Krenz und die chinesische Lösung." In *1989 und die Rolle der Gewalt,* edited by Martin Sabrow, 153–72. Göttingen: Wallstein Verlag, 2012.

Scheiper, Stephan. *Innere Sicherheit. Politische Anti-Terror-Konzepte in der Bundesrepublik Deutschland während der 1970er Jahre.* Paderborn: Schöningh, 2010.

Schildt, Axel. "'Berliner Republik'—harmlose Bezeichnung oder ideologischer Kampfbegriff? Zur deutschen Diskursgeschichte der 1990er Jahre." In *Teilungen überwinden. Europäische und internationale Politik im 19. und 20. Jahrhundert,* edited by Michaela Bachem-Rehm, Claudia Hiepel, and Henning Türk, 21–32. Munich: De Gruyter Oldenbourg, 2014.

Schildt, Axel, and Detlef Siegfried. *Deutsche Kulturgeschichte. Die Bundesrepublik von 1945 bis zur Gegenwart.* Munich: Carl Hanser Verlag, 2009.

Schmidt, Steffen, and Anne Wilhelm. "Nicht-institutionalisierte politische Beteiligung und Protestverhalten." In *Bundeszentrale für politische Bildung Online,* 10 June 2011. Retrieved 23 May 2018, http://www.bpb.de/geschichte/deutsche-einheit/lange-wege-der-deutschen-einheit/47408.

Scholtyseck, Joachim. *Die Außenpolitik der DDR.* Munich: Oldenbourg Verlag, 2003.

Schröter, Anja. "Eingaben im Umbruch. Ein politisches Partizipationselement im Verfassungsgebungsprozess der Arbeitsgruppe 'Neue Verfassung der DDR' des Zentralen Runden Tisches 1989/90." *Deutschland Archiv* 45, no. 1 (2012): 50–59.

Schröter, Ursula. "Abbruch eines Aufbruchs. Zur Frauenpolitik in der DDR." *Das Argument* 56, no. 3 (2014): 376–86.

Schüle, Annegret, Thomas Ahbe, and Rainer Gries, eds. *Die DDR aus generationengeschichtlicher Perspektive. Eine Inventur.* Leipzig: Leipziger Universitätsverlag, 2005.

Schwarz, Gislinde, and Christine Zenner, eds. *Wir wollen mehr als ein "Vaterland." DDR-Frauen im Aufbruch.* Reinbek: Rowolth TB-V, 1990.

Schwarz, Hans-Peter. *Helmut Kohl. Eine politische Biographie.* Munich: Deutsche Verlags-Anstalt, 2012.

Snyder, Sarah B. *Human Rights Activism and the End of the Cold War: A Transnational History of the Helsinki Network.* Cambridge: Cambridge University Press, 2011.

Solga, Heike. *Auf dem Weg in eine klassenlose Gesellschaft? Klassenlagen und Mobilität zwischen Generationen in der DDR.* Berlin: Oldenbourg Verlag, 1995.

———. "'Systemloyalität' als Bedingung sozialer Mobilität im Staatssozialismus, am Beispiel der DDR." *Berliner Journal für Soziologie* 4 (1994): 523–42.

Staritz, Dietrich, and Siegfried Suckut. "SED-Erbe und PDS-Erben." *Deutschland Archiv* 24 (1991): 1038–51.

Teipel, Jürgen. *Verschwende Deine Jugend*. Frankfurt a. M.: Suhrkamp Verlag, 2001.
Thaa, Winfried. *Die Wiedergeburt des Politischen. Zivilgesellschaft und Legitimitätskonflikt in den Revolutionen von 1989*. Opladen: Leske + Budrich, 1996.
Ther, Philipp. "1989—eine verhandelte Revolution," Version: 1.0. *Docupedia-Zeitgeschichte*, 11 February 2010. Retrieved 23 May 2018, http://dx.doi.org/10.14765/zzf.dok.2.604.v1.
Thumfart, Alexander. *Die Politische Integration Ostdeutschlands*. Frankfurt a. M.: Suhrkamp Verlag, 2002.
Vester, Michael. *Soziale Milieus im gesellschaftlichen Strukturwandel. Zwischen Integration und Ausgrenzung*. Frankfurt a. M.: Suhrkamp Verlag, 2001.
Weidner, Tobias. *Die Geschichte des Politischen in der Diskussion*. Göttingen: Wallstein Verlag, 2012.
Wentker, Hermann. *Außenpolitik in engen Grenzen. Die DDR im internationalen System*. Munich: Oldenbourg Verlag, 2007.
———. "Chance oder Risiko? Die Außen- und Deutschlandpolitik der DDR im deutsch-deutschen Kommunikationsraum." In *Außenpolitik im Medienzeitalter. Vom späten 19. Jahrhundert bis zur Gegenwart*, edited by Frank Bösch and Peter Hoeres, 191–209. Göttingen: Wallstein Verlag, 2013.
Wierling, Dorothee. *Geboren im Jahr Eins. Der Jahrgang 1949 in der DDR und seine historischen Erfahrungen*. Berlin: Christoph Links Verlag, 2002.
Wirsching, Andreas. *Abschied vom Provisorium. Die Geschichte der Bundesrepublik Deutschland 1982–1989/90*. Munich: Deutsche Verlags-Anstalt, 2006.
Wittner, Lawrence S. *The Struggle against the Bomb: A History of World Nuclear Disarmament Movement*. 3 vols. Stanford: Stanford University Press, 1993–2003.
Wolf, Christa. *Voraussetzungen einer Erzählung: Kassandra. Frankfurter Poetik-Vorlesungen*. Neuwied: Luchterhand, 1984.
Wolfrum, Edgar. *Rot-Grün an der Macht. Deutschland 1998–2005*. Munich: C.H. Beck, 2013.
Yurchak, Alexei, *Everything Was Forever, Until It Was No More: The Last Soviet Generation*. Princeton: Princeton University Press, 2006.
Zaremba, Marcin. *Im nationalen Gewande. Strategien kommunistischer Herrschaftslegitimation in Polen 1944–1980*. Osnabrück: fibre, 2011.
Zwahr, Hartmut. *Die erfrorenen Flügel der Schwalbe. DDR und Prager Frühling. Tagebuch einer Krise*. Bonn: Verlag J.H.W. Dietz Nachf., 2007.

CHAPTER 2

Economic Crises, Structural Change, and International Entanglements

Ralf Ahrens and André Steiner

German politicians and the general population on both sides of the Berlin Wall were always well aware that the rivalry between the systems in East and West was largely being fought out on the economic battlefield. Economic success or failure—which ordinary people judged directly in terms of consumption—primarily determined the extent of legitimacy afforded each system. At the same time, the two national economies that emerged out of a single economic area after World War II remained interconnected throughout the era of "divided Germany." These links extended well beyond the boundaries of direct foreign economic relations, although these were of greater importance in the German Democratic Republic than in the Federal Republic of Germany. Furthermore, both economies were faced with similar cross-system challenges, but their options for dealing with these issues were determined by their respective systems. At times, they even relied on similar instruments to address such problems. Yet each of these economic systems encompassed a different set of boundaries for political action, and the economic structures that surrounded them varied between East and West.

After taking a brief look at the initial postwar period, this chapter compares key aspects of economic development in East and West Germany while analyzing the "asymmetrical" entanglements between the two. A short sketch of the crisis-ridden macroeconomic changes of the 1970s is followed by an analysis of the cross-system problems that stemmed from structural change at an economic level, which were driven by technological innovations as well as the integration of both national economies in the international division of labor and their reciprocal trade relations. Finally, this chapter illustrates that even the economic upheavals following the collapse of the Eastern Bloc were still heavily influenced by the long-term structural change that had taken shape in the decades prior to the 1990s. All three sections focus on macroeconomic developments within the two Germanies.[1]

Crises in East and West Germany

The division of the German single economic area had different consequences for the two "new" Germanies that emerged after the war. In terms of economic structure, the Soviet Occupation Zone (SBZ)/GDR suffered from substantial disadvantages. It lacked raw materials as well as most basic industries, but it did have a strong manufacturing sector. The Western Zone, which later formed the Federal Republic, covered a larger and more economically homogeneous area. Additionally, the dismantling of industries and reparations payments that were demanded of East Germany in the early postwar period, which far outweighed those of the Western Zone, necessitated rather significant structural changes in the economy. Meanwhile, the nascent planned economy, with its tendency to hedge against foreign economic risks, further exacerbated the disadvantages that plagued the East German economy.[2]

The separate monetary reforms were not only supposed to eliminate the existing monetary surplus in 1948, but also set a divergent course for the economic systems in what would become East and West Germany.[3] The ordoliberal school of thought largely prevailed in the West, laying the foundation for what would later be termed a "social market economy," which ideally combined the economic efficiency of the markets with a minimum level of social security and a stable institutional framework.[4] The East, in contrast, began with the construction of a zone-wide planning apparatus while preparing economic plans along Soviet lines.[5] Spurred on by the Marshall Plan—which not only influenced foreign economic policy, but also had a psychological effect on politics and society—the economy in the Western Zone grew faster than in the SBZ/GDR. In turn, the West German level of welfare became the standard of comparison for the East German population. This comparison with "the West" thus remained an important parameter for economic policy decisions in the GDR. Simultaneously, the SED leadership always had to bear in mind that the GDR belonged to the Soviet bloc, which was what justified its existence in a political and ideological as well as military and economic sense. In West Germany, on the other hand, proponents portrayed the "social market economy" as the best way to move away from the controlled economy of the Nazi era and as an answer to the failure of the capitalist system during the Great Depression. It was also supposed to be part of the bulwark set up to stop the spread of communism. That said, however, the more the GDR's economic performance and standard of living lagged behind that of the FRG from the late 1950s onward, the less its system seemed to represent a viable economic alternative.

The foundation for the West German "Economic Miracle" with its stable growth not only lay in the emergence of mass consumerism in conjunction with increased income; rather, elements of the general economic framework, such as the new social partnership between capital and work, the gradual liberalization of foreign economic policy, or the first steps toward western European economic integration, also played a crucial role. In addition, this growth rested on the surplus of well-trained human capital, augmented by immigration from East Germany before 1961, which was very much a drain on the GDR economy. The ability of West German companies to quickly consolidate their export markets within the unusually rapidly expanding global economy also contributed to this economic boom. Moreover, the above-average percentage of the capital goods industry within the production structure proved to be beneficial because the respective products were quite in demand on the domestic as well as foreign markets. Likewise, recovery investments bolstered growth quantitatively and qualitatively to a significant degree.[6] At the same time, an unprecedented upswing in productivity swept over the agricultural sector, which also helped pave the way for mass consumption.[7]

The GDR could not keep up with this predominantly demand-based growth in the Federal Republic. The different shortcomings and defects associated with the way in which a classic planned economy functioned became more and more apparent as a result. Moreover, consumption levels continued to fall behind in light of the reparations that still had to be paid to the USSR and the reliance of SED industrial policies on the capital goods industry in keeping with Marxist theory and Stalinist industrialization policies; the uprising on 17 June 1953 did little to change the reality of this situation.[8] In order to generate stronger productivity-driven growth following the building of the Wall in 1961, which suppressed migration to the West and changed the general economic framework, the SED leadership introduced an economic reform. As part of this restructuring, more indirect and monetary-based instruments were supposed to be used to manage the economy in order to ensure more innovation and thereby increase the efficiency of the entire economy.[9] Concurrently, in response to the first economic crisis in 1966/67 following the "miracle years," the West German government sought to increase its interventions in the economy through what was referred to as "global management"

(Globalsteuerung) in the Federal Republic. A planning euphoria took hold in other parts of society as well, which was a manifestation of technocratic fantasies, but these measures had little in common with the Soviet-style mechanisms of a planned economy.[10] Such apparent parallels formed the basis of convergence theories that sprouted in the West at the end of the 1960s espousing the idea that the competing systems would move closer together as they faced similar industrial and social challenges. However, proponents of these theories often overlooked the fact that neither the West nor the East intended to alter their tenets of property ownership.

Nevertheless, by introducing reforms and raising its investment quota, the GDR was able to temporarily improve its economic situation, which also fostered consumption. After the rather austere years of the 1950s, the standard of living in the GDR improved considerably as a result. While the supply of foodstuffs stabilized and the range of available products expanded to an extent, the number of technical consumer goods in households multiplied, although their quality and number still lagged behind compared to West Germany. Regardless, the 1960s seemed to mark the "golden years" for many GDR citizens, thanks not only to the improving standard of living and steady growth rates, but also the temporary tenor of candor that emerged in the discussions about economic and social problems within the context of the economic reforms.[11]

Both of these models for economic growth faced massive crises around 1970, but the causes behind them came from very different directions. Toward the end of the 1960s, the SED leadership had launched a growth and technology offensive, concentrating its investments in those branches of the industry considered to be modern while neglecting suppliers and energy producers. As it had become clear that the GDR lagged behind, this strategy was supposed to accelerate structural change in order to finally "overtake without catching up" to the West, as the SED party leader Walter Ulbricht put it.[12] Similar attempts to boost economic development were made several times throughout the history of the GDR as part of the country's efforts to demonstrate the advantages of its economic system. Yet, each time, the faults inherent in the system of a planned economy clashed with the lofty goals of SED leaders, which far exceeded the potential of East Germany's economy. Combined with the inconsistency of previous economic reforms, these overblown growth policies led to another economic crisis, ultimately loosening Walter Ulbricht's hold on the SED while opening the door for Erich Honecker. Faced with the unrest in Poland in December 1970 as well as the increasing number of strikes in the GDR, Honecker then changed the tone of the country's economic policy. As in other Soviet bloc countries, the hope was that a boom in consumption, as well as improved social policies, would increase the motivation to work, thereby establishing the foundation for better productivity. Simultaneously, a "shift from a growth-based paradigm of progress to a security-based paradigm of consolidation" was introduced in order to ensure domestic peace and uphold the SED's monopoly on power.[13]

But, these policies also bore new risks. Significant extra costs burdened the GDR economy, especially between 1971 and 1976, and investments in new technologies were neglected as a result.[14] Even the explosion in prices for petroleum and other raw materials that hit the markets globally, which will be addressed later in this chapter, did not deter the SED leadership from its course. At first, the leaders of the GDR dismissed the international currency fluctuations and the collapse of the Bretton Woods global monetary system as a capitalist phenomenon that had little to do with their own economy; in the beginning they also ignored the growing debts owed to the West for political reasons.[15] In reality, these new debts signaled that the East German economic policies adopted since the early 1970s had heavily burdened the national economy.

Additionally, the SED leadership responded to the growth crisis at the end of the 1960s by backpedaling on its economic reforms and reintroducing "classic" steering mechanisms typical of a planned economy. This move was supposed to address the insecurities that had emerged as a result of the reforms and regain trust by returning to old institutions. Yet, this process increased centralism and dirigisme, thereby exacerbating all too familiar inefficiencies within the system while giving less priority to structural changes and innovation. Given these circumstances, targeted attempts to boost the development of microelectronics were only able to achieve rather unsatisfactory results later on. These failed efforts were mirrored by the dwindling strength of the Utopian hopes and visionary aspects of the socialist project. Combined with the progressive loss of substance and the deteriorating global economic situation, these factors steered economic policy in both the GDR and the FRG toward crisis management, although some measures were done just for the sake of it.[16] By the end of the 1970s at the latest, the trust of official elites and the population at large in the potential and the structures of the planned economy—to the extent that it still existed—had thus crumbled or disappeared entirely.[17]

In light of these developments and the crisis that then ensued in 1971, growth in the GDR took a nosedive once again in 1976 and 1982 before entering a final stage of steady decline in 1986. That said, however, it must be noted that it is more difficult to assess growth in East Germany than in West Germany due to the lack of sufficient data. Nonetheless, it can safely be said that East Germany's growth rates continually sank after the 1950s; they recovered slightly in the first half of the 1970s, but declined noticeably from then on.[18] Despite (or rather because of) the return of more state price-fixing measures from the 1970s onward, inflation sped up in the GDR in the 1970s and 1980s, leading to an appreciation of prices in the early 1980s in particular.[19] Thanks to this trend—as well as continuing supply shortages, state-ordered austerity measures, and a waning trust in the planned economy—most East Germans felt that the country was in a fluctuating state of permanent crisis by the early 1980s.[20]

Especially in light of the economic downturns in 1974/75 and 1981/82, as well as persistent structural unemployment, many West Germans also became aware of a general sense of crisis that seemed to linger in the air at the time. As in the East, the average growth rates in West Germany sank continually from the 1950s onward. From a long-term perspective, though, it can be said that they normalized rather than shrank in the wake of the extraordinary growth of the "Golden Age."[21] Nonetheless, twenty years of almost uninterrupted economic growth had a lasting impact on the expectations of the population in the years that followed. A steeper than usual rise in prices in the 1970s, combined with relatively weak economic growth, thus raised concerns among average West Germans. This constellation, which came to be known as stagflation, was an entirely new phenomenon for the FRG.

The short-term causes of the economic downturn in the FRG in the 1970s can be summed up in three main points. First, the existing increases in prices for raw materials and foodstuffs on the global market were followed by an explosion in oil prices in 1973, which put a damper on consumption. Second, the Bretton Woods international monetary system, with its fixed, yet adaptable exchange rates, collapsed in 1973. This heightened the volatility of the entire economic cycle, instigating a general feeling of insecurity within the societies affected. International capital mobility also continued to increase, which boosted international demand but also capital costs for national producers. Third, the perceived crisis in 1966/67, which was only a moderate downswing in hindsight, was relatively quickly overcome, but the upswing that followed on its heels brought labor shortages as well as growing inflation, which resulted in demands for higher wages. As a consequence, gross wages and salaries across the board climbed between 1969 and 1974 by a nominal annual average of 11.4 percent, further fueling inflation in turn. The jump in costs for primary production factors—capital, labor, and raw materials—effectively capped profits and investments. In response, the government introduced economic policies to combat these short-term causes (we will return to the long-term factors later) behind the economic downturn.[22]

The Bundesbank (the German central bank) took advantage of the leeway afforded in terms of currency and other monetary policies in the wake of the collapse of the Bretton Woods system, choosing to withdraw its support for the U.S. dollar in early 1973. It opted to raise interest rates in order to rein in inflation. Over the next few years, it came to adopt more and more monetarist policies. The federal government, on the other hand, sought to cool down the overheated economy along Keynesian lines, in part because its council of economic experts still forecasted growth even though the recession had already begun to set in. The result, in 1975, was the deepest economic slump that the FRG had yet to experience. Despite the rather surprising introduction of a program aimed at boosting the economy, which ultimately fueled inflation further, unemployment climbed. At the same time, growing budget deficits limited the options for additional fiscal injections. In response, the West German federal government passed its first Budget Structure Act (Haushaltsstrukturgesetz), which was supposed to help reduce the public deficit. The new phenomenon of stagflation accompanied by high unemployment and the government's uncertainty when it came to dealing with this problem thus account for the vacillations in economic policy in the years that followed. The government went back and forth between attempts to consolidate the budget and self-contradictory fiscal interventions with different agendas. But, these goals were only partially achieved, and the state deficit continued to grow.[23]

On a political level, West Germany lost its faith in the ability of reforms and political planning to live up to expectations—expectations that were linked in terms of economic policy to Globalsteuerung and the concerted action of employers and employees (Konzertierte Aktion) dating back to the second half of the 1950s.[24] Indeed it was one of the ironies of history that just as the extent of unemployment made it seem expedient to adopt Keynesian process policies for the first time since the 1930s, the weaknesses of these policies were criticized—or, rather, their theoretical basis was. In the end, not only the Christian-liberal government but also the social-liberal coalition already began to successively turn away from this approach.[25]

This loss of trust had two consequences: on the one hand, it created the basis for abandoning Keynesian-inspired demand-based politics in favor of a monetarist approach to combating inflation and business-friendly "supply-based" policies. To a certain extent, this corresponded to the general trend toward the adoption of neoliberal tendencies in Western industrialized nations, although the comparably radical economic turn taken in the United States and Great Britain only appeared in a much more moderate form in the FRG and continental Europe in general.[26] On the other hand, companies reduced their demand for capital goods in light of the ensuing uncertainty. Ultimately, it was the "cumulation of unintended consequences from certain actions" that led "the economy into crisis."[27]

Economic policy thus became a crisis management tool that was characterized by rather short-term reactions to changing circumstances.[28] The dilemma facing the social-liberal government was that the intra-industrial structural change that it accepted constantly produced social costs, but it hardly had any influence over the shape of this transformation. Its crisis management measures reached their limits as the social costs began to exceed the possibilities afforded through the welfare state and the willingness of the trade unions to make concessions. The conservative-liberal government that took over in 1982 also had to struggle with this problem. It also wanted to roll back on state intervention while strengthening entrepreneurship and the social market economy.[29] These efforts were successful in some respects in the 1980s, but relatively low real growth rates made it clear that the era of the "economic miracle" was over for good. Nonetheless, the shift toward supply-based economic policies had already begun under the social-liberal coalition. The "neoliberalism as a conservative project" approach adopted by the Christian Democratic Union (CDU) under Helmut Kohl successfully consolidated the budget and buffered inflation. At the same time, however, it led to some cuts in social services inspired by such supply-based policies and the spectacular privatization of some public companies. Simultaneously, the government kept up the tradition of structural policies that had evolved since the 1960s while limiting its business cycle policies. Ultimately, neither Keynesian nor neoclassic-monetarist concepts could generate a new growth dynamic on their own.[30]

In sum, the short-term factors fueling the crises in East and West Germany were indeed different. On one side of the Iron Curtain, they were primarily tied to a growth offensive forced by politicians; on the other side of the curtain, supply shortages and corresponding price hikes, which were also influenced by policy decisions, fed the flames. The political reactions to these crises also differed in terms of their novelty and content. Whereas East Germany primarily opted for a return to allegedly tried and true alternatives, West Germany chose to explore ostensibly new options. For a long time, the East weighed in on the side of certainty; in contrast, West German politicians and experts were uncertain how to proceed. However, one thing that both sides had in common was that they had not paid enough attention to the long-term factors behind the slump in growth and the perceived crises of the 1970s.

Furthermore, these factors were very much alike in East and West Germany. For both countries, the reconstruction and "catching up" potential stemming from the economy's disastrous years in the interwar period and World War II had generated the rapid growth of the Golden Age, which was exhausted over time. As a result, supply conditions deteriorated, and it became increasingly difficult to ensure technological progress. Moreover, the rise in real capital intensity decreased the marginal productivity of capital. This meant that the returns generated by the same investment quota kept decreasing. Although the prices of primary goods had risen only slowly during the boom years at first, this exorbitant growth ultimately pushed up the prices for raw materials. That said, the rise of some Asian economies not only intensified competitive pressure in developed industrial countries, but also drove up prices even before the oil price shock that hit in 1973.[31] These processes appeared in a similar form in the GDR, even though they were systemically transmitted in a different way. Despite slight improvements in the 1960s, East Germany was plagued over the long-term by waning investment efficiency stemming from the depletion of its reconstruction potential and rising capital intensity. The information and management problems associated with the planned economy further intensified these effects, as did the lack of interest in profits among the enterprises, as well as the fragmentation of the funds and resources used and the insufficient focus on economic criteria. Likewise, the low level of labor mobility due to the full employment guarantee also played a role.[32]

All told, both blocs experienced an analogous decrease in growth that was spurred on by cross-system factors, although the causal relationships between these factors varied by system. However, the stalled growth that hit the East a little bit later than the West was part of a lethal process developing behind the Iron Curtain.[33] Within this context, structural change proved to be a significant factor, which will be discussed in more detail in the next section.

Structural Change and Its Origins

In his influential book *Das technologische Patt*, which was published in the mid-1970s, the West German scholar of innovation Gerhard Mensch located the core of the crisis "in the drift of structural change." He argued that this transformation unleashed identity crises among the population that were based on fear and hope alike—fear of losing familiar ways of work and life, but hope in the new activities and perspectives that might result from innovation.[34] The continuous changes affecting economic structures were and remain a by-product of the industrial capitalist system. Yet, this transformation varies in its intensity at different points in time. Likewise, the actors involved, as well as the general public, often have different perceptions of such phases. In the FRG, for example, the 1970s and 1980s were seen primarily as a time of intense structural transformation. In the GDR, on the other hand, structural conservatism took the lead in politics as well as economics following the abandonment of forced structural policies in the late 1960s. At the same time, however, the SED leadership had to come to terms with the challenges of the "scientific-technological revolution" and develop corresponding economic structures.[35]

The three-sector model that is often used to analyze structural change in the economy, which breaks the national economy down into the three sectors of agriculture, industry, and service, has received much scholarly criticism since the 1970s; recently, it has also been historicized as a concept in and of itself.[36] If, for lack of a better alternative, employment trends in the primary, secondary, and tertiary sector are taken as an indicator of structural change, the FRG and the GDR followed a very similar path at the beginning of the 1970s.[37] In the early 1950s, approximately the same percentage of the work force—and the largest portion thereof—was employed in the industrial sector in both German states. The percentage employed in agriculture in the GDR—in keeping with the historically more agricultural-based economic structure in the eastern part of Germany—was higher than in the FRG, while a smaller percentage was employed in the service sector. The percentage employed in industry increased significantly in East and West Germany in the 1950s. This growth began to slow down in the 1960s, but the highest percentages employed in industry were reached in the FRG in 1965 and in the GDR in 1970. The service sector grew relatively quickly in the GDR in the 1950s, which was primarily a result of the expansion of the state bureaucracy and its economic management apparatus. During this period, the tertiary sector expanded more slowly in the FRG, but its significance increased much more quickly than in the GDR in the 1960s. That said, however, it did not grow as quickly as during the reconstruction phase after the war. In contrast, the importance of the primary sector shrank just as quickly in both systems in the 1950s and 1960s, although agricultural employment was somewhat higher in East Germany due to long-term factors. By and large, deagriculturalization was completed during the phase of rapid growth in the 1950s and 1960s in both Germanys, which meant that one of the major sources of productivity dropped away.

The share of industry in total employment in West Germany receded quite quickly in the 1970s, but this process slowed down noticeably in the 1980s. The service sector percentage grew rather constantly in comparison, primarily as a result of the boost in part-time employment in this sector.[38] As of 1973/74, more people were employed in the service sector than in industry; quantitatively, therefore, the West was indeed a "service society" from the 1970s onward. Relying on the results of a study that eliminated system-specific differences in the sectoral allocation of professional and occupational structure between the GDR and the FRG, a similar, yet delayed, process can be detected in the East.[39] Whereas employment in the primary sector dropped by almost half in East Germany in the 1970s and 1980s, the percentage of those employed in industry dropped by almost five percentage points; meanwhile, employment in the service sector gained more than ten points, climbing to 51.2 percent.[40] From this perspective, the structure of the GDR economy at the end of the 1980s resembled that of the FRG in 1981. If a higher service sector percentage is used as a benchmark for modernity, as was often done in studies inspired by modernization theory, the GDR lagged behind the FRG in the transition to a service-based society. However, the development of the service sector in the East had progressed further than has often been surmised. The view was sometimes skewed by the fact that many service jobs were to be found within the combinates (large state-run combines) and industrial companies, in part because of supply instability and scarcity within the planned economy, as well as the factory focus of state social policy.[41]

Beginning in the 1970s, employment in the industrial sector in the FRG declined in absolute and relative terms. The share of the secondary sector in the GDR, by comparison, began to sink in the 1970s, but absolute employment still continued to climb until the mid-1980s, which was related to the increasing overall number of employed individuals up to 1988. One of the major factors behind these changes in the West and the East—to a varying extent in each case—was rapid technological progress marked by the expansion of the information technology (IT) branch and the flexibilization of technical solutions associated with it. In turn, this advancement was fueled by increased competition on the domestic and international markets during times of crises. Due to the shape of the respective systems, however, this process unfurled differently in East and West, bearing with it disparate consequences. Ultimately, it was technological progress that made the tertiarization of material goods production, as well as the industrialization of the performance of services demanded by market competition, possible. This shift became readily apparent in the increasing number of jobs in research and development, management, administration, and comptrollership within the industrial sector. Furthermore, the growth in social services was accompanied by a rapid jump in production-related services in areas such as public transportation, credit and insurance business, consulting and tax advising, independent research and development, and data processing. At the same time, the industrial sector began to offer more knowledge-intensive products. Durable consumer goods such as washers, vacuums, and other home electronics, for example, reduced the time spent on household chores. Simultaneously, modern electronic devices also replaced market-related services in the trade, credit, and transportation branches, as well as in public administration. This then stimulated the production of capital goods in return, countering the trend toward deindustrialization.

The expansion of the service sector was also tied in part to the fact that certain services within the industrial sector were externalized—for example, marketing and legal counsel. A purely statistical effect was therefore also at work in this process. But this could account for only a small part of this general phenomenon. In fact, tertiarization primarily reflected the increased service intensity attached to production that rested on new technological innovations, especially in terms of the storage, processing, and transmission of information throughout the whole economy. It was also linked to a stronger intersectoral division of labor in which the traditional boundaries between different branches were increasingly blurred and more fluid.[42] Ultimately, the industrial and service sectors moved more and more toward "a symbiotic relationship"; it became increasingly difficult to differentiate between the secondary and tertiary sector, raising doubts as to the applicability of the three-sector model considering the developments of the previous forty years. Likewise, "deindustrialization" only applies to a limited extent because industry continued to hold a dominant position within the economic, political, and social structure of the Federal Republic.[43] Even the political responses to collapsing branches made this clear because the West German government was most interested in the preservation of industrial jobs. Interestingly, this intra-industrial structural change attracted political attention in relation to unemployment, but the waning significance of the industrial sector as a whole within the national economy went largely unnoticed.[44] Quite possibly, it was the cross-sector nature of the transformation within production structures that kept the sinking importance of the "pure" industrial economy in its nineteenth-century robes from being noticed.

One of the decisive, short-term factors behind this drop was that the recession in 1974/75 hit the industrial sector particularly hard. Additionally, the demise of the Bretton Woods system did away with the undervaluation of the German Mark, which had benefited the industrial sector in particular.[45] Simultaneously, these factors, together with mid-range and long-term aspects, ultimately slowed down structural change in the FRG beginning in the mid-1970s. On the whole, this deceleration resulted from the mostly complete deagriculturalization process mentioned above, the slower pace of welfare state expansion, and the partially deteriorating international selling conditions for West German industries stemming in part from competition coming from newly industrializing countries.[46]

The increasingly saturated consumer goods markets, with their ever more demanding consumers, also factored into this process during the "Golden Age" in the West. But the 1970s were also an age of ambivalence, in which the advent of mass consumption served as the counterpoint to economic crises accompanied by growing unemployment. Within this mass consumption society, moreover, consumer demands became more and more differentiated and refined from the 1970s onward. These developments proved to be a problem for the SED leadership, too, because as televisions became more commonplace in households, GDR residents learned more quickly about the newer and better quality products available in the West. Consumer society in the West had moved beyond the satisfaction of simple consumer demands as clothing labels and car brands became status symbols. The younger generation in the GDR that had not lived through the meager postwar and reconstruction years was also more susceptible to consumerism, which meant that young people came to expect that a similar array of goods would also become available in East Germany. But the SED leaders could not cave into these consumer cravings—nor did they want to—because their idea of consumption was shaped by what they considered to be essential to meet the needs of a working-class family during the Weimar Republic, which was the period in which most of them were socialized. In the 1970s and 1980s, therefore, it was no longer even theoretically possible for the East to achieve its alternative aspirations of generating its own pattern of consumption.[47]

In terms of production, the Fordist model had reached the limits of its expansion in the West. The growth stimuli that came through the third industrial revolution, with its flexibilization of technology and the emerging model of post-Fordist production that went along with it, were still too weak to counteract this development. Similarly, the new jobs being created in the service sector were not enough to offset the rapid increase in unemployment that was taking place. Especially since it was primarily the more capital-intensive areas of this sector that were expanding, hardly any jobs were being generated for low-skilled workers or those with training in specific industries. The statistics indicating a low level of labor mobility between the primary sector and the secondary and tertiary sectors reflected this development, confirming the segregation of the corresponding job markets. On the whole, the core of the tertiarization process in the FRG was not a sectoral structural shift, but rather a cross-sector transformation of production structures that was being propelled by fiercer competition on the domestic and international markets.[48]

In the GDR, the SED leadership continued to cultivate the nominal predominance of industry within the structures of the economy. The legitimizing ideology of the regime, which construed the working class as the ruling class and extolled the virtues of a working-class society, further reinforced this image. Yet, as outlined above, the share of the secondary sector within the economy was actually sinking. But this development was rather more than just an unintended consequence of the increasing problems that the regime faced in trying to manage different aspects of society. The service sector, for example, grew as a result of the ongoing expansion of the state and planning apparatuses, including the Stasi. Furthermore, the expansion of the welfare state that was pushed through under Honecker also contributed to the growth of the tertiary sector. However, the highly integrated economic units in the GDR had no interest in outsourcing service functions to external providers, as had been done to a certain extent in the FRG, because they valued internal autarchy. This can be interpreted as the "real socialist" equivalent to the symbiosis between the secondary and tertiary sectors characteristic of the FRG.

Moving beyond such intersectoral transformations, the changes occurring within the industrial sector itself also need to be taken into account. The branches that benefited most from this process of intersectoral structural change between 1970 and 1987 proved to be—in this order—automobile manufacturing, precision engineering/optics, plastics processing, energy, and office equipment/IT. Consequently, the trends that had emerged during the postwar boom years mostly stayed their course. That said, it was the automobile industry that gained the most ground. On the flip side of the coin, textile and leather goods, clothing, beverage and tobacco, steel construction, building materials, iron and steel, and mining were the big losers. Industrial decline thus shifted the regional balance of employment and added value, to the great detriment of the old mining regions, reinforcing the trend in favor of southern Germany that had been solidifying since the 1930s. In the GDR, the energy, electronics, coal mining, iron and steel, and mechanical engineering industries profited the most, but their relative growth still lagged behind that of their counterparts in the FRG. Employment declined the most (relatively) in textiles and leather, clothing, paper and printing, watches and toys, building materials, iron and metal goods, and plastics processing branches. Thus, the tendencies that had developed in the 1950s and 1960s also continued by and large in East Germany as well. But at the same time, this intersectoral structural transformation was much less intense in the GDR than in the FRG, and it exhibited other characteristics. The drop in employment in the textile and clothing industry, for example, was only half as much as in the Federal Republic. The automobile industry was not among the winners that dominated the structure of the economy in the East. Instead, it was the iron and steel industries that continued to grow in the GDR even while they were shrinking in the Federal Republic. Similarly diverging developments could also be traced in the plastics processing industry, which was one of the structural winners in the West, but on the losing side in the East, despite the fact that it at least temporarily profited from the SED's economic policies. In this respect, the employment structures within the manufacturing sectors in both Germanys differed quite considerably.[49]

More detailed assessments of the structure of the industrial sector in the FRG have shown that the industrial decline that had set in around 1973 did not result primarily from the increase in net redundancies within the shrinking iron and steel, textile, clothing, and shipbuilding industries. Rather, it stemmed from a decrease in net additions to the job markets in the growth sectors in particular; in the high-tech mechanical engineering industry, as well as within the microelectronics and aerospace industries, for instance, the number of jobs created was too low. The same applied to the mid-sized industries, such as chemical and plastic processing, optics and precision engineering, automobile, electrical engineering, and mechanical engineering (including office and computer equipment) industries.[50] Simultaneously, as mentioned above, this drop could not be counteracted by an increase in jobs in the service sector because it was mostly the capital-intensive areas of this sector that were expanding. Even within the manufacturing sector, low-skilled jobs were being eliminated, especially as a result of skill-biased technical change and not necessarily because of the increase in international trade, which were both at the core of the structural unemployment (Sockelarbeitslosigkeit) emerging at the time.[51] All told, the technological revolution that necessitated a more highly qualified workforce and the corresponding structural change in the economy that had begun in 1970s took on new proportions, ultimately becoming one of the long-term factors behind the development of mass unemployment. Although this transformation did not take place in the East at the same pace as in the West, it was nonetheless a factor behind the erosion of full employment looming in the GDR, which manifested itself in increasing downtime and idle periods as well as overqualified employees and a growing number of increasingly tolerated dropout livelihoods of different kinds.

Since full employment was considered to be one of the "basic values" of East German socialism, it thus remained one of the primary goals of economic and social policy. Economic policies appeared to be structural policies per se in the East, and they were governed by a Stalinist paradigm of industrialization until the bitter end. Simultaneously, an eye was always kept on the West in order to be able to follow some of its developments and avoid falling behind completely. The decisive factor influencing the GDR leadership in its decision on whether structural change was supposed to progress or rather be taken down a notch was whether or not it would undermine full employment. This consideration tended to block the transformation, and, ultimately, some of its unintended mid-range consequences were the erosion of the basis of full employment and, along with it, the collapse of state socialism. Structural change was likewise approached from a labor market perspective among policy makers in the West, especially given that full employment was also an essential aim of economic policy decisions, although it was never guaranteed (economically) by the state. Consequently, agrarian and industrial policies in the West were often driven by social policy goals and were not necessarily part of a conscious effort to boost the economy.[52] The costs and possibilities associated with such a policy line also factored into the decision-making process.

Economic structural change in the East and West were therefore only connected through the rivalry between the two systems. As this played a much greater role in the GDR during the period in question, the dynamics of this interaction were thus asymmetrical. Against its own claims of having created an alternative system, the GDR sought to reproduce the technological developments and consumption trends of the West, but was never able to reach the same qualitative or quantitative niveau. At the same time, however, both sides in this race to get ahead had to face increasing competition within international markets.

Foreign Trade, Economic Integration, and German-German Relations

A look at East and West German foreign trade relations perhaps most clearly reveals the tensions between demarcation and entanglement within the two German economies. This was particularly true regarding integration in the European Communities (EC) in the West and the Council for Mutual Economic Assistance (COMECON) in the East. According to estimates, about half of the industrial production coming from the territory of what would become the GDR and almost a fourth of the production in West Germany was shipped to other parts of the Reich in 1936; the corresponding ratios for imports were similar.[53] In contrast, by the end of the 1950s, so-called inter-German trade accounted for about 2.5 percent of the FRG's cross-border exchange of goods, although it was never officially recognized as regular foreign trade; ten years later, it only amounted to about 1.5 percent with a slight upward trend.[54] The East German economy was much more dependent on trade with West Germany and West Berlin, which had grown to over 10 percent of the GDR's foreign trade in the second half of the 1950s before dropping to about 8 percent as a result of a policy of independence (called Störfreimachung) adopted by the GDR after the West German government had suspended the trade agreement in reaction to political quarrels.[55]

The COMECON, which the GDR joined in 1950 and whose member states rapidly came to account for about two-thirds of East German foreign trade, ultimately transferred the systemic weaknesses of the participating planned economies—the lack of efficiency incentives in enterprises, the limited informative value of prices and currencies, and lagging innovation—onto the international stage. Moreover, since the level of industrialization varied greatly between its member states, the more industrialized states—the GDR and Czechoslovakia in particular—had to rely more heavily on Western trade partners when it came to importing innovative and high-quality industrial goods.[56] As a result of these problems within the Eastern Bloc, inter-German trade on the basis of "accounting units" that did not require foreign currency reserves and was supported by an interest-free overdraft proved to be much more significant for the GDR economy than for that of the FRG.[57] Consequently, as early as the 1950s, the GDR became dependent on the high-quality and relatively innovative products of the mechanical engineering, steel, chemical, and optical industries of the West. Over the course of the 1960s, the percentage of inter-German trade within its overall foreign trade volume began to increase slightly again.[58] Despite its growing overvaluation, the exchange rate between the GDR Mark and the D-Mark was officially kept at 1:1 due to political claims to equal status.[59]

The reform efforts of the 1960s did little to alleviate the fundamental problems of the inflexible foreign trade system that insulated production against the fluctuations of the international markets. Around 1970, debates over a reform of the COMECON by and large only served to reinforce existing mechanisms of division of labor compatible with central plan coordination. The GDR reacted to this stagnation with a turn to the West. The foreign trade share of the COMECON countries had already been gradually declining since the 1960s, if the trading volumes with the different currency areas are calculated in terms of the actual cost of production of export goods and the actual costs of imports (as opposed to the official statistics). This statistical trend corresponds to an unintended but then later consciously espoused policy of importing capital goods financed on credit from the West in order to modernize the industries in the GDR. After the East German industries had already lost the ability to compete in Western markets as a result of the lack of efficiency within the centrally planned economy as of the 1950s and the reforms of the 1960s had not been able to fundamentally reverse this trend, the GDR acquired a growing debt in Western currencies. Consequently, the GDR was structurally dependent on its "class enemy" as it entered into a phase of crisis in the 1970s and 1980s.[60]

Up to this point, the economic alignment of the FRG with the West had, by and large, proven to be a success story. Reconstruction after the war and the "economic miracle" were marked by two basic trends in foreign trade policy: the liberalization of the foreign trade system and the corresponding integration into the global economy as well as the incorporation of the country in the European Coal and Steel Community (ECSC) and the European Economic Community (EEC). Initially, the step-by-step transfer of West German exports and imports out of the hands of the Allies, and the facilitation of inter-European trade through the establishment of a multilateral clearing system and the reduction of volume-based import restrictions within the framework of the Organization for European Economic Cooperation (OEEC) pushed forward by the American occupation authorities, were largely responsible for bringing the West German industries back to the global market. Bilateral liberalization treaties allowed for a noticeable increase in the exchange of goods with Western and Northern European neighbors as of 1949 by dismantling quotas. Likewise, the integration of the FRG in the General Agreement on Tariffs and Trade (GATT) in 1951 boosted German exports, placing pressure on the domestic industries to compete with other countries. Simultaneously, the integration of the D-Mark in the European Payments Union (EPU) and the transition to currency convertibility in 1958, as well as the liberalization of capital trade, spurred growth in West German foreign trade from the monetary side.[61]

The economic potential attached to the FRG's integration in Western Europe has been quite apparent since the 1960s, if measured on the basis of trade flows. While West Germany in particular profited from the trade-generating effects of the customs union, the overall share of Western Europe in global trade also increased significantly.[62] As early as 1960, trade with the other five member countries accounted for almost 30 percent of West German foreign trade; this figure jumped to 46.7 percent (exports) and 39.9 percent (imports) by the time the union expanded in 1973. Trade with East European countries (not including the GDR), on the other hand, hovered around 4 percent. Before the war, however, about 15 percent of the exports from the territory that later became the FRG went to eastern and southeastern Europe. In terms of the breakdown of the types of goods being traded, the growing percentage of commercial finished products among the country's imports indicated that the industrialized Federal Republic had been able to take advantage of the benefits of economic specialization through its growing integration in the global economy.[63] Its progressive economic interdependence with Western national economies was reflected in the respective shares of intra-industry trade—that is, the reciprocal exchange of goods within the same industries.[64] Given these circumstances, inter-German trade was important in terms of German-German politics, but it was very much a subordinate economic policy concern.

Instead, West German foreign trade policy focused on dealing with the consequences of the erosion of the international monetary system that had been set up by the Bretton Woods Conference in 1944. The suspension of fixed exchange rates and the final dissolution of the system by the U.S. government in 1973 granted the West German government and the Bundesbank more flexibility because Bretton Woods had tightly limited autonomous monetary policies during crises situations and the options of the "magic square" stabilization policy instituted on the heels of the crisis of 1966/67. Yet because the harmonization of monetary policy remained a core element of Western European integration, efforts were made to stabilize the currency exchange rates within the EC through the "currency snake" introduced in 1972. Similarly, the European Monetary System of 1979 allowed exchange rates to fluctuate to a limited extent, and capital controls were still permitted in order to ensure monetary stability. Given the economic strength of West Germany, especially in terms of exports, the Deutsche Mark quickly became the European anchor currency.[65]

The appreciation of the D-Mark against the U.S. dollar increased the price of German products abroad, but it by no means brought an end to West Germany's regular trade balance surpluses. Although the earlier undervaluation had certainly promoted export surpluses, the country's competitive economic strength rested first and foremost on its manufacturing industry, which was doing well competitively in quality and innovation in human-capital-intensive goods.[66]

However, the internationalization of the West German economy was even more clearly reflected in direct foreign investments than it was in its foreign trade statistics. Between 1960 and 1980, direct foreign investments rose almost three times as fast as domestic equipment investments. Whereas foreign investments only slowly gained momentum in the postwar decades due to a lack of capital, they now took off, primarily in the form of shares acquired in foreign companies. As such, they could offset rising domestic costs as well as hedge against protectionism in the countries that imported German industrial goods.[67] From a macroeconomic perspective, growing capital exports were certainly one of the downsides associated with consistent trade balance surpluses. Export trade may have stimulated domestic investments and sometimes offset a sluggish domestic economy, but, at the same time, the FRG was transferring goods abroad whose equivalent value had to be invested as a credit or in the form of foreign investments. Simultaneously, the surpluses put upward pressure on the D-Mark and therefore drove up prices and costs, which in turn created a lasting problem given the country's increasing reliance on exports.[68]

Naturally, this high degree of integration within the global market was also a potential problem regarding imports during phases of tougher international competition. This was reflected most poignantly in the success of Japanese exports on the West German market in the 1970s and 1980s, but also in the growing share of newly industrializing countries in West German imports of industrial goods. As the joint foreign trade policy of the EEC was more or less in tune with the GATT tariff reductions, the protection afforded to German industry was significantly reduced on this front. Protectionism shifted, as in other countries, from customs duties to nontariff trade barriers, such as compulsory or "voluntary" import quotas as well as targeted subventions that varied greatly from sector to sector. In general, the Federal Republic counted among the countries that were less inclined toward protectionism. As by far the largest portion of the country's foreign trade took place within the EEC and the European Free Trade Association (EFTA), many sectors could hardly even contemplate possible ways to withdraw from competition through such measures, especially because the EC also controlled national subsidies and could prohibit certain state aid programs by court order.[69]

National reactions to the structural problems emerging in many of the member states varied noticeably, however, and the economic and monetary union outlined in the Werner Plan of 1970 seemed to retreat into the distance. In the 1980s, economists and journalists began to attribute this stagnation to a "eurosclerosis" of the EC and its member states. In part because of the pressure exerted by such claims, the Single European Act (SEA) was passed in 1986 with the aim of establishing a single market and unifying economic and monetary policy. As a result of this treaty, several concrete steps were taken toward a further liberalization of the cross-border movement of goods, labor, and capital.[70]

But, the economic effects of the single market should not be overestimated. Although trade within the EEC continued to grow, this political integration had only a minimal effect on the specialization of the individual national economies.[71] The success of European industrial policies in pioneering large-scale technologies in the IT and aerospace branches, for example, was fair to middling at best. In other sectors, such as agriculture or the steel industry, European policy had a tendency to preserve existing structures and often aimed to cushion the detrimental impact of the decline of older industrial regions on the social and labor markets.[72] Regardless of the difficulty of measuring success, these industrial policies demonstrate that Western Europe, including West Germany, did not intend to jettison its long tradition of state intervention in economic structures and business cycles. Despite such measures and other processes of adjustment plagued by crises, the economy of the Federal Republic was already deeply immersed in a new phase of internationalization when it unexpectedly gained new industrial regions through German reunification.

In the fall of 1989, the GDR was still solvent. But, trouble was definitely looming on the horizon: given its net debt in convertible currencies, which amounted to 175 percent of the export revenue coming from trade with Western industrialized countries, as well as the poor performance of its exports on the markets that worsened even further in the 1980s, there was hardly any perceivable way for the country to avoid falling into the debt trap.[73] The inefficient division of labor within COMECON was one factor behind this hopeless situation because the delayed industrialization of other bloc countries cost the GDR a substantial market share in the Eastern export markets. Although East Germany officially attempted to specialize in certain production lines on a bilateral level, which was reflected statistically in the rising share of corresponding products among the country's exports and imports, these goods did not meet Western standards of development and quality. Moreover, rising commodities prices on the global market, especially for crude oil, put a strain on the foreign exchange balance. As prices within the COMECON only adjusted to those on the global market with a substantial delay, the GDR profited quite considerably—despite accelerated adjustments beginning in 1975—from relatively inexpensive Soviet oil exports until the mid-1980s. Most of this oil was then processed and exported to the West, proving to be the most important source of foreign currency for a while. But, the GDR's real exports to the USSR almost had to be doubled to afford even this relatively inexpensive crude oil.[74]

In addition, after a brief interruption in the early 1970s, the GDR reinstated its targeted policy to import Western capital goods; at the same time, however, rising commodity prices strained the country's foreign currency balance even further. An assessment of East German foreign trade according to the actual cost of exports and the actual proceeds from the transfer of imports to the factories thus reveals a lasting shift in regional structure. Consequently, as of 1980, the share of COMECON countries in the imports and exports of the GDR was only about 56 percent, while that of the "non-socialist economic area" was about 41 percent.[75] The GDR, as well as other Soviet bloc countries, chose to take a direct path into the global market after it became apparent that the COMECON would not be able to come to grips with the challenges that went along with globalization.[76] The FRG remained by far the GDR's most important Western trade partner. Around half of East German exports to capitalist industrialized countries went to the Federal Republic, while West Germany's share in Eastern imports was somewhat lower.[77] Inter-German trade continued to be worthwhile for the GDR, especially since it was conducted in "accounting units," which meant that convertible currencies were not needed to import goods from the West. Furthermore, GDR exports to West Germany—as opposed to other non-EEC member countries—were subject to a lower value-added tax and exempt from import duties and levies as a result of political considerations related to the "German question."[78]

Moreover, the extension of the interest-free credit line to pay for the trade in goods between the two Germanys (the so-called "swing") in the 1970s all but begged for the GDR to increase its debt. Yet the growth of the country's debt in convertible currencies was ultimately far more dramatic. This deficit stemmed from the fact that the GDR was consuming more than it could afford under Honecker's "unity of economic and social policy"; at the same time, the country's investments were still not enough to make its manufactured export goods competitive. The GDR's trade balance only managed to shift out of the red in the early 1980s thanks to the economic pressures generated by the refusal of the West to grant loans to the entire Soviet bloc for a while in the wake of the national insolvency of Poland and Romania, as well as a sharp rise in international interest rates. However, this positive trade balance rested almost entirely on import cuts. Likewise, the two "Strauß loans" issued by West Germany in 1983 and 1984 (named after Bavarian prime minister Franz Josef Strauß, who had arranged them) and amounting to a total of about two billion D-Mark helped the GDR get out of this acute credit crunch. Yet, these loans were not significant in terms of the development of inter-German trade. Shortly thereafter, the GDR was no longer able to defer the imports it needed, which meant that its net debt in convertible currencies owed to other Western industrialized countries began to grow once again. Simultaneously, trade with these countries as well as with the FRG declined because the GDR could no longer compensate for sinking revenue from petroleum export products with other kinds of export goods.[79] The "Strauß loans" may also be interpreted as evidence of a "solidifying basis of trust between the two Germanies" that ran contradictory to the general political climate of the nuclear arms race between the two blocs.[80] This money coming from West Germany was not spent on imports, but rather invested in Western banks in order to demonstrate the creditworthiness of the GDR. The fact that the use of the swing was curtailed despite the parallel increase in the cost of currency loans was supposed to evoke an impression of normality and independence from West Germany.[81]

At the same time, the GDR intensified its attempts to cushion the burgeoning economic crisis by cultivating relationships with the FRG outside of regular trade relations. The production of Western consumer goods in the GDR, which increased in the 1980s in light of the currency crunch, brought East German society closer to West German standards of consumption, thereby boosting cultural integration to a certain degree. But the economic benefits of this trend were more than questionable. Cross-trade agreements that obligated Western exporters to buy products from the factories that they supplied or other GDR products were made in various industrial sectors. The stronger exploitation of the price differences for crude oil on the global market and within COMECON, for example, relied on the import of Western chemical systems whose products were primarily exported to West Berlin and Scandinavia. In the 1970s and 1980s, West Berlin's supply of gasoline, diesel fuel, and heating oil relied heavily on GDR exports. The building of so-called "foreign currency hotels" by Western construction companies was also part of this type of foreign exchange, as was the "licensed production" of Western consumer goods with imported machinery in which a portion of the products went to the West German manufacturers and another portion was sold—sometimes in exchange for West German Marks in the Intershops—to the East German population. The import of capital goods, paid for with all kinds of GDR products, was also intended to replace the dependence on prefabricated parts for manufacturing from the West. Yet the refinancing of machinery imports through countertrade by no means came close to the shares originally intended. The improved supply of the country with Western consumer goods therefore continued to put a strain on the foreign currency balance, and the cross-trade agreements effectively turned the GDR into a kind of subcontractor for Western companies.[82]

The transfers in "hard" West German currency that flowed in through other nontrade channels resulted primarily from the political entanglements between the two countries, yet they bore enormous economic significance for the GDR. Clocking in at about two billion D-Mark annually in the 1980s—which was roughly equivalent to the two Strauß loans put together—these revenues from prisoner bailouts, road tolls, transit fees for crossing the border, the minimum currency exchange required to cross into the GDR, and other transfer payments and private monetary gifts improved the country's foreign currency balance. On balance, this money flowed into interest payments and the repayment of outstanding loans. It even completely covered the net interest payments for foreign currency loans in some years; in others, it accounted for at least half of them.[83]

Finally, it should also be pointed out that the West German Mark gradually established itself as an illegal, yet tolerated, second currency in the GDR; the East German society experienced what might be termed the "silent victory of the D-Mark" even before 1989.[84] Despite the trends toward stagnation in reciprocal trade, the GDR economy became increasingly dependent on the Federal Republic in the 1980s. Thus, although the economic reunification of the two Germanies was not the only option available in the fall of 1989 when the SED leadership was looking bankruptcy in the face, the existing interdependencies, as well as trends, seemed to speak in favor of such a union.

Transformation and Continuities

The asymmetric and unequally interdependent relationship between East and West Germany continued beyond 1989 to a certain extent. Initially, this certainly applied to the government's ability to guarantee the standard of living in the East as the government under Modrow expanded the import of consumer goods from the West in order to stabilize the situation.[85] Furthermore, the extensive social transfers from the West that set in shortly after the economic and currency union also boosted the level of consumption in the new federal states.[86] East German exports to COMECON member countries were also supposed to be temporarily stabilized by West German subsidies. By the time the council was dissolved in 1991, however, these export figures had still declined by almost 60 percent. Having already plummeted steeply in the second half of 1990, imports to the new federal states coming from this region also amounted to less than a fourth of the volume of 1989. East German exports to Western countries and West Germany sank by about a third immediately following the currency union in mid-1990 because the competitive constraints caused by the overvaluation of the GDR Mark could not be compensated by cutting costs over the short term.[87]

The further development of East and West German foreign trade occurred within an extremely dynamic international context that is now referred to as the breakthrough phase of globalization.[88] In the 1990s, though, German foreign trade was still marked by a sustainable Europeanization rather than by globalization per se, especially since a significant portion of its export potential was directed initially toward the supply of the new federal states. Moreover, although the growth of the share of the service sector in foreign trade and foreign direct investments accelerated, Germany was ultimately considered to be a country in which the internationalization of the service sector was relatively low.[89]

From an institutional perspective, reunification only strengthened the domestic focus of the German economy for a short time, which was to be expected of a national market that expanded greatly almost overnight. The "reunification boom" that resulted from the high demand for modern capital and consumer goods in the new states, which was partially financed by government transfer payments, proved to be an enormous stimulus package for West German industry. In fact, it cushioned the blow of the international economic downturns that set in at the time. But this boom came to an end in 1992, when the West German states plunged into a longer phase of stagnation. At the same time, the geopolitical shift induced by the fall of the Wall gave the West European economic and monetary union a big boost, which benefited the new German federal states in the long run. The French in particular pushed for the union as a counterbalance to the sudden expansion of the German national economy. Through the introduction of the Euro, the economic power of a reunified Germany was supposed to be harnessed for the rest of Europe. Yet, in the end, the Bundesbank proved to be the model for the establishment of an independent European Central Bank whose monetary policy was committed to stabilization. In turn, this move proved to be crucial for the firm establishment of convergence criteria in attaining EU membership.[90]

Parallel to this intensification of European integration, globalization did more than just put individual companies under stronger pressure to compete internationally. It also questioned the model of what was referred to as Germany Inc. (Deutschland AG). This network of industrial corporations and their principal banks, which cultivated strong political connections and close ties, had been growing since the days of the German empire. A slight unraveling of the capital and personal ties began to appear as early as the 1970s, but it was not until the 1990s that drastic upheavals changed the facts of corporate governance in many of Germany's largest companies. The growth in capital market financing and the involvement of international institutional investors led to an increased reliance on shareholder value as the key benchmark for corporate governance in these joint-stock companies; at the same time, industrial relations organized along the traditional model of corporatism increasingly came under pressure.[91]

Shortly after reunification, the need to coordinate the privatization of the East German economy even seemed to give a boost to the "German model" of corporatist cooperation between the state, industry, and the unions. But it was not long before it became quite apparent that privatization, specific cost issues, and the reorganization of associational life definitely affected the changes taking place in the entire country. This certainly held true for the sale of major East German enterprises to non-German concerns, such as Elf Aquitaine or Arcelor, or the erosion of the collective wage agreement that had already begun in the metal industry in the new federal states in 1992, which had been actively fostered by the Treuhandanstalt, a "trust agency" that had been established to manage privatization. The shrinking importance of principle banks in corporate finance and the organizational and instrumental reforms pertaining to the financing of public budgets via the international capital market also pointed to overall changes.[92]

At the same time, the restructuring of the East put a heavy strain on the West German economy and the public budgets that relied on it. These budgets started off in good shape, but the final accounts of the Treuhand revealed that the privatization of the East German industry had not generated a profit of about 600 billion D-Mark for the coffers of the federal government as had been projected, but rather resulted in losses amounting to 264 billion.[93] This situation was further exacerbated by the social welfare costs associated with high unemployment, the financial strain put on the Western German welfare state through the integration of the new federal states, and the great need to modernize the East German infrastructure. Moreover, the costs of unification managed to nullify the consolidation of state finances that had been undertaken in the 1980s. The financing of public expenditures through credit once again increased, and the share of public debt in the gross domestic product (GDP) rose sharply. In reaction to these issues, the privatization of federal and state property increased at such a rapid pace in the 1990s that the sales of public property in the decades prior paled in comparison. Alongside the liberalization of the finance sector, the split-up and partial privatization of the Deutsche Bundespost (German federal post office) was also quite spectacular, especially since it was accompanied by the opening of the market for mail delivery and telecommunications. The Bundesbahn (the federal railway company) that merged with its GDR counterpart, the Deutsche Reichsbahn, adopted a private legal form, but it remained the property of the state.[94]

However, privatization and liberalization were not just reactions to the tight budgetary situation; rather, they were also linked to the demands for reform voiced in the 1980s that had never proceeded much beyond a rhetorical level. In the age of global competition, greatly accelerated flows of information, and increasingly international and flexible job markets, it was easier to justify and actually implement measures to eliminate real or supposed obstacles to growth.⁹⁵ These trends were most apparent in the finance sector, where a series of laws propelled the turn toward the marketization of financial relations, especially during the stock market euphoria in the 1990s.⁹⁶ During the recession that hit after the reunification boom, a debate erupted over Germany's ability to compete as a business location; it drew heavily on the criticism that had been launched against the seemingly obsolete Modell Deutschland (the German model of co-operative capitalism) in the 1980s. These discussions produced political results, including the Standortsicherungsgesetz (Business Location Safeguard Law) of 1993 that reduced the tax burdens on small and midsize enterprises. In keeping with the narrow perception of globalization as a competition over costs, it was quite logical to stylize cost reduction and flexibilization as the key challenges for companies and politics.⁹⁷ This was admittedly part of an international trend that coincided in the German context with disappointed expectations vis-à-vis reunification.

The combination of the need for private retirement provision and flexible employment models that were sometimes quite precarious was a new experience for all Germans, though the East German population definitely had more adapting to do. The job cuts in the enterprises that had been successfully privatized by the Treuhand and the layoffs in the liquidized factories added up to about 60 percent of the jobs that had still existed in the East in 1990.⁹⁸ At the same time, a more dramatic east-west divide in regional economic performance developed alongside the old north-south divide that had existed in former West Germany. Thus, it often took a long while for new industrial and service clusters to emerge in the eastern federal states after reunification. The deindustrialization that occurred throughout East Germany can at best be seen as part of a "catch-up modernization" process.⁹⁹ In reality, however, its roots lay in the SED's misguided industrial policies and its inability to steer the country's limited means of investment and its import of Western capital goods into the development of competitive capacities and products. The economic landscape of the late GDR was dotted here and there with modern "islands" of production surrounded by machinery with an extremely high amount of wear and tear.¹⁰⁰ This economic decay was often termed *Abbau Ost* (Dismantling the East) in order to emphasize the contrast to the economic reconstruction program known as *Aufbau Ost* (Developing the East), which had been put in place over the course of reunification in order to bring the East German economy up to speed with the West. It came about in part through the hasty move toward privatization because potential buyers had little interest in manufacturing companies in the East given the production capacity surpluses in the West. Not only the politically mandated time constraints and the lack of capital in East Germany but also practical errors hampered privatization. These included the shift of factual GDR state debts to the books of the enterprises that were to be privatized, as well as cases of corruption and fraud.[101]

Additionally, this transformation and the course it took varied greatly according to the respective structures of the different sectors. Most of the East German steel production sites, for example, were retained at first. They also benefited—as was also the case in the West in the 1980s—from extensive public funds that flowed into large investment projects within this highly concentrated industry, which were also motivated by regional political concerns or social policy issues. In contrast, the mechanical engineering industry lost an extremely high share of its employees, despite the fact that it had been one of the GDR's leading sectors with a smaller productivity gap. The relatively small average size of the companies and a fractured ownership structure that dampened public interest and increased the chances of "raisin-picking" for new owners largely accounted for this loss. Moreover, the strong focus on exports proved to be quite a strain because these companies were forced to enter the global market unprotected; they were also confronted by West German competitors who were already under pressure themselves. The net losses in employment proved to be much lower in the public service and retail trade sectors as well as in the chemical industry, even though it was not generally considered to be very modern.[102]

Overly optimistic political estimations certainly had something to do with the East German economy hitting rock bottom as the reunification boom took a downswing in 1991 and unemployment figures skyrocketed. The simple transfer of Western institutions and the West German currency onto the existing East German structures had not—as hoped—generated self-sustaining growth on a broad level. After bottoming out in the early 1990s, growth rates rebounded quite impressively at first, but they were heavily dependent on construction activity that soon dropped off again. Industry employment figures finally stabilized in the mid-1990s, but they still remained at a much lower level than in the GDR. In terms of productivity, the East was not quite able to achieve the same level as the West because large companies with a focus on innovation were still underrepresented. This catch-up process further stagnated in the second half of the 1990s, and, although it gained momentum slowly in the decade that followed, it still has not been completed even today.[103]

Lastly, with its transformation into a market economy and its corresponding integration into not only the West German but also the European and global economy, the East underwent structural transformations almost overnight that had taken decades in the West. Its outdated economic structures had hardly any way to protect themselves against the shock waves released by the need to adjust to new competition. Thus, the economic and social upheavals in the 1990s were first and foremost the result of GDR economic policy. Additionally, they stemmed from avoidable and unavoidable political errors made after 1990, as well as accelerated globalization in the wake of the collapse of the Soviet bloc. But methodological constraints make it difficult to separate these factors and specify their different implications.[104]

At the same time, the share of industry in overall employment dipped quite quickly in West Germany in the 1990s. Among other things, the real appreciation of the D-Mark after the reunification boom handicapped industry and facilitated an increase in the share of the service sector, which was akin to what happened in the mid-1970s.[105] Yet it has been apparent for some time that self-sufficient economic development in East Germany would not come about without functioning industrial companies. In any case, the prognoses regarding the transition of the Federal Republic to a service society did not hold up. Although industrial production is becoming more and more intertwined with the service sector, the persistence of industry and especially the insistence on its "modernity" since the economic and financial crisis in 2008/09 have fundamentally called into question the idea of a "post-industrial society."[106]

Although to a lesser degree than before, both the old and new federal states are still shaped by industrial structures (and their accompanying institutions such as trade unions), which had been suffering under pressure to adapt to the changing global situation since the 1960s. The ensuing upheavals not only bolstered the entanglements between the two Germanies, but also often intensified demarcation efforts on both sides. As part of the post-1989 transformation, the East Germans fought to achieve the consumption level of the West symbolized by the D-Mark, and to adopt the institutions and structures of the West German social market economy. Although it was very much a game of catch-up, the East was able to make huge jumps forward in prosperity and affluence. Yet a considerable portion of the population had to stand by and watch as their professional qualifications and skills lost value over the course of the massive restructuring of the economy.

Ultimately, this was one of the consequences of the inability of the East German planned economy to react adequately and flexibly to the new cross-system challenges that played an obvious role in the country's downfall in the 1980s. In contrast, the West German system, with its market-based economy, was actually able to adjust well enough to these changes in order to bring about a new upturn in the 1980s. Nonetheless, it was also plagued by structural and institutional problems affecting its ability to react to economic structural change and demographic shifts that had not received enough attention for far too long. The symptoms of this were rising unemployment and the perpetually overwhelming stress on the social welfare system, which were the contradictory results of a bundle of different developments. The growth in productivity required by an economy that had become increasingly globalized since the 1970s, as well as entrenched structures governing economic activity, for example, blocked substantial employment growth. The further expansion of social expenditures and the decline in the employable share of the population put a strain on the social welfare systems, which was further exacerbated by the way in which the costs of reunification were financed. Now, in the aftermath of the labor market reforms in the early twenty-first century, the German economy is doing much better than ever before. Whether this status can be maintained over the long run, however, is very much dependent on the further course of sectoral developments as well as the country's ability to deal with the smoldering crisis of the Euro and the challenges of globalization.

Ralf Ahrens studied modern history, political science, and economics at the universities in Frankfurt/Main and Freiburg/Breisgau. After receiving his doctorate in economic history at the Technische Universität Dresden, he held postdoctoral research positions in contemporary history at the universities in Dresden and Jena. He has been doing research at the Center for Contemporary History in Potsdam (ZZF) since 2009. His book publications include *Gegenseitige Wirtschaftshilfe? Die DDR im RGW—Strukturen und handelspolitische Strategien* (2000); *Flick: Der Konzern, die Familie, die Macht* (with Tim Schanetzky, Jörg Osterloh and Norbert Frei, 2009); *Die "Deutschland AG": Historische Annäherungen an den bundesdeutschen Kapitalismus* (ed. with Boris Gehlen and Alfred Reckendrees, 2013).

André Steiner is a senior research fellow at the Center for Contemporary History in Potsdam and professor of economic and social history at the University of Potsdam. His Ph.D. is from Humboldt-University in Berlin, where he studied history and economics. He is a former research fellow at the Institutes for Economic History in Berlin and Mannheim and interim professor for social and economic history at the Ruhr University Bochum. He has published *Die DDR-Wirtschaftsreform der sechziger Jahre: Konflikt zwischen Effizienz- und Machtkalkül* (1999) and *The Plans that Failed:'An Economic History of the GDR* (2010). He is coeditor of *Der Mythos von der postindustriellen Welt: Wirtschaftlicher Strukturwandel in Deutschland 1960 bis 1990* (2016).

NOTES

1. For an analysis of the sectoral level, see, for example, Werner Plumpe and André Steiner, eds., *Der Mythos von der postindustriellen Welt: Wirtschaftlicher Strukturwandel in Deutschland 1960 bis 1990* (Göttingen, 2016); Johannes Bähr and Dietmar Petzina, eds., *Innovationsverhalten und Entscheidungsstrukturen: Vergleichende Studien zur wirtschaftlichen Entwicklung im geteilten Deutschland* (Berlin, 1996); Lothar Baar and Dietmar Petzina, eds., *Deutsch-deutsche Wirtschaft 1945 bis 1990. Strukturveränderungen, Innovationen und regionaler Wandel: Ein Vergleich* (St. Katharinen, 1999).
2. Werner Abelshauser, *Deutsche Wirtschaftsgeschichte: Von 1945 bis zur Gegenwart*, 2nd ed. (Munich, 2011), 59–73; André Steiner, *The Plans That Failed: An Economic History of the GDR* (New York, 2010), 11–15.
3. Christoph Buchheim, "The Establishment of the Bank deutscher Länder and the West German Currency Reform," in *Fifty Years of the Deutsche Mark: Central Bank and the Currency in Germany since 1948*, ed. Deutsche Bundesbank (Oxford, 1999), 55–100; Frank Zschaler, "Die vergessene Währungsreform: Vorgeschichte, Durchführung und Ergebnisse der Geldumstellung in der SBZ 1948," *Vierteljahrshefte für Zeitgeschichte* 45, no. 2 (1997): 191–224.
4. Gerold Ambrosius, *Die Durchsetzung der Sozialen Marktwirtschaft in Westdeutschland 1945–1949* (Stuttgart, 1977); Anthony J. Nicholls, *Freedom with Responsibility: The Social Market Economy in Germany, 1918–1963* (Oxford, 2000).
5. André Steiner, "Die Deutsche Wirtschaftskommission—ein ordnungspolitisches Machtinstrument?," in *Das letzte Jahr der SBZ: Politische Weichenstellungen und Kontinuitäten im Prozeß der Gründung der DDR*, ed. D. Hoffmann and H. Wentker (Munich, 2000), 85–105.
6. For a summary, see Herbert Giersch, Karl-Heinz Paqué, and Holger Schmieding, *The Fading Miracle: Four Decades of Market Economy in Germany* (Cambridge, 1992), 16–116.
7. Arnd Bauerkämper, "Agrarwirtschaft und ländliche Gesellschaft in der Bundesrepublik Deutschland und der DDR. Eine Bilanz der Jahre 1945–1965," *Aus Politik und Zeitgeschichte* B38/97 (1997): 25–37.
8. For a summary, see Steiner, *Plans*, 83–90.
9. André Steiner, *Die DDR-Wirtschaftsreform der sechziger Jahre. Konflikt zwischen Effizienz- und Machtkalkül* (Berlin, 1999).
10. Giersch, Paqué, and Schmieding, *Fading Miracle*, 139–54.
11. For a summary, see Steiner, *Plans*, 126–32.
12. For a summary, see Steiner, *Plans*, 119–25.
13. Steiner, *Plans*, 141–144; Peter Hübner, "Fortschrittskonkurrenz und Krisenkongruenz? Europäische Arbeitsgesellschaften und Sozialstaaten in den letzten Jahrzehnten des Kalten Krieges (1970–1989)," *Zeitgeschichte* 34, no. 3 (2007): 144, 146.
14. Steiner, *Plans*, 145–47, 151–55.

15. Cf. Stephen Kotkin, "The Kiss of Debt: The East Bloc Goes Borrowing," in *The Shock of the Global: The 1970s in Perspective*, ed. Niall Ferguson, Charles S. Maier, Erez Manela, and Daniel J. Sargent (Cambridge, 2010), 80–94.
16. On the details, see Steiner, *Plans*, 142–54.
17. Andreas Malycha, *Die SED in der Ära Honecker: Machtstrukturen, Entscheidungsmechanismen und Konfliktfelder in der Staatspartei 1971 bis 1989* (Munich 2014), 264–69.
18. Cf. Albrecht Ritschl and Mark Spoerer, "Das Bruttosozialprodukt in Deutschland nach den amtlichen Volkseinkommens- und Sozialproduktstatistiken 1901–1995," *Jahrbuch für Wirtschaftsgeschichte* 38, no. 2 (1997): 27–54; Steiner, *Plans*, 160–61; Jaap Sleifer, *Planning Ahead and Falling Behind: The East German Economy in Comparison with West Germany 1936–2002* (Berlin, 2006).
19. Cf. Gerhard Heske, *Bruttoinlandsprodukt, Verbrauch und Erwerbstätigkeit in Ostdeutschland 1970–2000. Neue Ergebnisse einer volkswirtschaftlichen Gesamtrechnung* (Cologne, 2005), 185; André Steiner, "Preisgestaltung," in *Geschichte der Sozialpolitik in Deutschland seit 1945*, vol. 10, *Deutsche Demokratische Republik 1971–1989. Bewegung in der Sozialpolitik, Erstarrung und Niedergang*, ed. Christoph Boyer, Klaus-Dietmar Henke, and Peter Skyba (Baden-Baden, 2008), 304–23.
20. Steiner, *Plans*, 159–60, 185–89.
21. For a brief overview of the different explanations for this, see Rainer Metz, "Expansion und Kontraktion. Das Wachstum der deutschen Wirtschaft im 20. Jahrhundert," in *Geschichte der deutschen Wirtschaft im 20. Jahrhundert*, ed. Reinhard Spree (Munich, 2001), 78–87.
22. Giersch, Paqué, and Schmieding, *Fading Miracle*, 158–59, 176–90. Wage increases calculated according to Deutsche Bundesbank, *50 Jahre Deutsche Mark. Monetäre Statistiken 1948–1997* (Munich, 1998), CD-ROM, Tabelle DJ0429.
23. Giersch, Paqué, and Schmieding, *Fading Miracle*, 186–92. On the fundamental problem of forecasts and prognosis options in this context, see Tim Schanetzky, *Die große Ernüchterung. Wirtschaftspolitik, Expertise und Gesellschaft in der Bundesrepublik 1966 bis 1982* (Berlin 2007), 184–92.
24. Tim Schanetzky, "Sachverständiger Rat und Konzertierte Aktion: Staat, Gesellschaft und wissenschaftliche Expertise in der bundesrepublikanischen Wirtschaftspolitik," *Vierteljahrschrift für Sozial- und Wirtschaftsgeschichte* 91, no. 3 (2004): 324; Alexander Nützenadel, *Stunde der Ökonomen. Wissenschaft, Politik und Expertenkultur in der Bundesrepublik 1949–1974* (Göttingen 2005).
25. Hansjörg Siegenthaler, "Das Ende des Keynesianismus als Gegenstand Keynesianischer Interpretation," *Jahrbuch für Wirtschaftsgeschichte* 43, no. 1 (2002): 237–48.
26. For a more detailed account of the West German case, see Schanetzky, *Die große Ernüchterung*; for a more general perspective, see Hartmut Kaelble, *Kalter Krieg und Wohlfahrtsstaat. Europa 1945–1989* (Munich 2011), 181–83.

27. Siegenthaler, *Ende des Keynesianismus*, 243–45.
28. Edgar Grande, "West Germany: From Reform Policy to Crisis-Management," in *The Politics of Economic Crisis: Lessons from Western Europe*, ed. Erik Damgaard, Peter Gerlich, and Jeremy Richardson (Aldershot, 1989), 55–56; Gabriele Metzler, *Konzeptionen politischen Handelns von Adenauer bis Brandt. Politische Planung in der pluralistischen Gesellschaft* (Paderborn 2005), 412.
29. Grande, *West Germany*, 55–57.
30. Schanetzky, *Die große Ernüchterung*, 211–33; Andreas Wirsching, *Abschied vom Provisorium: 1982–1990* (Munich, 2006), 242–88; Ulrich Herbert, *Geschichte Deutschlands im 20. Jahrhundert* (Munich 2014), 967–78. Quote: Anselm Doering-Manteuffel, "Die deutsche Geschichte in den Zeitbögen des 20. Jahrhunderts," *Vierteljahrshefte* für Zeitgeschichte 62, no. 3 (2014): 341.
31. Herman van der Wee, *Prosperity and Upheaval: The World Economy 1945–1980* (Berkeley, 1986), 84; Ludger Lindlar, *Das mißverstandene Wirtschaftswunder. Westdeutschland und die westeuropäische Nachkriegsprosperität* (Tübingen, 1997), 331–33; Giersch, Paqué, and Schmieding, *Fading Miracle*, 223–25.
32. Steiner, *Plans*, passim.
33. The latter is also pointed out in Charles S. Maier, "'Malaise': The Crisis of Capitalism in the 1970s," in Ferguson, *Shock*, 45.
34. Gerhard Mensch, *Stalemate in Technology: Innovations Overcome the Depression* (Cambridge, 1979), 6–9, 90–94.
35. Cf. André Steiner, "Die siebziger Jahre als Kristallisationspunkt des wirtschaftlichen Strukturwandels in West und Ost?," in *Das Ende der Zuversicht? Die siebziger Jahre als Geschichte*, ed. Konrad H. Jarausch (Göttingen, 2008), 34–36; Ralf Ahrens, "Planning Priorities, Managing Shortages: Industrial Policy in the German Democratic Republic, from Stalinism to Welfare Dictatorship," in *Industrial Policy in Europe after 1945: Wealth, Power and Economic Development in the Cold War*, ed. Christian Grabas and Alexander Nützenadel (Basingstoke, 2014).
36. Cf. Rüdiger Graf and Kim Christian Priemel, "Zeitgeschichte in der Welt der Sozialwissenschaften. Legitimität und Originalität einer Disziplin," *Vierteljahrshefte für Zeitgeschichte* 59, no. 4 (2011): 479–508; Jan-Otmar Hesse, "Ökonomischer Strukturwandel. Zur Wiederbelebung einer wirtschaftshistorischen Leitsemantik," *Geschichte und Gesellschaft* 39, no. 1 (2013): 86–115.
37. On the following, with the corresponding figures and their problematics, see Steiner, "Die siebziger Jahre," 32.
38. On the former, see Marlene Nowack, "Der Strukturwandel und seine Begleiterscheinungen—Rückblick auf die Entwicklung ausgewählter Wirtschaftsbereiche im früheren Bundesgebiet," in *Wirtschaftsstruktur und Arbeitsplätze im Wandel der Zeit*, ed. Hans Günther Merk (Stuttgart, 1994), 39. Corresponding data is still lacking for the GDR.
39. Annegret Groebel, *Strukturelle Entwicklungsmuster in Markt- und Planwirtschaften* (Heidelberg, 1997), 105–15.
40. Groebel, *Strukturelle Entwicklungsmuster*, 118. Cf. the compilation in Steiner, "Die siebziger Jahre," 32–33.

41. Cf. Peter Hübner, "Betriebe als Träger der Sozialpolitik, betriebliche Sozialpolitik," in Boyer, Henke, Skyba, *Geschichte der Sozialpolitik*, 10:703–38.
42. Henning Klodt, Rainer Maurer, and Axel Schimmelpfennig, *Tertiarisierung der deutschen Wirtschaft* (Tübingen, 1997), 48, 56.
43. Gerold Ambrosius, "Ursachen der Deindustrialisierung Westeuropas," in *Umweltgeschichte. Umweltverträgliches Wirtschaften in historischer Perspektive*, ed. Werner Abelshauser (Göttingen, 1994), 221 (quote); Gerold Ambrosius, "Sektoraler Wandel und internationale Verflechtung: Die bundesdeutsche Wirtschaft im Übergang zu einem neuen Strukturmuster," in *Auf dem Weg in eine neue Moderne? Die Bundesrepublik Deutschland in den siebziger und achtziger Jahren*, ed. Thomas Raithel, Andreas Rödder, and Andreas Wirsching (Munich, 2009), 21.
44. Grande, *West Germany*, 52–53.
45. Klodt, Maurer, and Schimmelpfennig, *Tertiarisierung*, 23–26.
46. Gerold Ambrosius, "Agrarstaat oder Industriestaat—Industriestaat oder Dienstleistungsgesellschaft? Zum sektoralen Strukturwandel im 20. Jahrhundert," in Spree, *Wirtschaft*, 68.
47. Steiner, *Plans*, S. 185–89.
48. Klodt, Maurer, and Schimmelpfennig, *Tertiarisierung*, 35, 55–58, 205–07.
49. Steiner, "Die siebziger Jahre," 39–41; with reference to the data provided in Martin Gornig, *Gesamtwirtschaftliche Leitsektoren und regionaler Strukturwandel. Eine theoretische und empirische Analyse der sektoralen und regionalen Wirtschaftsentwicklung in Deutschland 1895–1987* (Berlin 2000), 78, 93. On the shifts in regional structure, see ibid., 108–113; Dietmar Petzina, "Standortverschiebungen und regionale Wirtschaftskraft in der Bundesrepublik Deutschland seit den fünfziger Jahren," in *Wirtschaftliche Integration und Wandel von Raumstrukturen im 19. und 20. Jahrhundert*, ed. Josef Wysocki (Berlin, 1994), 101–27.
50. Ambrosius, *Deindustrialisierung*, 209–10.
51. Carsten Ochsen, "Zukunft der Arbeit und Arbeit der Zukunft in Deutschland," *Perspektiven der Wirtschaftspolitik* 7, no. 2 (2006): 173–93.
52. Cf. Stefan Grüner, "Ensuring Economic Growth and Socioeconomic Stabilization: Industrial Policy in West Germany, 1950–1975," in Grabas and Nützenadel, *Industrial Policy in Europe*, 86–112; Stefan Goch, *Eine Region im Kampf mit dem Strukturwandel. Bewältigung von Strukturwandel und Strukturpolitik im Ruhrgebiet* (Essen, 2002).
53. Deliveries: 49 percent compared to 22 percent; imports: 55 compared to 21 percent; Bruno Gleitze, *Ostdeutsche Wirtschaft. Industrielle Standorte und volkswirtschaftliche Kapazitäten des ungeteilten Deutschland* (Berlin, 1956), 8.
54. Siegfried Kupper, *Der innerdeutsche Handel. Rechtliche Grundlagen, politische und wirtschaftliche Bedeutung* (Cologne, 1972), 65.
55. Heinz Köhler, *Economic Integration in the Soviet Bloc: With an East German Case Study* (New York, 1965), 61–70; Ralf Ahrens, *Gegenseitige Wirtschaftshilfe? Die DDR im RGW—Strukturen und handelspolitische Strategien 1963–1976* (Cologne, 2000), 115.

56. Cf. the detailed accounts in more recent studies: Ahrens, *Wirtschaftshilfe*; Randall W. Stone, *Satellites and Commissars: Strategy and Conflict in the Politics of Soviet-Bloc Trade* (Princeton, 1996); André Steiner, "The Council of Mutual Economic Assistance: An Example of Failed Economic Integration?," in *Geschichte und Gesellschaft* 39, no. 3 (2013): 240–58.
57. Cf. the overview provided in Maria Haendcke-Hoppe-Arndt, "Interzonenhandel/Innerdeutscher Handel," in *Materialien der Enquete-Kommission "Aufarbeitung von Geschichte und Folgen der SED-Diktatur in Deutschland,"* ed. Deutscher Bundestag (Frankfurt a. M., 1995), vol. V/2, 1543–71.
58. Jörg Roesler, "Handelsgeschäfte im Kalten Krieg. Die wirtschaftliche Motivation für den deutsch-deutschen Handel zwischen 1949 und 1961," in *Wirtschaftliche Folgelasten des Krieges in der SBZ/DDR*, ed. Christoph Buchheim (Baden-Baden, 1995), 193–220; Kupper, *Handel*, 65.
59. Cf. Oskar Schwarzer, *Sozialistische Zentralplanwirtschaft in der SBZ/DDR. Ergebnisse eines ordnungspolitischen Experiments, 1945–1989* (Stuttgart, 1999), 121–25; Armin Volze, "Die gespaltene Valutamark. Anmerkungen zur Währungspolitik und Außenhandelsstatistik der DDR," *Deutschland Archiv* 32, no. 2 (1999): 232–41.
60. Ralf Ahrens, "Debt, Cooperation, and Collapse: East German Foreign Trade in the Honecker Years," in *The East German Economy, 1945–2010: Falling Behind or Catching Up?*, ed. Hartmut Berghoff and Uta A. Balbier (Cambridge, 2013), 161–76.
61. Christoph Buchheim, *Die Wiedereingliederung Westdeutschlands in die Weltwirtschaft 1945–1958* (Munich, 1990); Reinhard Neebe, *Weichenstellung für die Globalisierung. Deutsche Weltmarktpolitik, Europa und Amerika in der Ära Ludwig Erhard* (Cologne, 2004).
62. Johannes Bähr, "Integrationseffekte und Integrationspotentiale in unterschiedlichen Wirtschaftssystemen: Das geteilte Deutschland im Vergleich," in *Wirtschaftliche und soziale Integration in historischer Sicht*, ed. Eckart Schremmer (Stuttgart, 1996), 245–46, 255.
63. Abelshauser, *Wirtschaftsgeschichte*, 257–58.
64. Giersch, Paqué, and Schmieding, *Fading Miracle*, 166, 172.
65. Cf. Harold James, *International Monetary Cooperation since Bretton Woods* (New York, 1996), 205–59, 289–303, 309–22; Giersch, Paqué, and Schmieding, *Fading Miracle*, 176–84, 250–55.
66. Abelshauser, *Wirtschaftsgeschichte*, 260.
67. Stefan Schreyger, *Direktinvestitionen deutscher Unternehmen im Ausland von 1952 bis 1980* (Cologne, 1994), 59–73, 94–97, 312; Harm G. Schröter, "Außenwirtschaft im Boom: Die Direktinvestitionen der Bundesrepublik Deutschland 1950–1975," in *Der Boom 1948–1973. Gesellschaftliche und wirtschaftliche Folgen in der Bundesrepublik Deutschland und in Europa*, ed. Hartmut Kaelble (Opladen, 1992), 82–106.
68. The share in the net national product at market prices climbed from 18.5 percent in 1970 to 29.4 percent in 1985, but the share of export-dependent jobs

rose even faster; Abelshauser, *Wirtschaftsgeschichte*, 217, 259–63; Wirsching, *Abschied*, 225.
69. Giersch, Paqué, and Schmieding, *Fading Miracle*, 223–35.
70. Cf. Mancur Olson, "The Varieties of Eurosclerosis: The Rise and Decline of Nations since 1982," in *Economic Growth in Europe since 1945*, ed. Nicholas Crafts and Giovanni Tonniolo (Cambridge, 1996), 73–94; John Gillingham, *European Integration, 1950–2003: Superstate or New Market Economy?* (Cambridge, 2003), 81–163, 228–58.
71. Werner Plumpe and André Steiner, "Dimensionen wirtschaftlicher Integrationsprozesse in West- und Osteuropa nach dem Zweiten Weltkrieg," *Jahrbuch für Wirtschaftsgeschichte* 49, no. 2 (2008): 36.
72. Abelshauser, *Wirtschaftsgeschichte*, 262–66; Arne Gieseck, *Krisenmanagement in der Stahlindustrie. Eine theoretische und empirische Analyse der europäischen Stahlpolitik 1975 bis 1988* (Berlin 1995); Mark Spoerer, "'Fortress Europe' in Long-Term Perspective: Agricultural Protection in the European Community, 1957–2003," *Journal of European Integration History* 16, no. 2 (2010): 143–62.
73. Steiner, *Plans*, 164, 192.
74. Ahrens, *Wirtschaftshilfe*, 249–343; André Steiner, "'Common Sense Is Necessary': East German Reactions to the Oil Crises of the 1970s," in *The Energy Crises of the 1970s: Anticipations and Reactions in the Industrialized World*, ed. Frank Bösch and Rüdiger Graf (Cologne, 2014), 231–50.
75. Ahrens, *East German Foreign Trade*, 164. "Other socialist countries" accounting for the remaining percentage.
76. Cf. André Steiner, "The Globalisation Process and the Eastern Bloc Countries in the 1970s and 1980s," *European Review of History/Revue européenne d'histoire* 21, no. 2 (2014): 165–81.
77. After adjustment of the statistics for an undervaluation of the D-Mark: Armin Volze, "Zur Devisenverschuldung der DDR—Entstehung, Bewältigung und Folgen," in *Die Endzeit der DDR-Wirtschaft—Analysen zur Wirtschafts-, Sozial- und Umweltpolitik*, ed. Eberhard Kuhrt (Opladen 1999), 178.
78. Cf. Detlef Nakath, "Die DDR—'heimliches Mitglied' der Europäischen Gemeinschaft? Zur Entwicklung des innerdeutschen Handels vor dem Hintergrund der westeuropäischen Integration," in *Aufbruch zum Europa der zweiten Generation. Die europäische Einigung 1969–1984*, ed. Franz Knipping and Matthias Schönwald (Trier, 2004), 461–70.
79. Haendcke-Hoppe-Arndt, *Interzonenhandel*, 1557, 1568; Volze, *Devisenverschuldung*, 180.
80. Herbert, *Geschichte*, 1026.
81. Haendcke-Hoppe-Arndt, *Interzonenhandel*, 1559; on the loans, see Jonathan R. Zatlin, *The Currency of Socialism: Money and Political Culture in East Germany* (Cambridge, 2007), 140–45.
82. Jörg Roesler, "Der Einfluss der Außenwirtschaftspolitik auf die Beziehungen DDR—Bundesrepublik. Die achtziger Jahre," *Deutschland Archiv* 26, no. 5

(1993): 566–68; Zatlin, *Currency*, 94–99; Matthias Judt, "Kompensationsgeschäfte der DDR—Instrumente einer europäischen Ost-West-Wirtschaftsintegration?," *Jahrbuch für Wirtschaftsgeschichte* 49, no. 2 (2008): 117–38.
83. Volze, "Zur Devisenverschuldung," 160–69, 182–83.
84. Werner Plumpe, "Die alltägliche Selbstzermürbung und der stille Sieg der D-Mark," in *Revolution und Vereinigung 1989/90. Als in Deutschland die Realität die Phantasie überholte*, ed. Klaus-Dietmar Henke (Munich 2009), 92–103; for details, see Zatlin, *Currency*.
85. Dieter Grosser, *Das Wagnis der Währungs-, Wirtschafts- und Sozialunion. Politische Zwänge im Konflikt mit ökonomischen Regeln* (Stuttgart, 1998), 128–30.
86. Gerhard A. Ritter, *The Price of German Unity: Reunification and the Crisis of the Welfare State* (New York, 2011), 91–99.
87. Grosser, *Wagnis*, 453–54, 465; Klaus Werner, "Die Integration der DDR-Wirtschaft im RGW und der Zusammenbruch der Ostmärkte," in *Herausforderung Ostdeutschland. Fünf Jahre Währungs-, Wirtschafts- und Sozialunion*, ed. Rüdiger Pohl (Berlin, 1995), 60–65; Gerlinde Sinn and Hans-Werner Sinn, *Jumpstart: The Economic Unification of Germany* (Cambridge, MA, 1992), 36–39.
88. Thomas W. Zeiler, "Opening Doors in the World Economy," in *Global Interdependence: The World after 1945*, ed. Akira Iriye (Cambridge, MA, 2014), 318–54.
89. Hans-Hagen Härtel and Rolf Jungnickel, eds., *Grenzüberschreitende Produktion und Strukturwandel—Globalisierung der deutschen Wirtschaft* (Baden-Baden, 1996), 81–83 (quotation), 98–99, 121–27.
90. Herbert, *Geschichte*, 1135 (quotation); Andreas Wirsching, *Der Preis der Freiheit. Geschichte Europas in unserer Zeit* (Munich, 2012), 155–56; see Harold James, *Making the European Monetary Union: The Role of the Committee of Central Bank Governors and the Origins of the European Central Bank* (Cambridge, 2014).
91. Cf. Wolfgang Streeck and Martin Höpner, eds., *Alle Macht dem Markt? Fallstudien zur Abwicklung der Deutschland AG* (Frankfurt a. M., 2003); Ralf Ahrens, Boris Gehlen, and Alfred Reckendrees, eds., *Die "Deutschland AG": Historische Annäherungen an den bundesdeutschen Kapitalismus* (Essen, 2013).
92. Roland Czada, "Das Erbe der Treuhandanstalt," in *Einheit—Eigentum—Effizienz. Bilanz der Treuhandanstalt*, ed. Otto Depenheuer and Karl-Heinz Paqué (Heidelberg, 2012), 137–42.
93. Karl Brenke and Klaus F. Zimmermann, "Ostdeutschland 20 Jahre nach dem Mauerfall: Was war und was ist heute mit der Wirtschaft?," *Vierteljahrshefte zur Wirtschaftsforschung* 78, no. 2 (2009): 33–35.
94. Wolfgang Streeck, *Re-Forming Capitalism: Institutional Change in the German Political Economy* (Oxford, 2009), 68–76; Abelshauser, *Wirtschaftsgeschichte*, 505–7.
95. Cf. Ritter, *Price*, 278–306; Herbert, *Geschichte*, 1207–12.

96. Susanne Lütz, *Der Staat und die Globalisierung von Finanzmärkten. Regulative Politik in Deutschland, Großbritannien und den USA* (Frankfurt a. M., 2002), 145–46, 234–48.
97. Wencke Meteling, "Internationale Konkurrenz als nationale Bedrohung—Zur politischen Maxime der 'Standortsicherung' in den neunziger Jahren," in *Konkurrenz in der Geschichte: Praktiken—Werte—Institutionalisierungen*, ed. Ralph Jessen (Frankfurt a. M., 2014), 289–315.
98. Karl-Heinz Paqué, *Die Bilanz. Eine wirtschaftliche Analyse der Deutschen Einheit* (Munich, 2009), 48–49, 67.
99. See, among others, Rainer Geißler, "Nachholende Modernisierung mit Widersprüchen—Eine Vereinigungsbilanz aus modernisierungstheoretischer Perspektive," in *Vom Zusammenwachsen einer Gesellschaft. Analysen zur Angleichung der Lebensverhältnisse in Deutschland*, ed. Heinz-Herbert Noll and Roland Habich (Frankfurt a. M., 2000), 45–46.
100. André Steiner, "Ausgangsbedingungen für die Transformation der DDR-Wirtschaft: Kombinate als künftige Marktunternehmen?," *Zeitschrift für Unternehmensgeschichte* 54, no. 2 (2009): 140–57.
101. Cf. in summary, André Steiner, "From the Soviet Occupation Zone to the 'New Eastern States': A Survey," in Berghoff and Balbier, *The East German Economy*, 41.
102. Roland Czada, "'Modell Deutschland' am Scheideweg: Die verarbeitende Industrie im Sektorvergleich," in *Transformationspfade in Ostdeutschland. Beiträge zur sektoralen Vereinigungspolitik*, ed. Roland Czada and Gerhard Lehmbruch (Frankfurt a. M., 1998), 368–72, 382–90.
103. Steiner, *Soviet Occupation Zone*, 42–47; Herbert, *Geschichte*, 1144–57.
104. Ritter, *Price*, 72–73; Stefan Schirm, "Deutschlands wirtschaftspolitische Antworten auf die Globalisierung," in *Die Bundesrepublik Deutschland—eine Bilanz nach 60 Jahren*, ed. Hans-Peter Schwarz (Cologne, 2008), 405–22; Christoph Kleßmann, "'Deutschland einig Vaterland'? Politische und gesellschaftliche Verwerfungen im Prozess der deutschen Vereinigung," *Zeithistorische Forschungen/Studies in Contemporary History* 8, no. 1 (2009): 85–104.
105. Klodt, Maurer, and Schimmelpfennig, *Tertiarisierung*, 23–26.
106. Birger P. Priddat and Klaus-W. West, eds., *Die Modernität der Industrie* (Marburg 2012).

BIBLIOGRAPHY

Ahrens, Ralf. "Debt, Cooperation, and Collapse: East German Foreign Trade in the Honecker Years." In *The East German Economy, 1945–2010: Falling Behind or Catching Up?*, edited by Hartmut Berghoff and Uta A. Balbier, 161–76. Cambridge: Cambridge University Press, 2013.

———. *Gegenseitige Wirtschaftshilfe? Die DDR im RGW—Strukturen und handelspolitische Strategien 1963–1976*. Cologne: Böhlau, 2000.

———. "Planning Priorities, Managing Shortages: Industrial Policy in the German Democratic Republic, from Stalinism to Welfare Dictatorship." In *Industrial Policy in Europe after 1945: Wealth, Power and Economic Development in the Cold War*, edited by Christian Grabas and Alexander Nützenadel, 300–20. Basingstoke: Palgrave Macmillan, 2014.

Ahrens, Ralf, Boris Gehlen, and Alfred Reckendrees, eds. *Die "Deutschland AG": Historische Annäherungen an den bundesdeutschen Kapitalismus*. Essen: Klartext, 2013.

Ambrosius, Gerold. "Agrarstaat oder Industriestaat—Industriestaat oder Dienstleistungsgesellschaft? Zum sektoralen Strukturwandel im 20. Jahrhundert." In *Geschichte der deutschen Wirtschaft im 20. Jahrhundert*, edited by Reinhard Spree, 50–69. Munich: Beck, 2001.

———. *Die Durchsetzung der Sozialen Marktwirtschaft in Westdeutschland 1945–1949*. Stuttgart: DVA, 1977.

———. "Sektoraler Wandel und internationale Verflechtung: Die bundesdeutsche Wirtschaft im Übergang zu einem neuen Strukturmuster." In *Auf dem Weg in eine neue Moderne? Die Bundesrepublik Deutschland in den siebziger und achtziger Jahren*, edited by Thomas Raithel, Andreas Rödder, and Andreas Wirsching, 17–30. Munich: Oldenbourg, 2009.

———. "Ursachen der Deindustrialisierung Westeuropas." In *Umweltgeschichte: Umweltverträgliches Wirtschaften in historischer Perspektive*, edited by Werner Abelshauser, 191–221. Göttingen: Vandenhoeck & Ruprecht, 1994.

Baar, Lothar, and Dietmar Petzina, eds. *Deutsch-deutsche Wirtschaft 1945 bis 1990: Strukturveränderungen, Innovationen und regionaler Wandel*. St. Katharinen: Scripta Mercaturae, 1999.

Bähr, Johannes. "Integrationseffekte und Integrationspotentiale in unterschiedlichen Wirtschaftssystemen: Das geteilte Deutschland im Vergleich." In *Wirtschaftliche und soziale Integration in historischer Sicht*, edited by Eckhart Schremmer, 241–58. Stuttgart: Steiner, 1996.

Bähr, Johannes, and Dietmar Petzina, eds. *Innovationsverhalten und Entscheidungsstrukturen: Vergleichende Studie zur wirtschaftlichen Entwicklung im geteilten Deutschland*. Berlin: Duncker & Humblot, 1996.

Bauerkämper, Arnd. "Agrarwirtschaft und ländliche Gesellschaft in der Bundesrepublik Deutschland und der DDR: Eine Bilanz der Jahre 1945–1965." *Aus Politik und Zeitgeschichte* B38/97 (1997): 25–37.

Brenke, Karl, and Klaus F. Zimmermann. "Ostdeutschland 20 Jahre nach dem Mauerfall: Was war und was ist heute mit der Wirtschaft?" *Vierteljahrshefte zur Wirtschaftsforschung* 78, no. 2 (2009): 32–62.

Buchheim, Christoph. *Die Wiedereingliederung Westdeutschlands in die Weltwirtschaft 1945–1958*. Munich: Oldenbourg, 1990.

———. "The Establishment of the Bank deutscher Länder and the West German Currency Reform." In *Fifty Years of the Deutsche Mark: Central Bank and the*

Currency in Germany since 1948, edited by Deutsche Bundesbank, 55–100. Oxford: Oxford University Press, 1999.

Czada, Roland. "Das Erbe der Treuhandanstalt." In *Einheit—Eigentum—Effizienz: Bilanz der Treuhandanstalt*, edited by Otto Depenheuer and Karl-Heinz Paqué, 125–46. Heidelberg: Springer, 2012.

———. "'Modell Deutschland' am Scheideweg: Die verarbeitende Industrie im Sektorvergleich." In *Transformationspfade in Ostdeutschland: Beiträge zur sektoralen Vereinigungspolitik*, edited by Roland Czada and Gerhard Lehmbruch, 365–410. Frankfurt a. M.: Campus, 1998.

Deutsche Bundesbank. *50 Jahre Deutsche Mark: Monetäre Statistiken 1948–1997.* CD-ROM. Munich: Beck, 1998.

Doering-Manteuffel, Anselm. "Die deutsche Geschichte in den Zeitbögen des 20. Jahrhunderts." *Vierteljahrshefte für Zeitgeschichte* 62, no. 3 (2014): 321–48.

Geißler, Rainer. "Nachholende Modernisierung mit Widersprüchen—Eine Vereinigungsbilanz aus modernisierungstheoretischer Perspektive." In *Vom Zusammenwachsen einer Gesellschaft: Analysen zur Angleichung der Lebensverhältnisse in Deutschland*, edited by Heinz-Herbert Noll and Roland Habich, 37–60. Frankfurt a. M.: Campus, 2000.

Giersch, Herbert, Karl-Heinz Paqué, and Holger Schmieding. *The Fading Miracle: Four Decades of Market Economy in Germany.* Cambridge: Cambridge University Press, 1992.

Gieseck, Arne. *Krisenmanagement in der Stahlindustrie: Eine theoretische und empirische Analyse der europäischen Stahlpolitik 1975 bis 1988.* Berlin: Duncker & Humblot, 1995.

Gillingham, John. *European Integration, 1950–2003: Superstate or New Market Economy?* Cambridge: Cambridge University Press, 2003.

Gleitze, Bruno. *Ostdeutsche Wirtschaft: Industrielle Standorte und volkswirtschaftliche Kapazitäten des ungeteilten Deutschland.* Berlin: Duncker & Humblot, 1956.

Goch, Stefan. *Eine Region im Kampf mit dem Strukturwandel: Bewältigung von Strukturwandel und Strukturpolitik im Ruhrgebiet.* Essen: Klartext, 2002.

Gornig, Martin. *Gesamtwirtschaftliche Leitsektoren und regionaler Strukturwandel: Eine theoretische und empirische Analyse der sektoralen und regionalen Wirtschaftsentwicklung in Deutschland 1895–1987.* Berlin: Duncker & Humblot, 2000.

Graf, Rüdiger, and Kim Christian Priemel. "Zeitgeschichte in der Welt der Sozialwissenschaften: Legitimität und Originalität einer Disziplin." *Vierteljahrshefte für Zeitgeschichte* 59, no. 4 (2011): 479–508.

Grande, Edgar. "West Germany: From Reform Policy to Crisis-Management." In *The Politics of Economic Crisis: Lessons from Western Europe*, edited by Erik Damgaard, Peter Gerlich, and Jeremy Richardson, 50–69. Aldershot: Avebury, 1989.

Groebel, Annegret. *Strukturelle Entwicklungsmuster in Markt- und Planwirtschaften.* Heidelberg: Physica, 1997.

Grosser, Dieter. *Das Wagnis der Währungs-, Wirtschafts- und Sozialunion: Politische Zwänge im Konflikt mit ökonomischen Regeln*. Stuttgart: DVA, 1998.

Grüner, Stefan. "Ensuring Economic Growth and Socioeconomic Stabilization: Industrial Policy in West Germany, 1950–1975." In *Industrial Policy in Europe after 1945: Wealth, Power and Economic Development in the Cold War*, edited by Christian Grabas and Alexander Nützenadel, 86–112. Basingstoke: Palgrave Macmillan, 2014.

Haendcke-Hoppe-Arndt, Maria. "Interzonenhandel/Innerdeutscher Handel." In *Materialien der Enquete-Kommission "Aufarbeitung von Geschichte und Folgen der SED-Diktatur in Deutschland,"* edited by Deutscher Bundestag, vol. V/2, 1543–571. Frankfurt a. M.: Suhrkamp, 1995.

Härtel, Hans-Hagen, and Rolf Jungnickel, eds. *Grenzüberschreitende Produktion und Strukturwandel—Globalisierung der deutschen Wirtschaft*. Baden-Baden: Nomos, 1996.

Herbert, Ulrich. *Geschichte Deutschlands im 20. Jahrhundert*. Munich: Beck, 2014.

Heske, Gerhard. *Bruttoinlandsprodukt, Verbrauch und Erwerbstätigkeit in Ostdeutschland 1970–2000: Neue Ergebnisse einer volkswirtschaftlichen Gesamtrechnung*. Cologne: Zentrum für Historische Sozialforschung, 2005.

Hesse, Jan-Otmar. "Ökonomischer Strukturwandel. Zur Wiederbelebung einer wirtschaftshistorischen Leitsemantik." *Geschichte und Gesellschaft* 39, no. 1 (2013): 86–115.

Hübner, Peter. "Betriebe als Träger der Sozialpolitik, betriebliche Sozialpolitik." In *Geschichte der Sozialpolitik in Deutschland seit 1945*, vol. 10: *Deutsche Demokratische Republik 1971–1989. Bewegung in der Sozialpolitik, Erstarrung und Niedergang*, edited by Christoph Boyer, Klaus-Dietmar Henke, and Peter Skyba, 703–38. Baden-Baden: Nomos, 2008.

———. "Fortschrittskonkurrenz und Krisenkongruenz? Europäische Arbeitsgesellschaften und Sozialstaaten in den letzten Jahrzehnten des Kalten Krieges (1970–1989)." *Zeitgeschichte* 34 (2007): 144–50.

James, Harold. *International Monetary Cooperation since Bretton Woods*. New York: Oxford University Press, 1996.

———. *Making the European Monetary Union: The Role of the Committee of Central Bank Governors and the Origins of the European Central Bank*. Cambridge, MA: Harvard University Press, 2014.

Judt, Matthias. "Kompensationsgeschäfte der DDR—Instrumente einer europäischen Ost-West-Wirtschaftsintegration?" *Jahrbuch für Wirtschaftsgeschichte* 49, no. 2 (2008): 117–38.

Kaelble, Hartmut. *Kalter Krieg und Wohlfahrtsstaat. Europa 1945–1989*. Munich: Beck, 2011.

Kleßmann, Christoph. "'Deutschland einig Vaterland'? Politische und gesellschaftliche Verwerfungen im Prozess der deutschen Vereinigung." *Zeithistorische Forschungen/Studies in Contemporary History* 8, no. 1 (2009): 85–104.

Klodt, Henning, Rainer Maurer, and Axel Schimmelpfennig. *Tertiarisierung der deutschen Wirtschaft*. Tübingen: Mohr, 1997.

Köhler, Heinz. *Economic Integration in the Soviet Bloc: With an East German Case Study*. New York: Praeger, 1965.

Kotkin, Stephen. "The Kiss of Debt: The East Bloc Goes Borrowing." In *The Shock of the Global: The 1970s in Perspective*, edited by Niall Ferguson, Charles S. Maier, Erez Manela, and Daniel J. Sargent, 80–94. Cambridge, MA: Harvard University Press, 2010.

Kupper, Siegfried. *Der innerdeutsche Handel. Rechtliche Grundlagen, politische und wirtschaftliche Bedeutung*. Cologne: Markus, 1972.

Lindlar, Ludger. *Das mißverstandene Wirtschaftswunder. Westdeutschland und die westeuropäische Nachkriegsprosperität*. Tübingen: Mohr Siebeck, 1997.

Lütz, Susanne. *Der Staat und die Globalisierung von Finanzmärkten. Regulative Politik in Deutschland, Großbritannien und den USA*. Frankfurt a. M.: Campus, 2002.

Maier, Charles S. "'Malaise': The Crisis of Capitalism in the 1970s." In *The Shock of the Global: The 1970s in Perspective*, edited by Niall Ferguson, Charles S. Maier, Erez Manela, and Daniel J. Sargent, 25–48. Cambridge, MA: Harvard University Press, 2010.

Malycha, Andreas. *Die SED in der Ära Honecker. Machtstrukturen, Entscheidungsmechanismen und Konfliktfelder in der Staatspartei 1971 bis 1989*. Munich: De Gruyter Oldenbourg, 2014.

Mensch, Gerhard. *Stalemate in Technology: Innovations Overcome the Depression*. Cambridge: Ballinger, 1979.

Meteling, Wencke. "Internationale Konkurrenz als nationale Bedrohung—Zur politischen Maxime der 'Standortsicherung' in den neunziger Jahren." In *Konkurrenz in der Geschichte: Praktiken—Werte—Institutionalisierungen*, edited by Ralph Jessen, 289–315. Frankfurt a. M.: Campus, 2014.

Metz, Rainer. "Expansion und Kontraktion. Das Wachstum der deutschen Wirtschaft im 20. Jahrhundert." In *Geschichte der deutschen Wirtschaft im 20. Jahrhundert*, edited by Reinhard Spree, 70–89. Munich: Beck, 2001.

Metzler, Gabriele. *Konzeptionen politischen Handelns von Adenauer bis Brandt. Politische Planung in der pluralistischen Gesellschaft*. Paderborn: Schöningh, 2005.

Nakath, Detlef. "Die DDR—'heimliches Mitglied' der Europäischen Gemeinschaft? Zur Entwicklung des innerdeutschen Handels vor dem Hintergrund der westeuropäischen Integration." In *Aufbruch zum Europa der zweiten Generation. Die europäische Einigung 1969–1984*, edited by Franz Knipping and Matthias Schönwald, 451–73. Trier: Wissenschaftlicher Verlag, 2004.

Neebe, Reinhard. *Weichenstellung für die Globalisierung. Deutsche Weltmarktpolitik, Europa und Amerika in der Ära Ludwig Erhard*. Cologne: Böhlau, 2004.

Nicholls, Anthony J. *Freedom with Responsibility. The Social Market Economy in Germany, 1918–1963*. Oxford: Clarendon, 2000.

Nowack, Marlene. "Der Strukturwandel und seine Begleiterscheinungen—Rückblick auf die Entwicklung ausgewählter Wirtschaftsbereiche im früheren Bundesgebiet." In *Wirtschaftsstruktur und Arbeitsplätze im Wandel der Zeit*, edited by Hans Günther Merk, 36–65. Stuttgart: Metzler-Poeschel, 1994.

Nützenadel, Alexander. *Stunde der Ökonomen. Wissenschaft, Politik und Expertenkultur in der Bundesrepublik 1949–1974*. Göttingen: Vandenhoeck & Ruprecht, 2005.
Ochsen, Carsten. "Zukunft der Arbeit und Arbeit der Zukunft in Deutschland." *Perspektiven der Wirtschaftspolitik* 7, no. 2 (2006): 173–93.
Olson, Mancur. "The Varieties of Eurosclerosis: The Rise and Decline of Nations since 1982." In *Economic Growth in Europe since 1945*, edited by Nicholas Crafts and Giovanni Tonniolo, 73–94. Cambridge: Cambridge University Press, 1996.
Paqué, Karl-Heinz. *Die Bilanz. Eine wirtschaftliche Analyse der Deutschen Einheit*. Munich: Hanser, 2009.
Petzina, Dietmar. "Standortverschiebungen und regionale Wirtschaftskraft in der Bundesrepublik Deutschland seit den fünfziger Jahren." In *Wirtschaftliche Integration und Wandel von Raumstrukturen im 19. und 20. Jahrhundert*, edited by Josef Wysocki, 101–27. Berlin: Duncker & Humblot, 1994.
Plumpe, Werner. "Die alltägliche Selbstzermürbung und der stille Sieg der D-Mark." In *Revolution und Vereinigung 1989/90. Als in Deutschland die Realität die Phantasie überholte*, edited by Klaus-Dietmar Henke, 92–103. Munich: dtv, 2009.
Plumpe, Werner, and André Steiner. "Dimensionen wirtschaftlicher Integrationsprozesse in West- und Osteuropa nach dem Zweiten Weltkrieg." *Jahrbuch für Wirtschaftsgeschichte* 49, no. 2 (2008): 21–38.
———, eds. *Der Mythos von der postindustriellen Welt. Wirtschaftlicher Strukturwandel in Deutschland 1960 bis 1990*. Göttingen: Wallstein, 2016.
Priddat, Birger P., and Klaus-W. West, eds. *Die Modernität der Industrie*. Marburg: Metropolis, 2012.
Ritschl, Albrecht, and Mark Spoerer. "Das Bruttosozialprodukt in Deutschland nach den amtlichen Volkseinkommens- und Sozialproduktstatistiken 1901–1995." *Jahrbuch für Wirtschaftsgeschichte* 38, no. 2 (1997): 27–54.
Ritter, Gerhard A. *The Price of German Unity: Reunification and the Crisis of the Welfare State*. New York: Oxford University Press, 2011.
Roesler, Jörg. "Der Einfluss der Außenwirtschaftspolitik auf die Beziehungen DDR—Bundesrepublik. Die achtziger Jahre." *Deutschland Archiv* 26, no. 5 (1993): 558–72.
———. "Handelsgeschäfte im Kalten Krieg. Die wirtschaftliche Motivation für den deutsch-deutschen Handel zwischen 1949 und 1961." In *Wirtschaftliche Folgelasten des Krieges in der SBZ/DDR*, edited by Christoph Buchheim, 192–220. Baden-Baden: Nomos, 1995.
Schanetzky, Tim. *Die große Ernüchterung. Wirtschaftspolitik, Expertise und Gesellschaft in der Bundesrepublik 1966 bis 1982*. Berlin: Akademie, 2007.
———. "Sachverständiger Rat und Konzertierte Aktion: Staat, Gesellschaft und wissenschaftliche Expertise in der bundesrepublikanischen Wirtschaftspolitik." *Vierteljahrschrift für Sozial- und Wirtschaftsgeschichte* 91, no. 3 (2004): 310–31.

Schirm, Stefan. "Deutschlands wirtschaftspolitische Antworten auf die Globalisierung." In *Die Bundesrepublik Deutschland—eine Bilanz nach 60 Jahren*, edited by Hans-Peter Schwarz, 405–22. Cologne: Böhlau, 2008.
Schreyger, Stefan. *Direktinvestitionen deutscher Unternehmen im Ausland von 1952 bis 1980*. Dissertation, University of Cologne, 1994.
Schröter, Harm G. "Außenwirtschaft im Boom: Die Direktinvestitionen der Bundesrepublik Deutschland 1950–1975." In *Der Boom 1948–1973. Gesellschaftliche und wirtschaftliche Folgen in der Bundesrepublik Deutschland und in Europa*, edited by Hartmut Kaelble, 82–106. Opladen: Westdeutscher Verlag, 1992.
Schwarzer, Oskar. *Sozialistische Zentralplanwirtschaft in der SBZ/DDR. Ergebnisse eines ordnungspolitischen Experiments, 1945–1989*. Stuttgart: Steiner, 1999.
Siegenthaler, Hansjörg. "Das Ende des Keynesianismus als Gegenstand Keynesianischer Interpretation." *Jahrbuch für Wirtschaftsgeschichte* 43 (2002): 237–48.
Sinn, Gerlinde, and Hans-Werner Sinn. *Jumpstart: The Economic Unification of Germany*. Cambridge, MA: MIT Press, 1992.
Sleifer, Jaap. *Planning Ahead and Falling Behind: The East German Economy in Comparison with West Germany 1936–2002*. Berlin: Akademie, 2006.
Spoerer, Mark. "'Fortress Europe' in Long-Term Perspective: Agricultural Protection in the European Community, 1957–2003." *Journal of European Integration History* 16 (2010): 143–62.
Steiner, André. "Ausgangsbedingungen für die Transformation der DDR-Wirtschaft: Kombinate als künftige Marktunternehmen?" *Zeitschrift für Unternehmensgeschichte* 54, no. 2 (2009): 140–57.
———. "'Common Sense Is Necessary': East German Reactions to the Oil Crises of the 1970s." In *The Energy Crises of the 1970s: Anticipations and Reactions in the Industrialized World*, edited by Frank Bösch and Rüdiger Graf (*Historical Social Research* 39 [2014]), 231–50. Cologne: GESIS, 2014.
———. *Die DDR-Wirtschaftsreform der sechziger Jahre. Konflikt zwischen Effizienz- und Machtkalkül*. Berlin: Akademie, 1999.
———. "Die Deutsche Wirtschaftskommission—ein ordnungspolitisches Machtinstrument?" In *Das letzte Jahr der SBZ. Politische Weichenstellungen und Kontinuitäten im Prozeß der Gründung der DDR*, edited by Dierk Hoffmann and Hermann Wentker, 85–105. Munich: Oldenbourg, 2000.
———. "Die siebziger Jahre als Kristallisationspunkt des wirtschaftlichen Strukturwandels in West und Ost?" In *Das Ende der Zuversicht? Die siebziger Jahre als Geschichte*, edited by Konrad H. Jarausch, 29–48. Göttingen: Vandenhoeck & Ruprecht, 2008.
———. "From the Soviet Occupation Zone to the 'New Eastern States': A Survey." In *The East German Economy, 1945–2010: Falling Behind or Catching Up?*, edited by Hartmut Berghoff and Uta A. Balbier, 17–49. Cambridge: Cambridge University Press, 2013.
———. "The Globalisation Process and the Eastern Bloc Countries in the 1970s and 1980s." *European Review of History/Revue européenne d'histoire* 21, no. 2 (2014): 165–81.

———. *The Plans That Failed: An Economic History of the GDR.* New York: Berghahn, 2010.

———. "Preisgestaltung." In *Geschichte der Sozialpolitik in Deutschland seit 1945,* vol. 10: *Deutsche Demokratische Republik 1971–1989. Bewegung in der Sozialpolitik, Erstarrung und Niedergang,* edited by Christoph Boyer, Klaus-Dietmar Henke, and Peter Skyba, 304–23. Baden-Baden: Nomos, 2008.

Stone, Randall W. *Satellites and Commissars: Strategy and Conflict in the Politics of Soviet-Bloc Trade.* Princeton: Princeton University Press, 1996.

Streeck, Wolfgang. *Re-Forming Capitalism: Institutional Change in the German Political Economy.* Oxford: Oxford University Press, 2009.

Streeck, Wolfgang, and Martin Höpner, eds. *Alle Macht dem Markt? Fallstudien zur Abwicklung der Deutschland AG.* Frankfurt a. M.: Campus, 2003.

van der Wee, Herman. *Prosperity and Upheaval: The World Economy 1945–1980.* Berkeley: University of California Press, 1986.

Volze, Armin. "Die gespaltene Valutamark. Anmerkungen zur Währungspolitik und Außenhandelsstatistik der DDR." *Deutschland Archiv* 32, no. 2 (1999): 232–41.

———. "Zur Devisenverschuldung der DDR—Entstehung, Bewältigung und Folgen." In *Die Endzeit der DDR-Wirtschaft—Analysen zur Wirtschafts-, Sozial- und Umweltpolitik,* edited by Eberhard Kuhrt, 151–83. Opladen: Leske + Budrich, 1999.

Werner, Klaus. "Die Integration der DDR-Wirtschaft im RGW und der Zusammenbruch der Ostmärkte." In *Herausforderung Ostdeutschland. Fünf Jahre Währungs-, Wirtschafts- und Sozialunion,* edited by Rüdiger Pohl, 53–66. Berlin: Analytica, 1995.

Wirsching, Andreas. *Abschied vom Provisorium: 1982–1990.* Munich: DVA, 2006.

———. *Der Preis der Freiheit. Geschichte Europas in unserer Zeit.* Munich: Beck, 2012.

Zatlin, Jonathan R. *The Currency of Socialism: Money and Political Culture in East Germany.* Cambridge: Cambridge University Press, 2007.

Zeiler, Thomas W. "Opening Doors in the World Economy." In *Global Interdependence: The World after 1945,* edited by Akira Iriye, 318–54. Cambridge, MA: Harvard University Press, 2014.

Zschaler, Frank. "Die vergessene Währungsreform. Vorgeschichte, Durchführung und Ergebnisse der Geldumstellung in der SBZ 1948." *Vierteljahrshefte für Zeitgeschichte* 45, no. 2 (1997): 191–224.

CHAPTER 3

Entangled Ecologies
Outlines of a Green History of Two or More Germanys

Frank Uekötter

Few would doubt that the significance of environmental issues has grown dramatically since 1970. We can find the consequences in virtually every sphere of life: in new ministries in East and West Germany; new civic organizations such as BUND, Greenpeace, and Attac; new lifestyles; and new ways to talk about mobility, food, and other essentials of modern life. Environmentalism has never been uncontested, and may never be, but there is no way to doubt that it has seeped into the very pores of German society, and environmental historians do not suffer from a dearth of topics. But the broad range of issues and perspectives is a challenge of the first order for those who want to write coherent narratives: how do you take stock of something that knows no limits? The green Germany is about politics and the economy, about social status and material legacies; we find its repercussions out in the countryside and inside nuclear power plants; and environmentalism has left its mark on ideas of German engineering as well as German patriotism. A widely held opinion is that Germans take environmental issues more seriously than the rest of the planet.

Environmental historians are not only wrestling with a broad range of issues, but also face more than one line of conflict. Different groups have been blamed for the state of the German environment—industrialists, farmers, experts, consumers—and we get different narratives with each of these culprits. Was environmentalism anti-industrial at its core, or is it a grandiose opportunity for German engineers in that it opens new markets for cutting-edge technology made in Germany? And then there is the inherent diversity of environmental concerns. How can one write an environmental history of the green Germany when bird lovers clash with renewable energy enthusiasts over wind power, when eco-farming is under threat from the quest for biofuels, and when the burgeoning climate change movement is viewed with deep suspicion among advocates of biodiversity? The unity of the environmental movement has always been more myth than reality, and several observers have been tempted to throw in the towel. As Anthony Giddens put it, "Strictly speaking, of course, there is no green movement—rather, there is a diverse range of positions, perspectives and recipes for action."[1]

For a while, environmental historians sought to marshal this diversity by merging it into a general narrative of phenomenal growth. According to these accounts, Western societies finally woke up around 1970—a bit late, but hopefully not too late—and the promise of environmentalism gradually pushed doubts and resistance to the margins.[2] The end of socialist rule in Eastern Europe was swiftly incorporated into this narrative: it was the collapse of an even more destructive alternative to Western capitalism, if not an act of ecocide, for socialism was doomed to fail on environmental terms as well. But triumphant narratives of the irresistible rise of environmentalism have come to ring hollow in the twenty-first century: the green happy ending of history is far less certain than conventional wisdom had it in the 1970s and 1980s. Simple teleological narratives clash with a reality where environmental sustainability is still very much elusive. Compared with the global triumph of neoliberalism, another cause that was ascendant in the 1970s, emphatic proclamations of an "age of ecology" look dubious at best.[3] It is entirely plausible that a few decades from now, scholars will view 1970s environmentalism as an ephemeral mood swing in complacent affluent societies of the West.

All of this speaks in favor of a circumspect approach that looks at different issues and explores a multitude of perspectives. A contemporary history of the environment looks very different depending on one's point of view: should we write from an urban or a rural perspective, against the background of the United States or the Global South—and what about the perspective of battery-cage chickens in solitary confinement? The state of research also calls for a tentative approach, as the gaps in our literature are still legion. The number of case studies is increasing, but few scholars have tried to identify running themes or sought to connect experiences on both sides of the Iron Curtain. It is a long way from isolated case studies to a complete picture, but we may never move beyond a set of fragments if we do not offer some ideas on how it might all fit together. That is what this essay attempts to do.

Unified Ecologies

From an ecological perspective, national borders have an air of arbitrariness, and particularly so in the case of the German-German border. Neither the FRG nor the GDR were self-contained realms of nature. Both had a multitude of regions from the coasts of the North Sea and the Baltic Sea to the peaks of the Ore Mountains (Erzgebirge) and the Alps in the south. The Wall was always permeable in an ecological sense, far more so than for people.

There was a dynamic trans-German exchange in the air and the water. Two large German rivers, the Elbe and the Werra, ran from East Germany into West Germany, bringing large amounts of water from one system to the other. The potential for conflict was especially great in the case of the Werra because its drainage basin was heavily affected by the central German potash industry. The processing of these salts produces waste lyes with a high salt content, which are not biologically degradable. Conflicts go back to Imperial Germany, when the potash industry was already facing serious objections from downstream interests. Shortly before World War I, for instance, the senate in the city of Bremen decided to oppose permits for new potash plants on the Weser River and its tributaries in order to protect its supply of drinking water.[4]

The GDR sought to expand its potash industry because it was a profitable source of foreign currency, and the Werra offered almost perfect opportunities for the externalization of the ensuing environmental costs. The negative effects of salt waste showed up mostly in West Germany, and while a joint East-West wastewater committee did exist, it met only twice after World War II. By the early 1970s, both the Werra and the upper Weser River were mostly dead as a result. In 1971, a pollution-induced fish kill triggered a shutdown at a West German nuclear facility, as tons of dead fish clogged up the cooling water inlet of the Würgassen nuclear power plant. West Germany pressured the GDR into several rounds of expert talks during the 1980s, but East Germans kept things up in the air until the collapse of socialist rule. However, governments reached an agreement on the Röden River on the border between Thuringia (East Germany) and Bavaria (West Germany), with the terms reflecting the imbalance of environmental sentiments and financial resources. The FRG pledged to provide the necessary technology and most of the funds for the construction of a water treatment plant in the Thuringian town of Sonnenberg.

Both states felt the consequences of two seismic events that were the result of potash mining. On 23 June 1975, scientists recorded an earthquake with a magnitude of 5.2 on the Richter scale, followed by a 5.5 event on 13 March 1989; both rank among the most powerful seismic events in the global history of mining. In order to maximize salt yields, the East German mining company had reduced the size of salt pillars beyond a critical point, resulting in the sudden collapse of an entire bed that stretched across several square kilometers. A number of historical buildings had to be torn down as a result.[5] These geological shock waves turned into political ones when the GDR sought to shift the blame to the Federal Republic. It falsely claimed that the injection of waste lyes into the ground had destabilized the GDR's underworld. As it happened, underground injection of waste lyes was in turn a response to GDR pollution, as it kept pollution levels in the river from rising even further.[6]

Whereas the rivers ran from East to West, the air mostly moved in the opposite direction because of prevailing winds. This became a matter of concern in the 1970s, when the long-range transport of air pollutants received growing attention. East Germans suffered tremendously from the emissions of domestic lignite coal mines, but West Germans added to the burden in no small measure. The FRG took advantage of their upwind location with a measure of chutzpa and commissioned the infamous Buschhaus power plant near Helmstedt in the 1980s. Built to burn particularly sulfuric high-salt lignite, the original design allowed Buschhaus to produce no less than 6 percent of the FRG's total power plant emissions by annually releasing 150,000 tons of sulfur dioxide into the air each year while contributing a paltry 0.4 percent to the country's electric power supply. Its 300-meter-high smokestack, West Germany's tallest, sent pollutants straight into the eastern part of the Harz mountains when the wind blew from the west. Environmentalists wondered aloud whether this was how the government of Lower Saxony envisioned reunification.[7] Buschhaus provoked a major demonstration and a special session of Germany's parliament in the summer of 1984, and the operators hurriedly retrofitted the new power plant with sulfur scrubbers.

However, winds do not always blow from the west in temperate zones. In late April 1986, for example, easterly winds blew air from Ukraine across central Europe. As a result, radioactive particles from the Chernobyl disaster fell to the ground on both sides of the Iron Curtain. Germans shared an experience of contamination that even made its way into sociological theory via Ulrich Beck's concept of a risk society.[8] Beck argued that environmental risks eliminated boundaries and inevitably endangered everyone, irrespective of class and political system, and this idea resonated widely in the general public for some time. But in reality, there was no uniformity in the exposure to Chernobyl's radioactive toll, as the degree of contamination differed enormously. It was highest in southern Bavaria, which was somewhat ironic, as the state faced a bitter conflict over a nuclear reprocessing plant in Wackersdorf at the time.[9]

Trash created another connection between ecosystems in East and West. In order to obtain foreign currency, the GDR imported four to five million tons of waste from the FRG and West Berlin in the mid-1980s, including more than half a million tons of hazardous waste. It also took on municipal and hazardous waste from the Netherlands, Italy, Austria, and Switzerland, and a Swiss company built a hazardous waste incineration facility near Berlin. The flow of waste was eminently one-directional; in fact, East German waste did not move much at all, as many GDR factories embraced wildcat on-site disposal. The one asset of GDR waste management was efficient recycling of "secondary raw materials" in what was called the SeRo-system, but that was entirely due to the country's notorious shortage of raw materials.[10] The entanglement of West and East German waste streams mattered beyond the German context. In negotiations over what would become the Basel Convention on the Control of Transboundary Movements of Hazardous Wastes and Their Disposal, the GDR and the FRG successfully lobbied for permission to make bilateral waste agreements outside the treaty's framework.[11]

In a somewhat ironic twist of fate, West Germans were reunited with their own waste in 1990. The GDR not only lacked orderly disposal practices, but also reliable information about the number of landfills. Initial estimates listed about fifty thousand sites, but this number had climbed to more than eighty thousand landfills by 1997, and a quarter of these sites did actually show signs of leakage.[12] Environmental restoration in the former GDR was a technological and administrative megaproject, and historian Günter Bayerl has argued that it can be "deemed a 'success story' for the most part."[13] However, the costs as well as the scientific and technical challenges were huge—little wonder in a project with plenty of unknowns. Sociologist Matthias Groß has shown how recultivation of open-cast lignite coal mines required improvisation and experimentation for problems such as the contamination of water with acids and heavy metals, or the stability of embankments. A popular recreation area near Leipzig, the Leipziger Neuseenland, is a result of recultivation.[14]

But when it comes to environmental restoration, all efforts pale in comparison to the contaminated sites of the SDAG Wismut, a Soviet-German corporation for uranium mining in Saxony and Thuringia. Uranium mining was carefully kept under wraps in the GDR, which meant that the full extent of the environmental damage came to light only after the collapse of socialist rule. By the end of 2010, billions had been spent on the restoration of 9,104 levees, the filling of 6.5 million cubic meters of cavities, and the safe disposal of almost 190,000 tons of scrap metal and

154 million cubic meters of solid waste. The clean-up project reached a milestone when a formerly devastated open-cast uranium mine hosted the national gardening fair (Bundesgartenschau) in 2007.[15] Nuclear waste is a more contested issue in West Germany, where the search for a permanent storage for spent nuclear fuel is ongoing. Clean-up is also pending for the Asse II mine near Wolfenbüttel, where a total of 125,787 barrels of low- and medium-level nuclear waste were stored in somewhat haphazard fashion between 1967 and 1978.

However, toxic waste was not the only environmental legacy of the GDR. It also left behind some largely untouched landscapes that became nature reserves. For example, a national park in the Müritz lake district was already being discussed at Landschaftstag, the first nature conservation conference, held in Neubrandenburg in 1966. If it had been implemented, this project would have made the GDR the creator of Germany's first national park.[16] The Müritz National Park became a reality in 1990 as part of the GDR's national park program, which brought a dramatic increase in protected areas. However, the German Green Belt (Grünes Band Deutschland) is perhaps more interesting from the perspective of an interwoven history. The German Green Belt sought to preserve the wasteland along the former Iron Curtain; it became Germany's largest system of linked biotopes with a total area of 177 square kilometers. Turning a landscape of death into a nature reserve was a vision that succeeded in spite of tremendous administrative obstacles. The project involved nine states, thirty-eight counties, and two independent cities—an administrative nightmare under ordinary circumstances. The Green Belt has been part of a European project since 2003.[17]

But for all the differences between East and West, it bears recognition that both German states had to deal with similar issues. Many environmental problems were the result of a large industrial sector in combination with the mobility and consumption requirements of advanced affluent societies. The East German shopping frenzy of 1989/90, when everything from bananas to used cars found grateful buyers, showed a convergence of consumerist desires. The hot topics were remarkably similar on both sides of the Iron Curtain: industrial chemistry, heavy industry, nuclear power, lignite coal. Only uranium mining remained an overwhelmingly East German experience, though just for lack of significant deposits in the FRG. The U.S. uranium mining experiences indicates that only a fortunate geology saved the Federal Republic from a disaster on par with the Wismut.[18]

These parallels raise questions about the sharp contrasts that prevail in accounts of East and West German environmentalism around 1990. The demise of the GDR was framed heavily in ecological terms: environmental devastation was part of what came across as history's final verdict on socialist rule.[19] Furthermore, environmental devastation was one of the few indictments that did not undergo critical reflection as the GDR moved into perspective. While enthusiasm about capitalism, consumerism, and democracy was fading, the GDR's environmental toll looked even more dramatic as the full extent of devastation became clear. As a 2014 article on GDR environmental policy put it, "from an ecological perspective, the GDR was a failed state."[20] It is high time to move this conventional wisdom into perspective: perhaps we remember the GDR's environmental sins so well because the promise of capitalism and democracy looked rather ambiguous in the twenty-first century.

For a capitalist system that did not treat the environment terribly well, it was deeply gratifying to discover a system of production that performed even more poorly. But many environmental problems did not grow into dramatic proportions until the last decade of the GDR, exactly the time when West German environmentalism took off. If the GDR had collapsed in 1980, retrospective criticism would have shown far less of a green tinge.

The Rise of Environmental Policy

Conventional wisdom has it that the years around 1970 were a transnational turning point for environmental policy. However, it is rewarding to look at events around 1970 against the background of older traditions. There was no "zero hour" (*Stunde Null*) in environmental policy. We can trace an interplay between new environmental problems and the search for new policies since the earliest days of industrialization. Most Western countries, including Germany, saw a first wave of institutional change with lasting repercussions in the two decades before World War I.

The environmental policies of the 1970s were thus embedded within longer-term reform trends. As early as the 1950s, both Germanys attempted to strengthen regulatory policies. The Federal Republic showed a clear preference for the evolutionary development of existing practices and approaches.[21] In 1954, the GDR passed a new nature protection law, which was followed by a law on the planned development of the Socialist landscape (*Gesetz über die planmäßige Gestaltung der sozialistischen Landeskultur*) in 1970. As of 1968, environmental protection was also enshrined in East Germany's constitution.[22] In the 1950s, the GDR launched a major assessment of the environmental state of the land (Landschaftsdiagnose) that covered the entire country; there was nothing comparable in the FRG. The project fused the trend toward landscape management that had been thriving since the 1930s with socialist planning.[23] In the early years, at least when it came to directives from above, the GDR looked more energetic and enthusiastic on the environmental policy front than the Federal Republic.

There was no conflict between the values underscoring environmental policy and growing consumption in the 1950s. As it stood, environmental protection was a complement to mass affluence, rather than a countervailing trend. Many problems were still apparent even for lay people at the time. It did not take any scientific equipment to see the smoke and dust in the air, the heaps of foam on rivers and streams, or the makeshift landfills. Protests were typically driven by individual concerns over living and working conditions, although one might rightly ask whether this changed all that much over subsequent decades. Scholars have emphasized the trend toward "postmaterial" values, but that must not obscure the persistence of protests that grew out of property interests. Even Ronald Inglehart had to admit in his path-breaking study on the "silent revolution" in affluent Western societies that he could not detect the dichotomy between material and postmaterial values quite as clearly when it came to environmental issues.[24]

The rise of environmental policy in the two German states was typical of transnational developments in the years after 1970. The creation of new institutions, such as the Ministry for Environmental Protection and Water Management in the GDR (1972), and the Expert Council for Environmental Questions (1971) and the Federal Department for the Environment (Umweltbundesamt, 1974) in the Federal Republic, were part of a general trend: never before had so many institutions been established with the word "environment" in their names in such a short period of time. The United States was a pioneer in the booming environmental movement, especially after millions of protesters took part in the nationwide Earth Day demonstrations on 22 April 1970. The United Nations proved to be another beacon of light, hosting its first Conference on the Human Environment in Stockholm in June 1972.[25] The goal to accumulate environmental credentials was a transnational concern in the run-up to the UN conference, though the Soviet bloc countries ultimately boycotted the event due to a conflict over the status of the GDR in international law. With twelve hundred delegates from 114 countries, the Stockholm summit remained the largest event of its kind until the legendary Rio de Janeiro Earth Summit in 1992.[26]

Thus, from the very beginning, reasserting state authority was a powerful factor in the range of political motivations that underpinned the boom of environmental policy. The mythology of environmentalism suggests that it was first and foremost the protests of outraged citizens that forced the powers that be to make concessions. The West German environmental movement shows the value of civic activism from the Green Party to Greenpeace, but in the early 1970s, pressure from public protest was weak. There was the social dynamism that culminated in the student movement of 1968, but it showed little interest in environmental issues. Likewise, there was no event in West Germany that was comparable to the American Earth Day celebrations that had been taking place since 1970. Quite tellingly, the buzzword "environmental protection" (*Umweltschutz*) was coined by the Federal Ministry of the Interior under the leadership of Hans-Dietrich Genscher, who had received jurisdiction for a division for water protection, air pollution control, and noise reduction when a new federal government was formed in 1969. Genscher transformed this "Division U" ("U" for Umweltschutz) into the engine behind an ambitious reform of environmental policy. Rather than being the rally cry of outraged citizens, the word *Umweltschutz* was actually "a bureaucratic creation par excellence."[27]

In the interplay between government policy and civil society that typically stands at the core of environmental policy, political insiders had a head start in the Federal Republic in the early 1970s. Remarkably, even the initial calls for powerful civic associations came from within the administration. As early as 1961, an enterprising civil servant working at the Ministry of Labor in North Rhine-Westphalia, which was responsible for emissions control at the time, asked in a meeting held with representatives of the city of Duisburg "whether an umbrella organization of citizens' associations might be willing to become a committed proponent of emissions reduction that could take up the fight against polluters."[28] Similarly, Genscher's Ministry of the Interior set about building networks, and it had a hand in the creation of the National Association of Citizens' Initiatives on Environmental Protection (Bundesverband Bürgerinitiativen Umweltschutz or BBU), whose leaders leaned toward Genscher's liberal party, the Freie Demokratische Partei (FDP). If one can speak of an environmental party in West Germany in the 1970s, then it was the FDP and specifically its left-liberal wing—a legacy that is all but forgotten due to the party's subsequent development. The BBU, for example, received financial support from the Friedrich Naumann Stiftung.[29] But as citizen's initiatives flourished during the 1970s, and particularly in the wake of radicalization over nuclear power, the role of the Federal Ministry of the Interior changed from puppet master to sorcerer's apprentice. The FDP's influence all but collapsed in 1977, when Hans-Helmuth Wüstenhagen, an FDP member, was forced to step down as the chairman of the BBU under pressure from leftist groups.[30]

Genscher was one of the first politicians to recognize the potential of environmental issues. These topics were full of opportunities for politicians to make a name for themselves, especially since the deficiency of existing regulatory policies was largely beyond debate. The career potential was particularly important in the years after the postwar boom. In an age of economic stagnation and growing doubts over state planning, environmental policy stood out as one of the few arenas where politicians could still hope for massive budget increases, expansion of jurisdictions, and new staff. There is ground to suspect that this was a general pattern in Western states at the time, but it was particularly successful in West Germany. We can compile an impressive list of politicians whose careers took off due to their involvement in environmental policy issues: Hans-Dietrich Genscher, Joschka Fischer, Jo Leinen, Klaus Matthiesen, Monika Griefahn, Jochen Flasbarth, Fritz Vahrenholt, Max Streibl, and Klaus Töpfer.[31]

Environmental policy was a remarkably effective springboard for a career in politics. The story of Joschka Fischer, the taxi driver from Frankfurt who became the vice chancellor of Germany, is a particularly spectacular example of how environmental policy could provide a heretofore nonexistent path into the political elite.[32] But at the same, we should not forget those who left or gave up at some point. When Wolfgang Sternstein, who had been a member of the board of the BBU for several years, visited Wüstenhagen in Freiburg years after the latter had stepped down from office, he encountered "a bitter old man who complained about everything under the sun."[33] The strength of the German environmental movement has often been admired from abroad, but some people paid a high personal price along the way.

Policies did not lack ambition in the 1970s, but a sense of disillusionment set in after a while. This was perhaps inevitable in an approach that adhered to the model of environmental policy "from above," which was one of the notable parallels between East and West. While political leaders specified far-reaching goals and couched them in bold rhetoric, implementation of policies was left to subordinates, whose fate was largely beyond the leaders' purview. Implementation was always complicated in environmental policy, but politicians were loath to hear too much about these complications.

Like the Federal Republic, the GDR's leaders were clear that environmental problems had to be taken seriously. The new general secretary of the central committee of the SED, Erich Honecker, mentioned environmental protection in his speech at the Eighth Party Congress in 1971. He even called upon the people to bring environmental problems to the attention of state authorities.[34] In the GDR, environmental policy fell under the rubric of the widely cited "unity of economic and social policy," which was given a green ideological complement with the "unity of economy and ecology."[35] In programmatic terms, this made for a striking parallel to the "quality of life" motif adopted by West German social democrats in their efforts to sharpen their political profile at the time—environmental policy was intended as part of the party's promise of prosperity for everyone.[36] The creation of the GDR's Ministry for Environmental Protection and Water Management (West Germany's Federal Ministry of the Environment was not established until the 1986 Chernobyl disaster[37]) was accompanied by the formation of a working group for "environmental protection and environmental management" at the East German Academy of Sciences. It was founded at the urging of the economic historian Hans Mottek, who also became the head of the environmental research commission at the academy.[38] But ambiguities soon found its way into the daily business of environmental policy, and they certainly did not diminish over time.

As Tobias Huff has pointed out, the pinnacle of GDR environmental policy was reached as Honecker came to power in May 1971.[39] But the noble intentions of the party leadership soon became stuck in the wheels of bureaucracy. While ministries typically received a corresponding body in the SED central committee party apparatus, no such parallel party institution was established for the Ministry of the Environment. Moreover, the Minister of the Environment as of March 1971, Hans Reichelt, had no access to the political resources of the SED because he belonged to the Democratic Farmers' Party of Germany (Demokratische Bauernpartei Deutschlands, or DBD).[40] All in all, the GDR's socialist environmental policy remained a fleeting vision due to the notorious lack of resources and the byzantine structures of the SED state. Environmental policy, like so many other aspects of the socialist system, also seemed to suffer from the worsening and ultimately terminal sclerosis in the GDR's final years. For example, when Dresden's sewage treatment plant was damaged by an Elbe river flood in 1987, it remained out of commission until after the fall of the Wall, and the city's untreated wastewater flowed directly into the river.[41] In the fight against sulfur dioxide emissions, which had been the subject of international negotiations since the early 1980s, the GDR resorted to the falsification of data in order to camouflage the government's impotence.[42] The failure of the administration to come to grips with such problems made environmental issues a fitting vehicle for protest movements, as did the official socialist ideology that defined environmental problems as a leftover of the capitalist past. According to dogma, socialism would overcome the exploitation of nature, a trope that provided dissidents with evidence of how the SED state was out of touch with reality.[43]

But in the 1970s, the differences between the two German states were matters of degrees, as both regimes were wrestling with implementation problems. West Germany's federalism made the task of turning new political programs into a reality no less complicated than the socialist bureaucracy in the East. Implementation was about political jockeying. When Genscher pressed ahead with his environmental agenda, for example, the Bavarian Ministry of Labor and Social Welfare internally called for "the most vocal resistance" because the initiative came from the other side of the political aisle.[44] And it was about authority and jealously guarded jurisdictions. By and large, the cooperation between the federal and state levels was one of the thorniest issues within the West German system of government, and it did not help that Genscher's environmental policy sought to expand the authority of the federal government at the expense of the states. In his memoirs, Genscher wrote that "never before had a minister tried to appropriate as much responsibility from the states in the name of the federal government," though he was still remorseful about the "lost 'water battle'"—that is, the fight for a stronger federal role in water policy.[45] If there was an advantage for West Germany over the GDR in matters of implementation, it was that the FRG could have an open conversation over lackluster enforcement. Negligent implementation of environmental legislation has been a running theme in West German debates ever since a 1974 landmark report of the Expert Council for Environmental Questions.[46] There was no similar rallying cry in the GDR, nor, for that matter, a place to discuss implementation in public.

Environmental policy lost much of its thrust in West Germany when Genscher moved on to the Foreign Ministry in 1974. In the same year, a new chancellor, Helmut Schmidt, shifted the emphasis away from visionary plans to "realistic cost-benefit calculations."[47] Even decades later, environmentalists were still talking about a closed-door meeting of the government held at Gymnich Castle in June 1975 that signaled this turning of the tide.[48] And then there was the divisive debate over nuclear power, where escalating protests and a hard-line government response provoked situations akin to civil war. Another striking parallel: both German states were remarkably stubborn when it came to nuclear power, and they both made a mockery of state planning with dramatic bureaucratic blunders.[49] In the GDR, a former salt mine at Morsleben became a deposit for radioactive waste in 1971, for example, but it was not granted a permanent operation permit from the State Office for Nuclear Safety and Radiation Protection until 1986.[50] And Morsleben was still superior in legal terms to the Asse II mine in West Germany. It fell under mining law until 2009, when the Federal Office for Radiation Protection (Bundesamt für Strahlenschutz) took charge of Asse II, which meant that disposal of nuclear waste was no different in legal terms from disposal of household waste.[51]

There was no general divergence on the level of environmental policy between GDR and FRG until 1979, when the prime minister of Lower Saxony, Ernst Albrecht, decided to cancel a reprocessing facility in Gorleben in response to hefty protests. It was the first decision of a West German politician that would have been inconceivable in the GDR. The gap widened over the 1980s, which became the environmental decade par excellence in the Federal Republic. It was during this decade that the self-perception and the global image of Germany as the model green country emerged. The dynamism in civil society was the driving force behind this development, which is a point that will be discussed in more detail in the next section. What needs to be emphasized here, however, is the sharp contrast to what was happening on the other side of the Wall at the time because the SED regime was dragging its feet on environmental issues. The decision of the Council of Ministers to declare all environmental data to be state secrets was the environmental policy equivalent to declaring bankruptcy.[52] By the end of the 1980s, the GDR was the "largest air polluter in Europe in terms of its size and population" due to its reliance on lignite coal.[53]

It all came down to a striking ideological inversion. The Federal Republic moved from a loosely regulated economy during the miracle years toward a comprehensive system of environmental controls that eventually covered virtually every aspect of industrial pollution. In contrast, the GDR went from comprehensive state planning to a laissez-faire approach to environmental issues, where the quest for hard currency trumped everything else. In other words, in West Germany capitalism was reined in to a remarkable degree under a green banner, while the GDR adopted a kind of ecological dog-eat-dog capitalism, where every environmental sacrifice was acceptable as long as it offered another breath of life for socialism. For anyone who sought to criticize the environmental toll of short-term maximization of profits, the late GDR provided far more fodder than contemporary West German capitalism.

The most dramatic event in GDR environmental policy came after the demise of SED rule. Literally with its last dying breath, the GDR's Council of Ministers decided to create five national parks, six biosphere reserves, and three nature parks, effectively placing no less than 4 percent of the country's land under protection.[54] East Germany also stuck to its iconic sign for nature reserves, a friendly-looking owl (West Germany had a flying eagle, which smacked of an act of state). But other than that, West German environmental law, institutions, and routines were just mapped onto the East, the common pattern in the wake of reunification. It looked like a matter of common sense at the time. In light of socialism's environmental toll, the idea that the West should learn from GDR environmental policy seemed patently absurd. However, things do not look quite so clear a few decades down the line.

In the early 1990s, environmental policy entered a new, eminently transnational orbit. Within a few years, environmental policy moved toward a new international framework. The Single European Act of 1987 expressly granted the European Community (soon to be called the European Union) a clear mandate for environmental policy. The EU used its newly gained powers with vigor in the decades that followed, even going so far as to consider an energy or carbon dioxide tax.[55] The EU's environmental achievements include the council directive concerning the protection of waters against pollution caused by nitrates from 1991 and the council directive on the conservation of natural habitats and of wild fauna and flora (known as the Habitats Directive) from 1992. Moreover, the UN Framework Convention on Climate Change and the Biodiversity Convention were signed in 1992, two treaties that, together with the Montreal Protocol for the protection of the ozone layer of 1987, define the framework of global environmental policy to this day. However, these ambitious initiatives stand in growing contrast to the rather cumbersome world of real politics in which environmental regulations often seem to be quite authoritarian. The link between democracy and environmental protection, which appeared to be self-evident in Germany in 1990, is not so obvious in current global environmental policy. It would seem that there are still lessons to be learned from GDR environmental policy in the twenty-first century.

Civil Societies

It seems rather arbitrary to draw a line between green politics and civil society in the Federal Republic. The careers of leading politicians such as Jürgen Trittin and Monika Griefahn, who went from being activists to ministers, suggest fluid borders between politics and protest. Particularly in the 1980s, there was a symbiotic relationship between these two realms. Environmental organizations and citizens' initiatives identified problems and pushed for solutions, while politicians tried their best to follow up and gain popular acclaim. But this de facto alliance began to crumble in the years after reunification. In 2000, for example, when the red-green coalition government made a deal to phase out nuclear energy, it found itself facing crowds of angry protesters.[56] Similarly, while civic mobilization reached new heights in the run-up to the Copenhagen Climate Summit in 2009, the conference itself proved to be a fiasco in terms of environmental policy. Renewable energy projects have met resistance from environmentally minded citizens. From a twenty-first century perspective, politics and civil society are two separate spheres, each with its own rules. As such, they must be analyzed according to their own logics.

Civil society is a rather difficult topic in an interwoven history of the two Germanys. Both countries had environmental movements that flourished in the 1980s, but that meant vastly different things. Whereas Michael Beleites's research study titled *Pechblende* (Pitchblende, also known as uraninite) on uranium mining at Wismut circulated as an underground samizdat publication in the GDR, several editions of Holger Strohm's *Friedlich in die Katastrophe* (Quietly into disaster) have been printed since its initial publication in West Germany in 1973, and the book became the defining compendium on the technical risks associated with nuclear energy that every leftist bookshelf in Germany had to have.[57] Furthermore, the West German environmental movement received much of its support from a political community that was lukewarm at best about East Germany. Among the major parties of West Germany, none was as uninterested in reunification as the Green Party. Party members such as Wilhelm Knabe and Petra Kelly entertained personal contacts with civil rights activists in the East, but that does not change the general picture.

All that makes for a conceptual imbalance in a cross-border approach. Whereas West German activists could write lengthy books warning of an impending apocalypse, for instance, East German concerns could only be expressed in petitions of limited scope.[58] While environmental activists in West Germany attacked megaprojects ranging from Kalkar to Startbahn West, East German environmental efforts had to focus on smaller projects and concerns that look rather petty in a naive German-German comparison. Activists in the FRG could stage mass demonstrations against the "nuclear state" whereas East German activists had to work hard just to create something akin to a "public sphere" in the first place. They never dreamed of staging mass protests. Organizing tree-planting actions or bike demonstrations was risky enough.[59]

At first glance, it seems rather easy to trace the institutional outlines of the change of civic activism in the West. New citizens' initiatives sprouted up everywhere, and national organizations such as BUND and Greenpeace were established. At the same time, venerable nature conservancy associations such as the League for Bird Protection (Bund für Vogelschutz) transformed into agile NGOs, albeit not without hefty internal debates in some cases. Similarly, the Green Party became a permanent fixture within the West German party spectrum. But looking at events more closely, the transformation becomes more and more diffuse. There were violent anti-nuclear protests and local eco-projects with municipal funding and all the necessary permits, bearded hippie types and establishment figures, globe-trotting charismatic celebrities such as Petra Kelly and dedicated local nature enthusiasts who took care of neglected grasslands. One cannot help but wonder what they had in common.[60]

But for all the divergences in political styles and worldviews, it is clear that diversity contributed greatly to the liveliness and persistence of the environmental movement. With topics ranging from the building of new highways to global climate change, from the protection of the horseshoe bat to protests against nuclear power plants, and from calls for a speed limit of one hundred kilometers per hour on the German Autobahn to combating the deforestation of the Amazon rainforest, the new environmentalism had plenty of entry points for concerned citizens. During the boom years of environmentalism, mutual support was key among activists: people were happy to go to a rally when the others were circulating one's own petition. These reciprocal relationships flourished best within what is referred to as the "alternative" or "counterculture" milieu.

This chapter does not allow for a comprehensive discussion of the underlying causes of the environmental revolution, but two points deserve special attention. First, West German environmentalism took off in the wake of the second oil price shock of 1979/80, an economic crisis that changed political lines of conflict in many Western countries.[61] To put it bluntly, while the British and the Americans discussed neoliberalism, and the French debated Mitterrand's brand of socialism, the Germans were up in arms over forest dieback. The enthusiasm with which West German citizens from different directions suddenly subscribed to the green movement bore the marks of sociopsychological evasion. It helped that debates over a fundamental shift in economic policy remained rather theoretical in the Federal Republic as long as the social-liberal coalition was in its death throes.

Unlike mass unemployment, people found some quick solutions for environmental problems. The 1970s upswing in environmental policy had fostered the development of new technologies, but many innovations were delayed due to costs. The technology for flue gas desulphurization in coal-fired power plants, for example, had been available since the early 1970s. Likewise, catalytic converters for automobile exhaust systems had been around for a while, but they were only being routinely built into German automobiles destined for the American market. When environmental concerns flourished in the early 1980s, the powers that be aggressively pushed for the use of such technological innovations, leaving the green movement to bask in the aura of success for a while. In hindsight, this was really nothing more than clearing a policy backlog, but in the contemporary context, the new environmental policy offensive seemed to be proof that civic protests could even bring large industrial corporations to their knees.

The power of environmental protest was particularly fascinating for contemporaries who had been influenced by Marxism as a result of their involvement in the student protest movement and the alternative milieu. Environmental issues were like a match made in heaven for Marxist buzz words. For example, "alienation" could also be found in nature, and the exploitation of the proletariat was vaguely similar to the exploitation of nature. Moreover, Marx himself spoke of the material interaction or "metabolism between man and nature" in Das Kapital.[62] Of course, this was really a case of vulgar Marxism at heart, but after the myriad disappointments that followed in the wake of the protests in 1968, many leftists were open to a bit of ideological flexibility. Doubts about such arguments were more or less relegated to the private sphere, as in the case of Rudi Dutschke, who wrote in his diary in March 1977 that "the whole anti-nuclear and mass demonstrations in B[rokdorf] a[nd] I[tzehoe] are theoretically and politically troublesome for me."[63]

Quite paradoxically, Marxism was more important for West German environmentalists than it was for their East German counterparts. Indeed, socialism as an ideology had very little relevance for GDR environmental history in the 1980s, apart from glossy rhetoric. But if socialism was largely meaningless for environmental issues, this also made them innocent—or, rather, as innocent as political issues can be in a totalitarian society. As a result, environmental issues offered a convenient vehicle for conveying East German dissatisfaction over unbridled industrial production, the notorious lack of resources that left little room for investing in environmental protection measures, and detached GDR leaders. Both within and beyond state-sanctioned circles, environmental protests served as a front for proxy conflicts. Complaints over ecological problems did not harbor the same political risks as, say, remarks about economic stagnation or the privileges of party bigwigs. As a result, seemingly trivial topics often bore great significance for East Germans. For instance, when the environmental working group in Halle, which operated under the protection of the Protestant Church, objected in 1988 to a road paving project through the local heath forest called the Dölauer Heide, speculations ran wild within the group as to whether a military agenda was behind the project. But, as it turned out in the end, the forest service was merely looking to use up some bitumen that it had been allotted. After the collapse of the GDR, the group later admitted that it had been chasing a ghost and that the whole matter had been more about venting frustration than achieving anything truly significant.[64]

The environmental community was inevitably fragmented in the GDR, but it had its hierarchies nonetheless, and the scholarly literature reflects these hierarchies to the present day. A great deal of attention has been devoted to the environmental library in the parish hall of the Zionskirche in East Berlin, in part because of the dramatic failure of a nighttime Stasi raid on 25 November 1987. The attempt to drive a wedge between the church and environmental groups backfired. While the parish council of the Zionskirche supported a vigil calling for the release of the imprisoned members of the environmental library, groups from other cities sent messages of solidarity.[65] A path can thus be traced from these events to the establishment of the green-environmental network called Arche in 1988, which linked together grassroots groups from all over the GDR.[66] International cooperation among Eastern European environmentalists was also fostered by the Greenway network that connected activists from Poland, Hungary, Czechoslovakia, and Yugoslavia in 1985 and had spread to all the Soviet bloc countries by 1989 (apart from Romania and Albania).[67] However, this boom in networks did not mean everything went smoothly; the movement was also plagued by considerable internal tensions. Internal strife was yet another parallel between the East and West German milieus, perhaps because new social movements in general are quite susceptible to quarrels thanks to their emphasis on grassroots democracy and their habitual aversion to hierarchies. In what seems like a bizarre example in hindsight, the tensions between the environmental library and the Arche network culminated in a formal declaration of incompatibility on 2 May 1998 that forced members to choose between the two organizations.[68]

For the most part, the green movements in both German states operated within their own distinct political universe until 1989. If cross-border exchange took place at all, it worked best through media channels. The East German author Monika Maron, for example, published her debut novel *Flugasche* (*Flight of Ashes*) in the West with S. Fischer Verlag in Frankfurt in 1981. It is the story of the journalist Josefa Nadler, who found herself in trouble with the SED and her colleagues after reporting on an aging power plant that was responsible for severe pollution in a town named "B." In one of the most cited passages in the novel, Maron calls the town of "B.," which was easily recognized as Bitterfeld, "the dirtiest town in Europe."[69] "Real socialism" in this region dominated by the chemical industry took yet another blow when the Soviet Union lost the European Football Championships final on 25 June 1988. Environmental activists took advantage of the fact that the football-loving state apparatus was temporarily distracted by the match and shot documentary film footage of the disastrous environmental situation. The film material was smuggled into the West, where it aired in September on the ARD

(Arbeitsgemeinschaft der öffentlich-rechtlichen Rundfunkanstalten der Bundesrepublik Deutschland, or Consortium of the Public Broadcasting Institutions) investigative reporting show *Kontraste*, cementing the image of Bitterfeld as a symbol of the environmental catastrophe in East Germany.[70] Similarly, the West German media was also mostly responsible for the popularization of Michael Beleites's *Pechblende*. While only a very few East Germans actually had a chance to read this samizdat publication, a great number of them saw a documentary based on this study that aired on West German television on 3 November 1987.[71]

But while West German television certainly reached both German audiences, there were notable divergences in the modes of perception. In the GDR, journalists from the West were a trump card in the struggle to create something akin to a public sphere. Despite all the legitimacy issues that arose from working with "Western media," this cooperation was still one of the few ways to raise public awareness.[72] The effect that such popularization could have can be seen, for instance, in the way the council of the Karl-Marx-Stadt (now Chemnitz) district reacted to *Pechblende*. It distributed its own "Informational Materials Concerning the Status of Radiation Protection in the Southern Districts of the GDR," which effectively meant that the district government felt the need to fight for public opinion on this issue.[73] In the West, by contrast, reports on the GDR's eco-problems established the impression of a late socialist environmental catastrophe, but the political purpose behind these reports was less clear. After all, it was easy to underscore the merits of West German environmental policy if Eastern Europe was used as a foil.[74]

After 1989, environmental activism differed greatly between East and West. On the whole, the green-environmental network Arche formed the basis of the Green Party that was founded in the GDR in November 1989. The party gained seats in the People's Chamber (Volkskammer) in March 1990 and then the Bundestag in December 1990. However, the Berlin Arche chapter took a somewhat different path as it began to care for the homeless in 1990, setting up a shelter in a parish in Treptow.[75] Shifts like these were a very typical phenomenon in the former Eastern Bloc states, where the prominence of environmental issues within the protest movements prior to the *Wende* contrasted sharply with the almost complete collapse of many environmental movements after 1990. By way of example, an estimated one hundred thousand Lithuanians protested against the Soviet nuclear power plant Ignalina in September 1988. The construction of a third reactor was canceled before the collapse of Soviet rule, but the two existing reactors remained in use until they were shut down at the request of the European Union during the negotiations over Lithuania's membership. It is difficult to say what actually led to the disintegration of environmental protest movements in Eastern Europe. Was it the general change of the political climate that paved the way for the erosion of the political and socioeconomic base of the East German environmental groups, which would mean that it was more or less the victory of neoliberalism that accounts for their demise? Or had environmental issues in Eastern Europe really only been a vehicle for other grievances, which meant that eco-camouflage was no longer required in an open society?[76]

Two points are clear. First, environmental issues were not cardinal topics in Eastern European societies at large in the 1980s. Second, environmental protests were tightly interwoven with other concerns. The protest against the Ignalina plant, for example, was not only directed against nuclear technology—whose risks had become quite apparent after Chernobyl—but also against a symbol of much-hated Soviet hegemony. Similarly, there was an affinity between environmental and peace activism within groups affiliated or close to the Church that was clearly reflected in phrases such as "the protection of God's creation" in which both strands were intertwined.[77] Likewise, the rubric of "urban ecology," which proved to be the most agile segment of GDR environmental activism within the state-sanctioned Society for Nature and the Environment (Gesellschaft für Natur und Umwelt), covered a variety of topics that were all compatible with the general idea of improving the quality of life.[78] The Thuringian environmentalist group in Knau-Dittersdorf, for one, drew attention to the complex problem of factory farming through its protests against a major pig farm, tapping into a topic that would not receive great attention in the German public until the twenty-first century.[79] Yet this link between environmental issues and other topics was not an Eastern European peculiarity. It corresponds to a widespread pattern within the Global South that Joan Martinez-Alier has referred to as the "environmentalism of the poor."[80]

West German environmentalists moved in the opposite direction. They saw environmental problems as distinct issues, disconnected from the broader context.[81] This allowed environmentalism to diffuse into various political milieus, leaving only a few stubborn conservative politicians who branded the protest movement a leftist conspiracy.[82] As a result, West German environmentalists remained insensitive to how environmental problems were tied to social injustices. It was hardly noticed, for example, that the discrimination against Turkish migrants in Günter Wallraff's controversial bestseller *Ganz Unten* from 1985 also showed in the excessive pollution to which they were exposed.[83]

Reunification thus resulted in the collision of the two distinct worlds of environmental activism that had existed in the East and the West. There were profound differences in terms of environmental thought and political style, and also a profound lack of interest in the views and routines of the other side. The West German Green Party drew many members from a political community where the question of reunification was meaningless because the persistence of a divided Germany was considered to be a suitable punishment for the evils of National Socialism. In East Germany, politicians from the Bündnis 90 and the Grüne in the GDR failed to take a position on the issue of German reunification leading up to the elections for the People's Chamber in March 1990.[84] In the federal election campaign after unification in 1990, the Green Party focused ostentatiously on climate change: "Everyone is talking about Germany. We're talking about the weather."[85] Needless to say, environmental activists were hardly the only ones who had trouble understanding their brothers and sisters in the "other" Germany. But few groups had to struggle quite as much to accept their new compatriots as fellow citizens in the first place.

The real turning point for the Greens after reunification came with the federal elections on 2 December 1990, when the party failed to achieve the 5-percent vote threshold necessary to make it into parliament. This came as a shock to the Greens, as it followed upon the heels of a decade filled with many electoral victories and ever growing public acclaim. Not surprisingly, therefore, its First National Party Congress for all of Germany took place in Neumünster in April 1991 under the banner of renewal. Petra Kelly failed dismally in her bid to become speaker, and the radical environmentalists who supported Jutta Ditfurth decided to split from the party shortly thereafter.[86] On the whole, the party became more disciplined, more professional, and more moderate. For the first time, a red-green coalition of social democrats and the Green Party survived an entire legislative term in Lower Saxony. The fact that it did so under the leadership of Gerhard Schröder, chancellor of a red-green federal government from 1998 to 2005, makes it tempting to draw simple teleological lines forward. The path toward the federal red-green coalition had far too many "ifs" and "buts" to depict it as the inevitable conclusion of the greening of Germany. But for all the caveats, it remains doubtful whether a stable red-green federal government would have been feasible without the internal reflection process that took place within the Green Party after 1990.

But before the Green Party could dream of taking over federal ministries, it had to unify two parties with distinct West German and East German flavors. It was a long and difficult process, particularly for the East German side. The fusion of the Greens with the remains of the East German civil rights movement dragged on until 1993, not necessarily because of organizational issues, but rather because many East Germans first had to go through the laborious process of bringing themselves up to speed on current debates. Different intellectual horizons were very much at play in these discussions: as one diagnosis from 1994 suggested, "The search for future models of society beyond capitalism and socialism—often referred to as a 'third way'—is being replaced by the pragmatic handling of specific problems as they arise."[87] There was also a tension between West German activism, where politicians were allowed to have a private life, and the comprehensive commitment with body and soul that dissident life in socialist authoritarian states brought with it.[88] At the same time, East German activists had to adapt to a new institutional and media context while overcoming their understandable exhaustion after having gone through four election campaigns in 1990. All in all, the fusion of East and West German Greens had an air of resigned commitment to what was inevitable. The upcoming federal elections of 1994 and the specter of the 5-percent hurdle were looming in the back of everyone's mind.[89]

The East German activists were able to achieve a small symbolic victory, namely the inclusion of Bündnis 90 as the first part of the official name of the party. The Bund für Vogelschutz was even willing to adopt the name of its East German counterpart, so it is now known as Naturschutzbund Deutschland. It should be noted, though, that one reason behind this move was that it also brought a convenient end to an internal squabble over the name and focus of the organization that had been going on for decades within the West German bird protection association.[90] Ever since reunification, the performance of the Greens in elections has been much weaker in the former GDR than in the West. Especially in state elections for about a decade, they often failed to achieve the necessary 5 percent to attain seats in the state parliaments. Furthermore, it needs to be borne in mind that the unification of the environmental movements in the East and West was never truly completed. A share of GDR activists joined together in the Green League (Grüne Liga), which was a loose network for decentralized grassroots activism. For all intents and purposes, the Green League was an extension of the Arche concept within a new political framework. As such, this organization has been the antithesis of the more strongly centralized, media-savvy, and politically well-connected environmental organizations characteristic of the West.[91]

More research is needed on the shrinking significance of the green movements in postsocialist Eastern Europe, especially in light of the energetic and rapid response of governments to these issues. The willingness of political leaders to tackle environment problems showed in investments in clean-up technology worth billions and the remediation of contaminated sites, but this had significant side effects in reducing the scope of civic environmental activism. We can see the result in environmental activism surrounding Energiewende (Energy Transition [to renewable sources]), a political-administrative mega-project that leaves scant room for enraged citizens. Protest takes place mostly in the form of local opposition against specific projects. It takes considerable knowledge and insider contacts to talk about renewable energy nowadays, and few average citizens can muster the time and expertise to join these debates.

A Different Life

Contemporary environmental history has mostly focused on the political sphere. But such a perspective looks only at fragments of what the environment has really meant since 1970. Environmentalism brought people to reconsider virtually every facet of everyday life. "Green thinking" influenced food choices and consumer routines in supermarkets—at least for those who still dared to enter these cathedrals of consumerism rather than the local organic co-op. Daily routines bear the marks of environmentalism, which may account for the movement's remarkable resilience, which is anything but self-evident. As Christopher Rootes has noted, the environmental movement is "the great survivor among the new social movements that arose in and since the 1960s."[92]

Dreams of a different life are a crucial part of contemporary environmental history. Yet historians who seek to write such narratives are constrained by two factors. First, they face a desolate state of research even by the generous standards of environmental history. A cultural history of the environment, as Michael Bess has done for France, has not yet been written for the German case, though the endeavor would not lack for interesting topics.[93] The rising popularity of muesli and whole grain bread, for example, says quite a bit about German sensitivities in the late twentieth century. Second, a German-German perspective presents peculiar challenges, as consumption and lifestyles differed greatly between East and West. Whereas West Germans tried to save energy in the wake of the oil crises by installing thermostats and double-glazed windows, East Germans simply opened windows in well-heated but poorly insulated rooms. Similarly, restaurants in the West offered a taste of new culinary worlds, while charcoal grills were fired up along the streets in East Germany after the *Wende*, a culinary monoculture even for those who like Thuringian bratwurst.

German critics of consumption could draw upon older intellectual traditions. It is quite striking, for example, that Vance Packard's American bestsellers quickly made their way across the pond to West Germany. In

1958 and 1961, two books appeared in translation just a year after their original publication, *Der geheimen Verführer* (*The Hidden Persuaders*) and *Die große Verschwendung* (*The Waste Makers*).⁹⁴ Furthermore, it is difficult to write West German consumer history without *Stiftung Warentest*, a kind of German equivalent to *Consumer Reports* in the United States, created in 1964. Tests of *Stiftung Warentest* have been a cornerstone of responsible consumption ever since. Just how far the critique of consumption resonated in East Germany is still up for debate: could average GDR citizens even begin to understand the concerns of Western consumers? Postconsumerist Westerners, at any rate, tended to be quite condescending of their Eastern neighbors on these matters, as Otto Schily showed on live television when he flashed a banana on the evening of the GDR's free election of 1990 as his no-word commentary to the election results. The legendary move reflected a deep suspicion of the consumerist spree that East Germans embarked on at the time.⁹⁵

The alternative milieu was a crucial incubator for the socialization of West Germans who were critical of consumerism. In his groundbreaking study, Sven Reichardt points out that environmentalism was more than just a political agenda because it was also a decision about lifestyles—even though, at the end of the day, smoke-filled neighborhood pubs may have been more popular than health food stores and green tea.⁹⁶ But the alternative milieu had its center in large cities and thrived on personal contacts, and that made it difficult to diffuse eastward. Even if it did make it across the Wall, East Germans who sought to adopt such a lifestyle faced political and social hurdles. A church organization, the Kirchliches Forschungsheim Wittenberg, published an alternative cookbook with vegetarian recipes in 1983, but that was an anomaly rather than a harbinger of new food choices.⁹⁷

According to Reichardt, the alternative milieu fell apart in the 1980s, but its cultural shock waves resonate in Germany to the present day. It lives on in the alternative farming community, whose growth has been strikingly steady ever since the heady days of 1970s counterculture. Given that organic products can now be found in every supermarket, it is hard to image what it must have been like as consumers and farmers found themselves confronted by ideas of alternative farming methods around 1980. It was a different world, far removed from the factory farming methods that changed agricultural production across Western Europe, and engaging with alternative farming was a vertigo-inducing experience. After visiting thirteen organic and biodynamic farms in West Germany and Austria in 1982, two officials from the Chamber of Agriculture in Westfalen-Lippe summed up their findings as follows: "In our democracy, people can still do business in any way they like. And it should stay this way."⁹⁸

Changing ideas of health and disease where another realm where environmentalism reshaped everyday life. While fears of infectious diseases waned in the postwar decades, cancer became the defining concern. Most Germans have found themselves confronted with the death of friends or relatives from cancer. For Petra Kelly, the loss of her half-sister Grace to cancer was a traumatic experience that her biographer Saskia Richter has identified as a "point of departure for her involvement in politics."[99] Kelly was not the only one to draw connections between cancer and environmental pollution, which was reflected by a whole discourse on this issue that cannot be boiled down to a simple dichotomy between material and postmaterial values. To many, it now seemed that pollution poisoned the human body. After the *Wende*, for example, a poll of leading doctors in East German hospitals revealed that the number of respiratory illnesses among children more than doubled between 1974 and 1989, despite a dropping birth rate.[100] As a result, a new sense of urgency seeped into the debates over pollution because it was no longer just about dirt and odors. Pollution was now about human survival.

This discursive shift was quite obvious in West Germany, but it could also be found in East Germany. A poll conducted in 1971, for example, indicated that more than 90 percent of those questioned believed that there was a link between air pollution and health.[101] After the Chernobyl incident, the fear of exposure to radioactivity was felt equally by East and West Germans, although it was expressed differently: the insistent questions about milk and sandboxes that West German parents posed to the authorities could not be asked in the GDR public.[102] Likewise, a German-German analysis of the fears associated with industrial chemicals, which came to a head in the FRG following the accidents in Seveso in 1976 and at Sandoz in 1986, would also be a worthwhile endeavor for future scholarship.[103] Such a project would bring together aspects of a cultural history of the environment and the yet unwritten history of the body within an environmental history perspective.

Of Wolves and Hens: The Subversive Power of Environmental History

According to West Germany's agricultural census of 1989, there were 5,368,577 milk cows, 14,659,627 pigs, and 38,226,140 laying hens in the country.[104] These figures mirror a trend with severe ethical and socioeconomic repercussions. Ever since factory farming began to change food production in the 1950s, most animals have seen a drastic reduction of the space in which they can move (including the infamous cages for laying hens). Factory farming also changed the bodies of these animals: they were bred systematically for maximum production and the artificial environment of industrial-style pens. Artificial insemination has made it possible to create a multitude of offspring born to selected high-performance animals, which has ultimately resulted in the unprecedented homogenization of the gene pool. Some top-performing bulls, for example, have produced over a million descendants.[105]

Factory farming marks a watershed in the long history of relations between humans and animals. Farm animals used to be recognized by their personalities and were given names, but factory farming treated them as anonymous cogs in a vast machinery: everything that mattered about these animals could be said in numbers. But perhaps even more shocking is the silence with which this transformation took place in both East and West Germany. It came across like a natural trend, devoid of alternatives or even serious debates. Consumers seemed only to be interested in reducing their grocery bills at first, and farmers had limited options. They could get bigger, get better, or get out.[106]

The industrialization of agricultural production also transformed plant production, which embraced monoculture in unprecedented fashion. We can see the result in rows and rows of perfectly manicured corn stretching far off into the horizon. From the perspective of biodiversity, the postwar period was a dark era on both sides of the Iron Curtain. Both German states used excessive amounts of chemical pesticides, and the overuse of fertilizers led to severe water pollution. From an environmental history perspective, agricultural history in East and West Germany shows some remarkable parallels.[107]

The twenty-first century will most likely be the first century in the history of the world in which the majority of the population lives in cities. Despite all their differences, the histories of the GDR and the FRG were both marked by a dramatic acceleration in urbanization that had a similar outcome with monumental consequences, namely the end of the countryside as the defining arena of socialization in "Old Europe." The implications of this are particularly dramatic within the context of the history of animals. The line separating livestock from pets, a fluid boundary just a hundred years ago, is now a firm border in moral and spatial terms.[108] When a bear crossed the German-Austrian border in the Alps in 2006, for example, German urbanites found that fears of wild nature left no other option than to shoot what was perceived as a "problem bear" (*Problembär*). On the other hand, wolves have migrated peacefully from Poland to Germany and came as far westward as the Lüneburg Heath, the gratifying case of a genuine East-West transfer in the unified Germany.

The gap in lifestyles between city and country has shrunk dramatically, but tensions can still be detected from an environmental history perspective. No other area of German society reacted as vigorously to new environmental policies than the agricultural sector. While the environmental report issued by the GDR in 1990 called for a "reduction of livestock numbers in over-sized facilities to an ecologically acceptable level and decentralized animal husbandry," for example, the actual trend toward ever-larger mass breeding farms continued unabatedly.[109] Concerted reform efforts such as the "agrarian reform" (Agrarwende), which the red-green coalition launched at the height of the BSE (*bovine spongiform encephalopathy*) crisis, were not able to reverse these developments, though they did achieve some improvements.[110]

In sum, environmental history brings us to reconsider received wisdoms of the literature. Maybe the countryside did not disappear as comprehensively as conventional readings suggest? And maybe the ultimate triumph of freedom was a relative thing when we look at the fate of animals in factory farms? Environmental history does not just claim a room of its own in the house of history—it also forces us to review the narratives and the perspectives that historians have embraced. Scholars have only begun to explore this subversive power of environmental history.

Reunited Ecologies

From an environmental history perspective, reunification took place on different levels at varying speeds and with varying amounts of hubbub. On a material level, reunification marked the beginning of a clean-up program in the GDR that would costs billions, but it occurred largely beyond the public's attention. Few people cared about the GDR's shoddy waste management practices, but many were angry about the new sewage treatment plants. They brought fees for house owners to unprecedented heights, and it did not help that many plants were oversized in anticipation of an economic boom that never materialized.[111] Political reunification proved to be more difficult, particularly when it required more than a bloc transfer of the West German state of the art to the new East German states.

The green 1980s were a time of mutually reinforcing actions in politics, civil society, and lifestyles. The 1990s were different: tensions grew between the different realms. A gap emerged between political imperatives and civic protest, as shown in events such as the protests against the sinking of the oil platform Brent Spar in 1995. While the Greenpeace-inspired protests drew widespread support and ultimately triggered the largest consumer boycott of postwar Germany, the campaign failed to take stock of the many causes of the worrisome state of the North Sea, many of which were more troublesome than Brent Spar.[112] The 1990s were also marked by an internet and high-tech euphoria that made environmental concerns look strangely old-fashioned by way of comparison.

The environmental movement disintegrated into a broad range of concerns in the 1990s. On the one end of the spectrum, there were entrepreneurial manifestos in favor of an "environmentally-friendly social market economy."[113] At the other end, heavily annotated eco-feminist books trumpeted the joint struggle against capitalism, patriarchy, and the control of nature, majestically emerging from the toil of everyday politics.[114] Disintegration had its limits, and the Fundi and Realo factions within the Green Party found ways to work with each other, but sometimes communication collapsed altogether. The nuclear phase-out of the red-green government drew vigorous protests from hard-core anti-nuclear activists, and no words could heal the divide until Merkel sought to renegotiate the agreement in 2010.

So what does one make of the red-green federal government that came into office in 1998? It was both a fitting conclusion of history and a mystery, and the latter had a lot to do with lukewarm scholarly interest. While the early Greens were virtually flooded with academic attention, their seven years in power have not been studied to a satisfactory degree.[115] In a book that focuses on the legacy of the two German states, it is crucial to recognize that Gerhard Schröder's government was an eminently West German affair. The cooperation between the Social Democrats and the Green Party was an idea that emerged in a specific West German context in the 1980s, and these coalitions never took root in East German states, apart from the minority government that was briefly formed in Saxony-Anhalt and disappeared after one term. In Schröder's first cabinet, Christine Bergmann (Ministry for Family, Senior Citizens, Women and Youth) was the only minister who had grown up in East Germany.

In the 1980s, the red-green coalition nurtured great hopes for a comprehensive ecological modernization project. The Schröder government soon looked more modest by way of comparison.[116] Continuities prevailed in the institutions and tools of environmental policy. For example, while the red-green government expanded support for renewable energy sources, it stuck to the general approach that the federal government had embraced with a law of 1990 (Einspeisegesetz).[117] Even the government's anti-nuclear stance is best understood as part of a long farewell to nuclear power in Germany: not a single reactor project got off the ground since reunification. Even East German states, otherwise desperate for investors, showed no appetite for new nuclear projects in the 1990s.[118]

Jürgen Trittin's infamous move to put a deposit on cans drew on a decree that was drafted more than a decade earlier under Klaus Töpfer.

The red-green government abandoned traditions in agricultural policy in dramatic fashion when it touted "changing agriculture as we knew it" (Agrarwende). Renate Künast became the first Green Minister of Consumer Protection, Food and Agriculture. It would have been impossible without the BSE crisis. If mad cow disease had not been looming on the horizon, the government's agrarian policy would likely have continued with "business as usual," as indicated by the appointment of Karl-Heinz Funke as the first Federal Minister of Agriculture under Gerhard Schröder. In terms of an ecological taxation, Germany was a European latecomer. By the time Schröder was sworn in as chancellor, ten states had already reformed their tax systems accordingly.[119] Nevertheless, the eco-tax turned into a political football.

If the CDU/CSU and FDP had won the federal election in 2005, it might have changed the course of environmental policy at the federal level. Neoliberal reformism was at the core of the opposition's campaign, which could have inspired a policy overhaul. But with a coalition of social democrats and the CDU/CSU under Merkel, the new government stuck to a cross-party consensus regarding environmental problems. Staunch antienvironmental rhetoric could be heard in the United States and Great Britain, and from the Czech Republic and its president Václav Klaus, but it never made much ground in Germany.[120] At the moment, it is hard to imagine a backlash against the environmental progress made in Germany since the 1970s. The problem facing environmental activists today is rather one of success, marked by the loss of atomic power as a rallying cry in the wake of the government's decision of 2011 to do away with nuclear power plants as well as the conflicts from the expansion of renewable energy.

The majority decision within the Bundestag to eliminate nuclear power in Germany on the heels of the Fukushima catastrophe bears the hallmarks of a "green" *Sonderweg* (special path). No other country reacted to the nuclear accident in Japan with as much resolve as Germany. But new reactor projects are few in numbers in Western countries, and perhaps the German decision is just the more determined version of a general farewell to nuclear power. Even in France, Europe's poster child for atomic power, there is only one current nuclear construction project underway—in Flamanville in Normandy—although at least forty reactors of this size need to be built in order to keep the country's nuclear power capacity at current levels. Contrasts between East and West Germany are fading. The environmental problems of factory farming in Mecklenburg-Vorpommern resemble those in the Oldenburg region in Lower Saxony, and the same holds true for the brown coal and chemical industries.

German environmentalism is changing, and many certainties of recent decades have come into question. The move toward renewable energy is happening, but it is also beset by uncertainties. Environmental organizations are changing, while the Green Party faces a rocky farewell of the founding generation. Environmental awareness among average Germans seems to be somewhat ambivalent at a time when they fly long distances to eco-resorts in order to eat organic food. There is no green happy ending of history in sight, and environmental sustainability lingers as an elusive goal. Environmental historians have little trouble with the notorious lopsidedness of intra-German comparisons, where the West thrives while the East fails. In terms of environmental sustainability, we have a GDR that failed in spectacular fashion and an FRG that failed in unspectacular fashion.

In other words, contemporary environmental history offers a number of loose ends. We are unsure about many dangers that we face and about the future of environmental policy. We are even unsure about the terms and concepts that we use in order to assess success and failure. Do recent decades mark the final stage of the age of fossil fuels? Or do we currently witness the beginnings of a radicalization of fossil fuel use, whose harbingers show in countries like Iraq and Nigeria? Will future historians primarily deplore our collective failure in terms of climate policy? Or will it be the horrible fate of animals in factory farms that makes them blush in shame? Perhaps they will praise the rise of politics and civil society — even though it was borne by sated affluent citizens—for opening the doors to a century that had to be environmental for lack of a choice? Or will future historians find it all terribly superficial? For the time being, historians will not be able to embrace one of these narratives with full confidence. The one certainty is that, no matter how the history of our times will be written one day, narratives will need to account for the environment. No history of late-twentieth century Germany will be complete without a good dose of green.

Frank Uekötter is reader in environmental humanities at the University of Birmingham (U.K.). His books include *The Green and the Brown: A History of Conservation in Nazi Germany* (2006), *The Age of Smoke: Environmental Policy in Germany and the United States, 1880–1970* (2009), *The Greenest Nation? A New History of German Environmentalism* (2014), and, as editor, *Exploring Apocalyptica: Coming to Terms with Environmental Alarmism* (2018). He is currently working on an environmental history of the modern world.

NOTES

1. Anthony Giddens, *The Politics of Climate Change* (Cambridge, 2009), 50.
2. Cf. Fred Pearce, *Die Grünen Macher* (Berlin, 1992).
3. Cf. Joachim Radkau, *The Age of Ecology: A Global History* (Cambridge, 2014); Daniel S. Jones, *Masters of the Universe: Hayek, Friedman, and the Birth of Neoliberal Politics* (Princeton, 2012).
4. Jürgen Büschenfeld, *Flüsse und Kloaken. Umweltfragen im Zeitalter der Industrialisierung (1870–1918)* (Stuttgart, 1997), 380.
5. Ulrich Eisenbach, "Kaliindustrie und Umwelt," in *Die Kaliindustrie an Werra und Fulda. Geschichte eines landschaftsprägenden Industriezweigs*, ed. Ulrich Eisenbach and Akos Paulinyi (Darmstadt, 1998), 210–12, 216 and 220; A. M. Eckert, "Geteilt, aber nicht unverbunden. Grenzgewässer als deutsch-deutsches Umweltproblem," *Vierteljahreshefte für Zeitgeschichte* 62 (2014): 69–100.
6. Hartmut Ruck, "Die Kali-Industrie an der Werra in Thüringen 1945–1989," in *Bunte Salze, weiße Berge. Wachstum und Wandel der Kaliindustrie zwischen Thüringer Wald, Rhön und Vogelsberg*, ed. Hermann-Josef Hohmann and Lothar Brückner (Hünfeld, 2004), 118f.
7. Rainer Grießhammer, *Letzte Chance für den Wald? Die abwendbaren Folgen des Sauren Regens* (Freiburg, 1983), 72.
8. Cf. Ulrich Beck, *Risk Society: Towards a New Modernity* (London, 1992).
9. Melanie Arndt, *Tschernobyl. Auswirkungen des Reaktorunfalls auf die Bundesrepublik Deutschland und die DDR* (Erfurt, 2011), 53.
10. Hannsjörg F. Buck, "Umweltbelastung durch Müllentsorgung und Industrieabfälle in der DDR," in *Die Endzeit der DDR-Wirtschaft. Analysen zur Wirtschafts-, Sozial- und Umweltpolitik*, ed. Eberhard Kuhrt (Opladen, 1999), 461, 468f., and 478.
11. Ulrich Petschow, Jürgen Meyerhoff, and Claus Thomasberger, *Umweltreport DDR. Bilanz der Zerstörung, Kosten der Sanierung, Strategien für den ökologischen Umbau. Eine Studie des Instituts für Ökologische Wirtschaftsforschung* (Frankfurt a. M., 1990), 84; Christian Möller, "Der Traum vom ewigen Kreislauf. Abprodukte, Sekundärrohstoffe und Stoffkreisläufe im 'Abfall-Regime' der DDR (1945–1990)," *Technikgeschichte* 81 (2014): 61–89.
12. Buck, "Umweltbelastung," 465 and 482.
13. Günter Bayerl, *Peripherie als Chance. Studien zur neueren Geschichte der Niederlausitz* (Münster, 2011), 439.
14. Cf. Matthias Gross, *Ignorance and Surprise: Science, Society, and Ecological Design* (Cambridge, MA, 2010), 121–62.
15. Michael Meissner, "Schichtende. Kontroversen um Rückbau und Sanierung," in *Uranbergbau im Kalten Krieg. Die Wismut im sowjetischen Atomkomplex*, vol. 1: *Studien*, ed. R. Boch (Berlin, 2011), 382 and 394f.
16. Jörg Roesler, *Umweltprobleme und Umweltpolitik in der DDR* (Erfurt, 2006), 22.
17. Bundesamt für Naturschutz, ed., *Erlebnis Grünes Band* (Bonn-Bad Godesberg, 2011), 11 and 13.

18. Frank Uekötter, "Bergbau und Umwelt im 19. und 20. Jahrhundert," in *Rohstoffgewinnung im Strukturwandel. Der deutsche Bergbau im 20. Jahrhundert*, ed. Dieter Ziegler (Münster, 2013), 560.
19. Cf. Petschow, Meyerhoff, and Thomasberger, *Umweltreport DDR*; Joachim Kahlert, *Der Einigungsprozess als Chance für die Umwelt. Aufgaben und Ziele auf dem Weg zu einer Umweltunion* (Bonn, 1990).
20. Tobias Huff, "Über die Umweltpolitik der DDR. Konzepte, Strukturen, Versagen," *Geschichte und Gesellschaft* 40 (2014): 523. See also Eckert, *Geteilt*, 69.
21. For a more detailed account, see Frank Uekötter, *The Age of Smoke: Environmental Policy in Germany and the United States, 1880–1970* (Pittsburgh, 2009).
22. Arnold Vaatz, "Umweltpolitik," in *Lexikon des DDR-Sozialismus. Das Staats- und Gesellschaftssystem der Deutschen Demokratischen Republik*, ed. Rainer Eppelmann, Horst Möller, Günter Nooke, and Dorothee Wilms (Paderborn, 1996), 630f.
23. Willi Oberkrome, *"Deutsche Heimat." Nationale Konzeption und regionale Praxis von Naturschutz, Landschaftsgestaltung und Kulturpolitik in Westfalen-Lippe und Thüringen (1900–1960)* (Paderborn, 2004), 341 and 522.
24. Ronald Inglehart, *The Silent Revolution: Changing Values and Political Styles among Western Publics* (Princeton, 1977), 43.
25. Adam Rome, *The Genius of Earth Day: How a 1970 Teach-In Unexpectedly Made the First Green Generation* (New York, 2013).
26. Thorsten Schulz-Walden, *Anfänge globaler Umweltpolitik. Umweltsicherheit in der internationalen Politik (1969–1975)* (Munich, 2013), 235–43; David Ekbladh, *The Great American Mission: Modernization and the Construction of an American World Order* (Princeton, 2010), 247–50.
27. Jens Ivo Engels, *Naturpolitik in der Bundesrepublik. Ideenwelt und politische Verhaltensstile in Naturschutz und Umweltbewegung 1950–1980* (Paderborn, 2006), 275.
28. Stadtarchiv Duisburg 503/689, Aktenvermerk über die Besprechung mit Herrn Oberregierungsrat Öls, Arbeits- und Sozialministerium NRW Düsseldorf am 3. Juli 1961 [Memorandum on the discussion with the Council for Oil, Labor, and Social Affairs NRW Dusseldorf on 3 July 1961], 2.
29. Sandra Chaney, *Nature of the Miracle Years: Conservation in West Germany, 1945–1975* (New York, 2008), 195–97; Engels, *Naturpolitik*, 287 and 334f.
30. Engels, *Naturpolitik*, 336f.
31. The career of German chancellor Angela Merkel, who was Federal Minister of the Environment from 1994 to 1998, followed a new pattern in that her time in office was marked by administration of the status quo rather than leadership. In the wake of numerous initiatives launched by her predecessor Klaus Töpfer, Merkel's term was like a calm after the storm, neither marred by scandals nor marked by resounding victories.
32. Paul Hockenos, *Joschka Fischer and the Making of the Berlin Republic: An Alternative History of Postwar Germany* (Oxford, 2008).

33. Wolfgang Sternstein, *"Atomkraft—nein danke!" Der lange Weg zum Ausstieg* (Frankfurt a. M., 2013), 106.
34. Andreas Dix and Rita Gudermann, "Naturschutz in der DDR: Idealisiert, ideologisiert, instrumentalisiert?," in *Natur und Staat. Staatlicher Naturschutz in Deutschland 1906–2006*, ed. Hans Werner Frohn and Friedemann Schmoll (Bonn, 2006), 574.
35. Tobias Huff, *Natur und Industrie im Sozialismus. Eine Umweltgeschichte der DDR* (Göttingen, 2015), 385.
36. Bernd Faulenbach, *Das sozialdemokratische Jahrzehnt. Von der Reformeuphorie zur Neuen Unübersichtlichkeit. Die SPD 1969–1982* (Bonn, 2011), 228f. and 261; Ulrich Herbert, *Geschichte Deutschlands im 20. Jahrhundert* (Munich, 2014), 915.
37. *Die Umweltmacher, 20 Jahre BMU—Geschichte und Zukunft der Umweltpolitik* (Hamburg, 2006).
38. Roesler, *Umweltprobleme*, 27.
39. Huff, "Über die Umweltpolitik der DDR," 540.
40. Ibid., 542.
41. Vaatz, "Umweltpolitik," 633f.
42. Huff, "Über die Umweltpolitik der DDR," 552.
43. Horst Barthel, *Umweltpolitik in beiden deutschen Staaten. Literaturstudie* (Berlin, 2001), 15f.
44. Bayerisches Hauptstaatsarchiv MArb 2596/II, *Vermerk vom 12. Mai 1970*.
45. Hans-Dietrich Genscher, *Erinnerungen* (Berlin, 1995), 130.
46. Deutscher Bundestag, 7. Wahlperiode, *Drucksache 2802*, 177. For a classic analysis of this problem, see Renate Mayntz, *Vollzugsprobleme der Umweltpolitik. Empirische Untersuchung der Implementation von Gesetzen im Bereich der Luftreinhaltung und des Gewässerschutzes* (Stuttgart, 1978).
47. Manfred Görtemaker, *Geschichte der Bundesrepublik Deutschland. Von der Gründung bis zur Gegenwart* (Munich, 1999), 581.
48. Georges Fülgraff, "Das Dilemma der Umweltpolitik—Eine Bilanz," in *Umweltpolitik in der Defensive. Umweltschutz trotz Wirtschaftskrise*, ed. Eberhard Schmidt and Sabine Spelthahn (Frankfurt a. M., 1994), 17.
49. For the major studies on German-German nuclear history, see Joachim Radkau and Lothar Hahn, *Aufstieg und Fall der deutschen Atomwirtschaft* (Munich, 2013); Mike Reichert, *Kernenergiewirtschaft in der DDR. Entwicklungsbedingungen, konzeptioneller Anspruch und Realisierungsgrad (1955–1990)* (St. Katharinen, 1999).
50. Falk Beyer, *Die (DDR-)Geschichte des Atommüll-Endlagers Morsleben* (Magdeburg, 2004), 34.
51. Anselm Tiggemann, *Die "Achillesferse" der Kernenergie in der Bundesrepublik Deutschland. Zur Kernenergiekontroverse und Geschichte der nuklearen Entsorgung von den Anfängen bis Gorleben 1955 bis 1989* (Lauf a. d. Pegnitz, 2014), 145.
52. Herbert Schwenk and Hainer Weißpflug, *Umweltschmutz und Umweltschutz*

in Berlin (Ost). Zu Auswirkungen der DDR-Umweltpolitik in Berlin (Berlin, 1996), 81.
53. Cord Schwartau, "Umweltschutz in der DDR," in *Veränderungen in Gesellschaft und politischem System der DDR. Ursachen, Inhalte, Grenzen. Einundzwanzigste Tagung zum Stand der DDR-Forschung in der Bundesrepublik Deutschland 24. bis 27. Mai 1988,* ed. Ilse Spittmann-Rühle and Gisela Helwig (Cologne, 1988), 51.
54. Hans D. Knapp, "Das Nationalparkprogramm der DDR," in *Die Krise als Chance—Naturschutz in neuer Dimension,* ed. Michael Succow, Lebrecht Jeschke, and Hans Dieter Knapp (Neuenhagen, 2001), 50.
55. Anita Wolf-Niedermaier, "Umweltpolitik," in *Europa von A bis Z. Taschenbuch der europäischen Integration,* ed. Werner Weidenfeld and Wolfgang Wessels (Bonn, 2000), 338f.
56. Edgar Wolfrum, *Rot-Grün an der Macht. Deutschland 1998–2005* (Munich, 2013), 240.
57. Holger Strohm, *Friedlich in die Katastrophe. Eine Dokumentation über Atomkraftwerke,* 10th ed. (Frankfurt a. M., 1982).
58. Cf. Felix Mühlberg, *Bürger, Bitten und Behörden. Geschichte der Eingaben in der DDR* (Berlin, 2004). On the indirect influence of the West German media on the population, cf. 137f.
59. Christian Halbrock, "Störfaktor Jugend. Die Anfänge der unabhängigen Umweltbewegung in der DDR," in *Arche Nova. Opposition in der DDR. Das "Grün-ökologische Netzwerk Arche" 1988–90,* ed. Carlo Jordan and Hans Michael Kloth (Berlin, 1995), 27; Nathan Stoltzfus, "Public Space and the Dynamics of Environmental Action: Green Protest in the German Democratic Republic," *Archiv für Sozialgeschichte* 43 (2003): 394f.
60. For an impressive look at this cacophony within the environmental movement, see Silke Mende, *"Nicht rechts, nicht links, sondern vorn." Eine Geschichte der Gründungsgrünen* (Munich, 2011).
61. Frank Bösch, "Umbrüche in die Gegenwart. Globale Ereignisse und Krisenreaktionen um 1979," *Zeithistorische Forschungen/Studies in Contemporary History* 9 (2012): 8–32.
62. Karl Marx and Friedrich Engels, *Das Kapital,* vol. 1 (Berlin [Ost], 1968), 57. Karl Marx, *Capital: Critique of Political Economy,* vol. 1 (London, 1990), 133.
63. Gretchen Dutschke, ed., *Rudi Dutschke. Jeder hat sein Leben ganz zu leben. Die Tagebücher 1963–1979* (Cologne, 2003), 278.
64. Wieland Berg, *Das Phantom. Die Aktivitäten der Ökologischen Arbeitsgruppe (ÖAG) Halle gegen die Asphaltierung der Heidewege 1988 und die Reaktion des MfS* (Halle, 1999), 58.
65. Detlef Pollack, *Politischer Protest. Politisch alternative Gruppen in der DDR* (Opladen, 2000), 108.
66. Carlo Jordan, "Akteure und Aktionen der Kirche," in *Arche Nova. Opposition in der DDR. Das "Grün-ökologische Netzwerk Arche" 1988–90,* ed. Carlo Jordan and Hans Michael Kloth (Berlin, 1995), 37–40.

67. Carlo Jordan, "Greenway. Das osteuropäische Grüne Netzwerk 1985–1990," *Horch und Guck* 15 (2006): 31–37.
68. Wolfgang Rüddenklau, *Störenfried. DDR-Opposition 1986–1989* (Berlin, 1992), 178.
69. Monika Maron, *Flugasche* (Frankfurt a. M., 2009), 32. For the English translation, see Monika Maron, *Flight of Ashes* (Columbia, 1986).
70. Rainer Hällfritzsch, Ulrike Hemberger, and Margit Miosga, *Das war Bitteres aus Bitterfeld*, DVD der Bundesstiftung zur Aufarbeitung der SED-Diktatur, 2009.
71. Manuel Schramm, "Strahlenschutz im Uranbergbau. DDR und Bundesrepublik Deutschland im Vergleich (1945–1990)," in *Uranbergbau im Kalten Krieg. Die Wismut im sowjetischen Atomkomplex*, vol. 1: *Studien*, ed. Rainer Karlsch and Rudolf Boch (Berlin, 2011), 322.
72. Hubertus Knabe, *Umweltkonflikte im Sozialismus. Möglichkeiten und Grenzen gesellschaftlicher Problemartikulation in sozialistischen Systemen. Eine vergleichende Analyse der Umweltdiskussion in der DDR und Ungarn* (Cologne, 1993), 344.
73. Schramm, "Strahlenschutz im Uranbergbau," 323.
74. The language and mental world of the Cold War also left its mark on environmental discourse, which could be quite clearly detected, for example, in Wolf Oschlies, *"Öko-Kriege" in Osteuropa. Ausgewählte Tatorte grenzüberschreitender Umweltzerstörung*, Berichte des Bundesinstituts für ostwissenschaftliche und internationale Studien 29 (Cologne, 1990). On this topic, see also Jacob Darwin Hamblin, *Arming Mother Nature: The Birth of Catastrophic Environmentalism* (Oxford, 2013).
75. Jordan, "Akteure," 69.
76. Frank Uekötter, "Environmentalism, Eastern European Style: Some Exploratory Remarks," in *Umweltgeschichte(n). Ostmitteleuropa von der Industrialisierung bis zum Postsozialismus*, ed. Horst Förster, Julia Herzberg, and Martin Zückert (Munich, 2013), 249, 251.
77. Cf. Maria Nooke, *Für Umweltverantwortung und Demokratisierung. Die Forster Oppositionsgruppe in der Auseinandersetzung mit Staat und Kirche* (Berlin, 2008), 334.
78. Knabe, *Umweltkonflikte im Sozialismus*, 230–32.
79. Jan Schönfelder, *Mit Gott gegen Gülle. Die Umweltgruppe Knau/Dittersdorf 1986 bis 1991. Eine regionale Protestbewegung in der DDR* (Rudolstadt, 2000).
80. Joan Martinez-Alier, *The Environmentalism of the Poor: A Study of Ecological Conflicts and Valuation* (Northhampton, MA, 2002).
81. The environmental decade of the 1980s took off characteristically just at the same time as the protest movement against NATO's rearmament fell apart. Cf. Susanne Schregel, *Der Atomkrieg vor der Wohnungstür. Eine Politikgeschichte der neuen Friedensbewegung in der Bundesrepublik 1970–1985* (Frankfurt a. M., 2011).

82. Rüdiger Graf, "Die Grenzen des Wachstums und die Grenzen des Staates. Konservative und die ökologischen Bedrohungsszenarien der frühen 1970er Jahre," in *Streit um den Staat. Intellektuelle Debatten in der Bundesrepublik 1960–1980*, ed. Dominik Geppert and Jens Hacke (Göttingen, 2008), 207–28.
83. Günter Wallraff, *Ganz unten* (Cologne, 1985).
84. Wolfgang Jäger, *Die Überwindung der Teilung. Der innerdeutsche Prozeß der Vereinigung 1989/90* (Stuttgart, 1998), 412.
85. Helge Heidemeyer, "(Grüne) Bewegung im Parlament. Der Einzug der Grünen in den Deutschen Bundestag und die Veränderungen in Partei und Parlament," *Historische Zeitschrift* 291 (2010): 88.
86. Joachim Raschke, *Die Grünen. Wie sie wurden, was sie sind* (Cologne, 1993), 924–25.
87. Hagen Findeis, Detlef Pollack, and Manuel Schilling, *Die Entzauberung des Politischen. Was ist aus den politisch alternativen Gruppen der DDR geworden? Interviews mit ehemals führenden Vertretern* (Leipzig, 1994), 5.
88. Ibid., 305.
89. Christoph Hohlfeld, "Bündnis 90/Grüne—eine neue Partei?," in *Die Grünen. Wie sie wurden, was sie sind*, ed. Joachim Raschke (Cologne, 1983), 839.
90. Cf. Helge May, *NABU. 100 Jahre NABU—ein historischer Abriß 1899–1999* (Bonn, 1999).
91. Hermann Behrens, "Umweltbewegung," in *Umweltschutz in der DDR. Analysen und Zeitzeugenberichte*, vol. 3, ed. Institut für Umweltgeschichte und Regionalentwicklung e. V. (Munich, 2007), 142f.
92. Christopher Rootes, "The Transformation of Environmental Activism: An Introduction," in *Environmental Protest in Western Europe*, ed. Christopher Rootes (Oxford, 2003), 1.
93. Michael Bess, *The Light-Green Society: Ecology and Technological Modernity in France 1960–2000* (Chicago, 2003).
94. Vance Packard, *Die geheimen Verführer. Der Griff nach dem Unbewussten in jedermann* (Düsseldorf, 1958); Vance Packard, *Die große Verschwendung* (Düsseldorf, 1961).
95. Ilko-Sascha Kowalczuk, *Endspiel. Die Revolution von 1989 in der DDR* (Munich, 2011), 540.
96. Sven Reichardt, *Authentizität und Gemeinschaft. Linksalternatives Leben in den siebziger und frühen achtziger Jahren* (Frankfurt a. M., 2014), 582f.
97. Knabe, *Umweltkonflikte im Sozialismus*, 304.
98. Hauptstaatsarchiv Düsseldorf NW 831 Paket 105 Bd. 13, Landwirtschaftskammer Westfalen-Lippe, Gruppe 21—Betriebswirtschaft an die Kreisstellen der Landwirtschaftskammer, 21. Juli 1982, S. 2.
99. Saskia Richter, *Die Aktivistin. Das Leben der Petra Kelly* (Munich, 2010), 60.
100. Kahlert, *Einigungsprozess*, 64.
101. Hans Michael Kloth, "Grüne Bewegung, Grünes Netzwerk, Grüne Partei. Ein politologischer Versuch," in *Arche Nova. Opposition in der DDR. Das*

"Grün-ökologische Netzwerk Arche" 1988–90, ed. Carlo Jordan and Hans Michael Kloth (Berlin, 1995), 146.
102. Arndt, Tschernobyl, 98.
103. Frank Uekötter and Claas Kirchhelle, "Wie Seveso nach Deutschland kam. Umweltskandale und ökologische Debatte von 1976 bis 1986," in *Archiv für Sozialgeschichte* 52 (2012): 317–34; Nils Freytag, "Der rote Rhein. Die Sandoz-Katastrophe vom 1. November 1986 und ihre Folgen," *Themenportal Europäische Geschichte* (2010).
104. Bundesministerium für Ernährung, Landwirtschaft und Forsten, ed., *Agrarbericht 1989. Agrar- und ernährungspolitischer Bericht der Bundesregierung. Materialband (Bundestagsdrucksache 11/3969)* (Bonn, 1989), 23.
105. Bernhard Hörning, *Auswirkungen der Zucht auf das Verhalten von Nutztieren* (Kassel, 2008), 31. On the methodology behind these remarks, see Edmund Russell, *Evolutionary History: Uniting History and Biology to Understand Life on Earth* (Cambridge, 2011); Susan R. Schrepfer and Philip Scranton, eds., *Industrializing Organisms: Introducing Evolutionary History* (New York, 2004).
106. Cf. Frank Uekötter, *Die Wahrheit ist auf dem Feld. Eine Wissensgeschichte der deutschen Landwirtschaft* (Göttingen, 2010), 331–89.
107. Arnd Bauerkämper, "The Industrialization of Agriculture and Its Consequences for the Natural Environment: An Inter-German Comparative Perspective," *Historical Social Research* 29 (2004): 124–49.
108. See Amir Zelinger, *Menschen und Haustiere im Deutschen Kaiserreich: Eine Beziehungsgeschichte* (Bielefeld, 2018).
109. Institut für Umweltschutz, ed., *Umweltbericht der DDR. Informationen zur Analyse der Umweltbedingungen in der DDR und zu weiteren Maßnahmen* (Berlin, 1990), 45.
110. Wolfrum, *Rot-Grün*, 249–53.
111. Oliver Hollenstein, *Das doppelt geteilte Land. Neue Einblicke in die Debatte über West- und Ostdeutschland* (Wiesbaden, 2012), 25.
112. Cf. Anna-Katharina Wöbse, "Die Brent Spar-Kampagne. Plattform für diverse Wahrheiten," in *Wird Kassandra heiser? Die Geschichte falscher Ökoalarme*, ed. Frank Uekötter and Jens Hohensee (Stuttgart, 2004), 139–60.
113. Jürgen Hopfmann and Georg Winter, *Zukunftsstandort Deutschland. Das Programm der umweltbewußten Unternehmer* (Munich, 1997).
114. Mary Mellor, *Wann, wenn nicht jetzt! Für einen ökosozialistischen Feminismus* (Hamburg, 1994).
115. For a first, politics-heavy synthesis, see Wolfrum, *Rot-Grün*.
116. Well-documented in Joachim Raschke, *Die Zukunft der Grünen. "So kann man nicht regieren"* (Frankfurt a. M., 2001).
117. Klaus-Dieter Maubauch, *Energiewende. Wege zu einer bezahlbaren Energieversorgung* (Wiesbaden, 2014), 47.
118. Frank Uekötter, "Fukushima and the Lessons of History: Remarks on the Past and Future of Nuclear Power," in *Europe after Fukushima: German Per-*

spectives on the Future of Nuclear Power, ed. Jens Kersten, Markus Vogt, and Frank Uekötter (Munich, 2012), 18.
119. Wolfrum, Rot-Grün, 217.
120. Cf. Václav Klaus, Blauer Planet in grünen Fesseln. Was ist bedroht: Klima oder Freiheit? (Vienna, 2007).

BIBLIOGRAPHY

Arndt, Melanie. Tschernobyl. Auswirkungen des Reaktorunfalls auf die Bundesrepublik Deutschland und die DDR. Erfurt: Landeszentrale für politische Bildung, 2011.

Barthel, Horst. Umweltpolitik in beiden deutschen Staaten. Literaturstudie. Berlin: Gesellschaftswissenschaftliches Forum, 2001.

Bauerkämper, A. "The Industrialization of Agriculture and Its Consequences for the Natural Environment: An Inter-German Comparative Perspective." *Historical Social Research* 29 (2004): 124–49

Bayerl, Günter. *Peripherie als Chance. Studien zur neueren Geschichte der Niederlausitz*. Münster: Waxmann, 2011.

Beck, Ulrich. *Risk Society: Towards a New Modernity*. London: Sage Publications, 1992.

Behrens, Hermann. "Umweltbewegung." In *Umweltschutz in der DDR. Analysen und Zeitzeugenberichte*, vol. 3, edited by Institut für Umweltgeschichte und Regionalentwicklung e. V., 131–48. Munich: Oekom, 2007.

Berg, Wieland. *Das Phantom. Die Aktivitäten der Ökologischen Arbeitsgruppe (ÖAG) Halle gegen die Asphaltierung der Heidewege 1988 und die Reaktion des MfS*. Halle: Druck-Zuck, 1999.

Bess, Michael. *The Light-Green Society: Ecology and Technological Modernity in France 1960–2000*. Chicago: University of Chicago Press, 2003.

Bösch, F. "Umbrüche in die Gegenwart. Globale Ereignisse und Krisenreaktionen um 1979." *Zeithistorische Forschungen/Studies in Contemporary History* 9 (2012): 8–32.

Beyer, Falk. *Die (DDR-)Geschichte des Atommüll-Endlagers Morsleben*. Magdeburg: Landesbeauftragte für die Unterlagen des Staatssicherheitsdienstes der ehemaligen DDR in Sachsen-Anhalt, 2004.

Buck, Hannsjörg F. "Umweltbelastung durch Müllentsorgung und Industrieabfälle in der DDR." In *Die Endzeit der DDR-Wirtschaft. Analysen zur Wirtschafts-, Sozial- und Umweltpolitik*, edited by Eberhard Kuhrt, 455–93. Opladen: Leske und Budrich, 1999.

Bundesamt für Naturschutz, ed. *Erlebnis Grünes Band*. Bonn-Bad Godesberg: Bundesamt für Naturschutz, 2011.

Büschenfeld, Jürgen. *Flüsse und Kloaken. Umweltfragen im Zeitalter der Industrialisierung (1870–1918)*. Stuttgart: Klett-Cotta, 1997.

Chaney, Sandra. *Nature of the Miracle Years: Conservation in West Germany, 1945–1975*. New York: Berghahn, 2008.
Die Umweltmacher. *20 Jahre BMU—Geschichte und Zukunft der Umweltpolitik*. Hamburg: Hoffmann und Campe, 2006.
Dix, Andreas, and Rita Gudermann. "Naturschutz in der DDR: Idealisiert, ideologisiert, instrumentalisiert?" In *Natur und Staat. Staatlicher Naturschutz in Deutschland 1906–2006*, edited by Hans Werner Frohn and Friedemann Schmoll, 535–624. Bonn: Bundesamt für Naturschutz, 2006.
Dutschke, G., ed. *Rudi Dutschke. Jeder hat sein Leben ganz zu leben. Die Tagebücher 1963–1979*. Cologne: Kiepenheuer & Witsch, 2003.
Eckert, A. M. "Geteilt, aber nicht unverbunden. Grenzgewässer als deutsch-deutsches Umweltproblem." *Vierteljahreshefte für Zeitgeschichte* 62 (2014): 69–100.
Eisenbach, Ulrich. "Kaliindustrie und Umwelt." In *Die Kaliindustrie an Werra und Fulda. Geschichte eines landschaftsprägenden Industriezweigs*, edited by Ulrich Eisenbach and Akos Paulinyi, 194–222. Darmstadt: Hessisches Wirtschaftsarchiv, 1998.
Ekbladh, David. *The Great American Mission: Modernization and the Construction of an American World Order*. Princeton: Princeton University Press, 2010.
Engels, Jens Ivo. *Naturpolitik in der Bundesrepublik. Ideenwelt und politische Verhaltensstile in Naturschutz und Umweltbewegung 1950–1980*. Paderborn: Schöningh, 2006.
Faulenbach, B., ed. *Das sozialdemokratische Jahrzehnt. Von der Reformeuphorie zur Neuen Unübersichtlichkeit. Die SPD 1969–1982*. Bonn: Dietz, 2011.
Findeis, Hagen, Detlef Pollack, and Manuel Schilling. *Die Entzauberung des Politischen. Was ist aus den politisch alternativen Gruppen der DDR geworden? Interviews mit ehemals führenden Vertretern*. Leipzig: Evangelische Verlagsanstalt, 1994.
Fülgraff, Georges. "Das Dilemma der Umweltpolitik—Eine Bilanz." In *Umweltpolitik in der Defensive. Umweltschutz trotz Wirtschaftskrise*, edited by Eberhard Schmidt and Sabine Spelthahn, 13–24. Frankfurt a. M.: Fischer, 1994.
Genscher, Hans-Dietrich. *Erinnerungen*. Berlin: Siedler, 1995.
Giddens, Anthony. *The Politics of Climate Change*. Cambridge: Polity Press, 2009.
Görtemaker, Manfred. *Geschichte der Bundesrepublik Deutschland. Von der Gründung bis zur Gegenwart*. Munich: Beck, 1999.
Graf, Rüdiger. "Die Grenzen des Wachstums und die Grenzen des Staates. Konservative und die ökologischen Bedrohungsszenarien der frühen 1970er Jahre." In *Streit um den Staat. Intellektuelle Debatten in der Bundesrepublik 1960–1980*, edited by Dominik Geppert and Jens Hacke, 207–28. Göttingen: Vandenhoeck & Ruprecht, 2008.
Gross, Matthias. *Ignorance and Surprise: Science, Society, and Ecological Design*. Cambridge, MA: MIT Press, 2010.
Grießhammer, Rainer. *Letzte Chance für den Wald? Die abwendbaren Folgen des Sauren Regens*. Freiburg: Dreisam-Verlag, 1983.

Halbrock, Christian. "Störfaktor Jugend. Die Anfänge der unabhängigen Umweltbewegung in der DDR." In *Arche Nova. Opposition in der DDR. Das "Grün-ökologische Netzwerk Arche"* 1988–90, edited by Carlo Jordan and Hans Michael Kloth, 13–32. Berlin: BasisDruck Verlag, 1995.

Heidemeyer, H. "(Grüne) Bewegung im Parlament. Der Einzug der Grünen in den Deutschen Bundestag und die Veränderungen in Partei und Parlament." *Historische Zeitschrift* 291 (2010): 71–102,

Herbert, Ulrich. *Geschichte Deutschlands im 20. Jahrhundert.* Munich: C.H. Beck, 2014.

Hockenos, Paul. *Joschka Fischer and the Making of the Berlin Republic: An Alternative History of Postwar Germany.* Oxford: Oxford University Press, 2008.

Hollenstein, Oliver. *Das doppelt geteilte Land. Neue Einblicke in die Debatte über West- und Ostdeutschland.* Wiesbaden: Springer VS, 2012.

Hörning, Bernhard. *Auswirkungen der Zucht auf das Verhalten von Nutztieren.* Kassel: Kassel University Press, 2008.

Huff, Tobias. "Über die Umweltpolitik der DDR. Konzepte, Strukturen, Versagen." *Geschichte und Gesellschaft* 40 (2014): 523–54.

Huff, Herbert. *Natur und Industrie im Sozialismus. Eine Umweltgeschichte der DDR.* Göttingen: Vandenhoek & Ruprecht, 2015.

Inglehart, Ronald. *The Silent Revolution: Changing Values and Political Styles among Western Publics.* Princeton: Princeton University Press, 1977.

Institut für Umweltschutz, ed. *Umweltbericht der DDR. Informationen zur Analyse der Umweltbedingungen in der DDR und zu weiteren Maßnahmen.* Berlin: Verlag Visuell, 1990.

Jäger, Wolfgang. *Die Überwindung der Teilung. Der innerdeutsche Prozeß der Vereinigung 1989/90.* Stuttgart: Deutsche Verlags-Anstalt, 1998.

Jordan, Carlo. "Akteure und Aktionen der Kirche." In *Arche Nova. Opposition in der DDR. Das "Grün-ökologische Netzwerk Arche"* 1988–90, edited by Carlo Jordan and Hans Michael Kloth, 37–70. Berlin: BasisDruck Verlag, 1995.

Jordan, C. "Greenway. Das osteuropäische Grüne Netzwerk 1985–1990." *Horch und Guck* 15 (2006): 31–37.

Kahlert, Joachim. *Der Einigungsprozess als Chance für die Umwelt. Aufgaben und Ziele auf dem Weg zu einer Umweltunion.* Bonn: Friedrich Ebert Stiftung, 1990.

Kloth, Hans Michael. "Grüne Bewegung, Grünes Netzwerk, Grüne Partei. Ein politologischer Versuch." In *Arche Nova. Opposition in der DDR. Das "Grün-ökologische Netzwerk Arche"* 1988–90, edited by Carlo Jordan and Hans Michael Kloth, 145–79. Berlin: BasisDruck Verlag, 1995.

Kowalczuk, Ilko-Sascha. *Endspiel. Die Revolution von 1989 in der DDR.* Munich: C. H. Beck, 2011.

Hamblin, Jacob Darwin. *Arming Mother Nature: The Birth of Catastrophic Environmentalism.* Oxford: Oxford University Press, 2013.

Hohlfeld, Christoph. "Bündnis 90/Grüne—eine neue Partei?" In *Die Grünen. Wie sie wurden, was sie sind,* edited by Joachim Raschke, 839-46. Cologne: Bund-Verlag, 1993.

Hopfmann, Jürgen, and Georg Winter. *Zukunftsstandort Deutschland. Das Programm der umweltbewußten Unternehmer.* Munich: Droemer Knaur, 1997.
Klaus, Václav. *Blauer Planet in grünen Fesseln. Was ist bedroht: Klima oder Freiheit?* Vienna: Gerold, 2007.
Knabe, Hubertus. *Umweltkonflikte im Sozialismus. Möglichkeiten und Grenzen gesellschaftlicher Problemartikulation in sozialistischen Systemen. Eine vergleichende Analyse der Umweltdiskussion in der DDR und Ungarn.* Cologne: Verlag Wissenschaft und Politik, 1993.
Knapp, Hans Dieter. "Das Nationalparkprogramm der DDR." In *Die Krise als Chance—Naturschutz in neuer Dimension,* edited by Michael Succow, Lebrecht Jeschke, and Hans Dieter Knapp, 35–56. Neuenhagen: Findling, 2001.
Maron, Monika. *Flugasche.* Frankfurt a. M.: Fischer, 2009.
Marx, Karl. *Capital: Critique of Political Economy,* vol. 1 (London: Penguin, 1990).
Marx, Karl, and Friedrich Engels. *Das Kapital,* vol. 1. Berlin (Ost): Dietz, 1968.
Maubach, Klaus-Dieter. *Energiewende. Wege zu einer bezahlbaren Energieversorgung.* Wiesbaden: Springer VS, 2014.
May, Helge. *NABU. 100 Jahre NABU—ein historischer Abriß 1899–1999.* Bonn: NABU, 1999.
Mayntz, Renate. *Vollzugsprobleme der Umweltpolitik. Empirische Untersuchung der Implementation von Gesetzen im Bereich der Luftreinhaltung und des Gewässerschutzes.* Stuttgart: Kohlhammer, 1978.
McNeill, John R., and Peter Engelke. "Mensch und Umwelt im Zeitalter des Anthropozäns." In *Geschichte der Welt. 1945 bis heute. Die globalisierte Welt,* edited by Akira Iriye and Jürgen Osterhammel, 357–534. Munich: C. H. Beck, 2013.
Mellor, Mary. *Wann, wenn nicht jetzt! Für einen ökosozialistischen Feminismus.* Hamburg: Argument-Verlag, 1994.
Mende, Silke. *"Nicht rechts, nicht links, sondern vorn." Eine Geschichte der Gründungsgrünen.* Munich: Oldenbourg, 2011.
Meissner, Michael. "Schichtende. Kontroversen um Rückbau und Sanierung." In *Uranbergbau im Kalten Krieg. Die Wismut im sowjetischen Atomkomplex,* vol. 1: *Studien,* edited by Rudolf Boch, 355–95. Berlin: Links, 2011.
Möller, Christian. "Der Traum vom ewigen Kreislauf. Abprodukte, Sekundärrohstoffe und Stoffkreisläufe im 'Abfall-Regime' der DDR (1945–1990)." *Technikgeschichte* 81 (2014): 61–89.
Mühlberg, Felix. *Bürger, Bitten und Behörden. Geschichte der Eingaben in der DDR.* Berlin: Dietz, 2004.
Nooke, Maria. *Für Umweltverantwortung und Demokratisierung. Die Forster Oppositionsgruppe in der Auseinandersetzung mit Staat und Kirche.* Berlin: Links, 2008.
Oberkrome, Willi. *"Deutsche Heimat." Nationale Konzeption und regionale Praxis von Naturschutz, Landschaftsgestaltung und Kulturpolitik in Westfalen-Lippe und Thüringen (1900–1960).* Paderborn: Schöningh, 2004.
Oschlies, Wolf. *"Öko-Kriege" in Osteuropa. Ausgewählte Tatorte grenzüberschreitender Umweltzerstörung.* Berichte des Bundesinstituts für ostwissenschaft-

liche und internationale Studien 29. Cologne: Bundesinst. für Ostwiss. und Internat. Studien, 1990.
Packard, Vance. *Die geheimen Verführer. Der Griff nach dem Unbewussten in jedermann*. Düsseldorf: Econ-Verlag, 1958.
———. *Die große Verschwendung*. Düsseldorf: Econ-Verlag, 1961.
Pearce, Fred. *Die Grünen Macher*. Berlin: Rotbuch-Verlag, 1992.
Pettenkofer, Andreas. *Die Entstehung der grünen Politik. Kultursoziologie der westdeutschen Umweltbewegung*. Frankfurt a. M.: Campus, 2014.
Petschow, Ulrich, Jürgen Meyerhoff, and Claus Thomasberger. *Umweltreport DDR. Bilanz der Zerstörung, Kosten der Sanierung, Strategien für den ökologischen Umbau. Eine Studie des Instituts für Ökologische Wirtschaftsforschung*. Frankfurt a. M.: Fischer, 1990.
Pollack, Detlef. *Politischer Protest. Politisch alternative Gruppen in der DDR*. Opladen: Leske + Budrich, 2000.
Radkau, Joachim. *The Age of Ecology: A Global History*. Cambridge: Polity Press, 2014.
Radkau, Joachim, and Lothar Hahn, *Aufstieg und Fall der deutschen Atomwirtschaft*. Munich: Gesellschaft für ökologische Kommunikation, 2013.
Raschke, Joachim, *Die Grünen. Wie sie wurden, was sie sind*. Cologne: Bund-Verlag, 1993.
———. *Die Zukunft der Grünen. "So kann man nicht regieren."* Frankfurt a. M.: Campus-Verlag, 2001.
Reichert, Mike. *Kernenergiewirtschaft in der DDR. Entwicklungsbedingungen, konzeptioneller Anspruch und Realisierungsgrad (1955–1990)*. St. Katharinen: Scripta-Mercaturae-Verlag, 1999.
Reichardt, Sven. *Authentizität und Gemeinschaft. Linksalternatives Leben in den siebziger und frühen achtziger Jahren*. Frankfurt a. M.: Suhrkamp, 2014.
Richter, Saskia. *Die Aktivistin. Das Leben der Petra Kelly*. Munich: Dt. Verl.-Anst., 2010.
Roesler, Jörg. *Umweltprobleme und Umweltpolitik in der DDR*. Erfurt: Landeszentrale für politische Bildung Thüringen, 2006.
Rome, Adam. *The Genius of Earth Day: How a 1970 Teach-In Unexpectedly Made the First Green Generation*. New York: Hill and Wang, 2013.
Rootes, Christopher. "The Transformation of Environmental Activism. An Introduction." In *Environmental Protest in Western Europe*, edited by Christopher Rootes, 1–19. Oxford: Oxford University Press, 2003.
Ruck, Hartmut. "Die Kali-Industrie an der Werra in Thüringen 1945–1989." In *Bunte Salze, weiße Berge. Wachstum und Wandel der Kaliindustrie zwischen Thüringer Wald, Rhön und Vogelsberg*, edited by Hermann-Josef Hohmann and Lothar Brückner. Hünfeld: Ulmenstein 2004, 101–34.
Rüddenklau, Wolfgang. *Störenfried. DDR-Opposition 1986–1989*. Berlin: Basis-Dr., 1992.
Russell, Edmund. *Evolutionary History: Uniting History and Biology to Understand Life on Earth*. Cambridge: Cambridge University Press, 2011.

Schönfelder, Jan. *Mit Gott gegen Gülle. Die Umweltgruppe Knau/Dittersdorf 1986 bis 1991. Eine regionale Protestbewegung in der DDR*. Rudolstadt: Hain-Verlag, 2000.

Schramm, Manuel. "Strahlenschutz im Uranbergbau. DDR und Bundesrepublik Deutschland im Vergleich (1945–1990)." In *Uranbergbau im Kalten Krieg. Die Wismut im sowjetischen Atomkomplex*, vol. 1: *Studien*, edited by Rainer Karlsch and Rudolf Boch, 271–328. Berlin: Links, 2011.

Schrepfer, Susan R., and Philip Scranton, eds. *Industrializing Organisms: Introducing Evolutionary History*. New York: Routledge, 2004.

Schregel, Susanne. *Der Atomkrieg vor der Wohnungstür. Eine Politikgeschichte der neuen Friedensbewegung in der Bundesrepublik 1970–1985*. Frankfurt a. M.: Campus, 2011.

Schulz-Walden, Thorsten. *Anfänge globaler Umweltpolitik. Umweltsicherheit in der internationalen Politik (1969–1975)*. Munich: Oldenbourg, 2013.

Schwartau, Cord. "Umweltschutz in der DDR." In *Veränderungen in Gesellschaft und politischem System der DDR. Ursachen, Inhalte, Grenzen. Einundzwanzigste Tagung zum Stand der DDR-Forschung in der Bundesrepublik Deutschland 24. bis 27. Mai 1988*, edited by Ilse Spittmann-Rühle and Gisela Helwig, 48–58. Cologne: Verlag Wissenschaft und Politik, 1988.

Schwenk, Herbert, and Hainer Weißpflug. *Umweltschmutz und Umweltschutz in Berlin (Ost). Zu Auswirkungen der DDR-Umweltpolitik in Berlin*. Berlin: Ed. Luisenstadt, 1996.

Stedman Jones, David. *Masters of the Universe: Hayek, Friedman, and the Birth of Neoliberal Politics*. Princeton: Princeton University Press, 2012.

Sternstein, Wolfgang. *"Atomkraft—nein danke!" Der lange Weg zum Ausstieg*. Frankfurt a. M.: Brandes & Apsel, 2013.

Stoltzfus, N. "Public Space and the Dynamics of Environmental Action: Green Protest in the German Democratic Republic." *Archiv für Sozialgeschichte* 43 (2003): 385–403.

Strohm, Holger. *Friedlich in die Katastrophe. Eine Dokumentation über Atomkraftwerke*. Frankfurt a. M.: Zweitausendeins, 1982.

Tiggemann, Anselm. *Die 'Achillesferse' der Kernenergie in der Bundesrepublik Deutschland. Zur Kernenergiekontroverse und Geschichte der nuklearen Entsorgung von den Anfängen bis Gorleben 1955 bis 1989*. Lauf an der Pegnitz: Europoforum-Verlag, 2004.

Uekötter, Frank. *The Age of Smoke: Environmental Policy in Germany and the United States, 1880–1970*. Pittsburgh: University of Pittsburgh Press, 2009.

———. "Bergbau und Umwelt im 19. und 20. Jahrhundert." In *Rohstoffgewinnung im Strukturwandel. Der deutsche Bergbau im 20. Jahrhundert*, edited by Dieter Ziegler, 539–70. Münster: Aschendorff, 2013.

———. *Die Wahrheit ist auf dem Feld. Eine Wissensgeschichte der deutschen Landwirtschaft*. Göttingen: Vandenhoeck & Ruprecht, 2010.

———. "Environmentalism, Eastern European Style: Some Exploratory Remarks." In *Umweltgeschichte(n). Ostmitteleuropa von der Industrialisierung bis zum*

Postsozialismus, edited by Horst Förster, Julia Herzberg, and Martin Zückert, 241–54. Munich: Vandenhoeck & Ruprecht, 2013.

———. "Fukushima and the Lessons of History: Remarks on the Past and Future of Nuclear Power." In *Europe after Fukushima: German Perspectives on the Future of Nuclear Power*, edited by Jens Kersten, Markus Vogt, and Frank Uekötter, 9–31. Munich: RCC Perspectives, 2012.

———. *The Greenest Nation? A New History of German Environmentalism*. Cambridge, MA: MIT Press, 2014.

Uekötter, Frank, and Claas Kirchhelle. "Wie Seveso nach Deutschland kam. Umweltskandale und ökologische Debatte von 1976 bis 1986." *Archiv für Sozialgeschichte* 52 (2012): 317–34.

Vaatz, Arnold. "Umweltpolitik." In *Lexikon des DDR-Sozialismus. Das Staats- und Gesellschaftssystem der Deutschen Demokratischen Republik*, edited by Rainer Eppelmann, Horst Möller, Günter Nooke, and Dorothee Wilms, 630–38, Paderborn: Schöningh 1996.

Wallraff, Günter. *Ganz unten*. Cologne: Kiepenheuer & Witsch, 1985.

Wöbse, Anna-Katharina. "Die Brent Spar-Kampagne. Plattform für diverse Wahrheiten." In *Wird Kassandra heiser? Die Geschichte falscher Ökoalarme*, edited by Frank Uekötter and Jens Hohensee, 139–60. Stuttgart: Steiner, 2004.

Wolf-Niedermaier, Anita. "Umweltpolitik." In *Europa von A bis Z. Taschenbuch der europäischen Integration*, edited by Werner Weidenfeld and Wolfgang Wessels, 337–41. Bonn: Bundeszentrale für politische Bildung, 2000.

Wolfrum, Edgar. *Rot-Grün an der Macht. Deutschland 1998–2005*. Munich: C. H. Beck, 2013.

Zelinger, Amir. *Menschen und Haustiere im Deutschen Kaiserreich: Eine Beziehungsgeschichte*. Bielefeld: transcript, 2018.

CHAPTER 4

Social Security, Social Inequality, and the Welfare State in East and West Germany

Winfried Süß

German reunification entailed more than just achieving the union of two separate states deeply embroiled in the system rivalry of the Cold War. Rather, it also necessitated the integration of two societies with antagonist models of economic and social order whose structures of social inequality had grown further and further apart since the division of Germany. Embedded as they were within their respective blocs, East and West Germany followed different trajectories in the postwar decades, especially when it came to their standards of living. As reunification commenced, GDR citizens lagged "clearly behind the West Germans" in almost "all objective and subjective dimensions related to quality of life."[1] Hardly any of the protesters from the East German citizens' movement who demanded the return of freedom and better prospects from a sclerotic communist dictatorship during the peaceful revolution of 1989/90 could have known just how much the people of East Germany would have to adapt as the two Germanys became one.

The welfare state played a significant role in this strenuous integration process. It was intrinsically tied to the expectations of affluence harbored in the East, especially since these kinds of hopes were consciously fueled by the Christian Democrat and Liberal coalition in the run-up to the GDR's last People's Chamber (Volkskammer) elections in March 1990. After all, Helmut Kohl's famous promise of rapidly "blooming landscapes" explicitly included the generous transfer of social benefits from West to East.[2] Thus, under the banner of a social union (the program was called *Sozialunion*), the welfare state became a significant component of the German reunification treaties.³ In the negotiations, however, the structure of social security proved to be a major bone of contention because it was intrinsically related to the larger conflict over how much of the old GDR system should become part of unified Germany. Simultaneously, though, the welfare state was an important mental link between the two German societies, especially during the difficult early phase of reunification. Although the divergent conceptions of a welfare state that had emerged on each side of the Wall were tainted by the system-specific attributes of each state, both German societies believed that social policy was the way to address social problems. Ultimately, it was also social security institutions that had to absorb some of the social shock waves unleashed by the reunification process.

In its guise as a key anti-crisis mechanism, the welfare state was thus called upon for a third time in twentieth-century German history to deal with the social consequences of the transformation of a political system (after 1918 and after 1945). Yet the social cushioning of this particular transformation was unprecedented in history because of the antagonistic relationship between the two German states in the system rivalry of the Cold War, the need to deal with the economic and social legacy left behind in the wake of a run-down socialist state, and the way in which German reunification was embedded within global economic transformations.

The promise that standards of life would be equalized across all of Germany as quickly as possible was certainly one of the mainstays of political rhetoric during the *Wende*. But, as recent studies in social science have pointed out, this goal has yet to become a reality, although it must be said that substantial progress has been made in the twenty-five years since reunification. As of 2009, households in the new federal states were less than half as wealthy on average than those in the West. Likewise, in spite of trends toward more equal wages and salaries, East Germans were still earning a fifth less than West Germans. Even today, people living in the former East face a greater risk of unemployment and poverty.⁴ Moreover, if normative attitudes are taken into account, two quite distinct subsocieties still seem to exist that differ in terms of their living standards and the persistence of inequalities, as well as in their respective notions of justice, expectations vis-à-vis the welfare state, and attitudes toward social inequality. In general, former citizens of East Germany expect more from the welfare state and possess a heightened sense of social polarization, but they are also more committed to equalization.⁵

Yet there is another side to the history of sociopolitical integration in reunified Germany. When it comes to key aspects of welfare, such as life expectancy, for example, the differences between East and West have largely been overcome. In 1990, life expectancy among men differed by

3.5 years and among women by 2.6 years, with East Germans on the low end. Just twenty years later, these differences had shrunk to 1.3 and 0.2 years, respectively.[6] Additionally, since the turn of the millennium, the varying attitudes toward the welfare state and social justice have become less pronounced as a result of changes on both sides of the old Wall. This chapter looks more closely at such ambivalent aspects of sociopolitical integration while seeking to situate the system change of 1989/90 within a longer social history perspective.

In places where the welfare state has put the brakes on the market, the politically regulated access to transfer incomes, social infrastructures, and social services has had a decisive impact on the livelihood of citizens. Alongside families and markets, welfare regimes are the third hub around which social relations revolve in modern societies, and their significance has increased steadily over the course of the twentieth century. Welfare regimes sculpt life courses and define the social positions of individuals in that they reduce, limit, legitimize, and even produce inequalities.[7] Given the centrality of such issues for the lives of citizens, it makes sense to analyze how the basic patterns of social security have changed in East and West Germany since the 1970s in terms of sociopolitical leitmotifs and management practices, as well as the awareness that problems exist. Going a step further, then, how did these changes impact the empirical development of social inequality? Such an analysis not only looks at a field of politics that was decisively shaped by the division and reunification of Germany, but also it examines sociohistorical developments that follow their own distinctive long-term rhythms of change. It thus provides insight into the relationship between transformation-related and long-term exogenous factors that have induced shifts in social inequality.

"The Golden Years"? Welfare and Work in East and West Germany around 1970: Two German Welfare States

After the fall of the Third Reich, both German states developed distinct welfare regimes that generally faced the same kinds of issues, but tried to deal with them differently. Especially during the formative years of the early postwar period, each side was strongly driven by the desire to clearly set itself apart from the other German state. In doing so, they drew on traditions that had coexisted "in tense juxtaposition to one another" during the Weimar Republic.[8] The West German welfare state began to expand steadily in the 1950s. By ensuring and then elevating the social status of employees, the growing welfare state made work less of a commodity, thereby reducing the underlying tensions between capital and work. West Germany thus introduced a welfare state regime that curbed the markets and evened out power imbalances—for example, through labor laws—but let the markets continue to be the central mechanism regulating the dissemination of social opportunities. Accordingly, the results of this market-induced distribution influenced social security in a watered-down form. In West Germany, this was reflected in the way in which social security was organized according to professions, which meant that the level of social benefits was often tied to the labor market position of the respective professions. As the West German social market economy did not eliminate the core independence of an entrepreneur whose actions still bore risks, it could not guarantee full employment. This was—and still remains—the Achilles heel of social order in the Federal Republic.

For the most part, the GDR moved in the opposite direction. It transformed the tiered system of social security into a uniform system and pushed private welfare providers to the wayside to make room for publicly run social services and infrastructures. At the same time, it sought to eliminate the risks of a market economy by adopting the principles of a planned economy within a socialist state. In turn, this made it possible to permanently secure jobs for employees in East Germany, which guaranteed a "right to work." Together with the prices fixed politically by the state, this job security offered a basic safety net that covered everyday necessities, effectively offering a much higher standard of existential security than in the FRG. This combination of job security and guaranteed basic provisions was a great source of legitimacy for the socialist model of society, especially for the generation that had experienced the Great Depression of the 1930s.

These particularities of GDR social policy, however, had far-reaching consequences. For one, this job security cost the planned economy some of its dynamic economic potential given that companies were burdened with additional politically mandated responsibilities otherwise covered by social security institutions or the family in market economies. In taking on these various functions, ranging from health and childcare to recreational activities, these enterprises turned into a "core of socialization and societal integration" (*Vergesellschaftungskern*) that had no equivalent in the Federal Republic.[9] Yet the accumulation of such extraneous responsibilities negatively affected productivity, which clearly lagged behind in the GDR compared to West Germany. GDR social policy was thus only able to overcome social problems on a very limited scale, without much conflict, by redistributing productivity gains; this had been possible to a much greater extent in the social market economy of the FRG during the postwar boom.

In East Germany, social policy was strongly defined by other political concerns. This constellation was particularly evident in cases in which GDR social policy appears to have been quite successful in retrospect, such as in health care and family policy, both of which served the primary interest of workforce mobilization. GDR social policy measures were also often tied to behavioral expectations of the state. In this sense, the GDR took up with the authoritarian governmental and patronal traditions of the German welfare state. The limits of these policies became quite clear when their success depended on the cooperation of those affected—for example, in the prevention of behavior-related illnesses, such as cardiovascular diseases.

Demarcation and Observation: The Rivalry between the German Welfare States during the Cold War

Entanglements and demarcations within the social policies of the two Germanys are key to a comparison of the "two worlds" of the German welfare state. Their mutual awareness of one another was embedded in the global bloc conflict of the Cold War and therefore shaped by an acute sense of rivalry. Indeed, some scholars have argued that this rivalry propelled the expansion of the welfare state on both sides of the Iron Curtain.[10] In its most simplified form, however, this thesis remains questionable, especially given the more complex and rather indirect nature of these interrelationships. The rivalry between the two Germanys did indeed play a particularly important role in West Germany in the early 1950s. The establishment of a uniform system of social insurance in the GDR, with its reduced range of services, worked to delegitimize corresponding plans in West Germany at the time, despite the fact that similar models had already been adopted in other Western countries, such as Great Britain. Moreover, the reconstruction of ambulant health care in a way that highly privileged self-employed doctors can be interpreted as a West German counterpoint to the move in the GDR to curb the bourgeois dominance of the health care professions. Over the course of the 1950s, however, the GDR became less of a reference point for West German social policy, primarily due to the clearly increasing gap in the resources allotted to the respective systems of social benefits and social services. At least until the beginning of the 1970s, the only exception to this growing divide proved to be health care.

In the GDR, social policy was at first relegated to the margins of the state's social project. It was supposed to repair the damage that had been caused by capitalist exploitation, which no longer existed in the official narrative of the "workers' and peasants' state." Consequently, the problems that were supposed to be remedied by the welfare state were seen as temporary manifestations of transition in the "construction of socialism." Not the level of social security but, rather, a higher standard of living was considered to be indicative of victory in the rivalry between the systems. As the superior productivity of the market economy became apparent in the wake of the West German "economic miracle," social security institutions in East Germany had to counter this by providing evidence of the advantages of state socialism. At the same time, the SED leadership increasingly sought to legitimize itself through social policy when it was no longer able to generate legitimacy through democratic rights of participation.[11] Social inequality, unemployment, and the return of poverty in West Germany beginning in the 1980s were topics repeatedly picked up by the media in the GDR in order to contrast the socialist leitmotif of a social safety net with the inevitably risk-laden industrial social order of West Germany that was subject to the whims of the market economy.

Whereas the competition between the two welfare states was merely a "by-product of Germany's division" for the Federal Republic in that the GDR was not a significant point of reference, the comparison between the two Germanys acquired an "existential dimension" for the legitimacy of the SED regime over time.[12] Such contrasts became highly problematic for the GDR when specific areas were concretely rather than abstractly compared. The GDR came away on top in only a few areas, such as subsidized prices for basic consumer goods or its vaccine program. In other areas, such as working hours, pension amounts, or social housing, the GDR did not perform nearly as well. As a result of this asymmetric rivalry with the West, the GDR leadership was greatly limited in its scope of action. Especially since the standard of living and social policy were so important as a source of legitimacy for the regime, the social order of the GDR and the power monopoly of its political leadership was put on the line whenever economic efficiency was prioritized over social needs.[13] Social policy also latently functioned as a source of legitimacy in the Federal Republic, but it was much less pervasive. It was bound up in the competition between two national parties that were proponents of the welfare state, namely the Christian Democratic Union (CDU) and the Social Democratic Party (SPD), making it difficult to carry through with any major cuts in social benefits despite the worsening economic situation of the mid-1970s.

Patterns of Inequality during Phases of Affluence and Upward Social Mobility

Just a few years after the collapse of the Nazi dictatorship, the "collapsed society" (*Zusammenbruchsgesellschaft*) of Germany, with its many damaged biographies and precarious living situations, was transformed into two increasingly affluent postwar German societies capable of a high degree of social integration (albeit in different ways and on different levels, but nonetheless to a surprisingly great extent in both cases). Both societies characteristically wove work, welfare, and patterns of social inequality tightly together. Consequently, work was much more than just a guiding principle of social order on both sides of the Iron Curtain. Standard, contract-based employment (*Normalarbeitsverhältnisse*), which structured income as well as gender roles, biographies, and recreational activities, shaped the realities of everyday life in both Germanys.[14] For a long time, West Germany adhered to the strong male breadwinner model, while female employment played a more decisive role alongside male employment much earlier on in the East. In both societies, though, work was the most important anchor for social security. Especially in the Federal Republic, however, social safeguards were heavily influenced by the markets. A German-German history of social inequality can thus hardly be written without taking the employment-related stratification of society into account. Yet, merely relying on class or social status primarily defined by position within the labor force cannot adequately account for the complex structures of social inequality.

Four fundamental processes shaped West Germany's work-oriented society around 1970:

1. Industrial society developed new contours. Employment in the so-called secondary sector of the production industry maxed out at about 49 percent in 1970 before it was overtaken by the service sector in the mid-1970s. However, this did little to change the industrial character of the West German economy. The percentage of civil servants and employees enjoying a privileged social security status among the total working population rose from about 20 percent to 36 percent. The percentage of self-employed individuals, on the other hand, declined. Although most jobs were still coupled with physical labor, the differentiations between manual and nonmanual occupations became less pronounced. In keeping with these developments, a single category of employees (as opposed to making legal distinctions between blue and white collar workers) had developed gradually since the 1960s that served as a social policy benchmark in the political realm.

2. Increasing labor productivity caused a singular rise in affluence. For most of the years between 1950 and 1970, the West German economy exhibited growth rates between 7 and 14 percent. The per capita income of the population increased fivefold during the same period. Especially for workers, this "explosion of wealth"[15] paved the way for improvements in their lives that were "spectacular, comprehensive, and revolutionary

from a social history perspective" because ordinary workers were able to overcome "the traditional narrowness and insecurity of the 'proletarian' way of life." It also made it easier for low-wage earners to move beyond a lifestyle that was solely directed at the immediate reproduction of their capacity for labor.[16] Continued improvements in the standard of living also generated an "elevator effect"[17] throughout many sectors of West German society that, among other things, resulted in a steady decline in poverty until the end of the 1970s. In 1973, not even 3 percent of West Germans whose household income was less than half of the average West German income level were considered to be poor, and social assistance was provided to only about 1 percent of the population in order to combat poverty. Using the idea of an "elevator" to describe this collective increase in affluence, however, can be problematic because it implies that all demographic groups and social strata profited equally from this prosperity boom. But, in fact, neither the degree of affluence nor the rate of growth was equally distributed. Rather than what contemporaries such as Helmut Schelsky saw as a "leveled middle-class society," West German society was really a welfare-based work-oriented society with a pluralization of social positions.[18] There were also people who lived in the "shadows of the economic miracle,"[19] such as those for whom work could not function as a mechanism of social integration (e.g., certain types of war victims and the mentally disabled) or those who did not meet the behavioral expectations that were the foundation for inclusion in the welfare state (the homeless, for example). The same held true for groups whose social integration was simply not part of the sociopolitical agenda, including foreign labor migrants, who have commonly been referred to as *Gastarbeiter* (guestworkers), a term which clearly underscores their temporary residency status in the country.

3. A fifteen-year phase of full employment between longer periods of low unemployment set in between 1959 and 1973 as part of the upswing in prosperity. Its implications for social history, as well as for the history of experience, cannot be underestimated, especially because it brought stability in work and lifestyle for most of the working population for the first time in decades. Full employment did away with one of the most defining and significant characteristics of a proletarian existence, namely high job insecurity. During this era of labor shortage, the rise in productivity brought higher real wages, thereby increasing the share of wealth that landed in the hands of employees; incomes reliant on entrepreneurial activity, however, slumped noticeably. In turn, this fostered the emergence of overarching patterns of consumption that leveled the differences between social classes as well as between the different European societies.

Moreover, the shortage of labor also boosted upward occupational mobility processes for almost all occupational groups, but for specially skilled workers in particular. Approximately two out of every five male skilled workers traded their blue collars for white ones between 1950 and 1970, moving from the shop floor up to the preproduction or production supervision levels.[20] Many children from working-class families were able to climb a rung or two up the social ladder into lower or mid-rank positions within the growing civil service during this time.[21] Switching to these kinds of jobs (nine hundred thousand of which had been newly created between 1950 and 1970) equaled a clear move up the social ladder from the lower to the middle class because of the high level of social security and benefits enjoyed by the civil service. Simultaneously, the expansion of the educational system loosened the tight bond between social background and educational achievement, even though there was less of a reduction in class-based differences than in other European countries.[22] The upward mobility of these groups was facilitated by the emergence of a new trifold lower class that had formed within the West German work force in companies. It was comprised of expellees, refugees from the Soviet Zone and the GDR, and foreign workers; the latter accounted for the majority of labor migrants after the Berlin Wall had gone up, and they also tended to take on low-skilled work.[23] Women only profited to a very limited extent from this sustained demand for labor. Part-time work did become a socially accepted professional model for married women in the Federal Republic over the course of the 1960s, and more than a small number of women managed to move from a socially disadvantageous position as family workers into gainful employment. But, women's employment stagnated at about 38 percent (1970), which was relatively low in international comparison.

4. In spite of the diminishing effects of market-related inequality on daily life in West Germany and increasing opportunities for consumption and career advancement, material inequality within West German society remained astonishingly stable. As in most other West European societies, West Germany experienced a modest reduction in economic inequality over the course of the economic upswing. It rested primarily on the detectable loss of status among affluent demographic groups in the 1960s. The percentage of total income earned by the highest-earning tenth of the population sank from 34.6 percent in 1950 to 32 percent in 1971, while the poorest-earning fifth of the population made slight gains.[24] This moderate decrease in income inequality indicates that performance-related differentiation within the labor market was a consistently high priority.

The data related to the development of wealth inequality suggests a less clear-cut picture. It indicates a much stronger concentration of assets within the richest fifth of the population and continuing disparities between self-employed individuals and those employed by others. This not only had to do with the way in which the currency reform of 1948 had favored those with real assets, but also with tax laws that were very investment-friendly. Companies were able to avoid having to pay taxes on a majority of their profits as long as these earnings were reinvested in production-related areas. When the economist Wilhelm Krelle published his research on the distribution of wealth in West German society at the end of the 1960s, he unleashed a veritable scandal with his findings that indicated that less than 2 percent of the population controlled over 35 percent of the country's total assets and over 70 percent of its productive assets. Accordingly, or at least it so appeared, the "hard core of social inequality, which stemmed from the distribution of income and wealth, remained mostly constant," even though it was overshadowed by a growth in prosperity.[25] When examined from a more nuanced perspective, however, this image of stable ratios of inequality turns out to be more complex. The years between 1962 and 1978, at least, marked a phase of substantial, wide-ranging reduction in income inequality as reflected by the decrease in the Gini coefficient, one of the most important measurements of distribution for analyzing inequality, from 0.29 to 0.25. In addition, the expansion of the welfare state effectively added a new dimension of distribution to the coordinate system of inequality. It fostered a new form of social wealth in a quantitative as well as qualitative sense, namely education as a form of social capital. This wealth, which had been primarily accumulated in the form of dynamic pension rights tied to prosperity, relativized the importance of traditional differences in income and wealth, especially in later phases of life.[26] Such pension rights served to offset the differences between generations, transferring the position that had been achieved during working life into a standard of living in retirement.[27] Clearly, the achievement of social equality was by no means a political priority in the Bonn Republic. Rather, the social order of West Germany fostered performance-related differentiation and sought to deal with the problem of social inequality by generalizing social security and limiting inequality at the bottom of the material distribution spectrum.

In the GDR, however, social equality was a very prominent leitmotif. This rested in part on the SED's promise to build a more socially just society. Indeed, the popular notion of leveling social differences and reducing the impact of social distinctions on society as much as possible was one of the most important sources of legitimacy for the socialist dictatorship. Moreover, with the goal of securing its political power, the SED regime initiated a policy that sought to strip away the privileges of aristocratic and bourgeois elites and foster the establishment of a class of socialist elites. Consequently, mobility within and across generations was extraordinarily high in the GDR in the 1950s and 1960s. By pushing out middle-class elites and promoting the emergence of a socialist counter-elite in the economy as well as in education, administration, and the state security apparatus, the SED regime provided plenty of options for politically loyal young workers and peasants to climb the social ladder to positions that would have otherwise been out of their reach based on their formal professional qualifications; this held true in particular for those born between 1918 and 1930, but it applied to women only to a limited extent. Most of the transformations in social structures that took place in the GDR from the 1950s onward can be seen as the results of dictatorial policy making. These attempts at political manipulation greatly influenced social inequality in the GDR, effectively politicizing the social structure of East German society in a variety of ways.

At the same time, East Germany was very much a "work oriented society," and even more so in certain respects than the FRG in the strictest sense of the word.[28] East Germany supposedly represented a social utopia in which society was ruled by workers for workers and work was devoid of the "alienation" and capitalist exploitation that had been predicted by Marx. However, the vision of a mostly socially homogeneous socialist work-oriented society free of conflicts permanently clashed with the fact that there was a serious gap between the actual resources available and those needed in order to achieve such a utopia. The socialist work society suffered from a chronic shortage of labor, thanks in part to an exodus to the West. In fact, some of its particularities, such as the high percentages of employment among women and retirees, actually stemmed from the need to increase the size of the workforce.

In contrast to the Federal Republic, agriculture and industry continued to be much stronger in the GDR. Correspondingly, the East German service sector grew more slowly, and it never reached the same level as in the West. Significant differences also existed between East and West in employment. Since most companies and large-scale agricultural enterprises were expropriated and members of the "old" industrial middle class were pushed into the manufacturing cooperatives, not more than 3.5 percent of employed individuals were self-employed or family workers in 1970. Similarly, the traditional differences between workers, employees, and civil servants that had been firmly embedded in social and labor law in Germany were leveled in the GDR. The civil service, with its firm attachment to the state, for example, had already been lumped into the general category of workers and employees by the Soviet military administration. As this category consisted of workers as well as the "intelligentsia," it encompassed two groups of working people who served different functions according to Communist theories of society. In 1970, for instance, approximately 83 percent of the workforce fit into this category. By and large, white-collar employees lost their income advantages over workers. Outside of the party sector, they earned less than skilled workers if they did not have a specialized diploma or university degree. To a certain extent, therefore, the contours of a uniform "employee society" (*Arbeitnehmergesellschaft*) appeared earlier in East Germany than in the Federal Republic. The meaning attached to the term "worker" thus changed accordingly, shifting from a category of employment and position in terms of social law to a quite flexible description of social background.

In general, differences in income were less pronounced in the GDR than in the FRG. This was tied to the fact that the mercantile middle class was pushed out of the uppermost income segment and also to the comparatively high wages that were paid for mundane jobs and the accelerated reduction of qualification-related income differences that had set in once the Wall had gone up. Furthermore, income levels were less of a factor in social inequality in the GDR than in the Federal Republic. The high state subsidies for rents, basic necessities, and select consumer goods put a damper on the effects of income-related differences. At the same time, this above-average buying power was often offset by the lack of goods available. This "doubled equality" of security and scarcity was a strong thread in the social fabric of the GDR.

How did this influence social inequality in the GDR around 1970 on the whole? The varying significance of income and professional qualifications for social inequality in the GDR underscores the fact that it makes little sense to map categories of social inequality that were developed with market economies in mind onto a society in which markets were nothing more than subordinate variables of social inequality because of the monopoly of politics over the production of goods. Heike Solga's model of a "socialist class society" addresses this problem by differentiating between a small party elite with unlimited authority over the provision of social goods, a service class with limited rights of access, and a working class without any corresponding rights.[29]

However, the SED leadership could by no means mold such social differences at will. Rather, the party's desire to control as much as possible clashed with its often contradictory and inconsistent regulatory practices, as well as the limited reach of its steering efforts. This was particularly true in cases in which plans for equality conflicted with the demands of rationality in a state-controlled socialist economy that could not mobilize sufficient social resources for the economic rivalry between the systems without a material incentive system. GDR sociologists intensively discussed this problem over the course of the "debate over driving forces"

(*Triebkräfte-Debatte*) in the 1980s. Its protagonists maintained that social inequality was indeed a factor in the development of a socialist society. To a certain extent, these theorists actually leaned toward the structural-functionalist social theories proposed by American sociologists such a Talcott Parsons, although they never really broke with historical materialism.[30] Private networks and family resources staked out another boundary hemming in state control. For example, the children of academics competing for access to a university education could counteract discrimination orchestrated by the SED with the cultural capital of their educated middle-class families. Indeed, such sociocultural differences, distinctions, and behavioral idiosyncrasies sometimes proved to be astonishingly tenacious within East German society. The government's attempts to equalize society in fact resulted in unintended side effects that actually worked as a third roadblock against the SED's influence. By putting strict limits on trade professions, for instance, craftsmen actually attained a very strong position on the informal market for services within the socialist economy of scarcity. Thus, the establishment of an alternative social order through the formation or restructuring of clearly demarcated larger groups was not really as particular to the GDR as it seemed. Rather, the truly distinguishing feature of East German society was the permanent tension that existed between the homogenizing attempts of the SED leadership to reshape society and the new social differentiations that emerged through overlapping and sometimes contrary social positions within the framework of "state-socialist intersectionality."[31]

Endangered Postwar Orders in the 1970s and 1980s: Consolidation, Restructuring, and the Self-Consuming Expansion of the Welfare State

The advent of a grand coalition government under the CDU and SPD in December 1966 heralded in a new phase of accelerated welfare-state growth in West Germany that lasted until the mid-1970s. The budget earmarked for social purposes climbed from just about a fourth to a third of the country's gross domestic product during this period. The percentages allocated to almost all areas of social policy—with the exception of family affairs—increased during these years.[32] Consequently, the period from 1966 to 1974 can be described as a second foundational era for West German social policy in which the main features of the emerging welfare state took shape. Simultaneously, a striking change in course occurred that was not necessarily reflected in institutional reforms, but rather in changes in the basic concept of the social state, the way of looking at sociopolitical problems, and the strategies adopted to deal with these issues. Three developments stand out in particular: first, subsequent interventions in social problems were supposed to be augmented by "active social policies" that would work to counteract such problems proactively. This generally more scientific approach to social policy was also geared toward finding long-term answers. Second, social policy was supposed to focus less on individual problems and more on society as a whole, which considerably increased the expectations that social policy should influence social relations. Third, social policy was tightly bound up in the Keynesian management of the economy. As a result, the welfare state came to be seen as a necessary prerequisite for stable, long-term economic growth rather than as a roadblock to economic development. From 1969 onward, the social-liberal coalition continued with this policy course, but it set a slightly different tone by focusing more on social participation and equal opportunity. This brought accelerated growth in social expenditures once again, although the political actors involved often underestimated the financial momentum of their reforms while overestimating their political steering potential. For example, this is what happened in health care with the hospital finance reforms of 1970/1972. Although these policies sought to modernize this long-neglected sector, they introduced a financing model that drove up costs but was not easy to alter easily given the federalism of the West German system.

For the most part, the expansion of the welfare state was financed by social security contributions deducted from earned income. So, despite favorable economic developments, employees' contributions to the social security schemes rose from 12.7 percent to 14.6 percent between 1966 and 1974. In a sense, this move was quite risky because it linked the funding of the welfare state even more closely to economic development and coupled it even more tightly to the male-dominated "normal employment" model. Above all, the ability to finance the welfare state in the long term was only secure if a few optimistic assumptions about the country's economic future held out over the long run: stable economic growth, full employment, a stable division of work along gendered lines, and stable demographic structures. In many respects, the Keynesian welfare state that emerged after 1966 was a fair-weather phenomenon that rested on unquestioned assumptions about the social, demographic, and economic stability of Western societies.

It became increasingly clear in the 1970s just how much the welfare state was affected by changes in these basic constellations. First, the pluralization of family types that had been fostered by social policy, changes in gender roles, and the demographic aging of the population forced the government to take action because it could no longer be assumed that families would be able to take care of their elderly members. Second, changes in global trade flows and the transition to a postindustrial economy led to a crisis in industrial employment that hit old industrial sectors, such as the steel and textile industries, particularly hard. Rising long-term unemployment also put pressure on social policy to deal directly with the roots of this problem. It also increased the dissonance between necessary social security expenditures that had been determined by long-term benefit schemes (which were not easy to retract within the German system of social insurance once they had been granted) and the amounts being paid into the social security system that were not growing as quickly as had been predicted. Consequently, almost all the branches of the social security system were running on a financial deficit as of the mid-1970s. At the same time, the globalization of the products and finance markets loosened the ties that bound the possibilities for capital appropriation to national economies. The costs of social security therefore became an important element in the international competition between countries. All together, these developments had a deep impact on the structural conditions of West German social policy. In a sense, the sociopolitical institutions suddenly seemed to have "aged" because they had to deal with conditions for which they had not been intended.[33]

The social security system was still expanded to a limited extent (especially in terms of family policy in the 1980s), but as of the mid-1970s, a "social policy of the second order" had taken over the political agenda.[34] The goal was not to tackle new social problems, but rather to adapt the growth of the social security system to the changed circumstances in order to ensure stability.[35] The priority for both the SPD-led and CDU-led governments in intervening in the system, however, was to consolidate the budget rather than stabilize social security contributions. Many of the reforms thus addressed separate aspects of larger problems or different subsystems within the social security system rather than the interdependencies between these subsystems. It is difficult to sum up the long-term effects of these policy reforms. At a macroeconomic level, this consolidation was at least partially successful. After 1975, the ratio between national income and social benefits expenditures in the Federal Republic, for example, tended to stagnate or drop slightly. It reached its highest point (prior to German reunification) in 1975, topping out at 33.4 percent of the GDP; by 1989, it had sunk to 30.2 percent, despite slower economic growth. Although the trend toward growth in social expenditures was not completely reversed, it was once again coupled more tightly to the development of the country's economic strength. This dampening effect was quite striking in a European comparison as it set in earlier in West Germany than in neighboring states. Yet, it should not be forgotten that these reforms never questioned the core idea of social security as had been the case in Anglo-Saxon democracies. For the politicians of both major political parties, social security was a key sociopolitical value that no one wanted to relinquish, especially in times of economic crisis, because of the poignant experiences with insecurity in the first half of the twentieth century. Indeed, the welfare state was seen as a bulwark against political extremism and social unrest. Consequently, the political and social upheavals during the period leading up to 1945 were more significant for the development of the West German welfare state than they were for what was happening on the other side of the Berlin Wall.

Ultimately, the reforms did not manage to decrease the financial dependency of the welfare state on the eroding model of normal employment. The lack of progress in adapting to shifting sociocultural and sociostructural circumstances continued to be problematic for West German social policy. The need for new social policies to deal with changing lifestyles and the demographic aging of the population was intensely discussed, but these debates resulted in political action in only a few isolated instances before 1989, such as in the introduction of a child-raising allowance and the parental leave clauses in the state pension scheme in 1986.[36] Reforms that were made therefore tended to underscore problematic structural particularities of the West German welfare state rather than modifying them to better address the changing social context, even though they did achieve a measure of financial consolidation.

Family and housing issues dominated social policy in the GDR in the 1970s and 1980s. In order to counteract the declining birth rate and overcome the continual labor shortage problem, policies directed at the situation of women and the family during the Honecker era not only sought to tap into the potential of the female workforce, but also reemphasized the generative function of the family. Alongside the expansion of the childcare system, the SED regime introduced preferential housing for young families and the so-called "baby year" in order to encourage childbearing. Although these policies put a drain on resources, their effects were rather ambiguous. In 1977, for example, about 80 percent of the women entitled to paid maternal leave took advantage of this policy, and women's employment climbed to over 90 percent (1989), which was quite high in international comparison. Yet, these policies made little progress when it came to women's equality in the workplace. Women were still overly represented in poorly paid professions such as in the health care sector, but underrepresented in management positions. Moreover, the persistence of the gendered division of labor at home subjected working women to a double burden. That said, the birth rate did increase more strongly than in West Germany, but not as much as was hoped, and not enough to guarantee the reproduction of the parent generation.

At the beginning of the 1970s, the SED leadership also launched a large-scale construction program to deal with the massive housing shortage and the enormous need to overhaul its existing housing, much of which was very outdated. The plan was to be able to provide 3.5 million apartments within two decades, including renovated older housing. But it took a bit of creative math in order to achieve this lofty goal. Nevertheless, the regime did increase the volume of new construction considerably for over a decade to over a hundred thousand apartments per year before construction began to wane again in the second half of the 1980s. Although the limited resources available were primarily put to use in a few development zones, which increased the disparities between the crumbling older buildings of the inner cities and new neighborhoods, this ambitious housing construction scheme became the second "attractive core of social policy during the Honecker era" from the people's point of view.[37]

These housing policy initiatives were part of a shift in social policy "from a growth-oriented paradigm of progress to a security-oriented paradigm of consolidation." This same shift was also detected in strategies designed to secure the power of the state in other socialist countries around 1970.[38] Consumer policy played a key role in steering this new course. Between 1971 and 1986/87, the percentage of state subsidies on consumption-related spending (not including rent for housing) climbed from 10 to over 26 percent. Without this artificial price capping, consumers would have had to pay almost double for food items during the late phase of the GDR.[39] For the East German population, these social and consumer policy initiatives during the Honecker era signaled a noticeable change in the temporal framework of SED politics: rather than pursuing a long-range vision of a communist society, the SED leadership promised that social energy would be channeled more heavily into fulfilling current consumer expectations. In doing so, the SED abandoned the promises of a social utopia that it had relied on to legitimize its social policy up to that point, but it countered this loss by increasing what it could concretely offer GDR consumers. Consumption thus became part of a new social contract—under the motto of "real existing socialism"—that tied the reassertion of party rule, a more centralized planned economy, and increased preventative surveillance of the population to the promise of a noticeably improved standard of life for GDR citizens.[40]

Honecker was the driving force behind this swing in the government's policy on consumption, which was pushed through despite reservations voiced by economic experts. Economists pointed to the lack of economic resources and to the negative effects that state's increase in subsidies would have on labor productivity. Their caution was not unfounded: increasing government price subsidies derailed the economy over the long term while fostering changes in consumer behavior and cracks in the foundation of political loyalty that proved to be disastrous in the end. Hopes for an increase in productivity were soon dashed in the wake of these policies because it had not been possible to link employee self-interest with the economic goals planned for the country as a whole.[41] Three aspects in particular proved to be problematic. First, the subsidies ate up an ever-larger percentage of the country's accrued wealth. In 1981, for example, approximately a fourth of the economic output of the GDR went into subsidies, which meant that it could not flow into productivity-enhancing investments. As a result, the percentage of the GDR's economic output that went toward investments sank noticeably from the mid-1970s onward (from approximately 33 percent in 1977 to 22 percent in 1985). Second, price subsidies led to rather dysfunctional consumer behavior because low prices did not encourage the thrifty use of limited resources (such as energy). Third, these subsidies did not encourage better performance because they were sprinkled about here and there in a scattershot approach that did not really take differences in need or demand into account. Rather, the combination of a strong social security system with slight improvements in living standards that could be achieved without individual effort put a damper on employee motivation.

In those areas in which the SED leadership focused on popular consumption, it drew attention to the living standards in West Germany as a reference point, propelling the rivalry between the two systems to the next level. As a result, the party found itself treading on thin ice. In reality, there was a wide discrepancy between the high-quality products typical of individualized consumption that were most desired by GDR consumers and the simple, standardized, and cheap goods that were available in East Germany.[42] Moreover, these policies raised expectations among the population that would have cost the SED leadership legitimacy if it began to backpedal on the consumption front. It therefore blocked any suggestions to deal with the intrinsic weaknesses of the GDR economy that would have shifted the focus toward more investment rather than consumption. In the end, the GDR's increasing social expenditures "capped economic capacity and presented a threat to the political system."[43]

Scholars have accordingly interpreted social policy developments in the GDR and the FRG as two different ways of responding to the industrial decline unleashed by the "third industrial revolution," which generated a new kind of rationalization crisis. While the West was generally able to overcome this slump following a series of severe adjustment crises, industrial decline only served to accelerate the collapse of state socialism in the East.[44] Such a political economy approach emphasizes the shared problems faced by both systems from the 1970s rather than stressing the differences between them. But a closer examination of the sociopolitical decision-making processes behind these developments on both sides of the Wall clearly reveals that the respective paths of the two Germanys were not necessarily shaped by different responses to globalization, tertiarization, and demographic shifts, but rather a mutual lack of response to these phenomena for reasons that varied. The fundamentally different nature of the link between social policy and the political system in the two Germanys certainly needs be taken into consideration. Although a strong bond exists between democracy and the welfare state, this link is quite flexible. The populations in market-economy democracies can come to terms with modifications in the trajectory of the social state and cuts in social security benefits, as was done in the Federal Republic after 1982 and again after 2003. Welfare state crises and social policy cutbacks thus tugged away at the political legitimacy of the elected government in power, but they did not undermine the legitimacy of the social order as a whole. In East Germany, however, the "real-existing socialism" of the Honecker era relied even more heavily on social policy as a source of legitimacy, which meant that the growing gap between the claims of a more comprehensive welfare system for GDR citizens and the limited financial means to uphold these promises heightened the sense that the system as such was failing. Ultimately, the SED state invested a large portion of the resources that it desperately needed to keep afloat the economy of "socialism on German soil" in social policy measures that aimed to solidify its political legitimacy. If consumption is defined as one of the basic needs served by a socialist welfare state, which was the assumption made by the leaders of the GDR, then the final crisis that hit East Germany can be deemed the result of a deliberate strain put on the welfare state. From this perspective, the 1970s left a much deeper cleft in social policy for the GDR than it did for the West German welfare state.

Patterns of Inequality "after the Boom"

The expansion of the welfare state in the reform era leveled social inequality in the FRG in a variety of ways. Not only those in the lowest income brackets benefited from these policies, but also victims of war whose pensions were index-linked. Likewise, self-employed individuals profited from being able to pay into the public pension fund under favorable conditions. In general, there was a basic move to reduce social differences and better sponsor social integration. The introduction of a legal framework regulating the continued payment of wages in the event that a worker became ill (1969), for example, removed one of the most symbolic differences between blue and white collar professions. Clear progress was also made in terms of the social integration of disabled people: around four million physically and mentally disabled individuals saw a noticeable increase in their social participation opportunities thanks to the expansion of social services and infrastructure institutions as well as the redefinition of their social rights. Similarly, the introduction of a minimum income pension in 1972 counteracted some of the gender-specific wage discrimination that had affected many women. Nonetheless, other disadvantages for women that stemmed from the still dominant strong male breadwinner model persisted. Very little was done within the system to foster the integration of foreign workers, who constituted about 10 percent of the employed population in 1974.

The precise effects of the retrenchment of the West German welfare state that began in 1975 on social inequality are difficult to determine, especially because important processes that impacted inequality were still ongoing. The momentum driving professional upward mobility, for example, continued despite slumping economic data; sometimes it even accelerated because the tertiarization of the economy brought about an "upward shift" toward qualified white collar jobs.[45] In contrast, however, the employment histories of those in the branches of the production sector that were heavily hit by industrial decline were much more discontinuous as more flexibility was required of the workforce. At the same time, a gap grew between the more experienced and often younger core of the workforce and the older and often less-skilled losers in this transformation process, who often found themselves facing unemployment or early retirement.[46]

Despite the economic crisis and the restructuring of the welfare state with the ad hoc retraction of some elements, the balancing and security mechanisms of the West German system of taxes and social transfers remained mostly intact. Although these cuts led to the relative impoverishment of the unemployed and those receiving social assistance, pensioners were able to slightly improve their income position.[47] Inequality among household net incomes—after taxes, social security contributions, and social benefits had been deducted—increased much later than it did for market-dependent incomes. This indicates that, at least at first, the sustainability of the social safety net suffered only slightly as the crisis set in. It was not until the mid-1980s and especially the 1990s that the leveling effects of the tax and transfer system waned.[48] The tight link between contributions and benefits in the German welfare state tradition offers one plausible explanation for this because the affluence acquired during the boom years thus came back to the recipients of pensions and unemployment support when the economic crisis hit.

The lower spike in the poverty rate in comparison to other European countries also indicates a rather moderate divergence of income levels. At the same time, though, it still points to new fault lines within the structure of social inequality. Three trends clearly emerge when the development of poverty is broken down according to different life situations: first, the poverty rate among the elderly sank below the average of that for the entire population after 1973. Second, the pension reforms considerably reduced the risk of poverty for women. However, the number of younger single mothers who fell below the poverty line began to increase in the 1970s. Consequently, a specific life situation became a poverty risk that did not stem from the position within the workforce, but rather resulted from processes of sociocultural transformation such as changed partnership forms. Third, beginning in the 1980s, long-term unemployment became more significant as a poverty-inducing factor, especially among those just starting out in their careers and among low-skilled workers.[49]

The attention devoted to poverty, however, increased far more than the poverty rate itself. In the wake of the economic crises of the 1970s, public interest in this topic grew, spurred on in particular by nongovernmental groups such as the Greens, social welfare organizations tied to the churches, and even researchers. Discussions also erupted over the links between processes of social structural change and new kinds of poverty (such as the poverty of older people in need of care, or one-parent families), in addition to the self-image of West Germany as a work-oriented society protected by a comprehensive welfare state. The debates over the "new social question" and "new poverty" transferred the poverty issue from the "third world" back to Germany. They interpreted poverty as a problem that was first and foremost caused by processes of economic and social change that were beyond the individual level and therefore needed to be addressed by the welfare state. In the GDR, on the other hand, the poverty question was split discursively in that a strict distinction was made between the *deserving* and *undeserving poor*. This and the partial individualization of the causes of poverty also exhibited more parallels to the discussion of poverty in Great Britain than it did to West German debates. Since poverty-generating conditions had been officially overcome in socialist society, social scientists and political actors expelled poverty from the realm of normality in GDR society by blaming deviant social behaviors such as alcoholism and a lack of discipline with regards to work for the poverty that still existed. The media also claimed that unemployment and poverty were structural problems inherent to capitalist societies in order to depict the GDR as the "better, more humane alternative to the Federal Republic" in which employees could count on social security and a safety net.[50]

One of the prices that people paid for this security in the GDR was a lack of professional development opportunities. Whereas the chances for upward professional mobility were comparably open in West Germany, people born after 1960 in the GDR did not have nearly as many career advancement chances. After the initial phase in which socialism was established in the GDR, many of the more prominent positions were occupied by relatives of the founding generation, who acquired positions of leadership at a relatively young age and held on to them until they were quite old. Accordingly, this increased the significance of political loyalty for professional careers. When the GDR was first getting started, membership in the SED was one way to compensate for other deficits in job qualifications, such as a lack of the appropriate degrees. For the age cohorts that came later, party affiliation became a necessary prerequisite for any kind of career development; since there were fewer career options, upward mobility in the GDR was beset with increasing pressure to become politicized.[51]

Although the SED leadership never gave up on its intention to grant privileges to the children of workers and peasants, and the uniform socialist state schools proclaimed to guarantee equal educational opportunities for all children regardless of their backgrounds, family resources continued to play a role in gaining access to the upper levels of education. In fact, they even sometimes seemed to be more important than ever before. Consequently, the rate of self-recruitment among the academically educated civil service was on the rise. While in the 1960s and 1970s the sons within this class had a three-times-higher chance of belonging to the civil service themselves than the sons of workers, the chances for the age cohorts born after 1960 increased by a factor of seven to eight. This meant that the chances for children of workers to acquire a higher level of education by attending university in the GDR were worse than in West Germany.

Of course, the income hierarchy was not only determined by education. A variety of political criteria, such as the function of certain professions in the apparatus of rule, were also quite decisive. The tip of this hierarchy was occupied by the predominantly male members of the apparatus of dictatorial power, while employees outside of production and retirees were relegated to the bottom.[52] Thanks to the relatively homogeneous income structure and limited consumption opportunities, the material differences in East Germany were less pronounced than in West Germany. In particular, the gap between mid-level incomes and the highest income brackets was much smaller than in the Federal Republic. Furthermore, the high subsidies for rents and basic necessities in the GDR cushioned the effects of low income on social stratification. However, almost a third of the GDR population, and especially retirees, were entirely dependent on these artificially cheaper everyday items.[53]

On the opposite end of the social hierarchy in GDR society, the elites favored by the SED state enjoyed access to more privileged living conditions. Special benefits—including better housing, the use of recreational facilities, and extra shopping options—took the notion of the classes that were privileged by the state-socialist welfare state[54] over the top in terms of exclusivity; this effectively compromised the ideal of equality that had framed East German society. Access to this kind of infrastructure and social services increasingly became a stratification factor. Not only were these benefits enjoyed by the approximately one thousand people who belonged to the circle of power-holding elites, but also a number of prestigious elites (such as artists) and privileged elite functionaries. This form of social inequality was not very formalized, nor was it really visible to the public. As a result, a public outcry ensued when the people of the GDR became aware of these practices as the SED lost its grip on power,

Figure 4.1. Information Brochure for Citizens of the GDR about the Establishing of the Social Union, Presented during a Meeting of the Last GDR Parliament (Volkskammer), June 1990 (source: Ulstern Bild - AIDN - Bildarchiv, used with permission)

although it must be said that the level of luxury enjoyed by the elite was still very modest according to Western standards. Its welfare state equivalent consisted of a complicated system of special and extra retirement pensions for individual professional groups and several different special health care systems that existed alongside the official egalitarian old age and health care provisions for privileged professional groups.[55]

Owning cash in foreign currency was yet another way to achieve a higher standard of living because it allowed people to take advantage of what was offered within the shadow economy; whoever had this kind of cash could buy luxury consumer goods or services that were otherwise in short supply. To some extent, the patterns of privilege typical of the SED also governed access to foreign currency. Yet, in this case, access was also regulated in other ways, creating a unique kind of inequality that escaped the control of the SED leadership. The people who profited most from being able to acquire extra consumer goods were those professional groups with contacts to the West (including some with little social prestige, such as the waitstaff in international hotels) who were able to earn extra informal payment for services that were in short supply, and families who had access to Western products and Western currency thanks to contact with relatives in the West.

The Path to the Present: Social Security and Social Stratification after the Collapse of State Socialism

Drained but Reinforced: The Transformation and Restructuring of the Welfare State since the 1990s

German Reunification shifted the priorities of social policy over the short term as well as at a more fundamental level. The enormous urgency with which the political actors had to negotiate the reunification process in early 1990 created a preference for consistent solutions, which affected a number of the basic decisions that shaped the sociopolitical framework for a unified Germany at an early stage.[56] First, a cross-party coalition of West German social politicians and GDR representatives pushed through the idea that the economic and currency union of the two countries should also be accompanied by a "social union." This was a decision in favor of a welfare-state approach to dealing with the consequences of the East German dictatorship, which had proven to be a successful tactic after World War II. Second, the political actors involved determined that this social union would consist of transposing West German institutions into the former East Germany, which was broken down into the new federal states. The reforms that had been planned in the West were not integrated into the reunification process; they were pushed back for the time being, only to be taken up again a decade later under more difficult circumstances. This vote in favor of the transfer of welfare state institutions was also a vote against keeping the sociopolitical traditions of the GDR, which proved to be a very controversial point. Indeed, it touched on the question of which elements of the GDR's sociopolitical identity would be brought into a reunified Germany. In particular, the right to work and the well-functioning system of childcare in the GDR had a high symbolic value within this context. Ultimately, only a portion of the GDR's achievements in terms of equality with respect to the employment of women with children were taken over after reunification. The notion that the GDR was a model society and point of reference when it came to this issue continued to hold sway, especially since it was easier to reconcile with cross-European trends than the strong male breadwinner model that had determined the path of the old West Germany.

When the decision was made in favor of the social union, however, the costs associated with this process were greatly underestimated. One point that was particularly problematic had to do with a third fundamental decision that was made, namely to finance reunification primarily through the coffers of the social security system. Even then, critics questioned this method of financing because it essentially meant that the costs of German unity would be covered by the contributions paid by those insured in the system. Business owners, independent professionals, and civil servants, on the other hand, were largely exempt from paying into this system, which meant that the financial burden of German unity was disproportionately put on the shoulders of the lower and middle income brackets.

Unlike the West German laws that offset such financial burdens in 1949 and 1952 (Lastenausgleich), there were hardly any measures introduced in 1990 that required wealthy individuals to make special contributions to finance reunification. In contrast to the way that West Germany had dealt with the victims of war and expellees, preexisting patterns of inequality were actually strengthened after 1990 because of various regulations, such as the priority given to the natural restitution of factories and property to old owners without instituting a property levy.[57] The problematic strain that the costs of reunification put on the social security system, given the increased cost of labor, was not a necessary consequence of German unity; rather, it was the result of a financing model that had been chosen for extrinsic reasons. The expectation was that it would be easier in a political sense to increase social security contributions as opposed to taxes.[58]

Despite these issues, however, the share of the German welfare state in the success of the reunification process was quite remarkable. The quick and unproblematic introduction of the sociopolitical institutions of the Federal Republic in the states of the former East helped to make the transformation of a planned economy into a market economy more bearable and therefore socially acceptable to the citizens in the new federal states. It aided in the reorganization of the circulation of money and goods in eastern Germany, making it possible for companies to share the burden of the costs related to the system transformation with the tax payers and the contributors to statutory social insurance schemes.[59]

The main social problem during the transformation period was dealing with mass unemployment. Just from 1990 to 1994, approximately three million employees lost their jobs in the new federal states. Many of these older individuals were forced to take early retirement, while the younger people affected were directed toward the state-financed "secondary job market"; very few of the latter actually managed to find their way back to the regular "primary job market" in the long term. In order to soften the blow of this economic transformation, the German government turned to tried-and-true measures that had been used to overcome social problems in the old Federal Republic. These policies had in fact already attracted a great deal of criticism since the 1980s because they shifted state financial burdens onto the social security system, which increased labor costs.

The impact of reunification on the sociopolitical institutional order was therefore quite uneven. Although the residents of the new federal states experienced a radical break in terms of the continuity of the welfare state, the sociopolitical institutions of the Federal Republic proved to be elastic enough to be able to deal with the special, historically unique situation of German reunification. Indeed, these institutions emerged from the fusion of the two states in a relatively unaltered form, and in many respects they were even strengthened by this period of transformation. On the path to German unity, the welfare state once again proved its astounding ability to adapt to changed circumstances and to absorb the impact of social problems on a very large scale. At the same time, however, social policy lost much of its autonomy, leaving behind the impression of an "exhausted welfare state."[60]

The way in which social policy developments are assessed very much depends on the time frame that is taken under consideration. Keynesian policies dominated until 1994, and their overarching aim was to deal with the social consequences of German reunification. They were coupled, however, with a massive increase in government debt, high wage costs, and strongly diminishing economic performance. The social expenditure ratio rose in the first few years after reunification in the new federal states to over 55 percent, and the aggregate social security contribution rate climbed by 7.6 percent, from 35.5 percent to 42.1 percent, between 1990 and 1998. This considerably weakened the competitiveness of the German economy in the international markets. As of the 1990s, Germany was no longer considered to be one of the motors of growth because it had become one of the weakest countries in terms of growth in Europe. This put new pressure on the Achilles' heel of the German welfare state, namely the tight link between the state of employment and the financial leeway afforded social policy.

Since the end of the 1990s, several governments have made a concerted effort to reverse these developments. From 1999 to 2007, the coalition government of the SPD and the Greens introduced its so-called Agenda Policy, which was then continued under the second grand coalition (SPD and CDU). This policy approach resulted in some rather deep clefts in the continuity of sociopolitical goals, management tactics, and sociopolitical practices. The crisis of the financial markets that hit in 2008, however, tripped off a countermovement and the renaissance of consensus-oriented crisis management policies. It was also accompanied by a "re-legitimation"[61] of the German welfare state model that had come under pressure with the introduction of the Agenda 2010. Some elements of these agenda policies have been revised as a result. Thanks to its welfare-state based "crisis Keynesianism," Germany has emerged from the recent economic disasters in much better shape than most of its European neighbors.[62]

Although it is still somewhat difficult to assess the key trends of more recent social policy, four main aspects should be emphasized:

1. The erosion of "national" social policy. Globalization and European integration have fundamentally changed the conditions, scope, and contexts of the impact of social policy. European integration, for example, has eroded what used to be a tight link between the welfare state and the nation-state by incrementally creating a cross-state social space that arches over national systems of solidarity and transfers responsibilities to the level of the European Union. This development has had ambiguous consequences for the EU member states. On the one hand, it has boosted the importance of social security as a separate goal of European integration. On the other hand, more traditional forms of national social policy now collide even more often with the basic economic liberties of the common market. Moreover, involvement in the Lisbon strategy adopted by the EU, with its focus on competitiveness, has demanded market-compatible social policy measures (such as private risk hedging), putting classic social benefit programs increasingly under pressure to prove their legitimacy.

2. Marketization and financialization. Since the 1990s, the balance between the state, the markets, and families has tipped a good bit in favor of the markets. These changes can be seen as a shift in emphasis rather than

a real structural break because private elements have always played a certain role in financing and providing social benefits in the German welfare state. The introduction of the compulsory long-term care insurance in 1994 institutionalized the financing of this system along the traditional lines of social security, but it also consciously made space for private providers to offer nursing care services within a state-regulated welfare market. Marketization trends are even more apparent in the health care system, where municipalities have given up much of their traditional role as hospital providers to profit-oriented clinic companies. That said, however, this marketization has not necessarily strengthened the position of private providers because the newly created welfare markets in Germany tend to be strictly regulated.[63] In some areas, the scope of autonomy afforded private actors has actually been reduced—for example, by turning the traditionally fine-lined system of regional public health insurance providers into a de facto single-provider insurance system offering comprehensive social protection to the detriment of private practice doctors and private insurance providers.

3. Security loss and deregulation. With the partial privatization of pension schemes through the "Riester reform" of 2002, an interest-based coalition, led by financial service providers as well as some of the unions and Green party politicians, did away with the idea that the main purpose of the public pension fund was to ensure standards of living, in favor of keeping the contributions to the system at a stable rate. The goal was to prepare the pension fund for the drop in the number of people paying into the system that was predicted to result from the major demographic shift in progress.[64] In order to achieve this, benefits were cut down to such an extent that future pensioners can no longer count on being able to maintain their previous standard of living. The ensuing gap was supposed to be filled by supplemental private pension schemes offering tax incentives, but it was virtually impossible for employees in low-income brackets with an unsteady employment history to pay into this system. Consequently, the danger of poverty in old age, which had basically disappeared from the spectrum of sociopolitical problems in West Germany after the pension reforms of 1957 and 1972, has returned to haunt the future prospects for old age in post-reunification Germany.

Job market policy was the second major field of deregulation in social policy alongside the pension system. In light of persistent mass unemployment, the Red-Green coalition, supported by the Bundesrat dominated by the CDU, introduced a series of reforms that were stylized as a break with the tradition of a welfare state whose primary aim was security. They marked a move toward a social policy agenda with a focus on the labor market that resembled the "New Labour" approach practiced in the

UK since 1997. These reforms, known as the Hartz reforms, combined a number of measures designed to encourage the unemployed to seek work, to foster the restructuring of the traditional labor administration system according to the guidelines of "New Public Management," and to make decisive changes to benefit legislation. Some of the measures intended to reactivate the desire to find work among the unemployed included providing support to former recipients of social assistance who were now required to actively seek employment, and stricter regulations about jobs that people could reasonably be expected to accept. Both of these policies were intended to increase the motivation to find a job among the unemployed. Changes in benefits legislation, moreover, dictated that—after a limited transitional period in which individuals would continue to be paid income-based unemployment benefits—social assistance and what used to be a de facto unlimited system of income-based unemployment benefits tied to the former standards of living were combined into a second stage of unemployment benefits, known as Arbeitslosengeld II, whose amount was the same across the board. Arbeitslosengeld II was conceived as a way to ensure a basic minimum of existence; it was also coupled with strict asset and needs assessments, little protection for existing wealth and property, and tough rules that applied to domestic partnerships.[65] This marked a far-reaching departure from some of the key principles of the German welfare state in one of the main fields of social policy. Prior to this point, income compensation as well as old age pensions and unemployment benefits had been governed by the idea that contributions and payouts should be equivalent, and, since the 1950s, that the goal should be to ensure a consistent standard of living.

In the old system, the principle of equivalence in terms of social security contributions and social benefit claims and the rules that determined what kind of job a person could reasonably be expected to accept took into account the previous occupational status of job seekers. It guaranteed that members of the middle class could continue to live a similar lifestyle over the long term, even if they lost their jobs. It is therefore misleading to interpret the Hartz reforms as a poverty policy measure that was mainly directed against the lower classes. In truth, the big losers were the members of the middle classes, who used to be particularly well protected by social policy, but now found themselves faced with a larger chance of falling down the social ladder if they lost their jobs. Many people who had been reliant on social assistance, on the other hand, now received support in trying to find work on the job market for the first time.

If only the issue of unemployment is taken into account, the Hartz reforms were indeed a success. Bolstered by an economic upswing, Germany has experienced a strong reduction in unemployment since 2006 that cannot be compared to anything other than the initial phase of the economic miracle. These policies also clearly motivated many long-term as well as short-term unemployed people to get back on the job market. Approximately eight hundred thousand people have found jobs with full social security benefits through this system since 2009. Most of these jobs, however, have been only part-time positions. This touches on the highly problematic downside of the "German job miracle," namely even more increases in social inequality and the considerable long-term problems related to the financial situation of the social security system. In particular, the Hartz reforms have strengthened the trend toward more part-time work and mini-jobs. With about 6.5 million employees (approximately 20 percent of the total workforce), post-reunification Germany has one of the largest low-wage sectors in Europe, which has exacerbated the problem of people with jobs who still suffer from poverty.

4. Changes in the leitmotifs of social policy. The move away from the principle of ensuring standards of living may very well be one of the most far-reaching social policy readjustments over the long term. Before 2005, social policy debates in Germany were mostly about the financial resources of individual branches of the social security system. Following the conflicts that surrounded the Hartz reforms, however, social policy has increasingly become more about ensuring a basic level of protection, which is reflected in the current debates over poverty in old age and the minimum wage. Put more bluntly, social assistance, which was originally intended to be a stop-gap measure for problematic situations that were not otherwise covered systematically within the German welfare state tradition, has shifted from the periphery to the center of social policy. If this trend ends up being permanent, it would imply a break in the continuity of the German welfare state tradition.

Although they have evolved, the leitmotifs of gender politics in social policy have also changed significantly. The male breadwinner model (which often appears in a modified form as a male breadwinner plus an extra female income) is still quite present in today's social reality, but family and social policy in Germany has been shifting more and more to the adult-worker model, which puts the focus on the working individual as opposed to the family as a social unit. This model also assumes that all adult family members are gainfully employed. Unlike the old West German child-raising allowance, the parental benefits policy that was introduced in 2007, for example, is calculated according to income, and both parents are required to reduce their employment in order to take advantage of the full length of benefits.

At least at a programmatic level, there has been a shift since the Red-Green coalition from a protective welfare state to one focused on bolstering the position of individuals vis-à-vis the job market, whereby activating labor market policies are augmented by a willingness to assist in the accumulation of human capital. Under the banner of other policies, whose goals are to level chances and increase education opportunities for children from socially deprived families or those with migrant backgrounds, older leitmotifs of social democratic politics have been revived, albeit with a stronger focus on integrating the recipients of these policy benefits into the labor force.

The welfare state has by no means lost its overwhelming significance in this interplay of different arenas of inequality; rather, its importance has tended to be reinforced. At present, alongside classic risk hedging functions, programs that aim to improve employability are on the rise. Within this deeply altered economic, sociostructural, and sociocultural context, the protective welfare state has shifted considerably toward a regulatory and activating welfare state.

Social Polarization in a Fragmented Competitive Society

Patterns of social inequality have changed more dramatically since 1990 than welfare state institutions. The development of social inequality since this point has been marked by a significant change in the balance of power between capital and work to the detriment of employees. There are, however, five other trends that merit particular attention:

1. The tight structure of standard, contract-based employment (Normalarbeitsverhältnisse) that was underpinned by the welfare state had been facing increased pressure since the 1970s. Less as a result of reunification and more as a result of the need to respond to global developments, the world of work in post-reunification Germany has been subjected to processes of deregulation, flexibilization, and deformalization related to employment, as well as a polarization of professional qualifications, which have reinforced inequality. Because of these developments, the contours of a uniform work-oriented society have become less clear.[66]

2. In the context of this knowledge-based industrial society, education is becoming a more significant factor in social inequality. The ongoing tertiarization of the economy in addition to the automation and digitalization of production have raised the bar in terms of employment qualifications. The number of jobs for low-qualified individuals without any occupational training has decreased considerably again since 1990. In addition, there is a plethora of poorly paid, precarious, "atypical" kinds of employment in this segment (such as mini-jobs, pseudo self-employment, and part-time work); but, at the same time, the percentage of highly

qualified employees has more than doubled since 1990. In light of these circumstances, earned educational qualifications no longer guarantee a secure career with chances for upward mobility. Instead, education has become an essential prerequisite for employability in a work environment in which professional qualifications need to be renewed at shorter and shorter intervals. This change has had a mixed effect on structures of inequality. On the one hand, highly qualified, highly driven employees in the service sector and those in the free professions, in particular, have been the winners in terms of social inequality since the 1990s. On the other hand, the wage gap between professions requiring a university education and those that do not has shrunk.

3. Since the mid-1990s, the income gap has been widening. The above-average growth among the highest-earning tenth of the population between 1998 and 2008, combined with the stagnating position of the lowest-earning 40 percent of the population, has fed this development. The unemployed have suffered in particular because their income situation worsened in both absolute and relative terms. Other relative losers were trainees, workers, and blue collar employees. The relative winners have been retirees, civil servants, well-qualified employees, and the heterogeneous group of freelancers and the self-employed. The poverty rate has moved in a similar direction. In the year before reunification, 11.8 percent of the West German population was considered to be in danger of becoming poor. Since the turn of the century, this figure has climbed sharply, hitting 15.1 percent in 2011. As a result, income disparity at the macro level has started to resemble the distribution patterns of the early 1960s, with the notable exception that most of the poor communities are no longer located in the South as they were in West Germany in the 1950s, but rather in eastern Germany.

This trend is even more evident in the development of inequalities of wealth. The poorest fourth of the population has suffered slight losses in this respect since 1992, while the wealthiest quarter of the population had made considerable gains until the financial market crisis hit in 2007. There are clear disparities between east and west as well as between north and south in terms of wealth. The intergenerational transfer of the wealth that had been accumulated in the years of prosperity after World War II has also contributed to the increasing inequality in the distribution of wealth. This transfer of wealth through inheritance has grown significantly over the last twenty years. Between 1999 and 2010, more than three trillion Euros were inherited in Germany, and economists are predicting an additional wave of inheritances in the coming years. Academics are more than three times as likely to inherit wealth than workers. As a result of fewer opportunities to accumulate wealth and the lesser importance of property ownership in the past, East Germans are not nearly as likely to profit from an inheritance as West Germans are. Inheritance, therefore, has continued to reinforce existing inequalities in wealth.[67]

4. Unlike the other former communist bloc states, the old East Germany was able to merge into a functioning system of welfare institutions after 1989/90. Thanks to the enormous influx of financial transfers and administrative expertise, the social implications of the system transformation in Germany's new federal states resulted in less harsh structures of inequality than in the majority of the other eastern European states. Despite high unemployment and increasing income disparity, the distribution of income in Germany is still much less unequal than in most European countries.[68] This can be seen as evidence for the continuing effective hedging of the markets by employment relations, fiscal policy measures, and the social security system. However, the social transformation process in the new federal states was radical, and it turned out to be much "more difficult and cumbersome than initially supposed by many."[69] The way in which this process was entangled with waves of global economic and sociostructural transformations sometimes resulted in changes in social inequality in post-reunification Germany that varied greatly by region and whose causes were not always easy to locate. Most of the citizens of the new federal states found themselves facing a significant increase in insecurity and inequality on the one hand, but also a substantial improvement in their standard of living on the other.

At the end of this reorganization process, in which the East German states lost approximately four million jobs, a social fabric comprised of different layers had emerged that more closely resembled that of West German society than before, but nonetheless retained some of its East German particularities. For example, gender inequality is still less pronounced in these states. Likewise, material inequality is not as strong as in the old West Germany. What cannot be overlooked, however, is that the overall level of affluence in the former East is still lower than in the West. The unemployment quota in the new federal states is much higher: it averaged about 11.6 percent in 2013, which was almost double that of the old federal states. Of course, this has implications in terms of poverty. A larger number of the regions with particularly high poverty rates are located in the eastern federal states.[70]

As part of the system transition, East Germany had only had a very short time to achieve the economic structural transformation that had taken more than twenty-five years in West Germany. Over the course of the deindustrialization process, a large number of companies had already been forced to close their doors or rush to adapt to market society. Many of these businesses, which were tightly knit social communities in and of themselves, disappeared during the difficult years of transition. For East Germans, this meant that they lost not only access to social services that had been provided through them, but also a place where the simultaneous increases in insecurity, the sometimes major drops in social status, and the pressure to adapt to a new kind of society could have been discussed.

In terms of individual biographies, the balance of gains and losses during this transformation phase were very unequally distributed across generations and social structures. Particularly those groups who had suffered as a result of the focus on economic production in the GDR, such as East German pensioners, were among the winners in this process. Their social situation improved significantly through the introduction of a dynamic pension scheme along West German lines. Some of the losers of the *Wende* were groups that had been well-protected in the social security system in the GDR, such as single parents, many of whom have since been faced with a much higher risk of poverty. Younger people paid for a larger variety of job options with growing insecurity during the entry-level career phase, although this was softened by migration within Germany. Other losers included employees who had been part of the core of the GDR's work society within the "older" industrial structures, especially unskilled and semi-skilled workers, many of whom suffered from long-term unemployment after 1990. The age cohort of forty-five to fifty-five-year-olds was hardest hit by the system transformation; members of this cohort were too young to retire in 1990, but they were often seen as too old to start again with new jobs by potential employers. Although this transformation process was also embedded in a historically unique surge of increased affluence and its impact was softened greatly by the welfare state, the social consequences of the biographical insecurity faced by the citizens of the East German federal states were quite dramatic on the whole. Indeed, from the perspective of the history of experience, the significance of this process simply cannot be overestimated. This was reflected not least in the steeply dropping birth rate in East Germany between 1990 and 1994.

In terms of social inequality, moreover, there were several problematic aspects related to German reunification. Some patterns of inequality, such as the high risk of poverty among poorly qualified employees and single-parent families, are less an expression of an East-West difference than a reflection of accumulated regional disparities that resulted from the transformation of work and other sociocultural changes. In this sense, they emerged from processes that were also taking place in other regions of Germany and in most European countries as well. The experiences of many people in the new federal states during this transformation phase, however, were marked by a sharp discrepancy between their high expectations and the reality of their social situations. This meant that disappointment with the German welfare state after reunification was really quite inevitable. Given the often tremendous demands that were made of people over the course of this transition, it is rather surprising that the overwhelming majority of East Germans believe that the *Wende* had a positive effect on their own lives. Nonetheless, in retrospect, the socio-political institutions of the GDR—in particular the health care system, the childcare system, and the high level of job security—are aspects of state socialism before its fateful demise that are still remembered in a particularly positive light.[71]

5. Although it is by no means easy to outline the complex development of income distribution and the risk of job loss, it is even more complicated to tease out the factors feeding into social inequality as it changes over time. Despite the fact that inequalities are now much more dependent on individual decisions than in the past, the great majority of these differences are still tightly coupled with the key principles of a wage-based employment society and the system of social security associated with it. Indeed, the greatest risk of poverty in modern society was and will continue to be unemployment. However, it is becoming increasingly more difficult to trace social inequality back to a few definitive dimensions of inequality, because its structure has acquired a number of different layers.[72] The distribution effects of the job market have been augmented by specific social stratifications such as ethnicity, as well as regrowth in the significance of age-related differences and stronger regional variations that have appeared since 1990 (not only in the form of a slowly decreasing split between east and west, but also a growing gap between north and south). Simultaneously, social positions that are relevant in terms of inequality are no longer as tightly linked to specific social classes because they are more heavily dependent on individual choices. As a result, for example, the poverty risk of single-parent families is now spread across almost all income brackets. Moreover, the welfare state is still very much mixed up in constellations of social inequality in Germany. Patterns of inequality that are not directly linked to the job market have thereby come to play a greater role. The trajectory of sociopolitical integration in the new federal states points to the fact that the effects of timing, such as the ability to take advantage of welfare state programs under favorable conditions, is becoming more important, as the developments in early retirement regulations suggest. The growth in female employment and the erosion of the male breadwinner model have not entirely leveled existing gender-based inequalities. There is still a striking inequality in income distribution, for instance, due to industry-specific wage practices and the

way in which family work is organized. However, these differences have become less pronounced since 1990. The welfare state has increasingly reshaped household inequalities through social services, thereby "de-privatizing" them.[73] Despite this trend, which has moved post-reunification Germany closer to the path of other states in western and northern Europe, the significance of households as arenas of inequality has by no means diminished. To the contrary, their importance has actually grown due to a greater array of available options.

How can we summarize all these changes in a nutshell? The development of income and wealth structures and the rising inequality in educational opportunities do in fact support the thesis that patterns of social inequality are becoming more and more polarized. On the other hand, unlike other European countries, Germany still has a broader middle class, which has been able to capitalize on the gains in affluence over the last two decades. The Hartz reforms affecting poverty and job market policy, combined with the Riester reforms in the pension system over the long term, marked a departure from the idea of guaranteed standards of living that had once been one of the constitutive elements of West Germany's identity as a welfare state. These moves effectively weakened the ability of the social security system to offset social inequalities. Nonetheless, the basic outline of the West German welfare state is still very much evident in post-reunification Germany. In some places, such as family and education policy, it has even become a bit stronger. The notion of an increasingly divided society therefore seems to be rather exaggerated on the whole. Paradoxically, it has been the spread of social vulnerability to mid-level skilled workers and university-educated service professionals due to downward professional mobility that has indicated a trend to the opposite. To put it more precisely, there is now greater equality, but it is greater equality in the guise of insecurity. It is still not clear whether words such as "precariousness" and "social exclusion" as a "new vocabulary of fear related to the transformation of work and social life" can in fact adequately describe these changes.[74] Rather, it seems to be more difficult to identify clear patterns of social inequality given the growing downward permeability of society and the blurring of the lines between secure and insecure jobs as the competition among employees has intensified.[75]

Winfried Süß is a senior research associate and head of the research group "Welfare States in Transition" at the Center for Contemporary History (ZZF) in Potsdam. He teaches modern European history at the

University of Munich. He taught as assistant professor at the University of Munich, as guest professor of comparative welfare state research at the University of Göttingen, and as guest professor of modern European history at the University of Wuppertal. He has written and edited books on the history of the Third Reich, such as *Der "Volkskörper" im Krieg: Gesundheitspolitik, medizinische Versorgung und Krankenmord im nationalsozialistischen Deutschland 1939–1945* (2003) and *Städte im Nationalsozialismus: Räume und soziale Ordnungen* (ed. with Malte Thießen, 2017), and on the history of the welfare state, such as *Von der Reform in die Krise: Der westdeutsche Wohlfahrtsstaat in der Großen Koalition und der Sozialliberalen Ära* (2018).

NOTES

1. Peter Krause and Ilona Ostner, "Einleitung: Was zusammengehört. Eine sozialwissenschaftliche Bilanzierung des Vereinigungsprozesses," in *Leben in Ost- und Westdeutschland. Eine sozialwissenschaftliche Bilanz der deutschen Einheit 1990–2010* (Frankfurt a.M., 2010), 19.
2. Helmut Kohl, Speech to the German Bundestag, 8 March 1989, as quoted in Dieter Grosser, *Das Wagnis der Währungs-, Wirtschafts- und Sozialunion. Politische Zwänge im Konflikt mit ökonomischen Regeln* (Stuttgart, 1998), 268.
3. For an overview, see Manfred G. Schmidt and Gerhard A. Ritter, *The Rise and Fall of a Socialist Welfare State: The German Democratic Republic (1949–1989) and German Unification (1989–1994)* (Heidelberg, 2013), 200–89.
4. Markus M. Grabka, "Private Vermögen in Ost- und Westdeutschland gleichen sich nur langsam an," *DIW Wochenbericht* 40 (2014): 965; Markus M. Grabka, Jan Goebel, and Jürgen Schupp, "Höhepunkt der Einkommensungleichheit in Deutschland überschritten?," *DIW Wochenbericht* 43 (2012): 6–8.
5. Bernd Wegner and Stefan Liebig, "Gerechtigkeitsvorstellungen in Ost- und Westdeutschland im Wandel: Sozialisation, Interessen, Lebenslauf," in *Leben in Ost- und Westdeutschland*, ed. Peter Krause and Ilona Ostner (Frankfurt a. M., 2010), 83–101; Ursula Dallinger, "Erwartungen an den Wohlfahrtsstaat. Besteht eine 'innere Mauer' zwischen West- und Ostdeutschen?," in *Leben in Ost- und Westdeutschland*, ed. Peter Krause and Ilona Ostner (Frankfurt a. M., 2010), 573–96.
6. Reinhard Busse and Annette Riesberg, *Health Care Systems in Transition: Germany. WHO Regional Office for Europe on behalf of the European Observatory on Health Systems and Policies* (Copenhagen, 2004), 10; Statistisches Bundesamt, ed., *Bevölkerung und Erwerbstätigkeit. Sterbetafeln: Früheres Bundesgebiet und neue Bundesländer 2009/2011* (Wiesbaden, 2012).

7. Hans Günter Hockerts, "Einführung," in *Soziale Ungleichheit im Sozialstaat. Großbritannien und die Bundesrepublik im Vergleich*, ed. Hans Günter Hockerts and Winifried Süß (München, 2010), 10–14.
8. Philip Manow-Borgwardt, "Entwicklungslinien ost- und westdeutscher Gesundheitspolitik zwischen doppelter Staatsgründung, deutscher Einigung und europäischer Integration," *Zeitschrift für Sozialreform* 43 (1997): 102.
9. Martin Kohli, "Die DDR als Arbeitsgesellschaft? Arbeit, Lebenslauf und soziale Differenzierung," in *Sozialgeschichte der DDR*, ed. Hartmut Kaelble, Jürgen Kocka, and Hartmut Zwahr (Stuttgart, 1994), 39.
10. Herbert Obinger and Carina Schmitt, "Guns and Butter? Regime Competition and the Welfare State during the Cold War," *World Politics* 63 (2011).
11. Hans Günter Hockerts, "Einführung," in *Drei Wege deutscher Sozialstaatlichkeit. NS-Diktatur, Bundesrepublik und DDR im Vergleich*, ed. Hans Günter Hockerts (Munich, 1998), 14.
12. Peter Hübner, "Die deutsch-deutsche Sozialstaatskonkurrenz nach 1945," in *Die Krise des Sozialstaats*, ed. Martin Sabrow (Leipzig, 2007), 31.
13. Hübner, "Sozialstaatskonkurrenz," 48.
14. On the historical background of the term "normal employment" (*Normalarbeitsverhältnis*), see Toni Pierenkemper and Klaus Zimmermann, "Zum Aufstieg und Niedergang des Normalarbeitsverhältnisses in Deutschland 1800–2010—ein Forschungsprojekt," in *Jahrbuch für Wirtschaftsgeschichte* 50 (2009): 232f.
15. Rainer Geißler, *Die Sozialstruktur Deutschlands. Ein Studienbuch zur sozialstrukturellen Entwicklung im geteilten und vereinten Deutschland* (Opladen, 2014), 59.
16. Josef Mooser, "Abschied von der 'Proletarität.' Sozialstruktur und Lage der Arbeiterschaft in der Bundesrepublik in historischer Perspektive," in *Sozialgeschichte der Bundesrepublik Deutschland. Beiträge zum Kontinuitätsproblem*, ed. Werner Conze (Stuttgart, 1983), 162.
17. Ulrich Beck, *Risikogesellschaft. Auf dem Weg in eine andere Moderne* (Frankfurt a. M., 1986), 124f.
18. Karl M. Bolte, "Strukturtypen sozialer Ungleichheit. Soziale Ungleichheit in der Bundesrepublik Deutschland im historischen Vergleich," in *Lebenslagen, Lebensläufe, Lebensstile*, ed. Peter A. Berger and Stefan Hradil (Göttingen, 1990), 36–49.
19. Wilfried Rudloff, "Im Schatten des Wirtschaftswunders: Soziale Probleme, Randgruppen und Subkulturen 1949 bis 1973," in *Bayern im Bund*, vol. 2: *Gesellschaft im Wandel 1949–1973*, ed. Thomas Schlemmer and Hans Woller (Munich, 2002), 347–467.
20. Burkart Lutz, "Integration durch Aufstieg. Überlegungen zur Verbürgerlichung der deutschen Facharbeiter in den Jahrzehnten nach dem Zweiten Weltkrieg," in *Bürgertum nach 1945*, ed. Manfred Hettling and Bernd Ulrich (Hamburg, 2005), 307.

21. Mooser, "Abschied," 172. On the significance of the expanding civil service section as a channel of upward mobility for the middle classes, see Berthold Vogel, *Wohlstandskonflikte. Soziale Fragen, die aus der Mitte kommen* (Hamburg, 2009), 116–69.
22. Cf. the essay by Emmanuel Droit and Wilfried Rudloff in this volume.
23. Cf. Maren Möhring's essay in this volume.
24. *The World Top Income Database* (Website); Irene Becker and Richard Hauser, "Wird unsere Einkommensverteilung immer ungleicher? Einige Forschungsergebnisse," in *Sozialstaat in der Globalisierung*, ed. Dieter Döring (Frankfurt am Main, 1999), 97. This assessment for the poorest-earning fifth of the population refers to the period between 1962–1978.
25. Hans Günter Hockerts, "Rahmenbedingungen. Das Profil der Reformära," in *Geschichte der Sozialpolitik in Deutschland seit 1945*, vol. 5: *Bundesrepublik Deutschland 1966–1974. Eine Zeit vielfältigen Aufbruchs*, ed. Hans Günter Hockerts (Baden-Baden, 2006), 143.
26. Pension rights in the 1970s were roughly equivalent to the doubled volume of the assets belonging to private households. Werner Abelshauser, *Deutsche Wirtschaftsgeschichte seit 1945* (Munich, 2004), 347.
27. For a recent account on this topic, see Cornelius Torp, *Gerechtigkeit im Wohlfahrtsstaat: Alter und Alterssicherung in Deutschland und Großbritannien von 1945 bis heute* (Göttingen, 2015), 88–107; Alfred C. Mierzejewski, *A History of the German Public Pension System. Continuity amid Change* (Lanham 2016), 200–4.
28. Kohli, "DDR," 38.
29. Heike Solga, *Auf dem Weg in eine klassenlose Gesellschaft? Klassenlagen und Mobilität zwischen Generationen in der DDR* (Berlin, 1995), 130, 236.
30. Thomas Mergel, "Soziologie und soziale Ungleichheit als Problem der DDR-Soziologie," in *Das Soziale ordnen. Sozialwissenschaften und gesellschaftliche Ungleichheit im 20. Jahrhundert*, ed. Christiane Reinecke and Thomas Mergel (Frankfurt a. M., 2012), 327–30.
31. Jens Gieseke, "Soziale Ungleichheit im Staatssozialismus. Eine Skizze," *Zeithistorische Forschungen/Studies in Contemporary History* 10 (2013): 4.
32. Hans Günter Hockerts and Winfried Süß, "Gesamtbetrachtung: Die sozialpolitische Bilanz der Reformära," in *Geschichte der Sozialpolitik in Deutschland seit 1945*, vol. 5: *Bundesrepublik Deutschland 1966–1974. Eine Zeit vielfältigen Aufbruchs*, ed. Hans Günter Hockerts (Baden-Baden, 2006), 948–54.
33. Hans Günter Hockerts, "Vom Problemlöser zum Problemerzeuger? Der Sozialstaat im 20. Jahrhundert," *Archiv für Sozialgeschichte* 47 (2007): 16–29; Winfried Süß, "Der bedrängte Wohlfahrtsstaat. Deutsche und europäische Perspektiven auf die Sozialpolitik der 1970er-Jahre," in *Archiv für Sozialgeschichte* 47 (2007): 103–26; Paul Pierson, "Post-industrial Pressures on the Mature Welfare States," in *The New Politics of the Welfare State*, ed. Paul Pierson (Baltimore, 1995), 82–91.

34. F.-X. Kaufmann, "Der Sozialstaat als Prozess. Für eine Sozialpolitik zweiter Ordnung," in *Verfassung, Theorie und Praxis des Sozialstaats. Festschrift für Hans F. Zacher zum 70. Geburtstag*, ed. Franz Ruland (Heidelberg, 1998), 307–22.
35. On this point and the following, see Winfried Süß, "Umbau am 'Modell Deutschland.' Sozialer Wandel, ökonomische Krise und wohlfahrtsstaatliche Reformpolitik in der Bundesrepublik 'nach dem Boom,'" *Journal of Modern European History* 9 (2011): 228–36.
36. M. H. Geyer, "Sozialpolitische Denk- und Handlungsfelder: Der Umgang mit Sicherheit und Unsicherheit," in *Geschichte der Sozialpolitik in Deutschland seit 1945, vol. 6: Bundesrepublik Deutschland 1974–1982. Neue Herausforderungen, wachsende Unsicherheiten*, ed. Martin H. Geyer (Baden-Baden, 2008), 226–31.
37. Axel Schildt, "Wohnungspolitik," in *Drei Wege deutscher Sozialstaatlichkeit. NS-Diktatur, Bundesrepublik und DDR im Vergleich*, ed. Hans Günter Hockerts (Munich, 1998), 185.
38. Peter Hübner, "Fortschrittskonkurrenz und Krisenkongruenz? Europäische Arbeitsgesellschaften und Sozialstaaten in den letzten Jahrzehnten des Kalten Krieges (1970–1989)," *Zeitgeschichte* 34 (2007): 144.
39. André Steiner, "Leistungen und Kosten: Das Verhältnis von wirtschaftlicher Leistungsfähigkeit und Sozialpolitik in der DDR," in *Sozialstaatlichkeit in der DDR. Sozialpolitische Entwicklungen im Spannungsfeld von Diktatur und Gesellschaft 1945/49–1989*, ed. Dierk Hoffmann and Michael Schwartz (Munich, 2005), 34f., 40.
40. Christoph Boyer, Klaus-Dietmar Henke, and Peter Skyba, "Gesamtbetrachtung," in *Die Geschichte der Sozialpolitik in Deutschland seit 1945, vol. 10: Deutsche Demokratische Republik 1971–1989. Bewegung in der Sozialpolitik, Erstarrung und Niedergang*, ed. Christoph Boyer, Klaus-Dietmar Henke, and Peter Skyba (Baden-Baden, 2008), 767f.
41. Detlev Pollack, "Die konstitutive Widersprüchlichkeit der DDR. Oder: War die DDR-Gesellschaft homogen?," *Geschichte und Gesellschaft* 24 (1998): 118f.
42. See the contribution to this volume by Christopher Neumaier and Andreas Ludwig.
43. Boyer, Henke, and Skyba, "Gesamtbetrachtung," 777.
44. See the brilliant attempt at such an explanation in Christoph Boyer, "Lange Entwicklungslinien europäischer Sozialpolitik im 20. Jahrhundert. Eine Annäherung," *Archiv für Sozialgeschichte* 49 (2009): 43, 49–56.
45. Rainer Geißler, *Die Sozialstruktur Deutschlands. Ein Studienbuch zur sozialstrukturellen Entwicklung im geteilten und vereinten Deutschland* (Opladen, 1992), 201.
46. Lutz Raphael, "Flexible Anpassungen und prekäre Sicherheiten. Industriearbeit(er) nach dem Boom," in *Die Anfänge der Gegenwart. Umbrüche in*

Westeuropa nach dem Boom, ed. Morten Reitmayer and Thomas Schlemmer (Munich, 2014), 55.
47. Jens Alber, Der Sozialstaat in der Bundesrepublik 1950–1983 (Frankfurt a. M., 1989), 299–304.
48. Becker and Hauser, "Wird unsere Einkommensverteilung," 98, 111; Christoph Birkel, "Einkommensungleichheit und Umverteilung in Westdeutschland, Großbritannien und Schweden 1950 bis 2000," Vierteljahrshefte zur Wirtschaftsforschung 75 (2006): 181f.
49. Winfried Süß, "Vom Rand in die Mitte der Gesellschaft. Armut als Problem der deutschen Sozialgeschichte 1961–1989," in Sozialstaat Deutschland. Geschichte und Gegenwart, ed. Ulrich Becker, Hans Günter Hockerts, and Klaus Tenfelde (Bonn, 2010), 125–30.
50. Süß, "Rand," 131–38; Christoph Lorke, Armut im geteilten Deutschland. Die Wahrnehmung sozialer Randlagen in der Bundesrepublik Deutschland und der DDR (Frankfurt a. M., 2015), 339–76, 363.
51. Heike Solga, "'Systemloyalität' als Bedingung sozialer Mobilität im Staatssozialismus, am Beispiel der DDR," Berliner Journal für Soziologie 4 (1994): 529–38.
52. Gieseke, "Ungleichheit," 6, 9–12.
53. Steiner, "Leistungen," 38.
54. R. M. Lepsius, "Soziale Ungleichheit und Klassenstrukturen in der Bundesrepublik Deutschland," in Klassen in der europäischen Sozialgeschichte, ed. Hans-Ulrich Wehler (Göttingen, 1979), 179–82.
55. Philip Manow-Borgwardt, "Die Sozialversicherung in der DDR und der BRD 1945–1990: Über die Fortschrittlichkeit rückschrittlicher Institutionen," Politische Vierteljahresschrift 35 (1994): 46f.
56. For a fundamental overview of this period, see Gerhard A. Ritter, ed., Geschichte der Sozialpolitik in Deutschland seit 1945, vol. 11: Bundesrepublik Deutschland 1989–1994. Sozialpolitik im Zeichen der Vereinigung (Baden-Baden, 2007).
57. Richard Hauser, "Zwei deutsche Lastenausgleiche—Eine kritische Würdigung," Vierteljahrshefte zur Wirtschaftsforschung 80 (2011): 121.
58. Gerhard A. Ritter, "Gesamtbetrachtung," in Geschichte der Sozialpolitik in Deutschland seit 1945, vol. 11: Bundesrepublik Deutschland 1989–1994. Sozialpolitik im Zeichen der Vereinigung, ed. Gerhard A. Ritter (Baden-Baden, 2007), 1110; Idem, "Sozialpolitische Denk- und Handlungsfelder im Einigungsprozess," in Geschichte der Sozialpolitik in Deutschland seit 1945, 11:290–294.
59. Ritter, "Denk- und Handlungsfelder," 281f.
60. Christine Trampusch, Der erschöpfte Sozialstaat. Transformation eines Politikfeldes (Frankfurt a. M., 2009), 107.
61. Frank Nullmeier, "Die Sozialstaatsentwicklung im vereinten Deutschland. Sozialpolitik der Jahre 1990 bis 2014," in Grundlagen und Herausforderun-

gen des Sozialstaats. Denkschrift 60 Jahre Bundessozialgericht. Eigenheiten und Zukunft von Sozialpolitik und Sozialrecht, ed. Ulrich Becker (Göttingen, 2014), 190.
62. Manfred G. Schmidt, "Noch immer auf dem 'mittleren Weg'? Deutschland seit den 1990er Jahren," in Grundlagen und Herausforderungen des Sozialstaats. Denkschrift 60 Jahre Bundessozialgericht. Eigenheiten und Zukunft von Sozialpolitik und Sozialrecht, ed. Ulrich Becker (Göttingen, 2014), 225f.
63. Hans Günter Hockerts, "Vom Wohlfahrtsstaat zum Wohlfahrtsmarkt? Privatisierungstendenzen im deutschen Sozialstaat," in Privatisierung. Idee und Praxis seit den 1970er Jahren, ed. Norbert Frei and Dietmar Süß (Göttingen, 2012).
64. Hans G. Hockerts, "Abschied von der Dynamischen Rente. Über den Einzug der Demografie und der Finanzindustrie in die Politik der Alterssicherung," in Sozialstaat Deutschland. Geschichte und Gegenwart, ed. Ulrich Becker, Hans Günter Hockerts, and K. Tenfelde (Bonn, 2010).
65. Anke Hassel and Christof Schiller, Der Fall Hartz IV. Wie es zur Agenda 2010 kam und wie es weitergeht (Frankfurt a. M., 2010), 26–54.
66. Dietmar Süß and Winfried Süß, "Zeitgeschichte der Arbeit. Beobachtungen und Perspektiven," in Nach dem "Strukturbruch." Kontinuität und Wandel von Arbeitsbeziehungen und Arbeitswelt(en) seit den 1970er Jahren, ed. Knud Andresen, Ursula Bitzegeio, and Jürgen Mittag (Bonn, 2011); Christoph Weischer, "Soziale Ungleichheit 3.0. Soziale Differenzierungen in einer transformierten Industriegesellschaft," Archiv für Sozialgeschichte 54 (2014).
67. Martin Kohli and Harald Künemund, "Verschärfen oder verringern Erbschaften die soziale Ungleichheit?," in Die Ökonomie der Gesellschaft, ed. Sylke Nissen and Georg Vobruba (Wiesbaden, 2009).
68. Philip Ther, Die neue Ordnung auf dem alten Kontinent. Eine Geschichte des neoliberalen Europa (Berlin, 2014), 136–73; United Nations, ed., Human Development Report. Overcoming Barriers: Human Mobility and Development (New York, 2009), 195–98.
69. Geißler, "Sozialstruktur," 457; 466–74.
70. Paritätischer Wohlfahrtsverband, ed., Zwischen Wohlstand und Verarmung: Deutschland vor der Zerreißprobe. Bericht zur regionalen Armutsentwicklung in Deutschland 2013 (Berlin, 2013), 10.
71. Infratest-dimap, ed., Repräsentativbefragung 25 Jahre Mauerfall: Systemvergleich BRD/DDR im Auftrag des MDR (Berlin, 2014), 4f.
72. Weischer, "Soziale Ungleichheit 3.0," 342.
73. Weischer, "Soziale Ungleichheit 3.0," 339.
74. Vogel, "Sicher—Prekär," 75, 89.
75. Stephan Lessenich and Frank Nullmeier, "Einleitung: Deutschland zwischen Einheit und Spaltung," in Deutschland—eine gespaltene Gesellschaft, ed. Stefan Lessenich and Frank Nullmeier (Frankfurt a. M., 2006), 7–27.

BIBLIOGRAPHY

Abelshauser, Werner. *Deutsche Wirtschaftsgeschichte seit 1945.* Munich: C. H. Beck, 2004.
Alber, Jens. *Der Sozialstaat in der Bundesrepublik 1950–1983.* Frankfurt a. M.: Campus, 1989.
Beck, Ulrich. *Risikogesellschaft. Auf dem Weg in eine andere Moderne.* Frankfurt a. M.: Campus, 1986.
Birkel, Christoph. "Einkommensungleichheit und Umverteilung in Westdeutschland, Großbritannien und Schweden 1950 bis 2000." *Vierteljahrshefte zur Wirtschaftsforschung* 75 (2006): 174–94.
Bolte, Karl Martin. "Strukturtypen sozialer Ungleichheit. Soziale Ungleichheit in der Bundesrepublik Deutschland im historischen Vergleich." In *Lebenslagen, Lebensläufe, Lebensstile,* edited by Peter A. Berger and Stefan Hradil, 27–50. Göttingen: Otto Schwartz & Co., 1990.
Boyer, Christoph. "Lange Entwicklungslinien europäischer Sozialpolitik im 20. Jahrhundert. Eine Annäherung." *Archiv für Sozialgeschichte* 49 (2009): 25–67.
Boyer, Christoph, Klaus-Dietmar Henke, and Peter Skyba. "Gesamtbetrachtung." In *Geschichte der Sozialpolitik in Deutschland seit 1945,* vol. 10: *Deutsche Demokratische Republik 1971–1989. Bewegung in der Sozialpolitik, Erstarrung und Niedergang,* edited by Christoph Boyer, Klaus-Dietmar Henke, and Peter Skyba, 765–94. Baden-Baden: Nomos, 2008.
Busse, Reinhard, and Annette Riesberg. *Health Care Systems in Transition: Germany.* Copenhagen: WHO Regional Office for Europe on behalf of the European Observatory on Health Systems and Policies, 2004.
Dallinger, Ursula. "Erwartungen an den Wohlfahrtsstaat. Besteht eine 'innere Mauer' zwischen West- und Ostdeutschen?" In *Leben in Ost- und Westdeutschland. Eine sozialwissenschaftliche Bilanz der deutschen Einheit 1990–2010,* edited by Peter Krause and Ilona Ostner, 573–96. Frankfurt a. M.: Campus, 2010.
Geißler, Rainer. *Die Sozialstruktur Deutschlands. Ein Studienbuch zur sozialstrukturellen Entwicklung im geteilten und vereinten Deutschland.* Opladen: Westdeutscher Verlag, 1992.
———. *Die Sozialstruktur Deutschlands. Ein Studienbuch zur sozialstrukturellen Entwicklung im geteilten und vereinten Deutschland.* 7th ed. Opladen: Westdeutscher Verlag, 2014.
Geyer, Martin H. "Sozialpolitische Denk- und Handlungsfelder: Der Umgang mit Sicherheit und Unsicherheit." In *Geschichte der Sozialpolitik in Deutschland seit 1945,* vol. 6: *Bundesrepublik Deutschland 1974–1982. Neue Herausforderungen, wachsende Unsicherheiten,* edited by Martin H. Geyer, 111–231. Baden-Baden: Nomos, 2008.
Gieseke, Jens. "Soziale Ungleichheit im Staatssozialismus. Eine Skizze." *Zeithistorische Forschungen/Studies in Contemporary History* 10 (2013): 171–98.

Grabka, Markus M. "Private Vermögen in Ost- und Westdeutschland gleichen sich nur langsam an." *DIW Wochenbericht* 40 (2014): 959–66.

Grabka, Markus M., Jan Goebel, and Jürgen Schupp. "Höhepunkt der Einkommensungleichheit in Deutschland überschritten?" *DIW Wochenbericht* 43 (2012): 3–15.

Grosser, Dieter. *Das Wagnis der Währungs-, Wirtschafts- und Sozialunion. Politische Zwänge im Konflikt mit ökonomischen Regeln.* Stuttgart: Deutsche Verlags-Anstalt, 1998.

Hassel, Anke, and Christof Schiller. *Der Fall Hartz IV. Wie es zur Agenda 2010 kam und wie es weitergeht.* Frankfurt a. M.: Campus, 2010.

Hauser, Richard. "Zwei deutsche Lastenausgleiche—Eine kritische Würdigung." *Vierteljahrshefte zur Wirtschaftsforschung* 80 (2011): 103–22.

Becker, Irene, and Richard Hauser. "Wird unsere Einkommensverteilung immer ungleicher? Einige Forschungsergebnisse." In *Sozialstaat in der Globalisierung*, edited by Dieter Döring, 89–116. Frankfurt a. M.: Campus, 1999.

Hockerts, H. G. "Abschied von der Dynamischen Rente. Über den Einzug der Demografie und der Finanzindustrie in die Politik der Alterssicherung." In *Sozialstaat Deutschland. Geschichte und Gegenwart*, edited by Ulrich Becker, Hans Günter Hockerts, and Klaus Tenfelde, 257–86. Bonn: Dietz-Verlag, 2010.

———. "Einführung." In *Drei Wege deutscher Sozialstaatlichkeit. NS-Diktatur, Bundesrepublik und DDR im Vergleich*, edited by Hans Günter Hockerts, 7–25. Munich: De Gruyter, 1998.

———. "Einführung." In *Soziale Ungleichheit im Sozialstaat. Großbritannien und die Bundesrepublik im Vergleich*, edited by Hans Günter Hockerts and Winfried Süß, 9–18. Munich: C. H. Beck, 2010.

———. "Vom Problemlöser zum Problemerzeuger? Der Sozialstaat im 20. Jahrhundert." *Archiv für Sozialgeschichte* 47 (2007): 3–29.

———."Rahmenbedingungen. Das Profil der Reformära." In *Geschichte der Sozialpolitik in Deutschland seit 1945*, vol. 5: *Bundesrepublik Deutschland 1966–1974. Eine Zeit vielfältigen Aufbruchs*, edited by Hans Günter Hockerts, 1–155. Baden-Baden: Nomos, 2006.

———. "Vom Wohlfahrtsstaat zum Wohlfahrtsmarkt? Privatisierungstendenzen im deutschen Sozialstaat." In *Privatisierung. Idee und Praxis seit den 1970er Jahren*, edited by Norbert Frei and Dietmar Süß, 70–87. Göttingen: Wallstein, 2012.

Hockerts, Hans Günter, and Winfried Süß. "Gesamtbetrachtung: Die sozialpolitische Bilanz der Reformära." In *Geschichte der Sozialpolitik in Deutschland seit 1945*, vol. 5: *Bundesrepublik Deutschland 1966–1974. Eine Zeit vielfältigen Aufbruchs*, edited by Hans Günter Hockerts, 942–63. Baden-Baden: Nomos, 2006.

Hübner, Peter. "Die deutsch-deutsche Sozialstaatskonkurrenz nach 1945." In *Die Krise des Sozialstaats*, edited by Martin Sabrow, 25–61. Leipzig: Leipziger Universitätsverlag, 2007.

———. "Fortschrittskonkurrenz und Krisenkongruenz? Europäische Arbeitsgesellschaften und Sozialstaaten in den letzten Jahrzehnten des Kalten Krieges (1970– 1989)." *Zeitgeschichte* 34 (2007): 144–50.

Infratest-dimap, ed. *Repräsentativbefragung 25 Jahre Mauerfall: Systemvergleich BRD/DDR im Auftrag des MDR.* Berlin: Infratest-dimap, 2014.

Kaufmann, Franz-Xaver. "Der Sozialstaat als Prozess. Für eine Sozialpolitik zweiter Ordnung." In *Verfassung, Theorie und Praxis des Sozialstaats. Festschrift für Hans F. Zacher zum 70. Geburtstag,* edited by Franz Ruland, 307–22. Heidelberg: Müller, 1998.

Kohli, Martin. "Die DDR als Arbeitsgesellschaft? Arbeit, Lebenslauf und soziale Differenzierung." In *Sozialgeschichte der DDR,* edited by Hartmut Kaelble, Jürgen Kocka, and Hartmut Zwahr, 31–61. Stuttgart: Klett Cotta, 1994.

Kohl, Martin, and Harald Künemund. "Verschärfen oder verringern Erbschaften die soziale Ungleichheit?" In *Die Ökonomie der Gesellschaft,* edited by Sylke Nissen and Georg Vobruba, 94–107. Wiesbaden: Verlag für Sozialwissenschaften, 2009.

Krause, Peter, and Ilona Ostner. "Einleitung: Was zusammengehört. Eine sozialwissenschaftliche Bilanzierung des Vereinigungsprozesses." In *Leben in Ost- und Westdeutschland. Eine sozialwissenschaftliche Bilanz der deutschen Einheit 1990–2010,* edited by Peter Krause and Ilona Ostner, 11–36. Frankfurt a. M.: Campus, 2010.

Lepsius, Rainer M. "Soziale Ungleichheit und Klassenstrukturen in der Bundesrepublik Deutschland." In *Klassen in der europäischen Sozialgeschichte,* edited by Hans-Ulrich Wehler, 166–209. Göttingen: Vandenhoek & Ruprecht, 1979.

Lessenich, Stephan, and Frank Nullmeier. "Einleitung: Deutschland zwischen Einheit und Spaltung." In *Deutschland—eine gespaltene Gesellschaft,* edited by Stefan Lessenich and Frank Nullmeier, 7–27. Frankfurt a. M.: Campus, 2006.

Lutz, Burkart. "Integration durch Aufstieg. Überlegungen zur Verbürgerlichung der deutschen Facharbeiter in den Jahrzehnten nach dem Zweiten Weltkrieg." In *Bürgertum nach 1945,* edited by Manfred Hettling and Bernd Ulrich, 284–305. Hamburg: Hamburger Edition, 2005.

Lorke, Christoph. *Armut im geteilten Deutschland. Die Wahrnehmung sozialer Randlagen in der Bundesrepublik Deutschland und der DDR.* Frankfurt a. M.: Campus, 2015.

Madaràsz-Lebenhagen, Jeannette, and Antja Kampf. "Prävention in zwei deutschen Staaten in den 1950er bis 1970er Jahren. Geschlechterbilder im Umgang mit chronischen Erkrankungen des Herz-Kreislauf-Systems." In *Asymmetrisch Verflochten. Neue Forschungen zur gesamtdeutschen Nachkriegsgeschichte,* edited by Udo Grashoff, Detlef Brunner, and Andreas Kötzing, 148–65. Berlin: Ch. Links, 2013.

Manow, Philip. "Die Sozialversicherung in der DDR und der BRD 1945–1990: Über die Fortschrittlichkeit rückschrittlicher Institutionen." *Politische Vierteljahresschrift* 35 (1994): 40–61.

———. "Entwicklungslinien ost- und westdeutscher Gesundheitspolitik zwischen doppelter Staatsgründung, deutscher Einigung und europäischer Integration." *Zeitschrift für Sozialreform* 43 (1997): 101–31.
Mergel, Thomas. "Soziologie und soziale Ungleichheit als Problem der DDR-Soziologie." In *Das Soziale ordnen. Sozialwissenschaften und gesellschaftliche Ungleichheit im 20. Jahrhundert*, edited by Christiane Reinecke and Thomas Mergel, 307–36. Frankfurt a. M.: Campus, 2012.
Mooser, Josef. "Abschied von der 'Proletarität.' Sozialstruktur und Lage der Arbeiterschaft in der Bundesrepublik in historischer Perspektive." In *Sozialgeschichte der Bundesrepublik Deutschland. Beiträge zum Kontinuitätsproblem*, edited by Werner Conze, 143–86. Stuttgart: Klett Cotta, 1983.
Mierzejewski, Alfred C. *A History of the German Public Pension System: Continuity amid Change*. Lanham: Lexington Books, 2016.
Nullmeier, Frank. "Die Sozialstaatsentwicklung im vereinten Deutschland. Sozialpolitik der Jahre 1990 bis 2014." In *Grundlagen und Herausforderungen des Sozialstaats. Denkschrift 60 Jahre Bundessozialgericht. Eigenheiten und Zukunft von Sozialpolitik und Sozialrecht*, edited by Ulrich Becker, 181–99. Göttingen: Erich Schmidt Verlag, 2014.
Obinger, Herbert, and Carina Schmitt. "Guns and Butter? Regime Competition and the Welfare State during the Cold War." *World Politics* 63 (2011): 246–70.
Paritätischer Wohlfahrtsverband, ed. *Zwischen Wohlstand und Verarmung: Deutschland vor der Zerreißprobe. Bericht zur regionalen Armutsentwicklung in Deutschland 2013*. Berlin: Paritätischer Wohlfahrtsverband, 2013.
Pierenkemper, Toni, and Klaus Zimmermann. "Zum Aufstieg und Niedergang des Normalarbeitsverhältnisses in Deutschland 1800–2010—ein Forschungsprojekt." *Jahrbuch für Wirtschaftsgeschichte* 50 (2009): 231–42.
Pierson, Paul. "Post-industrial Pressures on the Mature Welfare States." In *The New Politics of the Welfare State*, edited by Paul Pierson, 80–104. Baltimore: Johns Hopkins University Press, 1995.
Pollack, Detlev. "Die konstitutive Widersprüchlichkeit der DDR. Oder: War die DDR-Gesellschaft homogen?" *Geschichte und Gesellschaft* 24 (1998): 110–31.
Raphael, Lutz. "Flexible Anpassungen und prekäre Sicherheiten. Industriearbeit(er) nach dem Boom." In *Die Anfänge der Gegenwart. Umbrüche in Westeuropa nach dem Boom*, edited by Morten Reitmayer and Thomas Schlemmer, 51–64. Munich: De Gruyter, 2014.
Ritter, Gerhard A. "Gesamtbetrachtung." In *Geschichte der Sozialpolitik in Deutschland seit 1945*, vol. 11: *Bundesrepublik Deutschland 1989–1994. Sozialpolitik im Zeichen der Vereinigung*, edited by Gerhard A. Ritter, 1105–22. Baden-Baden: Nomos, 2007.
———. "Sozialpolitische Denk- und Handlungsfelder im Einigungsprozess." In *Geschichte der Sozialpolitik in Deutschland seit 1945*, vol. 11: *Bundesrepublik Deutschland 1989–1994. Sozialpolitik im Zeichen der Vereinigung*, edited by Gerhard A. Ritter, 107–349. Baden-Baden: Nomos, 2007.

Rudloff, Wilfried. "Im Schatten des Wirtschaftswunders: Soziale Probleme, Randgruppen und Subkulturen 1949 bis 1973." In *Bayern im Bund*, vol. 2: *Gesellschaft im Wandel 1949–1973*, edited by Thomas Schlemmer and Hans Woller, 347–467. Munich: De Gruyter, 2002.

Schildt, Axel. "Wohnungspolitik." In *Drei Wege deutscher Sozialstaatlichkeit. NS-Diktatur, Bundesrepublik und DDR im Vergleich*, edited by Hans Günter Hockerts, 151–89. Munich: De Gruyter, 1998.

Schmidt, Manfred G. "Noch immer auf dem 'mittleren Weg'? Deutschland seit den 1990er Jahren." In *Grundlagen und Herausforderungen des Sozialstaats. Denkschrift 60 Jahre Bundessozialgericht. Eigenheiten und Zukunft von Sozialpolitik und Sozialrecht*, edited by Ulrich Becker, 221–40. Göttingen: Erich Schmidt Verlag, 2014.

Schmidt, Manfred G., and Gerhard A. Ritter. *The Rise and Fall of a Socialist Welfare State: The German Democratic Republic (1949–1989) and German Unification (1989–1994)*. Heidelberg: Springer, 2013.

Solga, Heike. *Auf dem Weg in eine klassenlose Gesellschaft? Klassenlagen und Mobilität zwischen Generationen in der DDR*. Berlin: Akademie-Verlag, 1995.

———. "'Systemloyalität' als Bedingung sozialer Mobilität im Staatssozialismus, am Beispiel der DDR." *Berliner Journal für Soziologie* 4 (1994): 523–42.

Statistisches Bundesamt, ed. *Bevölkerung und Erwerbstätigkeit. Sterbetafeln: Früheres Bundesgebiet und neue Bundesländer 2009/2011*. Wiesbaden: Stat. Bundesamt, 2012.

Steiner, André. "Leistungen und Kosten: Das Verhältnis von wirtschaftlicher Leistungsfähigkeit und Sozialpolitik in der DDR." In *Sozialstaatlichkeit in der DDR. Sozialpolitische Entwicklungen im Spannungsfeld von Diktatur und Gesellschaft 1945/49–1989*, edited by Dierk Hoffmann and Michael Schwartz, 31–45. Munich: De Gruyter, 2005.

Süß, Dietmar, and Winfried Süß. "Zeitgeschichte der Arbeit. Beobachtungen und Perspektiven." In *Nach dem "Strukturbruch." Kontinuität und Wandel von Arbeitsbeziehungen und Arbeitswelt(en) seit den 1970er Jahren*, edited by Knud Andresen, Ursula Bitzegeio, and Jürgen Mittag, 345–68. Bonn: Dietz-Verlag, 2011.

Süß, Winfried. "Der bedrängte Wohlfahrtsstaat. Deutsche und europäische Perspektiven auf die Sozialpolitik der 1970er-Jahre." *Archiv für Sozialgeschichte* 47 (2007): 95–126.

———. "Umbau am 'Modell Deutschland.' Sozialer Wandel, ökonomische Krise und wohlfahrtsstaatliche Reformpolitik in der Bundesrepublik 'nach dem Boom.'" *Journal of Modern European History* 9 (2011): 215–40.

———. "Vom Rand in die Mitte der Gesellschaft. Armut als Problem der deutschen Sozialgeschichte 1961–1989." In *Sozialstaat Deutschland. Geschichte und Gegenwart*, edited by Ulrich Becker, Hans Günter Hockerts, and Klaus Tenfelde, 123–39. Bonn: Dietz-Verlag, 2010.

Ther, Philip. *Die neue Ordnung auf dem alten Kontinent. Eine Geschichte des neoliberalen Europa*. Berlin: Suhrkamp, 2014.

Torp, Cornelius. *Gerechtigkeit im Wohlfahrtsstaat: Alter und Alterssicherung in Deutschland und Großbritannien von 1945 bis heute.* Göttingen: Vandenhoeck & Ruprecht, 2015.

Trampusch, Christine. *Der erschöpfte Sozialstaat. Transformation eines Politikfeldes.* Frankfurt a. M.: Campus, 2009.

United Nations, ed. *Human Development Report: Overcoming Barriers: Human Mobility and Development.* New York: Palgrave Macmillan, 2009.

Vogel, Berthold. "Sicher—Prekär." In *Deutschland—eine gespaltene Gesellschaft,* edited by Stefan Lessenich and Frank Nullmeier, 73–91. Frankfurt a. M.: Campus, 2006.

———. *Wohlstandskonflikte. Soziale Fragen, die aus der Mitte kommen.* Hamburg: Hamburger Edition, 2009.

Wegner, Bernd, and Stefan Liebig. "Gerechtigkeitsvorstellungen in Ost- und Westdeutschland im Wandel: Sozialisation, Interessen, Lebenslauf." In *Leben in Ost- und Westdeutschland. Eine sozialwissenschaftliche Bilanz der deutschen Einheit 1990–2010,* edited by Peter Krause and Ilona Ostner, 83–101. Frankfurt a. M.: Campus, 2010.

Weischer, Christoph. "Soziale Ungleichheit 3.0. Soziale Differenzierungen in einer transformierten Industriegesellschaft." *Archiv für Sozialgeschichte* 54 (2014): 305–42.

CHAPTER 5

Rationalization, Automation, and Digitalization
Transformations in Work

Rüdiger Hachtmann

Many East German workers were hit by a shock just after the Wall fell. One employee at the pharmaceutical factory of the VEB Leipziger Arzneimittelwerke recalled that no one in 1990 "could even begin to come to terms with unemployment" and the idea that they "might actually be affected by it personally." Unemployment "simply didn't exist," he explained. In the GDR, he noted, people only "knew about unemployment through television." If all the talk of unemployment in the Federal Republic on West German television "had become too annoying"—especially since unemployment kept hitting record highs in the mid-1970s and eventually reached the two-million mark at the end of the 1980s—"we simply switched back to East German television. There was no unemployment there."[1]

Indeed, the guarantee of full employment in the GDR was one of the fundamental differences between East and West Germany before 1989. Even those East Germans who were able to retain their jobs after the Wall came down still noticed that "other issues took center stage" on the factory floor after reunification. As many former GDR residents noted, one was "under stress" in a different way after 1990, and one had to learn "not to make any mistakes" and that "people didn't help each other out as much." Rather than easing into the workday, they claimed, the pressure was on as soon as time cards were punched. East Germans who took up jobs in the West described the atmosphere at work as "cold" compared to their experiences in the GDR.[2] At the same time, however, many West

German employees also claimed that work had been less stressful in the 1970s and 1980s. Not only in the East, but also in the West, the workplace was changing rapidly in the 1990s thanks to technological innovations, deregulation, and flexibilization. But whereas increases in social pressure were seen as a consequence of reunification in the East, they tended to be attributed to globalization in the West.

Until 1989, both the East and West German worlds of work were bound by similar frameworks, and they faced similar challenges, which can be summed up under the rubrics of "rationalization," "automation," and "digitalization." Yet, thanks to the different natures of their respective systems, they followed separate trajectories prior to 1989. In terms of the organization of work and production technology, which were decisive factors for the individual workplace, both Germanys looked westward. The FRG closely tracked the developments in the United States, while the GDR was particularly interested in what was happening in West Germany. Why was the SED unable to achieve comparable results when it came to industrial rationalization? Why did the world of work seem to be so strangely static in East Germany, especially during the Honecker era, while rationalization was accelerating dynamically in the West at the same time? How did rationalization and globalization shape the structures of gainful employment in the "old" Federal Republic? Did older trends continue seamlessly in the whole of the Federal Republic (including the new East German states) after the *Wende* in 1989/90? Did some processes accelerate or perhaps take a new direction?

According to basic statistic indicators, most of the secular trends related to these questions seem to have continued unchanged. The percentage of Germans employed in the agricultural sector dwindled from 8.4 percent in 1970 (West Germany) to just 1.6 percent in 2010. Likewise, the percentage of industrial workers among the entire employed population sank considerably from 46.5 percent (West Germany) to 24.5 percent.[3] Based on rough figures, reunification seems to have had little or no effect on the shift toward a "service society" within the Federal Republic. For the wider service sector, the assessment that little changed in the world of work in the GDR appears to be overly hasty when the aggregate data is analyzed from a bird's eye point of view. It is therefore not only worthwhile to discuss the comparability of the constellations in the East and West on this level, but also in terms of all the elements that structured gainful employment. This chapter thus examines these similarities and differences while pointing out key trends that can be detected in post-reunification Germany.

The first section outlines the political and legal frameworks that were in place while casting light on broader trends. The second part looks at the implications of rationalization efforts on gainful employment in the industrial sector in West Germany as opposed to East Germany. The third section focuses on structural transformations in gainful employment within the service sector from the 1970s to the beginning of the twenty-first century, paying special attention to precarious job situations.

Frameworks

The constitutions of the two German states laid out fundamentally different frameworks for each society, beginning with their catalogs of basic rights. Whereas the GDR constitution established the right to work, the *Grundgesetz* (Basic Law) of the Federal Republic makes no mention of it. Instead, the government of the FRG expanded the social benefits system for the unemployed and fostered internal employee participation within companies and factories after 1949. Although the right to work was tied to a duty to work that was imposed in a politically repressive way in the GDR, which meant that *Werktätigen* ("working people") who opposed the political system could be demoted to lesser jobs, it was virtually impossible for employees to lose their jobs. The right to work anchored in the GDR constitution (Article 24) and the corresponding Law on Work (*Gesetz der Arbeit*) from 1950, as well as the Labor Code (*Gesetzbuch der Arbeit*) from 1962/1974, contained fundamental political concessions granted to workers and employees who were collectively referred to as *Werktätigen*. They were the key source of legitimization for the SED, which styled itself as the "avant-garde of the working class" and its "workers' and peasants' state."

The permanent employment guarantee that was tied to the right to work granted the working population in East Germany a great deal of leeway in their everyday work. The national economy put into place by the SED followed the model of a late-Stalinist style, centralized-command economy. Thus, since the party had the last word on all political, social, and economic questions, it had to bear the blame for any grievances, material shortages, or production stops, as well as the poor organization of labor resources or complaints about unfair wages. In Western market economies, on the other hand, companies and employers remained solely responsible for such issues, functioning as an intermediary institution that buffered dissatisfaction politically when it bubbled up to the top. Although government spending in the FRG already amounted to about 45 percent of the GDP in 1975 and continued to climb slightly, conflicts and labor disputes tended to be directed at different targets in the East than in the West.

Correspondingly, there was a tight surveillance network at work in GDR factories, as well as sociopolitical early warning systems in place, such as the company union committees (Betriebsgewerkschaftsleitung, or BGL), etc. Admittedly, however, this state apparatus of control and repression always had to keep in mind that the legitimacy of the SED state rested on the "working people." Nonetheless, those "who shied from work by stubbornly refusing to take a regular job despite being able to work" were stigmatized. In keeping with paragraph 249 of the GDR criminal code, they could also be sentenced to "remedial work education" and even "imprisonment for up to two years" in ostensibly severe cases. Yet this weapon was rather ineffective when it came to those who were disinclined to work, faked illnesses in order to call off work, or were just slackers in general. As the head of one of the largest GDR combines (factories) aptly lamented, "Of course [!] we had some slackers who didn't even bother to show up to the factory for two years, but we weren't allowed to fire them."[4] Such cases would never have been tolerated in West Germany, although employees did have more leeway and room to negotiate for quite a while during the phase of full employment. By the end of the 1970s, however, growing unemployment put a damper on this more open climate.

The structures of collective bargaining also differed at a basic level in the two Germanys. In the SED state, collective framework agreements were negotiated between the central committees of the individual unions organized within the Free German Trade Union Federation (Freier Deutscher Gewerkschaftsbund, or FDGB) and the respective state functionaries; these agreements were then supplemented by collective agreements for individual plants. More so than in Poland or Hungary, for example, self-employed people were a marginal group in the GDR, and politics played directly into collective bargaining. In the West, on the other hand, employers, who were themselves organized within umbrella organizations, exerted considerable influence over the collective wage agreements that were negotiated with the respective trade unions and regularly renewed or revised. Accordingly, these agreements were flexible, and they could be adapted to changing economic and political constellations. Moreover, they relieved the state of the responsibility for further sociopolitical demands and expectations in terms of wages, benefits, or contract negotiations. The state was not forced to intervene in order to achieve a settlement or another solution of some sort to resolve interest differences between employers and employees. However, an elaborate system of state social policy absorbed some of the tensions that resulted from the antagonism between capital and work. The federal government as well as the states exerted considerable influence over working conditions by establishing legal frameworks and institutions such as the Federal Institute for Occupational Safety and Health and its corresponding local supervisory offices (Gewerbeaufsicht).

But, the fact that the collective bargaining agreements for the different sectors have become less binding over time has torn away at the fabric of Germany's social constitution since the 1990s. The number of employers who have abandoned existing collective bargaining agreements or who seek to worm their way out of having to uphold minimum wage standards has been increasing at a considerable rate since 1989/90; this appeared first in the new federal states in particular, but it has now spread all over the country. In 2006, the percentage of German companies who were contractually obligated to follow collective bargaining agreements that applied to either the whole sector or their individual companies was only around 60 percent. Germany therefore lagged far behind countries such as Estonia and Italy (80 percent), as well as the Scandinavian and Benelux countries (over 80 percent).[5] Moreover, the number of loopholes and escape clauses built into these agreements continued to climb, while internal company "alliances for work" ate away at their core premises.

The federal German labor laws, however, set up the framework for a corrective to these trends, which was designed to cushion the impact of social conflicts, namely separate courts for labor issues that were reestablished after the collapse of the Nazi regime in West Germany. In the GDR, however, the municipal and district labor courts were dissolved in April 1961; in their place, "chambers for labor matters" were established within the municipal and district courts. The fact that only a small number of cases actually made their way to the labor courts before these changes took effect indicates that the internal "conflict resolution commissions" that had existed since April 1953 took care of most the issues that cropped up within individual companies. The declining importance of labor courts and the priority given to out-of-court arbitration and mediation authorities can be attributed to the fact that the SED generally denied the existence of social differences for ideological reasons. In the preamble of the procedural code for labor courts (*Arbeitsgerichtsordnung*) in the GDR from 29 June 1961, labor disputes were denounced as the "remnants of bourgeois ways of thinking and living habits."

Nonetheless, the place of work was a more important part of the lives of individual employees in the GDR compared to the FRG, especially since childcare options, vacation terms, and recreational activities were often dictated by the individual workplaces. Admittedly, the expansion of this infrastructure was not only politically and ideologically desirable, but also was fostered by the high percentage of female employment, which was considerably above that of the West. As of 1973, the Offices for Work and Wages (Ämter für Arbeit und Löhne) were responsible for the management of the workforce (until 1951, Employment Offices [Arbeitsämter]); 1951 to 1961, Departments of Labor (Abteilungen für Arbeit); 1961 to 1973, Offices for Work and Vocational Counseling (Ämter für Arbeit und Berufsberatung). The planning bureaucracy could mandate the transfer of employees from one plant to another, and even impose sanctions if these directives were not followed. Nonetheless, the "stockpiling" of extra workers was not uncommon. Ultimately, however, the full employment policy of the GDR was only a success on paper. Countless people were considered to be employed, although they were not really needed in the workflow or operating processes. This generally low level of labor productivity compared to Western industrial states can therefore be seen as an expression of an invisible form of mass unemployment. Moreover, the disproportionately inflated administrative and security apparatus of the SED state created superfluous jobs as well.

The FRG also experienced what was a de facto phase of full employment following the "Korea boom," which fostered rationalization of workforce organization and production technology, especially in the industrial sector. It also accounts for the state-sponsored stream of foreign "guestworkers" that flocked to West Germany well into the 1970s. Such measures were also largely designed to rein in the growing number of mothers who were becoming wage-earners. Notwithstanding, the percentage of women within the employment population rose from 37.1 percent in 1960 to 44.4 percent in 2005 (only in the "West"); there were clear jumps in these figures in the 1970s and 1980s, as well as after the turn of the twenty-first century, which were actually periods in which unemployment was on the upswing.[6] Consequently, the rising number of working women did not stem from the need for additional labor, but rather from the expansion of the educational system and a cultural transformation in women's self-images that was strengthening their desire to become economically independent.

Although unemployment reached an all-time statistical low in 1970, with approximately a hundred thousand (frictional) unemployed, it increased steadily from that point on; by 1989, it had climbed to around 2.3 million. According to the Federal Statistical Office (Statistisches Bundesamt), unemployment jumped to about five million (2005) following reunification before bouncing back nominally to about three million (see table 5.1). Naturally, these figures do not provide any qualitative information about the jobs that were counted statistically as "employment." Moreover, the rapidly growing structural unemployment in the "old Federal Republic" that had set in around the mid-1970s points to fundamental processes of transformation that engulfed the highly industrial societies of the West, affecting all sectors of the West German economy.

Table 5.1. Employment and Unemployment in Germany from 1970 to 2010 (the figures cited up to and including 1990 are only for West Germany)

Year	Number of employed individuals (in millions)	Employment rate	Number of unemployed individuals (in millions)	Unemployment rate
1970	26.8	44.2 percent	0.103	0.4 percent
1975	26.9	43.6 percent	0.613	2.3 percent
1980	28.0	45.4 percent	0.483	1.7 percent
1985	29.7	48.6 percent	1.976	6.7 percent
1990	31.8	50.3 percent	1.423	4.5 percent
1995	41.1	50.3 percent	3.205	7.8 percent
2000	42.9	52.2 percent	3.114	7.3 percent
2005	43.7	53.0 percent	4.506	10.3 percent
2010	43.8	53.6 percent	2.821	6.4 percent

Source: Statistisches Bundesamt, ed., Volkswirtschaftliche Gesamtrechnungen. Inlandsproduktsberechnung, Lange Reihen ab 1970. Fachserie 18 Reihe 1.5 (Wiesbaden, 2014), retrieved 25 May 2018, https://www.destatis.de/DE/Publikationen/Thematisch/VolkswirtschaftlicheGesamtrechnungen/Inlandsprodukt/InlandsproduktsberechnungLangeReihen PDF_2180150.pdf?__blob=publicationFile.

The significance of trade unions also varied between East and West Germany. In the GDR, all employees were de facto required to belong to a union, namely the FDGB, which was an appendage of the SED until 1989. In democratic societies, on the other hand, membership in trade unions is of course voluntary. The social and political significance of a trade union in such countries is therefore largely determined by the constellations of the labor markets. A high rate of structural unemployment normally leads to a lasting decline in their influence, while full employment typically strengthens the position of employees. This was very much the case in West Germany. The trade unions organized within the German Trade Union Federation (DGB) were at their strongest at the height of the full employment phase. Accordingly, their membership statistics thus reached a zenith in the 1970s and 1980s. The number of DGB members jumped from 5.4 million in 1950 to 8.0 million in 1981 (7.9 million in 1989). Reunification brought another boost in membership, bringing the number of DGB members up to 11.8 million in 1991. Since then, however, these figures have declined steadily, sinking to 9.8 million in 1994/95 and then 8.0 million just five years later. By 2013, the DGB had only 6.1 million members, which was almost half as many as in 1991.[7] The reasons behind these losses are myriad. In addition to the structural aspects already mentioned, others, such as the emergence of new service sectors just as the importance of traditional economic branches and vocational groups that had been highly organized in the past began to shrink, also factored into the shifts. Yet other types of factors also played a key role in this process. These included the increasing depoliticization of social life and the difficulties the unions faced in attracting younger people in particular. Similarly, the growing percentage of female workers within the working population who did not believe that their interests were well represented in the traditionally male-dominated unions also contributed to this decline.

Furthermore, the fundamentally varying labor laws and the substantially different position of the unions in both German states indicate a difference in the respective structures of conflict. The constitution of the GDR from 1949, for example, guaranteed the right to strike. Yet from the outset, the FDGB, which was dominated by the Communist parties (KPD and SED), refrained from engaging in any labor disputes in the state-owned companies and factories, which "belonged to the people" at least in name. It made no sense, the argument was made, for workers to strike against themselves, as they were supposedly the owners in the first place. This political and legal fiction was then debunked entirely in the wake of the events of 17 June 1953. Neither the Labor Code (*Gesetzbuch der Arbeit*) from 1961 and 1978, nor the constitution from 1968 recognized the right to strike. As a result, strikes were akin to a direct political attack against the SED in East Germany. Nonetheless, other lines of conflict still developed within the GDR. Plant managers and workers, including plant union leaders, often made an effort to combat excessive demands and expectations as well as other unreasonable requests from "above" with informal pacts from "below."[8]

In the Federal Republic, on the other hand, the right to strike and the right of association is guaranteed. However, the number of legal labor disputes remained relatively low in comparison to other West European states. This was due, in part, to the strong hold of neocorporatism, which encompassed a well-functioning mechanism for regulating conflicts within plants in the form of the work councils (*Betriebsräte*) that were introduced in 1952; this was augmented by the resulting relatively high share of employees who benefited from the growth in productivity.[9] Since the 1990s, moreover, the elevated level of structural unemployment has also mitigated the desire to strike.

In addition to this high unemployment, the lasting decline of the trade unions, as well as the increasing tendency of employers to ignore the wages set out in collective bargaining agreements, has shaped income and wage development since 1990. Nominal wages were not as decisive per se in the GDR given the subsidization of basic food items, the frequent shortages in consumer goods, and the great importance of informal "ties" when it came to be able to make purchases. Even the softening of the egalitarian wage structure through different types of wage bonus systems from the 1970s onward had only a minimal effect. In the Federal Republic before and after reunification, however, the development of wages is and has been a key indicator of workers' standards of living. While the growth in annual gross income was still about 8.5 percent on average in 1980, the yearly growth rates since the mid-1990s have increased at small intervals compared to previous decades (between 0.5 percent and 4 percent, with zero or negative "growth" in 1997, 2003, 2005, and 2009). There were even phases when annual net real incomes shrank noticeably: they decreased by about 7 percent across the country between 1993 and 1998 alone, slumping again between 2004 and 2009, and they have been dropping since 2011 yet again.[10] The clear increase in part-time work over the last two decades is undoubtedly partially responsible for this development. In and of itself, this has been part of a long-term trend that had assumed considerable proportions in Germany since the mid-1930s, but it has clearly been gaining speed since the beginning of the 1990s.[11] The rapid rise of half-day shifts and flexible working hours has led to a surge in part-time employment from 2.6 million (1991) to 3.5 million (1998) and then 5 million (2011). These figures also reflect the improved options for mothers and fathers to combine career and family. Simultaneously, though, these numbers are increasingly indicative of a trend toward more precarious employment situations. Although the average number of real working hours per week under full-time employees decreased in the 1980s, high structural unemployment and the fear of being laid off or fired contributed greatly to an increase in working time after reunification, from 39.7 hours in 1995 to 40.4 hours in 2008.[12]

The Industrial Sector

From Fordism to Toyotism: Rationalization on the March in the West

The pressure on company executives to rationalize was particularly dependent on the unemployment rate, as well as the level of the personnel costs. As early as the 1950s and 1960s, full employment and rising wage costs generated an enormous amount of pressure in this regard. This has only further increased since the 1970s, accompanied by the rapid globalization of foreign trade and capital flows, the accelerated internationalization of large corporations, and the tougher competition between national production sites. It has resulted in a steady increase in labor productivity in all economic sectors (see table 5.2). Admittedly, "labor productivity" is somewhat vague as a macroeconomic indicator. It not only obscures differences according to industry, plant size, etc., but also factors in the simple (raw) intensification of work. Additionally, it does not provide any indications about the degree and depth of the radical changes in production or information technology that have taken place, even though they were quite hefty in the last thirty years of the twentieth century.

The structural changes in the industrial sector have often been termed a "crisis" or the "end of Fordism" in economic and sociological discourse. These phrases involuntarily invoke the exceptional significance that was attached to "Fordism" (and "Taylorism") in the core industrial sectors for a long time. A key element of the ideal type of "classic" Fordism is the principle of a continually running yet relatively fixed system of mass production.[13] Both the Taylorist and Fordist models of production rely on mass distribution and a high level of standardization in workflow and finished products. At a conceptual level, factory Fordism is intrinsically dynamic because it (ideally!) functions through evermore perfect synchronization within an ever more complex machine "environment," accompanied by the tendency to replace an initially large number of unskilled workers engaged in a minimal number of monotone steps with "automated machines." The end of the road for Fordism, at least as a

Table 5.2. Labor Productivity in the Federal Republic of Germany per Employed Person and Hour of Work from 1970 to 2010 (Index 1970=100.0—the figures cited only apply for the former West Germany up to and including 1990)

Year	Labor productivity per	
	Employee	Hour of work
1970	100.00	100.00
1975	114.19	124.32
1980	128.98	144.87
1985	137.09	161.38
1990	146.40	182.51
1995	160.88	206.42
2000	168.15	227.03
2005	175.59	243.91
2010	178.96	252.41

Source: Statistisches Bundesamt, Volkswirtschaftliche Gesamtrechnungen (results calculated by the author).

model, is a fully automated factory staffed entirely by robots. Indeed, this tendency toward self-abrogation, or rather calculated obsolescence, is inherent within the Fordist model of production.

In turn, the dynamic unleashed by Fordism within individual plants exerts an enormous amount of influence on the structures of the workforce. When true to the model, skilled workers would fuse together into a small stratum at the outset. Their vocational profiles and assigned tasks would also change fundamentally, shifting more toward the setting up and surveillance of Fordist assembly lines. The majority of the production workers on the line would then (ideally) be trained for a short time. The proportion of skilled (supervisory) workers would then increase, while that of "simple workers" on the assembly line would shrink in accordance with the level of automation and perfection of the assembly line process. This general process was very much at work in West Germany as well as in other highly industrialized Western countries from the 1960s onward.

There were other elements that extended beyond the level of an individual factory that could be classified as "Fordist." Mass consumption, which rested on the three pillars of mass production, higher incomes, and mass distribution, as well as technological innovation—all of which made it possible to turn more and more luxury goods into mass products—was just one such aspect. The eight-hour day and the clear distinction between work and leisure time was a second element, while relatively long-term and secure employment was a third. Lastly, the idea of a "work-life balance," in which the center of life shifted toward leisure time and vacation, could also be considered a "Fordist" trend. Furthermore, specific types of corporate organization and culture, especially strong external control over employees and well-defined vertical integration, also fell under this rubric, as did the tendency toward so-called corporate self-sufficiency.

Global developments, however, have increasingly called the "Fordist" model into question since the mid-1970s. Japan's "economic miracle," for example, put a great deal of economic pressure on Western Europe. In particular, all eyes turned toward the major automaker Toyota, which had been developing a (seemingly) new production scheme since the beginning of the 1950s. Toyota quickly became the new act to follow. A key element of "Toyotism" is the just-in-time principle. It rests on the idea that the exact number of the right parts for each step in the production process is ready to go exactly when they are needed. The just-in-time principle also necessitates to the retraining of those workers (still) employed on the assembly line so that they can resolve any standstills resulting from production hold-ups or defects in machinery; workers also need to be able to operate different machines in order to be able to keep up with the planned flow rate. The just-in-time principle is augmented by the Kanban inventory control system. The latter deviates slightly from the classic assembly line idea because workers who are involved in a downstream production step pick up the parts that they need from the respective upstream production step. As a result, a limited type of teamwork becomes necessary. Although the Toyota production system has some flexibility, it is still very close to a Fordist model.[14]

For one or two decades, Toyotism dominated discourses on production, yet pragmatic considerations shaped how it was implemented in corporations. But then the even more radical teamwork model associated with the Swedish automaker Volvo came to dominate these discourses.[15] More so than in the Toyota production system, the members of the production group at Volvo carried out quite different tasks, which generally avoided lopsided workloads and allowed workers to act semi-autonomously (at least) within their teams.[16] Toyotism and the Volvo model became permanent fixtures within industrial discourse thanks not least to the political connotations of the debate over the "crisis of Fordism." This crisis seemed to stem from a variety of sources. In the wake of the long-lasting phase of full employment that held on into the 1970s, corporate managers began to worry about increasing labor turnover and the number of workdays lost due to illness. They saw both of these phenomena as indicative of widespread dissatisfaction with the monotony of working on the assembly line, which meant that alternatives needed to be found. But these were not the only factors that were fueling the fires behind the "crisis of Fordism." The 1968 students' movement also played an important role, although it did not attract apprentices and young workers on a large scale until a bit later. Provoked to a large extent by these protests, a discourse on alienation that drew on the early works of Karl Marx arose. It primarily targeted Fordism in a historical and empirical way, influencing the sometimes hefty debates that took hold of the trade unions in the 1970s. Some feminists within the New Women's Movement also objected to the monotony of the tasks assigned to women who worked on the assembly lines; traditionally, theories of work had discriminated against women in this respect, justifying the assignment of such menial tasks.

The "crisis of Fordism" took a virulent turn in the core Western industrial regions in the form of "attacks against supervisors, sabotage, shoddy work, go-slow protests and wild strikes," which, "in the eyes of experts" (according to *Der Spiegel* in early July 1973), had been unleashed by the "torture of the hamster wheel" that was the assembly line.[17] Naturally, though, these experts also noted, a "revolt against the assembly line" could only take place in times of full employment when no one feared being fired for their actions. The high rate of unemployment since the mid-1980s thus kept the lid on any overt protests, yet it did not herald a return to the primitive "old" kind of factory Fordism.

Patchwork Solutions and Improvisation instead of Production Flow—Industry in the GDR

The discourse and praxis of Fordism took a different course in the GDR. The production principles espoused by Taylor and especially Ford had been heartily embraced in the Soviet Union since the 1920s,[18] and the SED state followed in the footsteps of its "big brother." Notwithstanding, however, the SED basically failed in its attempts to introduce such a production regime even just in the core manufacturing sectors in East Germany. A whole slew of reasons blocked its efforts, cumulatively putting the brakes on production in general.

First, the centrally planned economy, by its very nature, did not allow the individual plants to introduce and implement fundamental innovations in production technology; this was not an issue for industrial corporations in a capitalist market-based economy. While West German companies found themselves facing global economic competition that forced them to invest in often quite expensive new technologies, East German companies were not subject to such capitalist stimulation. Any extensive rationalization projects always had to be "politically sanctioned," which meant that they had to be afforded political legitimacy by the respective supervisory body or the SED politburo as the final authority. This was even true for measures that had been instigated from "above." As Claus Krömke, the personal secretary of Günter Mittag from 1962 to 1989, commented in retrospect, "it wasn't possible to just say, now you should all do this and that." Furthermore, the fact that supervisory authorities always had to sanction any new measures considerably increased the level of bureaucratic red tape. It was therefore virtually impossible for the dynamism that made Fordism the industrial production regime that it was to develop in the GDR. Second, notwithstanding the static nature of GDR industry, the chronic lack of capital made the implementation of "at least somewhat modern means of production" one of the "major weaknesses of the combines." As the long-time general manager of Carl Zeiss Jena, Wolfgang Biermann, noted laconically, "You can't build modern assembly lines with old lathe machines."[19]

A third, no-less-important factor was that modernization of any kind was "never achieved along the entire chain, but rather only in certain links" within the overly political and heavily bureaucratic economic system of the GDR.[20] The publicly owned operations (referred to as VEB, which stood for Volkseigener Betrieb) that produced end goods were highly dependent on external suppliers, but they had virtually no recourse options in the event that suppliers did not properly fulfill the terms of their contracts. Consequently, suppliers often missed the delivery deadlines that had been agreed to or failed to deliver the right quantities; alternatively, the products they did supply were of substandard quality.[21] The larger and relatively autonomous combines in particular thus began to manufacture the semifinished products that they needed themselves. This resulted in greater vertical integration, which leaned in the direction of autarkic combines. At the same time in the West, however, numerous large corporations were quite successful in doing the opposite—namely, increasing their efficiency by reducing vertical integration.

The trend towards autarky was even stronger in production technology. Historical baggage left over from the division of Germany played into this development. Until 1945, almost all carmakers, for instance, depended on the West German mechanical engineering industry to produce the specialized and tailored machinery that they needed for highly developed assembly-line production systems. For a long time, there was not a single company in the GDR that was able to fill in this gap. Indeed, at no point did a functional division of work that could have compensated for this deficit emerge within the COMECON.[22] As a result, only partially suitable all-purpose machinery or outdated and unreliable specialized machines were used on the automobile manufacturing assembly lines in the GDR. However, in order to achieve a relatively efficient assembly line production system—after having narrowed production down to two basic models, namely the "Trabant" and the "Wartburg" in 1959—both car manufacturing plants began to produce their own machines in order to construct a Fordist-style system. Apart from the fact that this absorbed additional technical intelligence, neither of the publicly owned car-making factories in Zwickau and Eisenach was ever able to even partially fulfill its own demand for the right kind of specialized machinery; this situation was further exacerbated by the insufficient resources that the plants had been provided "from above."

Moreover, the condition of the outdated machinery in the factories in East Germany deteriorated even further in the 1970s and 1980s. According to Western standards, more than half of all the industrial production apparatuses in the GDR were considered to be "ready for the scrap heap" in 1989/90.[23] The lack of capital, as well as the priority that was given to housing construction during the Honecker era, also stood in the way of building new factory buildings that could properly accommodate modern assembly lines; at best, only a stripped-down version of such assembly lines could be installed in the old factory facilities. Thus, the Fordist production lines that did exist—almost always in fragmented form—never really ran smoothly. Except in a very few cases, none of the plans to import entire production facilities or partial manufacturing technology systems from providers in the West ever bore fruit.

Fourth, the GDR had a serious human resources problem. The planning commission sought to assign an additional number of planned employment positions to the individual factories within the framework of its investment in rationalization and expansion. Yet it remained to be seen whether or not the factories were truly able to hire additional personnel. Especially given the chronic competition to attract employees in the GDR and the tendency among all the larger operations to hold on to unnecessary workers so that they could rely on these extra hands when things broke down (which was not that seldom) in order to be able to still meet their quotas, efforts at modernization often failed because the necessary positions could not be filled.

Since it was virtually impossible to overcome the roadblocks standing in the way of substantial rationalization in production technology, it made sense to try to increase workloads by means of traditional Taylorist methods. But, even these endeavors faced insurmountable difficulties. For much of the industrial workforce, REFA, the German version of Taylorism and assembly-line manufacturing, had been tainted by the strong scent of capitalist exploitation since the 1920s. The general aversion to "stress and pressure at work" along Taylorist and Fordist lines survived the Nazi dictatorship, becoming even more virulent in the SBZ/GDR. The uprising on 17 June 1953 that had been provoked by more demanding work norms, which were really Taylorist-style measures that had been introduced administratively, hit the SED where it hurt, revealing one of its major sore points: it was not really possible to push through the increases in workloads that were necessary to force industrialization against the will of the "working people" because workers were considered to be the main pillar of support for the regime, and the SED claimed to represent their "objective" interests. After the uprising was put down, the fear of another wave of strikes akin to those of mid-1953, which has been termed the "June syndrome," made the SED more hesitant to introduce any kind of rationalization measures in the factories.

All the efforts to put "old wine into new wineskins" by changing the terminology used to describe the forms of rationalization and workload increases that the regime hoped to implement, which resembled those that had been developed before and after 1945 "in the West," proved to be futile. Since the 1960s, for example, the addition of "socialist" to the term "rationalization" was part of a calculated political attempt to "sell" this concept. Such ideas also included "technical-organizational measures" (TOM), which laid the groundwork for Fordist and Taylorist initiatives.

These, in turn, revived concepts that had been dominant prior to 1945, which reappeared in virtually unmodified forms at first. The Scientific Work Organization program (Wissenschaftliche Arbeitsorganisation, or WAO) bore a striking resemblance to classic Taylorist methods. In implementing this program, SED economists drew on the Methods-Time Measurement (MTM) system, which had been developed in the United States; this system was a more elaborate version of the Taylorist time measurement method.[24] All things considered, the recoding of these terms and the reliance on Western expertise when it came to modern forms of production technology and workflows did not have much use. On the whole, as scholarship on the automobile industry has illustrated, the supplier factories did not implement major internal rationalization measures "at all," while the factories responsible for final assembly in Zwickau and Eisenach only managed to do so "in a few exceptional cases."[25]

Likewise, not even older "American" production ideas were able to gain a firm foothold in most of the other industries in the GDR without major lag times. In the 1970s and 1980s, traditional Fordist structures were increasingly being replaced by more flexible production systems in West Germany, but the industrial sector in the GDR, as Peter Hübner noted, "was not even close to getting over the first hurdle."[26] For all intents and purposes, the leadership of the SED state effectively abandoned all of its initiatives to bring about a major modernization of production technology in manufacturing operations such as carmakers.[27] In 1989, productivity across the GDR was about a third less than in the FRG. The factories were only able to maintain their production volumes through constant "self-help" measures and economic as well as political juggling. Factory managers more or less became "masters of improvisation."[28] The same could also be said of their "subjects" who were also forced to hone their skills at improvisation in order to deal with the continual production hold-ups and machinery outages. The talented workmanship and advanced technical skills of both male and female workers employed in the East German industrial sector thus proved to be a major asset. The percentage of skilled workers and master craftsmen (not including those with advanced technical and university degrees) within the workforce as a whole increased from 53 percent in 1975 to 64 percent in 1985; correspondingly, the percentage of semiskilled and unskilled workers dropped from 33 percent down to 15 percent.[29]

Moreover, social pressure, as well as material incentives, were lacking on the shop floor in East German factories. As a result, most working people had accustomed themselves to an easy-going workday, and the number of absences was comparably high.[30] By the end of the 1970s, the demands that the DGB trade unions were making on the other side of the Wall had become a reality in the GDR. The legally defined workweek in East Germany went from 48 hours in 1949 to 43.5 in 1972, before dropping further to 42.9 in 1988; in the last decade before reunification, however, East Germans actually worked on average only about 36 hours per week.[31]

The Limits of Robotization

Around the same time, union demands for shorter work hours across the board began to disappear from the agenda again in the Federal Republic. The new buzz word was "flexible working hours," which was accompanied by the notion that the "end of Fordism," or even more fundamentally, the "end of our work society" (*"Ende der Arbeitsgesellschaft"* was a phrase coined by Ralf Dahrendorf in 1982 at the Bamberg Conference of Sociologists), was coming. In addition to the expansion of the service sector, the so-called Third Industrial Revolution fed into this discursive shift. This third wave of industrialization was reflected in the trends toward full automation and robotization, as well as digitalization, which were supposed to create a factory utopia without human workers. This vision for the future of industry, however, was very much rooted in the dynamics of Fordist production. After all, it was not a coincidence that the Ford factory in Detroit became home to the first robot in the car manufacturing industry in 1961. Ford had also been the first carmaker to establish its own automation department back in 1946.[32] In West Germany, it was the Volkswagen (VW) plant in Wolfsburg, which was the incarnation of Fordism and the economic miracle in the early postwar period, that developed a particular preference for the use of robots.

The move toward extensive robotization, however, met with unexpected difficulties.[33] Similar to FIAT, for example, VW had followed the Japanese model and automated parts of its car manufacturing system under the motto that "Robby"—which referred to robots—"does the dirty work" (as cited in the factory newsletter in 1982). In doing so, it hoped to significantly accelerate production times and reduce costs. But, by the end of the decade, the company's executives had to face the surprising fact that the standstill phases were even longer than before. The reason for this proved to be that the robots were unable to properly deal with any situations that deviated from the norm. They were only capable of reacting appropriately to foreseeable situations for which they had been programmed. The robots lacked the "tacit knowledge" of their human counterparts that came from socialization, "common sense," and experience; they did not know what to do when unexpected situations arose, nor could they improvise when necessary. Leading VW managers were forced to concede that humans "cannot just simply be traded for machines." In part for this reason, Toyotism kept a remarkably firm hold on production in large industrial companies. "A quiet return to strongly collaborative and standardized production systems" thus set in from the mid-1990s, and "Toyota—Asian discipline—has become the model to follow." With the onset of the financial crisis in 2008, the "work cycles on the assembly lines" at Mercedes-Benz, Bosch, and the Zahnradfabrik Friedrichshafen were "shortened even further." In the words of one of the workers' council members at the Zahnradfabrik Friedrichshafen, this resulted in "fewer and fewer movements, but always the same—'it's mind-deadening.'" The managers systematically reduced the number of more diversified steps. "Everything that is not strictly part of the production assembly line" the head of the workers' council at the Zahnradfabrik Friedrichshafen surmised in early 2009, is being "cut."[34]

Despite the unexpected rehabilitation of creative human labor and the continued existence of Toyota-style production regimes, the trend toward robotization in direct manufacturing has not been reversed. As the *Frankfurter Allgemeine Zeitung* headlined on 12 February 2015, robot manufacturers were "drowning in orders." In turn, innovative corporations in the main German industries operating on the global market have been hiring fewer and fewer unskilled production workers. Between 1993 and 2000 alone, the number of "plain workers" in the industrial sector nationwide sank by almost 30 percent, from 3.03 million to 2.15 million[35] (although their number increased in the growing service industry subsectors[36]). Repetitive jobs, which had been the norm for assembly line workers in the classic Fordist system, had been reduced down to the few shrinking "gaps" that were still left in the wake of full automation, especially in corporations with more capital, like those in the automotive and electronics industries. However, in other sectors of the manufacturing industry, such as wood and furniture making, simple forms of Fordist production systems and the unskilled labor needed to keep them going still continue to play a significant role in manufacturing.[37]

The fascination with industrial robots (IR) and the idea of a fully automated factory without human employees existed on both sides of the Wall. In the GDR, however, the failure of robotization did not necessarily lie in the fact that robots lacked "tacit knowledge"; rather, the "robot offensive" that was announced in 1980 never really got going in the first place because of system-related factors. The first devices that could be described as "robots" were installed in automotive and machine tool factories in 1976 and 1978, respectively.[38] But most of these exemplars were rather primitive "feed-in robots" that loaded pieces into factory machinery. More complex "technological robots," such as those that could carry out welding or assembly tasks autonomously, were very few and far between. Similarly, the spectrum of available uses for robots was mostly smaller than in the West, and the corresponding technology was often outdated in the East. Whereas GDR robots were still controlled through hydraulic systems, for example, most of their West German counterparts ran on microelectronic control systems. Moreover, many of the East German robots did not meet the demands and standards of the factories in which they were supposed to be put to use. The managers of the machine tool combinate Fritz-Hecker in Chemnitz (known as Karl-Marx-Stadt at the time), the most important IR manufacturer in the GDR, had to concede that "the functional reliability of the IR could not be guaranteed in the majority of the factories for which they had been intended" due to poorly conceived designs and constructions. Likewise, the calls to "develop, manufacture, and use simpler IR devices that would be more reliable and more readily available," rather than concentrating on complex high-tech robots, were often dismissed.[39] As a result, robotization only came to play a marginal role in industries that were otherwise well suited to this kind of technology, such as the automobile industry.

But, above all, the robot offensive resembled a "Potemkin village project," as Hübner put it, because the definition of a "robot" was stretched beyond recognition under the motto "more is better" for the production of industrial robots.[40] At the end of the five-year plan that ran from 1981 to 1985, official figures cited a grand total of sixty thousand industrial robots, which clearly exceeded the planned goal of forty-five thousand. According to these statistics, moreover, over seventeen thousand robots were already in use in the GDR by the end of 1982. These numbers, however, were nothing but exaggerated. In a memo addressed to the head of the public statistics office, the Staatliche Zentralverwaltung für Statistik, dated 6 December 1982, it was noted that the impressive figure of almost twenty thousand IR would be reduced down to just over one thousand if the official definition of a robot according to the International Organization for Standardization (ISO) was used.[41] The last annual statistical report (Statistische Jahrbuch) for the GDR in 1990, which contained more realistic data, lists the rather modest sum of 1,760 "industrial robots for flexible processes" that had been manufactured in the previous year in accordance with the corresponding ISO standards.[42]

Although the economic cadres of the SED regime constantly kept an eye on the state of affairs in the West, they were not in a position to turn what they saw into something that could benefit their own industries. This was especially true for many aspects of production organization and manufacturing technology. Experts from the Amt für Standardisierung, Messwesen und Warenprüfung (Bureau for Standardization, Metrology and Product Testing), for example, visited Japan in the 1980s in order to study the Toyotist production regime on site. Yet this visit does not seem to have left any visible marks on the GDR industry.[43] Likewise, the SED regime was very much the loser when it came to "the pursuit of the chip"—the attempt to catch up to the level of digitalization in the West.

Competition on Unequal Footing: The Digitalization of Industrial Production in East and West

The increasingly widespread introduction of digital information and communications technology (ICT) from the 1970s onward led to the disappearance of certain occupational groups, such as typesetters, who had been part of a proud working-class aristocracy before they were made redundant by phototypesetting machines. Although the elimination of certain occupational groups as a result of technological progress had been part of industrial history since the very beginning, the digital revolution fundamentally redefined the workplace for all employees. Its most important components were not only the ever-growing storage, information, and computing capacities of individual computers, but also the development of networks, initially channeled through external centers and then later provided via servers.

As early as the late 1970s, all major companies in West Germany with more than five hundred employees had their own mainframes.[44] During this decade, networked ICT also made its way into actual manufacturing processes. Production workers, whose work used to be relatively autonomous in individual production or within the framework of small-scale series production, found themselves increasingly dependent on external actors and factors. Microelectronic programs progressively came to control the workflows of lathe operators, for example; these programs, however, were largely managed externally, by a new, superior occupational group, namely the programmers. The qualifications and experience of lathe operators lost value as a result.[45]

Likewise, the job descriptions of those who were responsible for the digitalization of production continued to change. From the 1990s, the creative development activities, which had been tasks done by engineers in the automotive industry and its suppliers well into the 1970s, were pushed aside and replaced by communication and coordination tasks; accordingly, the engineers themselves were more strongly integrated into the "command chains" within the factories, changing their job profiles as a result. Business and management skills became the top priority over time, while, at the same time, engineers were assigned to an increasing number of steps within workflows. To the dismay of the engineers at the mercy of these processes, the great autonomy that they had once enjoyed eroded over the course of the 1970s, although they still retained a measure of freedom. Simultaneously, the expansion of ICT increased the flood of information pouring over their desks, as well as the volume of documentation requirements. This was accompanied by the feeling among those affected that their jobs were no longer secure given the on-going rationalization process and the constant demand to reduce costs.[46] Yet the ramifications of the digital revolution have not only been negative. The transformation of engineering jobs and, to an even greater extent, the new demands placed on skilled workers, for instance, has not necessarily led to standardized tasks and a loss of independence or deskilling. Sometimes they have also broadened the scope of many professions, transforming what were once just cutting machine operators into "pseudo-programmers." Similarly, this has fostered the development of new professional fields, such as mechatronic engineering, which became a separate trade.

Although the digital revolution and the dynamics that it unleashed shook up the industrial workplace in the West, little changed in the GDR, despite the East's myriad efforts to jump on the digital bandwagon. Leading East German economists were well aware of the fact that the GDR could not isolate itself from the global economy and that it had to keep up with the newest production systems in order to remain competitive internationally. Yet their abstract recognition of this point clashed with the political and mental inflexibility that prevailed in the East. When economic experts returned home from Western Europe or Japan completely fascinated by the modernization of "production workflows and workforce discipline" that was taking place abroad, their enthusiasm was crushed at home. As Christa Bertag, the director of the Berlin cosmetics factory noted, these ideas were rejected along the lines of "we didn't send you over there so that you can start a revolution at home." As there was little willingness to change the way that things were being done, Bertag, and presumably others who had been part of these travel groups, "never again" tried to make suggestions for optimizing production workflows within factories.[47]

Furthermore, external factors also contributed to the disappointing failure of the attempts by the SED leadership to promote the advancement of microelectronic computing, storage, and management technologies in industrial production along Western lines. These included the limited implementation of microelectronic systems in military technology in the COMECON countries at first, the lack of foreign currency, the technology embargo that had been put up by the West, and the poor quality of the processors that were being made in the Czechoslovak Socialist Republic in particular (which was part of the division of work between member countries). Although considerable investment funds had been made available to the Carl Zeiss Jena Kombinat since the end of the 1970s, the results of this increased funding for one of the key players in the research and production of microchips in the East were not very impressive.[48] In addition, the so-called "data processing centers" with "computer stations" that were set up in many of the GDR's large factories were apparently never used to their full capacity, or they proved to be prone to problems. The same applied to CNC (computerized numerical control) machines as well as CAD (computer-aided design) and CAM (computer-aided manufacturing) systems. They were put to use in a number of factories, but they still played only a peripheral role.

Sobering Experiences with the Market Economy

Until 1989, hardly anything had changed on the job for the great majority of East Germans. As a result, many were hit by a shock as the country joined the West. Up to this point, it was only through West German television that they had experienced mass unemployment and the fear of being fired. The idea that their jobs could be at risk during the transitional phase in 1990 never actually entered the minds of countless East Germans. According to one report, "it wasn't even possible for many of them to realize that everything was over so quickly." At first, a lot of them "who were still euphoric about unification" thought "that this could not really happen... then, after the first lay-offs, their faces fell and their smiles turned into frowns."[49]

Even today, unemployment figures still differ clearly between the old and the new German federal states. They dropped from 14.8 percent (1994) to 10.3 percent (2013) in the East, but from 8.1 percent to 6.0 percent in the West during the same time period. Correspondingly, the differences in income between both parts of Germany decreased in the 1990s, but they by no means disappeared.[50] With time, the shock experienced by the East Germans turned into fatalism and resignation, described by a worker here: "A certain kind of sadness set in over the fact that things had to end the way they did." Our social world, as one coworker put it, was split between those who still had jobs and those "who found themselves on the streets" and had to "take the other road." The latter, he continued, "did not want to keep in touch [with their former colleagues who were still employed] anymore, because they felt like they had been pushed to the margins" and they had become bitter about it. Colleagues also reported that those who had kept their jobs complained that the atmosphere at work had become "colder." Not surprisingly, this ripped apart many of the tightly woven networks among colleagues and neighbors that had existed until 1989. Since the *Wende*, one worker noted, his colleagues "have had nothing but cars and trips on their minds," and after work, they "prefer to withdraw and watch TV in the privacy of their own homes rather than talking with people in social situations."[51]

The demise of the SED regime also had consequences for West Germany. After the collapse of the Communist bloc, the elites in the West no longer found it necessary to ensure that their own social model would be more attractive than the social paternalism of the East. The acceleration of globalization since 1990, as well as the debates over production sites that had been unleashed by it, served to legitimize the "dismantling" of social benefits, and the weakened trade unions could do little to stop this. Likewise, the changing demographic composition of the population, combined with the sharply rising costs for unemployment insurance resulting from the growth in structural unemployment, led to a dramatic redistribution of funds within the budget for social services. Simultaneously, ways of doing business and property relations also changed. On the one hand, corporate decision-making became increasingly reliant on the current constellations of the financial markets and the stock exchanges. On the other hand, hedge funds that sought to achieve short-term increases in profitability gained more and more influence over corporate politics in their role as major shareholders.

All of these factors—forced globalization, the transition from "stakeholders" to "shareholders," a high rate of structural unemployment, the end of the Cold War, and the waning pressure to keep up a high standard of social services that went along with it—stripped away at the cooperative model of "Rhenish capitalism" that had prevailed in West Germany since the 1950s with its strong welfare state. A large percentage of the population was still employed along Fordist lines with well-paying, permanent, full-time jobs that had clearly regulated working hours and strictly separate spheres of work and private life. Yet, the percentage of people with precarious job situations grew. More than ever before, corporate executives focused on cutting their human resource costs. Indeed, the switch to the use of the term "nonwage labor costs" (*Lohnnebenkosten*) as opposed to "social security contributions" (*Sozialabgaben*) at the beginning of the 1990s was not a coincidence because it reflected this colder social climate. Around the same time, moreover, the talk of the "end of our work society" died down. In its place, everyone began talking about the "new complexity" of the times.[52]

The West German IT Sector as a Forerunner for "New" Corporate Cultures

Corporate worlds have always been complicated and in flux. Yet digitalization and the constantly shifting international division of labor have only further intensified this complexity. Even just a glance at the new leading sector, the IT "industry," drives home how difficult it can be to try to understand the intricate constellations that have formed. Since the 1970s, this booming sector has increasingly blurred the lines between "industry" and "service," two areas that used to be easy to tell apart.

Just between 1998 and 2001, the number of employees in all the branches associated with this sector in Germany grew by a good 15 percent, climbing from 710,000 to 819,000. There is, however, a striking difference in the trends in different segments of the IT industry. Software development and other IT services, for example, expanded at an above-average tempo; in this short period alone, the number of employees in this field increased by almost 45 percent. In contrast, the "classic" office equipment manufacturers and the producers of other data-processing devices lost considerable ground. Employment in these segments dropped from 128,000 (1998) to 104,000 (2001), slumping by almost 19 percent. Telecommunications (the manufacturing of intelligence equipment and telecommunication services), however, grew in keeping with the general trend of the entire industry. The IT sector also became increasingly diversified in terms of business size and employment qualifications. Whereas the software development and IT service sector were dominated by start-up companies and small businesses for the most part, with a comparatively high percentage of university graduates (60 to 90 percent), the three other sectors (intelligence equipment, telecommunications services, and office and data-processing equipment) were controlled by large corporations. Moreover, the percentage of highly qualified individuals in these sectors was only about a third, and it was only between 10 and 20 percent in the field of telecommunication services.[53]

But, IT did not become the leading industry because it had a higher percentage of employees (employment was in fact much higher in many of the more established industries), but rather because the internal structures of the software development and IT start-ups became the business model that everyone wanted to follow. Thanks to the often more manageable number of employees in these companies at first, as well as the specific nature of their "products," these companies could not achieve their goals using a Taylorist distribution of labor or any Fordist methods. Rather than adopting such models, many start-up companies focused on teamwork, project-oriented work, goal-setting, and flat hierarchies, as well as a (supposedly) more personal management style when it came to the relationship between employees and their bosses. A high level of intrinsic motivation and employee self-motivation were seen as the key to achieving job goals, and this was often nourished by the illusion of nonalienating work prevalent among employees. This new corporate culture was further romanticized by the aura of the hippie milieu of Silicon Valley, as well as the casual hipster vibe that surrounded many software companies.

However, the self-image that many start-up companies within the New Economy projected of themselves as the antithesis of more traditional production regimes veils the fact that key elements of this supposedly "new" corporate culture are not really all that new. A casual climate among colleagues and the need to work extra hours when the situation demands, for instance, have been quite commonplace on farms or in small shops for a long time. Likewise, craftsmen were quite familiar with the idea of flexible hours depending on the current contracted project, as well as room and board in the home of master craftsmen (which effectively blurred the boundaries between work and private life) well into the twentieth century.

Alongside the rise of software manufacturers with their special dynamics, high profit margins, and often egalitarian claims (at least in the beginning), the flexibility that had always been associated with working as a doctor or in small artisan or farm businesses became more attractive. Ultimately, the fascination that accompanied the global success of companies such as Microsoft or SAP in Germany has at least partially broken the hold of classic forms of Fordist organization, even in older industries. Likewise, well-established major industries have also abandoned the traditional idea of an autarkic corporate model since the beginning of the 1990s. Instead, they have opted for less vertical integration—coupled with outsourcing—in addition to decentralized, elastic corporate networks that tend to operate at a global level, as well as the often extensive reliance on financial service providers demanding high profitability over the short term. Furthermore, large portions of the New Economy became "no worker participation zones." New communications structures, such as electronic forums and informal types of participation, seemed to make institutionalized representation for employees obsolete.

At the same time, the illusions of "alternative" corporate cultures waned to the same extent that young IT companies grew into large industrial corporations and "normalized." However, a kind of convergence did occur because the new possibilities generated through the digital revolution reshaped hierarchies and power relations within established industries as well. Thanks to digitalization, company executives—and to a certain extent middle management levels—had access to an enormous amount of information that could be structured as needed, forming the basis for the reporting and controlling systems that have been introduced and successively expanded since the 1990s. This wealth of information not only makes it easier for corporate leaders to make strategic decisions, but also allows them to steer internal discourses and introduce new ways of managing performance.

Craft Trades, the "Creative Industry," and Pseudo Self-Employment

Digitalization has also transformed the one economic sector that seems to embody tradition and perseverance more than any other, namely the craft trades. For a long time, this trade was only undergoing a transition in the West. Until the *Wende* in 1989/90, the gap between East and West widened across this sector. Since the 1950s, self-employed master craftsmen in the GDR were encouraged to join the "production collectives" for their trade. After 1976, the remaining independent craftspeople were given better opportunities for development (cheaper loans, the appointment of apprentices, and new trade licenses) in order to meet the dire need for repairs and other services. As of 1988, only a minority of the country's craftsmen (165,000 employees) belonged to the production collectives, while 265,000 continued to practice their trade independently.[54] Fundamental problems plaguing this sector were that productivity remained low and trade practices were antiquated. If machines were used at all, then they were usually "pre-war models" or ones that had been built by the craftsmen themselves.[55]

In contrast, the West German trade sector went through a fundamental transformation after the mid-1980s. At the beginning of this decade, for example, 79 percent of all carpenters believed that electronic data processing was superfluous. By the turn of the century, only a "shrinking minority" of them were still "grumbling" about "the new marvels of the communication age." Beginning in the mid-1990s, digital information and communication technology made its way into the trades, and not just for bookkeeping. CNC machines and computer-aided construction software, for example, were put to use in the production process itself.[56] This resulted in a revolution within the internal structure of the craft trades that could only be compared in its intensity to the transformation of this sector that occurred in the last third of the nineteenth century. The need for capital (to acquire machinery or to remodel workshops, etc.) rose dramatically. In turn, the manifold increase in production output fostered by the use of modern machines forced an expansion of the market and intensified competition among craftsmen; standardization and typification also began to leave their marks on everyday production.

This "industrialization" (*Verindustrialisierung*) of the craft trades was reinforced by "outsourcing" in industry. Construction carpentry often mutated into the end of the chain in a production process dominated by industry. These companies degenerated into installation and service companies who merely assembled prefabricated parts, not only for major building construction projects, but also when it came to interior work, such as fitting a new kitchen. Alternatively, some of them also began to specialize in the production of supply parts.

Thus, even though the number of companies in the craft trades has grown since the 1990s, this cannot be seen as the advent of a new golden age for craftsmen. To the contrary, this boom in new companies is reflective of a crisis. In periods of high unemployment (regardless of whether structural or cyclical), craftsmen without jobs or those whose jobs are precarious have typically started small, pseudo self-employed companies in order to keep "their heads above water."[57] Indeed, the fact that many craftsmen's businesses became supply companies for industrial production or became part of these production chains themselves bears a remarkable resemblance to the widespread proto-industrial putting-out system and classic cottage industries of the early nineteenth century.

The introduction of CNC machines and CAD and CAM systems in the craft trades has had an ambiguous effect. On the one hand, the adaptation of quasi-industrial production processes has reduced the autonomy of the producers. It has also brought a separation between manual and mental work into the craft trades. When journeymen and master craftsmen just use CNC machines programmed "externally" or merely assemble industrially prefabricated parts, their qualifications and expert knowledge lose their value.[58] On the other hand, craftsmen have also become part of the "creative industry."[59] The growing proportion of time spent on planning, construction, and programming, as well as bookkeeping, has also marked a shift in daily work away from direct involvement in manual production toward tasks that can be best assigned to the service sector.

The Service Sector

More Gaps between East and West

The same trend, namely a shift in activity from the actual core of production to work that can be summed up as "services" (sales, financial services, public relations, marketing, etc.), can also be detected in the industrial sector.[60] Consequently, the service sector is actually gaining more ground in Western societies than statistics would seem to indicate (see table 5.3). A look at the data on the distribution of the GDP and the percentages of employees according to economic sector reveals a similar, yet less pronounced shift in the GDR (see table 5.4). This impression of seemingly analogous development trajectories, however, is quite misleading. Even the category of "service" itself is problematic: not only is it a vague term, but also it is very much open to interpretation. The service sector functions as a catch-all category that is used for everything that cannot be subsumed under "agriculture" and "industry." The categories of "service" and "service sector" are all the more problematic when they are used comparatively in relation to different political and economic systems.[61]

Table 5.3a. Employment in the Federal Republic of Germany according to Economic Sectors from 1970 to 2010 (in percent—the figures cited only apply for the former West Germany up to and including 1990)

Year	Primary (agriculture)	Secondary (industry)	Tertiary (service)	Total
1970	8.4	46.5	45.1	100.0
1975	6.6	42.4	51.0	100.0
1980	5.1	41.1	53.8	100.0
1985	4.4	38.1	57.5	100.0
1990	3.5	36.6	59.9	100.0
1995	2.3	32.0	65.8	100.0
2000	1.9	28.5	69.6	100.0
2005	1.7	25.7	72.6	100.0
2010	1.6	24.5	73.9	100.0

Source: Statistisches Bundesamt, ed., *Volkswirtschaftliche Gesamtrechnungen*, 70.

Table 5.3b. Gross Value Added in the Federal Republic of Germany according to Economic Sectors from 1970 to 2010 (in percent—the figures cited only apply for the former West Germany up to and including 1990)

Year	Primary (agriculture)	Secondary (industry)	Tertiary (service)	Total
1970	3.3	48.3	48.3	100.0
1975	2.8	42.4	54.8	100.0
1980	2.2	41.3	56.6	100.0
1985	1.7	39.4	58.9	100.0
1990	1.3	37.6	61.0	100.0
1995	1.1	32.7	66.2	100.0
2000	1.1	30.8	68.2	100.0
2005	0.8	29.3	70.0	100.0
2010	0.7	30.0	69.3	100.0

Source: Statistisches Bundesamt, ed., *Volkswirtschaftliche Gesamtrechnungen*, 58.

Table 5.4. Employees in the GDR according to Economic Sectors from 1950 to 1989 (in percent)

Year	Primary (agriculture and forestry)	Secondary (industry, craft trades, construction, and other production areas)	Tertiary (service) Total	Tertiary (service) including "non-production areas"	Total
1950	27.9	45.1	27.0	11.4	100.0
1960	17.0	49.0	34.0	15.5	100.0
1970	12.8	51.2	36.0	17.4	100.0
1975	11.3	51.5	37.2	19.0	100.0
1980	10.7	51.2	37.9	20.1	100.0
1985	10.8	50.7	38.5	21.0	100.0
1989	10.8	49.9	39.3	21.6	100.0

Source: *Peter Hübner, Arbeit, Arbeiter und Technik in der DDR 1971 bis 1989. Zwischen Fordismus und digitaler Revolution* (Bonn, 2014), S. 622f. (Tab. IV/2).

In the GDR, the percentage of workers compared to the total number of employed individuals actually stagnated or shrank in exactly those industries that have been and continue to be the motor behind the expansion of the tertiary sector in the West. This was certainly true for postal and telecommunications employees, who were at least initially responsible for installing the nationwide IT infrastructure needed in those countries in which the digital revolution had made inroads. The figures for this group actually dropped slightly in East Germany from 1.7 percent in 1970 to 1.5 percent in 1989. Throughout the Honecker era, almost 6 percent of all GDR employees worked in transportation, another important service industry. Surprisingly, the percentage of employees involved in trade did not change much: it rose from 9.4 percent in 1950 to 11 percent in 1970, before sinking back down slightly to 10.3 percent in 1989. Yet one specific area of the GDR's service sector did grow considerably, namely the "nonmanufacturing segment." What this means is that the increase in the percentage of employees in the GDR working in the so-defined service sector was primarily the result of the inflation of the political administrative apparatus, as well as the Stasi and other similar institutions, combined with the expansion of the social security system.

Thus, the growth trends for the service sector in the two German states could hardly have been more disparate. Whereas the private service sector gained ground on industry and the public sector in the West, the political/administrative segment of the tertiary sector kept expanding in the GDR.[62] In a similar vein, the nonpublic service sector in East Germany, unlike its West German counterpart, was only peripherally affected by rationalizations of any kind. Admittedly, larger stores belonging to the public trading organization (*Handelsorganisation,* or HO) and the *Kaufhallen* shops run by consumer collectives had been run like supermarkets since the 1960s, but the majority of the HO shops were still rather small in size and managed in an antiquated fashion.[63]

The introduction of computer technology in the 1970s did not result in a loss of jobs in the service sector industries in the West because labor demand increased at the same time. For example, the number of insured individuals grew for the insurance companies, and the number of account holders rose for the banks. In the banking and savings industry in the GDR, computer systems were brought in on a large scale at the beginning of the 1970s, in part to ease the transition from wages paid in cash to direct deposits. Apparently, however, these computers were not always used consistently. Since the production costs for these computers were so high, or rather the cost of importing them from the West (if this was actually even possible given the successively more restrictive embargoes that had been put into place), purchasing them would have eaten up too much foreign currency. Therefore, it seemed to be more cost-effective to rely on existing personnel in the GDR, despite the chronic shortage of labor.[64]

West Germany, however, followed a completely different path when it came to digitalization. Although the voices that were skeptical about the introduction of modern Internet and communication technologies at the beginning of the Digital Age were more numerous and louder than in the GDR, they could do nothing to halt the structural trend toward the digitalization of the tertiary sector over the long run. By the end of the 1970s at the latest, digitalization had made broad inroads in West Germany. The pioneers were the banking and savings institutions, which introduced ATMs in West Germany as of 1968, as well as the insurance companies and mail-order retailers. The Allianz AG insurance company, for example, had already acquired an IBM mainframe computer in 1956, paving the way for a comprehensive computerization of its office operations.[65] The mail-order department store Quelle also began using a gigantic computerized order processing and warehouse bookkeeping system at the end of 1957 that "digested" an average of twenty thousand orders a day. Previously, these orders had been processed laboriously by twelve hundred employees, most of whom were women. Likewise, the major European airlines began introducing electronic reservation systems in the 1960s in order to keep up with their American competitors.[66]

IT and computer technology found its way into the public service sector much more slowly. By the end of 1989, for example, only 22.5 percent of all public libraries in the state of North Rhine Westphalia were classified as "computer users."[67] Yet the West German libraries were much further on their way toward the implementation of IT and computer technology than their East German counterparts. It was not until after the *Wende* that both library systems were fully and "thoroughly digitalized." Interestingly, the effects of the introduction and ever more intensive use of IT technology overlapped with the simultaneous "managerialization" (*Verbetriebswitschaftlichung*) of the libraries. For librarians, this was very much a double-edged sword. From their point of view, however, the bad outweighed the good in many respects. For one, digitalization seemed to be a way to cut costs in light of municipal budget crises and university budget cuts.[68] Branch closings, job cuts, shorter opening hours, temporary employment contracts, and the introduction of flexible schedules according to user frequency created a feeling of insecurity among librarians; many of them complained about things such as "increasing stress" and "personal productivity assessments," or even "time allotments" for certain tasks.[69]

"Friendliness on Schedule" and McJobs: Neo-Taylorization in the Service Industry

Digitalization also led to the creation of entirely new industries and, with them, to the (neo) Taylorization of service jobs. The call centers that began popping up in the 1990s are one example of this phenomenon. The number of people employed in them (usually in low-paid, temporary, and part-time jobs) more than quadrupled from 45,000 in 1995 to over 225,000 in 2000, climbing up to 330,000 in 2005 and approximately 500,000 at the end of 2009.[70] The actual job tasks vary according to structure of the telephone calls that they make—that is, whether each call deals with personalized requests or follows a basic pattern. The significance of the latter call type has been growing, especially since it lends itself well to a Taylorist-style breakdown in tasks: calls are distributed automatically and dealt with according to a specific time schedule. Unlike workers in classic Fordist systems, who were kept in line by the running assembly line but at least had the freedom to let their minds wander, call center agents have to be mentally engaged in their work, and they are expected to conduct themselves in a certain way. They have to discipline their feelings and emotions. Of course, the controlling of affects has been just as important for countless employees in the service sector as well. After all, stores whose staff appear to be permanently bored, gruff, or incompetent always lose customers quickly. What is new about call centers—and fast food chains, supermarkets, and home and garden centers, just to name a few—is the ever-present demand for "friendliness on schedule," the need to control emotions in keeping with tightly scheduled and timed workflows, brief breaks, and standardized performance checks.

Yet the digital revolution is only one of the many factors that have been changing the world of work in the service sector at a fundamental level. For example, digitalization was accompanied by long-term sociopolitical trends, such as increases in vacation time, alongside rising income levels. These, in turn, have led to rapid growth in the significance of the "tourist industry."[71] In the land of the "world travel champions," the number of travel agencies jumped from 3,120 in 1970 to 9,500 in 1980, climbing up to 13,200 in 1990. This figure hit a peak in Germany in 1994 with 17,500 travel agencies, not including side businesses.[72] The fact that these numbers fell just as quickly from 14,235 in 2002 to 9,729 in 2013, however, has much more to do with an Internet trend:[73] travel agents are becoming redundant because it has become much easier for consumers to systematically search and book the best value for their money using "data highways" that provide direct access to the deals offered by "providers" (i.e., package tour companies, airlines, hotels, etc.).

Globalization also stirred up a number of areas within the tertiary sector, forcing German companies to make changes in order to keep up with the multinational corporations dominating the market. One example of this is the industrialization of the restaurant business thanks to fast-food chains, and McDonald's in particular, since 1971. McDonald's-style gastronomy relies on modern technology: large-size and easy-to-use freezers, refrigerators, and cooking equipment, plus the corresponding logistics, manufacturing, transport, storage, and preparation systems. Yet one of the defining characteristics of these self-service restaurants is, as Stephan Voswinkel puts it, the "modified adaptation of the Fordist model of production to the particular demands of interactive service."[74]

The McDonald's-style model of production rested on four pillars, or "MACs" (the ironic abbreviation for "minimal and calculable"). As the first Big MAC, "McSkill" represents the separation between the planning and instruction side of work and the actual execution of tasks in a classic Taylorist manner. It also covers the external preparation of foods outside of the actual restaurants. Cooking equipment dominates the production workflows in McDonald's restaurants, and the individual steps required to use this equipment and prepare food have been simplified so that unskilled workers are capable of using it all. As a result, McDonald's does not need to employ trained cooks. Furthermore, audio and visual signals make it easy for employees to follow the different warming and grilling procedures. Not only does this allow for training time to be kept to a minimum, but it also means that all employees have no trouble with these different tasks because they have been made as simple as possible. This leads into the "McJob" concept, the second Big MAC: most of McDonalds' employees have part-time jobs, and the majority are young and female; many of them also come from immigrant backgrounds (and therefore have an insecure position on the job market). For the most part, their hours tend to be flexible and are adjusted according to customer traffic, but they are not paid overtime. As a result, there is a high level of fluctuation among restaurant workers. The third main pillar, "McService," stands for the major reduction in the kind of service that is offered. Employees do not serve tables, but rather they stand behind cash registers where they assemble meals—also according to a Fordist building block principle—and collect payment or wipe tables between customers. The fourth Big MAC, "McFun," addresses customer acquisition and entertainment, which has targeted children in particular. Other elements, such as "drive-ins," also factor into the McDonald's-style model of production. Businesses like McDonald's have modified the basic Taylorist model defined according to F. W. Taylor's principles in one way in particular, namely through calculated lines of waiting customers: not supervisors but impatient customers make sure that employees consistently work at the steady, desired pace.

The "McDonald's model of production" has moved well beyond this particular fast food chain and mass gastronomy in general. Typically, this model is characterized by the employment of mostly unskilled workers and a neo-Taylorist workflow in which customers themselves take on some of the service functions and put together the goods they desire. Since the 1970s, such practices have become the norm in supermarkets and self-service gas stations, for example. The work of employees has thus been reduced to monitoring and cleaning up as well as sitting behind a cash register, skimming goods over a scanner at a regular pace, which sends a digital message to the warehouse so that the supply of goods is replenished continually and virtually automatically. Above all, however, the "McJob" idea, meaning "a low-pay, low-prestige, low dignity, low-benefit, no-future job in the service sector,"[75] has contributed considerably to the emergence of a steadily growing "secondary" labor market dominated by precarious jobs since the 1990s.

Lastly, fundamental changes in structures of work in the service sector were sometimes induced politically by means of government decisions. One example of this was the nursing care insurance system that was introduced at the beginning of 1995. Especially in light of rising life expectancy rates, it sprouted a new and rapidly growing market for private companies who could take over the care of the elderly. They were supposed to follow on the heels of the charitable and church welfare organizations who had been the main providers of this kind of care well into the 1980s in West Germany. Under the SED dictatorship, where social welfare was primarily for those able to work, the care of older people was mostly in the hands of the state, which handled it in a dilatory manner. The number of spaces in old people's homes was about 115,000 in the GDR's last year, compared to 88,500 in 1960; the percentage of hospital beds in the chronically overcrowded state nursing homes was about 85 percent in 1989. Given the lack of suitably qualified personnel, moreover, the ratio of caretakers to residents was still much worse than in West Germany. Likewise, the poor state of the homes themselves made "care aimed at active living" and true "geriatric rehabilitation" virtually impossible.[76]

Both the East and West German versions of nursing care were transformed by the law introduced in 1994. Although the first private nursing service companies popped up in the early 1990s, the market for private providers did not really take off until the nursing care insurance system was put into place, which firmly set out the preference for ambulatory elder care in section 3 of the SGB XI (German Social Code XI—Social Assistance).[77] As early as 1997, 1.2 million Germans in need of assistance, and especially older people, were being taken care of by nursing care services. By 2009, this figure had almost doubled to more than 2.3 million people. The dynamic way in which the market for nursing care developed in the 1990s is aptly reflected, at least in part, by the number of service providers that existed: in 1990, there were about 1,700 providers, but this number jumped quickly to 6,633 by 1993, hitting the 12,000 mark in 2009.[78] Approximately 60 percent of these service providers operated as private companies as of 2009. The number of employees working in the at-home nursing care industry grew from 36,000 in 1984 to 40,400 in 1993; after the advent of the nursing care insurance system, this figure catapulted to 107,200 in 1996 and more than doubled again to 269,000 in 2009.

The history of these kinds of nursing care services is very much a history of female employment. Since the introduction of the nursing care insurance system, almost 90 percent of all those employed in the ambulatory care sector have been women. Accordingly, the percentage of part-time employment has also been high. It rose from about 50 percent in 1994 to 71 percent in 2009.[79] Private service providers not only paved the way for part-time employment in this area, but also they were the forerunners when it came to "mini-jobs," coming in at 26 percent compared to 17 percent among the nonprofit nursing care providers.

One positive result of this privatization of the care of the elderly has been the professionalization of nursing care. Even among those working in "basic care," almost all of whom were women, almost two-thirds (65 percent) have completed formal vocational training (mostly as nurses or nursing aides). The other effects of this have been more ambivalent. Like all markets, the market for nursing care is driven by competition. Yet the prices have been set by a pseudo-monopoly, namely the health and nursing care insurance companies, which have a lot of clout over the service providers, most of whom are small companies. Thus, the great negotiating power of the insurance companies has resulted, according to Wilfried Kunstmann, in "agreements to subjugation" that set the tone for the way work is done in this business. Personnel scheduling and workflow organization are no longer being optimized to meet "patients' needs," but rather to maximize profits. This trend has intensified the work that needs to be done and limited the flexibility of the nursing staff. Many of these often-underpaid nurses and aides are overworked, prompting them to switch jobs or even professions. About 30 percent of them have been diagnosed with burn-out syndrome at least once. Meanwhile, the comparatively expensive cost of employing registered nurses is becoming a financial burden for many companies; the larger the nursing care provider, the lower the percentage of registered nurses they employ. As a result, there has been talk of a "gradual deprofessionalization of nursing care for the elderly" since the end of the 1990s.[80]

Tighter state and municipal budgets and the pressure to cut costs "from above" have only served to further strengthen the business side of care management and the focus on profits. On a completely different note, however, digitalization and the networking of information and communications structures has made it easier for nursing staff and care managers to keep up with the ever-growing mandate to maintain proper records. Time budgets (specifying the allotted time per patient) and increasing standardization have also led to a successive Taylorization of patient care. The stimulating and communicative aspects of care that are particularly beneficial for the elderly and help keep them active have mostly been deemed to be irrelevant in terms of profits, meaning that they are considered to be unnecessary in nursing care structured along Taylorist lines.

The Americanization of Paid Work?

"(Neo) Taylorization," "flexibility," and "insecurity" are different aspects of an all-encompassing process that has fundamentally transformed work in the service sector, industry, and agriculture, expressing itself ideologically in the form of neoliberal paradigms. The classic Fordist model, with its clearly fixed boundaries between work and leisure, is clearly eroding in its wake. The inclination to cut production costs—and therefore labor costs—as much as possible is very much intrinsic to the exploitation of capital. But it has been bolstered even more since the mid-1980s by chronic mass unemployment and underemployment, as well as the end of the Cold War, and it has been accompanied by an ever-accelerating process of globalization.

In the last two decades of the twentieth century, many countries actively tried to dismantle the legal, economic, and bureaucratic barriers faced by locating and relocating businesses. As a result, many international companies have engaged in what has been termed regime hopping since the 1990s, in which they play the different site locations against each other in order to obtain better deals.[81] Companies then choose the sites with what they see as the best terms for them in relation to labor laws, social standards, tax requirements, and political-administrative aspects. Simply threatening to move their locations has gained them an upper hand in collective bargaining and internal conflicts, proving to be the "joker that trumps the others in many situations."[82] This competition over business locations has brought about what Andreas Wirsching calls a "new kind of vulnerability" for employees, which is poorly disguised under the rather ambiguous heading of "flexibility" and which feeds into a downward spiral.

As working hours have become more flexible, the trade unions have become rather unwilling pacemakers. As part of their campaign to cut down working hours on the whole, they—from a position of relative strength—pushed companies to accept a limited form of flextime, which was contractually fixed for the first time at the end of June in 1984 in a collective wage agreement in the metal industry for the North Baden/ North Württemberg district. Although this agreement set out a nominal workweek of 38.5 hours, it has still been possible to institute special worktime arrangements for entire company workforces or individual groups of employees through internal company agreements. At the same time, the permitted compensation period for offsetting contract work hours was extended on average by about two months. This has meant that employers can adjust working hours to production needs without having to worry about paying overtime. Ten years later, these regulations were extended beyond the metal industry and sanctioned by the legislature in the German Working Hours Act (*Arbeitszeitgesetz*) that went into effect on 1 July 1994. This law was expressly intended "to improve the general conditions for flexible working hours" (section 1). By this time, however, the general constellation of society had changed fundamentally, not least because the trade unions and the workers' councils had fallen into a sustained position of weakness. As a result, the average working hours per week, along with Sunday, evening, and night shifts, have been on the rise. In Germany, for example, the number of employees who had to work longer than their usual daily number of hours, usually in the evenings, increased from 26.8 percent in 1995 to 43.8 percent in 2009; likewise, the percentage of (regular and sporadic) night-shift workers went from 13.1 percent to 15.2 percent over the same period.[83]

For a long time, part-time work, which was also very much associated with "flexibility," had been quite attractive for women in particular because it allowed them to combine paid work with motherhood. But there was also another trend that factored into the two-fold increase in the number of part-time employees to five million (2011) in the first twenty years after the *Wende*: since the turn of the century, the pressure on precariously employed and long-term unemployed people to accept "flexible" part-time work had grown because they could not find jobs offering other terms. Moreover, "flextime" has become more popular—especially since the turn of the millennium—despite the fact that it was a mostly foreign concept in Germany before then. This model rested on concepts largely appropriated from places like the United States, such as KAPOVAZ (capacity-oriented variable working time) or FREQUOVAZ, the latter of which couples working time to digitally tracked customer frequency in retail shops and shopping centers. In addition, "flexibility" is also tied to the ever-increasing trend toward contacting employees when they are off work.

Globalization and regime hopping, by fostering the omnipresence of "temporary workers," have also undermined the employee rights that had been hard fought for in earlier generations and protected by collective bargaining agreements or labor laws. The number of temporary employees has grown significantly since 1975 (see table 5.5). After the so-called "Hartz IV" legal regulations on second-stage unemployment benefits (Arbeitslosengeld II) took effect in 2002, the number of temporary workers peaked (at least for the time being) at 927,103 in August 2011. The number of employees with limited-term contracts also jumped from 1.8 million in 1991 to 2.8 million in 2011, while the number of people with "mini-jobs" quadrupled between 1991 and 2011 from 652,000 to 2.7 million.[84] In a nutshell, what used to be "atypical employment" is on the way to becoming the new norm. Whether these changes are interpreted in national terms and pejoratively deemed to be an "Americanization of the politics and culture of work" or a "downsizing of the German model"[85] is really a matter of taste and not important in the end. What is important about all this is that the competition between those

Table 5.5. Temporary Workers from 1970 to 2013 (absolute figures—only for West Germany up to and including 1990; number as of December each year)

Year	Absolute number
1970	19,417
1975	8,920
1980	33,227
1985	46,946
1990	118,875
1995	162,275
2000	337,845
2005	464,539
2010	823,509
2013	814,580

Source: Bundesagentur für Arbeit, "Arbeitnehmerüberlassung, Leiharbeitnehmer, Verleihbetriebe (1973–2014)," retrieved 29 May 2016, https://statistik.arbeitsagentur.de/Statistikdaten/Detail/Aktuell/iiia6/aueg-aueg-zr/aueg-zr-d-0-xls.xls.

with full-time jobs and those with less secure jobs has been intensifying (alongside a dramatic rise in burnout syndrome as well as other factors), leading to a multifaceted "dwindling solidarity of the workforce" within a company, but also between different locations of the same corporation.

Conclusion

In the 1960s and 1970s, East and West Germany were confronted by similar challenges: labor was short and the importance of the global market was growing, as was the pressure to develop production technology and optimize workplace organization. Yet this process followed very different paths in the two German states. Whereas rationalization began to make inroads toward automation (bought at the price of mass unemployment), and digitalization gained a foothold almost everywhere in West Germany, the GDR was able to tackle these challenges only on a very limited scale. It was not until after 1990 that the dynamics of this development—under the banner of flexibility—changed fundamentally in East and West Germany. The grievances experienced after the fall of the Wall by many East German employees, who complained about the "incredibly fast-moving pace" of work and life in general, were echoed by countless Germans across the entire Federal Republic just a few years later.[86] This feeling that has spread since the 1990s, that time has been speeding up and space is closing in—on a subjective as well as objective level—can only be compared to the fundamental upheavals that hit the European continent in the last third of the nineteenth century, when urbanization and industrialization turned society upside down. Back then, it was railroads and telegraphs that transformed perceptions of time and space. They embodied the revolutionary changes that were taking place and forced everyone to broaden their horizons in both a literal and metaphoric sense. Today, the Internet is this catalytic force.

Reunified Germany has been shaped by a dynamic sparked by globalization and digitalization, as well as the powerfully influential neoliberal paradigm of seemingly unharnessed markets that has shaken the world of work. Admittedly, the effects of this dynamic have differed depending on the particular sector, but they have nonetheless lent credence to the idea of a phase of "new complexity." In a broad sense, though, work has always been something "complex." Even during the West German "economic miracle," when Fordism was at its height, for example, manual production techniques were never completely eliminated in the manufacturing industries, not to mention the variety of paid jobs in the primary and tertiary sectors. Yet, these constellations have been more mottled than ever since the 1980s and 1990s. New markets emerged after the federal, state, and municipal governments openly or covertly privatized a growing number of infrastructure institutions (such as the postal service, the railroads, the utility companies, hospitals, public swimming pools, etc.) or sold off public properties. These formerly public institutions—and even those who are still nominally publicly owned—now function according to the logic of the "free" markets, which has had far-reaching effects on employment contracts, working conditions, and employee rights and entitlement in the workplace. But these areas were not the only ones affected by such transformations. Employees in more established economic sectors have also felt these same changes, which have been rolling in since the 1970s or even earlier in the "old" Federal Republic. In many places, farming has mutated into an agricultural industry, more and more of which has been partially, if not wholly, automated, and the employees in larger production facilities, especially meat factories, are subject to a quasi-Fordist production regime. The start-ups of the "New Economy" and the corporate culture that has developed along with them have become role models for portions of the industry and service sectors. They favor instituting new forms of flexible organization that represent an even harder break with the rigid Fordist flow-and-control system than the Toyota model. Fostered in part by the abandonment of collective bargaining agreements and the weakening of the trade unions over the long run, flextime and precarious forms of employment have become more and more commonplace in all three economic sectors since the end of the 1980s. Growing job insecurity, but also the desire for more personal fulfillment, have forced "entreployees"—a fashionable term that sums up this new kind of dependency in an offhand rather than truly analytical way—to engage in "self-marketing" and "self-optimization." Simultaneously, simple jobs have become more prominent in the tertiary sector in particular, where they have appeared in the context of the McDonald's production system, which leans strongly toward a (neo)Taylorist model.[87]

Yet the picture becomes even more complex because the different economic sectors and industries, as well as the different business segments (size, sales outlets, etc.), have developed their own particular structures. The large core companies in the automobile industry, for example, have been working toward the full automation of their final assembly lines as demanded within a Fordist production regime since the 1980s. The recognition of the fact that there are still roadblocks standing in the way of a completely robotic production line has only slightly curbed this trend. Simultaneously, Toyotist structures have also been kept. On the other hand, smaller companies (such as suppliers and businesses in those industries dominated by midsize companies, such as the woodworking industry) have often retained a stripped down form of Fordism or manual production techniques in the face of pressure to keep costs down. The resilience of older production systems has surely contributed to the fact that the *Wertewandel* (change in values) within the industrial workforce has not been nearly as radical since the 1970s as many sociologists and some historians have assumed, in part because older notions of work have persisted.[88]

Indeed, the lines of historical continuity are quite strong in general, despite all the major changes that have beset the East in particular over the last few decades. This consistency becomes all the more apparent if we do not limit ourselves to a regional focus, but rather shift our gaze beyond the borders of Germany and Europe. We can clearly see through such a wider lens that the digital revolution and automation have by no means done away with older kinds of manufacturing. Even in the IT hardware production industry, which is the backbone of the digital revolution, relatively primitive forms of a Fordist production regime are still being used, replete with "mass workers," most of whom are unqualified, female, highly segmented, and poorly paid. Of course, these kinds of employees are not often found in the industrial core of Europe these days because outsourcing and the international division of labor "regulated" by the markets has shifted production to other parts of the globe. Since the 1980s, for example, the production of this hardware has primarily taken place in what are often referred to as emerging or newly industrialized countries.[89] Yet even on the margins of Europe in places like Romania or Bulgaria, or even in some supply companies in Germany, this kind of "dirty Fordism" (as Alain Liepitz has called it) still persists in cases in which it is more cost-effective to pay low wages than invest in expensive production technology. The tendency of many sociologists and historians to focus on the frontrunners of modernization while neglecting the "grey zones" comprised of midsize and smaller businesses potentially overestimates the depth and breadth of the changes that have been unleashed by rationalization, automation, and digitalization, offering a skewed impression of a fundamental transformation in paid work. Consequently, the brief outline offered here should only be read as a work in progress because there is still much work to be done to understand all the many facets of the world of work.

Rüdiger Hachtmann is a senior research associate and project director at the Center of Contemporary History (ZZF) in Potsdam, and associate professor at the Technische Universität Berlin. He has published numerous monographs and essays on German and European history of the nineteenth and twentieth century. Recent monographs include *Das Wirtschaftsimperium der Deutschen Arbeitsfront* (2012), *Wissenschaftsmanagement im Dritten Reich* (2007), *Tourismus-Geschichte* (2007), and *1848/49: Epochenschwelle zur Moderne* (2002). Recent edited books include *Ressourcenmobilisierung. Wissenschaftspolitik und Forschungspraxis im NS-Herrschaftssystem* (with Sören Flachowsky and Florian Schmaltz, 2016), and *Detlev Peukert und die NS-Forschung* (with Sven Reichardt, 2015).

NOTES

1. Francesca Weil, *Herrschaftsanspruch und soziale Wirklichkeit: zwei sächsische Betriebe in der DDR während der Honecker-Ära* (Cologne, 2000), 172 (Interview colleague S.).
2. Ibid., 179 and 185 (colleagues I. and G., colleagues W. and Y.). On the background to experiences of unemployment in the GDR, see especially Berthold Vogel, *Die Spuren der Arbeitslosigkeit. Der Verlust der Erwerbsarbeit im Umbruch der ostdeutschen Gesellschaft zwischen Wohlstandssteigerung und neuer Ungleichheit*, in *Ostdeutsche Arbeitswelt im Wandel 1945–2015* (Dresden 2015), 58–73.
3. See "Labour Market: Employment (National Concept) by Industries. Germany," (Facts & Figures > National Economy & Environment), DEStatis

Statistiches Bundesamt, retrieved 28 May 2016, https://www.destatis.de/EN/FactsFigures/Indicators/LongTermSeries/LabourMarket/lrarb013.html.

4. Christa Bertag, managing director of the federal cosmetic combine in Berlin as of 1986, quoted in Theo Pirker and Mario Rainer Lepsius, *Der Plan als Befehl und Fiktion: Wirtschaftsführung in der DDR. Gespräche und Analysen* (Opladen, 1995), 253.
5. See Jelle Visser, "ICTWSS: Database on Institutional Characteristics of Trade Unions, Wage Setting, State Intervention and Social Pacts in 51 Countries between 1960 and 2014. Version 5.0," Amsterdam Institute for Advanced Labour Studies, University of Amsterdam, October 2015, retrieved 12 July 2016, www.uva-aias.net/208. On the background to this in West Germany, see Wolfgang Schroeder and Stephen J. Silvia, "Gewerkschaften und Arbeitgeberverbände," in *Handbuch Gewerkschaften in Deutschland*, ed. Wolfgang Schroeder, 2nd ed. (Wiesbaden 2014), 535–78, esp. 554–61.
6. See Institut der Deutschen Wirtschaft, ed., *Deutschland in Zahlen 2014* (Cologne, 2014), 11.
7. See Samuel Greef, "Gewerkschaften im Spiegel von Zahlen, Daten und Fakten," in Schroeder, *Handbuch Gewerkschaften*, 687.
8. Peter Hübner, *Arbeit, Arbeiter und Technik in der DDR 1971 bis 1989: Zwischen Fordismus und digitaler Revolution,* ed. Gerhard A. Ritter (Bonn, 2014).
9. See Friedhelm Boll and Viktoria Kalass, "Streik und Aussperrung," in *Handbuch Gewerkschaften in Deutschland* (Wiesbaden, 2014), 544.
10. Greef, "Gewerkschaften im Spiegel von Zahlen, Daten und Fakten," 673.
11. Rüdiger Hachtmann, "Industriearbeiterinnen in der deutschen Kriegswirtschaft 1936 bis 1944/45," *Geschichte und Gesellschaft: Zeitschrift für historische Sozialwissenschaft* 19 (1993): 338 and 364.
12. See Steffen Lehndorff, Alexandra Wagner, and Christine Franz, *Development of Working Time in the EU* (Fürth, 2010), 114 and 137, retrieved 12 July 2016, http://www.guengl.eu/uploads/_old_cms_files/Development_of_working_time_in_the_EU_(Pub___Thomas_Haendel___Dr__Axel_Troost_).pdf.
13. On the definition of Fordism and its history, see Rüdiger Hachtmann, "Fordismus," Version: 1.0, *Docupedia-Zeitgeschichte,* 27 October 2011, retrieved 25 May 2018, https://docupedia.de/zg/Fordismus; Rüdiger Hachtmann and Adelheid von Saldern, "Das fordistische Jahrhundert. Eine Einleitung," *Zeithistorische Forschungen/Studies in Contemporary History* 6 (2009): 174–85; Rüdiger Hachtmann and Adelheid von Saldern, "'Gesellschaft am Fließband': Fordistische Produktion und Herrschaftspraxis in Deutschland," *Zeithistorische Forschungen/Studies in Contemporary History* 6 (2009): 186–208.
14. See Steven Tolliday, "Diffusion and Transformation of Fordism: Britain and Japan Compared," in *Between Imitation and Innovation: The Transfer and Hybridization of Productive Models in the International Automobile Industry,* ed. Robert Boyer et al. (Oxford, 1998); Volker Elis, "Von Amerika nach Japan—und zurück. Die historischen Wurzeln und Transformationen des Toyotismus," *Zeithistorische Forschungen/Studies in Contemporary History* 6 (2009):

255–75; On the reception, see Christian Kleinschmidt, *Der produktive Blick: Wahrnehmung amerikanischer und japanischer Management- und Produktionsmethoden durch deutsche Unternehmer 1950–1985* (Berlin, 2002).

15. For the discussion and use of "Volvoism," see Peter Binkelmann, Hans-Joachim Braczyk, and Rüdiger Seitz, *Entwicklung der Gruppenarbeit in Deutschland. Stand und Perspektiven* (Frankfurt a. M., 1993); and Martina Heßler, *Kulturgeschichte der Technik* (Frankfurt a. M., 2012), 66–67.
16. Teamwork practices similar to those at Volvo had been invented in the 1920s by the psychologist Hellpach and were practiced at Daimler-Benz. See R. Lang and W. Hellpach, *Gruppenfabrikation* (Berlin, 1922).
17. "Manchmal schlage ich irgendwas kaputt," *Der Spiegel* 27 (1973): 98–100, retrieved 15 May 2018, http://www.spiegel.de/spiegel/print/d-41986623.html.
18. See Thomas P. Hughes, *American Genesis: A Century of Invention and Technological Enthusiasm 1870–1970* (Harmondsworth, 1989), 249–60; Stephen Kotkin, *Magnetic Mountain: Stalinism as a Civilization* (Berkeley, 1995), 364.
19. Quotes from Biermann and Krömke, in Pirker and Lepsius, *Der Plan als Befehl und Fiktion*, 46, 214.
20. Interview Krömke, in Ibid., 46.
21. See Reinhold Bauer, *Pkw-Bau in der DDR: Zur Innovationsschwäche von Zentralverwaltungswirtschaften* (Frankfurt a. M., 1999), 210–11.
22. For car production, see ibid., 216–32; for the GDR automobile manufacturer's attempts to install Fordist-like assembly lines, which are described in the following sentences, see ibid., 76–78, 186–199, 203, 273, 277.
23. As mentioned in Gernot Gutmann and Hannsjörg Buck, "Die Zentralplanwirtschaft der DDR—Funktionsweise, Funktionsschwächen und Konjunkturbilanz," in *Die wirtschaftliche und ökologische Situation der DDR in den 80er Jahren*, ed. Eberhard Kuhrt (Opladen, 1996), 9; for a brief introduction see André Steiner, *Von Plan zu Plan: Eine Wirtschaftsgeschichte der DDR* (Munich, 2004), 179–80, 213, 222–23.
24. See "DDR: Am Fließband," *Der Spiegel* 44 (1973), retrieved 15 May 2018, http://www.spiegel.de/spiegel/print/d-41898403.html; the implementation began in 1965, and in the 1970s and 1980s this procedure was "quite common," see Axel Bust-Bartels, *Herrschaft und Widerstand in den DDR-Betrieben: Leistungsentlohnung, Arbeitsbedingungen, innerbetriebliche Konflikte und technologische Entwicklung* (Frankfurt a. M., 1980), 75–77.
25. Bauer, *Pkw-Bau in der DDR*, 273.
26. See Hübner, *Arbeit, Arbeiter und Technik in der DDR 1971 bis 1989*, 16–17, 273–76, 448.
27. Bauer, *Pkw-Bau in der DDR*, 287.
28. Wolfgang Biermann, managing director of Carl Zeiss Jena, in Pirker and Lepsius, *Der Plan als Befehl und Fiktion*, 215.
29. Oskar Anweiler, "Bildungspolitik," in *Geschichte der Sozialpolitik in Deutschland*, vol. 10, *Deutsche Demokratische Republik 1971–1989: Bewegung in der Sozialpolitik, Erstarrung und Niedergang*, ed. Christoph Boyer, Klaus-Dietmar

Henke, and Peter Skyba (Baden-Baden, 2008), 567. On job-training programs in the GDR, see Hübner, *Arbeit, Arbeiter und Technik in der DDR 1971 bis 1989*, 77–79.

30. The official number of those who called in sick averaged around 6 percent—slightly higher than in West Germany.
31. See Anweiler, "Bildungspolitik," 652. See also André Steiner and Matthias Judt, *Statistische Übersichten zur Sozialpolitik in Deutschland seit 1945: Band SBZ/DDR* (Bonn 2006), 127.
32. See David Franklin Noble, *Forces of Production* (New York, 1984), 66–68.
33. On the following (including the quotes), see Martina Heßler, "Die Halle 54 bei Volkswagen und die Grenzen der Automatisierung: Überlegungen zum Mensch-Maschine-Verhältnis in der industriellen Produktion der 1980er-Jahre," *Zeithistorische Forschungen* 11 (2014): 56–76.
34. Quotes in Jonas Viering, "Taylors stille Rückkehr," *Die Zeit*, 15 January 2009, retrieved 12 July 2016, http://www.zeit.de/2009/04/Taylorismus/komplettansicht.
35. See Hartmut Hirsch-Kreiensen, "Industrielle Einfacharbeit," in *Arbeitswelten in Bewegung: Arbeit, Technik und Organisation in der "nachindustriellen Gesellschaft*," ed. Christian Schilcher and Mascha Will-Zocholl (Wiesbaden, 2012), 218–20.
36. From the total of 8.2 million "people employed in unskilled jobs,", about two-thirds (5.5 million) were employed in the service sector while only 27 percent (2.2 million) had jobs in industry. Ibid., 217.
37. See ibid., 213, 219, 225–28.
38. See Bauer, *Pkw-Bau in der DDR*, 275–76; Ralf Ahrens, "Rationalisierungseuphorie und Innovationsschwäche: Industrieroboter im Werkzeugmaschinenkombinat 'Fritz Heckert' um 1980," *Technikgeschichte* 79 (2012): 65.
39. See Ahrens, "Rationalisierungseuphorie und Innovationsschwäche," 67, 70–73.
40. Hübner, *Arbeit, Arbeiter und Technik in der DDR 1971 bis 1989*, 205; See also Reinhold Bauer, "Ölpreiskrisen und Industrieroboter. Die siebziger Jahre als Umbruchphase für die Automobilindustrie in beiden deutschen Staaten," in *Das Ende der Zuversicht? Die siebziger Jahre als Geschichte*, ed. Konrad Hugo Jarausch (Göttingen, 2008), 77; Bauer, *Pkw-Bau in der DDR*, 179, 275.
41. See Peter von der Lippe, "Die gesamtwirtschaftlichen Leistungen der DDR-Wirtschaft in den offiziellen Darstellungen: die amtliche Statistik der DDR als Instrument der Agitation und Propaganda der SED," in *Machtstrukturen und Entscheidungsmechanismen im SED-Staat und die Frage der Verantwortung*, vol. 2, *Materialien der Enquete-Kommission "Aufarbeitung von Geschichte und Folgen der SED-Diktatur in Deutschland*," ed. Deutscher Bundestag (Baden-Baden, 1995), 1973–2193; Ahrens, "Rationalisierungseuphorie und Innovationsschwäche," 72.
42. Statistisches Amt der DDR, ed., *Statistisches Jahrbuch der Deutschen Demokratischen Republik*, 35 (Berlin, 1990), 176. The annual statistical report is-

sued in 1989 listed 14,938 "individual industrial robots" produced in 1985, but the report from 1990 cited only 1,043 "process-flexible industrial robots" for the same year (1985). Statistisches Amt der DDR, ed., *Statistisches Jahrbuch der Deutschen Demokratischen Republik,* 34 (Berlin, 1989), 148.
43. See Hübner, *Arbeit, Arbeiter und Technik in der DDR 1971 bis 1989,* 217; Bauer, *Pkw-Bau in der DDR,* 178.
44. See Timo Leimbach, *Die Softwarebranche in Deutschland: Entwicklung eines Innovationssystems zwischen Forschung, Markt, Anwendung und Politik 1950 bis Heute* (Stuttgart, 2011), 88; Annette Schuhmann, "Der Traum vom perfekten Unternehmen: die Computerisierung der Arbeitswelt in der Bundesrepublik Deutschland (1950er- bis 1980er-Jahre)," *Zeithistorische Forschungen* 9 (2012): 231–56. For the current state of research on the history of digitalization in Germany, see Martin Schmitt and Julia Erdogan, "Digitalgeschichte Deutschlands: ein Forschungsbericht," *Technikgeschichte* 83 (2016): 33–70.
45. Schuhmann, "Der Traum vom perfekten Unternehmen," 232.
46. See Mascha Will-Zocholl, "Globalisierte Wirtschaft? Ingenieure in der Automobilindustrie," in *Arbeitswelten in Bewegung: Arbeit, Technik und Organisation in der "nachindustriellen Gesellschaft,"* ed. Christian Schilcher and Mascha Will-Zocholl (Wiesbaden, 2012), 159–84.
47. Interview Bertag, citation in Pirker and Lepsius, *Der Plan als Befehl und Fiktion,* 253.
48. In detail: Olaf Klenke, *Kampfauftrag Mikrochip: Rationalisierung und Sozialer Konflikt in der DDR* (Hamburg, 2008).
49. Quote from colleague S. in Weil, *Herrschaftsanspruch und soziale Wirklichkeit,* 172, 174.
50. See, for instance, Heiko Peters, "Ausblick Deutschland. Stillstand der Lohnkonvergenz zwischen Ost-und Westdeutschland seit Anfang der 2000er Jahre," ed. Deutsche Bank Research, April 2013, retrieved 25 May 2018, http://docplayer.org/32638413-Research-briefing-konjunktur.html.
51. Quotes from colleagues S., N., H., and B. in Weil, *Herrschaftsanspruch und soziale Wirklichkeit,* 172, 180–81.
52. See, e.g., Michael Schumann, "Industriearbeit zwischen Entfremdung und Entfaltung," *SOFI-Mitteilungen* 28 (2000): 111.
53. See Andreas Boes, "Arbeit in der IT-Industrie: Durchbruch zu einem neuen Kontrollmodus? Auf der Suche nach den Konturen eines postfordistischen Produktionsmodells," in *Das neue Marktregime: Konturen eines nachfordistischen Produktionsmodells,* ed. Klaus Dörre (Hamburg, 2003), 137.
54. See Clemens Büter, *Das Handwerk in der wirtschaftlichen Entwicklung der ehemaligen DDR und im Übergang zur sozialen Marktwirtschaft,* Europäische Hochschulschriften 1978 (Frankfurt a. M., 1997), 89, 131, 168.
55. See Christian F. Zander, *Vom Hobel zum Computer: Zur Wirtschaftsgeschichte des modernen Tischler- und Schreinerhandwerks in Deutschland* (Leinfelden-Echterdingen, 2008), 115–16. For the following remarks, see ibid., especially p. 138–59.

56. See ibid., 138–43.
57. The number of nominally independent craftsmen businesses in Germany during the Great Depression, for example, rose from 1.38 million in 1931 to 1.73 million in 1934, sinking back down to 1.47 million by April 1939. See Rüdiger Hachtmann, "Arbeitsmarkt und Arbeitszeit in der deutschen Industrie 1929 bis 1939," *Archiv für Sozialgeschichte* 27 (1987): 202–4.
58. Zander, *Vom Hobel zum Computer*, 140, 146, 148.
59. See for instance Birgit Huber, *Arbeiten in der Kreativindustrie: eine multilokale Ethnografie der Entgrenzung von Arbeits- und Lebenswelt* (Frankfurt a. M., 2012).
60. For an introduction, see Heiner Minssen, *Arbeit in der modernen Gesellschaft: Eine Einführung* (Wiesbaden, 2012), 109–11.
61. See also the chapter by André Steiner and Ralf Ahrens in this book.
62. This same development occurred earlier in the United States. Service sector percentage in 1960: 58.7 percent; 2003: 86.6 percent. See OECD Economic Surveys 2006: United States (Paris 2007).
63. In 1989, Konsum had more than twenty-one thousand stores under its umbrella that sold food and daily necessities, 544 of which were supermarket-style retail outlets and 399 of which were village general stores. See Jan Bösche, *Die Konsumgenossenschaften in der Wende von 1989/90: Von der Plan- zur Marktwirtschaft am Beispiel der Genossenschaft Sachsen-Nord, Eilenburg* (Norderstedt, 2007), 28–30.
64. See Martin Schmitt's current dissertation project, "Die Digitalisierung der Kreditwirtschaft" (ZZF/Section II).
65. See Leimbach, *Die Softwarebranche in Deutschland*, 84–86.
66. See, for instance, "BÜRO-AUTOMATION: Das Hirn," *Der Spiegel* 10 (1958), retrieved 15 May 2018, http://www.spiegel.de/spiegel/print/d-41760832.html; in detail: Schuhmann, "Der Traum vom perfekten Unternehmen."
67. See Siegfried Schmidt, "Siegeszug der EDV—Revolutionierung der Bibliotheken," in *Auf dem Wege in die Informationsgesellschaft: Bibliotheken in den 70er und 80er Jahren des 20. Jahrhunderts*, ed. Peter Vodosek and Werner Arnold (Wiesbaden, 2008), 257–84.
68. See Ulrich Thiem, "ADV—Nur für die Großen?," *Forum Bibliothek und Information* 33 (1981): 29–38.
69. See Schmidt, "Siegeszug der EDV—Revolutionierung der Bibliotheken," 280. On the opinions of the employees, see, for example, the surveys conducted by Ver.di at the beginning of 2011 (URL: http://www.verdi-gute-arbeit.de/upload/m4ddb5925991c6_verweis2.pdf).
70. Minssen, *Arbeit in der modernen Gesellschaft*, 97.
71. For a brief introduction, see Rüdiger Hachtmann, *Tourismus-Geschichte*, Grundkurs Neue Geschichte series (Göttingen, 2007), 140–72.
72. See Deutscher Bundestag, *Entwicklung und Folgen des Tourismus: Bericht zum Abschluss der Phase II*. Bericht des Ausschusses für Bildung, Forschung und Technikfolgenabschätzung, 14. Wahlperiode: Drucksache 14/1100, 25

January 1999, 46, retrieved 25 May 2018, http://dip21.bundestag.de/dip21/btd/14/011/1401100.pdf.
73. See Deutscher Reiseverband, "Fakten und Zahlen 2013," February 2014, 19, retrieved 25 May 2018, https://www.drv.de/fachthemen/statistik-und-marktforschung/fakten-und-zahlen-zum-reisemarkt.html.
74. See Stephan Voswinkel, "Das mcdonaldistische Produktionsmodell—Schnittstellenmanagement interaktiver Dienstleistungsarbeit," in *Begrenzte Entgrenzungen: Wandlungen von Organisation und Arbeit*, ed. Heiner Minssen (Berlin, 2000), 177–203, citation: 181.
75. Initially mentioned in Douglas Coupland, *Generation X: Tales for an Accelerate Culture* (New York, 1991).
76. See Gisela Hellwig, "Altenpolitik," in *Geschichte der Sozialpolitik in Deutschland seit 1945*, vol. 10, *Deutsche Demokratische Republik 1971–1989: Bewegung in der Sozialpolitik, Erstarrung und Niedergang*, ed. Christoph Boyer, Klaus-Dietmar Henke, and Peter Skyba (Baden-Baden, 2008), 535–40; Thomas Olk, "Soziale Infrastruktur und soziale Dienste in den 60er Jahren," in *Geschichte der Sozialpolitik in Deutschland seit 1945*, vol. 9, *Deutsche Demokratische Republik 1961–1971: politische Stabilisierung und wirtschaftliche Mobilisierung*, ed. Christoph Kleßmann (Baden-Baden, 2006), 671–73.
77. See, in particular, Wilfried Kunstmann, "Zur Entwicklung und Situation der häuslichen Alten- und Krankenpflege," in *Zwischenzeiten*, ed. Winfried Beck, *Jahrbuch für kritische Medizin* 30 (Berlin, 1998), 85–101.
78. Statistisches Bundesamt, ed., *Pflegestatistik 2009. Pflege im Rahmen der Pflegeversicherung* (Bonn, 2011), 6, 9; Kunstmann, "Zur Entwicklung und Situation der häuslichen Alten- und Krankenpflege," 88.
79. In 1994, the percentage of part-time employees amounted to 53 percent among the private companies, and 42 percent among the nonprofit providers. These figures and the following are drawn from Kunstmann, "Zur Entwicklung und Situation der häuslichen Alten- und Krankenpflege," 94; Maik Winter, "Qualifikationsprofile und -anforderungen im Rahmen der professionellen pflegerischen Versorgung demenzieller Kranker," in *Demenz als Versorgungsproblem*, ed. Heinz-Harald Abholz and Michael Essers, *Jahrbuch für kritische Medizin* 40 (Hamburg, 2008), 124; Statistisches Bundesamt, *Pflegestatistik 2009*, 9.
80. Winter, "Qualifikationsprofile und -anforderungen," 125–27.
81. Wolfgang Streeck calls this "Regime-Shopping": see Wolfgang Streeck, "National Diversity, Regime Competition and Institutional Deadlock: Problems in Forming a European Industrial Relations System," *Journal of Public Policy* 12, no. 4. (1992): 301–30.
82. Gert Schmidt, "Arbeit und Globalisierung," in *Nach dem "kurzen Traum": neue Orientierungen in der Arbeitsforschung*, ed. Norbert Altmann and Fritz Böhle (Berlin, 2010), 234.
83. Lehndorff, Wagner, and Franz, *Development of Working Time in the EU*, 141 and 143. For the background, see especially Dietmar Süß, "Stempeln,

Stechen, Zeit erfassen. Überlegungen zu einer Ideen- und Sozialgeschichte der 'Flexibilisierung' 1970–1990," *Archiv für Sozialgeschichte* 52 (2012): 139–62; Dietmar Süß, "Der Sieg der grauen Herren? Flexibilisierung und der Kampf um die Zeit in den 1970er und 1980er Jahren," in *Vorgeschichte der Gegenwart. Dimensionen des Strukturbruchs nach dem Boom*, ed. Anselm Doering-Manteuffel, Lutz Raphael, and Thomas Schlemmer (Göttingen, 2016), 109–27.

84. See Bundeszentrale für politische Bildung, "Atypische Beschäftigung | bpb," retrieved 28 May 2016, http://www.bpb.de/nachschlagen/zahlen-und-fakten/soziale-situation-in-deutschland/61708/atypische-beschaeftigung. For an introduction to the topic since the 1980s, see Christoph Weischer, "Soziale Ungleichheiten 3.0. Soziale Differenzierungen in einer transformierten Industriegesellschaft," *Archiv für Sozialgeschichte* 54 (2014): 305–43.
85. See Schmidt, "Arbeit und Globalisierung," 235; the following citation: Gert Schmidt, "Arbeit und Gesellschaft," in *Handbuch Arbeitssoziologie*, ed. Fritz Böhle, G. Günter Voß, and Günther Wachtle (Wiesbaden, 2010), 138.
86. Weil, *Herrschaftsanspruch und soziale Wirklichkeit*, 172, footnote 509 (Interview colleague L.).
87. According to Gerhard Bosch, the percentage of externally driven, Taylorist-style work in Germany has increased just between 1993 and 1998 from 37.8 percent to 39.3 percent. Gerhard Bosch, "Entgrenzung der Erwerbsarbeit—Lösen sich die Grenzen zwischen Erwerbs- und Nichterwerbsarbeit auf?," in *Begrenzte Entgrenzungen: Wandlungen von Organisation und Arbeit*, ed. Heiner Minssen (Berlin, 2000), 253–55.
88. On Daimler-Benz, see, for instance, Jörg Neuheiser, "Der 'Wertewandel' zwischen Diskurs und Praxis. Die Untersuchung von Wertvorstellungen zur Arbeit mit Hilfe von betrieblichen Fallstudien," in *Gab es den Wertewandel? Neue Forschungen zum gesellschaftlich-kulturellen Wandel seit den 1960er Jahren*, ed. Bernhard Dietz, Christopher Neumaier, and Andreas Rödder (Munich, 2014), 141–67.
89. See, for instance, Boy Lüthje, "Kehrt der Fordismus zurück? Globale Produktionsnetze und Industriearbeit in der 'New Economy,'" *Berliner Debatte Initial* 15 (2004): 62–73.

BIBLIOGRAPHY

Ahrens, Ralf. "Rationalisierungseuphorie und Innovationsschwäche: Industrieroboter im Werkzeugmaschinenkombinat 'Fritz Heckert' um 1980." *Technikgeschichte* 79 (2012): 61–77.

Anweiler, Oskar. "Bildungspolitik." In *Geschichte der Sozialpolitik in Deutschland seit 1945*, vol. 10: *Deutsche Demokratische Republik 1971–1989: Bewegung in der Sozialpolitik, Erstarrung und Niedergang*, edited by Christoph Boyer, Klaus-Dietmar Henke, and Peter Skyba, 541–82. Baden-Baden: Nomos, 2008.

Bauer, Reinhold. "Ölpreiskrisen und Industrieroboter. Die siebziger Jahre als Umbruchphase für die Automobilindustrie in beiden deutschen Staaten." In *Das Ende der Zuversicht? Die siebziger Jahre als Geschichte*, edited by Konrad H. Jarausch, 68–83. Göttingen: Vandenhoeck & Ruprecht, 2008.

———. *Pkw-Bau in der DDR : zur Innovationsschwäche von Zentralverwaltungswirtschaften*. Frankfurt a. M.: Lang, 1999.

Binkelmann, Peter, Hans-Joachim Braczyk, and Rüdiger Seitz. *Entwicklung der Gruppenarbeit in Deutschland. Stand und Perspektiven*. Frankfurt a. M.: Campus, 1993.

Boes, Andreas. "Arbeit in der IT-Industrie: Durchbruch zu einem neuen Kontrollmodus? Auf der Suche nach den Konturen eines postfordistischen Produktionsmodells." In *Das neue Marktregime: Konturen eines nachfordistischen Produktionsmodells*, edited by Klaus Dörre, 135–52. Hamburg: VSA, 2003.

Boll, Friedhelm, and Viktoria Kalass. "Streik und Aussperrung." In *Handbuch Gewerkschaften in Deutschland*, 535–78. Wiesbaden: Springer VS, 2014.

Bösche, Jan. *Die Konsumgenossenschaften in der Wende von 1989/90: Von der Plan- zur Marktwirtschaft am Beispiel der Genossenschaft Sachsen-Nord, Eilenburg*. Norderstedt: Books on Demand, 2007.

Bosch, Gerhard. "Entgrenzung der Erwerbsarbeit—Lösen sich die Grenzen zwischen Erwerbs- und Nichterwerbsarbeit auf?" In *Begrenzte Entgrenzungen: Wandlungen von Organisation und Arbeit*, edited by Heiner Minssen, 249–68. Berlin: Ed. Sigma, 2000.

Bundesagentur für Arbeit. "Arbeitnehmerüberlassung, Leiharbeitnehmer, Verleihbetriebe (1973–2014)." Retrieved 29 May 2016, https://statistik.arbeitsagentur.de/Statistikdaten/Detail/Aktuell/iiia6/aueg-aueg-zr/aueg-zr-d-0-xls.xls.

Bundeszentrale für politische Bildung. "Atypische Beschäftigung | bpb." Retrieved 28 May 2016, http://www.bpb.de/nachschlagen/zahlen-und-fakten/soziale-situation-in-deutschland/61708/atypische-beschaeftigung.

"BÜRO-AUTOMATION: Das Hirn." *Der Spiegel* 10 (1958). Retrieved 15 May 2018, http://www.spiegel.de/spiegel/print/d-41760832.html.

Bust-Bartels, Axel. *Herrschaft und Widerstand in den DDR-Betrieben: Leistungsentlohnung, Arbeitsbedingungen, innerbetriebliche Konflikte und technologische Entwicklung*. Frankfurt a. M.: Campus, 1980.

Büter, Clemens. *Das Handwerk in der wirtschaftlichen Entwicklung der ehemaligen DDR und im Übergang zur sozialen Marktwirtschaft. Europäische Hochschulschriften 1978*. Frankfurt a. M.: Lang, 1997.

Coupland, Douglas. *Generation X: Tales for an Accelerate Culture*. New York: St. Martin's Press, 1991.

"DDR: Am Fließband." *Der Spiegel* 44 (1973). Retrieved 15 May 2018, http://www.spiegel.de/spiegel/print/d-41898403.html.

Deutscher Bundestag. *Entwicklung und Folgen des Tourismus: Bericht zum Abschluss der Phase II*. Bericht des Ausschusses für Bildung, Forschung und Technikfolgenabschätzung, 14. Wahlperiode: Drucksache 14/1100, 25 January 1999. Retrieved 25 May 2018, http://dip21.bundestag.de/dip21/btd/4/011/1401100.pdf.

Deutscher Reiseverband. "Fakten und Zahlen 2013," February 2014. Retrieved 25 May 2018, https://www.drv.de/fachthemen/statistik-und-marktforschung/fakten-und-zahlen-zum-reisemarkt.html.

Elis, Volker. "Von Amerika nach Japan—und zurück. Die historischen Wurzeln und Transformationen des Toyotismus." *Zeithistorische Forschungen/Studies in Contemporary History* 6 (2009): 255–75.

Greef, Samuel. "Gewerkschaften im Spiegel von Zahlen, Daten und Fakten." In *Handbuch Gewerkschaften in Deutschland*, 657–755. Wiesbaden: Springer VS, 2014.

Gutmann, Gernot, and Hannsjörg Buck. "Die Zentralplanwirtschaft der DDR—Funktionsweise, Funktionsschwächen und Konjunkturbilanz." In *Die wirtschaftliche und ökologische Situation der DDR in den 80er Jahren*, edited by Eberhard Kuhrt. Opladen: Leske + Budrich, 1996.

Hachtmann, Rüdiger. "Arbeitsmarkt und Arbeitszeit in der deutschen Industrie 1929 bis 1939." *Archiv für Sozialgeschichte* 27 (1987): 177–227.

———. "Fordismus." Version: 1.0. Docupedia-Zeitgeschichte. 27 October 2011. Retrieved 25 May 2018, https://docupedia.de/zg/Fordismus.

———. "Industriearbeiterinnen in der deutschen Kriegswirtschaft 1936 bis 1944/45." *Geschichte und Gesellschaft: Zeitschrift für historische Sozialwissenschaft* 19 (1993): 332–66.

———. *Tourismus-Geschichte*. Grundkurs Neue Geschichte series. Göttingen: Vandenhoeck & Ruprecht, 2007.

Hachtmann, Rüdiger, and Adelheid von Saldern. "Das fordistische Jahrhundert. Eine Einleitung." *Zeithistorische Forschungen/Studies in Contemporary History* 6 (2009): 174–85.

———. "'Gesellschaft am Fließband.' Fordistische Produktion und Herrschaftspraxis in Deutschland." *Zeithistorische Forschungen/Studies in Contemporary History* 6 (2009): 186–208.

Hellwig, Gisela. "Altenpolitik." In *Geschichte der Sozialpolitik in Deutschland seit 1945*, vol. 10: *Deutsche Demokratische Republik 1971–1989: Bewegung in der Sozialpolitik, Erstarrung und Niedergang*, edited by Christoph Boyer, Klaus-Dietmar Henke, and Peter Skyba, 535–40. Baden-Baden: Nomos, 2008.

Heßler, Martina. "Die Halle 54 bei Volkswagen und die Grenzen der Automatisierung: Überlegungen zum Mensch-Maschine-Verhältnis in der industriellen Produktion der 1980er-Jahre." *Zeithistorische Forschungen* 11, no. 1 (2014): 56–76.

———. *Kulturgeschichte der Technik*. Historische Einführungen 13. Frankfurt a. M.: Campus, 2012.

Hirsch-Kreiensen, Hartmut. "Industrielle Einfachstarbeit." In *Arbeitswelten in Bewegung: Arbeit, Technik und Organisation in der "nachindustriellen Gesellschaft,"* edited by Christian Schilcher and Mascha Will-Zocholl, 211–40. Wiesbaden: Springer VS, 2012.

Huber, Birgit. *Arbeiten in der Kreativindustrie: eine multilokale Ethnografie der Entgrenzung von Arbeits- und Lebenswelt.* Frankfurt a. M.: Campus, 2012.

Hübner, Peter. *Arbeit, Arbeiter und Technik in der DDR 1971 bis 1989: Zwischen Fordismus und Digitaler Revolution.* Edited by Gerhard A. Ritter. Bonn: Dietz, 2014.

Hughes, Thomas P. *American Genesis: A Century of Invention and Technological Enthusiasm 1870–1970.* Harmondsworth: Viking, 1989.

Institut der Deutschen Wirtschaft, ed. *Deutschland in Zahlen 2014.* Cologne: Institut der Deutschen Wirtschaft, 2014.

Kleinschmidt, Christian. *Der produktive Blick: Wahrnehmung amerikanischer und Japanischer Management- und Produktionsmethoden durch Deutsche Unternehmer 1950–1985.* Berlin: Akad.-Verl., 2002.

Klenke, Olaf. *Kampfauftrag Mikrochip: Rationalisierung und Sozialer Konflikt in der DDR.* Hamburg: VSA-Verl., 2008.

Kotkin, Stephen. *Magnetic Mountain: Stalinism as a Civilization.* Berkeley: University of California Press, 1995.

Kunstmann, Wilfried. "Zur Entwicklung und Situation der häuslichen Alten- und Krankenpflege." In *Zwischenzeiten,* edited by Winfried Beck, 85–101, Berlin: Argument Verlag, 1998.

"Labour Market: Employment (National Concept) by Industries. Germany." (Facts & Figures > National Economy & Environment). DEStatis Statistiches Bundesamt. Retrieved 25 May 2016, https://www.destatis.de/EN/FactsFigures/Indicators/LongTermSeries/LabourMarket/lrarb013.html.

Lang, R., and W. Hellpach. *Gruppenfabrikation.* Berlin: Springer, 1922.

Lehndorff, Steffen, Alexandra Wagner, and Christine Franz. *Development of Working Time in the EU.* Fürth: GUE/NGL, Thomas Händel, Wolfgang-Abendroth-Stiftungs-Gesellschaft, 2010. Retrieved 12 July 2016, http://www.guengl.eu/uploads/_old_cms_files/Development_of_working_time_in_the_EU_(Pub___Thomas_Haendel___Dr__Axel_Troost_).pdf.

Leimbach, Timo. *Die Softwarebranche in Deutschland: Entwicklung eines Innovationssystems zwischen Forschung, Markt, Anwendung und Politik 1950 bis Heute.* Stuttgart: Fraunhofer Verlag, 2011.

Lippe, Peter von der. "Die gesamtwirtschaftlichen Leistungen der DDR-Wirtschaft in den offiziellen Darstellungen: Die amtliche Statistik der DDR als Instrument der Agitation und Propaganda der SED." In *Machtstrukturen und Entscheidungsmechanismen im SED-Staat und die Frage der Verantwortung,* vol. 2, *Materialien der Enquete-Kommission "Aufarbeitung von Geschichte und Folgen der SED-Diktatur in Deutschland,"* edited by Deutscher Bundestag, 1973–2193. Baden-Baden: Nomos, 1995.

Lüthje, Boy. "Kehrt der Fordismus zurück? Globale Produktionsnetze und Industriearbeit in der 'New Economy.'" *Berliner Debatte Initial* 15 (2004): 62–73.

"Manchmal schlage ich irgendwas kaputt." *Der Spiegel* 27 (1973). Retrieved 15 May 2018, http://www.spiegel.de/spiegel/print/d-41986623.html.

Minssen, Heiner. *Arbeit in der modernen Gesellschaft: Eine Einführung.* Wiesbaden: Verlag für Sozialwiss., 2012.

Neuheiser, Jörg. "Der 'Wertewandel' zwischen Diskurs und Praxis. Die Untersuchung von Wertvorstellungen zur Arbeit mit Hilfe von betrieblichen Fallstudien." In *Gab es den Wertewandel? Neue Forschungen zum gesellschaftlich-kulturellen Wandel seit den 1960er Jahren*, edited by Bernhard Dietz, Christopher Neumaier, and Andreas Rödder, 141–67. Munich: Oldenbourg, 2014.

Noble, David Franklin. *Forces of Production*. New York: Knopf, 1984.

OECD Economic Surveys 2006: United States (Paris, 2007).

Olk, Thomas. "Soziale Infrastruktur und soziale Dienste in den 60er Jahren." In *Geschichte der Sozialpolitik in Deutschland seit 1945*, vol. 9: *Deutsche Demokratische Republik 1961–1971: politische Stabilisierung und wirtschaftliche Mobilisierung*, edited by Christoph Kleßmann, 657–95. Baden-Baden: Nomos-Verl., 2006.

Peters, Heiko. "Ausblick Deutschland. Stillstand der Lohnkonvergenz zwischen Ost-und Westdeutschland seit Anfang der 2000er Jahre." Edited by Deutsche Bank Research. April 2013. Retrieved 25 May 2018, http://docplayer.org/32638413-Research-briefing-konjunktur.html.

Pirker, Theo, and Mario Rainer Lepsius. *Der Plan als Befehl und Fiktion: Wirtschaftsführung in der DDR. Gespräche und Analysen*. Opladen: Westdt. Verl., 1995.

Schmidt, Gert. "Arbeit und Gesellschaft." In *Handbuch Arbeitssoziologie*, edited by Fritz Böhle, G. Günter Voß, and Günther Wachtler, 127–47. Wiesbaden: Verlag für Sozialwiss., 2010.

———. "Arbeit und Globalisierung." In *Nach dem "kurzen Traum": neue Orientierungen in der Arbeitsforschung*, edited by Norbert Altmann and Fritz Böhle, 233–43. Berlin: Ed. Sigma, 2010.

Schmidt, Siegfried. "Siegeszug der EDV—Revolutionierung der Bibliotheken." In *Auf dem Wege in die Informationsgesellschaft: Bibliotheken in den 70er und 80er Jahren des 20. Jahrhunderts*, edited by Peter Vodosek and Werner Arnold, 257–84. Wiesbaden: Harrassowitz, 2008.

Schmitt, Martin, and Julia Erdogan. "Digitalgeschichte Deutschlands: ein Forschungsbericht." *Technikgeschichte* 83, no. 1 (2016): 33–70.

Schroeder, Wolfgang, and Stephen J. Silvia. "Gewerkschaften und Arbeitgeberverbände." In *Handbuch Gewerkschaften in Deutschland*, 2nd ed., edited by Wolfgang Schroeder, 535–78. Wiesbaden: Springer VS, 2014.

Schuhmann, Annette. "Der Traum vom perfekten Unternehmen: die Computerisierung der Arbeitswelt in der Bundesrepublik Deutschland (1950er- bis 1980er-Jahre)." *Zeithistorische Forschungen* 9, no. 2 (2012): 231–56.

Schumann, Michael. "Industriearbeit zwischen Entfremdung und Entfaltung." *SOFI-Mitteilungen* 28 (2000): 103–12.

Statistisches Amt der DDR, ed. *Statistisches Jahrbuch der Deutschen Demokratischen Republik*. Vols. 34 and 35. Berlin: Haufe, 1989, 1990.

Statistisches Bundesamt, ed. *Pflegestatistik 2009. Pflege im Rahmen der Pflegeversicherung*. Bonn: DEStatis, 2011.

———. *Volkswirtschaftliche Gesamtrechnungen. Inlandsproduktsberechnung. Lange Reihen ab 1970.* Fachserie 18 Reihe 1.5. Wiesbaden: DEStatis, 2014. Retrieved 25 May 2018, https://www.destatis.de/DE/Publikationen/Thematisch/Volks wirtschaftlicheGesamtrechnungen/Inlandsprodukt/Inlandsproduktsberechn ungLangeReihenPDF_2180150.pdf?__blob=publicationFile.

Steiner, André. *Von Plan zu Plan: eine Wirtschaftsgeschichte der DDR.* Munich: DVA, 2004.

Steiner, André, and Matthias Judt. *Statistische Übersichten zur Sozialpolitik in Deutschland seit 1945: Band SBZ/DDR.* Bonn: Bundesministerium für Arbeit und Soziales, Ref. Information, Publikation, Redaktion, 2006.

Streeck, Wolfgang. "National Diversity, Regime Competition and Institutional Deadlock: Problems in Forming a European Industrial Relations System." *Journal of Public Policy* 12, no. 4 (1992): 301–30.

Süß, Dietmar. "Der Sieg der grauen Herren? Flexibilisierung und der Kampf um die Zeit in den 1970er und 1980er Jahren." In *Vorgeschichte der Gegenwart. Dimensionen des Strukturbruchs nach dem Boom,* edited by Anselm Doering-Manteuffel, Lutz Raphael, and Thomas Schlemmer, 109–27. Göttingen: Vandenhoeck & Ruprecht, 2016.

———. "Stempeln, Stechen, Zeit erfassen. Überlegungen zu einer Ideen- und Sozialgeschichte der 'Flexibilisierung,' 1970–1990." *Archiv für Sozialgeschichte* 52 (2012): 139–62.

Thiem, Ulrich. "ADV—Nur für die Großen?" *Forum Bibliothek und Information* 33 (1981): 29–38.

Tolliday, Steven. "Diffusion and Transformation of Fordism: Britain and Japan Compared." In *Between Imitation and Innovation: The Transfer and Hybridization of Productive Models in the International Automobile Industry,* edited by Robert Boyer, Elsie Charron, Ulrich Jürgens, and Steven Tolliday, 57–96. Oxford: University Press, 1998.

Viering, Jonas. "Taylors stille Rückkehr." *Die Zeit,* 15 January 2009. Retrieved 12 July 2016, http://www.zeit.de/2009/04/Taylorismus/komplettansicht.

Visser, Jelle. "ICTWSS: Database on Institutional Characteristics of Trade Unions, Wage Setting, State Intervention and Social Pacts in 51 Countries between 1960 and 2014. Version 5.0." Amsterdam Institute for Advanced Labour Studies, University of Amsterdam. October 2015.

Vogel, Berthold. "Die Spuren der Arbeitslosigkeit. Der Verlust der Erwerbsarbeit im Umbruch der ostdeutschen Gesellschaft zwischen Wohlstandssteigerung und neuer Ungleichheit." In *Ostdeutsche Arbeitswelt im Wandel 1945–2015,* edited by Paul Kaiser, 58–73. Dresden: DIK-Verlag 2015.

Voswinkel, Stephan. "Das mcdonaldistische Produktionsmodell—Schnittstellenmanagement interaktiver Dienstleistungsarbeit." In *Begrenzte Entgrenzungen: Wandlungen von Organisation und Arbeit,* edited by Heiner Minssen, 177–203. Berlin: Ed. Sigma, 2000.

Weil, Francesca. *Herrschaftsanspruch und soziale Wirklichkeit: zwei sächsische Betriebe in der DDR während der Honecker-Ära.* Cologne: Böhlau, 2000.

Weischer, Christoph. "Soziale Ungleichheiten 3.0. Soziale Differenzierungen in einer transformierten Industriegesellschaft." *Archiv für Sozialgeschichte* 54 (2014): 305–43.

Will-Zocholl, Mascha. "Globalisierte Wirtschaft? Ingenieure in der Automobilindustrie." In *Arbeitswelten in Bewegung: Arbeit, Technik und Organisation in der "nachindustriellen Gesellschaft,"* edited by Christian Schilcher and Mascha Will-Zocholl, 159–84. Wiesbaden: Springer VS, 2012.

Winter, Maik. "Qualifikationsprofile und -anforderungen im Rahmen der professionellen pflegerischen Versorgung demenzieller Kranker." In *Demenz als Versorgungsproblem*, edited by Heinz-Harald Abholz and Michael Essers, 120–34. Berlin: Argument-Verlag, 2008.

Zander, Christian F. *Vom Hobel zum Computer: Zur Wirtschaftsgeschichte des modernen Tischler- und Schreinerhandwerks in Deutschland.* Leinfelden-Echterdingen: DRW, 2008.

CHAPTER 6

The Individualization of Everyday Life
Consumption, Domestic Culture, and Family Structures

Christopher Neumaier and Andreas Ludwig

The last thirty years of the twentieth century were marked by a phase of individualization. While class identities, milieus, and mostly universally valid norms had determined how people lived their lives prior to this point, all of the sudden there were more choices to be made when it came to individual lifestyles. Sociologists and the media in the Western world spoke of the "'me' decade" during the 1970s.[1] In West Germany, moreover, they claimed that "self-realization" had become the goal of life in an "ego society."[2] Such interpretations are certainly problematic, not only because of their pessimistic cultural outlooks, but also because they did not reflect mainstream opinion. At the same time, however, they point to the strong resonance of self-descriptions of Western societies bandied about in the 1970s and 1980s, such as in Daniel Bell's *The Coming of Post-Industrial Society*, Ronald Ingelhart's *The Silent Revolution*, or in the theory of individualization put forth by Ulrich Beck and Elisabeth Beck-Gernsheim.[3] These studies had a decisive influence on debates among scholars, politicians, and the public, but they also indicated that a broad sociocultural shift had occurred in a relatively short period of about ten to fifteen years in West Germany as in other Western countries. Although the GDR and other countries in East and Central Europe were not included in these contemporary analyses, the question remains as to whether they also experienced shifts in self-description and social practices. The emergence of a debate about the "socialist lifestyle" in the 1970s, for example, seems to indicate that East German society was also seeking to differentiate itself.[4]

This chapter looks at the fundamental changes in lifestyles that took place in West Germany, but it also brings East Germany into the picture.

It examines the degree to which the changes in both German states differed, exhibited parallels, bore relationships to one another, and even wove back and forth across the border. More specifically, it takes a look at two areas of life that stood at the heart of the debates about individualization back then, namely the satisfaction of individual desires through consumption, and the significance of the family.

Changes in family and private life took place mostly "undercover" (although they were often openly observed) and were part of an ongoing departure from traditional patterns of behavior at an individual level. Consumption, on the other hand, took place in public as it was very much a demonstrative and symbolic expression of the overcoming of scarcity and the victory of want over need. Since both of these aspects involve private desires, they offer a window into changing lifestyles and their qualitative transformation since the 1970s.

The move beyond traditional, normative contexts of life not only reflects a process of pluralization, but also one of individualization. The desire of individuals to determine their own lifestyles at this time has been articulated many times over. Yet analyzing the debates surrounding this issue reveals that social pressures and customary cultural norms were losing their firm grip on society, which was also accompanied by disintegration of certainties. Nevertheless, this pluralization also had its limits because not all lifestyle choices were available to everyone, and not everyone had the same opportunities in terms of consumption. Indeed, different social, spatial, and generational aspects directed the development of this differentiation process. At the same time, new homogenizing patterns emerged within social groups, as well as within certain age groups, that affected cultural norms and lifestyles.

Pluralization occurred in both Germanys, yet with a distinct cultural meaning and praxis in each case. The GDR may have set tight limits on individualization politically, but the inherent potential of individualization continued to develop. In particular, its influence was quite clear to see in the run-up to the peaceful revolution of 1989. As early as the beginning of the 1980s, contemporary West German observers, such as politicians, representatives of the Catholic and Protestant Churches, social scientists, and the media, had begun to discuss the perceived changes in everyday life, most notably in the arenas of consumption and then private lifestyles.

Consumption and Consumer Cultures

Any account of the development of consumption in Germany during the second half of the twentieth century has to start in 1945. The destruction brought about by World War II and the internal displacement that followed in its wake created a massive shortage of housing, furniture, and household goods. There was a grave lack of food, heating supplies, clothing, and consumer items, all of which were rationed. Quite often, trading on the black market was the only way to get what was desperately needed. It was not until the 1950s that increasing affluence allowed for consumption beyond that of basic necessities in both German states. Beginning in the 1970s, consumption became more differentiated across all social strata, especially as it became a way for many to express their individual personalities. As defined for the purposes of this article, consumption is more than just the purchase of goods. It encompasses the use of not only these goods, but also of services, as well as discourses about consumption, emotions, relationships, rituals, and forms of sociability and integration in society (*Vergesellschaftung*).[5] Consumption, therefore, is not passive: consumers take an active role in processes of negotiation. The shift toward a focus on consumers as the "center of gravity within 'modern consumer society'" was clearly evident in West Germany, reflected in market research conducted during the 1970s.[6] Although consumption was done by individuals coming from specific social milieus and generations, behavioral patterns were nonetheless collectively reproduced across society, resulting in the formation of relatively homogeneous social groups with a distinct habitus. The same was true of the GDR, even though it took place within a much smaller realm of economic possibilities and within the framework of a politically regulated arena of consumption. Nonetheless, there was a notion of a specific consumer society in East Germany associated with certain social practices, although it was quite obvious that the gaze of many East Germans was firmly fixed on the more affluent society of West Germany. The high level of bureaucratization and politicization in many areas of life, however, makes it difficult to draw comparisons to the developments in West Germany. Scholarship has often characterized the 1970s as a "transitional period"[7] in the history of consumption, but this scenario that was sketched out for Western industrialized societies may or may not be comparable with what was going on in the East.[8] Consequently, the aim of this chapter is to analyze the social goals, economic systems, issues of periodization, and private and public leitmotifs of consumption that pertained to East and West Germany within a comparative perspective. It looks at places of consumption and the actors involved—stores, advertising, and buyers—but also key areas of consumption, namely the home and household goods, food, clothing, and cars. By focusing on the postwar societies in the two Germanys, it traces a similar successive change in the priorities of consumption in each state: first food, then clothing, then the home, then cars.[9]

Consumption as a social praxis was embedded within larger developments in both countries. Most especially, it was firmly rooted in the formation of perpetually accelerating consumer societies in the developed industrial countries of the West and the COMECON countries in the postwar decades. The major differences between the market societies of the West and the planned economies of Eastern Europe will be dealt with on a selective basis, bearing in mind that divided Germany played a particular role in both blocs. Both German states developed into leading economic countries in Western as well as in Eastern Europe, and both were like a showcase (*Schaufenster*) offering a glimpse into life on the other side of the Iron Curtain. Germans on both sides of the border kept tabs on the level of consumption on the other side, which was then reflected in consumer politics. Although the consumer policy in the two Germanys showed clearly asymmetric tendencies, consumption itself was tied to the development of affluence in a similar way. Especially after the early 1970s, when West Germany had completed the transition to a mass consumer society, the GDR gave up its strategy of consumption-based competition between the two systems. In its place, it developed a model of social and consumer policy that was less tied to developments in the West, known as the "unity of economic and social policy," under Erich Honecker. The collapse of the GDR in 1989/90 then produced a distinctive kind of catch-up consumption in East Germany, albeit one that was shaped by particularities specific to East German culture.

Any attempt to outline the formation of specific consumer societies and the lifestyle aspects associated with them in the two German states is plagued by methodological issues that arise from different sociopolitical interpretations of consumption. Although it was quite straightforward that a consumer society would be part of the postwar democracy in West Germany, and corresponding sociological studies have been done to this end, the position of the GDR vis-à-vis consumption was as changeable as it was contradictory. The clear lack of any kind of contemporary analyses that went beyond the level of consumer policy in the GDR means that this analysis will have to rely more heavily on indirect information. This makes it all the more difficult to get at the subcutaneous praxis of consumption in alternative lifestyles. Given the different types of sources available for East and West, the following analysis is therefore also "asymmetric" in its methodology.[10]

Changes in Consumption and Their Interpretation

The 1950s marked a phase of catch-up consumption and the reconstruction of "normal" living conditions after World War II. Between the mid-1960s and the beginning of the 1980s, consumption and consumer culture clearly became more individualized and pluralized. During this period, consumer choice became an individualized form of socially relevant action that included the most different distinctive consumption options. This made it possible to identify different social groups of consumers with firm preferences.[11] The basis for this process had been laid in the second half of the 1950s and the early 1960s when West Germany and other Western European countries transitioned into mass consumer societies.[12] The 1960s brought a quantitative and qualitative expansion of consumption and diversification, feeding into a clear market penetration at the end of the decade.[13] Mass consumer goods could be found everywhere, even in lower-income households.[14]

The transformations that took place in the West can only be compared partially to what happened in the COMECON states. A wave of consumption did follow after the end of the Stalinist phase of industrialization that had focused on the expansion of heavy industry, but it occurred later than in the FRG and other Western European industrial countries such as Great Britain and France. Around 1960, consumption had just gotten a start in Eastern Europe. With the exception of the earlier spread of radios, there was a considerable consumption gradient within the COMECON.[15] The GDR at the time was very much a "society that met basic needs" (*Bedarfsdeckungsgesellschaft*).[16] Essentially, social policy in the GDR aimed to secure basic provisions. In 1958, as rationing finally came to an end and fixed prices were introduced, a gradual catch-up modus in terms of the "satisfaction of needs" set in, and mass consumption spread during the 1960s.[17] Consumer policy, as did design policy, followed a concept of egalitarian mass production in accentuated opposition to West Germany and in keeping with the idea of postwar "Socialist Modernity";[18] a distinctive kind of consumption only began to form at the beginning of the 1970s. From this point on, the GDR developed its own kind of consumerism, which was only partially comparable to what emerged in West Germany. As the core element of Honecker's political turn after the Eighth Party Congress of the SED in 1971, the "elevation of the material and cultural standard of life" stood at the heart of political decision-making.[19] This was only partly related to the availability of consumer goods because it placed a great emphasis on the improvement of "social consumption," which referred to family-related social services and the push to build more housing.[20] Referred to as the "departure from Utopia," this trend in consumption introduced in the GDR was seen as the intentional political abandonment of formerly existing paradigms that revolved around the satisfaction of needs, utility, and rational consumption. It led to an increase in distinct consumption choices, which will be discussed later.[21] In the GDR, there was a doubled system of reference when it came to the perception of consumption. Although the level of consumption in the country was one of the highest in the COMECON states alongside the Czechoslovak Socialist Republic itself,[22] the East German people were more interested in what was going on in West Germany. The GDR thus developed into an affluent society within this framework, but it did not become a Western-style consumer society. Citing this shift, historians have argued that the notion of a "consumer society" does not aptly reflect the specific way in which elements of consumption were adapted in East Germany under the Communist regime. Since a comparison of the two German states along these lines would only serve to point out the shortcomings of the GDR, they have suggested that speaking of a distinct East German "consumer culture" offers a more promising perspective.[23] Indeed, the lives of most East Germans reflected the lasting discrepancy between expectations and reality that had resulted from economic priorities and changing consumer policy strategies.

On another note, the transformation of sales outlets in both East and West points to the significance of sites of consumption as well as the extent to which they pervaded everyday life. After the mid-1950s, a major transition to self-service occurred within just a few years. By 1968, more self-service shops existed than stores offering full service in West Germany, most of which had been constructed by modifying retail stores. Within almost no time at all, supermarkets offering a steadily growing selection of goods became the primary place to buy food, as well as nonfood items. Between the second half of the 1960s and the end of the 1980s, superstores, cash-and-carry stores, and food discounters spread across the country, especially on the outskirts of towns and cities. Despite a vast variety of available brands, the range of goods and the manner in which goods were displayed were standardized. Thus, marketing strategies involving product presentation, package design, and advertising had to be developed in order to attract shoppers from different consumer groups.[24]

Retail sales outlets in the GDR went through a comparable modernization process. They generally fell into three different categories: the co-ops that had been revived back in 1945, the state-run stores, and private retailers. East Germany's first self-service store opened in 1956, and it was quickly followed by many others in the 1960s. Most of these stores were built by modernizing existing, usually smaller, shops. Among the co-ops, which accounted for about 30 percent of retails sales in the GDR, there were already 12,500 self-service stores by 1965.[25] Beginning in the mid-1960s, *Kaufhallen* were introduced as the East German equivalent of a supermarket. Many of them were built as standardized stores in new residential areas. In addition to adopting modern cultural leitmotifs from the West, economic planners hoped to establish a permanent assortment of goods in order to be better able to manage the range of products available. Not surprisingly, however, such plans often ran into difficulties. Quite often, there was not a sufficient selection of goods available, for example, nor was it easy to put the necessary infrastructure of cash registers, shelving, and, above all, proper packaging into place. Only 74 percent of the product assortment consisted of packaged goods in 1966; correspondingly, 10 percent of retail workers had packing jobs in the same year. When it came to the packaging of products, this delayed implementation of rationalization was quite typical of the dependence on what could be produced (in this case, the amount of paper) within the confines of the planned economy.[26] Simultaneously, however, it became quite apparent that policy had given priority to the rationalization of the retail sector. Since the focus was not intended to be on consumers, the stores themselves as well as their product displays were purely functional.[27]

The important role of the consumer was already a focal point in West Germany in the 1970s, where it clearly influenced advertising and marketing strategies. From the mid-1960s into the second half of the 1970s, Western market research was dominated by the hypothesis that consumers communicate social differences through consumption. The idea was that there was no uniform market as a whole that included every consumer, but rather market segments that were primarily divided along the lines of region, town size, age, gender, income, profession, educational background, social status, and lifestyle. The marketing strategies of manufacturers were pushed in a new direction, spurred on by several parallel processes at the beginning of the 1970s. First, market saturation was on the rise and the economic crises in 1967/68 and 1973/74 brought a slump in sales, both of which were further exacerbated by pessimistic analyses such as the study titled *The Limits to Growth* commissioned by the Club of Rome.[28] At the same time, however, consumers themselves began to set new priorities. The goal was no longer to show that social differences had been eroded, but rather to express (following the theory of Pierre Bourdieu) the "fine lines" between different social groups through individual cultures of consumption, which led to homogenizing patterns within these groups.[29] Simultaneously, the critique of consumption spread as a general criticism of society under the banner of "wastefulness" (*Verschwendung*), resulting in the establishment of a "leftist" and later "alternative" form of consumption that firmly denied an interest in profit.[30] Lastly, a decidedly generation-specific type of consumption could be detected in young people as early as the 1960s.[31]

In the second half of the 1970s and during the 1980s, the image of a "postmodern" consumer emerged who could no longer be defined by "class," "social status," or "profession." Postmodern consumers, therefore, consciously construct their identities with those consumer goods that they deem suitable and "therefore reflect the emotional and symbolic side of products in particular."[32] Consumers, according to scholars, can thus be seen as active users who weigh options. This theory thus mitigates the direct influence of the media and advertising on consumers.[33] Market researchers also identified new consumer groups such as "yuppies" (young urban professionals), "ultras" (ultraconsumers), and "dinkies" (double income, no kids). In the 1980s, the SINUS market research institute developed the idea of what they called "sinus-milieus" as part of a sociologically based structural analysis of society that primarily sees citizens as potential consumers.

West German companies, as well as social scientists, adapted this way of differentiating society according to consumer roles for their own social analyses in the 1980s. After 1990, this model was then applied to East Germany, revealing significant differences in comparison to the West. According to West German market researchers, a trend toward a retreat into private life, combined with increased "self-awareness," appeared across all levels of East German society, and was tied to a preference for "enjoyment" and "consumption" that was branded as Western in style. Likewise, these studies claimed that the middle-class milieus, especially those individualized by "'new' values" and focused on climbing the social ladder, were much less prevalent in the East.[34] Whereas they could identify a clearly postmaterialist population segment in 1980s West Germany, the studies apostrophized a "postsocialist" attitude in East Germany in 1997 that was evidenced by terms such as (enjoying) "life" and "trying out." It thus appeared that there was an image of society that had been introduced by a market research institute. Interestingly, however, this interpretation of society in very economic terms was only seldom questioned by social science research.[35]

These theoretical models were based on the theory of a "change in values" (*Wertewandel*), and they sought to understand the parallel processes of individualization and pluralization.[36] Yet these theories and models were themselves contemporary self-perceptions that need to be analyzed as part of a specific historical context; the selective model of society upon which they were built, for example, ignored other parameters such as work, age, and gender. They were "reflexive descriptions of an experienced process of transformation."[37] Therefore, by looking at the way in which consumer goods were used in everyday life, the malleability of these changing social worlds becomes all the more evident.[38] The following sections trace these processes in terms of the basic human needs for housing, food, and clothing.

Housing: Modern Lifestyles, Pleasure, and Aesthetics

The rise in affluence that was required for the spread of a new culture of consumption may be indicated by the increased square footage of the apartments in new residential construction projects. Whereas West Germans had an average of 592 sq. ft. (55 m²) in 1955, this figure had climbed to 753 sq. ft. (70 m²) by 1960, and to 926 sq. ft. (86 m²) by 1970. The construction of a huge number of new rental apartments that went on well into the 1970s laid the foundation for this enormous improvement in the housing situation.[39] During this time, the government also subsidized the construction of single-family homes.[40] One result of the better housing situation was that the children of middle- and lower-class families often got to have a room of their own. Although the average square footage of living space also increased in the GDR, it still fell well behind that of West Germany. Statistically speaking, each East German citizen had 222 sq. ft. (20.6 m²) to call their own in 1971; by 1989, this figure had jumped up to 297 sq. ft. (27.5 m²).[41] It was not until 1971 that new apartments were constructed on a large scale in the GDR as part of the government's social policy that aimed to remedy the housing shortage in the country by 1990. Simultaneously, there were distinctive signs that living space was becoming more individualized, such as the boom in the construction of single-family homes and the revival of the appeal of living in historic city neighborhoods, which had been on the rise since the 1980s.

Alongside these developments, the way in which people furnished and decorated their homes also changed dramatically. In the 1960s, separate kitchens of about 40 to 65 sq. ft. (4 to 6 m²) became the norm in social housing projects, replacing the open kitchens that had traditionally been favored in Germany. As a result, a growing number of consumers in East and West began to buy standardized built-in kitchens. This transition to the kitchen as a place of work was also linked to the idea of making housework easier by integrating appliances and other kinds of technology.[42] The trend toward the mechanization of household work could also be found in the GDR. By the end of the 1970s, the full supply of all major household items had been achieved, at least statistically.[43] Although most of the household-related consumer goods had already been introduced onto the market by the 1960s, the idea that a kind of catch-up consumerism set in during the Honecker era can clearly be seen in the greatly increasing production figures for some consumer goods and the stagnation or decline in the numbers for others.

As part of the idea that making housework easier would increase leisure time for women, the mechanization of the kitchen stood for a modern lifestyle. In reality, however, the amount of physical work may have decreased in well-equipped households, but women did not enjoy more free time, in part because more was expected in terms of hygiene and cleanliness.[44] Similar arguments appeared in the GDR, but the emphasis was put on relieving women from the duties of housework so that they could seek paid employment outside the home.[45]

Beginning in the 1960s, televisions, as a household consumer good, changed the everyday lives and domestic culture of entire families in West Germany. By 1968, 80 percent of all West German households already had a black-and-white TV.[46] In the GDR, it was not until the end of the 1970s that most households had a TV. The replacement of black-and-white models by color TVs mostly occurred in the 1980s in East Germany; the percentage of color televisions increased from 16.8 percent in 1980 (50 percent in West Germany) to 46.5 percent in 1987 (96 percent in West Germany).[47] The GDR only partially kept up with other new trends in consumer electronics. The first cassette recorder hit the market in East Germany as early as 1969 (1968 in the FRG), for example, but the GDR never manufactured video recorders. As part of a one-time deal, the GDR did import 50,000 VCRs from Japan, but they were sold at a price of 7,300 marks, which was equivalent to six or more monthly paychecks for most people.[48]

Telephone connections were yet another technological consumer good marked by this distinctive pattern of diffusion. Whereas only a fifth of all four-person-employee households had a telephone in 1970, 86 percent had one in 1980. West Germany, however, still lagged behind Sweden, Switzerland, and especially the United States. Compared to East Germany, on the other hand, the FRG was clearly in the lead. In 1973, 51 percent of West German households had a telephone compared to 9 percent in the East due to problems in providing the infrastructure; in 1983, the ratio was 88 percent in the West to 13 percent in the East.[49] All together, radios, televisions, and telephones changed the way people lived and communicated with one another: "The home became part of the world with the radio as its ear, the television as its eye, and the telephone as an interactive link."[50] Not too long thereafter in the 1980s, stereos, VCRs, and then PCs found their way into West German homes. The home developed a dual purpose as a place to retreat into the private sphere and to communicate with the outside world.[51] The spread of consumer electronics likewise turned living rooms from rarely used representative spaces into everyday living spaces.[52]

Household consumption by no means leveled social differences, but rather fed into pluralization and individualization. In turn, the reproduction of these two tendencies within generations and milieus created new social divides drawn along "fine lines" of difference. Taste and lifestyle—as social practices—made consumption-related social structures visible through facets such as brand names, product quality, design, symbolic elements, and prestige.

The Scandinavian furniture of the 1950s and early 1960s that was considered to be particularly modern in West Germany, for example, was mirrored on the other side of the Wall by the GDR's "602 furniture series" that came onto the market in 1957 as a modernized, Scandinavian-style system of the "combinable modular furniture" (komplettierungsfähige Anbaumöbel) originally introduced in 1930. These were "generational objects," just like the infamous wall units of the 1970s. While similar trends for kitchens in the GDR had led to a practical standardization of compatible elements, these same trends were less welcomed when it came to living room furniture because pieces mostly only differed in decor.[53] The development of the MDW (Montagemöbelprogramm Deutsche Werkstätten) modular furniture system was quite symptomatic of the cultural and political climate in which the production of consumer goods took place. It allowed for the self-assembly of all kinds of furniture by consumers themselves, years before the IKEA concept was introduced in the West.[54] Style trends tended to be similar in East and West Germany: whereas "functional" furniture was favored in the 1960s, warm fake wood pieces became more popular in the 1970s, followed at the end of the decade by a "new splendor" phase in which decorative trims and bull's-eye glass panes regained popularity. In the 1970s, furniture began to be seen as a mark of distinction. On the one hand, quality furniture such as leather chairs and solid wood pieces were much sought after. On the other hand, the popularity of functional and provisional furniture was on the rise, exemplified by the success of IKEA, which opened its first store in West Germany in 1974. The furniture manufacturer tapped into a trend among West Germans, namely a rejection of representational interiors.[55] The IVAR shelf system commercialized the "culture of re-use" and the desire to "do-it-yourself" that were popular among younger generations of consumers who wanted a decorating style that clearly differed from that of their parents' generation.[56] The introduction of the BILLY bookcases in 1978, however, indicated a shift toward functional and minimalist pieces.[57] Thus, in both East and West Germany, consumers developed distinctive, often contrasting decorating styles shaped by the changing fashions favored by different generations. Such consumer preferences and the growing mix of eclectic styles contributed significantly to the individualization of the home.

Plastics also evolved in both German states into symbols of modern life. A prime example of this trend in West Germany was the Panton chair, introduced in 1967 and made of a single piece of molded plastic.[58] A parallel rise in the popularity of plastics also emerged in the GDR. The petrochemical Kombinat Schwedt, for example, began producing tables and chairs made of polyurethane in 1974, using an Italian design, as part of the initiative to offer East Germans more consumer goods. In particular, the chair produced by the Kombinat became a popular mass consumer item, and it can still be found in a number of East German gardens. The plastic Gartenei folding chair was another particularly poignant example of the entwined history of the two Germanys; it was manufactured in East Germany under license for a West German company, and it is now considered to be an Eastern design icon.[59]

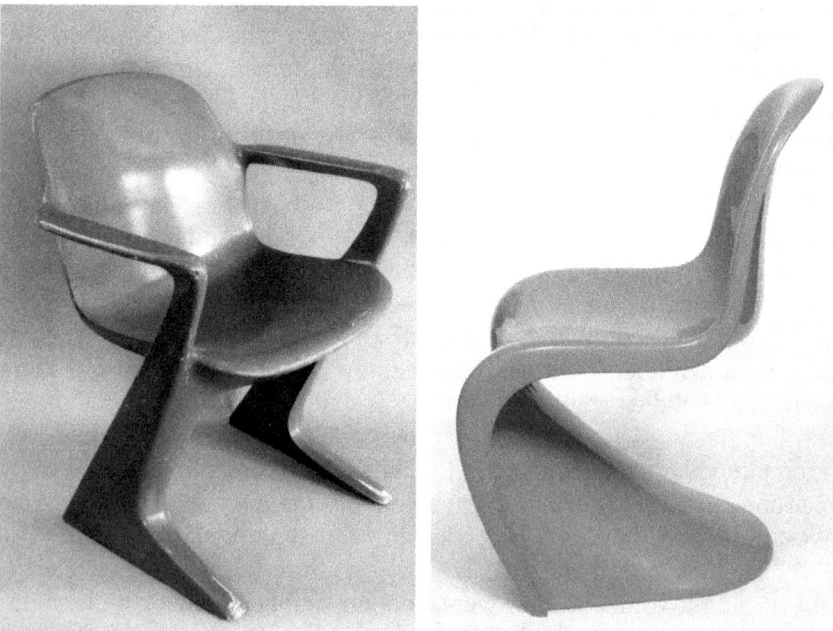

Figure 6.1. *Left,* PUR-Chair, VEB Petrolchemisches Kombinat Schwedt, 1974; *Right,* Panton Chair, Design by Verner Panton, Vitra AG, 1967 (photos: Südhoff, Dokumentationszentrum Alltagskultur der DDR; Werkbundarchiv/Museum der Dinge, used with permission)

Food and Clothing beyond the Basic Necessities

With the rise in affluence, food consumption from the 1950s to the 1970s had moved from a focus on nourishment and basic traditional dishes to increased culinary variety and nuanced food choices. This included the adoption and transformation of foreign food cultures, a process of "(self) ethnification" through food, and, more generally, the pluralization of food cultures.[60] In these developments, the period from the 1960s to the 1980s was a transitional phase. The first visitors to restaurants serving foreign food were migrants, but then these establishments attracted the younger, well-educated urban population in Germany who served as "innovators" by introducing the "the majority of West Germans to immigrant foods."[61] Thanks to their appealing prices, family-friendly atmospheres, and food selection, these kinds of restaurants quickly became mainstream.[62] In contrast, however, it cannot be said that a new consumer culture developed around food in the GDR. Foreign cuisine was served only in a few specialty restaurants in East Germany, and it tended to be either Eastern European or Asian-style food. For the most part, restaurants in the GDR served up standard German fare, in part because they were responsible for supplying a considerable portion of the "collective meals" in schools, offices, and smaller factories.

There were, however, clear parallels between East and West Germany in household food consumption. The end of the extreme postwar shortages fed into a "wave of bingeing" when food rationing was finally lifted in West Germany in 1950 and in the GDR in 1958. Yet differences in consumption cropped up when it came to goods that were not considered to be basic necessities, especially since consumer policy varied greatly between the two countries. Whereas the modernization of the food industry progressed slowly in the East, which meant that modern, prepackaged foods and ready-made products were in short supply, the East German government simultaneously increased the prices on certain goods that it determined to be luxury items.[63] The Delikat shops that were introduced in 1966 followed this principle. In addition to luxury food and drink, tobacco, and items of a high standard, they sold imports and products coming from what was referred to as "authorized manufacturing" at high prices.[64] Despite the costs involved, consumers frequented these stores more and more often.[65] As of the 1970s, therefore, a kind of parallel world of consumption had developed that was dependent on income levels. It grew to a rather substantial size due to the enormous surplus of buying power in the GDR. Even though the prices were set so high, there were still supply shortages in this consumer segment as well, the most famous of which was what has been termed "the coffee crisis" of 1977. Due to the rising price of coffee on the global market, the SED tried to limit the consumption of coffee beans in the GDR and raised the price of coffee accordingly. This sparked a significant public outcry over the fact that coffee should not be considered a luxury, but rather a basic grocery item.[66] As this example demonstrates, the consumption of "Western" brand-name products was a very sensitive political issue, as well as a core element of a specific East German consumer culture.

Clothing is the second basic area of consumption discussed here that evolved in distinctive ways since the 1950s. Beyond its protective function, clothing also has a symbolic function that is communicated through fashions and brand names. In the late 1960s, popular fashion and pop culture began to merge more and more, generating market segments exhibiting brand loyalty.[67] Most notably, the appearance of miniskirts and women wearing long pants are often cited as a typical expression of these kinds of changes. After blue jeans hit the market in the 1950s, the miniskirt that arrived in 1965 was seen as a "symbol of the sexual revolution," but it quickly established itself in mainstream society.[68] By 1970, more than half of young West German women wore them. Long pants for women had similar symbolic dimensions. The pantsuit permanently made its way into the wardrobes of professional women at the end of the 1960s, despite the fact that there had been protests and some women had actually lost their jobs because of it.[69] Clothing also became a way for young people to protest their parents' ideals and the dictates of conventional fashion, and consumers as well as designers consciously tapped into this symbolic power. The overall trend toward individualization and pluralization was reflected in the choices of individual actors. Some of these ideas were then copied a millions of times over across all of society, which meant that rather than having the intended effect of individualization, they always bore an element of homogenization. Later, especially from the 1980s onward, parallel youth cultures developed that often competed with each other and could be identified by a specific clothing style that was tied to an apparent preference for certain brands.[70]

Just as with other types of consumer goods, the clothing situation in the GDR was shaped by normative directives as well as production and supply issues. The ready-to-wear clothing industry was never able to offer a full range of clothing styles, despite some individual innovations. Nonetheless, clothing in the GDR had reflected some trends toward differentiation and individualization since the 1970s. The individual preferences of consumers were not only officially recognized, but also taken into consideration in the planned economy. For example, the concept of "young fashion" was introduced at the end of the 1960s. A chain of shops specialized in offering textiles for young people, and special contracts were made with manufacturers in order to provide a sufficient supply of garments.[71] Likewise, the one-time import of 150 thousand pairs of Western jeans into the GDR in the fall of 1971 indicates that the special fashion needs of the youth had been acknowledged.[72] A more distinctive selection of goods was also offered by the Exquisit shops for clothing and shoes, which had been introduced back in 1962. These stores were expanded considerably after 1971. Exquisit shops stocked Western and top-end Eastern clothing and shoes, and sold them at a high price, but in East German currency. The significance of this distinctive kind of consumption that necessitated a high level of income was clearly reflected in the sales figures for these stores. Whereas Exquisit goods accounted for only 3 percent of the textiles and shoes sold in 1970, they had climbed up to 18 percent by 1989.[73] Self-made clothing also came to be part of this trend toward more distinctive consumerism because it was a way for consumers to respond to the lack of selection in the shops and to craft their own individualized creations. In 1973, one-fifth of all women's outer garments in the GDR were self-sown and a third were self-knitted, and this upward trend continued until the end of the 1980s.[74]

This parallel world of food and clothing consumption in the GDR was also spurred on by the growing spread of Western goods within the country. The *Westpakete*—packages sent as gifts by friends and relatives in West Germany—accounted for a high percentage of consumer goods in the country, and about 20 percent of textiles in particular (in the 1970s/80s). In 1986, an estimated five million women's blouses were sent in these packages, whereas only 1.7 million blouses were actually made in the GDR; one-quarter of the coffee consumed in the GDR came from the West in the mid-1970s, but this had jumped to a half by 1989.[75] Consumer goods from the West also entered the country through the introduction and expansion of the Intershops and the Genex-Geschenkdienst, both of which relied upon payment in Western currencies. The Genex-Geschenkdienst offered consumer goods made in the GDR that were in short supply, such as cars, washers, and even single-family homes, in exchange for West German Marks. The Intershops, on the other hand, sold Western goods for Western currency. Initially established in the 1950s to serve foreign (i.e., Western) travelers, the Intershops became quite common in all the major East German cities in the 1970s; there were 221 Intershops in the GDR in 1974, but almost double as many (416) in 1988. These kinds of shops that sold goods for foreign currencies were also widespread in other parts of Eastern Europe, such as in Poland, where there were already 650 Pewex stores in 1983.[76] As of 1974, it was legal for East German citizens to possess Western money, which resulted in the development of a third culture of consumption that required access to foreign currencies in addition to the existing parallel consumer regimes based on fixed-priced goods and luxury items.

A look at consumer culture in the GDR thus reveals an increasing level of differentiation among lifestyles, but also a still-lagging kind of catch-up consumerism that was moving the country in the direction of a consumer society. This dynamic is reflected in the following table, which also gauges the chances of whether consumer desires could be met in the GDR. It also indirectly provides indications about consumer priorities in East Germany after 1990.

Table 6.1. Household Possessions and Planned Acquisitions in the GDR, 1988 (in percent of households)

Item	Owned	Planning to buy	Not available to purchase	Not needed
Color TV	53.0	13.9	24.6	8.5
Stereo	52.8	11.0	17.9	18.3
VCR	3.3	3.7	55.6	37.5
PC	5.9	4.5	34.6	55.1
Telephone	29.5	18.9	40.0	11.6
Weekend/vacation home	26.5	5.5	27.5	40.6

Source: Gunnar Winkler, ed., "Sozialreport DDR 1990. Daten und Fakten zur sozialen Lage in der DDR." Stuttgart: Bonn aktuell, 1990, 268.

The development of consumption in East Germany after reunification was in fact marked by a doubled frame of reference that sometimes clearly differed from that prior to 1989/90. Catch-up consumerism certainly applied when it came to cars, stereo systems, and then later furniture and household effects. The percentage of household expenses spent on transportation and mobility almost tripled between 1989 and 1991, but began to decline again slightly in 1992. The same figure for furniture and household effects also rose significantly between 1989 and 1992, almost doubling during this time. When it came to other consumer goods such as clothing, however, the amount spent remained stable for the most part.[77] A similar catch-up process took place in terms of people's living situations. After the push to build apartment housing within the framework of the planned economy came to an end, the preference shifted toward building one's own home in East Germany, despite the fact that Germany has typically been a "renters' country."[78] This, in turn, led to growing social segregation, especially since the number of empty apartments in East Germany doubled between 1995 and 1998 as a result of migration.

As early as the 1990s, however, products that had been bought in the GDR regained popularity and value. The cultural overvaluation of Western products that had taken place in the GDR because of the role that they had played in the satisfaction of personal desires and creating social distinctions in public dissolved after 1990 when these products became readily available. In fact, this actually reversed the trend: the desire for longevity and stability fed into a revaluation of GDR products since they were in fact known for their durability[79] and which were now called *Ostprodukte*. The revival in the popularity of GDR products that had been completely devalued in 1990 has evolved since the mid-1990s into a proper wave of nostalgia for the old East, known as *Ostalgie*, which has added a strong cultural element to consumerism.[80]

Automobile Culture: Trends towards Pluralization, Individualization, and Segmentation

The automobile was a consumer good that was particularly laden with personal emotions and social prestige. During the 1960s, it went from being a luxury item to a mass consumer good in West Germany, which lent it a special kind of social value at first. Cars became a "symbol of new democratic freedom"[81] and an expression of personal taste and social status.[82] The boom in automobiles in West Germany also led to traffic problems in cities, and the idea of a "car-friendly city" is simply the best example of the new automobile infrastructure that developed during this time and its ambiguous consequences. At the same time, the suburbanization process would have been impossible if not for the rise of car sales. Well into the 1970s, however, public opinion focused on the positive side. Cars continued to be status symbols, a practical necessity, a pastime, and a hobby object. In the course of the 1970s, the image of the car suffered in West Germany, both socially and privately, as the focus shifted toward its risks as opposed to its benefits. The number of road fatalities reached an all-time high of twenty thousand in 1970. Exhaust emissions and noise pollution were recognized as environmental and health hazards, which led to protective legislation in 1972 with the Gasoline Lead Act, followed by the Federal Immission Control Act in 1974. Similarly, the automobile was also criticized for its use of resources in the wake of the Club of Rome study in 1972 and the energy crises of 1973/74 and 1979/80. The (few) prohibitions against driving on Sundays that were introduced symbolized this critique.[83]

What happened with the automobile in West Germany can hardly be compared to its fate in the East. Although one of the main hubs of the automobile industry was located in the GDR, the SED did not devote much attention to personal transportation. As a result, production levels were low, and technological innovations were lacking. The production figures for 1971 indicate the degree to which the automobile industry in the GDR had fallen behind that of the FRG: whereas 3.6 million cars were built in West Germany that year, only 134 thousand left the factories in East Germany.[84] The only car models manufactured in the GDR were the Wartburg and the Trabant. Both models were last overhauled in the late 1950s and the mid-1960s, resulting in long wait times for new cars of over more than ten years. The car boom, as it were, did not hit the GDR until the 1970s, which was much later than in the West.[85]

On the other side of the Wall in West Germany, dramatic dips in sales, the arrival of foreign-made cars, and a changing demand structure fed into the transition from a seller's to a buyer's market. In response, the automobile industry tried to boost the purchase of replacement cars by reducing their average lifetime—in particular because it was not yet common for families to own a second car in the 1970s. Automakers also modified their product strategies in light of the fact that cars had become more of a way to distinguish social status. As part of this shift, the major manufacturers expanded their product ranges vertically and horizontally—that is, with a greater variety of makes and models. During this phase, brands, models, technology, and comfort features became all the more important in drawing lines of distinction because the main question was no longer about who owned a car, but rather what kind of car somebody drove. This reflected the general trend toward consumption as a means of making social distinctions and later becoming an expression of personalized consumer preferences.[86] Moreover, specific cultural values came to be associated with the respective brands and models. Ford and Opel stood for a kind of smug narrow-mindedness (*Spießigkeit*), while Mercedes cars were considered to be a symbol of "the establishment." Used French compact cars such as Citroën's Ente (2CV) or Renault's R4, on the other hand, were seen as symbols of an "automobile counter culture."[87] Consumer preference also changed to an extent in the 1970s because the trading-up principle—the idea that a new car had to be more expensive and more exclusive than the old one—was replaced for a short time by the trading-down principle at the beginning of the decade. Manufacturers also reacted to this trend and introduced new market segments, such as compact cars. Smaller, cheaper, and more efficient cars such as the VW Golf hence became the conscious preference of consumers.[88]

Nonetheless, such rational criteria were still mediated by symbolic, social, and psychological desires that were played upon in advertising and marketing.[89] The news of a technological product innovation, for example, was communicated via ads in terms of "symbolically inflated core indicators" such as motor performance in PS and fuel efficiency in liter per 100 km (the German equivalent of mpg).[90] This highlights the economic, cultural, and social status of advertising, which not only adapted to changing consumer desires, but was also attuned to processes of social change.

The marketing departments of the West German car manufacturers specifically tapped into the generally pessimistic social outlook in the country, targeting consumer fantasies and fears alike. Emotional appeals gave way to texts about safety, efficiency, and quality. Images highlighted innovative details up close and presented cost-efficient compact cars that were easy to park. "Driving fun" and "individuality," on the other hand, did not return as strong defining features in advertising until after the energy crises of the 1970s.[91] When the Golf diesel model was introduced in 1976, it was advertised as a "money-saver" (*Sparbüchse*)[92] with good motor performance in automobile magazines, which fostered its generally positive reception. This product discourse, which drew on scientific data, targeted heterogeneous and pluralized consumer groups with the aim of appealing to their individualized desires. After the energy crises in the 1970s, however, the "money-saving" argument became less attractive in the first half of the 1980s, and it was the sporty Golf GTI that caught the eye of consumers. Ads promoted this model by claiming it could go "from 0 to 50 in 3.3 seconds." For careful readers, the ad also explained that the GTI was not just "a hot rod," but also it was a "robust practical car made by Volkswagen that would keep running efficiently, day after day without fail."[93] As the ad claimed, it was the perfect car for everyday driving in the city because it could accelerate quickly to the normal speed limit of 50 km/h.

Consumer goods of short supply, such as cars, were rare items in the GDR. They were only really advertised until the 1960s; by the 1970s, they were simply touted as a lottery win. In comparison to the West, product advertising played a completely different role in East Germany. Around the same time as the years of the economic miracle in the West, the SED reacted to the uprising of 17 July 1953 with its "new course," and there was a revival of ads in popular magazines in the GDR. The number of ads rose significantly in the 1950s, topping out in the 1960s. As of the mid-1970s, however, product advertising was prohibited in East Germany. Since advertising was not about the market penetration of products in a planned economy, it needs to be read as a means to steer sales and communicate the socialist lifestyle that reflected the official ideas about what people should have within the regime of rational consumption.[94] Both in terms of style and content, East German advertising in the 1950s still drew on that of the 1920s/30s. It stressed the normalization of everyday life after World War II, calling for the return of elegance. In the 1960s, it was dominated by consumer information focused on product usage and creating an image of modern consumption. Then, in the 1970s, the actual consumer products gradually disappeared from ads. It seems puzzling that product advertising came to an end just as forms of consumerism that served to make distinctions between consumers were officially recognized and even sometimes fostered in the GDR.

A Comparison of the Two Consumer Societies

Having identified individualization, pluralization, and homogenization as a sign of social change since the 1970s, this chapter will next look at the related historical development of consumer society within a narrative that approaches consumption as a multifaceted process of satisfying needs and desires. From this perspective, the 1970s were very much a transitional period or *"Sattelzeit"*[95] for consumer society in West Germany. It marked the transition to a phase in which the satisfaction of the desire for individual self-realization became paramount. Yet it is just as readily apparent that consumption still served to satisfy the need to define social status, not to mention its role in providing for basic necessities. It has also been rightly pointed out that social position continued to have a lasting influence even after a consumer society had developed.[96] At the same time, however, the temporality of consumer society must not be neglected. The introduction of EC cards (debit cards) and ATMs during the 1970s, for instance, caused yet another significant dynamic rise in consumption.[97] The move from needs to desires in West Germany in the 1960s as part of a historical narrative of consumption rested on improved economic and social conditions, the separation of personal and social positions, and a discursive shift from the emphasis on the social connotations of consumption to a focus on its individual aspects.[98] In comparison to the West, the 1970s also marked a phase in the GDR in which the focus was on status; toward the end of the decade, albeit in a very confined milieu, there was also a phase of self-realization that took the form of alternative or "counteridentities."[99] Nonetheless, it is still controversial to refer to the GDR as a consumer society.

Despite the central focus on the consumer world of the FRG within East Germany, consumer society itself cannot be interpreted as the triumph of a successful Western model of society in the decades after 1945. While scholars point to the importance of the longue durée when it comes to consumer society,[100] they also stress the cultural differentiation among different societies overall. Accordingly, there is no single model of consumer society based on the paradigm of modernization, but rather many different consumer societies whose inner dynamics and various shades of differentiation need to be looked at more closely. For example, there are generational differences associated with consumption, such as the fact that retirees have become an important consumer group because they have had more money than young people since the 1990s. Such factors are augmented by variations in affluence, different leitmotifs of consumption (not just hedonistic ones), and the simultaneous internationalization and constriction of consumer markets.[101] Despite the fact that economic considerations are the driving force behind consumption, these factors were not necessarily homogeneous, nor were they always socially dominant.[102]

Types of Families and Daily Life

The following section offers a look at the family from a variety of perspectives. It begins with its sociostructural development as indicated by statistics before turning to changes in notions of the family and family policy. Then it examines shifts in family life over the last thirty years of the twentieth century, looking closely at how domestic partnerships among unmarried couples gained in popularity as a new way of life. As with consumption, there are two key leitmotifs that appear over and over again in these processes: individualization and pluralization. Finally, this section will identify the motors behind these developments toward the end of the twentieth century, bearing in mind that these processes had various facets that merit more attention. Although it is not possible to determine precisely who or what was behind these shifts, the role of women and small social groups living alternative lifestyles certainly played a key role. Sociological studies and very recent historical research have stressed the importance of both the student protest movement and the women's movement, or the leftist-alternative milieu. Yet there were indeed other decisive factors such as the legal reforms introduced in the 1970s, better contraception, improved access to education, and the growing percentage of women within highly qualified professions in particular. All told, it was employed female professionals with advanced degrees who were a central motor behind these changes.[103]

Statistics and the Family: The Gentle Pluralization of Private Lives

"Families Today—Three Different Ones" was the headline of an issue of the women's magazine *Für Sie* in July 1980. It compared the different lives of three kinds of nuclear families: a married couple with children, a childless married couple, and a married couple with an adopted child. Likewise, the magazine discussed the increasing prevalence of domestic partnerships, singles, and "one-parent families" (i.e., single parents). Based on examples, the article traced the appearance of entirely different familial and nonfamilial lifestyles alongside the traditional model of a nuclear family (a married couple with children). Despite divergent circumstances and desires, one thing united all these models: couples or individuals now seemed to be able to decide for themselves how they wished to live their lives, and if or how many children they wanted to have. Of course, better contraceptive methods, such as the birth control pill, which had become available in West Germany in 1961, aided this shift. But, more than anything else, it was also the result of a changed attitude toward personal lifestyle choices, which had become more differentiated and pluralized.[104]

The article in *Für Sie* summarized perceived changes in private lifestyles that had already begun to appear at the end of the 1960s, but gained a stronger foothold by the early 1980s at the latest. Research studies conducted at the time analyzed the scope of these trends on the basis of statistics about the number of marriages, births, and divorces. Their results indicated that both the birth rate and the inclination to marry were declining in East and West Germany. Parallel to this, the divorce rate was clearly on the rise. Although the decline in marriage was more gradual in the GDR than it was in West Germany, the divorce rate in East Germany was rising faster. Sociopolitical measures, such as financial support for mothers, actually helped to increase the birth rate for a short time in the second half of the 1970s.[105] In the 1980s, both Germanys entered into a phase of relative stability in which these sociostructural indicators no longer shifted fundamentally.

After reunification, on the other hand, another major shift occurred in the states of the former East Germany, reflected in particular by a noticeable decline in marriages and births. This trend resulted from the new social, political, and economic circumstances. The transition from a planned economy to a market-based system, for example, brought uncertainties into people's private lives, leading to a temporary slide in the birth rate, which contemporaries called "birth shock." Moreover, the fall of the Wall prompted many better-educated East German women to head to West Germany to look for jobs. This clearly had a detrimental effect on the number of marriages and births in the old GDR. Likewise, it also needs to be kept in mind that the decrease in the number of divorces at the beginning of the 1990s also reflected the legal changes associated with the adoption of the West German Civil Code (BGB) in the new federal states and not necessarily a short-term shift in attitudes about marriage.[106]

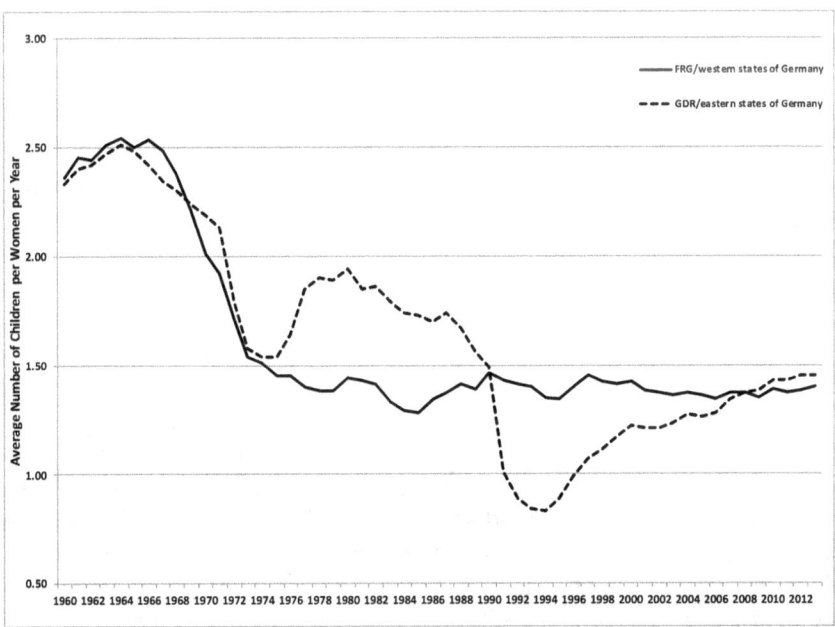

Figure 6.2. Overall Birth Rates in East and West Germany, 1960–2013 (source: Bundesinstitut für Bevölkerungsforschung [Federal Institution for Demographic Research])

Furthermore, the trends indicated by these statistics were not just a German phenomenon. Similar developments can be seen in almost all European countries. The specific national patterns do, however, differ in terms of when the shifts took place, the speed in which they progressed, and the degree to which the rates moved up or down. Broadly-speaking, things first began to change in the second half of the 1960s in northern Europe, hitting Central and Western Europe a few years later. Southern Europe was affected even later, and, apart from the decline in births, the shifts were less pronounced. In the former socialist countries of Eastern and Central Europe, there were clear shifts in the wake of the fall of Communism, such as a spike in divorces.[107]

Among contemporary observers, these very same demographic developments were taken as an indication that the "golden age of marriage" of the 1950s and early 1960s had come to an end.[108] They were also interpreted as a "crisis of the family," but this proved to be somewhat problematic because it clung to the rather narrow ideal of a middle-class nuclear family. According to this perspective, the nuclear family was implicitly defined as "normal," and all other lifestyles that did not correspond to this model were considered to be deviant. Consequently, many of the observations and interpretations made by contemporaries in the 1970s and 1980s have to be taken with a grain of salt and evaluated within their specific historical context. The collected aggregated data, however, can still be used to analyze trends. It indicates an increase in the number of singles, unmarried couples with and without children, couples without children, and single parents, as well as a decline in the number of married couples with children. Furthermore, they point to a "polarization of lifestyles into a family and nonfamily sector,"[109] which was exemplified in the growth of childless familial arrangements.[110]

Looking back, the changes that occurred between the 1970s and the 1990s can be interpreted as a "pluralization process within limits,"[111] a kind of gentle pluralization in which not every form of cohabitation could be freely chosen. The only age group in which most people could choose from several different lifestyles was that of the twenty- to thirty-five-year-olds. Thus, a significant pluralization and individualization only unfolded within a very narrowly defined social group. The majority of German citizens, especially those younger than twenty and older than thirty-five, lived in a traditional-style family. At the same time, however, this development does indicate that within this social group, desires and needs were initially supposed to be met on an individual level, but then later in the form of a family when they hit middle age.[112] This limited phase of pluralization in midlife was thus sandwiched between homogenized patterns of behavior in younger years and after starting a family.

A more differentiated perspective can also reveal the limits of this pluralization. The growth of the "singles" group, for example, resulted in part from increased life expectancy, especially because it counted a large proportion of older widowed women. Despite the fact that the transformation of the family was discussed at all levels of society in the 1970s, the majority of West Germans at the time still lived in a "traditional" family. It was not until the 1980s and 1990s that the prevalence of this kind of nuclear family shrank; by 2004, only 29 percent of families fit this model. Yet, it needs to be kept in mind that the category of "married couples without children" included married couples who may have had children (minors under 18) but, at the time of the survey, these children had already reached adulthood. The changes reflected in these statistics in fact only provided a "snapshot" of the ways things were, because they did not take into account the life cycle of a family.[113] If these points are factored into the analysis, then 53 percent of West Germans still lived in a nuclear family with children in 2005.[114] In this respect, the data collected clearly indicates that the middle-class nuclear family remained the dominant model well past the 1970s, although the public debates about the family would seem to suggest the opposite.

The Transformation of Family Ideals and Policy

A key shift in attitudes took place in West Germany in the second half of the 1970s as the role of marriage as an institution and goal in life was increasingly called into question. At the same time, an Allensbacher survey determined somewhat surprisingly that the family was still considered to be a significant aspect of people's lives.[115] It showed that a growing number of West Germans were decoupling marriage and family in their private lives. Yet many of them broke with this new outlook that had been articulated discursively and in praxis when it came to their own lives; the majority still married as soon as a baby was on the way.[116] These findings indicate that the main point of reference continued to be the traditional nuclear family.

Family policy in West Germany also reflected this shift in public opinion. Social Democrats pushed to define the family according to the relationship between children and parents in the 1970s. Consequently, parenthood was supposed to be the necessary qualification for a "family." By proposing this definition of the family, they sought to eliminate the legal discrimination against single mothers with children and unmarried couples with children. In doing so, the Social Democratic Party (SPD) was reacting to processes of social change that had been observed, but it continued to stick to the traditional model of married parents with joint children.[117] During this time, the definition of the family was also being discussed within the conservative Christian Democratic Union (CDU). In a draft of the basic party platform in 1977, for instance, single-parent homes were still defined as families, but in the version that was officially passed in 1978, this clause had been removed. It was not until 1994 that the CDU officially changed its view on the matter, recognizing single mothers and fathers as well as unmarried couples as families.[118]

There was at least a shift in what was being said about "the family" in West German society in the second half of the 1970s. More and more politicians and scholars were noting that the usual terms used for other types of families such as "half family" and "incomplete family" were normatively loaded and discriminatory. Even just this shift, which occurred over a few years, points to a fundamental change in society's acceptance of different types of families. Regardless, however, these normative terms by no means disappeared completely from use; academic publications, for instance, still spoke of "incomplete families."[119] As this all started to change, sociologists also began looking at the increasing prevalence of alternative forms of cohabitation. In order to assess this process using their methods, they introduced *Lebensform* (essentially "way of life") as an analytical concept at the beginning of the 1980s. This term was used to denote not only so-called familial lifestyles (traditional nuclear family, single parents, and unmarried couples with children), but also nonfamilial lifestyles (singles and unmarried couples without children).[120]

All together, these shifts fed into the evolution of a broader notion of the family between the late 1960s and the early 1980s that included not only single parents, but also unmarried couples with kids and remarried couples. This more flexible definition of the family gradually entered the mainstream, and it is now accepted by the majority of society.[121] Parallel to this process, *Lebensform* established itself as a more generic term that could be used to refer to the limited pluralization of familial and nonfamilial ways of life. Although the emergence of these new kinds of lifestyles did not result in a statistically proven mass phenomenon, it nonetheless had a considerable influence on the speeches, thoughts, and actions of politicians and researchers.

A shift also occurred in the GDR in the 1960s and 1970s, although the traditional nuclear family also continued to be the main point of reference. Single parents, however, already accounted for about 11 percent of families at this point in time, which does in fact point to a given rejection of the ideal of the middle-class nuclear family, especially in urban milieus.[122] On the whole, however, family lifestyles in East Germany changed less dramatically than in the FRG because the legal and sociopolitical frameworks were different. Moreover, the resources needed to create space for alternative lifestyles were missing. In particular, the lack of living space in the GDR made it considerably more difficult to adopt alternative lifestyles, thereby decreasing the potential for change.

Even before social practices began to change in East Germany, the introduction of the Family Code (Familiengesetzbuch) in 1965 outlined the political and legal framework for the model "socialist family." It set out a number of significant principles, including the idea that the basic interests of the family and society should be the same and that women and men were to be treated equally and share in the opportunity to work and participate in social life. Above all, this law emphasized the integration of the family in places of socialization outside of the home, such as the workplace, schools, and preschools. In essence, this ate away at the child-raising aspects of two-generation families. Of course, the Family Code established a set of ideals that did not necessarily reflect the realities of daily family life. Nonetheless, it can still be used to tease out differences between the two Germanys on a discursive level. Whereas social practices became more pluralized in both countries in the 1960s and 1970s, the differences in the way in which the topic of "family" was approached within society multiplied. For example, as the debate about the family took on a new plurality in West Germany, political discourse in East Germany focused strictly on the "socialist family."[123]

East German sociologists at the time intensely investigated these shifts with an eye to the significant differences between East and West. They saw the spread of new lifestyles as "'variations' of the traditional small family,"[124] noting that in the West, this process of pluralization had also expanded to nonfamilial ways of life.[125] As in the West, however, the idea of the family also became more pluralized and individualized in East Germany. This shift was finally acknowledged in 1970 and interpreted along the lines of a modified notion of society. Thus, at the end of the 1960s and the beginning of the 1970s, a recognition of individuality accompanied the idea of a "socialist way of life" that also affected family relationships and living habits.[126] The significance of this idea lies in its awareness of social realities. Yet its limits were to be found in the fact that it did not move away from the central paradigm of the convergence of personal and social developments; pluralization was duly recognized, but it had to be interpreted in terms of being functional vis-à-vis the socialist society as a whole.

The significance of the social and political consequences of this approach to marriage and the family should not be underestimated, for the accepted definition of the family determines which lifestyles are favored. In turn, this decides which kinds of lifestyles are protected and fostered and which kind bear the brunt of discrimination.[127] Such changes in thought also influenced political decision-making. In West Germany, the social-liberal coalition (1969 to 1982) took up these shifts and adapted its family policies accordingly, as demonstrated in the revision of the Federal Child Benefit Act (Bundeskindergeldgesetz): as of 1 January 1975, all parents regardless of income were to receive child benefit payments from the government. Furthermore, these changing notions of the family were reflected in the reform of the family and divorce laws in West Germany. As of 1977, the law did away with determining guilt, introducing the principle of the irretrievable breakdown of a marriage, which still applies today. At the same time, the reform of the law eliminated the model of housewife marriages (*Hausfrauenehe*) by declaring the legal equality of men and women in family law. Of course, the ideal of a family based on an equal partnership is not the equivalent of equality in social life, but the reform of the law did mark a turning point.[128]

Other noteworthy legal shifts occurred with the reform of the law on illegitimate children in 1969, the law on abortion in 1974, and the law on custody in 1979. These amendments resulted from the changing social framework, flanking the reform of family law as a whole. The new law on illegitimate children, for instance, granted children born outside of wedlock the same rights as children born within a marriage. The reformed abortion law established a legal time frame for abortions; abortions within the first twelve weeks, with the consultation of a physician, were no longer supposed to be punishable by law. In the end, however, a decision passed by the Federal Constitutional Court led to a weakening of these provisions, determining that abortions would only be tolerated in exceptional cases. The amendment of the custody laws replaced the traditional term of "parental authority" (*elterliche Gewalt*) with "parental custody" (*elterliche Sorge*). All of these reforms sought to promote other types of families alongside the traditional nuclear family while trying to live up to the promise of emancipation.[129]

Comparable public debates such as those that surrounded the reform of the West German laws on divorce did not emerge in the GDR. As of 1965, the Family Code established a consensus rule that applied to divorces, and claims for alimony or material support did not really play a role because the courts assumed that both partners in a marriage had jobs. Over the course of the 1970s, however, a paradigm shift occurred in the GDR's women's and family policy.[130] Whereas the government's earlier political measures sought to increase the female employment quota and the professional qualifications of women, they now sought to boost the birth rate, too. In 1972, maternity leave pay was extended from fourteen to eighteen weeks, and a reduced forty-hour workweek was introduced for mothers of three or more children under sixteen who were working full time.[131]

The Transformation of Family Life

Between the 1960s and the 1990s, family roles and practices changed in both German states, as did child-rearing methods. The bodily punishments and authoritarian parenting styles that had been typical up to the 1960s clearly went out of favor. Parallel to this shift, the goals for parenting changed, bringing in the idea of the "emancipation of the child."[132] This fostered a stronger emotional relationship between parents and children. In West Germany, norms such as obedience, good manners, cleanliness, and order lost ground to the aims of encouraging children to develop a sense of self-determination, independence, and responsibility. The goals related to cultivating "an appreciation for orderliness and hard work," on the other hand, were still highly valued. According to social science research, parenting remained more consistent in the GDR. On the one hand, the traditional primary virtues were still emphasized, but, on the other hand, parenting goals were geared more strongly at developing a sense of collectivity. At a political level, the overarching aim was to foster the ideal "socialist personality" that was supposed to be achieved by the programmatic inclusion of the family, or rather more precisely the parents, in the state child-raising system. Simultaneously, social scientists claimed, the social framework was different from that of the West because it fostered a considerably less emotional and more strongly objectified parent-child relationship.[133]

In contrast, the changes in the division of roles between husband and wife within the family were less pronounced. A hotly debated topic in West Germany in the 1970s was whether married women should work or whether they should just be housewives. Employment among married women was in fact on the rise between the 1960s and the late 1970s. Whereas 34.6 percent of married women worked outside the home in 1950, which remained quite consistent through 1965, this figure had jumped to 60.9 percent by 1979.[134] The employment quota among women with children under the age of six, on the other hand, hardly changed at all; it stayed at around 35 percent between 1973 and 1988. In contrast, 54 percent of women without children had jobs outside the home.[135] Consequently, the rise of the "double-income household"[136] was really only a reality for a minority of West German families in the 1970s and 1980s. According to studies conducted back at the time, this model was only found in certain social groups: young married couples, upper social strata, less religious families, and families living in cities. These families were considered to be the motors of social change because they had rejected patriarchal family roles in favor of a relationship based on partnership. In such households, both partners shared in the different responsibilities, tasks, duties, and rights. Accordingly, social change progressed at different speeds and strengths along four basic lines of distinction, namely city versus country, social milieu, religious denomination, and age. Other experts pointed to self-employed men and academics as innovators when it came to a new self-image of society because they supported their wives' employment outside the home.[137] Profession and education were thus two other important factors. In some West German milieus, at least, signs of a shift in the division of roles within the family appeared. Nonetheless, one role was not affected by these transformations, namely women's roles as mothers. For West German men, fatherhood was still at best a "weekend job."[138] There was no pluralization of social practices for these roles; rather, a relatively homogeneous behavioral pattern remained firmly in place.

As early as the 1950s, a long-lasting shortage of labor plus a trend toward a decline in female employment, combined with ideological reasons, led to a stronger push to foster women's work outside the home in

East Germany. During the 1970s, political measures focused on decreasing the quota of part-time work, which was about 32 percent in 1976.[139] Sociopolitical leverage was put to work here in particular because part-time work was especially prevalent among working mothers. Childcare options had been expanded since the 1960s, but there was a major boom in the 1970s. In 1970, for example, just 29 percent of children between one and three years of age were in daycare; by 1980, this figure had risen to 61 percent, and then 80 percent by 1989. In 1970, 47 percent of children aged six to ten went to after-school care, but by 1980, 75 percent were enrolled in these programs, topping out at 81 percent in 1989. On the other hand, around a fifth of parents did not take advantage of the state-run expanded childcare options for preschool and after-school care in the 1980s. By contrast, 65 percent of children attended kindergarten (preschool for ages four to six) in 1970, compared to 90 percent in 1989.[140]

Especially in terms of childcare, the differences between East and West Germany were quite significant. In the FRG, only about 1 or 2 percent of one- to three-year-olds were in daycare, and only 2 to 4 percent of elementary school children were enrolled in after-school care. Only the attendance figures for kindergarten were similar to those in the East, at around 39 percent in 1970 and 78 percent in 1980, which remained steady up to 1989. Yet, one has to note that kindergarten spaces were usually for all-day care in the GDR, but up to 88 percent of those in the FRG were half-day spots according to the figures presented by the Central Association of Catholic Kindergartens. According to these statistics, then, a lesser percentage of West German children were enrolled in full-time daycare.[141]

Clear discrepancies between propagated ideals and the world of everyday life could also be seen in terms of the division of work within the family in West Germany. For the most part, the ideal of a marriage based on equal partnership did not become a reality; it was wives who still bore the main burdens of housework. One reason behind the reticence of men to help at home had to do with the lack of prestige associated with household chores. Interestingly, however, there was also a difference between how men responded to this question on a theoretical level and what they actually did in practice. Whereas most men said that they were open to this new ideal of partnership and in fact supported it, they failed to make any corresponding changes in their daily lives. This discrepancy was by no means particular to the 1970s; it was still clearly evident in the 1980s as well.[142] One thing stands out about this in particular: data collected by social scientists between 1985 and 2007 indicates that even in those relationships in which both partners took care of household chores, there was a return to a traditional division of roles with the birth of the first child.[143]

The similarities to East Germany in terms of the division of housework are quite astonishing. As of 1985, women took care of the great majority of housework while men helped out only now and then by taking care of certain preferred tasks such as gardening or household repairs.[144] Due to this division of labor within the home, many women worked only part-time jobs or tried to find work as close to home as possible, even if this meant that their jobs were below their levels of qualification. East German women thus bore the triple burden of work, taking care of the household, and raising children.[145] This "traditionalization" that was observed led to a homogenization of family roles in Germany.[146] Since the late 1980s, however, ideas about gender roles have shifted considerably. At the end of the 1980s, a third of adults in West Germany said that women were responsible for the household and family while men were supposed to work to support their families. In 2012, by contrast, more than 90 percent of twenty- to thirty-nine-year-old Germans stated that both parents were responsible for raising children; 81 percent also maintained that both partners should contribute to the family income. At the same time, however, there were also striking differences between East and West. Whereas 21 percent of those questioned in the former West Germany favored the male-breadwinner model, only 9 percent in East Germany preferred this model.[147] According to the European Values Study in 2008, almost 60 percent of West Germans indicated that small children suffered when their mothers worked outside the home. In the old East Germany, on the other hand, only 35 percent of those asked shared this view. The so-called "myth of a mother's love" (*Mythos Mutterliebe*)—the idea that only mothers can build an intensive emotional relationship with their children because of their biological disposition—is therefore still much stronger in the West. As a result, there are still clear differences between East and West Germany even today when it comes to gender roles and the parent-child relationship. Yet these discrepancies have become less pronounced in the last twenty to twenty-five years.[148]

Women as a Driving Force behind the Popularity of Long-Term Domestic Partnerships

In West Germany, family roles changed the most among long-time couples who never married. Several factors contributed to the increasing popularity of such partnerships in the 1970s and 1980s, including the financial independence of partners, childlessness, low levels of religiosity, urban environments, and younger ages. Well-educated, employed women in particular tended to favor this kind of partnership as opposed to a traditional marriage, and this group grew over the course of the expansion of the university-based educational system in the 1970s. As early as 1980, it had become apparent that professional women with upper-level educations were consciously deciding against marriage and choosing unmarried partnerships because the traditional division of roles within a marriage did not leave room for self-realization outside the role of housewife and mother. The appeal that nonmarital partnerships developed as an alternative type of cohabitation was not necessarily reflected in the way it spread throughout society in the 1970s and 1980s, but rather in the rate of growth. According to estimates, there was a 277-percent increase in these kinds of partnerships between 1972 and 1982. Among those aged under twenty-four, the numbers of these relationships even multiplied tenfold. These developments boosted the social significance of unmarried couples enormously between the 1970s and the 1980s.[149]

In 1981, about 150 thousand unmarried couples lived together in the GDR, which meant that they were about as common as in West Germany. The number of single parents had also risen considerably, with an estimate of about 340 thousand unmarried mothers with minor-aged children in 1989. This statistically measured sociostructural transformation corresponds to the opinions of the population. In 1987, 70 percent of women agreed with the idea that a first child could be born out of wedlock, but that couples should marry if they had a second child. The changing attitude among citizens was encouraged particularly by the family policy framework in the GDR. Unmarried mothers, for example, were granted special benefits and preferred status in the assignment of living quarters with the birth of their first child. The introduction of a "baby year" for single mothers from the first child onward in 1976 further accelerated the spread of alternative lifestyles because this paid maternity leave was only granted to married women from the second child onward.[150] The effects of family policy decisions such as these can still be felt today in that the percentage of children born out of wedlock in East Germany went from 13 percent in 1970 to 61 percent in 2010 in the new federal states. In contrast, the percentage of children born to unmarried couples in West Germany was only 27 in 2010, which was considerably below the level of the East. Despite these differences, it is still clear that the percentage of children born out of wedlock in Germany increased on the whole, from just 7 percent in 1970 to 23 percent in 2000. This figure then jumped even further to 33 percent in the decade thereafter.[151]

As of the early twenty-first century, nonmarital partnerships were still more prevalent among groups with higher educational degrees, although this distinction has become less of a marker lately. Moreover, such a shift has also taken place in other European countries since the 1980s. In neighboring countries, such as France and the Netherlands, it has mainly been couples with university degrees who have opted not to marry, but to have children.[152]

What were the motors behind these changes? In West Germany, contemporary social scientists at the time focused on the role of women. They claimed that women themselves had initiated changes in opinion, thereby catapulting these issues onto the political agenda. Sociologists have interpreted this process as a democratic and publicly negotiated "emancipation 'from below'" that accounted for its broad social acceptance. In the GDR, on the other hand, the initiative seems to have come from male politicians who orchestrated an authoritarian and paternalistic "emancipation from above."[153] It was symbolized by the policy focus on mothers, often referred to as *Muttipolitik*, of the 1970s. Although women's burdens were lightened to an extent, especially through the expansion of childcare options, political decision-making largely reinforced traditional roles, thereby hindering emancipation. Yet, it needs to be kept in mind that women could also retreat to the private realm of the family, where they had more room to maneuver as individuals.[154] A truly differentiated look at daily lives in divided Germany in the 1970s and 1980s, however, has yet to be written to the end.

Conclusion

Consumption and family are two aspects of life that have changed enormously since the 1970s. The shifts in lifestyles outlined in this article developed parallel to each other in both East and West Germany. They were not interwoven per se, but rather they evolved up to 1990 in an environment of the mutual awareness of what was happening on the other side of the Wall—as part of a "shared but divided history" (*Geteilte Geschichte*). At the same time, however, there were fundamental differences between the Federal Republic and the GDR. Whereas a trend toward pluralization appeared in both countries, the effects of this process varied in strength due to the divergent social frameworks.

A strikingly dramatic shift occurred in consumer society in the FRG during this period that could be measured quantitatively in sales figures, but it was also reflected in changing social perceptions. The GDR also experienced a quantitative increase in private consumption, but it was accompanied by the simultaneous expansion of social policy initiatives, most especially the push to construct more apartment housing and expand family-related social services. The paradigm shift from the "modern consumerism" of the 1950s and 1960s to the "unity of economic and social policy" led to a boost in what was referred to as social consumption. Although this move allowed for private consumption, it was by no means the top priority. Consequently, there were considerable differences in the assessed sociopolitical and sociostructural value of consumption between East and West.

There were similar trends in family and lifestyle choices in the FRG and the GDR, but the responses to these shifts differed greatly. In West Germany, new types of families emerged as a result of the private choices made by many couples; these slowly gained social acceptance. Eventually, after a long and gradual process, the political realm took notice of these changes. Different family styles also became more prevalent in the GDR, but they did not spark nearly as much debate or negotiation as in West Germany. The political response to these shifts focused on increased financial support for sociopolitical programs with the goal of increasing the birth rate. Alternative lifestyles that did not fit into this model of a welfare state also appeared, especially in the 1980s, but they were deemed oppositional in nature and left out of the system.

There were clear shifts in family life in both East and West Germany, but they occurred at a different pace. The governments in both states reacted at a policy level to the pluralization of individual lifestyle choices and notions about ways of life in general. In West Germany, the focus went from supporting the traditional nuclear family to child-centered family policies that also applied to single mothers and unmarried couples with children. Social policies in the GDR, on the other hand, went from targeting women's issues to looking at ways to support families in light of demographic concerns. In the East, the normative ideals of a traditional nuclear family did not seem to be as firmly entrenched as in West Germany. When it came to consumption, there was a huge leap in private consumption in both states thanks to the improved financial situations, but this shift took place within two opposing economic frameworks. In West Germany, the long-term development of consumer society was very much a story of acceleration during this period; in the GDR, however, it marked a move away from the notion of East Germany's "special path" in consumer policy.

From the 1970s onward, the move to establish new kinds of private lifestyles pushed forward despite considerable resistance, resulting in a broad social acceptance of new ways of life in the 1980s. As a result of the general trend toward individualization, the political desire to regulate private lives, as well as the interpretive power of norms, waned over time. Individuals now have a wider variety of options when it comes to deciding how to live their lives, which has fostered the development of a kind of "live and let live" attitude that kept gaining ground in the

1990s. In terms of consumption, however, the lines of development have to be drawn differently over the long term because the collapse of the GDR brought a unique economic factor into the mix. Despite contrasting consumption habits in the 1990s—catch-up consumerism versus a specific East German style of consumption—as well as ongoing economic inequalities between East and West, the Western model of a consumer society triumphed across the divide in the end.

Christopher Neumaier is a research associate at the Center for Contemporary History (ZZF) in Potsdam, and he was visiting professor for the history of technology at the Technical University of Munich in 2017. He holds an M.Phil. in European Studies from the University of Cambridge and a Ph.D. from the Technical University of Munich. His research focuses on the history of consumption, environmental history, history of technology, and the history of the family in Germany.

Andreas Ludwig is a research associate at the Center for Contemporary History (ZZF) in Potsdam. He has published about the history of everyday life and in the fields of material culture, musealization, and urban history. He founded and directed the Documentation Centre of Everyday Culture of the GDR, for which he has edited several publications. His current research is about contemporary collecting in history museums.

NOTES

1. Tom Wolfe, "The 'Me' Decade and the Third Great Awakening," *New York Magazine*, 23 August 1976.
2. Refers to Ulrich Beck, "Tanz ums goldene Selbst," *Der Spiegel* 48, no. 22 (1994): 65.
3. See Daniel Bell, *The Coming of Post-Industrial Society: A Venture in Social Forecasting* (New York, 1973); Ronald Inglehart, *The Silent Revolution: Changing Values and Political Styles among Western Publics* (Princeton, 1977); Helmut Klages, *Wertorientierungen im Wandel: Rückblick, Gegenwartsanalyse, Prognosen* (Frankfurt a. M., 1984); Gerhard Schulze, *Die Erlebnisgesellschaft: Kultursoziologie der Gegenwart* (Frankfurt a. M., 2000); Ulrich Beck and Elisabeth Beck-Gernsheim, eds., *Riskante Freiheiten: Individualisierung in modernen Gesellschaften* (Frankfurt a. M., 1994).
4. See Georg Assmann, Wolfgang Eichhorn, and Erich Hahn, eds., *Wörterbuch der marxistisch-leninistischen Soziologie* (Berlin, 1977), s.v. "Lebensweise."
5. See Hannes Siegrist, "Konsum, Kultur und Gesellschaft im modernen Europa," in *Europäische Konsumgeschichte. Zur Gesellschafts- und Kulturge-*

schichte des Konsums (18. bis 20. Jahrhundert), ed. Hannes Siegrist, Hartmut Kaelble, and Jürgen Kocka (Frankfurt a. M., 1997), 16; Frank Trentmann, *The Empire of Things: How We Became a World of Consumers, from the Fifteenth Century to the Twenty-First* (London, 2016), 307.

6. Nepomuk Gasteiger, *Der Konsument: Verbraucherbilder in Werbung, Konsumkritik und Verbraucherschutz 1945–1989* (Frankfurt a. M., 2010), 10.
7. Alfred Reckendrees, "Die bundesdeutsche Massenkonsumgesellschaft. Einführende Bemerkungen," *Jahrbuch für Wirtschaftsgeschichte* 48 (2007): 27.
8. On the development of consumption in the GDR, see David F. Crew, "Consuming Germany in the Cold War: Consumption and National Identity in East and West Germany, 1949–1989. An Introduction," in *Consuming Germany in the Cold War*, ed. David F. Crew (Oxford, 2005), 1–19; Ina Merkel, "Consumer Culture in the GDR, or How the Struggle for Antimodernity was Lost on the Battleground of Consumer Culture," in *Getting and Spending: European and American Consumer Societies in the Twentieth Century*, ed. Susan Strasser, Charles McGovern, and Matthias Judt (Cambridge, 1998), 281–99; Paulina Bren and Mary Neuburger, eds., *Communism Unwrapped: Consumption in Cold War Eastern Europe* (Oxford, 2012). On the development of consumption in East Europe, see Donna Harsch, "Women, Family, and 'Postwar': The Gendering of the GDR's Welfare Dictatorship," in *Gender and the Long Postwar: The United States and the Two Germanys, 1945–1989*, ed. Karen Hagemann and Sonya Michel (Baltimore, 2014), 254–8.
9. See Jörg Roesler, "Privater Konsum in Ostdeutschland, 1950–1960," in *Modernisierung im Wiederaufbau: Die westdeutsche Gesellschaft der 50er Jahre*, ed. Axel Schildt and Arnold Sywottek (Bonn, 1993), 301.
10. For the methodological problem of reading "between lines," see Donna Harsch, "Society, the State, and Abortion in East Germany, 1950–1972," *American Historical Review* 102 (1997): 53–84.
11. See Axel Schildt and Detlef Siegfried, *Deutsche Kulturgeschichte: Die Bundesrepublik—1945 bis zur Gegenwart* (Munich, 2009), 246–47.
12. See Christian Kleinschmidt, *Konsumgesellschaft* (Göttingen, 2008), 32; Wolfgang König, *Geschichte der Konsumgesellschaft* (Stuttgart, 2000), 8.
13. See Wolfgang Ruppert, "Zur Konsumwelt der 60er Jahre," in *Dynamische Zeiten: Die 60er Jahre in den beiden deutschen Gesellschaften*, ed. Axel Schildt, Detlef Siegfried, and Karl Christian Lammers (Hamburg, 2000), 754; Ursula A. J. Becher, *Geschichte des modernen Lebensstils: Essen—Wohnen—Freizeit—Reisen* (Munich, 1990), 225–26.
14. See Kleinschmidt, *Konsumgesellschaft*, 140–43.
15. See the figures in Marie Elisabeth Ruban, "Der Lebensstandard in der DDR und in Osteuropa," in *DDR und Osteuropa: Wirtschaftssystem, Wirtschaftspolitik, Lebensstandard: Ein Handbuch* (Opladen, 1980), 350.
16. Ina Merkel, "Im Widerspruch zum Ideal: Konsumpolitik in der DDR," in *Die Konsumgesellschaft in Deutschland 1890–1990: Ein Handbuch*, ed. Heinz-Gerhard Haupt and Claudius Torp (Frankfurt a. M., 2009), 290.

17. Ibid.; Kleinschmidt, *Konsumgesellschaft*, 167–70. On this periodization, see Ina Merkel, *Utopie und Bedürfnis: Die Geschichte der Konsumkultur in der DDR* (Cologne, 1999).
18. Katherine Pence and Paul Betts, eds., *Socialist Modern: East German Everyday Culture and Politics* (Ann Arbor, 2008).
19. See Mary Fulbrook, *Power and Society in the GDR, 1961–1979: The Normalisation of Rule?* (New York, 2009).
20. See Eli Rubin, *Amnesiopolis: Modernity, Space, and Memory in East Germany* (Oxford, 2016).
21. See Merkel, *Utopie*, 17–20, 327.
22. See Ruban, "Lebensstandard"; Frank Trentmann, "The Long History of Contemporary Consumer Society," *Archiv für Sozialgeschichte* 49 (2009): 124.
23. See Merkel, *Utopie*, 24–27; Mary Nolan, "Negotiating American Modernity in Twentieth-Century Europe," in *The Making of European Consumption: Facing the American Challenge*, ed. Per Lundin and Thomas Kaiserfeld (Basingstoke, 2015), 36.
24. See Lydia Langer, *Revolution im Einzelhandel: Die Einführung der Selbstbedienung in Lebensmittelgeschäften der Bundesrepublik Deutschland (1949–1973)* (Cologne, 2013).
25. See Dokumentationszentrum Alltagskultur der DDR and Andreas Ludwig, eds., *KONSUM: Konsumgenossenschaften in der DDR* (Cologne, 2006), 25–61.
26. See Merkel, *Utopie*, 100.
27. For exceptions, see Patrick Hyder Patterson, "Risky Business: What Was Really Being Sold in the Department Stores of Socialist Eastern Europe?" in *Communism Unwrapped: Consumption in Cold War Eastern Europe*, ed. Paulina Bren and Mary Neuburger (Oxford, 2012), 116–39.
28. See Gasteiger, *Konsument*, 132, 137–39.
29. See ibid., 208–9; Helmut Schelsky, *Wandlungen der deutschen Familie in der Gegenwart: Darstellung und Deutung einer empirisch-soziologischen Tatbestandsaufnahme* (Stuttgart, 1955), 218; Pierre Bourdieu, *Distinction: A Social Critique of Judgement of Taste* (London, 1984).
30. Wolfgang F. Haug, *Kritik der Warenästhetik* (Frankfurt a. M., 1971); Sven Reichardt, *Authentizität und Gemeinschaft: Linksalternatives Leben in den siebziger und frühen achtziger Jahren* (Berlin, 2014), 319–50; Alexander Sedlmaier, *Consumption and Violence: Radical Protest in Cold War Germany* (Ann Arbor, 2014).
31. See Detlef Siegfried, *Time Is on My Side: Konsum und Politik in der westdeutschen Jugendkultur der 60er Jahre* (Göttingen, 2006).
32. Gasteiger, *Konsument*, 211.
33. See ibid., 143, 208–16.
34. Stefan Hradil, *Soziale Ungleichheit in Deutschland: Unter Mitarbeit von Jürgen Schiener* (Opladen, 2001), 432.
35. See ibid., 425–36.
36. See Gasteiger, *Konsument*, 226–29; Hradil, *Ungleichheit*, 428.

37. Maren Möhring, "Veränderungen der bundesdeutschen (Ess-)Kultur durch Migration und Tourismus," in *Mit dem Wandel leben: Neuorientierung und Tradition in der Bundesrepublik der 1950er und 60er Jahre*, ed. Friedrich Kießling and Bernhard Rieger (Cologne, 2011), 166.
38. See Oliver Kühschelm, Franz X. Eder, and Hannes Siegrist, "Einleitung: Konsum und Nation," in *Konsum und Nation: Zur Geschichte nationalisierender Inszenierungen in der Produktkommunikation*, ed. Oliver Kühschelm, Franz X. Eder, and Hannes Siegrist (Bielefeld, 2012), 12.
39. See Lidwina Kühne-Brüning, Werner Plumpe, and Jan-Otmar Hesse, "Zwischen Angebot und Nachfrage, zwischen Regulierung und Konjunktur: Die Entwicklung der Wohnungsmärkte in der Bundesrepublik, 1949–1989/1990–1998," in *Geschichte des Wohnens*, vol. 5: *1945 bis heute: Aufbau, Neubau, Umbau*, ed. Ingeborg Flagge (Stuttgart, 1999), 204.
40. See Clemens Zimmermann, "Wohnungspolitik—Eigenheim für alle?," in *Villa und Eigenheim: Suburbaner Städtebau in Deutschland*, ed. Tilman Harlander (Stuttgart, 2001), 64–75; Werner Polster and Klaus Voy, "Eigentum und Automobil: Materielle Fundamente der Lebensweise," in *Gesellschaftliche Transformationsprozesse und materielle Lebensweise*, ed. Werner Polster, Klaus Voy, and Claus Thomasberger (Marburg, 1993), 203–356.
41. See Statistisches Amt der DDR, ed., *Statistisches Jahrbuch der DDR 1990* (Leipzig, 1990), 201; for residential situation, see Rubin, *Amnesiopolis*.
42. See Axel Schildt, *Die Sozialgeschichte der Bundesrepublik Deutschland bis 1989/90* (Munich, 2007), 39; Ruppert, "Konsumwelt," 755, 760; Nolan, "Negotiating," 26–34. For the central role of the kitchen in consumption, see Karin Zachmann and Ruth Oldenziel, "Kitchen as Technology and Politics: An Introduction," in *Cold War Kitchen: Americanization, Technology, and European Users*, ed. Karin Zachmann and Ruth Oldenziel (Cambridge, MA, 2009).
43. See Bundesministerium für innerdeutsche Beziehungen, ed., *Materialien zum Bericht zur Lage der Nation im geteilten Deutschland 1987* (Bonn, 1987), 528.
44. See Schildt, *Sozialgeschichte*, 44; Martina Hessler, *Kulturgeschichte der Technik* (Frankfurt a. M., 2012), 88–89.
45. Donna Harsch argues to the contrary that a "second income" was desired in order to be able to buy high-quality consumer goods; see Donna Harsch, *Revenge of the Domestic: Women, the Family, and Communism in the German Democratic Republic* (Princeton, 2007), 188.
46. Statistisches Bundesamt, ed., *Statistisches Jahrbuch 1970 für die Bundesrepublik Deutschland* (Stuttgart, 1970), 467. For the link between television and social change, see Christina von Hodenberg, *Television's Moment: Sitcom Audiences and the Sixties Cultural Revolution* (New York, 2015), 1–15.
47. See Ruban, "Lebensstandard," 350; Statistisches Jahrbuch der DDR 1988, 291; Statistisches Bundesamt, ed., *Statistisches Jahrbuch für die Bundesre-*

publik Deutschland 1981 (Stuttgart, 1981) 452; *Statistisches Jahrbuch für die Bundesrepublik Deutschland 1988* (Stuttgart, 1988), 459.

48. See Peter Skyba, "Konsumpolitik in der DDR 1971 bis 1989: Die Verbraucherpreise als Konfliktgegenstand," in *Geschichte des Konsums: Erträge der 20. Arbeitstagung der Gesellschaft für Sozial- und Wirtschaftsgeschichte 23.–26. April 2003 in Greifswald*, ed. Rolf Walter (Stuttgart, 2004), 364.
49. The figures cited here are from Bundesministerium für innerdeutsche Beziehungen, ed., *Materialien zum Bericht zur Lage der Nation im geteilten Deutschland 1987* (Bonn, 1987), 528.
50. Arne Andersen, *Der Traum vom guten Leben: Alltags- und Konsumgeschichte vom Wirtschaftswunder bis heute* (Frankfurt a. M., 1997), 125.
51. See Schildt and Siegfried, *Kulturgeschichte*, 337.
52. See Herlinde Koelbl and Manfred Sack, eds., *Das deutsche Wohnzimmer* (Luzern, 1980).
53. See Andreas Lauber, *Wohnkultur in der DDR: Dokumentation ihrer materiellen Sachkultur: Eine Untersuchung zu Gestaltung, Produktion und Bedingungen des Erwerbs von Wohnungseinrichtungen in der DDR* (Eisenhüttenstadt, 2003).
54. See Andreas Ludwig, "'Hunderte von Varianten.' Das Möbelprogramm Deutsche Werkstätten (MDW) in der DDR," *Zeithistorische Forschungen/Studies in Contemporary History* 3, no. 3 (2006): 449–59.
55. See Petra Eisele, "Do-it-yourself-Design: Die IKEA-Regale IVAR und BILLY," *Zeithistorische Forschungen/Studies in Contemporary History* 3 (2006).
56. See Schildt and Siegfried, *Kulturgeschichte*, 408; Eisele, "Do-it-yourself-Design," 442–44.
57. Eisele, "Do-it-yourself-Design," 444.
58. See Ruppert, "Konsumwelt," 755–56, 760–62; "Panton Chair: Verner Panton, 1999," Vitra.com, retrieved 12 January 2018, http://www.vitra.com/de-de/product/panton-chair; Barbara Mundt, *Produkt-Design 1900–1990: Eine Einführung* (Berlin, 1990), 184–85.
59. See Jana Scholze, "Shifting Narratives of Things: The East/West German Garden Egg Chair," in *East German Material Culture and the Power of Memory*, ed. Uta A. Balbier, Cristina Cuevas-Wolf, and Joes Segal (Washington, DC, 2011), 87–98.
60. Maren Möhring, *Fremdes Essen: Die Geschichte der ausländischen Gastronomie in der Bundesrepublik Deutschland* (Munich, 2012), 29–31.
61. See König, *Geschichte*, 9, 136; Möhring, *Fremdes Essen*, 11–13, 148.
62. See Möhring, *Fremdes Essen*, 142–44.
63. See Roesler, " Privater Konsum," 299.
64. Western brand name products that were produced in the GDR in order to take advantage of the lower wages, portions of which remained in the GDR for sale.
65. See Merkel, *Utopie*, 274.

66. See Volker Wünderich, "Die 'Kaffeekrise' von 1977: Genußmittel und Verbraucherprotest in der DDR," *Historische Anthropologie* 11 (2003), 240–62; Monika Sigmund, *Genuss als Politikum. Kaffeekonsum in beiden deutschen Staaten* (Berlin, 2015).
67. See König, *Geschichte*, 387–88.
68. See Sabine Weißler, "Die Frau Die Mode Der Körper: Beweglichkeit und Bewegung," in *Um 1968: Die Repräsentation der Dinge*, ed. Wolfgang Ruppert (Marburg, 1998), 125–36.
69. See Petra Kipphoff, "Mutprobe in Hosen, na und? Bei uns bleibt der Protest aus (Der Kampf der Frau, Teil III)," *Die Zeit*, 22 May 1970, 57.
70. See Diana Weis, ed., *Cool aussehen: Mode und Jugendkulturen* (Berlin, 2012).
71. See Philipp Heldmann, "Konsumpolitik in der DDR: Jugendliche in den sechziger Jahren," in *Konsumpolitik: Die Regulierung des privaten Verbrauchs im 20. Jahrhundert*, ed. Hartmut Berghoff (Göttingen, 1999), 135–58.
72. See ibid., 153.
73. See Merkel, *Utopie*, 250, 263, 269; Trentmann, *Empire*, 334.
74. See Judd Stitziel, "Shopping, Sewing, Networking: Consumer Culture and the Relationship between State and Society in the GDR," in *Socialist Modern: East German Everyday Culture and Politics*, ed. Katherine Pence and Paul Betts (Ann Arbor, 2008), 261.
75. See ibid., 264; Annette Kaminsky, *Wohlstand, Schönheit, Glück: Kleine Konsumgeschichte der DDR* (Munich, 2001), 158; Wünderich, "Kaffeekrise," 243; Günter Manz, *Armut in der "DDR"-Bevölkerung, Lebensstandard und Konsumniveau vor und nach der Wende* (Augsburg, 1992), 49.
76. See Armin Volze, "Die Devisengeschäfte der DDR: Genex und Intershop," *Deutschland Archiv* 24, no. 11 (1991): 1145–59; Jonathan R. Zatlin, "Consuming Ideology: Socialist Consumerism and the Intershop, 1970–1989," in *Arbeiter in der SBZ/DDR*, ed. Peter Hübner and Klaus Tenfelde (Essen, 1999), 565.
77. *Unterrichtung durch die Bundesregierung: Materialien zur Deutschen Einheit und zum Aufbau in den neuen Bundesländern*, Deutscher Bundestag, Drs. 12/6854, 8 February 1994, 442–44; Elvir Ebert, *Einkommen und Konsum im Transformationsprozeß: Vom Plan zum Markt—vom Mangel zum Überfluß* (Opladen, 1997), 227–28.
78. 1993: 10,479; 1995: 30,574; 1998: 42,251. See Statistisches Bundesamt, *50 Jahre Wohnen in Deutschland: Ergebnisse aus Gebäude- und Wohnungszählungen, -stichproben, Mikrozensus-Ergänzungserhebungen und Bautätigkeitsstatistiken* (Wiesbaden, 2000), 51.
79. See Milena Veenis, "Consumption in East Germany: The Seduction and Betrayal of Things," *Journal of Material Culture* 4 (1999): 96–97; Patricia Hogwood, "'Red is for Love . . .': Citizens as Consumers in East Germany," in *East German Distinctiveness in a Unified Germany*, ed. Jonathan Grix and Paul Cooke (Birmingham, 2002), 45–60.

80. See Ebert, *Einkommen*, 251; Martin Blum, "Club Cola & Co.: Ostalgie, Material Culture and Identity," in *Transformations of the New Germany*, ed. Ruth A. Starkman (New York, 2006), 131–54.
81. König, *Geschichte*, 306.
82. See Christopher Neumaier, *Dieselautos in Deutschland und den USA: Zum Verhältnis von Technologie, Konsum und Politik, 1949–2005* (Stuttgart, 2010), 32; Kurt Möser, *Geschichte des Autos* (Frankfurt a. M., 2002), 193–94.
83. See Axel Schildt, "Vom Wohlstandsbarometer zum Belastungsfaktor—Autovision und Autoängste in der westdeutschen Presse von den 50er bis zu den 70er Jahren," in *Geschichte der Zukunft des Verkehrs: Verkehrskonzepte von der frühen Neuzeit bis zum 21. Jahrhundert*, ed. Hans-Liudger Dienel and Helmuth Trischler (Frankfurt a. M., 1997), 302–7; Ingo Köhler, "Marketing als Krisenstrategie: Die deutsche Automobilindustrie und die Herausforderungen der 1970er Jahre," in *Marketinggeschichte: Die Genese einer modernen Sozialtechnik*, ed. Hartmut Berghoff (Frankfurt a. M., 2007), 274–75.
84. See Reinhold Bauer, "Ölpreiskrisen und Industrieroboter: Die siebziger Jahre als Umbruchphase für die Automobilindustrie," in *Das Ende der Zuversicht? Die siebziger Jahre als Geschichte*, ed. Konrad H. Jarausch (Göttingen, 2008), 68–83.
85. Statistisches Jahrbuch der DDR 1988, 291.
86. See Köhler, "Marketing," 259–61, 266–68, 270–71; Stephanie Tilly and Dieter Ziegler, "Einleitung," *Jahrbuch für Wirtschaftsgeschichte* 51 (2010): 13.
87. Möser, *Geschichte*, 231.
88. See Peter Borscheid, "Agenten des Konsums: Werbung und Marketing," in *Die Konsumgesellschaft in Deutschland 1890–1990: Ein Handbuch*, ed. Heinz-Gerhard Haupt and Claudius Torp (Frankfurt a. M., 2009), 94; Köhler, Marketing, 281.
89. See Christopher Neumaier, "Eco-Friendly vs. Cancer-Causing: Perceptions of Diesel Cars in West Germany and the United States, 1970–1990," *Technology & Culture* 55 (2014): 430–34; König, *Geschichte*, 307–11.
90. Ulrich Wengenroth, "Gute Gründe: Technisierung und Konsumentscheidung," *Technikgeschichte* 71 (2004): 12.
91. Cf. Köhler, "Marketing," 290; Christopher Neumaier, "Vom Gefühl zum Kalkül? Autowerbung in Westdeutschland und den USA während der 1970er-Jahre," *Zeithistorische Forschungen/Studies in Contemporary History* 14 (2017): 541–59.
92. Helmut Eicker, "Sparbüchse," *Auto Motor und Sport* 20 (1976): 58.
93. Volkswagen advertisement, *Auto Motor und Sport* 8 (1982): 31.
94. See Rainer Gries, *Produkte als Medien: Kulturgeschichte der Produktkommunikation in der Bundesrepublik und in der DDR* (Leipzig, 2003); Simone Tippach-Schneider, *Messemännchen und Minol-Pirol: Werbung in der DDR* (Berlin, 1999); Helmut M. Bien and Ulrich Giersch, eds., *Spurensicherung: 40 Jahre Werbung in der DDR* (Frankfurt a. M., 1990).

95. Wolfgang König, "Die siebziger Jahre als konsumgeschichtliche Wende in der Bundesrepublik," in *Das Ende der Zuversicht? Die siebziger Jahre als Geschichte,* ed. Konrad H. Jarausch (Göttingen, 2008), 85.
96. See Claudius Torp and Heinz Gerhard Haupt, "Einleitung: Die vielen Wege der deutschen Konsumgesellschaft," in *Die Konsumgesellschaft in Deutschland 1890–1990: Ein Handbuch,* ed. Heinz-Gerhard Haupt and Claudius Torp (Frankfurt a. M., 2009), 13.
97. See König, " Die siebziger Jahre," 90.
98. See Peter Lohauß, "Marktgesellschaft und Individualisierungen: über den Wandel von Sozialstrukturen, Lebensstilen und Bewußtsein," in *Gesellschaftliche Transformationsprozesse und materielle Lebensweise,* ed. Werner Polster, Klaus Voy, and Claus Thomasberger (Marburg, 1993), 131.
99. Iris Häuser, *Gegenidentitäten: Zur Vorbereitung des politischen Umbruchs in der DDR: Lebensstile und politische Soziokultur in der DDR-Gesellschaft der achtziger Jahre* (Münster, 1996), 17, 70.
100. See Trentmann, *Empire.*
101. See Trentmann, "Long History," 109, 118, 121; Torp and Haupt, "Einleitung," 11, 19–21.
102. See König, " Die siebziger Jahre," 86.
103. Cf., Michael Wagner, "Entwicklung und Vielfalt der Lebensformen," in *Lehrbuch Moderne Familiensoziologie: Theorien, Methoden, empirische Befunde,* ed. Norbert F. Schneider (Opladen, 2008), 100; Reichardt, *Authentizität,* 351–60.
104. See "Familie heute—dreimal anders," *Für Sie,* 31 July 1980, Archive FFBIZ A Rep. 400 BRD 5, 56–58; Eva-Maria Silies, *Liebe, Lust und Last: Die Pille als weibliche Generationserfahrung in der Bundesrepublik 1960–1980* (Göttingen, 2010); Robert G. Moeller, "The Elephant in the Living Room: Or Why the History of Twentieth-Century Germany Should Be a Family Affair," in *Gendering Modern German History: Rewriting Historiography,* ed. Karen Hagemann and Jean H. Quataert (New York, 2007), 231–33.
105. See Norbert F. Schneider, "Grundlagen der sozialwissenschaftlichen Familienforschung—Einführende Betrachtungen," in *Lehrbuch Moderne Familiensoziologie: Theorien, Methoden, empirische Befunde,* ed. Norbert F. Schneider (Opladen, 2008), 15; Johannes Huinink and Dirk Konietzka, *Familiensoziologie: Eine Einführung* (Frankfurt a. M., 2007), 88–97.
106. See Dirk Konietzka and Michaela Kreyenfeld, "Nichteheliche Mutterschaft und soziale Ungleichheit im familialistischen Wohlfahrtsstaat: Zur sozioökonomischen Differenzierung der Familienformen in Ost- und Westdeutschland," *Kölner Zeitschrift für Soziologie und Sozialpsychologie* 57, no. 1 (2005): 32–61; Rüdiger Peuckert, *Familienformen im sozialen Wandel* (Wiesbaden, 2012), 166–67, 175–77, 305.
107. See Huinink and Konietzka, *Familiensoziologie,* 75.
108. Hartmann Tyrell, "Ehe und Familie—Institutionalisierung und Deinstiutionalisierung," in *Die "postmoderne" Familie: Familiale Strategien und Fami-*

lienpolitik in einer Übergangszeit, ed. Kurt Lüscher, Franz Schultheis, and Michael Wehrspaun (Konstanz, 1988), 151.
109. Peuckert, *Familienformen,* 155.
110. See ibid., 11, 20–23, 147, 151, 155.
111. Norbert F. Schneider, "Pluralisierung der Lebensformen: Fakt oder Fiktion?," *Zeitschrift für Familienforschung* 13, no. 2 (2001): 88.
112. See ibid.
113. Günter Burkart, *Familiensoziologie* (Konstanz, 2008), 29.
114. See ibid., 29–30.
115. See Renate Köcher, *Einstellungen zu Ehe und Familie im Wandel der Zeit: Eine Repräsentativuntersuchung im Auftrag des Ministeriums für Arbeit, Gesundheit, Familie und Sozialordnung Baden-Württemberg* (Stuttgart, 1985), 134, tables 73 and 74.
116. See "Ehe: Hat sie ausgedient? Oder wird sie jetzt erst richtig gut?," *Freundin,* 31 August 1978, Archive FFBIZ A Rep. 400 BRD 5.
117. See Elfriede Eilers, "Einleitung," in *Familienpolitik der SPD: Zweiter Entwurf, vorgelegt vom Familienpolitischen Ausschuß der SPD,* ed. Sozialdemokratische Partei Deutschlands (Bonn, 1975), 3.
118. See Frank Bösch, *Macht und Machtverlust: Die Geschichte der CDU* (Stuttgart, 2002), 39, 61.
119. See Alfons Cramer, *Zur Lage der Familie und der Familienpolitik in der Bundesrepublik Deutschland* (Opladen, 1982), 76.
120. Cf. Wagner, "Entwicklung," 101.
121. See Sabine Gründler and Katrin Schiefer, "Familienleitbilder unter dem Regenbogen—Akzeptanz von Regenbogenfamilien in Deutschland," *Bevölkerungsforschung Aktuell* 34, no. 4 (2013): 20.
122. See Gunnar Winkler, ed., *Sozialreport DDR 1990: Daten und Fakten zur sozialen Lage in der DDR* (Stuttgart, 1990), 264–65.
123. See Kanzlei des Staatsrates der DDR, ed., *Ein glückliches Familienleben—Anliegen des Familiengesetzbuches der DDR* (Berlin, 1965).
124. Jutta Gysi and Dagmar Meyer, "Leitbild: berufstätige Mutter. DDR-Frauen in Familie, Partnerschaft und Ehe," in *Frauen in Deutschland 1945–1992,* ed. Gisela Helwig and Hildegard Maria Nickel (Bonn, 1993), 150.
125. See Norbert F. Schneider, *Familie und private Lebensführung in West- und Ostdeutschland: Eine vergleichende Analyse des Familienlebens 1970–1992* (Stuttgart, 1994), 16; Gesine Obertreis, *Familienpolitik in der DDR 1945–1980* (Opladen, 1986), 286; Gisela Helwig, "Familienpolitik," in *Deutsche Demokratische Republik 1961–1971: Politische Stabilisierung und wirtschaftliche Mobilisierung,* ed. Christoph Kleßmann (Baden-Baden, 2006), 502–19.
126. See Günter Hoppe, "Über Wesen und Entwicklung der sozialistischen Lebensweise," *Einheit* 24, no. 4 (1969): 492–99; Bernd Bittighöfer, "Sozialistische Lebensweise—Errungenschaften und Aufgaben," *Einheit* 32, no. 1 (1977): 25–33; "Lebensweise, Sozialistische," in *DDR-Handbuch,* ed. Hartmut Zimmermann (Cologne, 1985), 1:817–18.

127. See Schneider, "Grundlagen," 13. For the role of family in West Germany and political debates during the 1950s and early 1960s, see Robert G. Moeller, *Protecting Motherhood: Women and the Family in the Politics of Postwar West Germany* (Berkeley, 1996).
128. See Christiane Kuller, *Familienpolitik im föderativen Sozialstaat: Die Formierung eines Politikfeldes in der Bundesrepublik 1949–1975* (Munich, 2004), 16–19; Ursula Münch, "Familien-, Jugend- und Altenpolitik," in *Bundesrepublik Deutschland 1966–1974: Eine Zeit vielfältigen Aufbruchs*, ed. Hans Günter Hockerts (Baden-Baden, 2006), 640–42, 646, 660–61, 666; Ursula Münch, "Familienpolitik," in *Bundesrepublik Deutschland 1974–1982: Neue Herausforderungen, wachsende Unsicherheiten*, ed. Michael H. Geyer (Baden-Baden, 2008), 658–60; Christopher Neumaier, "Ringen um Familienwerte: Die Reform des Ehescheidungsrechts in den 1960er/70er Jahren," in *Gab es den Wertewandel? Neue Forschungen zum gesellschaftlich-kulturellen Wandel seit den 1960er Jahren*, ed. Bernhard Dietz, Christopher Neumaier, and Andreas Rödder (Munich, 2014), 210–24.
129. See Münch, "Familien-, Jugend- und Altenpolitik (1966–1974)," 646, 650–54, 660–61, 666, 682–85; Münch, "Familienpolitik (1974–1982)," 650–52, 658–60; Sybille Buske, *Fräulein Mutter und ihr Bastard: Eine Geschichte der Unehelichkeit in Deutschland 1900–1970* (Göttingen, 2004), 343–45.
130. Gisela Helwig, "Familienpolitik," in *Deutsche Demokratische Republik 1971–1989: Bewegung in der Sozialpolitik, Erstarrung und Niedergang*, ed. Christoph Boyer, Klaus-Dietmar Henke, and Peter Skyba (Baden-Baden, 2008), 475.
131. See ibid., 475, 494–95.
132. Peuckert, *Familienformen*, 285.
133. See ibid., 285–87; Reichardt, *Authentizität*, 743.
134. See *Bericht der Bundesregierung über die Situation der Frauen in Beruf, Familie und Gesellschaft*, Deutscher Bundestag, Drs. 5/909 [Bonn, 1966], 61; Elisabeth Beck-Gernsheim, "Vom 'Dasein für andere' zum Anspruch auf ein Stück 'eigenes Leben': Individualisierungsprozesse im weiblichen Lebenszusammenhang," *Soziale Welt* 34 (1983): 316.
135. See Schneider, *Familie und private Lebensführung*, 81–82.
136. Sebastian Haffner, "Die Ehe wird anders: Sebastian Haffners Meinung," *Stern*, 24 January 1971.
137. Barbara Schmitt-Wenkebach, "Überlegungen und Beantwortung der Fragen zum Themenbereich 'Die Aufgabe der Frau für die Gesundheit in Familie und Gesellschaft,'" [Berlin, 24 November 1971], Archive BArch 189/3184, 132.
138. Helge Pross, *Gleichberechtigung im Beruf? Eine Untersuchung mit 7000 Arbeitnehmerinnen in der EWG* (Frankfurt a. M., 1973), 93.
139. Gabriele Gast, "Frauen," in *DDR-Handbuch*, ed. Hartmut Zimmermann (Cologne, 1985), 1:446–47. The employment rate of women reached 66.5 percent in 1964, 81.7 percent in 1973, 82.6 percent in 1976, and 82.8

percent in 1982. For employment rates see also Donna Harsch, "Industrialization, Mass Consumption, Post-Industrial Society," in *The Oxford Handbook of Modern German History*, ed. Helmut Walser Smith (Oxford, 2011), 666–8.
140. See Schneider, *Familie und private Lebensführung*, 163–64.
141. See ibid.
142. See ibid., 93–95; Sigrid Metz-Göckel and Ursula Müller, *Der Mann: Die BRIGITTE-Studie* (Weinheim, 1986), 16, 21, 24–26, 45–48.
143. See Annika Jabsen, Harald Rost, and Marina Rupp, *Die innerfamiliale Aufgabenteilung beim Wiedereinstieg von Müttern in den Beruf: Expertise für das Bundesministerium für Familie, Senioren, Frauen und Jugend* (Berlin, 2008), 4, 22–28.
144. See Winkler, *Sozialreport*, 268–69.
145. See Obertreis, *Familienpolitik*, 308; Gysi and Meyer, "Leitbild," 157–61; Donna Harsch, "Communism and Women," in *The Oxford Handbook of the History of Communism*, ed. Stephen A. Smith (Oxford, 2014), 488–9.
146. Jabsen, Rost, and Rupp, *Aufgabenteilung*, 4.
147. See Norbert F. Schneider, Sabine Diabaté, and Detlev Lück, "Gegenwärtige Familienleitbilder in Ost- und Westdeutschland im europäischen Vergleich," in *Familienleitbilder in Deutschland: Ihre Wirkung auf Familiengründung und Familienentwicklung*, ed. Christine Henry-Huthmacher and Konrad-Adenauer-Stiftung (Paderborn, 2014), 20.
148. See ibid., 20, 24–25.
149. See Sibylle Meyer and Eva Schulze, "Frauen in der Modernisierungsfalle: Wandel von Ehe, Familie und Partnerschaft in der Bundesrepublik Deutschland," in *Frauen in Deutschland 1945–1992*, ed. Gisela Helwig and Hildebard Maria Nickel (Bonn, 1993), 175.
150. See Helwig, "Familienpolitik (1971–1989)," 491; Ina Merkel, "Leitbilder und Lebensweisen von Frauen in der DDR," in *Sozialgeschichte der DDR*, ed. Hartmut Kaelble, Jürgen Kocka, and Hartmut Zwahr (Stuttgart, 1994), 373; Konietzka and Kreyenfeld, "Mutterschaft," 33.
151. See Olga Pötzsch, "Geburtenfolge und Geburtenabstand—neue Daten und Befunde," *Wirtschaft und Statistik* 2 (2012): 90.
152. See Peuckert, *Familienformen*, 104–5, 109.
153. See Rainer Geißler, *Die Sozialstruktur Deutschlands: Die gesellschaftliche Entwicklung vor und nach der Vereinigung: Mit einem Beitrag von Thomas Meyer* (Bonn, 2002), 365–66.
154. See Gunilla-Friederike Budde, *Frauen der Intelligenz: Akademikerinnen in der DDR 1945 bis 1975* (Göttingen, 2003), 315; Gunilla-Friederike Budde, "Alles bleibt anders: Die Institution 'Familie' zwischen 1945 und 1975 im deutsch-deutschen Vergleich," in *Verharrender Wandel: Institutionen und Geschlechterverhältnisse*, ed. Maria Oppen and Dagmar Simon (Berlin, 2004), 83–84, 94; Ute Schneider, *Hausväteridylle oder sozialistische Utopie? Die Familie im Recht der DDR* (Cologne, 2004), 23.

BIBLIOGRAPHY

Andersen, Arne. *Der Traum vom guten Leben: Alltags- und Konsumgeschichte vom Wirtschaftswunder bis heute.* Frankfurt a. M./New York: Campus, 1997.

Assmann, Georg, Wolfgang Eichhorn, and Erich Hahn, eds. *Wörterbuch der marxistisch-leninistischen Soziologie,* s.v. "Lebensweise." Berlin (DDR): Dietz, 1977.

Bauer, Reinhold. "Ölpreiskrisen und Industrieroboter: Die siebziger Jahre als Umbruchphase für die Automobilindustrie." In *Das Ende der Zuversicht? Die siebziger Jahre als Geschichte,* edited by Konrad H. Jarausch, 68–83. Göttingen: Vandenhoeck & Ruprecht, 2008.

Becher, Ursula A. J. *Geschichte des modernen Lebensstils: Essen—Wohnen—Freizeit—Reisen.* Munich: Beck, 1990.

Beck, Ulrich. "Tanz ums goldene Selbst." *Der Spiegel* 48, no. 22 (1994): 58–74.

Beck, Ulrich, and Elisabeth Beck-Gernsheim, eds. *Riskante Freiheiten: Individualisierung in modernen Gesellschaften.* Frankfurt a. M.: Suhrkamp, 1994.

Beck-Gernsheim, Elisabeth. "Vom 'Dasein für andere' zum Anspruch auf ein Stück 'eigenes Leben': Individualisierungsprozesse im weiblichen Lebenszusammenhang." *Soziale Welt* 34 (1983): 307–41.

Bell, Daniel. *The Coming of Post-Industrial Society: A Venture in Social Forecasting.* New York: Basic Books, 1973.

Bericht der Bundesregierung über die Situation der Frauen in Beruf, Familie und Gesellschaft. Deutscher Bundestag, Drs. 5/909 [Bonn, 1966].

Bien, Helmut M., and Ulrich Giersch, eds. *Spurensicherung: 40 Jahre Werbung in der DDR.* Frankfurt a. M.: Deutsches Werbemuseum, 1990.

Bittighöfer, Bernd. "Sozialistische Lebensweise: Errungenschaften und Aufgaben." *Einheit* 32, no. 1 (1977): 25–33.

Blum, Martin. "Club Cola & Co.: Ostalgie, Material Culture and Identity." In *Transformations of the New Germany,* edited by Ruth A. Starkman, 131–54. New York: Palgrave Macmillan, 2006.

Borscheid, Peter. "Agenten des Konsums: Werbung und Marketing." In *Die Konsumgesellschaft in Deutschland 1890–1990: Ein Handbuch,* edited by Heinz-Gerhard Haupt and Claudius Torp, 79–96. Frankfurt a. M.: Campus, 2009.

Bösch, Frank. *Macht und Machtverlust: Die Geschichte der CDU.* Stuttgart: Deutsche Verlags-Anstalt, 2002.

Bourdieu, Pierre. *Distinction: A Social Critique of Judgement of Taste.* London: Routledge & Kegan Paul, 1984.

Bren, Paulina, and Mary Neuburger, eds. *Communism Unwrapped: Consumption in Cold War Eastern Europe.* Oxford: Oxford University Press, 2012.

Budde, Gunilla-Friederike. "Alles bleibt anders. Die Institution 'Familie' zwischen 1945 und 1975 im deutsch-deutschen Vergleich." In *Verharrender Wandel: Institutionen und Geschlechterverhältnisse,* edited by Maria Oppen and Dagmar Simon, 69–98. Berlin: edition sigma, 2004.

———. *Frauen der Intelligenz: Akademikerinnen in der DDR 1945 bis 1975.* Göttingen: Vandenhoeck & Ruprecht, 2003.

Burkart, Günter. *Familiensoziologie*. Konstanz: UVK Verlagsgesellschaft, 2008.
Buske, Sybille. *Fräulein Mutter und ihr Bastard: Eine Geschichte der Unehelichkeit in Deutschland 1900–1970*. Göttingen: Wallstein, 2004.
Cramer, Alfons. *Zur Lage der Familie und der Familienpolitik in der Bundesrepublik Deutschland*. Opladen: Leske + Budrich, 1982.
Crew, David F. "Consuming Germany in the Cold War: Consumption and National Identity in East and West Germany, 1949–1989. An Introduction." In *Consuming Germany in the Cold War*, edited by David F. Crew, 1–19. Oxford: Berg, 2005.
Dokumentationszentrum Alltagskultur der DDR and Andreas Ludwig, eds. *KONSUM: Konsumgenossenschaften in der DDR*. Cologne: Böhlau, 2006.
Ebert, Elvir. *Einkommen und Konsum im Transformationsprozeß: Vom Plan zum Markt—vom Mangel zum Überfluß*. Opladen: Leske + Budrich, 1997.
"Ehe: Hat sie ausgedient? Oder wird sie jetzt erst richtig gut?" *Freundin*, 31 August 1978. Archive FFBIZ A Rep. 400 BRD 5.
Eicker, Helmut. "Sparbüchse." *Auto Motor und Sport* 20 (1976): 58–60.
Eilers, Elfriede. "Einleitung." In *Familienpolitik der SPD: Zweiter Entwurf, vorgelegt vom Familienpolitischen Ausschuß der SPD*, edited by Sozialdemokratische Partei Deutschlands, 3–4. Bonn, 1975.
Eisele, Petra. "Do-it-yourself-Design: Die IKEA-Regale IVAR und BILLY." *Zeithistorische Forschungen/Studies in Contemporary History* 3 (2006): 439–48.
"Familie heute—dreimal anders." *Für Sie*, 31 July 1980, 56–58. Archive FFBIZ A Rep. 400 BRD 5.
Fulbrook, Mary. *Power and Society in the GDR, 1961–1979: The Normalisation of Rule?* New York: Berghahn, 2009.
Gast, Gabriele. "Frauen." In *DDR-Handbuch*, edited by Hartmut Zimmermann, 1:443–49. Cologne: Verlag Wissenschaft und Politik, 1985.
Gasteiger, Nepomuk. *Der Konsument: Verbraucherbilder in Werbung, Konsumkritik und Verbraucherschutz 1945–1989*. Frankfurt a. M.: Campus, 2010.
Geißler, Rainer. *Die Sozialstruktur Deutschlands: Die gesellschaftliche Entwicklung vor und nach der Vereinigung: Mit einem Beitrag von Thomas Meyer*. Bonn: Bundeszentrale für politische Bildung, 2002.
Gries, Rainer. *Produkte als Medien: Kulturgeschichte der Produktkommunikation in der Bundesrepublik und in der DDR*. Leipzig: Leipziger Universitätsverlag, 2003.
Gründler, Sabine, and Katrin Schiefer. "Familienleitbilder unter dem Regenbogen: Akzeptanz von Regenbogenfamilien in Deutschland." *Bevölkerungsforschung Aktuell* 34 (2013): 18–24.
Gysi, Jutta, and Dagmar Meyer. "Leitbild: berufstätige Mutter. DDR-Frauen in Familie, Partnerschaft und Ehe." In *Frauen in Deutschland 1945–1992*, edited by Gisela Helwig and Hildegard Maria Nickel, 139–65. Bonn: Bundeszentrale für politische Bildung, 1993.
Haffner, Sebastian. "Die Ehe wird anders. Sebastian Haffners Meinung." *Stern*, 24 January 1971, 118–19.

Harsch, Donna. "Communism and Women." In *The Oxford Handbook of the History of Communism*, edited by Stephan A. Smith, 488–504. Oxford: Oxford University Press, 2014.

———. "Industrialization, Mass Consumption, Post-Industrial Society." In *The Oxford Handbook of Modern German History*, edited by Helmut Walser Smith, 663–88. Oxford: Oxford University Press, 2011.

———. *Revenge of the Domestic: Women, the Family, and Communism in the German Democratic Republic*. Princeton: Princeton University Press, 2007.

———. "Society, the State, and Abortion in East Germany, 1950–1972." *The American Historical Review* 102 (1997): 53–84.

———. "Women, Family, and 'Postwar': The Gendering of the GDR's Welfare Dictatorship." In *Gender and the Long Postwar: The United States and the Two Germanys, 1945–1989*, edited by Karen Hagemann and Sonya Michel, 253–73. Baltimore: Johns Hopkins University Press, 2014.

Haug, Wolfgang F. *Kritik der Warenästhetik*. Frankfurt a. M.: Suhrkamp, 1971.

Häuser, Iris. *Gegenidentitäten: Zur Vorbereitung des politischen Umbruchs in der DDR. Lebensstile und politische Soziokultur in der DDR-Gesellschaft der achtziger Jahre*. Münster: LIT, 1996.

Heldmann, Philipp. "Konsumpolitik in der DDR: Jugendliche in den sechziger Jahren." In *Konsumpolitik: Die Regulierung des privaten Verbrauchs im 20. Jahrhundert*, edited by Hartmut Berghoff. 135–58. Göttingen: Vandenhoek & Ruprecht, 1999.

Helwig, Gisela. "Familienpolitik." In *Deutsche Demokratische Republik 1961–1971: Politische Stabilisierung und wirtschaftliche Mobilisierung*, edited by Christoph Kleßmann, 496–522. Baden-Baden: Nomos, 2006.

———. "Familienpolitik." In *Deutsche Demokratische Republik 1971–1989: Bewegung in der Sozialpolitik, Erstarrung und Niedergang*, edited by Christoph Boyer, Klaus-Dietmar Henke, and Peter Skyba, 474–507. Baden-Baden: Nomos, 2008.

Hessler, Martina. *Kulturgeschichte der Technik*. Frankfurt a. M.: Campus, 2012.

Hodenberg, Christina von. *Television's Moment: Sitcom Audiences and the Sixties Cultural Revolution*. New York: Berghahn, 2015.

Hogwood, Patricia. "'Red is for Love . . .': Citizens as Consumers in East Germany." In *East German Distinctiveness in a Unified Germany*, edited by Jonathan Grix and Paul Cooke, 45–60. Birmingham: University of Birmingham Press, 2002.

Hoppe, Günther. "Über Wesen und Entwicklung der sozialistischen Lebensweise." *Einheit* 24, no. 4 (1969): 492–99.

Hradil, Stefan. *Soziale Ungleichheit in Deutschland: Unter Mitarbeit von Jürgen Schiener*. Opladen: Leske + Budrich, 2001.

Huinink, Johannes, and Dirk Konietzka. *Familiensoziologie: Eine Einführung*. Frankfurt a. M.: Campus, 2007.

Inglehart, Ronald. *The Silent Revolution: Changing Values and Political Styles among Western Publics*. Princeton: Princeton University Press, 1977.

Jabsen, Annika, Harald Rost, and Marina Rupp. *Die innerfamiliale Aufgabenteilung beim Wiedereinstieg von Müttern in den Beruf: Expertise für das Bundesministerium für Familie, Senioren, Frauen und Jugend.* Berlin: BMFSFJ, 2008.

Kaminsky, Annette. *Wohlstand, Schönheit, Glück: Kleine Konsumgeschichte der DDR.* Munich: Beck, 2001.

Kanzlei des Staatsrates der DDR, ed. *Ein glückliches Familienleben: Anliegen des Familiengesetzbuches der DDR.* Berlin (DDR): Staatsverlag der Deutschen Demokratischen Republik, 1965.

Kipphoff, Petra. "Mutprobe in Hosen, na und? Bei uns bleibt der Protest aus (Der Kampf der Frau, Teil III)." *Die Zeit,* 22 May 1970, 57.

Klages, Helmut. *Wertorientierungen im Wandel:* Rückblick, Gegenwartsanalyse, Prognosen. Frankfurt a. M.: Campus, 1984.

Kleinschmidt, Christian. *Konsumgesellschaft.* Göttingen: Vandenhoeck & Ruprecht, 2008.

Köcher, Renate. *Einstellungen zu Ehe und Familie im Wandel der Zeit: Eine Repräsentativuntersuchung im Auftrag des Ministeriums für Arbeit, Gesundheit, Familie und Sozialordnung Baden-Württemberg.* Stuttgart: Institut für Demoskopie Allensbach, 1985.

Koelbl, Herlinde, and Manfred Sack. *Das deutsche Wohnzimmer.* Luzern: Bucher, 1980.

Köhler, Ingo. "Marketing als Krisenstrategie. Die deutsche Automobilindustrie und die Herausforderungen der 1970er Jahre." In *Marketinggeschichte: Die Genese einer modernen Sozialtechnik,* edited by Hartmut Berghoff, 259–95. Frankfurt a. M.: Campus, 2007.

Konietzka, Dirk, and Michaela Kreyenfeld. "Nichteheliche Mutterschaft und soziale Ungleichheit im familialistischen Wohlfahrtsstaat: Zur sozioökonomischen Differenzierung der Familienformen in Ost- und Westdeutschland." *Kölner Zeitschrift für Soziologie und Sozialpsychologie* 57 (2005): 32–61.

König, Wolfgang. "Die siebziger Jahre als konsumgeschichtliche Wende in der Bundesrepublik." In *Das Ende der Zuversicht? Die siebziger Jahre als Geschichte,* edited by Konrad H. Jarausch, 84–99. Göttingen: Vandenhoeck & Ruprecht, 2008.

———. *Geschichte der Konsumgesellschaft.* Stuttgart: Franz Steiner, 2000.

Kühne-Brüning, Lidwina, Werner Plumpe, and Jan-Otmar Hesse. "Zwischen Angebot und Nachfrage, zwischen Regulierung und Konjunktur: Die Entwicklung der Wohnungsmärkte in der Bundesrepublik, 1949–1989/1990–1998." In *Geschichte des Wohnens,* vol 5: *1945 bis heute: Aufbau, Neubau, Umbau,* edited by Ingeborg Flagge, 153–232. Stuttgart: Deutsche Verlagsanstalt, 1999.

Kühschelm, Oliver, Franz X. Eder, and Hannes Siegrist. "Einleitung: Konsum und Nation." In *Konsum und Nation: Zur Geschichte nationalisierender Inszenierungen in der Produktkommunikation,* edited by Oliver Kühschelm, Franz X. Eder, and Hannes Siegrist, 7–44. Bielefeld: transcript, 2012.

Kuller, Christiane. *Familienpolitik im föderativen Sozialstaat: Die Formierung eines Politikfeldes in der Bundesrepublik 1949–1975.* Munich: Oldenbourg, 2004.

Langer, Lydia. *Revolution im Einzelhandel: Die Einführung der Selbstbedienung in Lebensmittelgeschäften der Bundesrepublik Deutschland (1949–1973)*. Cologne: Böhlau, 2013.

Lauber, Andreas. "Wohnkultur in der DDR: Dokumentation ihrer materiellen Sachkultur: Eine Untersuchung zu Gestaltung, Produktion und Bedingungen des Erwerbs von Wohnungseinrichtungen in der DDR." Manuscript. Eisenhüttenstadt: Dokumentationszentrum Alltagskultur der DDR, 2003.

Lohauß, Peter. "Marktgesellschaft und Individualisierungen: über den Wandel von Sozialstrukturen, Lebensstilen und Bewußtsein." In *Gesellschaftliche Transformationsprozesse und materielle Lebensweise*, edited by Werner Polster, Klaus Voy, and Claus Thomasberger, 89–140. Marburg: Metropolis, 1993.

Ludwig, Andreas. "'Hunderte von Varianten': Das Möbelprogramm Deutsche Werkstätten (MDW) in der DDR." *Zeithistorische Forschungen/Studies in Contemporary History* 3 (2006): 449–59.

Manz, Günter. *Armut in der "DDR"-Bevölkerung: Lebensstandard und Konsumniveau vor und nach der Wende*. Augsburg: Maro-Verlag, 1992.

Merkel, Ina. "Consumer Culture in the GDR, or How the Struggle for Antimodernity Was Lost on the Battleground of Consumer Culture." In *Getting and Spending: European and American Consumer Societies in the Twentieth Century*, edited by Susan Strasser, Charles McGovern, and Matthias Judt, 281–99. Cambridge: Cambridge University Press, 1998.

———. "Im Widerspruch zum Ideal: Konsumpolitik in der DDR." In *Die Konsumgesellschaft in Deutschland 1890–1990: Ein Handbuch*, edited by Heinz-Gerhard Haupt and Claudius Torp, 289–304. Frankfurt a. M.: Campus, 2009.

———. "Leitbilder und Lebensweisen von Frauen in der DDR." In *Sozialgeschichte der DDR*, edited by Hartmut Kaelble, Jürgen Kocka, and Hartmut Zwahr, 359–82. Stuttgart: Klett-Cotta, 1994.

———. *Utopie und Bedürfnis: Die Geschichte der Konsumkultur in der DDR*. Cologne: Böhlau, 1999.

Metz-Göckel, Sigrid, and Ursula Müller. *Der Mann: Die BRIGITTE-Studie*. Weinheim: Beltz, 1986.

Meyer, Sibylle, and Eva Schulze. "Frauen in der Modernisierungsfalle: Wandel von Ehe, Familie und Partnerschaft in der Bundesrepublik Deutschland." In *Frauen in Deutschland 1945–1992*, edited by Gisela Helwig and Hildegard Maria Nickel, 166–89. Bonn: Bundeszentrale für politische Bildung, 1993.

Bundesministerium für innerdeutsche Beziehungen. *Materialien zum Bericht zur Lage der Nation im geteilten Deutschland 1987*. Bonn: Eigenverlag, 1987.

Möhring, Maren. *Fremdes Essen: Die Geschichte der ausländischen Gastronomie in der Bundesrepublik Deutschland*. Munich: Oldenbourg, 2012.

———. "Veränderungen der bundesdeutschen (Ess-)Kultur durch Migration und Tourismus." In *Mit dem Wandel leben: Neuorientierung und Tradition in der Bundesrepublik der 1950er und 60er Jahre*, edited by Friedrich Kießling and Bernhard Rieger, 157–83. Cologne: Böhlau, 2011.

Moeller, Robert G. "The Elephant in the Living Room: Or Why the History of Twentieth-Century Germany Should Be a Family Affair." In *Gendering Modern German History: Rewriting Historiography*, edited by Karen Hagemann and Jean H. Quataert, 228–49. New York: Berghahn, 2007.

———. *Protecting Motherhood: Women and the Family in the Politics of Postwar West Germany*. Berkeley: University of California Press, 1996.

Möser, Kurt. *Geschichte des Autos*. Frankfurt a. M.: Campus, 2002.

Münch, Ursula. "Familien-, Jugend- und Altenpolitik." In *Bundesrepublik Deutschland 1966–1974: Eine Zeit vielfältigen Aufbruchs*, edited by Hans Günter Hockerts, 636–707. Baden-Baden: Nomos, 2006.

———. "Familienpolitik." In *Bundesrepublik Deutschland 1974–1982. Neue Herausforderungen, wachsende Unsicherheiten*, edited by Michael H. Geyer, 640–66. Baden-Baden: Nomos, 2008.

Mundt, Barbara. *Produkt-Design 1900–1990: Eine Einführung*. Berlin: Dietrich Reimer, 1990.

Neumaier, Christopher. *Dieselautos in Deutschland und den USA: Zum Verhältnis von Technologie, Konsum und Politik, 1949–2005*. Stuttgart: Franz Steiner, 2010.

———. "Eco-Friendly vs. Cancer-Causing: Perceptions of Diesel Cars in West Germany and the United States, 1970–1990." *Technology & Culture* 55 (2014): 429–60.

———. "Ringen um Familienwerte. Die Reform des Ehescheidungsrechts in den 1960er/70er Jahren." In *Gab es den Wertewandel? Neue Forschungen zum gesellschaftlich-kulturellen Wandel seit den 1960er Jahren*, edited by Bernhard Dietz, Christopher Neumaier, and Andreas Rödder, 201–25. Munich: Oldenbourg, 2014.

———. "Vom Gefühl zum Kalkül? Autowerbung in Westdeutschland und den USA während der 1970er-Jahre." *Zeithistorische Forschungen/Studies in Contemporary History* 14 (2017): 541–59.

Nolan, Mary. "Negotiating American Modernity in Twentieth-Century Europe." In *The Making of European Consumption: Facing the American Challenge*, edited by Per Lundin and Thomas Kaiserfeld, 17–44. Basingstoke: Palgrave Macmillan, 2015.

Obertreis, Gesine. *Familienpolitik in der DDR 1945–1980*. Opladen: Leske + Budrich, 1986.

Patterson, Patrick Hyder. "Risky Business: What Was Really Being Sold in the Department Stores of Socialist Eastern Europe?" In *Communism Unwrapped: Consumption in Cold War Eastern Europe*, edited by Paulina Bren and Mary Neuburger, 116–39. Oxford: Oxford University Press, 2012.

Pence, Katherine, and Paul Betts, eds. *Socialist Modern: East German Everyday Culture and Politics*. Ann Arbor: University of Michigan Press, 2008.

Peuckert, Rüdiger. *Familienformen im sozialen Wandel*. Wiesbaden: Springer VS, 2012.

Polster, Werner, and Klaus Voy. "Eigentum und Automobil: Materielle Fundamente der Lebensweise." In *Gesellschaftliche Transformationsprozesse und materielle Lebensweise*, edited by Werner Polster, Klaus Voy, and Claus Thomasberger, 203–356. Marburg: Metropolis, 1993.

Pötzsch, Olga. "Geburtenfolge und Geburtenabstand: neue Daten und Befunde." *Wirtschaft und Statistik* 2 (2012): 89–102.

Pross, Helge. *Gleichberechtigung im Beruf? Eine Untersuchung mit 7000 Arbeitnehmerinnen in der EWG*. Frankfurt a. M.: Athenäum, 1973.

Reckendrees, Alfred. "Die bundesdeutsche Massenkonsumgesellschaft: Einführende Bemerkungen." *Jahrbuch für Wirtschaftsgeschichte* 48 (2007): 17–27.

Reichardt, Sven. *Authentizität und Gemeinschaft: Linksalternatives Leben in den siebziger und frühen achtziger Jahren*. Berlin: Suhrkamp, 2014.

Roesler, Jörg. "Privater Konsum in Ostdeutschland, 1950–1960." In *Modernisierung im Wiederaufbau: Die westdeutsche Gesellschaft der 50er Jahre*, edited by Axel Schildt and Arnold Sywottek, 290–303. Bonn: J. H. W. Dietz Nachf., 1993.

Ruban, Maria Elisabeth. "Der Lebensstandard in der DDR und in Osteuropa." In *DDR und Osteuropa: Wirtschaftssystem, Wirtschaftspolitik, Lebensstandard: Ein Handbuch*, 319–65. Opladen: Leske + Budrich, 1981.

Rubin, Eli. *Amnesiopolis: Modernity, Space, and Memory in East Germany*. Oxford: Oxford University Press, 2016.

Ruppert, Wolfgang. "Zur Konsumwelt der 60er Jahre." In *Dynamische Zeiten. Die 60er Jahre in den beiden deutschen Gesellschaften*, edited by Axel Schildt, Detlef Siegfried, and Karl Christian Lammers, 752–67. Hamburg: Hans Christians, 2000.

Schelsky, Helmut. *Wandlungen der deutschen Familie in der Gegenwart: Darstellung und Deutung einer empirisch-soziologischen Tatbestandsaufnahme*. Stuttgart: Ferdinand Enke, 1955.

Schildt, Axel. *Die Sozialgeschichte der Bundesrepublik Deutschland bis 1989/90*. Munich: Oldenbourg, 2007.

———. "Vom Wohlstandsbarometer zum Belastungsfaktor: Autovision und Autoängste in der westdeutschen Presse von den 50er bis zu den 70er Jahren." In *Geschichte der Zukunft des Verkehrs: Verkehrskonzepte von der frühen Neuzeit bis zum 21. Jahrhundert*, edited by Hans-Liudger Dienel and Helmuth Trischler, 289–309. Frankfurt a. M.: Campus, 1997.

Schildt, Axel, and Detlef Siegfried. *Deutsche Kulturgeschichte: Die Bundesrepublik—1945 bis zur Gegenwart*. Munich: Carl Hanser, 2009.

Schmitt-Wenkebach, Barbara. "Überlegungen und Beantwortung der Fragen zum Themenbereich Die Aufgabe der Frau für die Gesundheit in Familie und Gesellschaft." [Berlin, 24 November 1971] 132, Archive BArch 189/3184.

Schneider, Norbert F. *Familie und private Lebensführung in West- und Ostdeutschland: Eine vergleichende Analyse des Familienlebens 1970–1992*. Stuttgart: Enke, 1994.

———. "Grundlagen der sozialwissenschaftlichen Familienforschung—Einführende Betrachtungen." In *Lehrbuch Moderne Familiensoziologie: Theorien, Methoden, empirische Befunde*, edited by Norbert F. Schneider, 9–21. Opladen: Barbara Budrich, 2008.

———. "Pluralisierung der Lebensformen: Fakt oder Fiktion?" *Zeitschrift für Familienforschung* 13 (2001): 85–90.

Schneider, Norbert F., Sabine Diabaté, and Detlev Lück. "Gegenwärtige Familienleitbilder in Ost- und Westdeutschland im europäischen Vergleich." In *Familienleitbilder in Deutschland. Ihre Wirkung auf Familiengründung und Familienentwicklung*, edited by Christine Henry-Huthmacher and Konrad-Adenauer-Stiftung, 18–25. Paderborn: Bonifatius, 2014.

Schneider, Ute. *Hausväteridylle oder sozialistische Utopie? Die Familie im Recht der DDR*. Cologne: Böhlau, 2004.

Scholze, Jana. "Shifting Narratives of Things: The East/West German Garden Egg Chair." In *East German Material Culture and the Power of Memory*, edited by Uta A. Balbier, Cristina Cuevas-Wolf, and Joes Segal, 87–98. Washington, DC: GHI, 2011.

Schulze, Gerhard. *Die Erlebnisgesellschaft: Kultursoziologie der Gegenwart*. Frankfurt a. M.: Campus, 2000.

Sedlmaier, Alexander. *Consumption and Violence: Radical Protest in Cold War Germany*. Ann Arbor: University of Michigan Press, 2014.

Siegfried, Detlef. *Time Is on My Side: Konsum und Politik in der westdeutschen Jugendkultur der 60er Jahre*. Göttingen: Wallstein, 2006.

Siegrist, Hannes. "Konsum, Kultur und Gesellschaft im modernen Europa." In *Europäische Konsumgeschichte: Zur Gesellschafts- und Kulturgeschichte des Konsums (18. bis 20. Jahrhundert)*, edited by Hannes Siegrist, Hartmut Kaelble, and Jürgen Kocka, 13–48. Frankfurt a. M.: Campus, 1997.

Sigmund, Monika. *Genuss als Politikum: Kaffeekonsum in beiden deutschen Staaten*. Berlin: de Gruyter/Oldenbourg, 2015.

Silies, Eva-Maria. *Liebe, Lust und Last: Die Pille als weibliche Generationserfahrung in der Bundesrepublik 1960–1980*. Göttingen: Wallstein, 2010.

Skyba, Peter. "Konsumpolitik in der DDR 1971 bis 1989. Die Verbraucherpreise als Konfliktgegenstand." In *Geschichte des Konsums: Erträge der 20. Arbeitstagung der Gesellschaft für Sozial- und Wirtschaftsgeschichte 23.–26. April 2003 in Greifswald*, edited by Rolf Walter, 343–66. Stuttgart: Franz Steiner, 2004.

Statistisches Amt der DDR, ed. *Statistisches Jahrbuch der DDR 1988, 1990*. Berlin (DDR): Staatsverlag, 1988 and 1990.

Statistisches Bundesamt. *50 Jahre Wohnen in Deutschland: Ergebnisse aus Gebäude- und Wohnungszählungen, -stichproben, Mikrozensus-Ergänzungserhebungen und Bautätigkeitsstatistiken*. Stuttgart: Metzler-Poeschel, 2000.

Statistisches Bundesamt, ed. *Statistisches Jahrbuch für die Bundesrepublik Deutschland 1970, 1981, 1988*. Stuttgart: Kohlhammer, 1970, 1981, and 1988.

Stitziel, Judd. "Shopping, Sewing, Networking: Consumer Culture and the Relationship between State and Society in the GDR." In *Socialist Modern: East German Everyday Culture and Politics*, edited by Katherine Pence and Paul Betts, 253–86. Ann Arbor: University of Michigan Press, 2008.

Tilly, Stephanie, and Dieter Ziegler. "Einleitung." *Jahrbuch für Wirtschaftsgeschichte* 51, no. 1 (2010): 11–17.

Tippach-Schneider, Simone. *Messemännchen und Minol-Pirol: Werbung in der DDR*. Berlin: Schwarzkopf & Schwarzkopf, 1999.

Torp, Claudius, and Heinz Gerhard Haupt. "Einleitung: Die vielen Wege der deutschen Konsumgesellschaft." In *Die Konsumgesellschaft in Deutschland 1890–1990: Ein Handbuch*, edited by Heinz-Gerhard Haupt and Claudius Torp, 9–24. Frankfurt a. M.: Campus, 2009.

Trentmann, Frank. *Empire of Things: How We Became a World of Consumers, from the Fifteenth Century to the Twenty-First*. London: Allen Lane, 2016.

———. "The Long History of Contemporary Consumer Society." *Archiv für Sozialgeschichte* 49 (2009): 107–28.

Tyrell, Hartmann. "Ehe und Familie—Institutionalisierung und Deinstitutionalisierung." In *Die "postmoderne" Familie: Familiale Strategien und Familienpolitik in einer Übergangszeit*, edited by Kurt Lüscher, Franz Schultheis, and Michael Wehrspaun, 145–56. Konstanz: Universitätsverlag Konstanz, 1988.

Unterrichtung durch die Bundesregierung: Materialien zur Deutschen Einheit und zum Aufbau in den neuen Bundesländern, Deutscher Bundestag, Drs. 12/6854, 8 February 1994, 442–44.

Veenis, Milena. "Consumption in East Germany: The Seduction and Betrayal of Things." *Journal of Material Culture* 4 (1999): 79–112.

Volkswagen advertisement. *Auto Motor und Sport* 8 (1982): 31.

Volze, Armin. "Die Devisengeschäfte der DDR: Genex und Intershop." *Deutschland Archiv* 24 (1991): 1145–59.

Wagner, Michael. "Entwicklung und Vielfalt der Lebensformen." In *Lehrbuch Moderne Familiensoziologie: Theorien, Methoden, empirische Befunde*, edited by Norbert F. Schneider, 99–120. Opladen: Barbara Budrich, 2008.

Weis, Diana, ed. *Cool aussehen: Mode und Jugendkulturen*. Berlin: Archiv der Jugendkulturen, 2012.

Weißler, Sabine. "Die Frau Die Mode Der Körper: Beweglichkeit und Bewegung." In *Um 1968: Die Repräsentation der Dinge*, edited by Wolfgang Ruppert, 125–36. Marburg: Jonas, 1998.

Wengenroth, Ulrich. "Gute Gründe. Technisierung und Konsumentscheidung." *Technikgeschichte* 71 (2004): 3–18.

Winkler, Gunnar, ed. *Sozialreport DDR 1990: Daten und Fakten zur sozialen Lage in der DDR*. Stuttgart: Akademie der Wissenschaften der DDR, 1990.

Wolfe, Tom. "The 'Me' Decade and the Third Great Awakening." *New York Magazine*, 23 August 1976. Retrieved 6 June 2016, www.nymag.com/news/features/45938/.

Wünderich, Volker. "Die 'Kaffeekrise' von 1977: Genußmittel und Verbraucherprotest in der DDR." *Historische Anthropologie* 11 (2003): 240–62.
Zachmann, Karin, and Ruth Oldenziel. "Kitchen as Technology and Politics: An Introduction." In *Cold War Kitchen: Americanization, Technology, and European Users*, edited by Karin Zachmann and Ruth Oldenziel, 1–29. Cambridge, MA: MIT Press, 2009.
Zatlin, Jonathan R. "Consuming Ideology: Socialist Consumerism and the Intershop, 1970–1989." In *Arbeiter in der SBZ/DDR*, edited by Peter Hübner and Klaus Tenfelde, 555–72. Essen: Klartext, 1999.
Zimmermann, Clemens. "Wohnungspolitik—Eigenheim für alle?" In *Villa und Eigenheim: Suburbaner Städtebau in Deutschland*, edited by Tilman Harlander, 64–75. Stuttgart and Munich: Deutsche Verlagsanstalt, 2001.
Zimmermann, Hartmut, ed. *DDR-Handbuch*, s.v. "Lebensweise, Sozialistische.", 1:817–18. Cologne: Verlag Wissenschaft und Politik, 1985.

CHAPTER 7

Paths to Digital Modernity
Computerization as Social Change

Jürgen Danyel and Annette Schuhmann

By the time microelectronics first appeared on the scene in the early 1970s, computers and all related information and communications technologies were well on their way to becoming a decisive factor in the development of modern industrial societies. Over the course of the 1980s, the computer, and new media formats associated with it, spread irrevocably into the deepest corners of society. The digital revolution touched virtually all aspects of life—from work, social communications, political culture, education, consumption, and leisure time all the way to personal lifestyle choices. Yet scholars of contemporary history in Germany have paid very little attention thus far to the phases and turning points within this process, nor have they analyzed the role of computerization within the context of the economic, social, and political upheavals in the last thirty years of the twentieth century.

Although the Internet revolution was very much a phenomenon of the 1990s, when state socialism had already collapsed (not counting the early beginnings of the web), the history of computerization was very much embedded in the political and social constellations of the Cold War. Since the late 1960s, technological innovation in microelectronics, computers, and software development had been one of the major fields of competition between Western industrialized societies and the Eastern Bloc countries. In addition to its very technological aspects, this rivalry also had sociopolitical and cultural dimensions. Whereas technological progress in electronic data processing in the 1950s and 1960s occurred primarily within the isolated arcane confines of military and scientific research, or at best in the major computing centers in large companies and government agencies, computerization entered a new phase in the 1970s as it reached a growing number of people in Western Europe and the United States. The mass availability of computers in the 1980s and the firm establishment of computer technology within the changing world of work and in new modes of communication became some of the major benchmarks of performance in rivalry between the opposing economic and political systems of the Cold War.

Consequently, any attempt to write a history of computerization in East and West Germany cannot ignore these comparative dimensions. Yet it also has to look past the system rivalry with its lines of demarcation and considerable asymmetries between the two countries to locate direct relationships and detect elements of entanglement within divided Germany. The reasons for adopting such a perspective are myriad. First, the rivalry between the two systems played out on a field where the dynamics were increasingly shaped by international connections. The use of computer technology in fact fostered global ties and cross-border communication. This created new problems for both systems within the political constellations of the Cold War. In Western industrialized societies, for example, the sales interests of the booming computer and software industry clashed with the politically mandated embargoes on advanced technologies put in place by some countries, especially the United States. The political strategies of "change through rapprochement" that sought to boost the economic links between East and West, however, conflicted with ideologically driven demarcation strategies, such as those forced by the United States after 1980 in the wake of the Soviet march into Afghanistan.

The difficulties faced by the countries of the Eastern Bloc were even larger. National models of self-sufficiency, which were repeatedly introduced vis-à-vis technology out of necessity, proved to be quite unpromising.[1] When it came to computerization, the state socialist regime could not get around the competition by offering ideologically postulated alternatives. Rather, all the Eastern Bloc countries followed the lead of the Soviet Union and put the introduction of modern information technology high up on their list of official priorities from the early 1970s onward. From the very beginning, however, the ailing and technologically backward people's economies of the COMECON states relied on ties to the West in both a technological and financial sense. They found themselves unable to provide the funds necessary for the desired computerization of industrial production, apart from a few isolated instances of political privilege. Consequently, they had to rely on the transfer of computer technology, as well as imported production systems and loans from the West. It had been intended and even concretely planned to develop collaborative solutions within the COMECON, but limited production capacities and differing levels of development in microelectronics detracted from the feasibility of these initiatives.[2]

Furthermore, the highly subsidized welfare system and promises of full employment in the GDR could not really be sacrificed in the name of computerization with the goal of rationalization. Well up the party ladder, officials were well aware of just how ruinous this stance might be in the long run. Moreover, rationalization and intensification had already become the new mantra of the SED's economic policy, although there was never any intention to give up on the idea of full employment.

Both German states certainly kept a close watch on one another until the collapse of the GDR, although East Germany undoubtedly kept better track of computerization developments in West Germany than vice versa. This essay looks specifically at the extent to which the special economic and financial policy relationship between the two Germanys offered a limited framework for ties that ran back and forth across the Wall in the area of computerization. New entanglements and dependencies, for example, also emerged in the gray areas of illegal technology transfers and industrial espionage. Although the East sought to use such methods to overcome its deficits, this only increased its dependence on the West in the end.

Technology was nevertheless one of the most important areas in which both sides kept tabs on each other from the very beginning. Well into the 1970s, however, only a limited number of experts within the field who were "in the know" could actually see that the West was outperforming the East in IT and computer technology. This changed as the computer became a device that could be used by mainstream individuals, making it a prime consumer good. By the mid-1980s, a large portion of West German society had come to realize that computers were very likely the technology of the future because they had used them at work or in their free time. At the same time, computer performance could be experienced and measured, which made it easier to draw comparisons between East and West. As in other fields of consumption, the media and advertising played an important cross-border role when it came to the evolution of computers as a consumer good. In addition, a growing number of economic experts, researchers, technicians, and private people had been able to see for themselves what the state of technology was like in both East and West Germany thanks to more opportunities for travel and interaction. These entanglements were also marked by the asymmetries so typical of the relationship between East and West. By the 1970s and 1980s, computerization in the societies governed by state socialism had long since ceased to represent any kind of competition for the West. When it came to technological advancements, West Germany had its gaze firmly affixed on the United States and Japan. The only people who seemed to be interested in whether the Eastern Bloc could keep up with computerization in the West were political observers and companies in those industries that saw the potential to tap into new sales markets or set up production facilities with licensing agreements.

Computerization, Information Society, and Digital Modernity

Computerization was associated with different terminology and social concepts in East and West Germany. The classic analyses by Daniel Bell,[3] Alain Touraine,[4] or Karl W. Deutsch,[5] as well as Manuel Castells' *The Information Age*,[6] which was published later, share the idea that the transformation brought about through computer technology constitutes a new historic era. The subsequent evolution of the Internet then added further fuel to the fire of such assessments of the time and predictions of the future. Metaphors of a revolution driven by technological progress also appeared in the Eastern Bloc countries within the context of the reform and modernization efforts of the 1960s. This then fed into the inflationary use of the term "scientific-technical revolution" in political propaganda at the time.[7] The idea of freeing up labor resources through rationalization was thus portrayed as a new chance for a Communist future that could be brought about through technological progress. In the Richta Report inspired by the Prague Spring, this vision of a scientific and technological utopia was interlaced with a fundamental critique of the alienating tendencies of state socialism.[8] Drawing on the early writings of Marx, it pointed to the liberation of the individual within a renewed socialist utopia while maintaining that civilization had come to a crossroads. As part of the cybernetics craze that hit most of the Eastern Bloc countries in the 1960s, this utopia was reduced in a technocratic sense to the level of data-driven social management and forecasting. After a short heyday, however, the party leadership within the bloc suppressed these visions.[9]

In spite of the various differences in detail, these notions all rested on the idea that industrial society would have to make way for a postindustrial society strongly shaped by information technology. Even in the GDR and the other Eastern Bloc countries, the expectation was that the current path of industrial development could be redirected through the computer-supported intensification of production. At the core, these rather optimistic interpretations were essentially inspired by a new dynamic of advancement. From this perspective, the social transformation that occurred on the cusp of the 1980s was therefore embedded within a new way of thinking about progress. In keeping with this line of thought, the theses claiming that an end had come to modernity—and the expectations of progress associated with it—need to be revised in terms of the history of computerization.[10]

Such optimistic interpretations of computerization as the historic root of information society stand in contrast to a whole series of contemporary interpretations that described the 1970s and the early 1980s as a period of social crisis.[11] The latter drew on the experiences of the oil crises in 1973 and 1979, which fed into a far-reaching structural transformation of the economy and a long-lasting recession after the boom of the postwar era. A high level of structural unemployment, the crises of the welfare state, environmental destruction, the negative consequences of the progressive mediatization of society, and the emergence of terrorism all called the faith in progress of the modern era into question. Computerization, which had become quite extensive since the second half of the 1970s, was also part of this perceived crisis because it was seen as a job killer, a means of alienation, and a method of control and surveillance with potentially Orwellian proportions.[12] It seems plausible that the influence of these perceptions of crisis can also be mapped on to the situation in the societies of state socialism. Indeed, the development of "information society" was ultimately given a high political priority. Yet it did not lead to a second socialist era of modernity, but rather it propelled the Communist bloc into financial ruin.

The history of computerization has therefore been integrated into completely different, or rather totally contradictory, interpretations of the transformation that took place on the cusp of the 1980s. Additional empirical analyses are needed in order to resolve these conflicting narratives by looking at the individual phases of the digital transformation in a long-term perspective while also accounting for its social significance. Such an approach reveals that the advancement of information and computer technology is still very much tied to positive expectations for the future, indicating that many of the fears and threat scenarios that had emerged in the early phase of computerization had waned quite quickly. The negative effects of rationalization and the way automation had alienated and accelerated work played a major role in the public debates over the implications of computerization in West Germany in the 1980s. Although these issues still received critical attention in the decades that followed, the computer was no longer directly addressed as technology. One exception to this trend had been the entire field of control and surveillance. Even today, debates still rage over the uncontrollable power of computers. But, first and foremost, this criticism has been aimed at intelligence services, the military, or large financial corporations and not necessarily at the computer or modern communications technology itself. In the

GDR, moreover, the critique against the surveillance of the Stasi had very little to do with computer technology; rather, it was directed at the omnipresence of the huge apparatus of the Ministry for State Security.

The successful establishment and global spread of the Internet might very well have given rise to more fantasies about progress and the future than the advancement of computer technology itself. Moreover, digital communications technologies and social networks have become vehicles of mobilization in situations of social upheaval and protest, although the limits of their reach were clear to see after the "Arab Spring."

The general revival of technological models of progress suggests that the term "modernity" might be used to describe the development of society that set in with computerization and has been further propelled by the arrival of the Internet. Indeed, although a more precise definition is warranted, the notion of "digital modernity" offers a way to bundle different aspects and dimensions of these processes of technological and sociocultural change that began in the mid-1970s. It also makes it possible to trace the outline of a separate historical era, characterized by the computerization of society; the digital production of goods and provision of services; the transfer of economic, political, and social communication, as well as decision-making processes, to the virtual spaces of the Internet; the digitalization and electronic availability of knowledge and cultural heritage on a larger scale; and the connectivity of the accompanying effects of globalization. Two further points speak in favor of using the concept of "digital modernity": first, the political upheavals of 1989 and the fall of state socialism do not mark a caesura in terms of digitalization, at least for the West; these events actually accelerated the trend toward an information society in the postcommunist countries. Second, it makes sense to reformulate the idea of "modernity" with respect to the Digital Age because these developments have been taking place within the framework of a capitalist economic order all along.

In contrast to this broadly defined use of "digital modernity," the term "computerization" will be used in a more narrow sense. It will be used in reference to the introduction of electronic data processing in the 1950s and the phase in which microelectronics and personal computers made inroads into society after the mid-1970s. It also encompasses the information and communications technologies that computers have fostered in different areas of society. As such, computerization describes a phase of digital modernity that can be isolated historically because it is tied to the establishment of a specific type of technology.

The notion of "information society" has also proven to be a flexible concept that can be used vis-à-vis contemporary history because it can bring different interwoven technological and social developments under one umbrella. Originally, "information society" was used to reflect the growing role of information processing (and, above all, electronic data processing) in conjunction with the increasing tertiarization of the economy (service society), which was tied to the need for different professional qualifications. Defined in such a narrow way, this term can certainly be used to analyze the social transformations that were tied to computerization in both East and West Germany. Yet, "information society" has come to be used in a much broader sense to describe a type of society in which information and communication technology has infiltrated every nook and cranny. As a relatively open concept, it also offers a way to think about the technological and cultural transition of computer society into the era of the Internet, whereby the Internet becomes the main media within a network and knowledge-based society. However, this term needs to be critically resituated within its own specific historical context on a regular basis in order to truly evaluate its half-life.

Consequently, the history of computerization since the mid-1980s can no longer be written as simply a history of technology as has been possible for 1960s and 1970s, but rather it must be embedded within a narrative of social history in the Information Age. The political, social, and cultural modes of computerization can only be explained within the context of the crisis management of Western industrialized societies, the functional differentiation of these societies as modern societies of consumption and leisure, and the accompanying individualization and pluralization processes.

The era of digital modernity can be broken down into several phases, marked by defining moments. The first phase began at the end of the 1950s with the use of the first mainframe computers in banks, government administrations, companies, large research facilities, and especially the military. The development and use of computer technologically was limited to a few sectors in society and strongly embedded within the political logic of the Cold War. It largely fell under the rubric of social engineering because it was designed to effectively manage processes and avoid conflict situations through the aggregation of mass data and its electronic processing. Massive state-sponsored programs were the primary motors behind the advancement of computers.[13] Huge mainframe computers that initially still relied on tube and relay technology were the dominant form of technology during this phase.

The second phase began in the early or perhaps mid-1980s. Personal computers and microprocessors were the technical icons of this period. In terms of social and cultural aspects, this phase was defined by the extensive rationalization of work and the spread of computers in private life that had been fostered initially by the commercial success of computer games (at least in the West). The personal computer, be it in the form of home computers or video game consoles, opened the floodgates for information society in the modern, pluralized, consumer and leisure societies that had differentiated themselves by this time. A new phase began in the mid-1990s with the advent of the Internet and the spread of digital mobile communications.

The Triumph of the Computer in Modern Industrial Societies

If there was one major myth about the future propagated in the twentieth century, then it was the myth that all of a society's problems could be fixed with technology. Especially in the early phase of the Nuclear and Space Age after 1945, this myth fostered a vision of the year 2000 in which everything would be automated. As in all other eras, the respective state of technology primarily influenced the world of work, often redefining its parameters entirely. Whenever a new wave of technology became established, it unleashed dramatic transformations. Looking back at the history of such technological revolutions, there always appear to be a few recurring factors that influenced how and to what extent technological innovations affected the societies in question.[14] In particular, the speed at which new technology spread and the number of people affected by it largely determined how extreme the ensuing changes would become.[15]

Computerization noticeably affected all areas of life, especially work, and the rate at which its effects were felt differed significantly from other technological innovations—for example, the spread of electricity or the invention and production of synthetic fabrics by the chemical industry. That said, the vision of machines (or other replacements of some kind) that could do our work for us or at least make it easier has been a historical constant. Likewise, it has always been accompanied by expectations and fears on the one side, and euphoric scenarios on the other.[16]

Images of paperless offices and factories without humans have been recurring metaphors in visions about the future of work in West Germany since the 1960s.[17] Technology experts and entrepreneurs envisaged euphoric scenarios in which the element of human error could be eliminated in the production process. Volkswagen, in particular, attempted to implement a fully automated assembly line in its famous "Halle 54" production area in Wolfsburg.[18] This technology push first appeared on a larger scale in industrial production. Clear outlines of the attempts to establish a fully automated factory of the future that would be devoid of humans can be traced in the history of the automobile industry in the United States, Japan, and Western Europe, where they often appeared under the catchphrase "Fabrik 2000" (Factory 2000).[19]

As computerization progressed, the discourses in East and West were preoccupied with the goal of achieving perfected production workflows that were free of disruptions. In fact, the introduction of computer technology was actually celebrated in both blocs with arguments about the "humanization of work," sometimes with reference to the same theorists such as Marx or Bernal.

This wave of technological information also wormed its way into theories of postindustrial society and ideologically tinged political commentaries, such as those propagated by Herman Kahn at the right-wing conservative Hudson Institute from the 1960s onward. Predictions of the future ranging in tone from euphoric to alarmist also emerged across the political spectrum.[20] In West Germany, for example, the futurologist and cyberneticist Karl Steinbuch admonished that the neglect of the natural sciences would threaten the chances of being able to keep up with the development of newer technologies.[21] In the early 1970s, some critics also pointed to the "costs" that a society would have to pay for concentrating on the development and use of advanced technologies.[22]

Cautionary voices that spoke of a "technological gap" or warned that the potential of advanced technologies might not be exhausted were also heard in the GDR. By the early 1970s, during the Ulbricht era, experts noticed that the GDR was falling behind in electronic data processing. Apparently, a great uncertainty still plagued the question of how and to what extent this new technology had to be dealt with in the GDR at the beginning of the 1970s. Although the political leadership agreed on the importance of the electronics industry for its program of forced rationalization, there were no efforts specifically designed to support the microelectronics industry to speak of around 1970.[23]

Representatives of the politburo first addressed this issue more concretely at the congress of the Central Committee in September 1976. They estimated that the state of technology in the GDR lagged about four years (analog circuits) to nine years (microprocessors) behind that of the West. At the same time, it was clear that this gap could not be closed over the next few years, so they also discussed the possibilities for counter trades and license agreements, which had already been done in other states in the Communist bloc.[24] The Communist power elite, especially in the Soviet Union, was very well aware of the fact that technological progress would decide the outcome of the rivalry between the systems.

Outside the boundaries of the Cold War confrontation, feature articles published at the time fueled fears that other countries were pulling ahead in technology, pointing at the Americans, alternating with the Soviets (Sputnik shock), then the Japanese (automobile industry, consumer electronics, ship building), the South East Asians (communications technology), and then later the Chinese (all areas). This talk of falling behind reappeared over and over again, until it began to fade after the first crisis in the so-called "tiger economies."

The socialist counterpart to the Western term "third industrial revolution" was "scientific-technical revolution" (Wissenschaftlich-technische Revolution, or WTR). This idea became a key rhetorical phrase throughout the Eastern Bloc within the context of the system rivalry. A look at its genesis and metamorphoses reveals the strategies that politicians and functional elites in the state socialist countries adopted to deal with the issue of technology. The idea of the "scientific-technical revolution" had been introduced by the Irish physicist John Desmond Bernal, whose 1954 work *Science in History* appeared in the GDR in 1961. It later made its way to other state socialist countries and soon became a classic work in scientific literature. Bernal sought to use this term to describe a revolutionary process that took place in the twentieth century in which most areas of life in industrialized societies underwent what might be termed a process of "scientification" (*Verwissenschaftlichung*). Essentially, as early as the 1950s Bernal predicted that the manual labor done by workers would be taken over by machines and electronically controlled devices, thereby doing away with hard and monotonous tasks.[25] One of the defining characteristics of this WTR was the use of electronic control systems in production. In 1970, moreover, Walter Ulbricht wrote in a draft proposal for the politburo that the success of this revolution "would make it possible for the GDR economy to catch up to the level of productivity in West Germany."[26]

Despite the system rivalry and the different trajectories of technology policy in both systems, the visions for the future in East and West Germany were quite similar until the end of the 1960s. The dream of factories devoid of humans and people liberated from having to do hard manual labor was just as prevalent in the theoretical writings of socialist technical visionaries as in the theories of Western European Marxists.[27] Unmistakably, however, by the beginning of the 1970s, these optimistic visions of the future had lost their appeal in the West. The introduction of computer science as a university subject, in contrast, indicated an at least somewhat positive attitude toward electronic data processing. Nevertheless, computers and microelectronics appeared rather seldom in popular science literature and the press until the end of the 1970s because the majority of the population did not seem to be interested in most of the uses for this technology. The optimistic faith in the socialist future also waned among the citizens of the GDR, but computerization was not an indicator of this in the East.

In the Communist bloc countries, official statements proclaimed that "socialist automation," together with the planned economy, would bring the victory of communism, claiming that such a process would lead to the demise of capitalism because of the discontinuous nature of production tied to the flexibility of the markets in the West. By the 1980s, a pragmatic way of dealing with this kind of technological propaganda had prevailed, but it had already ceased to be regarded as an expression of common sense by the 1970s.

In West Germany, misdirected rationalization strategies in the 1980s and the state's subvention policies, which leaned strongly toward lobby interests, led to an enormous overestimation of automation and, in turn, crises in some economic sectors. From the late 1960s, the competition, particularly from Asia, edged closer in the automobile industry, consumer electronics, and shipbuilding. Government and independent commercial institutions thus kept their eyes fixed first and foremost on Japan.[28] One of the most important realizations that came through observing developments in Japan was that technological factors played a secondary role, whereas factors such as personnel management, industrial relations, workforce organization, and job commitment were much more important when it came to explaining Japan's superiority. This realization reinforced the management philosophies that had been recommended, especially by business consultants who stressed the need for new forms of workforce organization and dealing with "human resources."

Over the course of the 1950s and 1960s, the visionary notions about the future of automation processes in the East and West were quite similar. Despite the competition between the two systems and different paths of development, the elites in both systems, if not others, believed that the computerization of science and work was revolutionary and necessary. In both countries, the first use of computers in production formed the foundation for a high degree of optimism. Both sides saw the development of microelectronics as a significant factor in the rivalry between the systems. Especially in terms of advanced technologies, however, this bipolar constellation was asymmetric. To the West, the Eastern Bloc hardly seemed to be much competition anymore, but it was seen as a potential future sales market. For the leaders of the GDR, however, West Germany remained a focal point and a frame of reference, as well as a rival, until 1989.

Computerization in East and West Germany: From the Mainframe to the Personal Computer

The expensive mainframe computers that had been used in the military, scientific institutes, administrative offices, insurance companies, and industrial facilities since the 1950s still continued to dominate the market until the early 1970s. However, there were a limited number of scenarios in which they could be used. The resulting misjudgments about the future development of this technology in the upper executive levels at the computing giant IBM, for example, are well known. IBM had mistakenly believed that only a small number of mainframes had any real chance on the market at first, but this was not surprising because, at this point in time, new information technologies, just like the early stages of the Internet in the early 1970s, were still firmly embedded in the constellations of the military rivalry and arms race between East and West. The exception to this proved to be the tradition of using technology to optimize computational processes in mathematics and the natural sciences or to collate mass statistical data.[29] It is therefore all the more surprising that the computer and other technological innovations using microprocessors were able to break out of the sphere of secret government programs and military facilities with such force that they were able to spread to all corners of society just a short time later.

The industrial production and mass import of microprocessors, without which the triumph of the PC within society would have been unthinkable, began in West Germany at the beginning of the 1970s. It was linked to the successive miniaturization of processing and storage units, which was primarily made possible through advancements in the semiconductor industry and the dropping prices for parts.

Initially, electronic data processing was mostly done in centralized computing facilities, but a stronger push toward decentralization set in during the 1970s. This trend had already begun in West Germany with the transition from punched cards to data entry using visual display units.[30] Although integrated circuits had been around in the West since 1960, they were hardly used, or rather used only in military aerospace research, because of their incredibly high production costs.[31] By the end of the 1970s, microchips had become more reliable, and the energy required for chip production sank enormously. The only thing that still stood in the way of the rapid spread of this technology was its still-high price. The standardization of hardware was primarily responsible for making the production of microprocessors on a large scale possible and cheaper in the United States and Western Europe.[32] The development tempo of the computer industry accelerated to such a rate at the end of the 1960s that it no longer seemed unreasonable to speak of a revolution, although the term tended to be used in an inflationary way. In the GDR, on the other hand, microelectronics—and the potential for rationalization associated with this technology—did not become a core focus within the scientific technical revolution until the end of the 1970s.[33]

Nonetheless, the costs for what was referred to as midrange data technology remained high in the West, which meant that most of the small and midsize production companies in West Germany could hardly afford to buy it. Although the prices for microprocessors had dropped significantly by 1980s, the costs for a microcomputer stand-alone system were still high, mostly because of the extremely expensive peripheral devices that were needed. The microprocessor only accounted for 0.5 percent of the cost of a computer in 1980, whereas peripheral devices and software were the main factors contributing to the high price tag.[34]

Accordingly, the story of the birth of the personal computer has often been told in retrospect like a modern fairy-tale. At first, as the narrative goes, this technological revolution took place silently: In a garage in Silicon Valley in 1976, Steve Wozniak and Steve Jobs began to build a computer based on the "Altair" and then sold it to a local computer store.[35] A similar story is told about the origins of Microsoft, which led to the rise of a new economic sector in the guise of the software industry.[36] Like the founders of Apple, Bill Gates and Paul Allen, who rewrote the software BASIC into an operating system for the new microcomputers, were creative outsiders. The name "personal computer" was given to the new computer generation put out by IBM, which had jumped onto the scene and commercialized what would become the new standard in computers.

Apart from creating legends, these popular stories about the origins of digital modernity exemplify just how quickly this new technology was able to gain a strong foothold in a variety of areas and milieus within society. Just a look at the computer hippies, nerds, and hackers in California back in the beginning points to the way in which this technology emerged and spread within very specific social and cultural contexts. For this reason, it is important to take the different actors involved into account, as well as their influence on the dynamics of technological innovation. Alongside the military, the high-tech industry, and government funding programs supporting electronic data processing, it was often subcultures and countercultures that used computers for their own purposes, contributing to their further technical development and generating new applications for their use. These types of cultures were lacking in the GDR, leaving little room for the creative appropriation of digital technology. "Hackers" in the Western sense were hard to find in the East, although there were some computer hobbyists who found creative ways to use the computers in some factories and schools.

The constellations in which these different actors interacted with one another in the West have been unusual since the very beginning. Large technology corporations and creative outsiders frequently develop symbiotic relationships with one another, but they are also just as likely to give up on them.

At the end of the 1970s, West Germany began to expand its entire telecommunications infrastructure on a large scale. If it had not done so, the rapid spread of the Internet since the 1990s would not have been possible. The first step in this direction was screen text (known as BTX, which stood for *Bildschirmtext*), which was presented in West Germany at the Internationale Funkausstellung (International Radio Exhibition, known as IFA) in Berlin. After a few initial field tests, it was then introduced across the country beginning in 1983. Although this new service did not at all live up to the initial euphoric expectations about the number of users, especially in private households, it broke new ground once different media were connected together. It linked communication over the telephone network with computer monitors and televisions in an interactive way that made a plethora of information available. Advancements in the modem technology that were designed to support this communication made it possible to connect different end devices (BTX terminals or a television with a BTX decoder) over the telephone network.[37]

This service was officially discontinued in December 2001 after almost twenty years in use. In terms of multimediality, BTX can be seen as a precursor to Internet communication. It was particularly popular in companies, government offices, and institutions, but not nearly as widespread in private homes. Although it was possible for households to subscribe to this service, it failed to catch on because, unlike its French counterpart "Minitel," it was quite expensive due to the monopoly that the Bundespost had over the prices. Despite these difficulties, BTX nonetheless contributed to the infiltration of computer and network-driven forms of communication into daily life in West Germany. Over the long term, BTX and videotext, which was introduced at about the same time, as well as cable television, functioned as the motors behind the expansion and modernization of the network and telecommunications infrastructure. A whole slew of new service providers popped up in order to provide content for this service, and they later supplied data and content for new types of media. Computers at work or in industrial production, however, were greeted rather skeptically or even seen as a threat at first, despite their advantages. Yet it did not take long for new types of media and communication that were made possible through computer technology to become accepted in everyday life in the private sphere. Computers clearly differed in this respect from the other new technologies that were being discussed in public debates in the 1970s and 1980s. Whereas computers came to be seen as less of a danger, for instance, the broader public and most politicians became increasingly skeptical about nuclear energy, and the tide of public opinion really began to turn against it after the reactor meltdowns in Harrisburg in 1979 and Chernobyl in 1986.[38]

The Eastern Bloc states also tried to launch themselves into the Information Age by tapping into enormous financial and human resources in the 1970s and 1980s. These countries—most especially the USSR—had been developing computing and data processing technology since the 1950s. They had also created similarly ambitious scientific programs and innovation project cycles comparable to those in the West. In the GDR, computer science and the development of "electronic computing technology" flourished under the technocratic reforms that were undertaken in the 1960s and the additional support that came through the cybernetics boom. Yet, before long, the SED put a political damper on the technology-friendly social climate that had welcomed rationalization and improved efficiency, as well as the cultures of expertise that had accompanied it. It had become clear rather quickly that it would not be easier and faster to mobilize the resources necessary to support technological innovations and their implementation within a centralized planned economy. Political trends and poor decisions, bureaucratic planning mechanisms, rivalries between local and regional authorities, difficulties in cooperation and the division of labor with the COMECON, not to mention a simple lack of investment funds, plagued computerization in the Eastern Bloc at the everyday level.[39]

All the countries of the Communist bloc were dependent on the transfer of technology from the West in order to further their own development of computer and software technology.[40] It proved to be extremely difficult to ensure this transfer given the conditions of the American embargo on advanced technologies and the politically motivated move toward isolation vis-à-vis the West. Without the special conditions that applied to German-German trade, and the acquisition activities and industrial espionage practiced by the main reconnaissance office (Hauptverwaltung Aufklärung, or HVA) of the Ministerium für Staatssicherheit (the Stasi), the GDR would never have been able to achieve its fully fledged microelectronics development program with its prestigious one-megabyte memory chip project.[41] In fact, it was an open secret that the privileged key microelectronics factories in the GDR, such as VEB Carl Zeiss Jena, often took technology that had been acquired from IBM in the West and either replicated it or just put a new label on it.[42] The GDR also made several attempts to circumvent the embargoes in the West in order to acquire production documents and licenses to manufacture memory chips and even entire printed circuit boards. A planned deal that had taken a great deal of negotiation with the Japanese corporation Toshiba in 1986 broke down in 1987 before it even really got going. The Japanese broke off the negotiations under pressure coming from the U.S. government.[43]

When the one-megabyte memory chip, which had been developed by the Zentrum für Mikroelektronik in Dresden, was handed over to Erich Honecker with much pomp and circumstance in 1988, it was actually already outdated. A popular joke at the time laced with a bit of sarcasm commented on this moment, claiming that the GDR had developed "the first microchip in the world that you can walk through" because of its larger size. The idea of mass producing this memory chip, for which only a limited number of prototypes had been made, was entirely unfeasible, though, because there was a lack of suitable production facilities. The introduction of new technologies in the economic sector, scientific research, or the state apparatus was therefore limited to a few highly subsidized, isolated applications. Much of the country's ailing industry, with its outdated manufacturing processes, was very ill equipped to deal with computerization on a large scale. Although almost all of the Communist parties of the Eastern Bloc had put the development of microelectronics at the top of their political agendas by the end of the 1970s, a point that they proclaimed loudly, the state of technology in their countries lagged about a decade behind that of the West at the beginning of the 1980s.

By the beginning of the 1970s, the transition to the Computer Age had overtaxed the GDR economy on all counts.[44] In addition to the technology embargo that had been put in place by the West, one of the major factors that stood firmly in the way of computerization was the long-standing restriction of microelectronic applications and development capacities for military purposes. The neglect of basic industrial research made things even more difficult, as did the huge increases in expenditures for consumption and social services in the Honecker era.[45]

Computer technology was introduced only in select areas of the military, the economy, the government administration, and scientific research. Priority was also given to the use of information technology in the Stasi's surveillance efforts.[46] It was therefore virtually impossible for computers to spread throughout society, which meant that the cultural aspects that went along with the integration of computers in people's everyday lives were also missing. The microelectronics manufacturers were not in a position to produce the necessary number of personal computers, nor were they able to sell them at halfway decent prices. It was not until 1984 that the first so-called home computers were produced for the domestic market in the GDR by Robotron in Dresden and VEB Mikroelektronik Mühlhausen. But this did not actually mean that people could buy them. Most of the computers that were produced were designated for "social use," which meant for use in the education and science sector, the army, or the economy. Consequently, it did not take long for the term "home computer" to disappear from official language. Once these computers hit the shelves in radio and TV stores in the major cities, private buyers had to pay 4,000 DDR Marks at first, which later dropped down to about 2,000 DDR Marks. Additionally, these users still had to buy a small television screen, such as those made by the Soviet brand Junost, and other peripheral devices. Not more than a total of 30,000 exemplars from the different series of low-end small computers were produced in the GDR between 1984 and 1989.[47] There are no records available that provide detailed information about how many of them were actually sold in stores. For the most part, these computers were acquired by schools, so that at least most of the young people in the GDR came into contact with computers in the 1980s. Moreoever, just as in the West, there were also radio and television programs about computers in the GDR, as well as computer magazines that were designed to pique the interest of hobbyists.

In light of this situation, it is astonishing that a lively computer scene actually developed in the GDR and the other Eastern Bloc countries. Computer fans often had to improvise electronic components or make the best out of the few, highly sought-after computers or parts that they could get from the West. The estimated two hundred thousand home computers (a figure that cannot be corroborated with concrete evidence) that were sent as gifts from relatives in West Germany or sold in the GDR at the Intershops were worth enormous amounts of money, equivalent to a family car.[48] Although this cross-border transfer of computers from the West was more or less tolerated, software imports were strictly prohibited. The state and the party sought to keep such subculture trends under control. By regulating access to software as well as hardware technology, they could keep a finger on private computer use. For the most part, the few computers that were available outside industry and government offices could only be accessed through the computer clubs and cabinets that were part of so-called social organizations, such as the Society for Sport and Technology (GST), that strictly controlled their use.

The Communist regimes were always suspect of the idea of privately owned computers because they presented a way to have free access to information and its dissemination. From their perspective, even simple technology such as the typewriter potentially opened the door for oppositional activities. Consequently, a key dynamic element of "Information Society" was lacking in the last years of the Communist bloc, namely computerization "from below" characterized by the mass cultural appropriation of this technology. The states of Eastern and Central Europe did not enter into the Internet Age until after the collapse of Communism.

The dynamics of a networked society, moreover, presented them with greater technical, cultural, and, above all, political problems than the early phase of computerization. Therefore, without a doubt, the failure to live up to the challenge of modern communication and information technologies must be put at the top of the list of factors that contributed to the demise of state socialism.

The Computerization of Work in Both German States

The computerization of work began as early as the 1950s in West Germany, spreading to more and more areas in industry and administration as time went on. In the GDR, on the other hand, the smallest technological measures of rationalized work were celebrated by the media. There was no shortage of propaganda images depicting the desired automation of production, but there was a major dissonance between propaganda and reality.[49] Over the course of the 1970s and 1980s, the main goal in many fields of production was to establish the basis for the automation of production and, in many places, just to mechanize production workflows in the first place. The SED leadership, however, still reckoned that at least the Soviet Union would achieve the full computerization of its national economy by the turn of the century.

Whereas the discourse in the West had been preoccupied with the question of whether microelectronics were a blessing or a curse for the workplace since the early 1970s, the rhetoric of progress espoused by the SED continued unabated. Of course, it must be kept in mind that there were not very many noticeable consequences of technological innovation that were felt in the GDR in the first place.

Since the mid-1970s, industrial production, many administrative branches, and the service sector in the Western industrialized countries had been revolutionized by the large-scale use of increasingly powerful microchips for all kinds of applications. Contemporary observers were quick to speak of a "third industrial revolution," while singing the praises of this "colossal tiny device."[50] Indeed, the microchip unleashed a domino effect that changed the world of work. One of the first branches to feel the repercussions of rationalization and restructuring was the watch industry, which had a long tradition in Southern Germany and Switzerland: it was hit particularly hard by the import of digital quartz watches from East Asia. The manufacturers of cash registers and office equipment met a similar fate, especially because many of them had failed to keep up with technological innovations.[51] The entire printing industry was subject to a particularly rapid technological transformation in which formerly powerful groups of employees, such as the typesetters, were made redundant by photosetting. The first major protests and strikes related to computerization in fact took place at newspaper publishers and large printing facilities. Microelectronics had an even more far-reaching effect on the metalworking industry and the automobile manufacturers in particular. CNC (Computerized Numerical Control) machines and industrial robots made it possible for the automation of entire production workflows, which pushed people out of their jobs. The list could go on and on, ranging from office work and public administration to the entire banking and insurance industries.[52]

In West Germany, the new catch word of the decade was "streamlined out of a job" (*wegrationalisiert*; literally, rationalized away). Yet the job crisis that hit the countries of the OECD in the early 1970s had more to do with a decisive structural change than just the introduction of new technologies. But this feeling of threat left an indelible mark on the public debates about the computer revolution. Since the end of the 1970s, the media had provided striking images and headlines for the ongoing debates over the growing clout of computer technology; it thereby amplified the fears and dangers associated with the advent of computers. In these debates and predictions that appeared in the major West German media outlets, the main leitmotif was the effects of computer technology on industrial work. As *Der Spiegel* wrote in 1978, "Tiny electronic components are threatening millions of jobs in industry and service companies. Neither the government nor the unions have any idea how to keep the consequences of progress in check."[53]

In comparison, little attention was paid to the "revolution"—or, better said, "evolution"—of office work that had been taking place for a long time as seen in the example of the West German social services administration in the 1970s.[54] In the 1980s, most of the administrative offices within the West German industrial factories were outfitted with what were called "terminals" on a large scale. Above all, this affected the payroll, bookkeeping, purchasing, and sales departments, as well as most other administrative departments. The use of new "intelligent" electronic data processing systems primarily changed workflow processes that involved repetitive steps governed by logical rules. This sparked an enormous wave of rationalization in administrative offices across West Germany. By the late 1970s, computers could not only process, save, and combine data, but also they could take over many tasks that had previously been done by bookkeepers. A huge number of jobs were cut as a result, and many administrative professions were almost completely wiped out. Over the course of the 1980s, the jobs of some employees at the mid-management level also came under threat for the first time.[55]

Simultaneously, however, the number of employees in other service and administrative areas increased despite the use of computers (such as in banks, insurance companies, and government administration) because the job demands, as well as the need for labor, increased.

Lastly, the Soviet bloc countries also found themselves faced with questions about the future of work and its social consequences in light of the "scientific-technical revolution." Thanks to the troublesome demographic situation, the GDR had been suffering from an enormous shortage of labor for a long time. Rationalization measures and automation therefore seemed to be the best strategy at the time. Moreover, there was really no job crisis to speak of in the GDR.[56] Yet the expectation that rationalization could overcome the labor shortage in the country proved to be overly ambitious. Although some automated and computerized assembly lines were created in parts of the steel and chemical industries, not to mention at Carl Zeiss Jena, the need for repair and maintenance personnel increased, offsetting the labor gains that had been made by modernizing production. Furthermore, more personnel were needed from year to year in order to keep up production levels in the country's antiquated production facilities.[57] Research has shown that the machine tool industry already met with considerable difficulties as it tried to transition to NC (numerically controlled) systems that read orders from data carriers, which meant that it never moved on to the next phase of automatic CNC-controlled industrial handling and production processes.[58]

The introduction of the Quelle system in 1957 serves as an indicator of just how far ahead West Germany was at a very early point.[59] The Informatik-System-Quelle, developed by the German company Standard Elektrik Lorenz (SEL), which patented the name "Informatik," marked the advent of information processing.[60] The system attracted attention worldwide because it proved that computers could not only calculate, but also "control processes." This opened a whole realm of new possibilities for the application of computers in industry and administration. At about the same time that the Quelle system came onto the scene, the foundation for data processing outside of the universities was laid with the installation of the Univac computer by Remington Rand in Frankfurt am Main. Thirty-five courses were offered in 1957 in order to train the first five hundred "operators."[61] Shortly thereafter, the insurance company Allianz began using the first IBM computer in the country.

From the mid-1960s, the number of computers installed in companies increased considerably. A gap emerged between the few major large-scale users on the one hand and a growing group of mid-level data technology users on the other. Generally speaking, until the beginning of the 1980s, the larger the company, the more likely it was to have its own mainframe. Smaller companies tended to rely on mid-level data technology or external computing centers. Banks and insurance companies, in contrast, were usually among the users of large mainframe systems because these branches were strongly centralized.

At the beginning of the 1980s, the big automobile manufacturers launched investment initiatives. They pushed through the computerization of the assembly process, sometimes quite aggressively. The presence of industrial robots in the production halls of car factories came to symbolize this development. The concepts of such perfected production systems carried many different names, the most common of which was Computer Integrated Manufacturing, or CIM. For some, CIM was a nightmare; for others, it was the ultimate ideal because it was always tied to the image of a factory almost entirely devoid of people. In a CIM factory, the idea was to take advantage of all the possibilities for technical rationalization, including the automation of processes that used to be considered mental work in places like construction offices. According to this theory, all production and administrative processes would be networked and controlled centrally in the future. The production of the Golf II that began in 1983 in the legendary "Halle 54" of the Volkswagen plant was considered to be the prime example of a CIM facility.[62]

The installation of systems such as those in a fully automated factory required a very high level of investment, but the profitability of these ventures was difficult to prove. The extremely high amount of time and energy that had to be put into the development of the necessary software led to long timelines for projects, but the state of information technology was continually advancing. Projects that seemed viable at first were often outdated by the time that they were actually put to use. Despite the awareness of the shortcomings of CIM projects that had developed in the 1980s, the West German government continued to subsidize these projects between 1987 and 1992 with 580 million German Marks. In addition, it provided over 300 million German Marks for pilot projects of this kind, as well as for projects that were already further down the line in twelve hundred companies.[63]

Despite a delayed start, microelectronics also found their way into the factories and administrative offices of East Germany in the early 1970s. First and foremost, these mainframes and office computers impacted the everyday work of employees. Even production workers found themselves confronted more and more with this new technology, especially those who worked in the manufacturing and supply plants that were part of the microelectronics program. Other portions of the workforce first came into contact with industrial robots as rationalization efforts were introduced.

At the end of the 1970s, approximately 130 industrial robots had been put to use in GDR factories, twenty-five of which had been imported from the West. The microelectronics program that was adopted in 1977 gave high priority to the production and use of industrial robots. The goal was to launch a robot initiative to produce seven thousand robots by 1980. Official statistics in 1980, however, listed only 2,189 industrial robots.[64]

In contrast to the skeptical and fearful way in which the West German public reacted to the use of this new technology, the official rhetoric in the GDR was accompanied only by positive expectations. In practice, however, the introduction of computers did bring with it problems that led to more than just minor social conflicts. Many of the workers affected by it reacted with subtle forms of resistance.[65]

As a result of the forced large-scale introduction of automation in West Germany, companies were already facing entirely different problems than their East German counterparts. The basic tenets of factory organization became more streamlined as a result of the strong fixation on technology and automation over the course of the 1970s and early 1980s. Other sources of productivity and efficiency were increasingly ignored. Production processes that were organized along these lines not only downgraded the importance of the expertise of employees to next to nothing, but also chipped away at flexibility, responsibility, and initiative within the workplace. The qualifications and experience of skilled workers diminished in value, which ultimately resulted in a loss of innovation potential. On the other hand, the generally high level of production technology had led to a certain renaissance in skilled work since the 1970s because there was a shortage of well-trained and experienced experts. Many workers saw an increase in the value of their jobs using complex machinery as opposed to that of hard manual labor.

Yet the peak phase of computerization took place within the context of a growing global economic crisis. Surprisingly, this situation did not at all hinder the advancement of computers and related communication technologies, but rather fostered it. Indeed, computerization had not only made inroads in industrial production, administration, and banking, but also had made its way, either simultaneously or a bit later, into many other areas of society. The individual effects of this technology and the way in which it was received differed from case to case. In the West, computerization soon brought new economic sectors that created more jobs, such as the software industry.[66] More detailed research is needed in order to determine the extent to which there were similar effects in the Communist bloc states and how state institutions steered career specialization and job placement accordingly.

Cultural Dimensions of the Digital Transformation

The cultural dimensions of the social transformation tied to computerization in the 1980s are reflected most clearly in the onset of the era of home computers and computer games.[67] As with earlier media transitions, the needs and demands at a societal level stimulated further technological advancements. Personal computers, which could be turned into personalized instruments for creativity and play, became a welcome object of desire in an increasingly differentiated and individualized society of consumption and leisure. It is no coincidence that small computers and gaming computers marched into private households, and especially children's rooms, in the first half of the 1980s. As of 1982, the Commodore 64 ushered in a new generation of home computers that came to replace the video game consoles and arcade games that had dominated the market up to that point. The new computers had three distinct advantages: they could be used to play an unlimited number of games, they offered a whole series of possible extensions and additions, and they could be used for a number of other purposes other than just games, ranging from programming and word processing to learning and making music. The computer magazine *Chip*, which had been in circulation since 1978, praised the "breadbox design" of the C 64 that was being sold for approximately 1,400 DM in 1983, calling it a "very strong model" offering a high level of performance and versatility.[68] Manufacturers, department stores, and electronics stores, in turn, kept coming up with new offers and incentives. The commercialization of the computer became an important factor in its conquest of society. Estimates suggest that seventeen million of the legendary C 64 computers, which were manufactured up to 1994, had been sold worldwide.[69] Other models, such as Commodore's Amiga or the devices sold by Atari, were similarly successful, achieving cult status like the C 64.

All of the sudden, computers were found everywhere, giving rise to the spread of computer stores, the appearance of computer advice shows on TV, and the publication of specialist magazines. Media headlines that proclaimed that the computer was invading private households further fueled the hype. Video games, *Der Spiegel* wrote in 1983, were the "gateway drug" luring children and teenagers into the world of computers. It went on to claim that the industry "was bombarding this target group."[70] It did not take long before public debates broke out over this trend and its dangers. These discussions reflected the divergent experiences of the population with computers, and the fronts were usually drawn along generational lines. One clear indication of this controversy surrounding computers was that the Bundesprüfstelle für jugendgefährdende Schriften

(Federal Review Board for Media Harmful to Minors) began to focus more on computer games. The year 1984 marked the first time a computer game (River Raid) landed on the list put out by the board. Whereas positive experiences with the new digital world became a permanent element of socialization for children and teenagers, parents remained rather skeptical. This older generation had largely been exposed to computers as a threat to their jobs, and they were alarmed by the horror stories about the electronic surveillance possibilities associated with computer technology. Although public opinion continued to sway between euphoria and fear, the dam had long since been broken. In the GDR, on the other hand, computers were only marginally used for games. Newspapers reported that some employees were using their computers to play games and sometimes secretly took them home over the weekend for their families. Likewise, East German teenagers copied games onto cassettes and then used them to play games on school computers.

The great extent to which computers and electronic data processing had advanced in the Western industrialized societies in the early 1980s was clearly reflected by the fact that there was hardly any area of society in which fiery debates surrounded by all kinds of media attention had not erupted over the consequences of computerization. Whereas parents, educational experts, psychologists, and politicians were fighting over the dangers that computer games presented for children and teenagers, schools were beginning to experiment with the use of computers in the classroom. As early as the mid-1980s, a debate raged over the question of whether mandatory computer science instruction should be introduced into schools in West Germany. These discussions were populated with images of the newly created computer rooms in many schools. Stories also emerged about computer whiz kids who could program what were still rather unwieldy computers to play games.[71] Suddenly, nobody wanted to miss the boat when it came to this new technology. A real fear of being left behind seemed to set in among educators and officials in the cultural ministries. The computer issue also fed into the more generalized education debates, which put additional pressure on the educational system to react to these developments.[72] Enthusiastic proponents of digital learning in the classroom saw computers as an essential cultural technology that children and teenagers needed to know how to use, just like they needed to learn reading, writing, and mathematics. The Federal Ministry of Education, headed by Dorothee Wilms, and the Federal Ministry of Research, led by Heinz Riesenhuber, began a large-scale Computer and Education campaign in 1984. This program called upon companies, associations, and research institutions to support the computerization of schools.[73] This unleashed a fierce competition among computer manufacturers who hoped to gain access to this important new sales market through the positive publicity generated by computer donations.

A discussion among computer scientists, mathematicians, and educators about the stronger integration of computer science in schools also emerged in the mid-1980s in the GDR. Although the first computers were installed in schools as early as 1983 in the other Eastern Bloc states, the computerization of the classroom in the GDR was initially limited to special schools focused on mathematics, the natural sciences, and technology. Furthermore, instruction in mathematics and computer science was expanded, especially at the extended upper secondary schools. Computer technology was also supposed to be promoted in the polytechnic high schools by including more electronic data processing content in the subject area called "Introduction to Socialist Production." In 1986, the Ministry of Education (Ministerium für Volksbildung) decided to introduce computer science as a subject, but it held that the full-scale introduction of this subject would not be possible until the beginning of the 1990s. The reasons behind this were clear: the GDR microelectronics factories were simply not in a position to supply the computers necessary for this undertaking.[74]

Of course, the establishment of computer science as a university discipline was also a part of these changes in education. As early as the 1960s, it was being taught at universities in the United States. During the 1970s, a program launched by the Federal Ministry of Research fostered the creation of computer science departments at West German universities. By the beginning of the 1980s, the initial construction phase had largely been completed.[75] In 1986/87, the new subject of computer science came to replace the courses that had previously been offered under "information processing" in East Germany. Corresponding official decisions made by the party and the council of ministers determined that computer science would be offered as a major at several East German Universities as part of the degree program to become a computer science engineer.

Many people could hardly imagine the extent to which computer technology would revolutionize industrial work and office jobs, nor that it would force entire sectors of industry to adopt entirely new production processes or that these sectors in their traditional form would disappear entirely. The rapid pace of these advances naturally instilled fear at first.

The process of computerization had always been accompanied by critical self-reflection in West German society since the 1960s, but the official rhetoric of progress remained in place in the GDR until the very end, despite the country's failures in this regard. In both German states, expectations and fears about the economic and sociostructural consequences of these developments in microelectronics clashed with one another at a discursive level. The general idea was that technology was supposed to provide solutions for present-day problems in society.[76] At the beginning of the 1970s, however, a debate broke out in West Germany about the "limits of growth." In 1976, the American computer scientist Joseph Weizenbaum published his critique of the research on artificial intelligence in a book called *Computer Power and Human Reason: From Judgment to Calculation*.[77]

The widespread sense of insecurity surrounding new technologies does not necessarily imply a rejection of scientific-technical advancement on the whole. Although studies are lacking on this issue, there are still clear indications that there was a relatively broad level of consensus in all Western countries concerning the paradigm of progress associated with computerization. Indeed, much of the insecurity did not stem from computers themselves, but rather from a "loss of trust" in political structures to be able to control these technologies and keep them on a development trajectory that was acceptable to all of society.[78]

Doubts about the feasibility of technological progress also surfaced in the GDR, but they by no means resulted in a kind of technological pessimism. Rather, the reality of economic and technological stagnation increasingly contradicted the official political rhetoric of advancement.[79] There were no signs, for example that microelectronics would present any danger to the existence of East German workers. In fact, to the contrary, the difficulties in dealing with technological progress and the worn-out state of production facilities due to a lack of investment funds were akin to a guarantee for workers. The right to work was never questioned, not by anyone. The implicit job guarantee that went along with this generated a sense of security, which should not be underestimated as a stabilizing factor.[80]

Yet computerization and the advancements in electronic data processing that went along with it also generated fears outside the world of work. In the mid-1980s, these threat scenarios unleashed hefty public debates in West Germany. The film *Alles unter Kontrolle: Notizen auf dem Weg in den Überwachungsstaat* (Everything under control: Notes on the way to a 'Big Brother' state) appeared in West German cinemas in April 1983.[81] With a mix of documentary material and staged scenes, the filmmakers presented a shocking panorama of all the methods of electronic surveillance over the population and personal data collection practiced by the Bundeskriminalamt (BKA, akin to the FBI in the Unites States), the police, and other government authorities. Before the film premiered, the disclosures made by the BKA engineer Bernd Rainer Schmidt had caused an uproar in the press and on TV. Schmidt revealed the methods of computer-aided video surveillance that he had developed, which the BKA used to keep an eye on endangered objects and public trouble spots. The film hit a nerve at the time because it tapped into the growing unease among much of the population. With the Orwellian year of 1984 on the horizon, the extent to which the police, the authorities, and companies collected data about individual people and groups to use for their own purposes caught the attention of the general public. This was compounded by further technological improvements in the methods of video surveillance that were used by the police during protests to keep tabs on groups such as those opposed to nuclear power. The head of the BKA, Horst Herold, had pointed things in this direction by developing the dragnet investigation method to search out the RAF (Red Army Faction) terrorists.[82]

The mistrust of the growing hunger of the state for more data that was spreading throughout West Germany manifested itself on the stage of the census that was scheduled for April 1983.[83] A broad movement to boycott the census quickly came together within the peace movement and among environmentalists' and citizens' initiatives that had formed in opposition to large projects such as the construction of the western take-off runway at the airport in Frankfurt am Main. It was by no means surprising that these alternative groups and other protesters would be quite sensitive to the misuse of electronically stored data and new surveillance methods. Indeed, they were the first people to have direct experience with the new technologies that were being tried out by the police and the authorities. The fear was that stored data could be used to identify and control politically undesirable people and groups. The boycott movement culminated in hundreds of constitutional complaints.[84] The main point of contention was the scope of the census and the plan to check the data collected in the census against the population registers. The fear was that a complete electronic record of all citizens would have an unimaginable number of possibilities for combining different data sets, thereby completely obliterating the protection of the private sphere. The growing power of the computer in the hands of the state was seen as a threat to basic human rights.[85]

With its decision passed on 15 December 1983, the Bundesverfassungsgericht (Federal Constitutional Court) put a stop to the census because it violated the basic rights of citizens as it was planned. The protests against the census were the first social movement to directly respond to the computerization of society. Data protection and the right of self-determination over personal data brought a new element to political debate that would prove to be highly contested in the decades to come. The implications of the success of the protests against the census in prompting a recodification of citizenship and basic rights in the digital revolution should not be underestimated. This was a positive experience for civil society because it demonstrated that the political use of the computer and information technology could be subjected to democratic checks and balances. In the end, data protection rights were strengthened considerably in West Germany at the federal and state levels, and the corresponding laws have become increasingly differentiated. Simultaneously, watch groups emerged within civil society that kept critical tabs on the further development of electronic data processing. The Chaos Computer Club (CCC), which was founded in West Berlin in 1981, is a good example of such a group. With spectacular initiatives designed to expose the major security holes in computer networks, the CCC sharpened public awareness of data security and data protection issues. The history of this club and its changing function is one of the major desiderata in the otherwise very detailed research that has been done on new social movements.[86]

In the state socialist countries, the respective state security and intelligence services also sought to perfect their extensive surveillance over the population through the use of electronic data processing. The Stasi's surveillance efforts have already attracted scholarly attention. Yet it was not a topic of conversation in the controlled public sphere of the GDR, although it was discussed throughout society, especially in the circles of the oppositional milieus, youth cultures, and art scenes that were most affected by it. Unlike in the West, concerns about the potential use of modern computer technology in collecting mass data did not surface in East. Apparently, the assumption was made at the time that these efforts were kept in check by the tech lag in the East. In fact, however, the MfS began using computers for surveillance on a large scale in the 1970s, and even used Siemens computer technology.[87] In addition, the Stasi was able to intercept data transmissions to infiltrate many sensitive Western computer networks, including those of the INPOL police system, companies such as Siemens, and even the Bundespatentamt (Federal Patent Office).[88]

The need to integrate very different data sets created some major problems over the course of reunification. For example, the pension benefit information of the GDR was stored in a central mainframe in Leipzig. Trying to combine this data with the completely different kind of data sets that were used in West Germany proved to be a challenge, and one that could have had very real material consequences for citizens in the East. Moreover, over four million new social security numbers had to be assigned in a short period of time in order to cover just the pensioners in the GDR.[89] As of yet, there has been no research done on the digital remapping of East German information and the integration of these data sets, whether it be for resident registration offices, saving accounts, or the intelligence agencies.

The Seeds of the Internet in Germany

The Internet, which is indeed a globalized medium of information and communication, has been spreading since the mid-1990s. As with microprocessor technology and personal computers, the development and introduction of this global network occurred on several parallel tracks at the same time.[90] It got its start in the United States, where the idea of a far-reaching network of military research institutions, leading American universities, and technology companies had been pursued since the beginning of the 1970s. The technological innovations that became the basis for the Internet—the TCP/IP standard, the HTML mark-up language, and local computer network connections (LAN)—had been made possible through generous funding grants provided by the state and the highly developed research infrastructure in the United States. Alongside these technological elements, there were also social and cultural factors that fed into the further differentiation of the network idea associated with the Internet. The Internet as both a concept and technology emerged in an innovative network milieu "whose dynamics and goals became largely autonomous from the specific purposes of military strategy or supercomputing linkups."[91] Thanks to this liberal idea of networked communication without hierarchies, the Internet was already poised for social acceptance even in its very early stages. Its dynamic has often come from unintended offshoots, such as email, that have established themselves and then influenced the trajectory of further technological development.

As in the United States, the university milieu and not necessarily the large technology corporations proved to be the motor behind the establishment of the Internet in West Germany.[92] A first network hub had already been set up at the computer center at the University of Karlsruhe in the mid-1980s, which made it possible to communicate via email with universities in the United States and other countries that were connected to it. Scientists in Dortmund took a different path and came up with a concept for an IP network designed to make connections within Europe. Both projects achieved the first stable dedicated lines, one to New York and the other to Amsterdam. At the end of the 1980s, the state of Baden-Württemberg invested a great deal of money and energy in order to create a network that connected the universities and research institutes in the state. The result of these efforts was the first regional IP-based network outside of the United States.

In the early 1990s, the Deutsches Forschungsnetz (German Research Network, or DFN) began working to create its own IP service. By opting for the TCP/IP model as opposed to others, Germany followed the general international trend. The first commercial Internet providers also emerged in the first half of the 1990s within the context of academic projects funded by third parties. Smaller independent providers proved to be the major force behind the spread of Internet access in Germany.

The costs for Internet access were very high at this time. Thanks to its monopoly, only Deutsche Telekom was able to provide the necessary dedicated connections for Internet service. Consumers therefore had to pay twice for Internet access, one fee to a provider and one fee to the Telekom for the use of the phone line. The liberalization of the telephone market in the mid-1990s did little to change this situation. Deutsche Telekom still dominated the market for local calls, which was what people used to connect their modems to their Internet service providers. In response to this pricing policy, different initiatives called for an Internet strike in Germany in 1998, but, according to Deutsche Telekom, not many users took part.[93] Competing providers either had to build up their own infrastructure or lease telephone lines from Deutsche Telekom. At the end of the 1990s, the market was thinned out in this sector, leaving many of the smaller providers in particular out in the cold.

The transfer of the administration of German Internet addresses to the DE-NIC (German Network Information Center, manager of the ".de" domain) in the first half of the 1990s also laid another element of the foundation needed to support the spread of the Internet in Germany. After years of temporary solutions in which the University of Dortmund and then the University of Karlsruhe took over this task, the most important German Internet providers banded together in 1996 to create an association that would be responsible for the technical sales and administration related to DE domains.

The GDR, of course, did not live to see the arrival of the Internet Age, which makes the question of how the SED leadership would have dealt with this technology a moot point. But, even if the SED had permitted the controlled development of the Internet, East Germany would have still lacked the basic infrastructure that was needed in order to use it. The other points that can be made about the Internet in the GDR are rather anecdotal: some of the East German universities did have local networks that were IP ready, and there was a dedicated line between Humboldt University and the Free University of Berlin at the end of the 1980s, which was the only one of its kind to cross the border between the two German states. The top-level domain reserved for the GDR, namely ".dd," was never used because there was never an East German Internet address. Communication via computers was limited to remote data transmission (RDT) over a few, fragile telephone lines. Over the course of unification, East German institutions were then connected to the existing West German network infrastructures. The refurbishment of the telecommunications infrastructure was one of the most important and most expensive elements of the reconstruction of East Germany.

All in all, the rise of the Internet further propelled the trend toward digital modernity. Economically, this gave a boost to the computer and software industries before the first signs of a crisis in this classic sector of the digital economy appeared. The changes that the Internet brought in terms of the world of work and social communications, as well as the availability and acquisition of knowledge, could only be dealt with cursorily here. The same can also be said for the new round of conflicts between commercial and democratic interests that have come about through the use of this medium. The social developments that accompanied the advent of the Internet, moreover, were not really tied up in the rivalry between the systems, nor the division of Germany. Consequently, the year 1989 was not as momentous for the path to digital modernity as it was in other areas because it merely marked the end of the attempts in the Communist bloc to steer computerization in keeping with a state-controlled planned economy and a closed society. After all, the GDR and the other states of the Eastern Bloc were nothing more than a small episode in the history of the Internet.

Conclusion

The path of Western industrialized societies and the Eastern Bloc states into digital modernity mostly followed a parallel history until the collapse of Communism. In the East as well as the West, computerization and the social changes associated with it became the focus of visions of the future as well as actual economic policy strategies. Well into the 1970s, the GDR and the other countries in the Communist bloc offensively tried to differentiate themselves by stressing their political, social, and cultural alternatives to the prevailing orders in the West. In doing so, they also tried to gloss over, or rather reinterpret, how they were lagging behind in many respects. But this mechanism no longer worked for computerization after the failed attempts to reform the centralized economy and the violent suppression of the Prague Spring. Whereas the political rhetoric of expectations surrounding technological advancement did not waiver, the ability of these countries to keep up with the digital revolution became a question of economic and, ultimately, political survival. Although many of the ideological structures that propped up the faith in state socialism had begun to erode in the 1970s, including those that were tied to technological advancement, the SED still clung to its commitment to modernity without interruption. The norms for better work and a better way of life, however, had long since been determined by the West, especially in terms of the rapidly developing world of computers. For the East German party and government elites who had to deal with this technology and for those East Germans who were interested in the computer as a consumer project, the goal was to share in some of the progress that had been achieved in the West. East Germans were not necessarily skeptical about this technology itself, but rather about the ability of their own system to effectively deal with the digital transformation. At the same time, the established norm of full employment put the brakes on the rationalization effects of computerization in the GDR economy, which meant that a debate over the computer as a "job killer" akin to the one raging in the West never even got started in the East. Indeed, to the contrary, computerization often brought new jobs because the challenges of the outdated industrial infrastructure in many areas of the East Germany economy had to be compensated through manpower.

The losses suffered by the East in terms of the digital transformation reinforced the modernity of the self-image of the West. Despite the broad public debates over the price of progress and possible alternatives that had been going on in West Germany and other Western countries since the 1970s, the generally positive attitude toward the digital transformation shared among politicians, economic experts, managers, and broad portions of the population never wavered. Even the recurring debates in the media over digital surveillance did not shake this faith in technological progress. The many daily uses for computers, as well as the games and other entertainment options that this technology made available, only further fueled the hunger for new and improved applications for computers in the 1980s, stimulating further technological advancement in turn. In the East, however, these kinds of extra motors that drove the digital transformation forward were much weaker, if they existed at all. Although the spread of computers throughout East German society was in fact desired, the GDR was always lacking the necessary resources. Furthermore, the political fears of the SED leadership about the links between computer technology and counterculture trends kept the computer and the forms of communication associated with it from becoming commonplace in the everyday lives of GDR citizens.

On the whole, the trajectory of social change driven by computerization in the West has proven to be irreversible thus far. Unlike in other areas where the existence of a socialist alternative had evoked political and social effects in the West, the digital revolution was not affected by developments in the East. Computerization would not have followed a fundamentally different course in the absence of the system rivalry and the Cold War, apart from the long-lasting dominance of military uses for this technology that had resulted from the arms race. On the flip side, this meant that the East was largely following the pattern of the West in its efforts to foster the computerization of the economy and society. This also helps to explain why the collapse of Communism in 1989 and the subsequent transformation of the former Eastern Bloc countries did not represent a real break of any kind in the history of digital modernity. Moreover, the huge extent to which these countries had to catch up to the West in terms of their communications infrastructures as well as computer and software development actually stimulated further advancements in digitalization and global networks. The scientific potential and technological expertise that had been cultivated in the Eastern Bloc before 1989 survived in those places and production facilities in which they could be easily adapted to fit the state of technology and development in the West, such as in Dresden or Jena.

What role did computerization play in the "asymmetrically entwined parallel history" of the two Germanys? The digital transformations that occurred in East and West Germany were related to one another. This was particularly true to the extent that the two Germanys permanently kept tabs on one another as part of the rivalry between the systems, although this mutual awareness was increasingly asymmetrical in nature. West Germany become less preoccupied with technological developments in the East, shifting its gaze more and more toward the United States and Japan as time went on. The GDR, on the other hand, had its eyes firmly fixed on West Germany until the end. The history of computerization therefore confirms the trend that historians have already pointed out in developments related to other aspects of society.[94]

Alongside this mutual awareness of one another, there were also close relationships between the two German states in terms of the economy, scientific research, and technology development, whose effects on computerization still need to be looked at in even more detail. Most likely, such analyses will detect simultaneous trends toward entanglement and disentanglement: by participating in the efforts of the COMECON to develop joint standards for electronic data processing, for example, the GDR partially cut itself off from other international developments. Yet it also kept ties to the developments in the West through its special economic relationship with West Germany.

The drastic growth of the gap in computer technology between East and West in the 1980s also led in part to a decoupling of the problems and deficits in the development of technology and the use of computers in industry and administration. The practical problems of computerization were therefore simply different on each side of the wall. Although West Germany had already turned toward the West when it came to technological advancements, it still had a great political interest in keeping tabs on the problems that the East faced with computerization. The West believed that progress in modernization within the crisis-plagued GDR economy might have a positive effect in bringing the two countries closer together. There were indeed some entanglements in the narrower sense of the word, especially the economic activities undertaken by the Kommerzielle Koordinierung (Commercial Coordination Office) in the West, which came to play a more important role in providing Western computer technology to the GDR in the 1980s. Of course, there were also the many illegal transfers of technology set up by the Stasi with the help of West German companies that circumvented the embargo regulations, but also unintentionally increased the GDR's dependence on the West. The advent of digital modernity in Germany was therefore very much a *geteilte Geschichte* in both senses of the term, marked by entanglements and disentanglements alike.

Jürgen Danyel is deputy director and head of the section "Contemporary History in Media and Information Society" at the Center for Contemporary History (ZZF) in Potsdam. His research focuses on the ways in which both German states dealt with their respective pasts, the elites in the Soviet Occupation Zone/GDR, the social history of state socialism, and the Prague Spring in 1968. He has published numerous studies on these topics.

Annette Schuhmann is a research associate and editor of the Internet portal "Zeitgeschichte-online" at the Center for Contemporary History (ZZF) in Potsdam. She studied history and political science at the Freie Universität Berlin. Her research focuses on industrial history in the societies of state socialism.

NOTES

1. Cf. Ralf Ahrens, "Spezialisierungsinteresse und Integrationsaversion im Rat für Gegenseitige Wirtschaftshilfe: Der DDR-Werkzeugmaschinenbau in den 1970er Jahren," *Jahrbuch für Wirtschaftsgeschichte* 49, no. 2 (2008): 73–92. See also *Olaf Klenke, Ist die DDR an der Globalisierung gescheitert? Autarke Wirtschaftspolitik versus internationale Weltwirtschaft—Das Beispiel Mikroelektronik* (Frankfurt a. M., 2001).
2. Ahrens, "Spezialisierungsinteresse"; Peter Hübner, *Arbeit, Arbeiter und Technik in der DDR, 1971 bis 1989* (Bonn, 2014), 45ff.; Simon Donig, "Vorbild und Klassenfeind. Die USA und die DDR-Informatik in den 1960er Jahren," *Osteuropa* 59, no. 10 (2009): 89–100.

3. Daniel Bell, *The Coming of Post-Industrial Society: A Venture in Social Forecasting* (New York, 1973). See also Ariane Leendertz, "Schlagwort, Prognostik oder Utopie? Daniel Bell über Wissen und Politik in der 'postindustriellen Gesellschaft,'" *Zeithistorische Forschungen/Studies in Contemporary History* 9, no. 1 (2012): 161–67.
4. Alain Touraine, *The Post-Industrial Society. Tommorow's Social History: Classes, Conflicts, and Culture in the Programmed Society* (London, 1974).
5. Karl W. Deutsch, *The Nerves of Government: Models of Political Communication and Control* (New York, 1963). See also Benjamin Seibel, "Berechnendes Regieren. Karl W. Deutschs Entwurf einer politischen Kybernetik," *Zeithistorische Forschungen/Studies in Contemporary History* 9, no. 2 (2012): 334–39.
6. Cf. Manuel Castells, *The Information Age: Economy, Society and Culture*, 3 vols. (Oxford, 2001).
7. As for the GDR, see André Steiner, *Von Plan zu Plan. Eine Wirtschaftsgeschichte der DDR* (Munich, 2004), 123ff.
8. Radovan Richta et al., *Civilization at the Crossroads: Social and Human Implications of the Scientific and Technological Revolution*, trans. Marian Šligová (New York, 1969).
9. See Slava Gerovitch, "Die sowjetische Kybürokratie," *Zeitschrift für Ideengeschichte* 6, no. 3 (2012): 19–25.
10. See some of the suggestions that have been made, such as "postmodernity," "reflexive modernity," or "new modernity," in Thomas Raithel, Andreas Rödder, and Andreas Wirsching, eds., *Auf dem Weg in eine neue Moderne? Die Bundesrepublik Deutschland in den siebziger und achtziger Jahren* (Munich, 2009).
11. On locating the self-perceptions and external perceptions of crises in a historical perspective, see K. H. Jarausch, "Krise oder Aufbruch? Historische Annäherungen an die 1970er-Jahre," *Zeithistorische Forschungen/Studies in Contemporary History* 3, no. (2006): S. 334–41; Frank Bösch, "Umbrüche in die Gegenwart. Globale Ereignisse und Krisenreaktionen um 1979," *Zeithistorische Forschungen/Studies in Contemporary History* 9, no. 1 (2012): 8–32.
12. Marcel Berlinghoff, "Computerisierung und Privatheit—Historische Perspektiven," *Aus Politik und Zeitgeschichte* 15–16 (2013): 14–19.
13. On the West German case, see Hartmut Petzold, *Rechnende Maschinen: Eine historische Untersuchung ihrer Herstellung und Anwendung vom Kaiserreich bis zur Bundesrepublik* (Düsseldorf, 1985); Annette Schuhmann, "Der Traum vom perfekten Unternehmen. Die Computerisierung der Arbeitswelt in der Bundesrepublik Deutschland (1950er- bis 1980er-Jahre)," *Zeithistorische Forschungen/Studies in Contemporary History* 9, no. 2 (2012): 231–56.
14. Dirk Baecker, *Studien zur nächsten Gesellschaft* (Frankfurt a. M., 2007), 10, 16ff.
15. Ibid.; see also Jürgen Kocka, "Mehr Last als Lust. Arbeit und Arbeitsgesellschaft in der europäischen Geschichte," *Zeitgeschichte-online*, January 2010, retrieved 17 May 2016, http://www.zeitgeschichte-online.de/thema/mehr-

last-als-lust, originally published in *Jahrbuch für Wirtschaftsgeschichte* 46, no. 2 (2005); Peter Hertner and Dieter Schott, "Zukunftstechnologien der (letzten) Jahrhundertwende: Intentionen—Visionen—Wirklichkeiten," *Jahrbuch für Wirtschaftsgeschichte* 40, no. 2 (1999): 9–16.

16. Dieter Schott, "Das Zeitalter der Elektrizität: Visionen—Potentiale—Realitäten," *Jahrbuch für Wirtschaftsgeschichte* 40, no. 2 (1999): 31–49; Peter Hertner, "Die Stoffe, aus denen die Träume wurden: Zukunftstechnologien der Jahrhundertwende. Aluminium und Kunstseide als Beispiele," *Jahrbuch für Wirtschaftsgeschichte* 40, no. 2 (1999): 17–29.
17. Margret Schwarte-Amedick, "Von papierlosen Büros und menschenleeren Fabriken," in *Zukünfte des Computers*, ed. Claus Pias (Zürich, 2005), 67–86.
18. Martina Heßler, "Die Halle 54 bei Volkswagen und die Grenzen der Automatisierung. Überlegungen zum Mensch-Maschine-Verhältnis in der industriellen Produktion der 1980er-Jahre," *Zeithistorische Forschungen/Studies in Contemporary History* 11, no. 1 (2014): 56–76.
19. Peter Brödner, *The Shape of Future Technology: The Anthropocentric Alternative* (London, 1990) (Orig. *Fabrik 2000. Alternative Entwicklungspfade in die Zukunft der Fabrik* [Berlin, 1985]); Richard Vahrenkamp, *Von Taylor zu Toyota. Rationalisierungsdebatten im 20. Jahrhundert* (Lohmar, 2010); Ulrich Jürgens and Thomas Malsch, *Breaking from Taylorism: Changing Forms of Work in the Automobile Industry* (Cambridge, 1993); Thomas Malsch, Knuth Dohse, and Ulrich Jürgens, *Industrial Robots in the Automobile Industry: A Leap towards "Automated Fordism"?* (Berlin, 1984).
20. Cf. Jochen Steinbicker, *Zur Theorie der Informationsgesellschaft. Ein Vergleich der Ansätze von Peter Drucker, Daniel Bell und Manuel Castells* (Opladen, 2001).
21. Karl Steinbuch, *Mensch, Technik, Zukunft. Basiswissen für die Probleme von morgen* (Stuttgart, 1971).
22. An interesting example of the dilemma between expectations and fears of the future, especially in terms of the unsolved problems of the present (transportation, armaments, environmental pollution, etc.) can be found in the three-part series that aired on ZDF (German public television channel) in 1972: Arno Schmuckler and Peter Kerstan, "Richtung 2000—Vorschau auf die Welt von morgen," retrieved 24 May 2016, http://www.youtube.com/watch?v=kaGnBNhE2xI, https://www.youtube.com/watch?v=WiOaN5RbCBk, and https://www.youtube.com/watch?v=StxNtLIhf4k.
23. Hübner, *Arbeit, Arbeiter und Technik*, 197ff.
24. Ibid., 199f.
25. John D. Bernal, *Science in History* (London, 1954); Uwe Fraunholz, "'Revolutionäres Ringen für den gesellschaftlichen Fortschritt.' Automatisierungsvisionen in der DDR," in *Technology Fiction. Technische Visionen und Utopien in der Hochmoderne*, ed. Uwe Fraunholz and Anke Woschech (Bielefeld, 2012), 197f.
26. Hübner, *Arbeit, Arbeiter und Technik*, 47.

27. Ibid, 47ff.
28. "Dai Ichi," *Der Spiegel* 9 (1968): 92; "Grausam aber gut," *Der Spiegel* 22 (1969): 118–37; "Number one," *Der Spiegel* 41 (1980): 174–76; Klaus von Dohnanyi, *Japanische Strategien oder Das deutsche Führungsdefizit* (Munich, 1969); Christian Kleinschmidt, *Der produktive Blick: Wahrnehmung amerikanischer und japanischer Management- und Produktionsmethoden durch deutsche Unternehmer 1950–1985* (Berlin, 2002).
29. See, for example, Klaus Gestwa and Stefan Rohdewald, "Verflechtungsstudien. Naturwissenschaft und Technik im Kalten Krieg," *Osteuropa* 59, no. 10 (2009): 5–15.
30. Cf. Michael Hartmann, *Rationalisierung der Verwaltungsarbeit im privatwirtschaftlichen Bereich. Auswirkungen der elektronischen Datenverarbeitung auf die Angestellten* (Frankfurt a. M., 1981), 163.
31. According to Hartmann, the first application using a microprocessor was a navigation computer on the intercontinental rocket Minutemann II: Hartmann, *Rationalisierung*, 157.
32. Ibid.
33. Hübner, *Arbeit, Arbeiter und Technik*, 197.
34. Hartmann, *Rationalisierung*, 157.
35. On the history of Apple, see *Revolution in the Valley: The Insanely Great Story of How the Mac Was Made* (Beijing, 2005); J. S. Young and W. L. Simon, *iCon: Steve Jobs, the Greatest Second Act in the History of Business* (Hoboken, 2005); Michael Moritz, *The Little Kingdom: The Private Story of Apple Computer* (New York, 1984); O. W. Linzmayer, *Apple Confidential: The Real Story* (San Francisco, 1999); Steve Wozniak and Gina Smith, *iWoz. Computer Geek to Cult Icon: How I Invented the Personal Computer, Co-Founded Apple, and Had Fun Doing It* (New York, 2006); Michael Moritz, *Return to the Little Kingdom: Steve Jobs, the Creation of Apple, and How It Changed the World* (London, 2009); Walter Isaacson, *Steve Jobs* (New York, 2013). On the cult surrounding the brand, see Leander Kahney, *The Cult of the Mac* (San Francisco, 2004).
36. See Paul Allen, *Idea Man: A Memoir by the Cofounder of Microsoft* (New York, 2011); Bill Gates, *The Road Ahead* (New York, 1995). The extensive literature on the biography of Bill Gates and the history of Microsoft are mostly journalistic in nature. See, for example, Jim Wallace and James Erickson, *Hard Drive: Bill Gates and the Making of the Microsoft Empire* (New York, 1992).
37. See Stefan M. Gergely, *Mikroelektronik. Computer, Roboter und Neue Medien erobern die Welt* (Munich, 1983), 145ff.
38. Compare, for example, Thomas Raithel, "Neue Technologien: Produktionsprozesse und Diskurse," in *Auf dem Weg in eine neue Moderne? Die Bundesrepublik Deutschland in den siebziger und achtziger Jahren*, ed. Thomas Raithel, Andreas Rödder, and Andreas Wirsching (Munich, 2009), 31–44.
39. See, for example, Gerhard Merkel, "Computerentwicklungen in der DDR—Rahmenbedingungen und Ergebnisse," in *Informatik in der DDR—eine Bi-*

lanz. Symposien 7. bis 9. Oktober 2004 in Chemnitz, 11. bis 12. Mai 2006 in Erfurt, ed. Friedrich Naumann and Gabriele Schade (Bonn, 2006), 40–54.

40. See Felix Herrmann, "Zwischen Planwirtschaft und IBM. Die sowjetische Computerindustrie im Kalten Krieg," *Zeithistorische Forschungen/Studies in Contemporary History* 9, no. 2 (2012): 212–30; see also Donig, "Vorbild und Klassenfeind."
41. A publication written by former members of the Science and Technology Sector of the Stasi's HVA provides insight into the extent of this illegal transfer of technology: Horst Müller, Manfred Süß and Horst Vogel, eds., *Die Industriespionage der DDR. Die wissenschaftlich-technische Aufklärung der HVA* (Berlin, 2008).
42. On the role of the Stasi in the microelectronics program at VEB Carl Zeiss Jena, see Reinhard Buthmann, *Kadersicherung im Kombinat VEB Carls Zeiss Jena. Die Staatssicherheit und das Scheitern des Mikroelektronikprogramms* (Berlin, 1997).
43. See Gerhard Barkleit, *Mikroelektronik in der DDR. SED, Staatsapparat und Staatssicherheit im Wettstreit der Systeme* (Dresden, 2000), 97ff.; Matthias Judt, *Der Bereich Kommerzielle Koordinierung. Das DDR-Wirtschaftsimperium des Alexander Schalck-Golodkowski—Mythos und Realität* (Berlin, 2013).
44. Ahrens, "Spezialisierungsinteresse," 78.
45. Ibid., 78f.; Hübner, *Arbeit, Arbeiter und Technik,* 198f.
46. See Christian Booß, "Der Sonnenstaat des Erich Mielke. Die Informationsverarbeitung des MfS. Entwicklung und Aufbau," *Zeitschrift für Geschichtswissenschaft* 60, no. 5 (2012), 441–57.
47. Cf. Klaus-Dieter Weise, *Erzeugnislinie Heimcomputer, Kleincomputer und Bildungscomputer des VEB Kombinat Robotron* (Dresden, 2005), 13f.
48. See Sven Stillich, "Mit Kilobytes gegen den Klassenfeind," *Spiegel-Online,* 22 December 2009. Reliable data about this private transfer of technology is still lacking.
49. The idea of a factory devoid of humans was a prominent motif in visions of the future of work. See Fraunholz, "Revolutionäres Ringen," 196.
50. See, among others, Dieter Balkhausen, *Die dritte industrielle Revolution. Wie die Mikroelektronik unser Leben verändert* (Düsseldorf, 1978), 12.
51. See the example of the "AEG Olympia Büromaschinenwerk" in Meinolf Dierkes and Lutz Marz, *Leitbildzentriertes Organisationslernen und technischer Wandel* (Berlin, 1998), 20ff.
52. For a more detailed account, see Schuhmann, "Traum vom perfekten Unternehmen," 231–56.
53. "Uns steht eine Katastrophe bevor," *Der Spiegel* 16 (1978): 80; "Mikroelektronik—Fluch oder Segen?," *Der Spiegel* 5 (1982): 126–29. See also Meinolf Dierkes and Lutz Marz, "Technikakzeptanz, Technikfolgen und Technikgenese. Zur Weiterentwicklung konzeptioneller Grundlagen der sozialwissenschaftlichen Technikforschung," in *Die Technisierung und ihre Folgen. Zur Biographie eines Forschungsfeldes,* ed. Meinolf Dierkes (Berlin, 1993), 18f.

54. Schuhmann, "Traum vom perfekten Unternehmen," 252f.
55. Hartmann, *Rationalisierung*, 115.
56. Hübner, *Arbeit, Arbeiter und Technik*, 494ff.
57. Ibid., 189f.
58. Ahrens, "Spezialisierungsinteresse," 88.
59. Schuhmann, "Traum vom perfekten Unternehmen," 244f.
60. Petzold, *Rechnende Maschinen*, 459ff.
61. Detlef Borchers, "Vor 50 Jahren: Beginn der DV-Ausbildung in Frankfurt/Main," *Heise online*, 19 October 2006.
62. Heßler, "Halle 54," 56–76.
63. Timo Leimbach, *Die Softwarebranche in Deutschland. Entwicklung eines Innovationssystems zwischen Forschung, Markt, Anwendung und Politik 1950 bis heute* (Stuttgart, 2011); Vahrenkamp, *Von Taylor zu Toyota*, 122.
64. Hübner, *Arbeit, Arbeiter und Technik*, 203f.
65. See Olaf Klenke, *Kampfauftrag Mikrochip. Rationalisierung und sozialer Konflikt in der DDR* (Hamburg, 2008).
66. On West Germany, see Leimbach, *Softwarebranche*.
67. Cf. Werner Faulstich, "Die Anfänge einer neuen Kulturperiode: Der Computer und die digitalen Medien," in *Die Kultur der 80er Jahre*, ed. Werner Faulstich (Paderborn, 2005), 231f.
68. Björn Schwarz, "Ein ganz starker Typ," *Chip* 6 (1983): 48.
69. On the different sales figure estimates for the C 64, see Michael Steil, "How Many Commodore 64 Computers Were Really Sold?," *Pagetable.com*, 1 February 2011.
70. "Computer—das ist wie eine Sucht," *Der Spiegel* 50 (1983): 177.
71. Cf. "Alarm in den Schulen: Die Computer kommen," *Der Spiegel* 47 (1984): 97–129.
72. See Klaus Haefner, *Die neue Bildungskrise. Lernen im Computerzeitalter* (Reinbek bei Hamburg, 1985).
73. Cf. Heinz Riesenhuber, "Computer und Bildung," *Wirtschaft und Erziehung* 36, no. 5 (1984), 153–55.
74. See Tom Schnabel and Lars Leppin, "Informatik und Rechentechnik in der DDR," Seminar paper, Humboldt University, Berlin, 1999.
75. Cf. Wolfgang Coy, "Was ist Informatik? Zur Entstehung des Faches an den deutschen Universitäten," in *Geschichten der Informatik. Visionen, Paradigmen, Leitmotive*, ed. Hans Dieter Hellige (Berlin, 2004), 473–98.
76. An interesting example of this coupling of visions of the future and the problems of the present is the ZDF TV production "Richtung 2000" from 1972.
77. Joseph Weizenbaum, *Computer Power and Human Reason: From Judgment to Calculation* (San Francisco, 1976).
78. Dierkes and Marz, "Technikakzeptanz," 19f. See also Ernst Kistler, "Die Technikfeindlichkeitsdebatte—Zum politischen Missbrauch von Umfrageergebnissen," *Technikfolgenabschätzung. Theorie und Praxis* 14, no. 3 (2005), 13–19.

79. Hübner, *Arbeit, Arbeiter und Technik*, 27.
80. Ibid., 27f.
81. *Alles unter Kontrolle: Notizen auf dem Weg in den Überwachungsstaat*, directed by Klaus Dzuck, Barbara Etz, and Niels Bolbrinker (West Germany, 1983).
82. For a more detailed account, see Achim Saupe, "Von 'Ruhe und Ordnung' zur 'inneren Sicherheit.' Eine Historisierung gesellschaftlicher Dispositive," *Zeithistorische Forschungen/Studies in Contemporary History* 7, no. 2 (2010): 170–87; Lea Hartung, *Kommissar Computer. Horst Herold und die Virtualisierung des polizeilichen Wissens* (Berlin, 2010).
83. See Larry Frohman, "'Only Sheep Let Themselves Be Counted': Privacy, Political Culture, and the 1983/87 West German Census Boycotts," *Archiv für Sozialgeschichte* 52 (2012): 335–78.
84. See also Andreas Wirsching, *Abschied vom Provisorium. Geschichte der Bundesrepublik Deutschland 1982–1990* (Munich, 2006), 393ff.; Peter Schaar, *Das Ende der Privatsphäre. Der Weg in die Überwachungsgesellschaft* (Munich, 2009), 99ff.
85. See Beate Rössler, *The Value of Privacy* (Cambridge, 2005).
86. A good source of information about the development of the CCC is its newsletter *Die Datenschleuder* (http://ds.ccc.de). See also Daniel Kulla, *Der Phrasenprüfer. Szenen aus dem Leben von Wau Holland, Mitbegründer des Chaos Computer Clubs* (Löhrbach, 2003); Jürgen Wieckmann, ed., *Das Chaos Computer Buch: Hacking Made in Germany* (Reinbek bei Hamburg, 1988).
87. Roger Engelmann et al., eds., *Das MfS-Lexikon: Begriffe, Personen und Strukturen der Staatssicherheit der DDR* (Berlin, 2012), 27. Initial considerations regarding the use of mass personal data by the Stasi can be found in Booß, "Der Sonnenstaat des Erich Mielke."
88. Klaus Marxen and Gerhard Werle, eds., *Strafjustiz und DDR-Unrecht*, vol 4/2: *Spionage* (Berlin, 2004), 740.
89. See Gerhard Ritter, *The Price of German Unity: Reunification and the Crisis of the Welfare State* (Oxford, 2011), 255. For eyewitness testimony, see Herbert Mrotzek and Herbert Püschel, *Krankenversicherung und Alterssicherung* (Opladen, 1997), 240.
90. On the history of the Internet, see Kathrin Rothemund, "Internet—Verbreitung und Aneignung in den 1990ern," in *Die Kultur der 90er Jahre*, ed. Werner Faulstich (Munich, 2010), 119–36; Torsten Braun, "Geschichte und Entwicklung des Internets," *Informatik-Spektrum* 33, no. 2 (2010): 201–7; Michael Friedewald, "Vom Experimentierfeld zum Massenmedium: Gestaltende Kräfte in der Entwicklung des Internet," *Technikgeschichte* 67, no. 4 (2000): 331–62.
91. See Castells, *Information Age*, vol 1: *The Rise of the Network Society* (Oxford, 2001), 49.

92. See the overview in Besim Karadeniz, "Das Internet in Deutschland," *Netplanet*, retrieved 24 May 2016, http://www.netplanet.org/geschichte/deutschland.shtml.
93. "Internet-Streik: Unterschiedliche Stellungnahmen zum Protest," *Computerwoche*, 10 November 1998.
94. See K. H. Jarausch, "'Die Teile als Ganzes erkennen.' Zur Integration der beiden deutschen Nachkriegsgeschichten," *Zeithistorische Forschungen/Studies in Contemporary History* 1, no. 1 (2004): 10–30; Christoph Kleßmann, "Verflechtung und Abgrenzung. Aspekte der geteilten und zusammengehörigen deutschen Nachkriegsgeschichte," *Aus Politik und Zeitgeschichte* 29–30 (1993): 30–41; Hermann Wentker, "Zwischen Abgrenzung und Verflechtung. Deutsch-deutsche Geschichte nach 1945," *Aus Politik und Zeitgeschichte* 1–2 (2005): 10–17.

BIBLIOGRAPHY

Ahrens, Ralf. "Spezialisierungsinteresse und Integrationsaversion im Rat für Gegenseitige Wirtschaftshilfe: Der DDR-Werkzeugmaschinenbau in den 1970er Jahren." *Jahrbuch für Wirtschaftsgeschichte* 49, no. 2 (2008): 73–92.

Allen, Paul. *Idea Man: A Memoir by the Cofounder of Microsoft*. New York: Portfolio/Penguin, 2011.

Alles unter Kontrolle. Notizen auf dem Weg in den Überwachungsstaat. Directed by Klaus Dzuck, Barbara Etz, and Niels Bolbrinker. West Germany: Film Verlag der Autoren, 1983.

Baecker, Dirk. *Studien zur nächsten Gesellschaft*. Frankfurt a. M.: Suhrkamp, 2007.

Balkhausen, Dieter. *Die dritte industrielle Revolution. Wie die Mikroelektronik unser Leben verändert*. Düsseldorf: Econ, 1978.

Barkleit, Gerhard. *Mikroelektronik in der DDR. SED, Staatsapparat und Staatssicherheit im Wettstreit der Systeme*. Dresden: Hannah-Arendt-Institut für Totalitarismusforschung e.V. an der Technischen Universität Dresden, 2000.

Bell, Daniel. *The Coming of Post-Industrial Society: A Venture in Social Forecasting*. New York: Basic Books, 1973.

Berlinghoff, Marcel. "Computerisierung und Privatheit—Historische Perspektiven." *Aus Politik und Zeitgeschichte* 15–16 (2013): 14–19.

Bernal, John D. *Science in History*. London: Watts, 1954.

Booß, Christian. "Der Sonnenstaat des Erich Mielke. Die Informationsverarbeitung des MfS. Entwicklung und Aufbau." *Zeitschrift für Geschichtswissenschaft* 60, no. 5 (2012): 441–57.

Bösch, Frank. "Umbrüche in die Gegenwart. Globale Ereignisse und Krisenreaktionen um 1979." *Zeithistorische Forschungen/Studies in Contemporary History* 9, no. 1 (2012): 8–32.

Braun, Torsten. "Geschichte und Entwicklung des Internets." *Informatik-Spektrum* 33, no. 2 (2010): 201–7.

Brödner, Peter. *The Shape of Future Technology: The Anthropocentric Alternative.* London: Springer, 1990.

Buthmann, Reinhard. *Kadersicherung im Kombinat VEB Carl Zeiss Jena. Die Staatssicherheit und das Scheitern des Mikroelektronikprogramms.* Berlin: Chr. Links Verlag, 1997.

Castells, Manuel. *The Information Age: Economy, Society and Culture.* 3 vols. Oxford: Blackwell, 2001.

Coy, Wolfgang. "Was ist Informatik? Zur Entstehung des Faches an den deutschen Universitäten." In *Geschichten der Informatik. Visionen, Paradigmen, Leitmotive,* edited by H. D. Hellige, 473–98. Berlin: Springer, 2004.

Deutsch, K. W. *The Nerves of Government: Models of Political Communication and Control.* New York: Free Press, 1963.

Dierkes, Meinolf, and Lutz Marz. *Leitbildzentriertes Organisationslernen und technischer Wandel.* Berlin: Wissenschaftszentrum Berlin für Sozialforschung, 1998.

———. "Technikazeptanz, Technikfolgen und Technikgenese. Zur Weiterentwicklung konzeptioneller Grundlagen der sozialwissenschaftlichen Technikforschung." In *Die Technisierung und ihre Folgen. Zur Biographie eines Forschungsfeldes,* edited by Meinolf Dierkes, 17–44. Berlin: Ed. Sigma, 1993.

Dohnanyi, Klaus von. *Japanische Strategien oder Das deutsche Führungsdefizit.* Munich: Piper, 1969.

Donig, Simon. "Vorbild und Klassenfeind. Die USA und die DDR-Informatik in den 1960er Jahren." *Osteuropa* 59, no. 10 (2009): 89–100.

Engelmann, Roger, Bernd Florath, Helge Heidemeyer, Daniela Münkel, Arno Polzin, and Walter Süß, eds. *Das MfS-Lexikon: Begriffe, Personen und Strukturen der Staatssicherheit der DDR.* Berlin: Chr. Links Verlag, 2012.

Faulstich, Werner. "Die Anfänge einer neuen Kulturperiode: Der Computer und die digitalen Medien." In *Die Kultur der 80er Jahre,* edited by Werner Faulstich, 231–45. Paderborn: Fink, 2005.

Fraunholz, Uwe. "'Revolutionäres Ringen für den gesellschaftlichen Fortschritt.' Automatisierungsvisionen in der DDR." In *Technology Fiction. Technische Visionen und Utopien in der Hochmoderne,* edited by Uwe Fraunholz and Anke Woschech, 195–219. Bielefeld: Transcript, 2012.

Friedewald, Michael. "Vom Experimentierfeld zum Massenmedium: Gestaltende Kräfte in der Entwicklung des Internet." *Technikgeschichte* 67, no. 4 (2000): 331–61.

Frohman, Larry. "'Only Sheep Let Themselves Be Counted': Privacy, Political Culture, and the 1983/87 West German Census Boycotts." *Archiv für Sozialgeschichte* 52 (2012): 335–78.

Gates, Bill. *The Road Ahead.* New York: Viking, 1995.

Gergely, S. M. *Mikroelektronik. Computer, Roboter und Neue Medien erobern die Welt.* Munich: Piper, 1983.

Gerovitch, Slava. "Die sowjetische Kybürokratie." *Zeitschrift für Ideengeschichte* 6, no. 3 (2012): 19–25.

Gestwa, Klaus, and Stefan Rohdewald. "Verflechtungsstudien. Naturwissenschaft und Technik im Kalten Krieg." *Osteuropa* 59, no.10 (2009): 5–14.
Haefner, Klaus. *Die neue Bildungskrise. Lernen im Computerzeitalter.* Reinbek bei Hamburg: Rowohlt, 1985.
Hartmann, Michael. *Rationalisierung der Verwaltungsarbeit im privatwirtschaftlichen Bereich. Auswirkungen der elektronischen Datenverarbeitung auf die Angestellten.* Frankfurt a. M.: Campus-Verlag, 1981.
Hartung, Lea. *Kommissar Computer. Horst Herold und die Virtualisierung des polizeilichen Wissens.* Berlin: Free University, 2010. Retrieved 17 May 2016, http://www.edocs.fu-berlin.de/docs/receive/FUDOCS_document_000000005003.
Herrmann, Felix. "Zwischen Planwirtschaft und IBM. Die sowjetische Computerindustrie im Kalten Krieg." *Zeithistorische Forschungen/Studies in Contemporary History* 9, no. 2 (2012): 212–30.
Hertner, Peter. "Die Stoffe, aus denen die Träume wurden: Zukunftstechnologien der Jahrhundertwende. Aluminium und Kunstseide als Beispiele." *Jahrbuch für Wirtschaftsgeschichte* 40, no. 2 (1999): 17–29.
Hertner, Peter, and Dieter Schott. "Zukunftstechnologien der (letzten) Jahrhundertwende: Intentionen—Visionen—Wirklichkeiten." *Jahrbuch für Wirtschaftsgeschichte* 40, no. 2 (1999): 9–16.
Hertzfeld, Andy. *Revolution in the Valley: The Insanely Great Story of How the Mac Was Made.* Beijing: O'Reilly, 2005.
Heßler, Martina. "Die Halle 54 bei Volkswagen und die Grenzen der Automatisierung. Überlegungen zum Mensch-Maschine-Verhältnis in der industriellen Produktion der 1980er-Jahre." *Zeithistorische Forschungen/Studies in Contemporary History* 11, no. 1 (2014): 56–76.
Hübner, Peter. *Arbeit, Arbeiter und Technik in der DDR, 1971 bis 1989.* Bonn: Dietz, 2014.
Isaacson, Walter. *Steve Jobs.* New York: Simon & Schuster, 2013.
Jarausch, Konrad H. "'Die Teile als Ganzes erkennen.' Zur Integration der beiden deutschen Nachkriegsgeschichten." *Zeithistorische Forschungen/Studies in Contemporary History* 1, no.1 (2004): 10–30.
———. "Krise oder Aufbruch? Historische Annäherungen an die 1970er-Jahre." *Zeithistorische Forschungen/Studies in Contemporary History* 3, no. 3 (2006): 334–41.
Judt, Matthias. *Der Bereich Kommerzielle Koordinierung. Das DDR-Wirtschaftsimperium des Alexander Schalck-Golodkowski—Mythos und Realität.* Berlin: Chr. Links Verlag, 2013.
Jürgens, Ulrich, Thomas Malsch, and Knuth Dohse. *Breaking from Taylorism: Changing Forms of Work in the Automobile Industry.* Cambridge: Cambridge University Press, 1993.
Kahney, Leander. *The Cult of the Mac.* San Francisco: No Starch Press, 2004.
Karadeniz, Besim. "Das Internet in Deutschland." *Netplanet.* Retrieved 15 May 2015, http://www.netplanet.org/geschichte/deutschland.shtml.

Kistler, Ernst. "Die Technikfeindlichkeitsdebatte—Zum politischen Missbrauch von Umfrageergebnissen." *Technikfolgenabschätzung. Theorie und Praxis* 14, no. 3 (2005): 13–19.

Kleinschmidt, Christian. *Der produktive Blick: Wahrnehmung amerikanischer und japanischer Management- und Produktionsmethoden durch deutsche Unternehmer 1950–1985*. Berlin: Akademie-Verlag, 2002.

Klenke, Olaf. *Ist die DDR an der Globalisierung gescheitert? Autarke Wirtschaftspolitik versus internationale Weltwirtschaft—Das Beispiel Mikroelektronik*. Frankfurt a. M.: Lang, 2001.

———. *Kampfauftrag Mikrochip. Rationalisierung und sozialer Konflikt in der DDR*. Hamburg: VSA-Verlag, 2008.

Kleßmann, Christoph. "Verflechtung und Abgrenzung. Aspekte der geteilten und zusammengehörigen deutschen Nachkriegsgeschichte." *Aus Politik und Zeitgeschichte* 29–30 (1993): 30–41.

Kocka, Jürgen. "Mehr Last als Lust. Arbeit und Arbeitsgesellschaft in der europäischen Geschichte." *Zeitgeschichte-online,* January 2010. Retrieved 17 May 2016, http://www.zeitgeschichte-online.de/thema/mehr-last-als-lust. Originally published in *Jahrbuch für Wirtschaftsgeschichte* 46, no. 2 (2005).

Kulla, Daniel. *Der Phrasenprüfer. Szenen aus dem Leben von Wau Holland, Mitbegründer des Chaos Computer Clubs*. Löhrbach: Pieper und The Grüne Kraft, 2003.

Leendertz, Ariane. "Schlagwort, Prognostik oder Utopie? Daniel Bell über Wissen und Politik in der 'postindustriellen Gesellschaft.'" *Zeithistorische Forschungen/Studies in Contemporary History* 9, no. 1 (2012): 161–67.

Leimbach, Timo. *Die Softwarebranche in Deutschland. Entwicklung eines Innovationssystems zwischen Forschung, Markt, Anwendung und Politik 1950 bis heute*. Stuttgart: Fraunhofer-Verlag, 2011.

Linzmayer, O. W. *Apple Confidential: The Real Story*. San Francisco: No Starch Press, 1999.

Malsch, Thomas, Knuth Dohse, and Ulrich Jürgens. *Industrial Robots in the Automobile Industry: A Leap towards "Automated Fordism"?* Berlin: International Institute for Comparative Social Research, 1984.

Marxen, Klaus, and Gerhard Werle, eds. *Strafjustiz und DDR-Unrecht. Dokumentation*. Vol. 4/2: *Spionage*. Berlin: De Gruyter Recht, 2004.

Merkel, Gerhard. "Computerentwicklungen in der DDR—Rahmenbedingungen und Ergebnisse." In *Informatik in der DDR—eine Bilanz. Symposien 7. bis 9. Oktober 2004 in Chemnitz, 11. bis 12. Mai 2006 in Erfurt,* edited by Friedrich Naumann and Gabriele Schade, 40–54. Bonn: Gesellschaft für Informatik, 2006.

Moritz, Michael. *The Little Kingdom: The Private Story of Apple Computer*. New York: W. Morrow, 1984.

———. *Return to the Little Kingdom: Steve Jobs, the Creation of Apple, and How It Changed the World*. London: Duckworth Overlook, 2009.

Mrotzeck, Herbert, and Herbert Püschel. *Krankenversicherung und Alterssicherung*. Opladen: Leske + Budrich, 1997.

Müller, Horst, Manfred Süß, and Horst Vogel, eds. *Die Industriespionage der DDR. Die Wissenschaftlich-Technische Aufklärung der HVA*. Berlin: Ed. Ost, 2008.

Petzold, Hartmut. *Rechnende Maschinen. Eine historische Untersuchung ihrer Herstellung und Anwendung vom Kaiserreich bis zur Bundesrepublik*. Düsseldorf: VDI-Verlag, 1985.

Raithel, Thomas. "Neue Technologien: Produktionsprozesse und Diskurse." In *Auf dem Weg in eine neue Moderne? Die Bundesrepublik Deutschland in den siebziger und achtziger Jahren*, edited by Thomas Raithel, Andreas Rödder, and Andreas Wirsching, 31–44. Munich: R. Oldenbourg Verlag, 2009.

Raithel, Thomas, Andreas Rödder, and Andreas Wirsching, eds. *Auf dem Weg in eine neue Moderne? Die Bundesrepublik Deutschland in den siebziger und achtziger Jahren*. Munich: R. Oldenbourg Verlag, 2009.

Richta, Radovan (and a research team). *Civilization at the Crossroads: Social and Human Implications of the Scientific and Technological Revolution*. Translated by Marian Šligová. New York: International Arts and Sciences Press, 1969.

Riesenhuber, Heinz. "Computer und Bildung." *Wirtschaft und Erziehung* 36, no. 5 (1984): 153–55.

Ritter, Gerhard. *The Price of German Unity: Reunification and the Crisis of the Welfare State*. Oxford: Oxford University Press, 2011.

Rössler, Beate: *The Value of Privacy*. Cambridge: Polity Press, 2005.

Rothemund, Kathrin. "Internet—Verbreitung und Aneignung in den 1990ern." In *Die Kultur der 90er Jahre*, edited by Werner Faulstich, 119–36. Munich: Fink, 2010.

Saupe, Achim. "Von 'Ruhe und Ordnung' zur 'inneren Sicherheit.' Eine Historisierung gesellschaftlicher Dispositive." *Zeithistorische Forschungen/Studies in Contemporary History* 7, no. 2 (2010): 70–187.

Schaar, Peter. *Das Ende der Privatsphäre. Der Weg in die Überwachungsgesellschaft*. Munich: Goldmann, 2009.

Schmuckler, Arno, and Peter Kerstan. *Richtung 2000—Vorschau auf die Welt von morgen*. 3 parts. ZDF, 1972. Video clip. Retrieved 24 May 2016, http://www.youtube.com/watch?v=kaGnBNhE2xI, https://www.youtube.com/watch?v=WiOaN5RbCBk, and https://www.youtube.com/watch?v=StxNtLIhf4k.

Schnabel, Tom, and Lars Leppin. *Informatik und Rechentechnik in der DDR*. Seminar paper, Humboldt University, Berlin, 1999. Retrieved 17 May 2016, http://waste.informatik.hu-berlin.de/diplom/robotron/studienarbeit/files/frames.html.

Schott, Dieter. "Das Zeitalter der Elektrizität: Visionen—Potentiale—Realitäten." *Jahrbuch für Wirtschaftsgeschichte* 40, no. 2 (1999): 31–49.

Schuhmann, Annette. "Der Traum vom perfekten Unternehmen. Die Computerisierung der Arbeitswelt in der Bundesrepublik Deutschland (1950er- bis 1980er-Jahre)." *Zeithistorische Forschungen/Studies in Contemporary History* 9, no. 2 (2012): 231–56.

Schwarte-Amedick, Margret. "Von papierlosen Büros und menschenleeren Fabriken." In *Zukünfte des Computers*, edited by Claus Pias, 67–86. Zürich: Diaphanes, 2005.

Schwarz, Björn. "Ein ganz starker Typ." *Chip* 6 (1983): 48.

Seibel, Benjamin. "Berechnendes Regieren. Karl W. Deutschs Entwurf einer politischen Kybernetik." *Zeithistorische Forschungen/Studies in Contemporary History* 9, no. 2 (2012): 334–39.

Steinbicker, Jochen. *Zur Theorie der Informationsgesellschaft. Ein Vergleich der Ansätze von Peter Drucker, Daniel Bell und Manuel Castells*. Opladen: Leske + Budrich, 2001.

Steinbuch, Karl. *Mensch, Technik, Zukunft. Basiswissen für die Probleme von morgen*. Stuttgart: Deutsche Verlags-Anstalt, 1971.

Steiner, André. *Von Plan zu Plan. Eine Wirtschaftsgeschichte der DDR*. Munich: Deutsche Verlags-Anstalt, 2004.

Vahrenkamp, Richard. *Von Taylor zu Toyota. Rationalisierungsdebatten im 20. Jahrhundert*. Lohmar: Eul, 2010.

Wallace, Jim, and James Erickson. *Hard Drive: Bill Gates and the Making of the Microsoft Empire*. New York: Wiley, 1992.

Weise, Klaus-Dieter. *Erzeugnislinie Heimcomputer, Kleincomputer und Bildungscomputer des VEB Kombinat Robotron*. Dresden: Förderverein für die Technischen Sammlungen der Stadt Dresden e.V., 2005. Retrieved 17 May 2016, http://robotron.foerderverein-tsd.de/322/robotron322a.pdf.

Weizenbaum, Joseph. *Computer Power and Human Reason: From Judgment to Calculation*. San Francisco: W.H. Freeman, 1976.

Wentker, Hermann. "Zwischen Abgrenzung und Verflechtung. Deutsch-deutsche Geschichte nach 1945." *Aus Politik und Zeitgeschichte* 1–2 (2005): 10–17.

Wieckmann, Jürgen, ed. *Das Chaos Computer Buch: Hacking Made in Germany*. Reinbek bei Hamburg: Wunderlich, 1988.

Wirsching, Andreas. *Abschied vom Provisorium. Geschichte der Bundesrepublik Deutschland 1982–1990*. Munich: Deutsche Verlags-Anstalt, 2006.

Wozniak, Steve, and Gina Smith. *iWoz. Computer Geek to Cult Icon: How I Invented the Personal Computer, Co-Founded Apple, and Had Fun Doing It*. New York: W.W. Norton & Co., 2006.

Young, J. S., and W. L. Simon. *iCon: Steve Jobs, the Greatest Second Act in the History of Business*. Hoboken, NJ: Wiley, 2005.

CHAPTER 8

Educational Rivalries
The Transition from a German-German Contest to an International Competition

Emmanuel Droit and Wilfried Rudloff

Since the eighteenth century, the concept of *Bildung* has been considered an untranslatable term because it describes a very "German invention and institution."[1] Generally speaking, Bildung equates to education, but also a kind of intellectual cultivation; it can be seen as a lifelong process of human development wherein individuals develop their spiritual and cultural sensibilities to become more free due to a higher level of self-reflection. In the age of high modernity and nation-states, educational institutions were therefore more than just places where knowledge was acquired. From a systematic perspective, educational institutions have four key social functions:[2] first, they contribute to the cultural reproduction of society and the cultural socialization of individuals by transmitting systems of meaning, values, and cultural heritage throughout society. Second, educational systems equip individuals with the knowledge and skills that they need in order to take part in work and economic life, a function that is essential to the successful performance of economies and administrations. Third, the different degrees that can be obtained at specific steps within the educational system are a major determinant of social opportunity, influencing upward and downward mobility within society. Educational participation and educational careers are some of the most important factors that affect individual life choices and social status as well as the reproduction of social structures. Last, educational systems—in very different ways depending on the political nature of a given society—foster political integration and the stabilization of political order. Indeed, educational systems occupy a very central position within the cultural, economic, social, and political systems of a given society. These four key functions associated with educational processes can be seen in societies ordered along democratic as well as authoritarian or dictatorial lines. They provide the theoretical framework for this chapter's analysis of the two educational systems with fundamentally different basic coordinates in East and West Germany.

Not long after 1945, the educational systems in the two German states began to develop in very divergent directions. Despite a shared heritage and some ongoing points of interaction, two entirely different educational systems emerged within the context of the Cold War and the division of Germany. This process of increasing disentanglement progressed considerably in the 1950s. In West Germany, education became a core element of the federalist system that was erected after 1945. From the very beginning, the individual states (*Länder*) in West Germany insisted on the importance of their "cultural sovereignty." Although the federal government was granted some jurisdiction of educational policy for the first time by a change in the *Grundgesetz* in 1969, its ability to shape the educational system was still limited.[3] In contrast, the educational system in the GDR was highly regulated by the centralized state and subject to the control of the SED's political apparatus; the states themselves were dissolved in 1952. As of 1963, Margot Honecker, the wife of Erich Honecker, stood at the helm of the Ministry of Education (Ministerium für Volksbildung). Consequently, the ministry had a stronger, more inviolable position vis-à-vis the educational section within the party apparatus.[4]

Not surprisingly, therefore, schools in the GDR were called upon to help secure the ideological rule of the SED from the very beginning, while education in West Germany was bound up in the country's basic pluralistic order. Educational policy in the West served as an arena for the general competition between the parties, which had, however, largely been toned down through the consensus demands of "cooperative federalism." The East German dictatorship, in contrast, not only infiltrated the realm of education, but also it went as far as to infuse ideology into the basic upbringing of its citizens (*Erziehungsdiktatur*).[5] It pursued the Promethean goal of cultivating "fully developed socialist personalities."[6,7] Meanwhile, schooling in West Germany after 1945 followed in the institutional footprints of the system that had existed before 1933. According to assumed aptitude types and levels, children were usually divided among three different school types at the end of fourth grade, namely the *Hauptschule* ("traditional" education), the *Realschule* (intermediate education), and the *Gymnasium* (the most prestigious form of secondary school, which provides the pathway to university education). The three types of schools differed in their learning goals as well as their educational niveaus. Since they were designed to prepare pupils for different occupations and levels of qualifications, these three school types were part of a hierarchy of entitlements. In East Germany, however, much of the traditional school system was cast aside. The contrast between the three-tiered West German school system, which had been reaffirmed and extended in the first two decades after 1949, and the newly created comprehensive state schools (*Einheitsschule* model) for all children in East Germany until eighth grade (and later tenth grade) was the most poignant expression of the ever more divergent paths taken by the two states. However, the school model adopted in the GDR did draw on the educational tradition that had developed within the socialist workers' movement. The reinforcement of the elitist education offered by the *Gymnasien* in West Germany contrasted with the idea that the "bourgeois monopoly on education had to be broken" in the GDR in the 1950s. The goal in East Germany was to develop an educational policy that actively counteracted the middle-class dominance of the educational system by privileging the "children of workers and farmers." In many respects, the contrasts between both systems can be drawn out in more number and detail, but the main point remains that the structural coordinates of both educational systems had developed contrasting contours in the 1960s. On both sides of the Berlin Wall, the rhetoric of demarcation left an indelible mark on educational policy, further underscoring the opposition between the two systems.

There were, however, older lines of the German educational tradition that continued in analogous structures in some parts of the educational systems in both states. One of these traditions was the dual vocational training path, although the word "dual" was avoided in the GDR.[8] The fact that companies and vocational schools were both involved in the occupational training process in East and West Germany (despite differences in detail) was, in many respects, rather unique when compared to other structures of vocational education. In the socialist countries that were members of the COMECON, for example, the entire vocational training process took place in schools. Both Germanys also continued to use the *Abitur* (akin to a high school leaving exam), which was yet another structural difference particular to the German context. While the *Abitur* regulated access to the university in East and West Germany, university aptitude tests were the decisive hurdle that had to be overcome in order to gain admission to the university system in the Anglo-Saxon world as well as in the Soviet and Eastern Bloc countries.[9] It needs to be borne in mind, however, that neither the opposition between federalism and centralism, nor that between a three-tier and an integrated school system, were, in and of themselves, distinctly representative of the respective ideological systems in question. Examples of centralized and integrated schools systems can also be found in great number in other Western industrialized states after 1945—for example, England, Italy, or originally Sweden. The major difference between the two German contexts was rather that East German educational system was supposed to do its part to contribute to the monist worldview and goal of ideological homogenization that prevailed in GDR society.

Not only was educational policy part of the demarcation process, but also historical scholarship on education in postwar Germany has tended to reproduce these lines of separation rather than writing a *geteilte* narrative of a shared and divided history. The following chapter aims to offer such a more integrated approach.[10] It does not intend to narrate a story of entanglements in the sense of a *histoire croisée* dedicated to outlining the relatively rare aspects of the contacts and exchanges between the two German states.[11] Rather, it seeks to explore the question of how both German societies dealt with cross-system problems that emerged prior to reunification. There were four main areas in which both educational systems had to grapple with issues that were not specific to their own respective systems. The first aspect was the particular social dynamic attached to increasing educational aspirations within society and the calls for an expansion of participation in the educational systems—as well as the limitations within this process, especially in the coordination of the educational and employment systems (section 1). Second, there was the issue of the conditions that allowed people to take advantage of educational opportunities in both educational systems, which was linked to the degree of equality and inequality within the educational system on the whole (section 2). The debates over the "scientification" (*Verwissenschaftlichung*) of the curriculum reflected a third constellation of problems that had to be dealt with in both systems, along with the question of which new areas of knowledge (such as information technology or environmental education) should be incorporated in the canon of school instruction (section 3). Last, the perpetual problem of the purpose of political education plagued both states (section 4). These four constellations also correspond to the four functions of educational systems mentioned above.

Following an analysis of these aspects, a look at the transformation processes that took place within educational policy after German reunification traces the complex threads of development that were drawn over a period of two decades. On the heels of the structural adjustments that took place between the new and the old federal states, the beginnings of a joint German transformation appeared, merging into a new cycle of reform whose dynamics were no longer defined by the division of Germany, but rather by the international contexts in which they were embedded, especially European integration.

Educational Expansion and the Coordination of the Educational and Employment Systems

The enormous increase in educational participation, which both German states experienced at different phases, was one of the most substantial aspects of social transformation after 1949. In both countries, the standard shifted from general basic education to an intermediate-level diploma, which meant that the majority of pupils no longer completed just the basic *Hauptschule* curriculum, but rather went a step above the old standard. This process took place in the West through the expansion of secondary schooling within the traditional three-tiered system, while it evolved in the GDR as part of the introduction of the standard *Polytechnische Oberschule* (POS, akin to a polytechnic high school). Strikingly, however, despite this similar expansion of participation, these developments took place in different phases.[12] Whereas more than a few West German observers noted that the GDR was pulling ahead in the 1960s in equal opportunity and transparency, as well as the reform of rural schools and the mobilization of talent reserves, this trend seemed poised to reverse at the beginning of the 1970s: as the expansion of the universities stopped abruptly in the GDR, resulting in a freeze on the quota for *Abiturienten* (those seeking to pass the *Abitur* and thereby gain access to a university education), participation began to take an upswing in West Germany, which was reflected by the increasing number of successful *Abitur* exams and students at the universities. These numbers continued to climb in West Germany, despite the considerable changes to the general situation brought about by a decrease in the birth rate, tight budgets, and a worsening crisis on the job market.

Moreover, this expansion of educational participation in the Federal Republic was reflected in the enrollment and graduation figures for the different schools. In 1960, 27 percent of West Germans left school with at least a mid-level diploma. By 1980, this number had doubled to about 56.2 percent of school graduates; in 1987, two-thirds of graduates had at least acquired an intermediate school leaving certificate.[13] However, the upward trend in pupils attending *Realschule* and gaining these intermediate diplomas that had begun in the 1950s began to flatten out considerably in the 1980s. The number of pupils opting for the *Gymnasium* and completing the *Abitur*, in contrast, continued to climb: As of 1960, only 6 percent of a respective age cohort completed the *Abitur*, but by 1990, this figure jumped to 24 percent (plus 9 percent who graduated with a technical school diploma, or *Fachhochschulreife*).[14] Admittedly, the loosening of the selection process restrictions most likely contributed to the growing number of pupils who enrolled in the secondary schools. On the whole, the expansion of the educational system was not primarily the result of any political steering efforts, but rather it emerged to a large extent from a self-propelling social process that fed on rising educational aspirations among parents and pupils.

In the GDR, the situation was reversed in many respects. Political steering measures had a comparatively stronger influence on the trajectory of educational participation in East Germany: at first, the aim of these policies was expansion, but then the goal became to put the brakes on this process. The decision to introduce the polytechnic high school with ten grade levels as the standard school was made at a time when not even a ninth year of *Hauptschule* had been instituted in all of the West German states. Although this shift to the polytechnic high schools was not without its hiccups, 90 percent of pupils had attended both the ninth and tenth grades at the POS as of the 1980s.[15] For a time, the GDR also seemed to be pulling ahead of the Federal Republic in the expansion of university education. The quota of school graduates with an *Abitur* was 15 percent in 1965, which was twice as high as in West Germany. It must be noted, though, that there were more alternative ways to complete an *Abitur* in East Germany, especially in the form of the dual diploma combining vocational education and an *Abitur* at the same time.[16] But, this was by no means a phenomenon that was limited to the two German states: in general (with a few individual exceptions, of course), the number of students rose more strongly in the states to the east of the Iron Curtain in the 1960s than to the west. As of 1960, the ratio of students was above the average of the West European states in most of the communist bloc countries.[17] The East seemed to have taken over the lead in what might be termed the educational rivalry between the systems.

But then, after the transition from Ulbricht to Honecker, the expansion of the educational system suddenly came to a halt in the GDR. An abrupt stop was put on the rising student quota in 1971, and then the quota was pushed back down; it then stabilized at about 12 to 14 percent. The optimism of educational economists in the Ulbricht era, which was based on the assumption that the demand for academic qualifications would continue to grow, had dissipated by the 1970s. The link between the output of the education system and the demand for highly qualified labor forces seemed to be splitting apart.[18] Ulbricht had announced at the Ninth Congress of the Central Committee in October 1968 that the GDR needed to become the global leader in terms of scientific-technical cadres by 1975.[19] But then Margot Honecker, as education minister, declared that instead of preparing pupils to study at universities and technical colleges, the main purpose of schooling was to provide new generations of highly qualified skilled workers.[20] From this point on, the socially induced dynamic of expansion in the West stood in contrast to the educational participation rates that had largely been frozen in place by the state in the East. Participation in education was subordinated to the imperatives of centralized planning, for which the major determinant was a largely stable qualification demand. Since individual educational needs no longer seemed to mesh with the labor needs of the economy, access to the upper secondary school levels (namely grades eleven and twelve, referred to as *Erweiterte Oberschule*, which came after the ten-year mandatory period of schooling as preparation for the *Abitur*), as well as to university studies, was restricted, effectively putting the brakes on educational expansion.

This kind of steering of the system from above in order to meet central planning needs was not at all compatible with the prevailing notions of state and sociopolitical order in West Germany. In 1972, in a case that came before the Bundesverfassungsgericht (Federal Constitutional Court) on the numerus clausus (which regulated university admission requirements), the court declared that capping the capacity of the universities merely on the basis of demand considerations was not permissible. The court cited Article 12, Paragraph 1 of the *Grundgesetz*, which reads, "All Germans shall have the right freely to choose their occupation or profession, their place of work and their place of training," as the basis for its decision.[21] Additionally, the West German educational planners had acquired little faith in the forecasting capabilities of the economists of education, at least with regard to those branches of the occupational system in which manpower requirements were governed by highly complex market processes. The West German planners therefore opted to rely on flexible adaption and adjustment processes on the job market. Thus it was assumed that the existing stock of qualifications would generate the corresponding demand on the labor market through mobility processes that crossed professional boundaries and created new labor market segments for people with these qualifications.[22] The goal of the planners in the GDR, on the other hand, was to eliminate these kinds of ambiguities and uncertainties when it came to the coordination of the educational and employment systems as much as possible.

In the planned economy of the GDR, discrepancies between the supply of educational qualifications and the demand for qualified labor could not be treated primarily as a problem of the individuals on the labor markets, as it was the case in market societies. Rather, these discrepancies indicated problems within the planning system itself. By backpedaling on educational expansion in order to avoid such disproportions, the SED in fact increasingly repudiated the individual educational expectations of families who, bit by bit, had begun to push their children toward the *Abitur* and university studies. In 1971, 11 percent of an age cohort attended the *Erweiterte Oberschule* (EOS), which climbed to 17 in 1973, but then fell to 9 percent in 1975 and 8 percent in 1980.[23] On average only two to three pupils in each tenth grade class were selected to go on to the EOS. This intensified the competition for these spots considerably, especially since the selection was often made according to political criteria. Some pupils actually committed to becoming professional soldiers in order to be able to enroll in the EOS, regardless of how well they had performed at school in the past.

At about the same time that the GDR considerably restricted access to the universities and reined in the "emission" of university graduates, a new debate emerged in West Germany. Although this discussion in the Federal Republic arose within a fundamentally different context, here, too, the question was whether and how to better correlate the number and type of qualification profiles emerging from the educational system with the needs of the occupational system.[24] Whereas West German educational policymakers had complained of the lack of graduates with higher qualifications in the 1960s, this mismatch between the educational and employment systems now seemed to have flipped. Within a comparative perspective, East and West seemed to be moving in opposite directions again. While the GDR tried to tighten the link between its educational and employment systems, one of the major sources of debate on educational policy in the West was actually whether the two systems were increasingly disassociating themselves from one another. As early as 1972, the frightful notion of the "academic proletariat"[25] appeared in West German education debates, and by the middle of this decade, more and more voices were warning of a sharp rise in unemployment among academics. At the political level, the Christian Democratic Union applauded the criticism directed at the continual expansion of educational participation, calling for less focus on academic educational tracks and more emphasis on vocational education.

In the 1980s, however, it became apparent that the "proletarianization theory" had not played out as many had predicted because mass unemployment among academics had never reached such a threatening level as had once been feared.[26] Just as always, job security continued to increase with each additional level of education.[27] Within the different economic sectors, however, there were considerable imbalances: the more university graduates were dependent on employment in civil service, the more their risk of unemployment. The percentage of university graduates employed in the civil service shrank in the 1970s, from about 68 percent in 1971 to just 26 percent in 1978.[28] In particular, this decline was the result of the shrinking employment chances that affected aspiring teachers.[29] Whereas the baby boomers had created a dire need for more teachers in the 1960s, the sinking birthrate in the 1970s further exacerbated the drop in demand for teachers that followed once the baby boomers graduated. Nonetheless, at the end of the 1970s, a fifth of unemployed academics were engineers, but this percentage dropped considerably in the 1980s.[30]

Once the federal government changed hands in 1982, the Ministry for Education and Science tried to put the brakes on the rush to the academic professions by redirecting the focus toward vocational training and education. In contrast to the GDR, the West German state could use only "soft" steering instruments, such as the numerus clausus, providing insufficient funds to the universities, or offering vocational counseling, etc. The restructuring of the student loan program, known as Bafög, in 1982, which required full repayment of the amounts awarded, combined with the rising job risks for university graduates, led to tendencies of social closure at the universities.[31] Unlike in the GDR, however, the absolute number of university students in West Germany continued to rise. The age cohorts with higher birth rates had reached university age. In expectation that the number of students would decline afterward, the "opening resolution" of the minister-president of the universities in 1977 had allowed for a temporary "overload" until, as was assumed, the "pile of students" would "tunnel out at the bottom" when the cohorts with lower birth rates reached the universities. The image of a "doubled bottleneck," which had been circulating in the second half of the 1970s, reflected the two-edged problem that the job market could not absorb the growing number of graduates, just as the universities could not deal with the ongoing mass rush to enroll.[32] The conditions for studying at the universities worsened, not least because they had not been able to fully adjust their capacities to deal with mass enrollment earlier. It was not until the end of the 1980s that the federal and state governments responded to the lack of necessary funding for the West German universities with joint "special university programs." In the GDR, on the other hand, the student-teacher ratio improved at the universities thanks to a considerable increase in teaching positions despite the stable level of students. Since the degree programs themselves were more strictly organized than in West Germany, students took less time to complete their degrees, and they did not change majors as often; there were also fewer dropouts. As a result, the difference in the number of graduates between East and West Germany universities in the 1980s was much less than that between the total numbers of students.[33] As calculations have shown, the higher quotas for admission and enrollment in West Germany compared to the GDR from the 1970s onward were leveled out to some degree by the high number of dropouts and incomplete degrees at West German universities.[34]

An often forgotten aspect of this growth in education that appeared alongside the expansion of the universities and higher educational qualifications was the decrease in the percentage of young people who left the educational system without having completed their leaving certificates for school or vocational training. There were, of course, clear differences between East and West Germany here as well. At the beginning of the 1970s, almost everyone who left the POS and did not enroll in a further secondary school institution began an apprenticeship (even if it was only partial vocational training for the very few who dropped out early without a leaving certificate); in the 1980s, this still amounted to three-quarters of the youth in the GDR.[35] In terms of the overall level of qualification among employed individuals, the greatest difference between the two societies could be found at the very bottom level. Whereas only 13 percent of all employed individuals in the GDR had not completed formal vocational training of some kind in 1988, this figure was still almost a quarter in the FRG.[36] Likewise, in the mid-1980s, less than 2 percent of those who left the POS had not attained a leaving certificate of some kind in the GDR.[37] In West Germany, however, 7 percent of those who dropped out of the general education schools never finished any formal training or schooling at the beginning of the 1980s. Yet the weaker performance in the West also had something to do with the growing problem of trying to integrate pupils whose families had come from foreign countries; a third of these pupils left school without completing their diplomas in 1983.[38] The schools in the GDR were not confronted with the question of how to integrate the children of immigrants, especially because there were no such children. In sum, although West Germany had taken the lead over the GDR in the production of higher-qualified graduates, the East German educational and training system was ahead of the West when it came to reducing the number of people at the bottom of the qualifications scale.

In West Germany, one consequence of the growth of the educational system that began to become more apparent was the cascade-like process of crowding out that took place on the job market. Highly qualified individuals were pushing less-qualified individuals out of the running for jobs that they used to be able to get. Educational expansion therefore eliminated some older educational hurdles, but it also created new ones. The job market proved to be more able to take on the growing number of highly skilled and better qualified individuals than had often been assumed, and the sustained growth of the service sector benefited university graduates in particular. Yet, at the same time, the transformation of occupational structures lagged behind the dynamic of educational expansion, and the competition among applicants on the job market continued to be stiff up and down the ladder of the vocational training and employment systems.³⁹ In the GDR, however, the proportions between the qualification levels for both the educational and the employment systems remained frozen at the point they had reached in the early 1980s; the supply and demand in terms of qualifications was officially stabilized and balanced out through the state-run educational and employment planning agendas. Nonetheless, discrepancies between job classifications and the actual demands of a job were still quite prevalent.⁴⁰ This often meant that people were working in jobs that were below their qualifications. Accordingly, the tight formal link between education and employment was accompanied by an informal disassociation.

Equal Opportunity

Education policy sometimes took on the function of social policy in both German states, although at different points in time in each country. In its early phase, East German educational policy was clearly seen as a way to redistribute educational opportunities within society. Within the context of a conscious attempt to replace the old elites with loyal socialist cadres and in response to the massive migration to the West that took place before the Wall went up, the "children of workers and farmers" were able to compensate for the educational deficits associated with their social background by demonstrating their loyalty to the new system.⁴¹ As the SED dictatorship was becoming established, the "bourgeois monopoly on education" was broken through efforts such as the creation of "worker and farmer" faculties and positive discrimination policies in upper secondary schools.⁴² At the universities, the social composition of the faculty as well as the student body had lost its "bourgeois" character, a process that picked up pace in the late 1960s alongside a generational shift. According to official statistics, the "children of workers" accounted for 52.7 percent of the students studying at East German universities in 1958.⁴³ Even though the category of "workers" was very broadly defined to include the children of salaried employees and of parents who worked for the security forces or held party offices, this figure nonetheless indicates that the GDR was moving closer toward its goal of "proportional equal opportunity." The idea was that the ratio of educational participation among the social classes should correspond to their respective percentages of the population.⁴⁴ By the late 1960s, children of production workers accounted for almost 60 percent of the students enrolled in the section on philosophy and scientific socialism at the Karl-Marx-Universität in Leipzig.⁴⁵

Compared to the GDR and other Western European states, the unequal distribution of educational opportunities was addressed a bit later in

West Germany. Whereas the issue of inequality was still virtually absent from educational discourse in the 1950s, this topic became one of the major points of discussion in education policy debates over the course of the 1960s. The search for "untapped talent reserves," whose exploitation became a maxim not only of economic reason but also social justice, heightened public awareness for the striking inequalities within the educational system that ran along social, regional, gender, and religious lines. The worst aspect, at least in the minds of the public, seemed to be the social discrimination that accompanied educational differences. The percentage of workers' children among those attending *Gymnasium*, for example, had hardly changed for the better between the end of the Weimar Republic and the early 1960s.[46] As indicated by the micro census data from 1972, the percentage of pupils over fifteen years old attending *Gymnasium* from civil service families was 18 percent, although they only accounted for 7 percent of the total population of the same age (the children of salaried employees made up 35 percent and 19 percent, respectively). The children of skilled workers comprised 23 percent of the population in their age groups, but only 12 percent of *Gymnasium* attendees; the percentage of the children of unskilled workers within this age group was about the same, but they made up only 6 percent of *Gymnasium* pupils.[47] Many of the plans for reform or restructuring that dominated the debates over this period were justified on the basis that they would correct these social imbalances. Some of these ideas included more flexible rules of admission within the three tiers of the secondary school system, the increase in the support available to finance a university education, and the introduction of the *Gesamtschule* model of an integrated comprehensive school (which was the subject of a highly controversial debate on the reform of the school structures). Educational policy was regarded as an instrument that could be used to change the social structures of opportunity.

Meanwhile, the educational system in the GDR came to function less and less as a channel of social mobility and more and more as a machine of differentiated sociopolitical reproduction and positioning. In contrast to the earlier educational offensive in the GDR, whose primary aim had been to cultivate a new socialist intelligentsia, the new goal as of the 1970s was to train and educate a broad-based, well-qualified working class employed in production, and a small but politically reliable class of elites. The educational system in the GDR determined the social position that would be accorded to young people upon achievement of a certain level of education. For the country's decision-makers, there was no dissonance between individual needs and skills on the one hand and the socioeconomic necessities of the planned economy on the other. Young people were thus reduced to "social entities" whose sole purpose was to serve society.

The East German school system in fact produced social difference: the POS was socially mixed, but it was primarily supposed to be for working class children; the EOS, on the other hand, largely remained in the hands of a political, economic, and academic elite, who were the "inheritors of education"[48] or the children of university graduates and members of the civil service class—in short, those who were the bearers of legitimate culture. The EOS became the stronghold of the socialist intelligentsia and civil service. By performing very well at school and mastering the expected socialist habitus (i.e., the internationalization of behaviors, language, judgment, and *Weltanschauung*, as well as commitment in youth organizations), children from these families were able to gain access to university education. The "bourgeois monopoly on education" had therefore been replaced by the "socialist privileges of education."[49] The most important criteria for being admitted to the EOS were academic performance and loyalty to the system. The children of civil servants profited the most from the growing importance of these criteria. Despite the official discourse about equal educational opportunities, "equal opportunity" was no longer the regime's first priority. This reality clashed with the expectations of most families, especially since they were almost always told that the East German schools fostered upward social mobility. On the one hand, an increasing number of teenagers successfully completed the ten grades at the POS, yet the doors of the EOS kept closing in the face of the children of production workers at a higher rate. Thus, contrary to official propaganda, social reproduction processes came to play more of a role. The GDR hardly differed in this respect to other Western European countries such as West Germany or France, where the republican schools also rested on the "myth of equal opportunity" just as in East Germany.[50]

In West Germany, too, the politics of equal opportunity lost some of its shine in the mid-1970s. The main reason behind this shift was the realization that social background still continued to play a decisive role in educational opportunities, despite the expansion of the educational system. Interpretations that claimed that schools did little to change existing patterns of inequality (such as those put forth by James Coleman, Christopher Jencks, Pierre Bourdieu and Jean-Claude Passeron, etc.) began to set the tone within international debates over education.[51] This shift from optimism to skepticism about reforms in educational policy did not fail to reverberate in West Germany as well. The political fronts between the parties had hardened since about 1973, making it more and more difficult to push through educational reforms that addressed social policy matters in the complicated negotiation processes that surrounded educational policy like a tight net. Attempts made by social-liberal state governments—especially those in Hesse or North Rhine Westphalia—to counteract the socially selective nature of the existing school system by implementing the *Gesamtschule* model, only exacerbated the political polarization that had set in. Likewise, these efforts were met with considerable resistance among parents. On the other side of the political spectrum, the Christian Democrats distanced themselves from the idea of "equal opportunity" in their cultural policy platform in 1976. Instead, they spoke of their goal as *Chancengerechtigkeit,* which was a similar concept, but one that emphasized fairness rather than equality. This switch in terminology reflected a programmatic shift in emphasis away from the goal of reducing inequalities across the board to a stronger insistence on properly addressing the differences in aptitude and talent among individuals in schools.[52] The idea of "equal opportunity," its critics suspected, aimed to level out individual talents; in their eyes, the reform efforts that were being championed under this banner were actually part of an attempt to misuse the schools in order to achieve a change in social order.[53]

All in all, the expansion of education in West Germany up to the end of the 1980s improved the chances for all social groups to send their children to upper secondary schools, but there was still an imbalance in the system and no major structural changes had been achieved. The percentage of students in the first year of study among those of the same age and respective social background climbed between 1969 and 1989 by 16 percent (to 43 percent) for the children of civil servants, by 9 percent (to 24 percent) for the children of salaried employees, and by just 2 percent (to 5 percent) for the children of workers.[54] For the lower classes, the redistribution of structures of opportunity was felt most in the *Realschulen*. At the university level, the *Fachhochschulen* (universities of applied sciences) that were established at the beginning of the 1970s served as a channel to move up the social ladder. Although inequality was lessened to a certain extent, a variety of indications point to the fact that this trend stagnated in the 1970s and 1980s.[55] Even more than the occupational family background of an individual, it was the cultural capital of parents—a family's educational background—that retained its constitutive significance for the structures of social inequality governing access to education.[56] Of the four dimensions of inequality related to educational participation, namely social class, gender, religion, and region, it was definitely social background that persisted most strongly.

Additionally, the educational chances for boys and girls had become more equal, or even flipped in favor of girls, in both German states (albeit in a different time frame) as part of what might be termed a "silent revolution" in education. At the beginning of the 1970s, girls were still underrepresented at the *Gymnasium* level in West Germany. But just a decade later, they had taken the lead over the boys, accounting for 52.1 percent of *Gymnasium* students in 1990.[57] The situation was quite different at the *Realschulen*, where female pupils had been in the majority since the early postwar years. Indeed, it was not long before girls performed better than the boys in earning diplomas or leaving certificates. As early as 1981, 21.9 percent of girls left school with an *Abitur*, compared to only 16.3 percent of boys.[58] For a time, however, there still seemed to be a gender gap that had to be overcome at the university level. Even at the end of the 1980s, three in five first-year students at West German universities were still male.[59]

By contrast, East German women had profited much earlier from the SED's sponsorship of female education. Whereas it had not become a matter of fact that boys and girls would be taught in the same classes in West German *Gymnasien* until the 1960s,[60] coeducation had already been introduced in the 1950s in the GDR with the establishment of the *Einheitsschule*, which was a comprehensive school for all. Moreover, the gender-based differences that had been part of the curriculum were eliminated with the *Einheitsschule*. Girls were already overrepresented at the EOS level in the 1960s.[61] The percentage of female students at the universities grew from 27 to 48 percent just between 1965 and 1975, and from 31 to 57 percent for the technical colleges over the same period.[62] Ever since this point, the expansion of academia has been weighted heavily toward a high percentage of women.[63] Moreover, the GDR was more successful than West Germany in winning over women for technical professions. The so-called third university reform led to the dismantling of the homogeneous male culture that had come to define advanced and university-level technical education.[64] When the planned quota for the desired percentage of women at the engineering schools was not met despite intensive propaganda campaigns, this deficit mainly stemmed from the rather stubborn notions still held by families and the often negative experiences that women had in the production halls on instruction days.[65] In 1987, the percentage of women among students studying mathematics and natural sciences was about 31 percent in West Germany, but 51 percent in East Germany. The percentage of women among engineering students was just 12 percent in West Germany, compared to 20 percent in the technical sciences in the East.[66]

Scientification (*Verwissenschaftlichung*) and New Demands on the Canon of Knowledge

In 1971, the introduction to the *Materialien zum Bericht zur Lage der Nation*, a report on the state of the Federal Republic, determined that both of the German economic and social systems were "characterized by the increasing significance of science, research, education, and vocational training."[67] The "mastery of the scientific-technical revolution" (STR) was seen as the key to modernization in the GDR.[68] The West German counterpart to this STR was the "second industrial revolution." It was associated with the expectation that economic growth could be planned with the help of science, which meant that it was possible to ensure that this process was socially balanced. The challenges of a knowledge-based society on both sides of the Wall had fed into the conviction that further expansion of the educational system was necessary, and that it needed to be brought up to date with the current times.

The SED had already appointed a commission in 1963 that had identified a number of weaknesses in the educational system, especially with respect to knowledge of mathematics and natural science.[69] Since schooling was a state, not a federal, matter in West Germany, it is difficult to compare curricula of the different states with the centralized curricula of the East German POS that were introduced in 1959. Generally, East German elementary school children (grades 1 to 4) spent more time learning math than their West German counterparts in the 1980s. In the GDR, they spent 821 hours studying math, compared to 753 hours in Bavaria and 618 hours in North Rhine Westphalia. Furthermore, they were generally further along in terms of curricula than West German schoolchildren. For example, division and multiplication were already being taught in first grade in the POS.[70]

Under Honecker, the notion of the STR lost much of its significance. The SED regime shifted its focus to the primary goal of "building up a stock of workers according to plan,"[71] and especially to training well-qualified, highly skilled workers. At the same time, in the early 1970s, the main goal of many West German educational reformers was to improve the correlation between schooling and science at all levels. According to the "structural plan" put out by the German Educational Council in 1970, which was one of the key documents in the debates over education reform, the "conditions of life in modern society demand that teaching and learning processes become more scientific."[72] It was often said in West German debates on education at the time that the scientific determination of society (*Wissenschaftsbestimmtheit*) necessitated "science-based learning" in schools. Others, however, objected to this dominance of science and pleaded for a stronger emphasis on practical experience in the classroom.[73]

The *Verwissenschaftlichung* of education was one of the main goals behind the reform of the upper grade levels of the *Gymnasium* in 1976.[74] But this was also one aspect in which the trajectories of the West and East

German school systems diverged. Whereas the differentiation of teaching in the GDR, including more choices for pupils, was often discussed internally, it was hardly implemented. The introduction of the West German upper grade–level reform in 1976, however, marked a decisive turning point in the history of the *Gymnasium*. It did away with the traditional idea of a firm canon of subjects and knowledge, as well as the existing hierarchies between main subjects and electives. These features were supposed to be replaced by an introduction to basic scientific skills, learning by example, and more room for an individualized choice of subjects for each pupil. In general, the hope was that this reform would lead to a new, more strongly self-determined culture of learning focused on scientific propaedeutics. Nonetheless, the tension between individualization, the freedom of choice, and compulsory subjects continued to be controversial.

The "orientation toward science" that was supposed to infuse classroom materials, as well as methods of learning, was intended as a guiding principle for "all ages" and for every "stage of mental development."[75] It was also supposed to be implemented in the *Hauptschule*. Since the 1960s, the idea that the *Hauptschule* was supposed to offer a popular and practical form of education (*volkstümliche Bildung*) was considered to be passé. Practical learning with real-life situations was no longer thought to be adequate in order to be able to deal with the demands of the technical-scientific age.[76] Consequently, the expected level of education that pupils of the *Hauptschule* were supposed to receive rose considerably. Teachers specializing in particular subjects replaced general education teachers assigned to a class for all subjects, and more emphasis was put on teaching specific topics in specially equipped classrooms for different subjects. But this restructuring of the *Hauptschule* intersected with the tendency of more and more parents to send their children to a higher school than the *Hauptschule*. The *Hauptschule* thus lost its status as the "main school" of the three-tier system; over the long run, moreover, it has developed into the catch-all school for pupils with an immigrant background.[77] At the beginning of the 1970s, the majority of the pupils in a given age cohort still attended the *Hauptschule*, but enrollment began to dwindle more and more.

The university system also found itself facing new demands and challenges. As "sites of research," the universities in the GDR attracted an increasing amount of political attention, eventually becoming a key element of a strategy of steered economic modernization.[78] Together with the reform package introduced in the 1960s (including the third university reform of 1968), a strengthening of the ideological education of everyone involved in the universities was fostered and promoted, despite the persistence of a leftover bourgeois milieu in medicine and theology.

The East Germany universities were each supposed to develop a specific research profile. Scholarship was supposed to be subject to the primacy of the economy and organized in such a way that the universities could address "key national economic issues" and catch up with West Germany in technology development. There was also a push to integrate students more heavily in the research process. One important aspect of the SED's modernization project for the universities was the introduction of third-party financing for research at the beginning of the 1960s in the form of commercial contracts with socialist industry partners.[79] In addition to the economic focus and stronger research profiles, this contract financing of research was supposed to correlate the potential for innovation at the university with the specific needs of the socialist industry. A prime example of such a cooperative effort was the partnership between Friedrich-Schiller-Universität Jena and the Zeiss factories.[80] At the same time, these joint programs were supposed to make use of available state budget funds for steered industrial research projects within the framework of the "major socialist research program."[81] This clear focus on production in the organization of scientific research not only applied to the universities, but also to nonuniversity research at the Germany Academy of Sciences (DAW) and industry institutes.[82] Since the industrial combinates were more interested in short-term joint projects for specific applications, this led to a systematic neglect of fundamental research at the universities for a long time. Meanwhile, the DAW was able to develop itself into the main site for fundamental research, especially in physics and chemistry. Early in the 1970s, it seemed that the industrial focus within research and the contract projects were becoming victims of their complexity. By 1972, the SED once again made fundamental research at the GDR's universities a major political priority, and significant funding was provided to them from the national budget. Despite this ambitious attempt to modernize socialist science and research by coupling it with the increasing scientification of the industrial sector, the problems and deficits in the GDR's academic system mounted in the 1980s. Indeed, no further noteworthy changes were made before the collapse of the SED regime.

In West Germany, the debate about the overhaul of the university system was hardly less heated than the discussions over the reform of the upper secondary school level, although it proved to have much less of an effect over the long run. The passing of a new legislative framework, the *Hochschulrahmengesetz*, in 1976 seemed to open a new chapter in the troublesome history of the reform of university studies. Ever since the Wissenschaftsrat (Council of Science and Humanities), which was the most important advisory body for West German university policy, had suggested the adoption of a consecutive system for the degree programs, this issue had been a persistent topic in the debate over university reform in the Federal Republic. Since the task of reforming the system was put into the hands of joint study reform commissions on the state and federal levels, the foundation had been laid for a stronger involvement of the state in the reform of university studies. The plan was to increase the efficiency of teaching, streamline and reduce the content of the degree programs, and strengthen the praxis-related aspects of courses. The ultimate goal, of course, was to deal with the transition of the university from an elite to a mass institution.[83] Likewise, this new process was supposed to set the course for a national standardization of study regulations at the different universities. Despite the major efforts that were made, the results were rather mediocre, so the commission was dissolved in the 1980s. Given the continuing influx of students, however, the question of how to reduce the number of semesters that students were taking to finish their degrees remained on the agenda.

As systems of knowledge, both the East and West German educational institutions faced the question of how to deal with a whole series of new technological and scientific challenges. They had to respond to these overarching developments that affected both states with answers that were specific to their respective systems. For example, discussions over the place of environmental education and information technology instruction in the classroom, as well as the changes that needed to be made in curricula and instruction to accommodate them, had evolved in both Germanys since the 1970s.[84] The socialist educational system in the GDR was tasked with fostering "the development of a commitment and sense of responsibility toward the environment and environmental protection."[85] In 1975, the Akademie der Pädagogischen Wissenschaften (APW), which was an academy of pedagogical sciences, created a research group for "environmental education in general schools." Similarly, "ecological" working groups were set up as part of a program in the late 1970s and the "environment" appeared as a topic in the book *Vom Sinn unseres Lebens* (The meaning of our life) distributed by the SED regime. However, there were still only mediocre attempts to include environmental education in curricula at the end of the 1980s.

In West Germany, on the other hand, environmental education had made considerable inroads in school curricula in the 1980s. A joint recommendation issued by the cultural ministers of all of the federal states in 1980 had called on schools to educate pupils to be environmentally conscious. Topics such as "ecosystems" in biology, "the air" in chemistry, and "energy" in physics made up the core of the curricula elements dealing with environmental problems in the mid-1980s. Environmental topics also appeared in other subjects, although not much was done with environmental policy in instruction on politics and economy. A comprehensive empirical survey conducted in 1985, however, came to the conclusion that environmental education did not account for more than twenty to twenty-four hours of instruction per year, distributed over eight subjects. The authors of this study also posited that although this environmental education was often taught with a problem-based didactic approach, much of the instruction remained rather abstract, without much reference to real-life practice.[86]

Additionally, both German states had faced the same challenge presented by the computerization of society since the 1970s. The statement by the Politburo of the Central Committee of the SED on the consequences of the development of information technology and information processing technology for the educational system that was issued in November 1985 was the most comprehensive response by the GDR leadership to the computer revolution.[87] As of 1985/86, "computer science" was introduced as a new main subject for ninth grade and above. There was still the problem, however, that the schools did not have enough computers to support this initiative.[88] In the consultations between the state planning commission and the ministries of the national economic sectors, it became clear that it would take until at least 1992 to introduce computer science instruction across the board. The decision was made to grant priority to the EOS; computer science was also supposed to be taught at the POS, but as a partial course in "computing and information technology" in the subject "Introduction to Socialist Production." In West Germany, the Federal and State Commission for Educational Planning and Research Promotion (Bund-Länder-Kommission für Bildungsplanung und Forschungsförderung) developed a "Comprehensive Concept for Information Technology Education" in the mid-1980s that was supposed to guide the different state ministries of education in developing corresponding programs.[89] Distinctions were made between "basic information technology instruction" for all pupils that was incorporated into the curricula of the existing subjects, the creation of a separate subject of "computer science" mostly for the last two grades (*Oberstufe*) at the *Gymnasium* level, the inclusion of job-related information technology instruction at the vocational schools that was tailored to specific occupations, and degree courses in computer science at the university level.[90] The state ministers of education had initially approved instruction in computer science for the *Gymnasium Oberstufe* in 1972. Yet the necessary hardware could not be found in sufficient number at most schools until the 1980s, when the computer industry began to donate computers to schools on a larger scale. As of 1989, approximately 72 percent of all schools had enough computers for an entire class, most of which had been installed in special computer rooms; usually, however, two to three children had to share one computer during lessons.[91] But just because schools had computers does not mean that they were regularly used in classroom teaching.[92] An expert report written for the Special Committee on the Future of Education Policy of the German Bundestag came to the conclusion at the end of the 1980s that West Germany had achieved a standard comparable to that of other advanced industrial societies in Western Europe in terms of computer science education, although the same could not be said for the use of modern media and transmission systems.[93]

Civic and Political Education

From the very beginning, both German school systems placed a high priority on civic and political education. In the 1970s, hefty public debates erupted over this subject in West Germany. With the move of some protagonists to adopt a definition of civic education highly informed by conflict theories that focused on emancipation, self-determination, and critical thinking abilities, the tone of the debate took on an unprecedented edginess. Especially the "General Guidelines for Social Studies Instruction" for the lower secondary school level[94] in Hessen had created quite a political stir since 1972. It established a new subject that was supposed to integrate what used to be the separate subjects of civics, history, and geography. Critics such as Hermann Lübbe and Thomas Nipperdey accused the authors of these guidelines of pursing a one-sided agenda that was interested only in revealing particular aspects of power, class, and domination in order to expose social inequality and situations of conflict while ignoring the necessary basic consensus about the political order as well as the general commitment to freedom, rule of law, and tolerance that underpinned society.[95] In particular, they objected to the comparatively uncritical presentation of the GDR as a neutral alternative system. The fight over these guidelines in countless newspaper articles, discussion events, letters to the editor, parliamentary debates, and pamphlets contributed to the sore losses suffered by the SPD in the election in Hesse in 1974, as well as to the replacement of the state's minister of education, Ludwig von Friedeburg. In the end, a distinctly milder version of these guidelines actually took effect.[96]

As in Hesse, the guidelines proposed for political science instruction in North Rhine-Westphalia in 1973/74 were also pulled into the whirlwind of political debate. Here again, critics charged that the understanding of politics adopted in this proposal was too narrowly focused on a critique of social constraints and power relations, with the ultimate goal of emancipation. They also argued that this approach ignored the legitimacy of the constitutional institutions and the rules of the game in a democratic state governed by the rule of law. In the face of political and media opposition—and deterred by what had happened in Hesse—Minister President Kühn asked the ministry of culture to revise the guidelines before the coming elections and to soften the language and the political tone of its contents.[97] Afterward, the conflict over civic and political education seemed to die down a bit. The "Beutelsberger Consensus," which was founded by civic education experts in 1976 and called for a "ban on strong-arming" as well as paying attention to controversial positions, seemed to indicate a pragmatic turn in civic education that would also survive in the less turbulent 1980s.

In the GDR, one of the main goals of educational policy was to increase the political efficacy of schooling and education, which concretely meant the intensification of ideological indoctrination and discipline through the FDJ (Free German Youth),[98] Communist youth groups, and the Pioneer organizations.[99] However, the country's political leadership had long since recognized that the reality of East German society no longer coincided with its ideological convictions.[100] For this reason, even after the Eighth SED Party Congress in 1971, the ideologization of the education system was pushed forward,[101] culminating, for example, in the introduction of military instruction in the POS in 1978.[102] The SED demanded the involvement of not only schools but also universities and colleges in its ideological indoctrination. Its appeals to this end appeared constantly in the statements of the Politburo of the SED, in official speeches, and in the talks delivered at pedagogical congresses. This omnipresent discourse, however, should not be interpreted as merely paying lip service to doctrine, because it was a real expression of a constant paternalist concern on the part of the SED leadership, which was not able to think of the country's youth as an autonomous and specific group.[103] The East German youth was supposed to serve the political project of the founding generation. On the basis of studies conducted by the Central Institute for Research on Youth (Zentralinstitut für Jugendforschung) in Leipzig and the working materials of the APW, the Ministry of Education regularly made note of serious and long-term deficits in socialist ideological education. In particular, it identified a weak level of social commitment among the youth (especially those in the workers' milieu[104]) in the youth organizations, which it identified as a problem. The extreme politicization of educational content and the constant expectations that the youth should be mobilized had an opposite effect than what was intended. Above all, this led to a kind of depoliticization and ideological demobilization, which can be read as a political response against the regime itself. Indeed, the great difficulty that a political youth organization such as the FDJ had in trying to mobilize young people for the socialist cause in the 1970s and 1980s resulted from an irrevocable loss of trust in the official institutions of the regime. Ideological cohesion disappeared in the 1970s, regardless of all the ways in which the youth still had to concede to the expectations of the SED regime, for example by participating in the ritualized flag-raising ceremonies commemorating anti-fascism or celebrating labor day on the first of May. In strongly politicized institutions such as the schools and the universities, it was basically necessary to pretend to play along. School children as well as university students had to get used to playing a certain social role and to do what was expected of them. Yet young people in the GDR also learned to test the limits of political expression, but without crossing the line. As time went on, they also sought more opportunities for individual and collective experiences outside official frameworks. Sociologists and psychologists in the GDR also realized in the 1970s that peer groups could function as a positive secondary instance of socialization.[105] In West Germany at the time, by contrast, sociologists stressed the significance of peer groups for the personal development of the individual.[106]

Asymmetric Turning Points, Cotransformation, and Europeanization (1989–2002)

Without a doubt, the events of 1989/90 marked a clear turning point for the entire educational system in the GDR.[107] West German education hardly changed at all, however, so that this was very much an asymmetrical caesura. The "peaceful school revolution" in the GDR was a very decisive experience for East German educators in schools and universities because it marked a twist in the careers of many, as well as an important break in the role of the educational system as a whole.[108] Despite all the criticism directed against the *Erziehungsdiktatur*, newly established independent interest groups, such as the one called Democratic Education and Schooling, wanted to preserve some of the structural elements of the GDR school system, including the idea of a uniform comprehensive school.[109] As the transformation process progressed, however, little remained of what had been discussed (equal opportunity, reform of pedagogy, *Einheitsschule*) around the country and even at the round tables in Berlin, Erfurt, Leipzig, and Rostock. Nonetheless, reunification did pave the way for a mutual cotransformation process over the next fifteen years.[110] To a large extent, this process was spurred on by international frames of reference and the influence of European cooperation at the political level.[111]

"Build a new school system, but don't do everything like the West." (Kurt Biedenkopf)

Reunification in the 1990s marked the failure of the GDR as a political project. Its achievements in the educational sector were therefore no longer seen as legitimate in either East or West Germany. The justified criticism of the ideological indoctrination and militarization of the education system in the GDR had disqualified it within the international context, which meant that there was no room to make finer points about its merits or pitfalls. Even within the Joint Education Commission FRG/GDR, which had been set up in May 1990 as the advisory body tasked with coordinating the cooperation and merger of the two educational systems, the main goal of the GDR negotiators soon became the "alignment of the school system with the states of the Federal Republic."[112] The GDR *Einheitsschule*, apart from a few significant finer points, was replaced by the tiered West German school system, which meant that approximately 5,000 POS had to be restructured. Likewise, countless preschools and daycare facilities, which had been attended by almost 80 percent of the children in the GDR between one and three years of age (compared to 1.6 percent in West Germany),[113] were closed down.[114] The new federal states largely, but not entirely, modeled their school systems after those in West Germany, and in particular the system in their respective partner states, which assisted the new states in the East in creating new administrative structures. At the same time, the new states cautiously took advantage of some of the freedom afforded by the federalist nature of the educational system in the Federal Republic to develop their own solutions and models for reform. Between 1991 and 1993, new laws on education and schooling in the East German federal states were passed. In Saxony, the *Hauptschule* and the *Realschule* were put together into the "middle school" (*Mittelschule*), in Saxony-Anhalt into the "secondary school" (*Sekundarschule*), and in Thuringia into the "regular school" (*Regelschule*). The *Abitur* in twelfth grade (instead of thirteenth grade as in West Germany) was reintroduced in East Germany, and Saxony also introduced the subject of *Wirtschaft-Technik-Haushalt* (economy-technology-household), which resembled the GDR subject that was called "practical work." All told, this process resulted in the creation of "very different school systems adapted to regional circumstances that were only comparable in terms of their move away from the *Einheitsschule*."[115] State legislators established the legal framework for the new systems, but the actual implementation of these reforms had to take place in the schools themselves. This process led to unprecedented experiments with new administrative norms, as well as new content and methods in the classroom in the early 1990s.

After the Wende, most East German teachers found themselves in a precarious situation. The system of coordinates around which many East German teachers had built their lives collapsed in their faces. Many of them were forced to acquire new teaching credentials (switching from teaching Russian to teaching French, for example), but all of them had to adapt to new curricula. Some of them were also pushed out because of their previous ideological commitment, or they were "de-stasified" (entstasifiziert).[116]

In the 1990s, East German teachers had to reshape their identity as a professional group.[117] Their commitment to education and their high level of expertise in their respective subjects made them a valuable resource for mastering the post-reunification transition. Yet this transformation process was more or less difficult depending on the school subject in question. Their function as communicators of knowledge and norms, which was part of their professional identity as teachers, played a key role in helping them to cope with the system change and its effect on their personal lives. From the perspective of these teachers, education was no longer "partisan" in any way, but rather it entailed the dissemination of general norms and values of living together as a society.

The Transition and Liquidation Process for the University System in the New Federal States

Reunification became a far-reaching, if not dramatic, turning point for the East German universities. The unification treaty foresaw the dismantling of the Academy of Building, the Agricultural Academy, and, most importantly, the Academy of Sciences (with its sixty institutes and about twenty-four thousand employees). The Institutes for the Education of Teachers were dissolved, and the pedagogical colleges were either shut down or integrated into other universities. While many research institutes also closed their doors, some were given new names and continued to operate. The old East German centers for cancer, cardiovascular, and molecular biology research, for example, were brought together to establish the Max-Delbrück Center for Molecular Medicine in Berlin in 1992, but a fourth of the staff was let go in the process.

As was done in the school system, representatives of the East and West German universities had already begun to meet and talk in early 1990. During the academic year 1991/92, moreover, numerous well-known experts from West German universities accepted visiting professor appointments at East German universities as part of a concerted effort to ensure the restructuring of course offerings in the East. Despite all the issues that arose with changing course requirements, the students at East German universities were still able to finish their degrees. This necessitated a major effort on the part of all those involved, especially since the local infrastructures of the East German universities left much to be desired. The state of the universities in the East was even worse than that of the West German universities suffering from major underfunding.

At a relatively early point, the East German universities began an internal evaluation and selection process. In order to work through these structural and personnel changes, Structure and Appointment Commissions (*Struktur- und Berufungskomissionen,* or SBK) were founded, as had been recommended by the Wissenschaftsrat. Renowned and experienced West German professors chaired these commissions. In many disciplines—especially the humanities and social sciences—these evaluations led to a liquidation process. These personnel changes were a particular painful dimension of the overhaul of the East German universities because it spelled the end of many academic careers. Only a select few of those who were already older than forty were able to catch up with the state of international research and publish their own findings in the relevant academic forums.[118] This liquidation process therefore led to a radical exchange of elites: most of the East German professorships were given to young West German academics as the universities were reconstructed; East Germans did not really have much chance of being appointed until the next hiring generation.[119] As a result, the majority of East German university professors and instructors faced a rather abrupt end to their academic careers. Most of the East Germans who were permitted to stay as mid-level assistant professors and lecturers in their respective departments were given only temporary contracts. At the Humboldt University in Berlin, for example, only about 10 percent of mid-level academics who had been employed as of 1993 still had a position when the first round of temporary contracts expired in 1998.[120] In light of this situation, many of the younger mid-career academics chose to leave the university and seek jobs in the private sector.

The Cotransformation of the School System in the Old Federal States

When the new federal states opted for a two-tiered school system rather than just copying the West German schools system, they turned out to be ahead of the game rather than behind. Naturally, it was much easier to conflate the *Hauptschule* and the *Realschule* into one school in the East, without keeping the separate tracks, than in the West, where there was a more stubborn structural and political resistance to such measures. In the new federal states, moreover, the legacy of the integrated GDR school system still played a considerable role. Since 80 percent of POS pupils had earned a diploma equivalent to that of the mid-level *Realschule* qualification in the West, it was not likely that the idea of setting up a *Hauptschule* would have been welcomed in the East.[121] Yet the two-track model that was adopted was primarily a response to two fundamental social processes at work in both East and West Germany. On the one hand, demographic changes stemming from dropping birth rates (which bottomed out for a while in the new federal states after 1989) factored into this consideration. On the other hand, the spiral of expectations that had been unleashed by the expansion of the education system meant that not only the educational background of the parent generation but also the aspirations of these parents to send their children to higher-level schools increased (as has been clearly reflected in parental decisions related to school choice). The sinking birthrate, for example, indicated that it was going to become even more difficult to maintain both a *Hauptschule* and a *Realschule*, especially in rural areas. Moreover, rising educational aspirations continued to feed the ongoing exodus from the *Hauptschule*, which was in danger of becoming nothing more than a catch-all school for the *Bildungsverlierer*, the pupils who lost out in the educational system.[122] Not only with the two-track system, but also the twelve-grade model, the *Abitur* exams centralized at the state level, the expansion of full-day schools, the call for more educational preschools, and the push to better promote highly talented pupils, the old federal states found themselves confronted with reform aspects that were rather familiar to the politicians and educationalists who knew about the institutional structures of the defunct GDR.

The two-pillar model that was developed speaks to a process of cautious cotransformation: at the beginning of the new millennium, the school structures in the Western federal states, too, began to change.[123] The majority of the old federal states set up a second pillar in their schools systems at the stage of the *Sekundarstufe I* (secondary education first stage), that stands alongside the first, inviolable pillar of the *Gymnasium*. Whereas the *Gymnasium* has proved to be the sole immutable commonality within the federalist jungle of the school system, the *Hauptschule* and the *Realschule* have been moved under one roof in the old states, which was similar to what had happened in the former East. Many of these new schools still offer separate tracks that lead to different diplomas or leaving certificates. Since they were not introduced in a uniform way across the different states, however, they have appeared in several variations and under different names depending on the state. This two-tiered system was touted as a trial compromise that aimed to make peace in the trenches of the hefty conflict between the proponents and opponents of integrated and tiered schools systems. By 2012, just two decades after reunification, only five of the federal states still had independent *Hauptschulen*.[124]

Europeanization: The Bologna Reforms and the Transformation of the Universities

The transformation of the higher education system in the new federal states was not seen as a chance to take on a large-scale reform of the universities in all of Germany. Yet the voices in favor of a more comprehensive reform of the universities grew louder and louder in the 1990s.[125] The most important impetus behind these calls for more extensive changes ultimately came from the European level. In 1998, the education ministers of France, England, Germany, and Italy announced the joint goal of creating a European higher education area; a year later in Bologna, the education ministers from twenty-nine European states committed to developing comparable degree programs in Europe by 2010. This marked the beginning of what has come to be known as the "Bologna process" or the "Bologna reforms." Germany introduced a system of study that followed the Anglo-Saxon model, which consisted of a two-stepped degree sequence, first the three- or four-year bachelor's degree and then the master's degree. As part of the transition process, the German universities had to go through a new accreditation process for their courses of study, and the degree programs had to be fundamentally reorganized according to modules, credit points, interim exams, etc. Higher education policy, at about the same time as school policy, began to become much more international in its outlook as a result of the debates over globalization and competitiveness.[126]

The Bologna process accomplished a series of reforms over a short period of time that otherwise would never have made it past the strong wall of resistance within the universities. The main goal of the higher education policy makers was to cut down on the time it took for students to receive their degrees. For a long time, complaints had circled around the lengthy amount of time that German university graduates needed to complete their degrees, which also meant that they entered the job market at an older age than many of their counterparts in other parts of the world. Proponents of the Bologna process argued that the German universities finally had to come to terms with the fact that they had become institutions of mass higher education as the educational system had expanded. In this sense, the Bologna reforms presented a new European argument in favor of an old solution for an even older problem.

The nature of university study was supposed to change in fundamental ways as the result of this process. But, as of the late 1990s, the German universities found themselves facing an even more extensive transformation process that fed into a deeper caesura marked by a plethora of changes that can only be touched upon briefly here.[127] For one thing, the university admissions process was changed, putting the selection and admission of applicants primarily in the hands of the university itself. The universities also became more responsible for their own management: the position of the presidents or rectors was strengthened while the self-administrating bodies lost power, and new "university councils," comprised of external members, were created as supervisory boards. As part of the reform of German federalism, the federal government was pushed out of its role in financing the building of the universities and legislating the higher education system.[128] The Excellence Initiative that was started by the federal and state governments in 2005 paved the way for state-regulated competition among the universities to achieve elite status, which would then entitle them to additional funds as a reward for top university research. Autonomy, competition, and differentiation have thus become the new lodestars of Germany's university policy firmament.

Internationalization: PISA and Its Consequences

The media attention that surrounded the "PISA Shock" at the beginning of the twenty-first century resembled the Sputnik shock of 1957 and the West German debates over the "education catastrophe" in the mid-1960s. In the PISA report, which compared the performance of pupils in thirty-one OECD countries, Germany came in at twenty-first place in reading skills, and it was also in the lowest third for mathematics and natural sciences.[129] The sociologist Wolf Lepenies commented on the PISA results in the *Süddeutsche Zeitung* rather ironically: "It's a shame that the GDR no longer exists. If it did, it would have scored better than the Federal Republic in the school test for the OECD countries called the PISA study."[130] The results of the supplemental PISA studies comparing the states within Germany detected a considerable gap in performance between the different states, and especially between north and south. Saxony and Thuringia did relatively well in comparison, but the rest of the former Eastern states performed poorly.[131] In addition to demonstrating the low average skill levels of pupils, the PISA study also brought to the light the tight link between social background and the acquisition of skills.[132]

After about two decades of fairly static school policy, the PISA study put the public spotlight on educational policy in the country. The study's results did not create nearly as much of a stir in any of the other participating countries.[133] In Germany, however, the school policy makers of the states were bombarded with criticism; the Kultusministerkonferenz (KMK), which is the standing assembly of the state educational ministries, felt compelled to respond in its guise as the national coordinating body for school policy. This sudden, newly awakened interest in educational policy opened a window of opportunity for reforms. The PISA report sparked a strong interest in the question of which factors in the "winning states" had contributed to their success. Education experts and policy makers trekked in great herds to the Scandinavian countries and especially Finland, the much-admired "PISA winner," in order to take a look at the particularities of the respective school systems. It did not take long before an entire catalog of reforms were put on the table.[134] The introduction of national "education standards" stood at the heart of these plans. Once passed by the ministries of culture, the new standards were supposed to be obligatory for all states. The standards determined the skills that pupils were supposed to have acquired in a given subject by the end of each year of schooling.[135] Not only was the entire school system now subject to continual evaluation, but also comparative testing was supposed to assess the performance of the single schools and individual pupils according to these standards. "Quality assurance" thus became the name of the game in school policy, and educational standards and performance evaluations were seen as two sides of the same coin.

The federal government also took advantage of this opportunity to become more involved in school policy, although the federal states were still very wary of large-scale federal initiatives. The Red-Green coalition government, for example, set aside four billion euros to fund an increase in full-day schooling options. Such efforts were accompanied by other reforms, such as the introduction of a centralized *Abitur* at the level of the federal states, which had already been put in place in four of the five new states, as well as in Bavaria, Saarland, and Baden-Württemberg, in addition to cutting the length of the *Gymnasium* attendance to eight years. By instituting a centralized *Abitur*, the idea was to ensure the comparability of the leaving certificates across the different states, and even the SPD-led states went from being opponents to proponents of this reform. Shortening the length of the *Gymnasium* track, on the other hand, was sympathetic to the finance ministers who saw a chance to save money. The eight-year *Abitur*, however, was not very popular in the West and was therefore quickly repealed in many places.[136] All told, a noticeably larger number of changes were made in a relatively short period compared to what had been done in the two decades prior to PISA. In subsequent PISA studies, German pupils slowly began to improve their position in the rankings and the social disparities have become less pronounced.[137]

Conclusion

The history of German-German education after 1945 was shaped by increasing disentanglements. Whereas West Germany reestablished the basic coordinates of the educational system of the Weimar Republic after 1945, education in the SBZ (Sowjetische Besatzungszone, Soviet Occupation Zone)/GDR departed from this shared German legacy, sometimes very quickly. The history of education in Germany remained nonetheless—albeit in an asymmetrical way—interwoven at different levels. These links ranged from the shared cultural legacy that could still be found in the canon of knowledge for schools, the exodus of highly qualified individuals from the East to the West before the Wall went up in 1961, or the persistence of some institutional commonalities. Moreover, the two educational systems were interrelated as a result of the mutual observation and oppositional demarcation processes that existed between the two countries. Likewise, both educational systems had to respond to overarching challenges that arose in the decades that followed with answers that were specific to their own systems. These common challenges included the issue of how to guarantee equal educational opportunities or how to deal with the anticipated and unexpected consequences of educational expansion. Similarly, schools and universities on both sides of the Wall found themselves grappling with the tension between talent differentiation and uniformity, as well as the correlation between education and the job market.

Furthermore, there was a political dimension to these educational entanglements. These political aspects appeared clearly in the discourse on education in the late 1950s and 1960s that honed in on the *Bildungswettlauf* (educational contest)[138] between East and West Germany, which was itself a part of the wider framework of the international and German-German rivalry between the systems. Yet, especially in the educational boom years of the 1960s and early 1970s in West Germany, the desire not to fall behind the educational systems of the other Western industrialized states proved to be even stronger. The quantitative parameters of educational expansion put about by the OECD, which were seen as a factor of economic growth, had a considerable influence in the Federal Republic.

In the 1970s, both German educational systems came to a turning point, albeit in different ways. Educational policy in both states lost much of its character as an instrument of social reform. If we consider that the East had sought to provide a superior school model by "breaking the monopoly on education" of the middle classes, this change in character was even more true for the GDR than for West Germany. Education was seen as less and less of a lever for regulating social changes, and less and less as a space for the dissemination and redistribution of social opportunity. Rather than focusing on privileging the "children of workers and farmers," the GDR moved toward the self-recruitment of a socialist intelligentsia. While educational participation continued to increase in West Germany, the brakes were put on educational expansion in the GDR (as measured by the chances of completing an *Abitur* and going on to a university). In this respect, East Germany deviated from the general international trend. A different logic also governed the steering mechanisms in both systems. In the East, educational opportunities for individuals were subordinated to the economic planning calculations within the employment system. In West Germany, by contrast, the social demand for education took priority over any predictions about labor demands, and the coordination of the employment and educational systems was supposed to be left up to the compensation and adjustment processes of the job market. Until its collapse, though, the GDR did stay in the lead when it came to women's education.

Moreover, changing economic and demographic frameworks shifted the basic coordinates of educational policy. Education lost ground to social policy on the political policy agendas in both German states.[139] Over time, education also lost a considerable amount of significance as a form of demarcation between the systems. The successes of the expansive GDR education policies in the 1960s that were seen as a leap in modernization were no longer a barb in the side of the West German system because it had begun to catch up with the expansion of its own educational system. West Germans proponents of the comprehensive school system, however, were still better off politically if they refrained from making references to the ideologically contaminated Einheitschule model in the GDR and opted to point out the merits of the numerous other integrated school systems that had been established in the West. In education, the 1980s were generally marked by a "phase of immobility and cooling off" on both sides of the Wall, which differed from the ongoing modernization efforts that could be found in a number of Anglo-Saxon states as well as countries in Northern and Western Europe.[140]

The educational rivalry between East and West came to an end in 1989 with the peaceful revolution in the GDR. The East German educational system was in tatters and fell into *damnatio memoriae* in public discourse. Despite the often painful restructuring of the educational system in the new federal states, many East German teachers and instructors were able to pick up the pieces and overcome this turning point in their lives thanks to their professional ethos.

Three transformation processes took place in the two decades after reunification that had different scopes as well as directional coordinates. First, the East German educational system was radically restructured along West German lines, but the federalist culture of education allowed for the development of an independent concept of institutional order in the new federal states. This process was followed a decade later by the beginnings of a structural reorganization process in a number of West German states in which the West looked to the East instead of the other way around. The clearest indication of this reversal was the spread of the two-pillar school model. Since the turn of the millennium, moreover, the European and international frames of reference have become all the more important for the German educational system. The Bologna process that was initiated in 1999 with the active engagement of the German federal government ultimately led to a far-reaching structural reorganization of the higher education system. Judged on the basis of the PISA shock and its consequences, international frames of reference have become all the more important in Germany, and school policy reform agendas are now highly informed by successful models from other countries around the world.

Emmanuel Droit is professor of international history at the Institute of Political Studies of the University of Strasbourg. His research focuses on the sociopolitical history of the GDR, Eastern European political polices during the Cold War, and the transnational history of the Eastern Bloc. His publications include *Vorwäts zum neuen Menschen ? Die sozialistische Erziehung in der DDR 1949–1989* (2014).

Wilfried Rudloff is a research associate at the Academy of Science and Literature Mainz. His main research interests include the history of the welfare state and the history of education since 1945.

NOTES

1. Aleida Assmann, *Arbeit am nationalen Gedächtnis: Eine kurze Geschichte der deutschen Bildungsidee* (Frankfurt a. M., 1993), 9.

2. Helmut Fend, *Neue Theorie der Schule: Einführung in das Verstehen von Bildungssystemen*, 2nd, revised ed. (Wiesbaden, 2008), 49ff.
3. Jürgen Raschert, "Bildungspolitik im kooperativen Föderalismus: Die Entwicklung der länderübergreifenden Planung und Koordination des Bildungswesens der Bundesrepublik Deutschland," in *Bildung in der Bundesrepublik Deutschland*, ed. Max-Planck-Institut für Bildungsforschung (Stuttgart, 1980), 1:103–215.
4. Gert Geißler, "Schulreform von oben: Bemerkungen zum schulpolitischen Herrschaftssystem in der SBZ/DDR," in *Erinnerung für die Zukunft II: Das DDR-Bildungssystem als Geschichte und Gegenwart* (Ludwigsfelde-Struveshof, 1997), 49–60; Gert Geißler and Ulrich Wiegmann, *Pädagogik und Herrschaft in der DDR: Die parteilichen, geheimdienstlichen und vormilitärischen Erziehungsverhältnisse* (Frankfurt a. M., 1996), 152ff.
5. Dorothee Wierling, "Die Jugend als innerer Feind. Konflikte in der Erziehungsdiktatur der sechziger Jahre," in *Sozialgeschichte der DDR*, ed. Hartmut Kaelble, Jürgen Kocka, and Hartmut Zwahr (Stuttgart, 1994), 404–25.
6. Gerhart Neuner, *Sozialistische Persönlichkeit—ihr Werden, ihre Erziehung* (Berlin-Ost, 1975).
7. Emmanuel Droit, *Vers un homme nouveau? L'éducation socialiste en RDA (1949–1989)* (Rennes, 2009) [German translation: *Vorwärts zum neuen Menschen? Die sozialistische Erziehung in der DDR* (Cologne, 2014)].
8. Dietmar Waterkamp, "Berufsbildung," in *Handbuch der deutschen Bildungsgeschichte*, vol. 6: *1945 bis zur Gegenwart. Zweiter Teilband: Deutsche Demokratische Republik und neue Bundesländer*, ed. Christoph Führ and Carl-Ludwig Furck (Munich, 1998), 257.
9. See Wolfgang Mitter, "Wandel und Kontinuität im Bildungswesen der beiden deutschen Staaten," in Wolfgang Mitter, *Schulen zwischen Reform und Krise. Zu Theorie und Praxis der vergleichenden Bildungsforschung* (Cologne, 1987), 283ff.; see also Heinz-Elmar Tenorth, "Die Bildungsgeschichte der DDR—Teil der deutschen Bildungsgeschichte?," in *Bildungsgeschichte einer Diktatur. Bildung und Erziehung in SBZ und DDR im historisch-gesellschaftlichen Kontext*, ed. Sonja Häder and Heinz-Elmar Tenorth (Weinheim, 1997), 80–81.
10. See Oskar Anweiler, "Grundzüge der Bildungspolitik und der Entwicklung des Bildungswesens seit 1945," in *Vergleich von Bildung und Erziehung in der Bundesrepublik Deutschland und in der Deutschen Demokratischen Republik*, ed. Oskar Anweiler (Cologne, 1990), 11–33; Oskar Anweiler, "Ergebnisse und offene Fragen," in ibid., 685–706; Anne Rohstock, "Ist Bildung Bürgerrecht? Wege zur Bildungsexpansion im doppelten Deutschland," in *Das doppelte Deutschland. 40 Jahre Systemkonkurrenz*, ed. Udo Wengst and Hermann Wentker (Bonn, 2008), 135–59; Gert Geißler, "Bildungs- und Schulpolitik," in *Deutsche Zeitgeschichte von 1945 bis 2000. Gesellschaft—Staat—Politik. Ein Handbuch*, ed. Clemens Burrichter, Detlef Nakath, and Gerd-Rüdiger Stephan (Berlin, 2006), 911–46; Ingrid Miethe and Birthe Kleber, "'Bildungs-

wettlauf zwischen West und Ost'—Ein retrospektiver Vergleich," in *Bildung, Gesellschaftstheorie und soziale Arbeit*, ed. Rita Braches-Chyrek, Dieter Nelles, Gertrud Oelerich, and Andreas Schaarschuch (Opladen, 2013), 155–74.

11. Michael Werner and Bénédicte Zimmermann, "Vergleich, Transfer, Verflechtung. Der Ansatz der Histoire croisée und die Herausforderung des Transnationalen," *Geschichte und Gesellschaft* 28 (2002): 607–36.
12. Gero Lenhardt and Manfred Stock, *Bildung, Bürger, Arbeitskraft. Schulentwicklung und Sozialstruktur in der BRD und der DDR* (Frankfurt a. M., 1997), 202ff.
13. Helmut Köhler and Gerhard Schreier, "Statistische Grunddaten zum Bildungswesen," in Anweiler, *Vergleich*, 132.
14. Helmut Köhler and Peter Lundgreen, *Datenhandbuch zur deutschen Bildungsgeschichte*, vol. 7: *Allgemein bildende Schulen in der Bundesrepublik Deutschland 1949–2010* (Göttingen, 2014), 81, 306–307, 328.
15. Gert Geißler, *Schulgeschichte in Deutschland. Von den Anfängen bis in die Gegenwart* (Frankfurt a. M., 2013), 991.
16. Arbeitsgruppe Bildungsbericht am Max-Planck-Institut für Bildungsforschung, *Das Bildungswesen in der Bundesrepublik Deutschland. Strukturen und Entwicklungen im Überblick* (Reinbek bei Hamburg, 1994), 212ff., 487–488, and 494ff.
17. Hartmut Kaelble, *Sozialgeschichte Europas. 1945 bis zur Gegenwart* (Munich, 2007), 392 and 403.
18. Dietmar Waterkamp, *Handbuch zum Bildungswesen der DDR* (Berlin, 1987), 40ff.
19. Roland Köhler, *Geschichte des Hochschulwesens der Deutschen Demokratischen Republik (1961–1980)*, part 1: *Überblick* (Berlin-Ost, 1987), 79.
20. Helmut Köhler and Manfred Stock, *Bildung nach Plan? Bildungs- und Beschäftigungssystem in der DDR 1949 bis 1989* (Opladen, 2004), 61.
21. Christoph Oehler, *Hochschulentwicklung in der Bundesrepublik Deutschland seit 1945* (Frankfurt a. M., 1989), 36.
22. Manfred Kaiser, "Zur Flexibilität von Hochschulausbildungen. Ein Überblick über den Stand der empirischen Substitutionsforschung," *Mitteilungen aus der Arbeitsmarkt- und Berufsforschung* 8 (1975): 203–21.
23. Siegfried Baske, "Die Erweiterte Oberschule in der DDR," in Anweiler, *Vergleich*, 215.
24. See Hedwig Rudolph and Rudolf Husemann, *Hochschulpolitik zwischen Expansion und Restriktion. Ein Vergleich der Entwicklung in der Bundesrepublik Deutschland und der Deutschen Demokratischen Republik* (Frankfurt a. M., 1984).
25. Winfried Schlaffke, *Akademisches Proletariat?* (Osnabrück, 1972).
26. See Hans-Peter Blossfeld, *Bildungsexpansion und Berufschancen. Empirische Analysen zur Lage der Berufsanfänger in der Bundesrepublik* (Frankfurt a. M., 1985), 98ff.

27. Manfred Tessaring, "Beschäftigungssituation und -perspektiven für Hochschulabsolventen," *Aus Politik und Zeitgeschichte* 50 (1989): 14–24.
28. Jens Naumann, "Entwicklungstendenzen des Bildungswesens der Bundesrepublik Deutschland im Rahmen wirtschaftlicher und demographischer Veränderungen," in Max-Planck-Institut für Bildungsforschung, *Bildung*, 1:88.
29. Beate Pieper, *Vom Lehrermangel zur Lehrerarbeitslosigkeit. Bildungspolitik als geschichtliches Dilemma* (Münster, 1984), 135ff.
30. Dirk Hartung and Beate Krais, "Studium und Beruf," in *Das Hochschulwesen in der Bundesrepublik Deutschland*, ed. Ulrich Teichler (Weinheim, 1990), 191; Friedemann Stooß, "Der Akademiker-Arbeitsmarkt bis zum Jahr 2000," in *Studium—und danach?*, ed. Egbert Kahle and Hermann J. Weihe (Frankfurt a. M., 1988), 7.
31. Oskar Anweiler, "Bildungspolitik," in *Geschichte der Sozialpolitik in Deutschland seit 1945*, vol. 7: *1982–1989: Bundesrepublik Deutschland. Finanzielle Konsolidierung und institutionelle Reform*, ed. Manfred G. Schmidt (Baden-Baden, 2005), 592ff.
32. Gerhard E. Ortner, "Gestaltung und Steuerung der Tertiären Bildung: Problemeinführung und Problemstrukturierung," in *Die deutsche Hochschule zwischen Numerus clausus und Akademikerarbeitslosigkeit. Der doppelte Flaschenhals*, ed. Ulrich Lohmar and Gerhard E. Ortner (Hannover, 1975), 18–19; Hansgert Peisert, *Das Hochschulsystem in der Bundesrepublik Deutschland. Funktionsweise und Leistungsfähigkeit* (Stuttgart, 1979), 70 and 118.
33. Helmut Köhler, "Qualifikationsstruktur und Hochschulentwicklung in der Deutschen Demokratischen Republik und der Bundesrepublik Deutschland," *Mitteilungen aus der Arbeitsmarkt- und Berufsforschung* 28 (1995): 104.
34. Klaus Klemm and Michael Weegen, "Wie gewonnen, so zerronnen. Einige Anmerkungen zum Zusammenhang von Bildungsexpansion und Akademikerangebot," *Jahrbuch der Schulentwicklung* 11 (2000), 129–50.
35. Arbeitsgruppe Bildungsbericht, *Das Bildungswesen*, 578.
36. Köhler and Stock, *Bildung*, 50; Rainer Geißler, *Die Sozialstruktur Deutschlands*, 2nd ed. (Opladen, 1996), 251–52.
37. Helmut Köhler, *Datenhandbuch zur deutschen Bildungsgeschichte*, vol. 9: *Schulen und Hochschulen in der Deutschen Demokratischen Republik 1949–1989* (Göttingen, 2008), 37.
38. Heike Solga, "Jugendliche ohne Schulabschluss und ihre Wege in den Arbeitsmarkt," in *Das Bildungswesen in der Bundesrepublik Deutschland. Strukturen und Entwicklungen im Überblick*, ed. Kai S. Cortina et al. (Reinbek bei Hamburg, 2003), 712–713.
39. Rudolf Tippelt and Bernd von Cleve, *Verfehlte Bildung? Bildungsexpansion und Qualifikationsbedarf* (Darmstadt, 1995), 150ff.
40. Köhler and Stock, *Bildung*, 74ff.; Geißler, *Sozialstruktur*, 252; Fred Klinger, "Wirtschaftsentwicklung, Beschäftigungssystem und Bildungswesen," in Anweiler, *Vergleich*, 68; Waterkamp, *Handbuch*, 190.

41. Heike Solga, *Auf dem Weg in eine klassenlose Gesellschaft? Klassenlagen und Mobilität zwischen Generationen in der DDR* (Berlin, 1995).
42. Ingrid Miethe and Martina Schiebel, *Bildung—Biografie—Institution. Die Arbeiter-und-Bauern-Fakultäten der DDR* (Frankfurt a. M., 2008).
43. Oskar Anweiler, "Bildungspolitik," in *Geschichte der Sozialpolitik seit 1945*, vol. 8: *1949–1961: Deutsche Demokratische Republik. Im Zeichen des Aufbaus des Sozialismus*, ed. Dierk Hoffmann and Michael Schwartz (Baden-Baden, 2004), 585.
44. Rainer Geißler, "Entwicklung der Sozialstruktur und Bildungswesen," in Anweiler, *Vergleich*, 91.
45. GESIS, B 6 146, Student 69, 1969, unpag.
46. Helmut Köhler, *Bildungsbeteiligung und Sozialstruktur in der Bundesrepublik. Zu Stabilität und Wandel der Ungleichheit von Bildungschancen* (Berlin, 1992), 78.
47. Luitgard Trommer-Krug, "Soziale Herkunft und Schulbesuch," in Max-Planck-Institut für Bildungsforschung, *Bildung*, 1:229 and 256.
48. Pierre Bourdieu, *Les héritiers. Les étudiants et la culture* (Paris, 1964).
49. Heike Solga, "Bildungschancen in der DDR," in Häder and Tenorth, *Bildungsgeschichte*, 293.
50. Pierre Bourdieu and Jean-Claude Passeron, *La reproduction. Eléments pour une théorie du système d'enseignement* (Paris, 1970); see also François Dubet, *Les places et les chances. Repenser la justice sociale* (Paris, 2010).
51. James Coleman, *Equality of Educational Opportunity* (Washington, 1966); Christopher Jencks, *Inequality: A Reassessment of the Effect of Family and Schooling in America* (New York, 1972); Bourdieu and Passeron, *La reproduction*.
52. "'Freiheit, Solidarität, Gerechtigkeit.' Grundsatzprogramm 1978," in Jörg-Dieter Gauger, *Kontinuität und Wandel—Bildungsbegriff und Bildungssystem in den Grundsatzerklärungen der CDU zwischen 1945 und 2011* (St. Augustin, 2011), 223.
53. See also Lutz-Rainer Reuter and Bernhard Muszynski, *Bildungspolitik. Dokumente und Analysen* (Opladen, 1980), 22.
54. Geißler, *Sozialstruktur*, 261.
55. Walter Müller, "Erwartete und unerwartete Folgen der Bildungsexpansion," in *Die Diagnosefähigkeit der Soziologie* (KZSS Sonderheft 38), ed. Jürgen Friedrichs, M. Rainer Lepsius, and Karl Ulrich Mayer (Opladen, 1998), 91; Walter Müller and Dietmar Haun, "Bildungsungleichheit im sozialen Wandel," *Kölner Zeitschrift für Soziologie und Sozialpsychologie* 46 (1994), 1–42; Walter Müller and Dietmar Haun, "Bildungsexpansion und Bildungsungleichheit," in *Einstellungen und Lebensbedingungen in Europa*, ed. Wolfgang Glatzer (Frankfurt a. M., 1993), 225–68.
56. Bernhard Schimpl-Neimanns, "Soziale Herkunft und Bildungsbeteiligung. Empirische Analysen zu herkunftsspezifischen Bildungsungleichheiten zwischen 1950 und 1989," *Kölner Zeitschrift für Soziologie und Sozialpsychologie* 52 (2000): 659ff. and 664.

57. Köhler and Lundgreen, *Datenhandbuch*, 7:242–244.
58. Köhler and Lundgreen, *Datenhandbuch*, 7:314.
59. Köhler and Schreier, "Statistische Grunddaten," 140.
60. Rita Wirrer, *Koedukation im Rückblick. Die Entwicklung der rheinland-pfälzischen Gymnasien vor dem Hintergrund pädagogischer und bildungspolitischer Kontroversen* (Essen, 1996).
61. Dorothee Wierling, *Geboren im Jahr Eins. Der Jahrgang 1949 in der DDR. Versuch einer Kollektivbiographie* (Berlin, 2002), 269.
62. Köhler and Stock, *Bildung*, 46.
63. Köhler, "Qualifikationsstruktur und Hochschulentwicklung," 99.
64. Karin Zachmann, "Frauen für die technische Revolution. Studentinnen und Absolventinnen Technischer Hochschulen in der SBZ/DDR," in *Frauen arbeiten. Weibliche Erwerbstätigkeit in Ost- und Westdeutschland nach 1945*, ed. Gunilla-Friederike Budde (Göttingen, 1997), 121–56.
65. Emmanuel Droit, "Die 'Arbeiterklasse' als Erzieher? Die Beziehung zwischen Schulen und Betrieben in der DDR (1949–1989)," in *Die ostdeutsche Gesellschaft. Eine transnationale Perspektive*, ed. Emmanuel Droit and Sandrine Kott (Berlin, 2006), 35–52.
66. Köhler and Schreier, "Statistische Grunddaten," 140f.
67. Deutscher Bundestag, *Materialien zum Bericht zur Lage der Nation 1971* (Bonn, 1971), 26.
68. Hubert Laitko, "Produktivkraft, Wissenschaft, wissenschaftlich-technische Revolution und wissenschaftliches Erkennen. Diskurse im Vorfeld der Wissenschaftswissenschaft," in *Denkversuche. DDR-Philosophie in den 60er Jahren*, ed. Hans Christoph Rauh and Peter Ruben (Berlin, 2005), 459–540.
69. Oskar Anweiler, "Bildungspolitik," in *Geschichte der Sozialpolitik in Deutschland seit 1945*, vol. 9: *1961–1971: Politische Stabilisierung und wirtschaftliche Mobilisierung*, ed. Christoph Kleßmann (Baden-Baden, 2006), 561–608.
70. Heinz Griesel, "Vergleich grundlegender Konzeptionen der Mathematikdidaktik in der BRD und in der DDR," *Zentralblatt für Didaktik und Mathematik* 35, no. 4 (2003), 166–71.
71. Wierling, *Geboren im Jahr Eins*, 119.
72. Deutscher Bildungsrat, *Strukturplan für das Bildungswesen. Empfehlungen der Bildungskommission* (Stuttgart, 1970), 33.
73. Klaus Klemm, Hans-Günter Rolff, and Klaus-Jürgen Tillmann, *Bildung für das Jahr 2000. Bilanz der Reform, Zukunft der Schule* (Reinbek bei Hamburg, 1985), 39–44; for the critical voices see *Mut zur Erziehung: Beiträge zu einem Forum am 9./10. Januar 1978 im Wissenschaftszentrum* (Bonn-Bad Godesberg, 1978), 163–65 (Thesis 8).
74. Werner Zimmermann and Jörg Hoffmann, *Die gymnasiale Oberstufe. Grundzüge—Reformkonzepte—Problemfelder* (Stuttgart, 1985); Hans-Werner Fuchs, *Gymnasialbildung im Widerstreit. Die Entwicklung des Gymnasiums seit 1945 und die Rolle der Kultusministerkonferenz* (Frankfurt a. M., 2004).
75. Deutscher Bildungsrat, *Strukturplan*, 33.

76. Sabine Engelhardt, *Von der Volkstümlichen Bildung zum Wissenschaftsorientierten Lernen. Untersuchungen zum Wandel des Bildungsbegriff,* Ph.D. diss. (University of Göttingen, 1988); Hans Göckel, *Volkstümliche Bildung? Versuch einer Klärung* (Weinheim, 1964).
77. Fritz Kraft, "Die Hauptschule in Nordrhein-Westfalen," in *Die Hauptschule. Erfahrungen—Prozesse—Bilanz,* ed. Udo Franz and Michael Hoffmann (Kronberg, 1975); Jürgen Bennack, "Der Lehrplan der Volks- und Hauptschule in der Bundesrepublik Deutschland nach 1945—aufgezeigt am Beispiel Nordrhein-Westfalen," in *Geschichte und Gegenwart des Lehrplans,* ed. Rudolf W. Keck and Christian Ritzi (Baltmannsweiler, 2000), 317–41.
78. Tobias Schulz, *Sozialistische Wissenschaft. Die Berliner Humboldt-Universität (1960–1975)* (Cologne, 2010).
79. Köhler, *Geschichte des Hochschulwesens.*
80. Uwe Hoßfeld, Thomas Kaiser and Heinz Mestrip, eds., *Hochschule im Sozialismus. Studien zur Geschichte der Friedrich-Schiller-Universität Jena (1945–1990)* (Cologne, 2007).
81. Schulz, *Sozialistische Wissenschaft,* 274.
82. Ibid., 273.
83. George Turner, *Hochschule zwischen Vorstellung und Wirklichkeit. Zur Geschichte der Hochschulreform im letzten Drittel des 20. Jahrhunderts* (Berlin, 2001), 116f.; Ulrich Schreiterer, *Politische Steuerung des Hochschulsystems. Programm und Wirklichkeit der staatlichen Studienreform 1975–1986* (Frankfurt a. M., 1989).
84. Wolfgang Hörner, "Informationstechnische Bildung," in Anweiler, *Vergleich,* 620–37.
85. Rudolf Hundt, "Pädagogische Aspekte des Umweltschutzes," *Hercynia N. F.* 13, no. 2 (1976): 193.
86. Dieter Bolscho, "Umwelterziehung in den Lehrplänen der allgemeinbildenden Schulen," *Die Deutsche Schule* 71 (1979): 663–70; Dieter Bolscho, "Umwelterziehung in der Schule. Ergebnisse einer empirischen Studie," *Die Deutsche Schule* 81 (1989): 61–72; Reinhold E. Lob, "Umwelterziehung in deutschen Schulen: Eine Bilanz nach 20 Jahren," *Die Deutsche Schule* 91 (1999): 102–13; Günter Eulefeld, Dietmar Bolscho, and Jürgen Rost, *Praxis der Umwelterziehung in der Bundesrepublik Deutschland. Eine empirische Untersuchung* (Kiel, 1988); Günter Eulefeld et al., *Entwicklung und Praxis schulischer Umwelterziehung in Deutschland. Ergebnisse empirischer Studien* (Kiel, 1993).
87. Hans-Jürgen Fuchs and Eberhard Petermann, eds., *Bildungspolitik in der DDR 1966–1990: Dokumente* (Berlin, 1991), 251–63.
88. *Informatik und Allgemeinbildung. Materialien der 6. Plenartagung der APW am 28. März 1988.* Info APW 2/1988.
89. Bund-Länder-Kommission für Bildungsplanung und Forschungsförderung, *Gesamtkonzept für die informationstechnische Bildung* (Bonn, 1987).
90. Hörner, "Informationstechnische Bildung."

91. Manfred Lang, *Computer in Schule und Lehrerbildung. IEA-Studie 1992 in westdeutschen Bundesländern* (Kiel, 1995), 24f.; see also Klaus-Henning Hansen and Manfred Lang, *Computer in der Schule. Ergebnisse der deutschen IEA-Studie, Phase I, 1989* (Kiel, 1993).
92. Oskar Anweiler, "Bildungspolitik," in *Geschichte der Sozialpolitik*, vol. 7: *1982–1989*, 583.
93. Winfried Sommer, "Neue Medien/Informations- und Kommunikationssysteme und Bildungswesen—für die Bildungspolitik des Bundes nutzbare internationale Erfahrungen und Informationen," in *Zukünftige Bildungspolitik—Bildung 2000. Schlußbericht der Enquete-Kommission des 11. Deutschen Bundestages und parlamentarische Beratung am 26. Oktober 1990*, ed. Deutscher Bundestag (Bonn, 1990), 439.
94. Der Hessische Kultusminister, *Rahmenrichtlinien Sekundarstufe I Gesellschaftslehre* (Wiesbaden, 1972); see also Gerd Köhler and Ernst Reuter, eds., *Was sollen Schüler lernen? Die Kontroverse um die hessischen Rahmenrichtlinien für die Unterrichtsfächer Deutsch und Gesellschaftslehre* (Frankfurt a. M. 1973).
95. Thomas Nipperdey and Hermann Lübbe, *Gutachten zu den Rahmenrichtlinien Sekundarstufe I Gesellschaftslehre des Hessischen Kultusministers* (Bad Homburg, 1973).
96. Waltraud Schreiber, *Schulreform in Hessen zwischen 1967 und 1982. Die curriculare Reform der Sekundarstufe I. Schwerpunkt Geschichte in der Gesellschaftslehre* (Neuried, 2005).
97. Hans-Helmuth Knütter and Klaus Dieter Ziehmann, "Die Richtlinien für den Politik-Unterricht in Nordrhein-Westfalenm," in *Der Streit um die politische Bildung*, ed. Peter Gutjahr-Löser and Hans-Helmuth Knütter (Munich and Vienna, 1975), 123–52; Jorg Gemein and Hartmut Kiensel, eds., *Politik und Unterricht. Wer bestimmt, was Schüler lernen? Richtlinien für den Politik-Unterricht in der Diskussion* (Essen, 1975); Walter Gerschler, "Reaktionen der Öffentlichkeit. Dokumentation der Presseberichte über die Richtlinien für den Politikunterricht," in *Zwischen Politik und Wissenschaft. Politik in der öffentlichen Diskussion*, ed. Walter Gagel and Rolf Schörken (Opladen, 1975), 105–32.
98. On the early history of the FDJ, see Peter Skyba, *Vom Hoffnungsträger zum Sicherheitsrisiko. Jugend in der DDR und Jugendpolitik der SED 1949–1961* (Cologne, 2000).
99. On the early history of the pioneer organization, see Leonore Ansorg, *Kinder im Klassenkampf. Die Geschichte der Pionierorganisation von 1948 bis Ende der 1950er Jahre* (Berlin, 1997); see also Heinz-Elmar Tenorth, Sonja Kudella, and Andreas Paetz, *Politisierung im Schulalltag der DDR. Durchsetzung und Scheitern einer Erziehungsambition* (Weinheim, 1996).
100. Mark Fenemore, *Sex, Thugs and Rock'n'Roll: Teenage Rebels in Cold-War East Germany* (New York, 2007); see also Marc-Dietrich Ohse, *Jugend nach*

dem Mauerbau. Anpassung, Protest und Eigensinn (DDR 1961–1974) (Berlin, 2003).
101. Erich Honecker, Bericht des ZK der SED an den VIII. Parteitag der SED (Berlin, 1971).
102. Geißler and Wiegmann, Pädagogik und Herrschaft; Christian Sachse, Aktive Jugend—wohlerzogen und diszipliniert. Wehrerziehung in der DDR als Sozialisations- und Herrschaftsinstrument (1960–1973) (Münster, 2000).
103. Walter Friedrich, Peter Förster, and Kurt Starke, eds., Das Zentralinstitut für Jugendforschung Leipzig 1966–1990. Geschichte, Methoden, Erkenntnisse (Berlin, 1999).
104. Wiebke Janssen, Halbstarke in der DDR. Verfolgung und Kriminalisierung einer Jugendkultur (Berlin, 2010).
105. Emmanuel Droit, "Les 'peer groups' dans l'espace public en RDA: de la stigmatisation à la reconnaissance? (1960–1980)," Histoire@Politique. Politique, culture, société 7 (2009): 9.
106. Sabine Hoffmann, "Freundschaftsgruppen," Elternhaus und Schule 4 (1982): 18–19.
107. Heike Knaack, "Schule im Umbruch. Unterrichtende und Unterricht in den neuen Bundesländern während und nach der Wiedervereinigung," Deutschland Archiv 36 (2003): 296–303.
108. On the typology of turning points, see Martin Sabrow, "Zäsuren in der Zeitgeschichte," Version 1.0, Docupedia-Zeitgeschichte, 3 June 2013, http://docupedia.de/zg/sabrow_zaesuren_v1_de_2013.
109. Matthias-Domaschk-Archiv, unpag.
110. Philipp Ther, Die neue Ordnung auf dem alten Kontinent: Eine Geschichte des neoliberalen Europa (Berlin, 2014).
111. On the former Eastern Bloc countries, see Dorota Dakowska, with Ioana Cîrstocea and Carole Sigman, "Les transformation des espaces académiques centre est-européens depuis 1989," Revue d'études comparatives Est-Ouest 45, no. 1 (2014), 5–19.
112. Gabriele Köhler, Anders sollte es werden. Bildungspolitische Visionen und Realitäten der Runden Tische (Cologne, 1999), 24.
113. Karl Zwierner, Kinderkrippen in der DDR (Munich, 1994).
114. Sandrine Kott, "Die Kinderkrippe," in DDR-Erinnerungsorte, ed. Martin Sabrow (Munich, 2009).
115. Axel Gehrmann, "Gewandelte Lehrerrolle in Ost und West? Erste Ergebnisse aus vier Befragungen (1994–1996–1998–1999)," in Transformation in der ostdeutschen Bildungslandschaft, ed. Hans Döbert, Hans-Werner Fuchs, and Horst Weishaupt (Opladen, 2002), 64.
116. Alexander von Plato, "Entstasifizierung im Öffentlichen Dienst der neuen Bundesländer nach 1989," Jahrbuch für historische Bildungsforschung 5 (1999): 313–42.
117. Doris Köhler, "Professionelle Pädagogen? Zur Rekonstruktion beruflicher Orientierungs- und Handlungsmuster ostdeutscher Lehrer der Kriegsgene-

ration," in *Konflikt und Konsens: Transformationsprozesse in Ostdeutschland*, ed. Martin Brussig, Frank Ettrich, and Raj Kollmorgen (Opladen, 2003), 169–92.
118. Dieter Zimmer, "Sag mir, wo die Forscher sind," *Die Zeit*, no. 32, 31 July 1992.
119. Roland Bloch and Peer Pasternack, *Die Ost-Berliner Wissenschaft im vereinigten Berlin. Eine Transformationsfolgenanalyse* (Halle-Wittenberg, 2004).
120. Oliver Günther and Sibylle Schmerbach, "Deutsche Universitäten im Umbruch—20 Jahre nach der Wende," in *Deutschland 20 Jahre nach dem Mauerfall. Rückblick und Ausblick*, ed. Franz Keuper and Dieter Puchta (Wiesbaden, 2010), 410.
121. Benjamin Edelstein and Rita Nikolai, "Strukturwandel im Sekundarbereich. Determinanten schulpolitischer Reformprozesse in Sachsen und Hamburg," *Zeitschrift für Pädagogik* 59 (2013): 488.
122. Gabriele Köhler, *Diskurs und Systemtransformation. Der Einfluss diskursiver Verständigungsprozesse auf Schule und Bildung im Transformationprozess der neuen Bundesländer* (Göttingen, 2009), 409–10 (re. Thüringen); Markus Weilandt, *Schule der Frühaufsteher. 20 Jahre Bildungspolitik in Sachsen-Anhalt* (Cologne, 2011), 36ff.; Edelstein and Nikolai, "Strukturwandel" (re. Sachsen); Hans-Werner Fuchs, *Bildung und Wissenschaft seit der Wende. Zur Transformation des ostdeutschen Bildungssystems* (Opladen, 1997), 173ff.
123. Klaus Hurrelmann, "Das Schulsystem in Deutschland: Das 'Zwei-Wege-Modell' setzt sich durch," *Zeitschrift für Pädagogik* 69 (2013): 455–68; Klaus Hurrelmann, "Thesen zur Entwicklung des Bildungssystems in den nächsten 20 Jahren," *Die Deutsche Schule* 105 (2013): 305–21.
124. Klaus-Jürgen Tillmann, "Das Sekundarschulsystem auf dem Weg in die Zweigliedrigkeit," *Pädagogik* 64, no. 5 (2012): 8–12.
125. Turner, *Hochschule*; George Turner, *Von der Universität zur university. Sackgassen und Umwege der Hochschulpolitik seit 1945* (Berlin, 2013).
126. Thomas Walter, *Der Bologna-Prozess. Ein Wendepunkt europäischer Hochschulpolitik?* (Wiesbaden, 2006); Philipp Eckardt, *Der Bologna-Prozess. Entstehung, Strukturen und Ziele der europäischen Hochschulreformpolitik* (Norderstedt, 2005); Johanna Witte, "Die deutsche Umsetzung des Bologna-Prozesses," *Aus Politik und Zeitgeschichte* 48 (2006): 21–27.
127. Christine Burtscheidt, *Humboldts falsche Erben. Eine Bilanz deutscher Hochschulreform* (Frankfurt a. M., 2011).
128. See also Gerd F. Hepp, *Bildungspolitik in Deutschland. Eine Einführung* (Wiesbaden, 2011), 226–64.
129. Deutsches PISA-Konsortium, *PISA 2000. Basiskompetenzen von Schülerinnen und Schülern im internationalen Vergleich* (Opladen, 2001).
130. Wolf Lepenies, "Mittelmaß in Europas Mitte," *Süddeutsche Zeitung*, 8/9 December 2001.
131. Deutsches PISA-Konsortium, *PISA 2000—Die Länder der Bundesrepublik Deutschland im Vergleich* (Opladen, 2002).

132. Jürgen Baumert and Gundel Schümer, "Familiäre Lebensverhältnisse, Bildungsbeteiligung und Kompetenzerwerb," in Deutsches PISA-Konsortium, *PISA 2000. Basiskompetenzen*, 323–410.
133. Dennis Niemann, "Deutschland—Im Zentrum des PISA-Sturms," in *Das PISA-Echo. Internationale Reaktionen auf die Bildungsstudie*, ed. Philipp Knodel et al. (Frankfurt a. M., 2010).
134. Klaus-Jürgen Tillmann et al., *PISA als bildungspolitisches Ereignis. Fallstudien in vier Bundesländern* (Wiesbaden, 2008).
135. Hubert Ertl, "Educational Standards and the Changing Discourse on Education: The Reception and Consequences of the PISA Study in Germany," *Oxford Review of Education* 32 (2006): 619–34.
136. Rainer Bölling, *Kleine Geschichte des Abiturs* (Paderborn, 2010), 119–31.
137. Eckhard Klieme et al., "PISA 2000–2009: Bilanz der Veränderungen im Schulsystem," in *PISA 2009. Bilanz nach einem Jahrzehnt*, ed. Eckhard Klieme et al. (Münster, 2010); Timo Ehmke and Nina Jude, "Soziale Herkunft und Kompetenzerwerb," in Klieme et al. *PISA 2009*, 231–54.
138. Hermann Gross, *Internationaler Wettbewerb in Wissenschaft und Bildungswesen zwischen West und Ost* (Essen-Bredeney, 1960); Leonhard Froese, Rudolf Haas, and Oskar Anweiler, *Bildungswettlauf zwischen West und Ost* (Freiburg, 1961); Hartmut Vogt, *Bildung für die Zukunft. Entwicklungstendenzen im deutschen Bildungswesen in West und Ost* (Göttingen, 1967); see also Oskar Anweiler, "Bildungswettstreit zwischen West und Ost—Schlagwort und Realität," *Die Deutsche Schule* 58 (1966): 721–29.
139. See Ralph Jessen, "Massenausbildung, Unterfinanzierung und Stagnation. Ost- und Westdeutsche Universitäten in den siebziger und achtziger Jahren," in *Gebrochene Wissenschaftskulturen. Universitäten und Politik im 20. Jahrhundert*, ed. Michael Grüttner et al. (Göttingen, 2010), 271f.
140. Jürgen Baumert, Kai S. Cortina, and Achim Leschinsky, "Grundlegende Entwicklungen und Strukturprobleme im allgemeinbildenden Schulwesen," in Cortina, *Das Bildungswesen*, 53.

BIBLIOGRAPHY

Ansorg, Leonore. *Kinder im Klassenkampf: Die Geschichte der Pionierorganisation von 1948 bis Ende der 1950er Jahre*. Berlin: Akademie Verlag, 1997.

Anweiler, Oskar. "Bildungspolitik." In *Geschichte der Sozialpolitik in Deutschland seit 1945*, vol. 7: *1982–1989: Bundesrepublik Deutschland. Finanzielle Konsolidierung und institutionelle Reform*, ed. Manfred G. Schmidt, 563–600. Baden-Baden: Nomos, 2005.

———. "Bildungspolitik." In *Geschichte der Sozialpolitik in Deutschland seit 1945*, vol. 8: *1949–1961: Deutsche Demokratische Republik. Im Zeichen des Aufbaus des Sozialismus*, edited by Dierk Hoffmann and Michael Schwartz, 553–88. Baden-Baden: Nomos Verlag, 2004.

———. "Bildungspolitik." In *Geschichte der Sozialpolitik in Deutschland seit 1945*, vol. 9: *1961–1971: Politische Stabilisierung und wirtschaftliche Mobilisierung*, edited by Christoph Kleßmann, 561–608. Baden-Baden: Nomos Verlag, 2006.

———. "Bildungswettstreit zwischen West und Ost—Schlagwort und Realität." *Die Deutsche Schule* 58 (1966): 721–29.

———. "Ergebnisse und offene Fragen." In *Vergleich von Bildung und Erziehung in der Bundesrepublik Deutschland und in der Deutschen Demokratischen Republik*, edited by Oskar Anweiler, 685–706. Cologne: Verlag Wiss. und Pol., 1990.

———. "Grundzüge der Bildungspolitik und der Entwicklung des Bildungswesens seit 1945." In *Vergleich von Bildung und Erziehung in der Bundesrepublik Deutschland und in der Deutschen Demokratischen Republik*, edited by Oskar Anweiler, 11–33. Cologne: Verlag Wiss. und Pol., 1990.

Arbeitsgruppe Bildungsbericht am Max-Planck-Institut für Bildungsforschung. *Das Bildungswesen in der Bundesrepublik Deutschland: Strukturen und Entwicklungen im Überblick*. Reinbek bei Hamburg: Rowohlt, 1994.

Assmann, Aleida. *Arbeit am nationalen Gedächtnis: Eine kurze Geschichte der deutschen Bildungsidee*. New York: Campus, 1993.

Bartz, Olaf. *Der Wissenschaftsrat: Entwicklungslinien der Wissenschaftspolitik in der Bundesrepublik Deutschland 1957–2007*. Stuttgart: Franz Steiner Verlag, 2007.

Baske, Siegfried. "Die Erweiterte Oberschule in der DDR." In *Vergleich von Bildung und Erziehung in der Bundesrepublik Deutschland und in der Deutschen Demokratischen Republik*, edited by Oskar Anweiler, 210–17. Cologne: Verlag Wiss. und Pol., 1990.

Baumert, Jürgen, Kai S. Cortina, and Achim Leschinski. "Grundlegende Entwicklungen und Strukturprobleme im allgemeinbildenden Schulwesen." In *Das Bildungswesen in der Bundesrepublik*, edited by Jürgen Baumert, Kai S. Cortina, and Achim Leschinski. 52–147. Berlin: Rowohlt Verlag, 2008.

Baumert, Jürgen, and Gundel Schümer. "Familiäre Lebensverhältnisse, Bildungsbeteiligung und Kompetenzerwerb." In *PISA 2000. Basiskompetenzen*, edited by Deutsches PISA-Konsortium, 323–410. Opladen: Leske + Budrich, 2001.

Bennack, Jürgen. "Der Lehrplan der Volks- und Hauptschule in der Bundesrepublik Deutschland nach 1945—aufgezeigt am Beispiel Nordrhein-Westfalen." In *Geschichte und Gegenwart des Lehrplans*, edited by Rudolf W. Keck and Christian Ritzi, 317–41. Baltmannsweiler: Schneider Verlag, 2000.

Blessing, Benita. *The Antifascist Classroom: Denazification in Soviet-Occupied Germany, 1945–1949*. New York: Palgrave, 2006.

Bloch, Roland, and Peer Pasternack. *Die Ost-Berliner Wissenschaft im vereinigten Berlin: Eine Transformationsfolgenanalyse*. Halle-Wittenberg: HoF-Arbeitsbericht, 2004.

Blossfeld, Hans-Peter. *Bildungsexpansion und Berufschancen: Empirische Analysen zur Lage der Berufsanfänger in der Bundesrepublik*. New York: Campus Verlag, 1985.

Bölling, Rainer. *Kleine Geschichte des Abiturs*. Paderborn: Ferdinand Schöningh, 2010.

Bolscho, Dieter. "Umwelterziehung in den Lehrplänen der allgemeinbildenden Schulen." *Die Deutsche Schule* 71 (1979): 663–70.

———. "Umwelterziehung in der Schule: Ergebnisse einer empirischen Studie." *Die Deutsche Schule* 81 (1989): 61–72.

Bourdieu, Pierre. *Les héritiers: Les étudiants et la culture*. Paris: Ed. de Minuit, 1964.

Bourdieu, Pierre, and Jean-Claude Passeron. *La reproduction. Eléments pour une théorie du système d'enseignement*. Paris: Ed. de Minuit, 1970.

Bund-Länder-Kommission für Bildungsplanung und Forschungsförderung. *Gesamtkonzept für die informationstechnische Bildung*. Bonn: BLK Geschäftsstelle, 1987.

Burtscheidt, Christine. *Humboldts falsche Erben: Eine Bilanz deutscher Hochschulreform*. Frankfurt a. M.: Campus Verlag, 2011.

Coleman, James. *Equality of Educational Opportunity*. Washington, DC: John Hopkins University, 1966.

Dakowska, Dorota, with Ioana Cîrstocea and Carole Sigman. "Les transformation des espaces académiques centre est-européens depuis 1989." *Revue d'études comparatives Est-Ouest* 45, no. 1 (2014): 5–19.

Deutscher Bildungsrat. *Strukturplan für das Bildungswesen*. Stuttgart: Klett-Cotta, 1970.

Deutscher Bundestag. *Materialien zum Bericht zur Lage der Nation 1971*. Bonn: Bundesministerium für innerdeutsche Beziehungen, 1971.

Deutsches PISA-Konsortium. *PISA 2000. Basiskompetenzen von Schülerinnen und Schülern im internationalen Vergleich*. Opladen: Leske + Budrich, 2001.

———. *PISA 2000—Die Länder der Bundesrepublik Deutschland im Vergleich*. Opladen: Leske + Budrich, 2002.

Dubet, François. *Les places et les chances: Repenser la justice sociale*. Paris: Seuil, 2010.

Droit, Emmanuel. "Die 'Arbeiterklasse' als Erzieher? Die Beziehung zwischen Schulen und Betrieben in der DDR (1949–1989)." In *Die ostdeutsche Gesellschaft: Eine transnationale Perspektive*, edited by Emmanuel Droit and Sandrine Kott, 35–52. Berlin: Links Verlag, 2006.

———. "Les 'peer groups' dans l'espace public en RDA: de la stigmatisation à la reconnaissance? (1960–1980)." *Histoire@Politique. Politique, culture, société* 7 (2009).

———. *Vers un homme nouveau? L'éducation socialiste en RDA (1949–1989)*. Rennes: Presses Univ. de Rennes, 2009 (German translation: *Vorwärts zum neuen Menschen? Die sozialistische Erziehung in der DDR*. Cologne: Böhlau, 2014).

Eckardt, Philipp. *Der Bologna-Prozess: Entstehung, Strukturen und Ziele der europäischen Hochschulreformpolitik*. Norderstedt: Books on Demand, 2005.

Edelstein, Benjamin, and Rita Nikolai. "Strukturwandel im Sekundarbereich: Determinanten schulpolitischer Reformprozesse in Sachsen und Hamburg." *Zeitschrift für Pädagogik* 59 (2013): 482–94.

Engelhardt, Sabine. *Von der Volkstümlichen Bildung zum Wissenschaftsorientierten Lernen: Untersuchungen zum Wandel des Bildungsbegriff.* Ph.D. diss.,University of Göttingen, 1988.
Ehmke, Timo, and Nina Jude. "Soziale Herkunft und Kompetenzerwerb." In *PISA 2009: Bilanz nach einem Jahrzehnt,* edited by Eckhard Klieme, Cordula Artelt, Johannes Hartig, Nina Jude, Olaf Köller, Manfred Prenzel, Wolfgang Schneider, and Petra Stanat, 231–54. Münster: Waxmann Verlag, 2010.
Ertl, Hubert. "Educational Standards and the Changing Discourse on Education: The Reception and Consequences of the PISA Study in Germany." *Oxford Review of Education* 32 (2006): 619–34.
Eulefeld, Günter, Dietmar Bolscho, and Jürgen Rost. *Praxis der Umwelterziehung in der Bundesrepublik Deutschland: Eine empirische Untersuchung.* Kiel: IPN, 1988.
Eulefeld, Günter, D. Bolscho, H. Rode, J. Rost, and H. Syebold. *Entwicklung und Praxis schulischer Umwelterziehung in Deutschland: Ergebnisse empirischer Studien.* Kiel: IPN, 1993.
Fend, Helmut. *Neue Theorie der Schule: Einführung in das Verstehen von Bildungssystemen.* 2nd, revised ed. Wiesbaden: Verlag für Sozialwissenschaften, 2008.
Fenemore, Mark. *Sex, Thugs and Rock'n'Roll: Teenage Rebels in Cold-War East Germany.* New York: Berghahn, 2007.
Friedrich, Walter, Peter Förster, and Kurt Starke, eds. *Das Zentralinstitut für Jugendforschung Leipzig 1966–1990: Geschichte, Methoden, Erkenntnisse.* Berlin: Edition Ost, 1999.
Froese, Leonhard, Rudolf Haas, and Oskar Anweiler. *Bildungswettlauf zwischen West und Ost.* Freiburg: Herder, 1961.
Fuchs, Hans-Jürgen, and Eberhard Petermann, eds. *Bildungspolitik in der DDR 1966–1990: Dokumente.* Wiesbaden: Harrassowitz, 1991.
Fuchs, Hans-Werner. *Gymnasialbildung im Widerstreit: Die Entwicklung des Gymnasiums seit 1945 und die Rolle der Kultusministerkonferenz.* Frankfurt a. M.: Peter Lang, 2004.
Gauger, Jörg-Dieter, *Kontinuität und Wandel—Bildungsbegriff und Bildungssystem in den Grundsatzerklärungen der CDU zwischen 1945 und 2011.* St. Augustin: Konrad-Adenauer-Stiftung, 2011.
Gehrmann, Axel. "Gewandelte Lehrerrolle in Ost und West? Erste Ergebnisse aus vier Befragungen (1994–1996–1998–1999)." In *Transformation in der ostdeutschen Bildungslandschaft,* edited by Hans Döbert, Hans-Werner Fuchs, and Horst Weishaupt, 63–83. Opladen: Leske + Budrich, 2002.
Geißler, Gert. "Bildungs- und Schulpolitik." In *Deutsche Zeitgeschichte von 1945 bis 2000: Gesellschaft—Staat—Politik,* edited by Clemens Burrichter, Detlef Nakath, and Gerd-Rüdiger Stephan, 911–46. Berlin: Karl Dietz Verlag, 2006.
———. *Schulgeschichte in Deutschland: Von den Anfängen bis in die Gegenwart.* Frankfurt a. M.: Peter Lang, 2013.

———. "Schulreform von oben: Bemerkungen zum schulpolitischen Herrschaftssystem in der SBZ/DDR." In *Erinnerung für die Zukunft II: Das DDR-Bildungssystem als Geschichte und Gegenwart,* 49–60. Ludwigsfelde-Struveshof: Pädagogisches Landesinstitut Brandenburg, 1997.

Geißler, Gert, and Ulrich Wiegmann. *Pädagogik und Herrschaft in der DDR: Die parteilichen, geheimdienstlichen und vormilitärischen Erziehungsverhältnisse.* Frankfurt a. M.: Lang, 1996.

Geißler, Rainer. *Die Sozialstruktur Deutschlands.* 2nd ed. Opladen: Springer, 1996.

———. "Entwicklung der Sozialstruktur und Bildungswesen." In *Vergleich von Bildung und Erziehung in der Bundesrepublik Deutschland und in der Deutschen Demokratischen Republik,* edited by Oskar Anweiler, 83–111. Cologne: Verlag Wiss. und Pol., 1990.

Gemein, Jorg, and Hartmut Kiensel, eds. *Politik und Unterricht: Wer bestimmt, was Schüler lernen? Richtlinien für den Politik-Unterricht in der Diskussion.* Essen: Neue Deutsche Schule Verlagsgesellschaft, 1975.

Gerschler, Walter. "Reaktionen der Öffentlichkeit. Dokumentation der Presseberichte über die Richtlinien für den Politikunterricht." In *Zwischen Politik und Wissenschaft. Politik in der öffentlichen Diskussion,* edited by Walter Gagel and Rolf Schörken, 105–32. Opladen: Springer, 1975.

Göckel, Hans. *Volkstümliche Bildung? Versuch einer Klärung.* Weinheim: Julius Beltz, 1964.

Griesel, Heinz. "Vergleich grundlegender Konzeptionen der Mathematikdidaktik in der BRD und in der DDR." *Zentralblatt für Didaktik und Mathematik,* 35 (2003): 166–71.

Gross, Hermann. *Internationaler Wettbewerb in Wissenschaft und Bildungswesen zwischen West und Ost.* Essen-Bredeney: Stifterverband für die deutsche Wissenschaft, 1960.

Günther, Oliver, and Sibylle Schmerbach. "Deutsche Universitäten im Umbruch—20 Jahre nach der Wende." In *Deutschland 20 Jahre nach dem Mauerfall: Rückblick und Ausblick,* edited by Franz Keuper and Dieter Puchta, 399–417. Wiesbaden: Gabler, 2010.

Hansen, Klaus-Henning, and Manfred Lang. *Computer in der Schule: Ergebnisse der deutschen IEA-Studie, Phase I, 1989.* Kiel: IPN, 1993.

Hartung, Dirk, and Beate Krais. "Studium und Beruf." In *Das Hochschulwesen in der Bundesrepublik Deutschland,* edited by Ulrich Teichler, 179–209. Weinheim: Dt. Studienverlag, 1990.

Hepp, Gerd F. *Bildungspolitik in Deutschland: Eine Einführung.* Wiesbaden: Springer, 2011.

Der Hessische Kultusminister. *Rahmenrichtlinien Sekundarstufe I Gesellschaftslehre.* Wiesbaden: Hessisches Kultusministerium, 1972.

Hoffmann, Sabine. "Freundschaftsgruppen." *Elternhaus und Schule* 4 (1982): 18–19.

Honecker, Erich. *Bericht des ZK der SED an den VIII. Parteitag der SED.* Berlin (Ost): Dietz Verlag, 1971.

Hörner, Wolfgang. "Informationstechnische Bildung." In *Vergleich von Bildung und Erziehung in der Bundesrepublik Deutschland und in der Deutschen De-*

mokratischen Republik, edited by Oskar Anweiler, 620–37. Cologne: Verlag Wiss. und Pol., 1990.

Hoßfeld, Uwe, Thomas Kaiser, and Heinz Mestrip, eds. *Hochschule im Sozialismus: Studien zur Geschichte der Friedrich-Schiller-Universität Jena (1945–1990)*. Cologne: Böhlau Verlag, 2007.

Hundt, Rudolf. "Pädagogische Aspekte des Umweltschutzes." *Hercynia N. F.* 13, no. 2 (1976): 193–201.

Hurrelmann, Klaus. "Das Schulsystem in Deutschland: Das 'Zwei-Wege-Modell' setzt sich durch." *Zeitschrift für Pädagogik* 69 (2013): 455–68.

———. "Thesen zur Entwicklung des Bildungssystems in den nächsten 20 Jahren." *Die Deutsche Schule* 105 (2013): 305–21.

Janssen, Wiebke. *Halbstarke in der DDR: Verfolgung und Kriminalisierung einer Jugendkultur*. Berlin: Links Verlag, 2010.

Jencks, Christopher. *Inequality: A Reassessment of the Effect of Family and Schooling in America*. New York: Basic Books, 1972.

Jessen, Ralph. "Massenausbildung, Unterfinanzierung und Stagnation: Ost- und Westdeutsche Universitäten in den siebziger und achtziger Jahren." In *Gebrochene Wissenschaftskulturen: Universitäten und Politik im 20. Jahrhundert*, edited by Michael Grüttner, Rüdiger Hachtmann, Konrad H. Jarausch, Jürgen John, and Matthias Middell, 261–78. Göttingen: Vandenhoeck & Ruprecht, 2010.

Kaelble, Hartmut. *Sozialgeschichte Europas: 1945 bis zur Gegenwart*. Munich: Beck Verlag, 2007.

Kaiser, Manfred. "Zur Flexibilität von Hochschulausbildungen: Ein Überblick über den Stand der empirischen Substitutionsforschung." *Mitteilungen aus der Arbeitsmarkt- und Berufsforschung* 8 (1975): 203–21.

Klemm, Klaus, Hans-Günter Rolff, and Klaus-Jürgen Tillmann. *Bildung für das Jahr 2000: Bilanz der Reform, Zukunft der Schule*. Reinbek bei Hamburg: Rowohlt, 1985.

Klemm, Klaus, and Michael Weegen. "Wie gewonnen, so zerronnen: Einige Anmerkungen zum Zusammenhang von Bildungsexpansion und Akademikerangebot." *Jahrbuch der Schulentwicklung* 11 (2000): 129–50.

Klieme, Eckhard, Nina Jude, Jürgen Baumert, and Manfred Prenzel. "PISA 2000–2009: Bilanz der Veränderungen im Schulsystem." In *PISA 2009. Bilanz nach einem Jahrzehnt*, edited by Eckhard Klieme, Cordula Artelt, Johannes Hartig, Nina Jude, Manfred Prenzel, Wolfgang Schneider, and Petra Stanat, 277–300. Münster: Waxmann Verlag, 2010.

Klinger, Fred. "Wirtschaftsentwicklung, Beschäftigungssystem und Bildungswesen." In *Vergleich von Bildung und Erziehung in der Bundesrepublik Deutschland und in der Deutschen Demokratischen Republik*, edited by Oskar Anweiler, 57–82. Cologne: Verlag Wiss. und Pol., 1990.

Knaack, Heike. "Schule im Umbruch: Unterrichtende und Unterricht in den neuen Bundesländern während und nach der Wiedervereinigung." *Deutschland Archiv* 36 (2003): 296–303.

Knütter, Hans-Helmuth, and Klaus Dieter Ziehmann. "Die Richtlinien für den

Politik-Unterricht in Nordrhein-Westfalen." In *Der Streit um die politische Bildung*, edited by Peter Gutjahr-Löser and Hans-Helmuth Knütter, 123–52. Munich: Olzog Verlag, 1975.

Köhler, Doris. "Professionelle Pädagogen? Zur Rekonstruktion beruflicher Orientierungs- und Handlungsmuster ostdeutscher Lehrer der Kriegsgeneration." In *Konflikt und Konsens: Transformationsprozesse in Ostdeutschland*, edited by Martin Brussig, Frank Ettrich, und Raj Kollmorgen, 169–92. Opladen: Leske + Budrich, 2003.

Köhler, Gabriele. *Anders sollte es werden: Bildungspolitische Visionen und Realitäten der Runden Tische*. Cologne: Böhlau Verlag, 1999.

———. *Diskurs und Systemtransformation: Der Einfluss diskursiver Verständigungsprozesse auf Schule und Bildung im Transformationprozess der neuen Bundesländer*. Göttingen: Vandenhoeck & Ruprecht, 2009.

Köhler, Gerd, and Ernst Reuter, eds. *Was sollen Schüler lernen? Die Kontroverse um die hessischen Rahmenrichtlinien für die Unterrichtsfächer Deutsch und Gesellschaftslehre*. Frankfurt a. M.: Fischer Verlag, 1973.

Köhler, Helmut. *Bildungsbeteiligung und Sozialstruktur in der Bundesrepublik: Zu Stabilität und Wandel der Ungleichheit von Bildungschancen*. Berlin: Max-Planck-Institut für Bildungsforschung, 1992.

———. *Datenhandbuch zur deutschen Bildungsgeschichte*, vol. 9: *Schulen und Hochschulen in der Deutschen Demokratischen Republik 1949–1989*. Göttingen: Vandenhoeck & Ruprecht, 2008.

———. "Qualifikationsstruktur und Hochschulentwicklung in der Deutschen Demokratischen Republik und der Bundesrepublik Deutschland." *Mitteilungen aus der Arbeitsmarkt- und Berufsforschung* 28 (1995), 96–108.

Köhler, Helmut, and Peter Lundgreen. *Datenhandbuch zur deutschen Bildungsgeschichte*. Vol. 7: *Allgemein bildende Schulen in der Bundesrepublik Deutschland 1949–2010*. Göttingen: Vandenhoeck & Ruprecht, 2014.

Köhler, Helmut, and Gerhard Schreier. "Statistische Grunddaten zum Bildungswesen." In *Vergleich von Bildung und Erziehung in der Bundesrepublik Deutschland und in der Deutschen Demokratischen Republik*, edited by Oskar Anweiler, 112–55. Cologne: Verlag Wiss. und Pol., 1990.

Köhler, Helmut, and Manfred Stock. *Bildung nach Plan? Bildungs- und Beschäftigungssystem in der DDR 1949 bis 1989*. Opladen: Leske + Budrich, 2004.

Köhler, Roland. *Geschichte des Hochschulwesens der Deutschen Demokratischen Republik (1961–1980)*. Part 1: *Überblick*. Berlin-Ost: Institut für Hochschulbildung, 1987.

Kott, Sandrine. "Die Kinderkrippe." In *DDR-Erinnerungsorte*, edited by Martin Sabrow, 281–90. Munich: Beck Verlag, 2009.

Kraft, Fritz. "Die Hauptschule in Nordrhein-Westfalen." In *Die Hauptschule. Erfahrungen—Prozesse—Bilanz*, edited by Udo Franz and Michael Hoffmann, 95–119. Kronberg: Cornelsen, 1975.

Laitko, Hubert. "Produktivkraft, Wissenschaft, wissenschaftlich-technische Revolution und wissenschaftliches Erkennen: Diskurse im Vorfeld der Wissenschaftswissenschaft." In *Denkversuche: DDR-Philosophie in den 60er Jahren*, edited by Hans-Christoph Rauh and Peter Ruben, 459–540. Berlin: Links Verlag, 2005.

Lang, Manfred. *Computer in Schule und Lehrerbildung: IEA-Studie 1992 in westdeutschen Bundesländern*. Kiel: IPN, 1995.

Lenhardt, Gero, and Manfred Stock. *Bildung, Bürger, Arbeitskraft: Schulentwicklung und Sozialstruktur in der BRD und der DDR*. Frankfurt a. M.: Suhrkamp, 1997.

Lepenies, Wolf. "Mittelmaß in Europas Mitte." *Süddeutsche Zeitung*, 8/9 December 2001.

Lob, Reinhold E. "Umwelterziehung in deutschen Schulen: Eine Bilanz nach 20 Jahren." *Die Deutsche Schule* 91 (1999): 102–13.

Miethe, Ingrid, and Birthe Kleber. "'Bildungswettlauf zwischen West und Ost'—Ein retrospektiver Vergleich." In *Bildung, Gesellschaftstheorie und soziale Arbeit*, edited by Rita Braches-Chyrek, Dieter Nelles, Gertrud Oelerich, and Andreas Schaarschuch, 155–74. Opladen: Verlag Barbara Budrich, 2013.

Miethe, Ingrid, and Martina Schiebel. *Bildung—Biografie—Institution: Die Arbeiter- und-Bauern-Fakultäten der DDR*. Frankfurt a. M.: Campus Verlag, 2008.

Mitter, Wolfgang. "Wandel und Kontinuität im Bildungswesen der beiden deutschen Staaten." In *Schulen zwischen Reform und Krise: Zu Theorie und Praxis der vergleichenden Bildungsforschung*, 277–94. Cologne: Böhlau, 1987.

Müller, Walter. "Erwartete und unerwartete Folgen der Bildungsexpansion." In *Die Diagnosefähigkeit der Soziologie* (KZSS Sonderheft 38), edited by Jürgen Friedrichs, M. Rainer Lepsius, and Karl Ulrich Mayer, 81–112. Opladen: Springer, 1998.

Müller, Walter, and Dietmar Haun. "Bildungsexpansion und Bildungsungleichheit." In *Einstellungen und Lebensbedingungen in Europa*, edited by Wolfgang Glatzer, 225–68. Frankfurt a. M.: Campus Verlag, 1993.

———. "Bildungsungleichheit im sozialen Wandel." *Kölner Zeitschrift für Soziologie und Sozialpsychologie* 46 (1994): 1–42.

Mut zur Erziehung: Beiträge zu einem Forum am 9./10. Januar 1978 im Wissenschaftszentrum. Stuttgart: Klett-Cotta, 1978.

Naumann, Jens. "Entwicklungstendenzen des Bildungswesens der Bundesrepublik Deutschland im Rahmen wirtschaftlicher und demographischer Veränderungen." In *Bildung in der Bundesrepublik Deutschland*, edited by Max-Planck-Institut für Bildungsforschung, 1:21–201. Reinbek bei Hamburg: Rowohlt, 1980.

Neuner, Gerhart. *Sozialistische Persönlichkeit—ihr Werden, ihre Erziehung*. Berlin-Ost: Dietz-Verlag, 1975.

Niemann, Dennis. "Deutschland—Im Zentrum des PISA-Sturms." In *Das PISA-Echo: Internationale Reaktionen auf die Bildungsstudie*, edited by Philipp Knodel, Kerstin Martens, Daniel de Olano, and Marie Popp, 59–90. Frankfurt a. M.: Campus Verlag, 2010.

Nipperdey, Thomas, and Hermann Lübbe. *Gutachten zu den Rahmenrichtlinien Sekundarstufe I Gesellschaftslehre des Hessischen Kultusministers*. Bad Homburg: Hessischer Elternverein, 1973.

Oehler, Christoph. *Hochschulentwicklung in der Bundesrepublik Deutschland seit 1945*. Frankfurt a. M.: Campus Verlag, 1989.

Ohse, Marc-Dietrich. *Jugend nach dem Mauerbau: Anpassung, Protest und Eigensinn (DDR 1961–1974)*. Berlin: Links Verlag, 2003.

Ortner, Gerhard E. "Gestaltung und Steuerung der Tertiären Bildung: Problemeinführung und Problemstrukturierung." In *Die deutsche Hochschule zwischen Numerus clausus und Akademikerarbeitslosigkeit: Der doppelte Flaschenhals*, edited by Ulrich Lohmar and Gerhard E. Ortner, 18–40. Hannover: Schroedel, 1975.

Peisert, Hansgert. *Das Hochschulsystem in der Bundesrepublik Deutschland: Funktionsweise und Leistungsfähigkeit*. Stuttgart: Klett-Cotta, 1979.

Pieper, Beate. *Vom Lehrermangel zur Lehrerarbeitslosigkeit: Bildungspolitik als geschichtliches Dilemma*. Münster: Wurf Verlag, 1984.

Raschert, Jürgen. "Bildungspolitik im kooperativen Föderalismus: Die Entwicklung der länderübergreifenden Planung und Koordination des Bildungswesens der Bundesrepublik Deutschland." In *Bildung in der Bundesrepublik Deutschland*, edited by Max-Planck-Institut für Bildungsforschung, 1:103–215. Reinbek bei Hamburg: Rowohlt Taschenbuch Verlag, 1980.

Reuter, Lutz-Rainer, and Bernhard Muszynski. *Bildungspolitik. Dokumente und Analysen*. Opladen: Leske + Budrich, 1980.

Rohstock, Anne. "Ist Bildung Bürgerrecht? Wege zur Bildungsexpansion im doppelten Deutschland." In *Das doppelte Deutschland: 40 Jahre Systemkonkurrenz*, edited by Udo Wengst and Hermann Wentker, 135–59. Berlin: Links Verlag, 2008.

Rudolph, Hedwig, and Rudolf Husemann. *Hochschulpolitik zwischen Expansion und Restriktion: Ein Vergleich der Entwicklung in der Bundesrepublik Deutschland und der Deutschen Demokratischen Republik*. Frankfurt a. M.: Campus Verlag, 1984.

Sabrow, Martin. "Zäsuren in der Zeitgeschichte." Version 1.0. *Docupedia-Zeitgeschichte*, 3 June 2013. http://docupedia.de/zg/sabrow_zaesuren_v1_de_2013.

Sachse, Christian. *Aktive Jugend—wohlerzogen und diszipliniert: Wehrerziehung in der DDR als Sozialisations- und Herrschaftsinstrument (1960–1973)*. Münster: LIT Verlag, 2000.

Schimpl-Neimanns, Bernhard. "Soziale Herkunft und Bildungsbeteiligung: Empirische Analysen zu herkunftsspezifischen Bildungsungleichheiten zwischen 1950 und 1989." *Cologneer Zeitschrift für Soziologie und Sozialpsychologie* 52 (2000): 636–69.

Schlaffke, Winfried. *Akademisches Proletariat?* Osnabrück: Fromm, 1972.

Schulz, Tobias. *Sozialistische Wissenschaft: Die Berliner Humboldt-Universität (1960–1975)*. Cologne: Böhlau Verlag, 2010.

Schreiber, Waltraud. *Schulreform in Hessen zwischen 1967 und 1982: Die curriculare Reform der Sekundarstufe I. Schwerpunkt Geschichte in der Gesellschaftslehre*. Neuried: Ars Una, 2005.

Schreiterer, Ulrich. *Politische Steuerung des Hochschulsystems: Programm und Wirklichkeit der staatlichen Studienreform 1975–1986.* Frankfurt a. M.: Campus Verlag, 1989.

Skyba, Peter. *Vom Hoffnungsträger zum Sicherheitsrisiko. Jugend in der DDR und Jugendpolitik der SED 1949–1961.* Cologne: Böhlau, 2000.

Solga, Heike. *Auf dem Weg in eine klassenlose Gesellschaft? Klassenlagen und Mobilität zwischen Generationen in der DDR.* Berlin: Akademie Verlag, 1995.

———. "Bildungschancen in der DDR." In *Bildungsgeschichte einer Diktatur: Bildung und Erziehung in SBZ und DDR im historisch-gesellschaftlichen Kontext,* edited by Sonja Häder and Heinz-Elmar Tenorth, 275–94. Weinheim: Deutscher Studien Verlag, 1997.

———. "Jugendliche ohne Schulabschluss und ihre Wege in den Arbeitsmarkt." In *Das Bildungswesen in der Bundesrepublik Deutschland: Strukturen und Entwicklungen im Überblick,* edited by Kai S. Cortina, Jürgen Baumert, Achim Leschinsky, Karl Ulrich Mayer, and Luitgard Trommer, 710–54. Reinbek bei Hamburg: Rohwolt, 2003.

Sommer, Winfried. "Neue Medien/Informations- und Kommunikationssysteme und Bildungswesen—für die Bildungspolitik des Bundes nutzbare internationale Erfahrungen und Informationen." In *Zukünftige Bildungspolitik—Bildung 2000: Schlußbericht der Enquete-Kommission des 11. Deutschen Bundestages und parlamentarische Beratung am 26. Oktober 1990,* edited by Deutscher Bundestag, 431–44. Bonn: Deutscher Bundestag, 1990.

Stooß, Friedemann. "Der Akademiker-Arbeitsmarkt bis zum Jahr 2000." In *Studium—und danach?,* edited by Egbert Kahle and Hermann J. Weihe, 5–27. Frankfurt a. M.: Thun, 1988.

Tenorth, Heinz-Elmar. "Die Bildungsgeschichte der DDR—Teil der deutschen Bildungsgeschichte?" In *Bildungsgeschichte einer Diktatur: Bildung und Erziehung in SBZ und DDR im historisch-gesellschaftlichen Kontext,* edited by Sonja Häder and Heinz-Elmar Tenorth, 69–96. Weinheim: Deutscher Studien-Verlag, 1997.

Tenorth, Heinz-Elmar, Sonja Kudella, and Andreas Paetz. *Politisierung im Schulalltag der DDR: Durchsetzung und Scheitern einer Erziehungsambition.* Weinheim: Beltz, 1996.

Tessaring, Manfred. "Beschäftigungssituation und -perspektiven für Hochschulabsolventen." *Aus Politik und Zeitgeschichte* 50 (1989): 14–24.

Ther, Philipp. *Die neue Ordnung auf dem alten Kontinent: Eine Geschichte des neoliberalen Europa.* Frankfurt a. M.: Suhrkamp, 2014.

Tillmann, Klaus-Jürgen. "Das Sekundarschulsystem auf dem Weg in die Zweigliedrigkeit." *Pädagogik* 64, no. 5 (2012): 8–12.

Tillmann, Klaus-Jürgen, Kathrin Dedering, Daniel Kneuper, Christian Kuhlmann, and Isa Nessel. *PISA als bildungspolitisches Ereignis: Fallstudien in vier Bundesländern.* Wiesbaden: Springer, 2008.

Tippelt, Rudolf, and Bernd von Cleve. *Verfehlte Bildung? Bildungsexpansion und Qualifikationsbedarf.* Darmstadt: Wiss. Buchgesellschaft, 1995.

Trommer-Krug, Luitgard. "Soziale Herkunft und Schulbesuch." In *Bildung in der Bundesrepublik Deutschland*, edited by Max-Planck-Institut für Bildungsforschung, 1:217–81. Reinbek bei Hamburg: Rohwolt, 1980.

Turner, George. *Hochschule zwischen Vorstellung und Wirklichkeit: Zur Geschichte der Hochschulreform im letzten Drittel des 20. Jahrhunderts*. Berlin: Duncker & Humblot, 2001.

———. *Von der Universität zur University: Sackgassen und Umwege der Hochschulpolitik seit 1945*. Berlin: BWV Berliner Wissenschaftsverlag, 2013.

Vogt, Hartmut. *Bildung für die Zukunft: Entwicklungstendenzen im deutschen Bildungswesen in West und Ost*. Göttingen: Vandenhoeck & Ruprecht, 1967.

von Plato, Alexander. "Entstasifizierung im Öffentlichen Dienst der neuen Bundesländer nach 1989." *Jahrbuch für historischen Bildungsforschung* 5 (1999): 313–42.

Walter, Thomas. *Der Bologna-Prozess: Ein Wendepunkt europäischer Hochschulpolitik?* Wiesbaden: Springer, 2006.

Waterkamp, Dietmar. "Berufsbildung." In *Handbuch der deutschen Bildungsgeschichte*, vol. 6: *1945 bis zur Gegenwart. Zweiter Teilband: Deutsche Demokratische Republik und neue Bundesländer*, edited by Christoph Führ and Carl-Ludwig Furck, 257–79. Munich: C.H. Beck, 1998.

———. *Handbuch zum Bildungswesen der DDR*. Berlin: BWV Berliner Wissenschaft, 1987.

Werner, Michael, and Bénédicte Zimmermann. "Vergleich, Transfer, Verflechtung: Der Ansatz der Histoire croisée und die Herausforderung des Transnationalen." *Geschichte und Gesellschaft* 28 (2002): 607–36.

Wierling, Dorothee. "Die Jugend als innerer Feind. Konflikte in der Erziehungsdiktatur der sechziger Jahre." In *Sozialgeschichte der DDR*, edited by Hartmut Kaelble, Jürgen Kocka, and Hartmut Zwahr, 404–25. Stuttgart: Klett-Cotta, 1994.

———. *Geboren im Jahr Eins: Der Jahrgang 1949 in der DDR. Versuch einer Kollektivbiographie*. Berlin: Links Verlag, 2002.

Witte, Johanna. "Die deutsche Umsetzung des Bologna-Prozesses." *Aus Politik und Zeitgeschichte* 48 (2006): 21–27

Wirrer, Rita. *Koedukation im Rückblick. Die Entwicklung der rheinland-pfälzischen Gymnasien vor dem Hintergrund pädagogischer und bildungspolitischer Kontroversen*. Essen: Die Blaue Eule, 1996.

Zachmann, Karin. "Frauen für die technische Revolution: Studentinnen und Absolventinnen Technischer Hochschulen in der SBZ/DDR." In *Frauen arbeiten. Weibliche Erwerbstätigkeit in Ost- und Westdeutschland nach 1945*, edited by Gunilla-Friederike Budde, 121–56. Göttingen: Vandenhoeck & Ruprecht, 1997.

Zimmer, Dieter. "Sag mir, wo die Forscher sind." *Die Zeit*, no. 32, 31 July 1992.

Zimmermann, Werner, and Jörg Hoffmann. *Die gymnasiale Oberstufe. Grundzüge—Reformkonzepte—Problemfelder*. Stuttgart: Klett-Cotta, 1985.

Zwiener, Karl. *Kinderkrippen in der DDR*. Munich: Verlag Deutsches Jugendinstitut, 1994.

CHAPTER 9

Mobility and Migration in Divided Germany

Maren Möhring

Migration and mobility, as well as the desire to move within and between the two Germanys, contributed significantly to the decisive political, social, and cultural transformations that took place in the last three decades of the twentieth century. Calls for the freedom to travel, for example, were one of the major catalysts behind the upheavals that engulfed Eastern Europe at the end of the 1980s. Similarly, public awareness of the great number of people moving around in the wake of these transitions was particularly high. Furthermore, the topic of migration between East and West Germany embodies the idea of "entanglement" almost more so than any other, although it leaned more heavily in one direction than the other.[1] This chapter therefore looks not only at the myriad forms of mobility that bound East and West Germany together, but also those that divided them. It examines the migration that occurred between East and West Germany, as well as the immigration of people from other countries to the Federal Republic and the GDR, and then later to reunified Germany. In doing so, it contextualizes these two kinds of migration within a larger framework that encompasses other forms of mobility, such as travel.[2] Although the number of foreigners living in East Germany is still rather low even today, this chapter nonetheless compares how both German states dealt with non-German labor migrants in particular and how the growing number of non-Germans has influenced debates about national identity. The following analysis will not only address the socioeconomic motives and effects of migration, but also look at the cultural implications of these processes of mobility, the transformation of society, and the semantics of the debates over migration.

At the end of World War II, postwar Germany was a "hub" of international migration due to the almost seven million displaced persons and approximately twelve million German refugees and expellees within its borders.[3] Whereas a large number of the former prisoners of forced labor camps and concentration camps left Germany for Great Britain, the United States, or Israel, the huge numbers of German refugees who remained within the territory of what would become East and West Germany presented a great challenge to the two fledgling states. By the time the Berlin Wall had been put up, around nine hundred thousand of the approximately 4.3 million expellees who were in the Soviet Occupation Zone as of 1948 had migrated to the Federal Republic.[4] At the same time, the movement of migrants and refugees from East to West Germany fueled an ongoing conflict between the two states. It also aptly reflects the violent yet helpless way in which the GDR leadership reacted to practices that persisted despite prohibitions and were therefore always interpreted as a critique against the system. Migration in both directions, moreover, was an unparalleled politically loaded issue during the Cold War.

Tourism and the freedom to travel were also very much a controversial political topic within the context of the rivalry between the systems. Travel has been quite popular among East and West Germans alike, both before and after the collapse of Communism. Although Germans were relatively immobile in terms of changing jobs or moving house for other reasons well into the 1990s (apart from during the immediate postwar years), they often spent short-term stays in different places. In addition to looking at domestic and foreign tourism, this chapter will also deal with the touristic exchanges that took place between East and West Germany, and especially family visits across the German-German border.

Whereas employers in West Germany often complained about the lack of mobility among West German citizens, there was another group that was highly mobile and flexible, namely the foreign labor migrants.[5] Even before the construction of the Wall put a stop to the influx of East Germans who came to work in West Germany, the West German government had already begun efforts to attract foreign workers in order to meet the ever increasing demand for labor that accompanied the economic upswing. The GDR also tried to encourage foreign workers to come to the country, but the influence of labor migrants on East German society and culture remained very limited. By comparing the West German *Gastarbeiter* (guestworker) system and the East German *Vertragsarbeiter* (contract worker) system, this chapter will examine mutual processes of demarcation as well as commonalities in the way in which both countries dealt with non-Germans. It will also touch on similarities and differences in

East and West German asylum policies, which can be seen as a reaction to common global challenges.

Two very specific forms of (labor) migration are usually left out, namely study abroad and the stationing of foreign troops in Germany. In fact, around ten million Soviet soldiers had been stationed in East Germany at some point before 1994.[6] In the history of migration, the British and American troops that occupied the West also need to be taken into consideration because they contributed to an often neglected wave of marriage migration in which about twenty thousand German women emigrated to the United States and another ten thousand or so left for Great Britain.[7]

The late 1980s were therefore very much a turning point in German migration history. The new waves of migration unleashed by the collapse of the Soviet Union represented a very direct confrontation with the transformations that were taking place in Eastern Europe. In addition to dealing with the wave of emigration from the GDR in 1989 and the huge number of East Germans who immigrated to the western regions of post-reunification Germany in the years that followed, this chapter also traces the discussions that surrounded the *Aussiedler*, the members of German minorities living for the most part in Eastern Europe who came to West Germany and, later, reunified Germany under the Federal Expellees Act (*Bundesvertriebenengesetz*). It will look at the contours of the asylum debates in the early 1990s that played an important role in the national reordering processes brought about through the upheavals in Eastern Europe as well as new global challenges. Moreover, the increasing Europeanization of migration policy will also be factored into this context. Over the course of reunification, as one theory suggests, the non-German migrants represented the figure of a "third other" that allowed for German-German reconciliation and the negotiation of a new German identity. For migrants who had been living in Germany for a while, reunification resulted in insecurity and a loss of status. The increasing processes of exclusion that even went as far as the violent pogroms at the beginning of the 1990s have realigned the relationship between Germans and non-Germans in reunified Germany. Accordingly, this chapter contributes to an analysis of the simultaneity of pluralization and homogenization as well as present-day politics of difference within a contemporary history perspective.

Migration and Mobility: Current Research Perspectives

Since a great surge in migration research has taken place over the last few decades, a great number of theories and empirical studies have been developed to deal with this topic.[8] In the 1990s, transnational approaches began to replace earlier analytical frameworks that concentrated on emigration and immigration, thereby defining migration as a one-time transition from a clear location of origin to a clear destination.[9] Although such new conceptual perspectives have proven to be very effective in furthering research on international migration, the movement of people that took place between East and West presents a very particular case that needs to be handled differently. Thanks to the prohibitions and tightly limited opportunities that made leaving the countries in Eastern Europe difficult, the decision to move to the West was often a very final one. It was usually difficult for those who left the East to maintain contacts across the border, and it was virtually impossible for them to visit their old home country. The migration regime in Eastern Europe after 1945 was therefore very unique in that the strict regulations on leaving the country separated it from most other systems of migration.[10] Correspondingly, "transnationality" is a problematic term with respect to the migration movements analyzed in this chapter, because although those East German citizens who fled or left the GDR for the FRG crossed a state border, they were considered to be German nationals when they arrived in the West and treated as citizens immediately. Even those migrants known as *Aussiedler*, which was a term used to refer to ethnic Germans who "came back" to Germany from Eastern Europe sometimes after several generations, were still considered to be German by descent. Consequently, although the *Aussiedler* essentially migrated from Russia to West Germany, their migration fostered the development of a new kind of Russian-German identity. Nonetheless, this was a singular kind of transnational migration because the *Aussiedler* did not fall under the category of "foreigners." Transnationality, therefore, cannot be presumed in these cases, but rather it must be interrogated as a problem within debates over nationality and belonging within its respective historical contexts.

Two other current trends in migration research inform the approach adopted within this chapter: first, the notion of the "autonomy of migration," which downplays the role of government migration policy as a key factor behind migration by stressing that these policies were more of an answer to migrant practices, sheds new light on migratory movements.[11] Actions undertaken by the state—such as closing borders—therefore clearly appear to be responses to self-willed practices, such as the desire of some GDR citizens to defect to the West. Such an approach shifts the focus to the "perseverance of migration movements" and their practices as well as aspects of materiality despite the enormous hurdles that had to be overcome. The tenacity of such migration often forces the permanent reformulation of state migration policies or even leads to their retraction, as in the case of the mass exodus from the GDR in the summer of 1989.[12] The praxis of migration can therefore be analyzed as a driving force in history.

Second, migration research can profit from the perspectives offered by mobility studies that examine different forms of mobility in relation to one another.[13] Such approaches investigate the transitions and entanglements between tourism and migration while interpreting travel as an overarching praxis, which ultimately questions the separation of seemingly clear categories such as tourists and migrants.[14] This does not mean that all forms of mobility should be treated as equivalent, but rather that the continuities between different types of mobility should be taken into account. For example, an East German visiting relatives in the West might decide to stay in that country, which meant that what was once a tourist trip became a permanent act of migration. Similar transitions also occurred among non-German labor migrants in West Germany, many of whom entered the country on a tourist visa, but then sought work and often remained as illegal or sometimes legal immigrants in the country. Moreover, although the political and legal classifications that make distinctions between tourism and migration, but also between labor migration and refugee movements, as well as voluntary and involuntary mobility, need to be taken into account, they also need to be critically interrogated.[15]

Migration and Mobility in Divided Germany from the 1950s to the 1980s

The loss of the former eastern German territories and the division of Germany led to mass migration across these new borders after 1945. Whereas the millions of people who had to leave their homes in Eastern Europe in 1945 and the years that followed came to be referred to commonly as *(Heimat)vertriebene* (expellees) in West Germany, they were called *Übersiedler* (akin to "resettlers")—and as early as 1950 as former *Übersiedler*—in the GDR, the latter of which suggested that the problem of integration had been overcome. Similarly, each of the two German states went about the process of integration in its own particular and clearly separate way. In the GDR, the *Neubürger* (new citizens) were supposed to be integrated, or rather assimilated, into work and daily life as quickly as possible. Whereas the GDR granted only short-term sociopolitical support for this group, the politically mandated restructuring of society that took place well into the 1960s offered greater chances for upward social mobility. In West Germany, however, the government instituted a comprehensive aid program within the framework of the *Lastenaus-*

gleichsgesetz (Equalization of Burdens Act) that was passed in 1952.[16] Yet neither of these approaches necessarily led to the "rapid integration" of this group.[17] Over the course of the 1970s, it was really only the younger generation of *Vertriebene* that was "integrated" in terms of jobs, income, and housing.[18] As with other migrants, age played a key role in the ability to successfully adapt and take advantage of opportunities in the new home country.

Migration between East and West Germany

Many of the refugees who came from the former eastern German territories did not stay where they first arrived, but rather moved multiple times within the FRG and the GDR. They accounted for a large proportion of the annual six-figured number of people who emigrated from the GDR to West Germany in the 1950s; approximately ten thousand emigrated in the opposite direction. All told, approximately 2.6 million East Germans left the GDR between 1951 and the building of the Berlin Wall; approximately 550 thousand opted to move in the other direction between 1949 and 1989.[19] At first, this immigration was not welcomed at all. Since West Germany was preoccupied with integrating refugees and *Vertriebene*, it was hardly in a position to take on more people, and the fear of Communist agents was quite rampant at the time. Moreover, West Germany did not want the GDR to be drained of people to the extent that only those who were in favor of the regime remained, which would have decreased the chances for reunification over the long run.[20]

In 1952, however, West Germany changed its attitude toward this immigration in light of the rivalry between the systems. At this point, the rejection quota for migrants from East Germany sank accordingly to about 21 percent.[21] From then on, West Germany saw emigration from the GDR to the Federal Republic as "voting with your feet."[22] It explicitly staged this influx of East Germans to attract a great deal of media attention in order to publicly reaffirm its own political system. The Federal Republic claimed to be the sole representation for all Germans, which was a claim that it could easily back up by pointing to the care provided to immigrants coming from the Soviet Occupation Zone (SBZ) and then later the GDR.[23] In light of the mass exodus that took place in 1952 and 1953, it is not possible to keep up the usual distinction made between those who came to the West as political refugees and those who immigrated primarily for socioeconomic reasons. Motives for immigrating that were not explicitly political successively gained legitimacy and were increasingly judged to be political in nature; in this sense, moreover, these motives were seen as further proof of the superiority of the Western system.[24]

On the other side of the border, the GDR leadership referred to this East-West migration as *Republikflucht* (fleeing the Republic), thereby emphasizing the lack of loyalty among these "dissidents" (*Abtrünnige*).[25] As of 1957, the *Republikflucht* Act made emigration a crime punishable by law. Furthermore, this exodus to the West was depicted as a targeted attempt by West German companies to attract workers. Indeed, "human capital" had become a highly sought-after resource because it was increasingly considered to be the key factor for boosting the economy. As a disproportionately high number of younger people (and children) migrated from the West to the East, the newspaper *Neues Deutschland*, which was the organ of the SED, countered in 1956, "Young people are voting with their feet."[26] West Germany, in contrast, tried only to paint the migration from East to West as politically motivated, and it attempted to downplay the migration from West to East as "normal" internal migration.[27]

Many of these German migrants—in both directions—were not at all or hardly motivated by explicitly political considerations, but rather they opted for migration because of familial reasons or hopes for a better livelihood. About two-thirds to 75 percent of the migrants going from West to East, for example, were return migrants who had not achieved what they had hoped to achieve by heading to the West and therefore decided to return for multiple reasons.[28] An increasing number of unskilled workers were found among this group because they had not been able to profit from the economic upswing in West Germany.[29] In particular, many return migrants named the secured existence and low cost of living offered in the GDR as the reasons behind their decision to come back.[30] However, there were political motives in a narrower sense, such as the officially proclaimed anti-fascism of the GDR, that incited some people to go over to the East.[31]

As in West Germany, people who wanted to immigrate to the GDR had to go through special registration offices in which they were questioned about their motives by the secret intelligence services. Although the SED did increase its efforts to attract immigration, or rather the return of East Germans who had emigrated after the exodus in 1952/53, East Germany had very strict entry regulations that were designed in particular to exclude those who the state determined to be criminal or "asocial" from being permitted into the country.[32] Leftist artists and intellectuals, on the other hand, were welcomed by the GDR with open arms.[33]

The immigrants who did settle in the GDR were often met with suspicion. Due to security concerns, they were often denied work in many companies. Consequently, they had to take jobs that were below their qualifications in areas such as farming, construction, or mining.[34] Many of the citizens who migrated from West to East, but also from East to

West, in the 1950s did not feel at home in the other part of Germany for quite some time. This reflected the early point at which these two states began to grow apart and the mistrust for one another that went along with it.[35] Moreover, people in the two Germanys felt that they were drifting even further apart over the course of the 1970s and 1980s.

The construction of the Berlin Wall in August 1961 brought an abrupt end to the mass emigration from the GDR. The leaders of the GDR thus signaled that they were prepared to establish as tight a controlled border and migration regime as possible. Migration in the years and decades that followed usually came about only through official permission to leave the country, the exiling of dissidents who had been stripped of their citizenship (especially in the wake of the expulsion of Wolf Biermann in 1976), political prisoners whose freedom had been bought by the West German government, or people who had dared to try to flee over the border or decided never to return from a trip to the West (the latter of whom were referred to as *Verbleiber* [stayers]).

Although the GDR constitution from 1949 guaranteed the right to emigrate, this clause was eliminated in the second constitution of 1968. Permission to leave the country was only granted in the form of a petition to relinquish East German citizenship.[36] An application to receive permission to leave was often answered with an employment ban, imprisonment, the marginalization of children, and other forms of discrimination.[37] Moreover, because there was no option for return as there was with other types of migration, those who submitted applications had to be very sure of their decisions.

The types of strongly regulated East to West migration listed above had been developed and arranged in (arduous) negotiations with West Germany. Not only were political leaders and migrants themselves involved in these processes, but also other actors. Almost half of the so-called *Sperrbrecher* (barrier breakers) who crossed the border despite the prohibitions relied on the support of West Germans to help them flee. In the jargon of the SED, these helpers were spoken of as "subversive bands of human smugglers."[38] Beginning in 1963, the FRG bought the freedom of five hundred to fifteen hundred political prisoners each year, paying up to 200,000 DM per head; the usual rate was about 40,000 DM, but this jumped to almost 96,000 as of 1977.[39] A total of more than thirty-three thousand political prisoners were released this way between 1963 and 1989, and the West German government also paid for over two hundred thousand people to leave the country. All in all, the West Germans spent about 3.4 billion DM on these efforts.[40] A high percentage of the political prisoners were people who had failed in their attempts to cross over the border of the GDR. Between the construction of the Wall and reunification, approximately seventy-five thousand attempts to flee the GDR failed, with an estimated death toll at the border of about one thousand.[41]

With the signing of the Helsinki Accords in 1975, the legitimacy of East Germany's isolationist policies, including the prohibitions against leaving the country, came under more pressure. East German citizens used this document in order to try to gain permission to leave. Although the East German government interpreted upholding the Final Act as a "may but not a must," it could really no longer withhold permission when it came to reuniting families.[42] The directive on the regulation of questions pertaining to family reunification and marriages between citizens of the GDR and foreigners from 1983 created the first official means to apply to leave the country for familial reasons. In 1984, thirty-two thousand petitions to leave were approved.[43] The number of such applications continued to grow, surpassing the one hundred thousand mark in 1987.[44] Not least the reforms introduced in the Soviet Union under Gorbachev encouraged many GDR citizens to insist on their right of personal freedom without relation to family reunification.[45] By the mid-1980s at the latest, the lack of travel opportunities in the GDR had come to play a key role in the reasons listed for wanting to leave the country.[46]

Visits and Tourism across the East/West Divide

GDR citizens were only free to travel within the borders of East Germany. As of 1954, they could also visit the other socialist countries in Eastern Europe with a visa, apart from Yugoslavia and Albania.[47] East Germans made extensive use of their limited freedom to travel. Indeed, GDR citizens can be described as the "'world travel champions' of the East."[48] Both the GDR and the FRG exhibited a similar and very high level of travel frequency compared to other countries around the world.

Not only did the number of trips in general begin to increase as of the 1970s, but also the number of trips taken abroad by East as well as West Germans. Between 1975 and 1989, the GDR Travel Office booked over a million trips outside the country per year.[49] In West Germany, where tourism had reached mass proportions in the 1960s, non-German travel destinations had taken over the lead by the late 1960s.[50] Whereas only a few East Germans could afford to take trips to places outside of Europe, these kinds of destinations had become all the more popular among West Germans in the 1980s.[51] As in other socialist countries, travel to Western countries was open only to a very small, politically reliable class of elites.

GDR tourism in the country's socialist neighbors also had a special function—namely, it provided a way for East Germans to meet up with their relatives and friends who had gone over to the West.[52] Socialist foreign countries were therefore akin to a third space where it was possible to keep up contacts that were otherwise barred. If, following Hill and Williams, "return travel" to the old home country is an integral element of migration, then the significance of these substitute locations in light of the lack of freedom to travel can be seen as a combination of migration and tourism.[53] Both these forms of mobility were in fact interlaced in a symptomatic way because "staying" in the West was one way for travelers from the Eastern Bloc to bring their trip to an end.

Official travel was permitted between East and West Germany, especially in the case of trips that were organized for young people on both sides of the Wall to meet one another, as well as exchanges for academic, cultural, and sport purposes.[54] In 1982, eleven thousand West German teenagers visited the GDR, and this figure jumped to 36,500 by 1984. Visits to relatives accounted for a large proportion of the travel between East and West. Not only were such visits a perpetual topic of negotiation between the two countries, but also they were a key form of German-German interaction.

The first travel permit agreement was made in 1963, which allowed residents of West Berlin to visit their families in the eastern part of the city for the first time since the Wall had been put up. In 1964, the SED introduced the first minimum currency exchange requirement for West Germans traveling to the GDR; as of 1968, a fee-based visa was needed for trips to West Berlin. Applications for vacation trips were seldom approved. Approvals were granted when relatives in the GDR sent an invitation or trips were planned to the Leipziger Messe (Leipzig Trade Fair). As part of the Four Power Agreement on Berlin in 1971, the two German states worked out a transit treaty that was supposed to regulate the unimpeded transport of goods and people, which led, among other things, to the construction of the Hamburg-Berlin transit route. This major German-German infrastructure project, which served as a bridge of sorts—depending on the perspective—created a very specific space of German-German experience. It was opened to traffic in 1982, and the flat rate transit fees helped the GDR to acquire badly needed cash in foreign currency.[55] Visits across the border were made easier with the Basic Treaty of 1972: close relatives were permitted to enter West Germany in the event of family emergencies, even if they were not yet of retirement age. Pensioners (whose loss the GDR thought it could bear) had been allowed to make such family visits since as early as 1964. Within the framework of what was referred to as minor border crossing, West Germans who lived near the border to the GDR were permitted to travel for thirty days a year in the nearby border region of the GDR. As part of the billion-dollar loan that the Federal Republic granted to the GDR in 1983, the GDR took further steps to make visits easier, including the reduction of the minimum amount of currency that had to be exchanged. Beginning in 1984, moreover, pensioners were not only permitted to visit relatives, but also friends and acquaintances in West Germany. Some of these East German retirees took advantage of the opportunity to apply for a West German passport while in the FRG with which they could then travel to other countries. This kind of tourism had been strictly prohibited by the GDR leadership.[56]

Thanks to these looser travel regulations, the number of visitors crossing the German-German border increased significantly. Whereas approximately six hundred thousand West Germans traveled to the GDR in 1962, this number rose to 1.25 million in 1970 and then 3.5 million in 1980.[57] Approximately one million East Germans traveled in the opposite direction in 1970, and 1.4 million in 1979.[58] As tourism became a part of everyday life, which was supposed to help stabilize the system, it further encouraged the desire for the freedom to travel, and ultimately contributed to the collapse of the GDR.

Travel to socialist countries was also particularly appealing to West Germans because of their high level of purchasing power. The same applied to other foreign destinations, especially those in southern Europe. The tight link between migration and tourism in West Germany was also reflected by the fact that the most popular travel destinations among West Germans were the home countries of the *Gastarbeiter*. Whereas migration and tourism differed in terms of the length of stays and the motivations behind them, both forms of mobility implied a transfer of people, goods, and images, as well as the creation of new entanglements. During the Cold War, these ties were formed primarily within the Eastern Bloc or between northwest and southern Europe.

Foreign Labor Migration in West and East Germany

Until the outbreak of World War II, the eastern and western countries of Europe were woven together in all kinds of ways due to different forms of labor migration. Italian workers sought jobs north of the Alps (*Transalpini*[59]), and countless Polish farmworkers headed to the Eastern provinces of Prussia in search of work on an estate.[60] Many laborers from Poland and Masuria were drawn to the Ruhr Valley in West Germany, which had even earned them the nickname *Ruhrpoles* by 1900 because a significant portion of the local population consisted of Poles.[61] After France signed a treaty on migration with Italy and Poland in 1919, a system of bilateral agreements began to develop over the course of the 1920s, paving the way for the influx of labor migrations to Western Europe after World

War II. Referred to as the *Gastarbeiter* system, these treaties led to strong entanglements between the European countries that were on the sending or receiving ends of these migration patterns.[62] After 1945, Eastern Europe formed its own separate migration regime. Here, too, some of the COMECON states who had been facing labor shortages since the late 1950s tried to attract foreign workers. In contrast to the West, however, they sought to recruit labor resources exclusively from other Eastern European countries or non-European countries run by governments that were either socialist or leaning in this direction.

By the early 1950s, West German job market experts had already begun to predict a labor shortage in certain sectors. As a result, the West German government tightened its emigration policies and began to set things in motion to recruit foreign workers. In 1955, it signed its first bilateral treaty with Italy, and this agreement was supposed to set a precedent for later labor recruitment agreements.[63] Accordingly, treaties were signed with Spain and Greece in 1960 and then Portugal in 1964. The recruitment agreement signed with Turkey in 1961 was the first treaty with a state whose territory was not mostly on the European continent. This treaty differed from the others insofar as the recruitment period was supposed to be limited to two years, and families were not permitted to follow. Although it was not mentioned in the actual agreement, but only in the correspondence surrounding it, this treaty was not supposed to encourage other non-European countries to try to send workers to the FRG.[64] West Germany did sign a treaty with Morocco in 1963 and Tunisia in 1965, but both of these agreements excluded the families of recruits from following. There were, therefore, first-class and second-class recruitment treaties.[65]

Despite the fact that almost a third of these labor migrants were women, the image of the *Gastarbeiter* that prevailed among the public was that of a male labor migrant.[66] In the first few years of recruitment, the term *Gastarbeiter* had quickly come to replace the term *Fremdarbeiter* (foreign worker, but very much in the sense of "alien worker") that was still in use despite the fact that it had become tainted by its association with the Nazis' forced labor programs. At the time, however, objections were already being raised about the term *Gastarbeiter*. The trade unions, for example, preferred "foreign employees." Initially, by referring to this labor migration as *Gastarbeit* (guest work), the West German recruitment policies stressed the fact that these workers were supposed to come to the FRG only for a short time, and they were expected to return home when they were no longer needed. Once the Berlin Wall had gone up, stopping the flow of immigration from the GDR, efforts were made to recruit more foreign labor migrants. At the beginning of the 1970s, this migration regime, which rested on bilateral treaties, was put to an end, not only in West Germany, but also in all other northern and western European countries who had engaged in this kind of recruitment. Scholarship has come to doubt the significance of the oil crisis in 1973 for this abrupt end to recruitment; the crisis seems to have been just the "last in a series of different reasons."[67] As early as the late 1960s, it had already become clear that what was intended to be a temporary form of labor migration was turning into full-fledged immigration. This led to intense debates over the integration and assimilation of these workers, which only seemed to be acceptable to the countries that had been recruiting foreign workers if the brakes were put on any further immigration.[68] Yet the goal behind this stop on recruitment, namely to end the influx of immigrants who were not from the EEC countries, was never met. Indeed, because the recruitment stop eliminated the chance to return to West Germany in the future, it actually motivated many of the migrants who were already in the country to put down roots and stay. In turn, this meant that even more of the families who had been left behind in the home country began to follow their relatives to West Germany. Only the Italian workers could claim more leniency because Italy belonged to the EEC.

The Western model of "Gastarbeit" was sharply criticized in the GDR as a prime example of capitalist-imperialist exploitation and proof of the lingering legacy of the Nazis in the Federal Republic.[69] Nonetheless, the GDR began to make its own effort to attract foreign workers at the beginning of the 1960s in order to counteract the labor shortage in the country. In 1957, the Soviet Union and Czechoslovakia had already brought in Bulgarian workers, and as of the mid-1960s, the idea of redistributing workers from socialist states with a labor surplus to those with a labor shortage was bandied about more and more.[70] In 1963, for example, the GDR signed what was referred to as an "occupational qualifications treaty" with Poland, which was followed by a commuter treaty in 1966. The latter allowed workers from the Polish border areas to commute to the GDR on a daily basis in order to work in the processing industry or hospitality sector.[71] A treaty with Hungary followed in 1967 that provided for "employment while completing vocational training," which was supposed to develop a new model that would bring Hungarian workers to the GDR for three years.[72] The GDR legitimized these bilateral treaties under the motto of vocational training and "international solidarity."[73] There was no official mention of a labor shortage or labor transfers, however, and the treaties were kept under wraps.

Until the mid-1970s, the GDR primarily recruited workers from other European COMECON states. When these neighboring countries began to put more demands on the GDR, the GDR began to sign treaties with non-European socialist or nonaligned countries in the mid-1970s. The workers recruited from these countries were supposed to stay in the country only on a temporary basis. For instance, the GDR came to an agreement with Algeria in 1974, Cuba in 1978, and Mozambique in 1979. In light of the worsening economic situation and the growing dependence on foreign workers in order to maintain production, a "mass import" of labor migrants occurred in the 1980s that brought the number of labor migrants up to about ninety-four thousand in 1989.[74] A large portion of these workers came from Vietnam; the GDR had already signed an agreement with Vietnam on schooling in 1973, which was followed in 1976 by a treaty that provided for job training only in production. Within the socialist bloc, Vietnam was one of the largest labor exporters. As of 1989, the majority of the labor migrants in the GDR came from Vietnam; fifty-nine thousand of the ninety-four thousand labor migrants were Vietnamese.[75] The GDR also signed treaties with Mongolia in 1982 and Angola in 1984, which were followed by treaties with China and North Korea in 1986. The justification that was originally provided for these treaties, namely to provide training and development aid to these countries, had become worthless by the 1980s.

In comparison to West Germany, labor migration set in much later in the GDR—at a point in time when the recruitment stop had already put an end to the *Gastarbeiter* system in Western Europe. Labor migration also differed quantitatively between East and West Germany: Whereas approximately 2.6 million foreigners were working in the FRG in 1973, there were only about twelve thousand in the GDR in 1970; this figure jumped in the GDR to twenty-six thousand in 1980, then sixty-one thousand in 1986, before topping out at almost ninety-four thousand in 1989.[76] At the end of 1989, foreigners accounted for 1.1 percent of the population in the GDR, compared to 7.7 percent in the Federal Republic.[77]

Despite all the official claims that the use of foreign labor in the GDR had nothing to do with the recruitment policies of the West, there are diverse parallels that can be drawn between these two practices. In both countries, for example, this labor recruitment was ultimately a one-sided transfer to a country with a more developed industrial sector; these transfers took place on the basis of bilateral treaties between countries that belonged to the respective blocs, but were nonetheless independent nation-states. The interests of the countries who provided the labor recruits were also similar; they sought to reduce their unemployment rates, decrease the national debt through wage transfers, or tap into a source of foreign currency.[78] In the East as well as the West, labor migrants were mostly recruited for relatively poorly paid jobs that were often associated with health risks and hard physical labor, as well as shift work. German workers tended to avoid these jobs in car manufacturing, the chemical industry, or the hospitality sector. Moreover, both states found a similar answer to a similar problem; in both cases, it can be rather justly said that an "underclass" of foreign labor migrants was created.[79] However, foreign policy and foreign trade considerations also played a role in these processes; the bilateral treaties served to stimulate the integration process in Western Europe as well as in the COMECON.[80]

Both German states initially granted migrants a work permit only for a job at a specific company, but these workers mostly enjoyed the same status as German workers in terms of wage agreements and social benefits. The West German welfare state and the East German "welfare dictatorship" had a considerable influence on migration policy in this respect.[81] Whereas the migrants in the GDR had to stay at the job to which they had been assigned and were not permitted to quit, many of the migrant workers in West Germany tried to find better jobs on their own accord.[82] In addition, protests against the poor working and living conditions among these workers also took place in both countries. In the mid-1970s, for example, Algerian workers went on strike several times in East Germany, despite the prohibitions against strikes. Simultaneously, Turkish workers led a strike at Ford in Cologne that hit the headlines, as did a strike by migrant and German women in Pierburg-Neuss.[83] The West German government as well as the GDR leadership reacted to these strikes in a similar way, namely by identifying the supposed ringleaders and sending them back to their countries of origin.

Another commonality shared by both labor migration regimes was that the West German employers and the East German state paid for the travel expenses to get to Germany, and the foreign workers were housed in dormitories provided by the respective factories and companies. In these housing facilities, workers had to comply with certain rules, including quite strict regulations on visitations. Residents, though, found ways around the entry checks and prohibitions about spending the night away from the dormitories in both countries. Although life in these residences was subject to surveillance and control, many migrants still managed to make friends among their colleagues. Indeed, the significance of these friendships cannot be underestimated, particularly in the GDR where the formation of migrant associations was prohibited. Foreigners were not granted freedom to practice their religion in the GDR, nor were they allowed to establish their own press outlets. In West Germany, on the other hand, many migrants relatively quickly sought out their own apartments (which was not allowed in the GDR), especially when their families later came to stay, but they often faced discrimination on the housing market. Labor migrants in both Germanys were often not permitted to enter dance clubs or restaurants.[84] Racist images of "hot-headed, knife-wielding southerners," "philistine" Eastern European, and Africans "from the bush"[85] circulated virulently in both German states, attesting to the lasting influence of colonial as well as Nazi traditions and racist mechanisms of exclusion. Even though racism was a crime in East Germany—unlike in the Federal Republic—there were criminal attacks against migrants in East Germany as well, especially in the 1980s as part of a rise in right-wing extremist groups on both sides of the Wall. The press, however, maintained its internationalist, friendly paternalist tone until the collapse of the GDR, and mentioning conflicts was taboo.[86] In the heated debates in West Germany, on the other hand, migration had predominantly been seen as a problem from the 1970s onward.

In spite of the parallels traced above, the situation of labor migrants in East and West Germany clearly differed in many respects. Recruitment in the GDR was always done collectively, and the groups that came together often stayed together for their entire stay in the East. West German companies, on the other hand, recruited people by name. In West Germany, individual labor migrants entered into the country with a work permit that had been acquired in advance from the German consulate or with a tourist visa, and then they looked for work once they got to Germany, but this was never the case in the GDR. These unofficial ways of entering the country were consciously made available in the Federal Republic in order to save on recruitment costs and avoid becoming dependent on the countries that were sending workers.[87] Similarly, the freedom of these labor migrants to choose whether or not to migrate and decide about their options in the GDR were much more limited than in West Germany, especially since the Stasi kept tabs on foreign migrants.[88] The isolated nature of the dormitories, most of which were located on the outskirts of town, also prevented labor migrants from interacting much with the East German population.[89] The GDR was also very consistent in rotating workers in and out, and there were no plans to have families follow their relatives to the GDR. In fact, it was not even possible for labor migrants to extend their stay up to ten years until the 1980s, but this by no means implied that they were to be granted permanent residency.[90] The only foreigners who were permitted to become permanent residents in the GDR were those who married East German citizens. That said, however, binational marriages had to be approved by the state, which did not welcome such unions. In addition, labor migrants who became pregnant were sent home.[91] Yet it should be noted that the GDR leadership did make a clear distinction between women from Mozambique or Vietnam and Polish women, for example, who were not subject to these discriminatory regulations.[92] Apparently, therefore, there was also a two-class system among foreign workers in the GDR that differentiated between Europeans and non-Europeans, which also affected the negotiating position of the countries who supplied labor recruits.

Even though neither East nor West Germany saw itself as a country of immigration, the Federal Republic was forced to permit families to follow their migrant worker relatives into the country and leave open the door for permanent residence permits because of its professed commitments to social and humanitarian rights. For this reason, as well as the significantly high amount of labor migration into the country, West Germany de facto became a country of immigration over the course of the 1970s. Neighborhoods full of migrants with their own shops, restaurants, and mosques made it clear that these labor migrants who were only supposed to stay in the country over the short-term were there to stay, which would change the face of West German society forever. The GDR, however, did not experience anything like this pluralization or transformation of urban space and society through migration.

Refugee and Asylum Policy in the Federal Republic and the GDR

Whereas World War I first brought the problem of refugees to the international political stage, it was National Socialism and World War II that prompted the affirmation of the right of asylum within the framework of the Universal Declaration of Human Rights passed by the United Nations in 1948. In West Germany, the experience of political and racist persecution between 1933 and 1945 led to the inclusion of a right of asylum in the *Grundgesetz* that was very liberal when compared internationally.[93] The Federal Republic granted asylum not only on the basis of the Geneva Convention relating to the Status of Refugees, as in other European countries, but also on the basis of Article 16, Paragraph 2, Section 2 of the *Grundgesetz* ("Persons persecuted on political grounds shall have the right of asylum") until 1993. Consequently, individuals could petition for the right to protection against political persecution on the basis of constitutional law.

The GDR Constitution of 1949 granted those foreigners asylum who had been persecuted for fighting for the basic principles that were outlined within it (Article 10, Paragraph 2). The GDR, which did not guarantee its citizens the right to leave the country, was not a signatory to the Geneva Refugee Convention.[94] In the GDR Constitution of 1968, the right of asylum was only formulated as "may grant asylum" and not "shall," and the decision to take on refugees was in the hands of the politburo, or rather the secretariat of the Central Committee of the SED.[95]

The right of asylum and refugee policy was therefore of major political importance in both German states. The GDR's refugee and asylum policy was clearly driven by its foreign policy interests: on the one hand, in keeping with international solidarity, it supported foreign Communist parties and their members; on the other hand, emigrants from the so-called young nation-states, which was the term used to refer to former colonies that had recently become independent, were taken in by the GDR.[96] For example, refugees from the Greek civil war, and Spanish Communists who had been expelled from France, came to the GDR in 1949 and 1950, respectively. Among those who were admitted to the GDR because of their participation in national liberation struggles were individual functionaries of the Algerian FLN, the Palestinian PLO, the South African ANC, and the Namibian SWAPO.[97]

The people who fled the Eastern Bloc for the West were considered to be the "real" political refugees in West Germany for the most part.[98] They were guaranteed the right to stay in West Germany during the Cold War, even if no grounds for asylum existed.[99] In general, the refugees who fled to West Germany in the wake of the Hungarian Uprising in 1956 and the Prague Spring in 1968/69 were welcomed with open arms, not only by the responsible authorities, but also the population at large. Likewise, refugees from Tibet, once it had been annexed to China, were also admitted without trouble to West Germany, and a great number of them were also accepted by Switzerland, France, and Sweden. Without a doubt, the "axiomatic Cold War configuration" determined the course of refugee and asylum policy.[100] This did not begin to change until the 1980s, when West Germany adopted an increasingly defensive approach toward refugees from Eastern Europe. For example, the approximately 250 thousand Poles who fled to the West after martial law was declared in Poland in December 1981 were no longer treated automatically as political refugees.[101] The legitimation that had been provided to justify the admission of refugees up to this point began to erode quickly. The willingness to accept asylum-seekers from the so-called Third World had already been very limited in decades prior, not just in the FRG, but across all of Europe.

Specific political events around the globe, such as the military coup against Allende's socialist government in Chile in 1973, prompted East and West Germany to take on political refugees from the country affected.[102] The GDR almost immediately permitted about two thousand members and followers of Chile's left-wing Unidad Popular to enter the country. It then used this gesture to tout its international solidarity and reaffirm its moral legitimation.[103] In West Germany, on the other hand, a heated debate broke out between the social-liberal government and the Christian Union parties over whether or not this group of Chileans should be granted asylum.[104] Despite the Christian Democrats' worries about Communist infiltration, the government decided in favor of admitting these refugees. All over West Germany—apart from Bavaria—the refugees were not selected on the basis of their political views. This appears to have reflected a "trend towards the universal principle of providing protection for victims of political persecution under dictatorship of all political hues" that was not dictated by the axiomatic constellations of the Cold War—at least in the Federal Republic.[105]

Both German states reacted to the same situation in Chile by accepting refugees, but they did so using different legal bases that were linked to divergent political goals; they did, however, share the common aim of providing humanitarian relief. Whereas these refugees evoked ambivalent feelings among portions of the West German population because of their left-wing political affiliation, the supposed and real privileges granted to these emigrants in East Germany unleashed rejection and even jealousy within the GDR.[106] The Chilean émigrés were given 2,500 to 3,000 Marks upon entry, plus they were granted interest-free loans, and, above all, highly sought-after housing in new apartment blocks.[107] In particular, the chance to travel to the West that was usually only granted to certain *Kader* (cadres) irked many East Germans, especially since these opportunities were sometimes used as a way to then stay in West Germany or other Western countries.[108] Many of the Chilean émigrés, most of whom were put to work in jobs in production that fell well below their actual qualifications, also petitioned for permission to go to the Federal Republic.[109] As early as 1968, moreover, several hundred Greeks resettled to the FRG as a result of the repression of those Greek civil war refugees who the Stasi considered to be "Eurocommunist" and therefore too Western in their political orientation.[110]

In light of the wary surveillance of the refugees by the Stasi and the general mistrust among the population, the political refugees in the GDR were by no means "equal members of a socialist collective that was transnational in its outlook," but rather they were only "tolerated guests in a nationally defined German community."[111] Unlike the so-called temporary contract workers, they were permitted to bring their families with them, and they were not housed in isolated dormitories. It was therefore at least theoretically possible for them to take part in the everyday life of the GDR. Ultimately, however, there were really not very many people who came to the GDR as political émigrés; they were, in fact, the smallest group of foreigners living in the GDR.[112]

In West Germany, too, asylum-seekers played only a marginal role in migration to the country until the recruitment stop in 1974. Only a few thousand of them entered the Federal Republic each year, and the majority came from Eastern Europe.[113] Over the course of the 1970s, the number of asylum-seekers increased, as it did all over Western Europe, and the countries of origin became more diversified. In addition to the military coup in Chile, the end of the Vietnam War and Khomeini's seizure of power in Iran tipped the scales so that by the late 1970s, the majority of refugees and asylum-seekers came from non-European countries.[114] This trend remained in place until the late 1980s. After this point, most of the asylum-seekers once again came from southern and eastern Europe, first Poland, and then Yugoslavia as the country began to collapse.[115] West Germany and Austria were popular destinations for these migrants because of their geographic locations, but also because of the migrant networks that had been set up during the era of the *Gastarbeiter*.

The number of asylum-seekers climbed steadily in the FRG from the 1970s onward, reaching the hundred thousand mark for the first time in 1980. West Germany was the recipient of seven hundred thousand of the 1.7 million petitions for asylum that were submitted between 1983 and 1990 in Europe. When compared to the country's population in 1985, there was one asylum-seeker for every 827 West Germans, whereas this figure was one to 567 in Sweden, and one to 666 in Switzerland.[116]

Not only the increasing number of asylum seekers was significant in terms of migration history, but also the fact that the only people who could still immigrate to West Germany after the recruitment stop in 1973 were either ethnic German *Aussiedler* or those who submitted petitions for asylum. As a result, petitions for asylum after this point, as Klaus Bade puts it, functioned as a partial "substitute for absent regular options for immigration."[117] But this by no means meant that the majority of asylum-seekers had exclusively economic motives, as the polemic talk of "economic refugees" would suggest. This buzzword, which soon came to dominate the debates on asylum in the FRG and elsewhere, was used to differentiate between supposedly legitimate and illegitimate asylum-seekers. Often, however, there was a mix of economic, social, and political reasons that motivated people to seek asylum. Politically persecuted Kurds often came to West Germany as *Gastarbeiter* during the recruitment phase, for example, but after 1974 the only way for them to enter the country was to petition for asylum. For people without relatives in the FRG or without German ancestors, the only legal migration channel was as refugees escaping persecution, which led to a rapid widening of this immigration route. The increasing numbers of asylum-seekers also led to an increase in the politicking that surrounds immigration issues. The low recognition quotas, for instance, were touted as proof of the supposed misuse of the right of asylum, even though many asylum-seekers were successful with their appeals or could not be deported because they were given a de facto status as refugees although they were not legally classified as such.

To sum up the asylum and refugee situation in divided Germany, it can safely be said that the number of refugees in the GDR was really quite low. Things changed in the Federal Republic over the course of the 1970s and 1980s as asylum became, in a certain sense, an "irregular channel for labor migration."[118] In 1975, the priority granted to West Germans as opposed to foreign workers on the job market was lifted for asylum-seekers. Along with the official permission to work that was provided to asylum-seekers, this partial lifting of the primacy of nationals on the labor market made it clear that not only the migrants themselves, but also the Federal Ministry of Labor had not lost its interest in the employment of foreign workers after the *Gastarbeiter* regime had been brought to an end.[119] As a result of the growing number of refugees, however, increasingly restrictive measures were adopted over the course of the 1980s in order to put a damper on this migration. Contrary to the provisions of the Geneva Refugee Convention, for instance, a visa requirement was issued for the main countries of origin in 1980. From 1982 onward, the social aid that had to be provided to these refugees because of the two-year prohibition against work was primarily paid out in the form of noncash benefits; all the federal states also introduced housing in camps, as well as residency restrictions for refugees. In the mid-1980s, the debates on asylum intensified, focusing more and more on the changes to the right of asylum that were being demanded by the Christian Democratic Union (CDU) and the Christian Social Union (CSU). These parties called for passing a law that, akin to the time limit put on labor migration, would redefine the country's policy on asylum to limit immigration only to exceptional cases. Yet asylum is in fact based on a "logic of exception": as political scientist Elias Steinhilper puts it, "The emphasis on the real need to protect a few has legitimized closing the door to many."[120]

Migration, Migration Policy, and the Redefinition of the Nation in the late 1980s and the 1990s

For the history of migration, the end of the Cold War represented a "major break."[121] The minimal amount of migration that had gone on between Eastern and Western Europe due the prohibitions against leaving the East quickly turned into mass migration within a relatively short amount of time in the late 1980s. In part, this migration resembled what was happening before World War II, and it drew upon this earlier experience.[122] Simultaneously, migration played a key role in tearing down the "Iron Curtain." In the case of Germany, for example, the mass exodus of GDR citizens in 1989 via Hungary and the embassy in Prague ultimately brought an end to the GDR and led to the revival of mass emigration from East to West Germany.

Asylum-seekers and ethnic German *Aussiedler* primarily shaped the contours of this movement of peoples that took place in the late 1980s and early 1990s. Due to Soviet reform policies in the mid-1980s, the number of *Aussiedler* who came to the FRG grew quickly, and these ethnic Germans were considered to be equal to German citizens as soon as they arrived in West Germany. Yet this privileged status granted to the *Aussiedler*, which rested not only on the West German understanding of the nation, but also the system rivalry of the Cold War, increasingly came under fire. The politically defined categorization of different migrant groups was also extremely controversial in the context of the debates on asylum in the early 1990s.

As part of the reunification process, the restrictive migration policy of the Federal Republic was extended to the new federal states, but without taking into account the special situation of the foreigners who were living in the former East. For many of the foreign labor migrants, the collapse of the GDR spelled the loss of their jobs and their residence permits; the majority of these former "contract workers" had to leave the country. Over the course of reunification, which was accompanied by the search for a new unified German identity, foreigners were not only excluded discursively, but also confronted with racist violence on a large scale. The pogroms directed at foreigners in the early 1990s also made it quite clear to migrants living in West Germany that the inclusion in German society for which they had fought so hard during the 1970s and 1980s was under threat. From the perspective of many migrants, reunification was therefore very much a decisive turning point that dramatically changed their self-image and the way in which they were perceived by others.

The Mass Exodus from East Germany in 1989 and Migration to the West after Reunification

The significant role of the East German exodus movement in the collapse of the GDR has often been pointed out. The desire to travel and the decision to migrate were very tightly linked in this context, which seems to have been something specific to the situation in the GDR at the time. There was a connection between travel visits to the West and emigration (as well as staying in the West without planning it beforehand) in other socialist states. But the fact that the calls for the freedom to travel in the GDR became such a central demand on the state differs at least from the trends in places such as the Soviet Union, where the more generalized struggle for the recognition of human rights played a much greater role during the reform and upheaval phase.[123]

At the beginning of 1989, under pressure from the Soviets, the GDR signed the Vienna Agreement of the Commission on Security and Cooperation in Europe (CSCE, later the Organization for Security and Cooperation in Europe, or OSCE), thereby committing itself to guaranteeing its citizens the right to leave the country. But the GDR did not live up to its word, and even in February 1989, Chris Gueffroy was shot trying to cross the Berlin Wall. Then, in the summer of 1989, some ten thousand East Germans, especially younger and well-educated ones, used their vacations in Hungary to flee across the border between Austria and Hungary to get to the West. On 10 September, Hungary announced that it would no longer work with the GDR to control its borders, which meant that the GDR cracked down on issuing travel permits to Hungary. From then on, East Germans were permitted to go to Hungary only in exceptional cases. At the beginning of October, fourteen thousand GDR citizens who had occupied the West German Embassy in Prague were sent on special closed trains across the territory of the GDR so that they could enter West Germany. The Soviet reform policies and the oppositional movements calling for the freedom to travel in the GDR by staging mass demonstrations exposed the crisis of the SED state for all to see. Finally, on 9 November 1989, Günter Schabowski announced the new travel regulations that were actually supposed to apply to those who wanted to emigrate, but his statement turned into a declaration of the immediate freedom to travel.[124]

In terms of the history of migration and tourism, this freedom to travel possessed a very high level of symbolic importance. Alon Confino has referred to the right to travel aptly as "an entitlement that reflects on the ability of the system to keep the promise of a better life."[125] The SED's restricted understanding of vacation, which was limited to the purpose of fostering collective identity and regeneration, was out of touch with the needs of the GDR public, and it could not rein in the desires for a better life that tourism had generated.[126]

A particularity in the history of divided Germany, which was in fact partly responsible for the strong movement to leave the country that ultimately helped to dismantle the SED state, was the way in which nationality laws were set up in West Germany and how they factored into the FRG's claims that it was responsible for the wellbeing of GDR citizens. Unlike the new citizenship law that was introduced in the GDR in 1967, replacing the German citizenship law (*Reichs- und Staatsangehörigkeitsgesetz*) that had been on the books since 1913, West Germany's citizenship laws clung to a unified notion of German citizenship. As a result, it was a place that East Germans could turn to in times of trouble, an option that did not exist in this form for the residents of other Eastern Bloc states. As a result, it was easy for West Germany to become the destination for a mass exodus from the GDR in 1989.

Approximately 360 thousand people left the GDR for West Germany in 1989, and almost 80 percent of them were younger than forty years old.[127] There had not been such a massive wave of migration from East to West since the 1950s. At the same time, reunification also brought migration in the other direction, especially as tens of thousands of administrative civil servants in particular moved from West to East Germany.[128] Some of the total 1.5 million West Germans who went to the new federal states between 1989 and 2001 hoped to make quick profits for their companies, while others had been given material incentives to become residents of the former East.[129] These payments, which were referred to as a *Buschzulage* (akin to a special allowance for living in less desirable places such as the African bush), indicate that there was a clear hierarchy between West and East as well as an aspect of "foreignness" and "otherness" at play. The topos of the "bush" not only cropped up when GDR citizens were talking about African labor migrants, but also came to be used within a process of "othering" that was taking place with respect to East Germany. Although there was not really much of a language barrier between the two Germanys, both states had grown so far away from one another in other respects that their supposed "shared cultural heritage" proved to be a rather shaky foundation.[130]

Aussiedler, Refugees, and the Asylum Debates of the Early 1990s

In addition to the westward migration of East Germans, West Germany experienced another significant wave of East to West migration in the late 1980s and 1990s, namely the immigration of *Aussiedler* (which were referred to as "late *Aussiedler*" or "*Spätaussiedler*" from 1993). This group of migrants was comprised of German nationals, or rather *Volkszugehörige* who were considered to be ethnic Germans (and their children and spouses), who had been residents of the former eastern territories of Germany or other (south)east European territories prior to 8 May 1945 and had remained there for a while before later emigrating to the Federal Republic. The *(Spät-)Aussiedler* fell under the provisions of the Federal Law on Expellees, and they enjoyed special privileges, such as comprehensive integration assistance and the right to immediate naturalization and coverage within the welfare system. The basis for their recognition as Germans was the one-sided reliance on the principle of ethnic descent, *ius sanguinis*, in the citizenship laws of the Federal Republic until 1999.

Aussiedler (or *Übersiedler*, as they were known in the GDR) had already been coming to West Germany, mostly from Poland, since the first decades after World War II; a far fewer number went to East Germany. The GDR had been much more cautious than West Germany when it came to encouraging the emigration of German relatives from Poland. In fact, the GDR no longer officially recognized any German minorities abroad.[131] Consequently, only a few thousand *Übersiedler* came to the GDR in the 1950s to join their families, while around 250 thousand people emigrated from Poland to the FRG.[132] For East Germany, the *Übersiedler* were not just ethnic Germans but also a source of labor. The SED used this form of migration to recruit workers; this subject thus overlaps with the topic of Polish labor migration that was touched on above.

The countries of origin that West Germany declared to be *Aussiedler* areas clearly reflected the influence of the system rivalry on the state's policy toward the *Aussiedler*: the members of German minorities in the Western world were not eligible for integration aid when they came to the Federal Republic, for example, because they were not considered oppressed. China, in contrast, was declared to be an *Aussiedler* area in 1957, despite the fact that West Germany did not need to step in to help cushion any blows left over from World War II in the country in keeping with the West German law on war restitutions (*Kriegsfolgengesetz*). The goal of this policy was therefore to make it as easy as possible for West Germany to take on Germans who were living under Communist rule.[133]

In terms of *Aussiedler* immigration, the year 1989 did not mark a clear break of any kind, although this kind of migration had picked up dramatically over the course of the transformation of Eastern Europe from the mid-1980s onward.[134] Until 1990, the majority of *Aussiedler* came from Poland, followed by the Soviet Union and then its successor states. Between 1988 and 1989, a total of almost 1.6 million *Aussiedler* emigrated to the Federal Republic, and two thirds of them came from the Soviet Union.[135]

Although these Polish and Russian *Aussiedler* were considered to be German from an administrative point of view, they were nonetheless confronted with various forms of discrimination in daily life. The majority of locals thought of them as foreigners: according to a survey done in 1989, only 31 percent of the German population considered them to be German.[136] Many locals moreover, were often envious of new arrivals, not least because some of these Russian-Germans were retirees who received pensions from the German state without ever having paid into the German social security system.[137] Despite, or rather because of, these tensions, the federal government did not want to openly deal directly with the issue of the immigration of *(Spät-)Aussiedler*. Even though these minorities hardly any longer faced the threat of expulsion in their home countries that came in the form of discrimination and oppression directed against ethnic Germans—which meant that one of the "basic assumptions behind the admission of the *Aussiedler*" no longer existed—they were hesitant to make any policy changes.[138] The SPD and the FDP called for a revision of the *Bundesvertriebenengesetz,* which regulated the rather liberal requirements for accepting *Aussiedler* into the country, a revision that would introduce quotas, but their suggestions were blocked by the Christian Democratic Union. Nonetheless, the CDU/CSU was later forced to agree to these changes to the law as part of what was called the Asylum Compromise of 1992/93. In accordance with another piece of legislation, only people of German descent from the former Soviet Union were recognized as *Aussiedler* as of early 1993, in part because it was assumed that they were still being pressured to leave the former Communist bloc.[139] The actual practice of accepting the *Aussiedler* into Germany had already changed successively since 1989. The *Wohnortszuweisungsgesetz* of 1989 regulated the assignment of where the *Aussiedler* were supposed to live once they entered the country, providing for an equal distribution of this migrant group across the whole country. This meant that these immigrants were rather limited in choosing where to live. Moreover, in keeping with the *Aussiedleraufnahmegesetz* of 1990, they were also required to submit their petition for permission to enter Germany before they left their countries of origin. This was followed in 1996 by an obligatory language test.[140] The government and the opposition had fought bitterly over these tightened restrictions when it came to dealing with the *Aussiedler* at a practical level.

The parties were only in agreement when it came to another group of migrants from the Soviet Union, and then later its successor states, who were permitted to immigrate to the Federal Republic as of 1991, namely the "Jewish quota refugees." In this case, migration policy drew on the country's historic responsibility for the expulsion and murder of the European Jews. Consequently, these policies were never called into question publicly, especially since Jewish immigrants were proof that the country was overcoming its Nazi past and that the integrity and trustworthiness of the new Germany was very much intact.[141] Between 1989 and 2005, a total of about two hundred thousand Russian Jews came to the Federal Republic on the basis of the *Kontingentflüchtlingsgesetz* (the law that regulated quota refugees), which had been passed in 1980 to allow for the rapid entry of the Vietnamese boat people. These Jewish immigrants accounted for almost a quarter of those Jews who emigrated from the (former) Soviet Union between 1989 and 2005.[142]

Rather than focusing on *Aussiedler* migration, the Union parties concentrated on the asylum issue. They were quite successful in pushing through this agenda, which meant that migration policy in the 1990s revolved around asylum regulations for the most part. The debates surrounding the asylum question, which was shaped by asylum-seekers coming from outside the country as well as the German nation itself, was a central element in the process of self-redefinition that took place in Germany after reunification. In these debates—as well as the discussions over the *Aussiedler*—the question of who was understood to be German and who in Germany could claim which rights was always implicitly, if not explicitly, negotiated.

The big issue in the early 1990s was not reunification, but rather the abuse of the right of asylum. As of summer 1991, surveys indicated that almost 80 percent of the population saw the "asylum/foreigner" issue as the most important problem facing the country.[143] Even before 1989/90, horror stories were bandied about in the West German press that Europe might soon be overrun by asylum-seekers. Interestingly, however, the refugee movement was on the rise around the world during this time, but compared to other places, Europe was only minimally affected by it. The majority of this migration driven by poverty and persecution played out in the Global South. Yet the consciously fueled debates over asylum quickly became more populist in tone. The term *Asylant* that appeared more often, as opposed to the more politically correct *Asylbewerber* (asylum-seeker), was quite derogatory. Other terms such as *Asylschmarotzer* (asylum spongers) or *Scheinasylanten* (bogus asylum-seekers) leaned even further toward denunciation. Not only were they used by right-wing radical parties such as "The Republicans," but also politicians from the CDU and CSU spoke of the "abuse of asylum status." The talk of *Asylanten* was tightly linked to the "flood" metaphors that became a decisive element of the debates. It implicitly stripped these immigrants of their individuality, pointing to the idea that Germany could no longer take on more refugees: "The boat is full!"—was the successful slogan of "The Republicans" who gained ground in the elections of 1991. As a result, it was not out of the question that a majority could be formed to push through dramatic changes such as an amendment to the *Grundgesetz*.

Even at the time, people made the connection between the asylum debates and the high number of racist acts of violence in the early 1990s.[144] In Hoyerswerda in 1991, as well as in Rostock-Lichtenhagen in 1992, pogrom-like attacks were made against foreigners—asylum-seekers as well as "contract workers"—under the watch of an applauding crowd and without any decisive action taken by the state authorities.[145] This violence was not limited to East Germany, but the public generally judged racism to be a predominantly East German problem. In the media, East Germans were therefore depicted as "generally backward, extreme right-wing, and violent," which made the West appear to be more advanced and more tolerant in comparison.[146] Whereas the asylum debates contributed to German-German integration by creating a cleft between Germans and non-Germans, "the debate over [the supposedly East German] origins of racist attacks reproduced the opposition between East and West Germany."[147] The violent attacks in Mölln in 1992 and Solingen in 1993 made it clear, however, that foreigners were also being murdered in the West, and that this racist violence was not only directed against refugees and asylum-seekers, but also against the (Turkish) migrants who had been living in the country for a long time. Between 1990 and 1993, a total of at least forty-nine non-Germans were murdered in the Federal Republic, although the number of unreported incidents is surely quite high.

This violence, however, did not change the hard tone of the asylum debates at all. To the contrary: after the pogrom in Rostock-Lichtenhagen, a politician from the Union parties claimed that this violence was not an expression of racism, but rather of "the fully justified resentment over the mass abuse of the right of asylum."[148] Friedrich Bohl from the Chancellor's Office issued an announcement that it would only be possible to bring an end to the excessive pressure on the people by putting limits on asylum rights.[149] As chancellor, Helmut Kohl ultimately threatened to declare a state of emergency, which was the most extreme measure that could be undertaken in order to bring an end (as was desired by the CDU) to domestic conflicts. He also promised that he would convince the SPD that a constitutional amendment was needed. At a special party congress in November 1992, the SPD approved what was called the Asylum Compromise. Among other points, this compromise included the establishment of the principle of safe third-party foreign states (free of persecution) as well as safe countries of origin. In addition, it introduced an accelerated asylum process for airports in which asylum-seekers were not considered to have officially entered the country and could therefore be deported within two days if their petition for asylum was not approved. The corresponding legislation (*Asylbewerberleistungsgesetz*) made cuts to the social benefits provided to asylum-seekers to bring them below the level of the country's standard welfare benefits, and it introduced the principle of providing vouchers for goods as opposed to cash support. The number of people petitioning for asylum did decrease considerably in the wake of the constitutional amendment. But, these legislative changes did not bring an end to the heated social climate and racist violence, which was clearly demonstrated by the attack in Solingen just a day after the Bundestag voted on the amendment.

By making this change to its constitution and eliminating the liberal West German provisions for asylum, Germany moved to align itself more closely with its European neighbors. In some countries of Europe, the idea of a safe third country had been put in place earlier. Some of the new regulations that were negotiated at the European level included the clause on the first country of registration that only allows asylum-seekers to submit their petition for asylum in the first safe country that they enter within Europe. For a few years now, the countries on the Mediterranean have become the main ports of entry for asylum migration because of their geographic position.

The amendments to the right of asylum in West Germany were not only part of a process of German-German reconciliation that, among others, came about through the exclusion of non-Germans, but also were embedded within the context of the Europeanization of migration policy. Since the late 1970s, states across Europe had become more restrictive in the way in which they dealt with the right of asylum. Correspondingly, asylum policy came to be seen more as a security issue that had to be negotiated between the ministers of the interior in the individual European countries.[150] This Europeanization of migration policy has therefore transferred elements of national sovereignty to supranational actors, but this by no means implies that we can speak of a uniform migration policy in the EU. Europeanization has also meant that European migration policy is no longer restricted to the EU territory. Readmission agreements such as those between the Federal Republic and Poland (before Poland joined the EU) have brought an increasing number of European states that are not part of the Schengen border system into the new European migration regime. Other forms of advance border controls, some of which are located hundreds of kilometers beyond Europe's borders, have also been part of this process, in addition to the shifting of borders within countries, such as the extraterritorial zone that has been established at Frankfurt Airport.[151] For these reasons as well as others, many authors have described the turn of the millennium as a transition to a new migration regime.[152] They do not point to the isolationism implied by the idea of the "For-

Figure 9.1. Still from *Duvarlar-Mauern-Walls* (2000, dir. Can Candan)

tress Europe," but rather to a new form of migration management that has made borders more permeable for certain people, such as highly qualified professionals, but also led to a steady increase in the number of illegal migrants whose (underpaid) labor has become essential for large portions of the European economy.

Post-reunification Germany from the Perspective of Foreign Migrants

Many historical accounts of the period after 1990 focus on the conflicts and differences between East and West Germans. They have rarely looked at the way in which foreigners living in Germany or people with immigrant backgrounds have perceived the reunification process. A considerable portion of the migrants living in West Germany had come to feel like a genuine part of society over the course of the 1980s, especially from a retrospective viewpoint after 1990. There have hardly been any academic studies on migrant responses to the migration debates that heated up after the *Wende*, even though these discussions called into question their place in German society. Some initial research has indicated that reunification, and especially the racist pogroms of the early 1990s, was a "shocking experience" for many migrants, who have come to see this as a decisive turning point in their own lives.[153] Most of the Turkish people interviewed in the 2000 documentary *Duvarlar-Mauern-Walls*, by the Turkish-American director Can Candan, stressed that they were overjoyed at first with the fall of the Wall, but that the violent racism that emerged thereafter had called into question the work that they had done, as well as their hard-won rights.[154] Since professional success no longer seemed to provide a path into mainstream society, some of them chose to withdraw back into the confines of the Turkish community.[155]

Not only East Germans, but also many migrants found themselves facing a loss of social status after reunification, which they responded to with different strategies. One option for West German migrants was to try to boost their image over that of the East Germans by depicting themselves as "well-educated, highly motivated, and reliable workers as well as demanding consumers with a great deal of purchasing power."[156] In doing so, they implied that they were harder workers and better consumers than the East Germans, thereby justifying their right to stay in the country. At the same time, however, this implicitly questioned the seemingly automatic acceptance of East Germans and *Aussiedler* as part of society in the Federal Republic. By calling on the shared experience of the West and pointing out the extent of their integration within society, these migrants sought to defend their position within a new unified Germany.[157]

Reunification thus created a situation in which West Germans without an immigrant background, migrants who had come to West Germany long before 1989, "new arrivals" from the GDR, and *Aussiedler* competed to prove that they belonged in the country, albeit under varying conditions and with different legal positions.[158] In fact, the inclusion of citizens of the former GDR was not as clear-cut as official statements made it seem. The forty years of a divided Germany had indeed affected national identity.

Yet the exclusion of foreigners through the emphasis on a shared German identity appeared in various forms on both sides of the old Wall. In particular, the racist attacks directed against non-Germans in the early 1990s that were most prevalent in East Germany can be seen as a transfer of an experienced devaluation.[159] The determination that a kind of shift occurred here in which a conflict was taken out on "a foreign body or a body made foreign for the purpose,"[160] neither attempts to justify racist violence through the potential exclusion experienced by the perpetrators in any way, nor to depict racism as a purely East German problem.

In this competition for social inclusion in the Federal Republic, another criterion of difference soon came to play a role alongside German nationality: whereas Portuguese migrants, for example, could understand themselves as Europeans and increasingly be perceived and accepted as such,[161] "the" Turkish migrant, like non-European asylum-seekers, was stylized as a threatening "other." Especially in the case of Turkish migrants, this position as outsiders in German society was becoming firmly established. More frequently than ever before, they were being construed as a Muslim threat, regardless of their actual religious affinity.[162] An increasing culturalization of the "foreigner question" had been detected since the 1970s, to the extent that Etienne Balibar spoke of a kind of cultural racism in 1990 that was not defined by "race" itself.[163] After the fall of the Iron Curtain, and especially since 9/11, this cultural racism has been directed more and more against Muslims.

Symptomatically, the perspective of foreigners who were living in East Germany during the *Wende* is largely missing in migration scholarship. In 1990, the West German government renounced the bilateral treaties that had been made by the GDR, or at least sought to dissolve them through monetary settlements and repatriation aid.[164] At first, there was no intention to treat East German labor migrants as equal to West German labor migrants, but they were granted the same status in 1997. The new name given to these workers known as "foreign working people" (*ausländische Werktätige*) in the GDR, namely "contract workers," stressed the limited nature of their work contracts. Accordingly, it also emphasized the temporariness of their stay because no place had been made for them in post-reunification Germany.[165]

Some of these foreign labor migrants were ordered to return to their home countries immediately after the Wall came down, such as those from North Korea, China, or Cuba. The ones who remained in East Germany found themselves in an extremely precarious legal and socioeconomic situation because of the many lay-offs (contrary to the terms of the respective contracts) that were made even before reunification. Although there had never been an issue with giving job priority to German workers because of the permanent shortage of labor in the GDR up to this point, all of the sudden the protection of jobs for Germans became a pressing issue; the vehement calls for action sometimes even led to strikes and threats of violence.[166] As early as May 1990, far more than half of the foreign workers in East Germany no longer had jobs. Many of them willingly returned to their home countries or were deported. By the end of 1990, only twenty-eight thousand of the former "contract workers" were still in the country.[167] They had been given the choice of either to leave the country or to stay in Germany until the end of their original contract period if they could provide proof that they had a job and a permanent residence. A large portion of the labor migrants who stayed in the country came from Vietnam, and they kept their heads above water by running different kinds of small shops because they had been permitted to receive business permits if they wanted to stay. Some of them went to neighboring countries such as Czechoslovakia. In general, there was a great deal of migration among Vietnamese workers between different states of the former Eastern Bloc after 1989/90, despite the fact that Vietnamese workers had also lost their jobs in these countries as well.[168] Even today, most Vietnamese are self-employed.[169] Present-day wholesale markets such as Dong Xuan Center/Asiatown in East Berlin were started up by former *Vertragsarbeiter* from Vietnam. The fact that these workers were able to rely on contacts that they had made back in the GDR, however, made it clear that despite all the attempts to isolate foreigners, Vietnamese immigrants and Germans had not lived entirely separate lives.[170]

After reunification, the former East German labor migrants from Vietnam came face-to-face with the boat people living in West Germany, but the two groups hardly have any contact with one another. This split within the Vietnamese minority in present-day Germany resulted in part from the different legal status enjoyed by these two groups, which is clearly reflected in differences in social status. Whereas the approximately twenty-three thousand boat people who came to West Germany as quota refugees between 1979 and 1982 had been promised the chance to become permanent residents,[171] many of the former "contract workers" from Vietnam do not have valid residence permits. This example points to the fact that so-called integration issues do not stem from "the culture" of the migrants, but rather they primarily result from the legal status of these groups and their prospects for a future in Germany.[172] At the same time, a difference has clearly persisted between East and West that is connected to the varying life stories of the Vietnamese in the two Germanys. To a certain extent, the Cold War has continued in that the boat people came from South Vietnam while most "contract workers" came from the North. As a result, many of the Vietnamese who came to West Germany were often active in anti-communist circles and therefore still see their countrymen who went to East Germany as "followers of the Hanoi Communists."[173] The difference or otherness that has been felt between East and West Germans was not just part of the process of German-German rapprochement; rather, it has also affected the migrants in the country, not least because as people living in Germany, sometimes with German citizenship, they had been an integral part of the reunification process, or at least they should have been part of it.

Conclusion

Over the course of reunification, the question of the identity of the German nation, which had begun to fade into the background in East and West Germany by the 1970s, became virulent once more; the lines of inclusion and exclusion had to be renegotiated. On the one hand, as this chapter has argued, the rapprochement between East and West Germany was fostered to a considerable extent through the exclusion of migrants, and most especially asylum-seekers. On the other hand, a clear distinction emerged in the debates over migration in the early 1990s between the supposedly tolerant West Germans and the ostensibly racist East Germans lacking experience with immigration. In reality, the clear pluralization of society that had come about through the presence of immigrants and their lifestyles in West Germany since the 1960s had not taken place in the GDR. Instead, East Germans experienced the displacement that was typical of migration processes after 1990 because they had to come to terms with a system of society that they did not know—without having to physically change location. In light of the existing differences between East and West, the goal became to achieve "unity within" by growing together (in an organic sense), which was ultimately conceived as a "project of creating a collective German identity."[174] Immigrants were not part of this scenario, despite the fact that questions of internal heterogeneity and plurality, as well as competing or supplementary forms of inclusion in the nation, actually had to be dealt with, not least because of the ever-increasing effect that Europeanization and globalization has had on the process of identity formation in the new Federal Republic. As it had done with the dramatic limitation of the right of asylum, Germany moved closer to European standards by altering its citizenship laws in 1999. With the immigration legislation (*Zuwanderungsgesetz*) passed in 2005, Germany finally had to admit that it was a country of immigration and that migration could not be stopped. Having conceded this point, it was only logical for the German state to try to channel and regulate this persistent immigration. Since this shift, economic and demographic factors (as well as others) have shaped German migration management, which has once again allowed for seasonal and commuter migration patterns. One of these new patterns has fostered the influx of Eastern European women who have been part of a rapidly growing sector of household-related services in what can be seen as a prime example of the feminization of migration appearing at a global level. Furthermore, these new migration patterns have clearly shown that Germany has reacquired its key position in terms of east to west migration since 1989. Germany, however, is also a popular destination country for south to north migration patterns. Immigrants have been moving north from non-European regions for a while, but due to the economic and financial crises, an increasing number of Europeans from the Mediterranean region have been heading northward.

Whereas both East and West used migration as a political instrument during the Cold War, cost-benefit calculations have become much more dominant today. Such considerations were of course nothing new because they had certainly surfaced in the debates on expellees, foreign *Gastarbeiter* and *Vertragsarbeiter*, *Aussiedler*, and asylum-seekers. Indeed, they have been a constant element in dealing with migration since at least the late nineteenth century when Germany went from being a country of emigration to one of immigration. Likewise, the constitutive role played by foreigners, or rather their exclusion, in nationalization processes is not something specific to Germany, but rather a general feature of modern states. The large-scale racist attacks directed at non-Germans over the course of reunification clearly revealed the violent side of exclusion processes. At the same time, they were an expression of the historic failure to recognize the reality that Germany was a country of immigration and to act accordingly. Moreover, the freedom of movement and travel inherent to migration has proven to be significant for German history before and after the fall of the Berlin Wall. Despite the current fascination with mobility that has characterized both migration and mobility studies, however, the right to come to a place and to *stay* there should not be brushed aside.

Maren Möhring is professor of comparative cultural and social history of modern Europe at the University of Leipzig. Her research focuses on the history of migration, consumption, the body, and gender as well as food studies. Her publications include *Fremdes Essen: Die Geschichte der ausländischen Gastronomie in der Bundesrepublik Deutschland* and *Marmorleiber: Körperbildung in der deutschen Nacktkultur (1890–1930)*.

NOTES

1. Detlev Brunner, Udo Grashoff, and Andreas Kötzing, "Asymmetrisch verflochten? Einleitung," in *Asymmetrisch verflochten? Neue Forschungen zur gesamtdeutschen Nachkriegsgeschichte*, ed. Detlev Brunner, Udo Grashoff, and Andreas Kötzing (Berlin, 2013), 15.
2. This chapter focuses exclusively on spatial mobility and not social mobility; on the latter, see the contribution by Winfried Süß in this book.
3. Johannes-Dieter Steinert, "Drehscheibe Westdeutschland: Wanderungspolitik im Nachkriegsjahrzehnt," in *Deutsche im Ausland—Fremde in Deutschland: Migration in Geschichte und Gegenwart*, ed. Klaus J. Bade (Munich, 1992), 386–92.
4. Helge Heidemeyer, "Vertriebene als Sowjetflüchtlinge," in *Vertriebene in Deutschland: Interdisziplinäre Ergebnisse und Forschungsperspektiven*, ed. Dierk Hoffmann, Marita Krauss, and Michael Schwartz (Munich, 2000), 237–49.
5. Ulrich Herbert and Karin Hunn, "Gastarbeiter und Gastarbeiterpolitik in der Bundesrepublik: Vom Beginn der offiziellen Anwerbung bis zum Anwerbestopp (1955–1973)," in *Dynamische Zeiten: Die 60er Jahre in den beiden deutschen Gesellschaften*, ed. Axel Schildt, Detlef Siegfried, and Karl-Christian Lammers (Hamburg, 2000), 286, 293.
6. The Soviet soldiers and their families were the largest group of foreigners living in the GDR. Cf. Silke Satjukow, *Besatzer. "Die Russen" in Deutschland 1945–1994* (Göttingen, 2008).
7. Sylvia Hahn, *Historische Migrationsforschung* (Frankfurt, 2012), 182–83. Jan Philipp Sternberg, *Auswanderungsland Bundesrepublik: Denkmuster und Debatten in Politik und Medien 1945–2010* (Paderborn, 2012), 163.
8. Klaus J. Bade, Pieter C. Emmer, Leo Lucassen, and Jochen Oltmer, eds., *The Encyclopedia of Migration and Minorities in Europe: From the 17th Century to the Present* (Cambridge, 2011).
9. Nina Glick-Schiller, Linda Basch, and Cristina Blanc-Szanton. "Transnationalism: A New Analytic Framework for Understanding Migration." *Annals of the New York Academy of Sciences* 645 (2009), 1–24.
10. The exception to this rule was Yugoslavia, which was the only socialist state to permit labor migration to Western countries.

11. Serhat Karakayalı and Tsianos Vassilis, "Movements that Matter: Eine Einleitung," in *Turbulente Ränder: Neue Perspektiven auf Migration an den Grenzen Europas*, 2nd ed., ed. Transit Migration Forschungsgruppe (Bielefeld, 2007), 13.
12. Manuela Bojadžijev and Serhat Karakayalı, "Autonomie der Migration. 10 Thesen zu einer Methode," in Transit Migration Forschungsgruppe, *Turbulente Ränder*, 207f.
13. John Urry, "Mobilities and Social Theory," in *The New Blackwell Companion to Social Theory*, ed. Bryan S. Turner (Malden, 2009), 477–95.
14. Maren Möhring, "Tourism and Migration: Interrelated Forms of Mobility," *Comparativ* 24, no. 2 (2014): 116–23.
15. Rainer Ohliger also calls for a joint approach to forced migration and other forms of migration: see Ohliger, "Menschenrechtsverletzung oder Migration? Zum historischen Ort von Flucht und Vertreibung der Deutschen nach 1945," *Zeithistorische Forschungen/Studies in Contemporary History* 2, no. 3 (2005), retrieved 27 February 2012, http://www.zeithistorische-forschungen.de/site/40208471/default.aspx.
16. Michael Schwartz, "Vertreibung und Vergangenheitspolitik: Ein Versuch über geteilte deutsche Nachkriegsidentitäten," *Deutschland Archiv* 30 (1997): 195.
17. Paul Lüttinger, "Der Mythos der schnellen Integration: Eine empirische Untersuchung zur Integration der Vertriebenen und Flüchtlinge in der Bundesrepublik Deutschland bis 1971," *Zeitschrift für Soziologie* 15 (1986): 20–36.
18. Michael Schwartz, "Vertriebene im doppelten Deutschland: Integrations- und Erinnerungspolitik in der DDR und der Bundesrepublik," *Vierteljahrshefte für Zeitgeschichte* 56, no. 1 (2008): 122.
19. Jörg Roesler, *"Rübermachen": Politische Zwänge, ökonomisches Kalkül und verwandtschaftliche Bindungen als häufigste Motive der deutsch-deutschen Wanderungen zwischen 1953 und 1961* (Berlin, 2004): 9; Bernd Stöver, *Zuflucht DDR: Spione und andere Übersiedler* (Munich, 2009), 9.
20. Volker Ackermann, *Der "echte" Flüchtling: Deutsche Vertriebene und Flüchtlinge aus der DDR 1945–1961* (Osnabrück, 1995), 282.
21. Roesler, "Rübermachen," 16.
22. On the history of this phrase, see Henrik Bispinck, "'Republikflucht': Flucht und Ausreise als Problem für die DDR-Führung," in *Vor dem Mauerbau: Politik und Gesellschaft in der DDR der fünfziger Jahre*, ed. Dierk Hoffmann, Matthias Schwartz, and Hermann Wentker (Munich, 2003), 285.
23. Helge Heidemeyer, "Flüchtlingslager im Nachkriegsdeutschland," *H-Soz-Kult*, 12 April 2013.
24. Helge Heidemeyer, *Flucht und Zuwanderung aus der SBZ/DDR 1945/1949–1961: Die Flüchtlingspolitik der Bundesrepublik Deutschland bis zum Bau der Berliner Mauer* (Düsseldorf, 1994), 336.
25. Bispinck, "Republikflucht," 288.
26. *Neues Deutschland*, 17 July 1956, as quoted in Jörg Roesler, "'Abgehauen':

Innerdeutsche Wanderungen in den fünfziger und neunziger Jahren und deren Motive," *Deutschland Archiv* 4 (2003): 566.
27. Andrea Schmelz, *Migration und Politik im geteilten Deutschland während des Kalten Krieges: Die West-Ost-Migration in die DDR in den 1950er und 1960er Jahren* (Opladen, 2002), 21. Heidemeyer, *Flucht*, 192.
28. Schmelz, *Migration*, 14, 321. On family-related chain migration, see Manfred Gehrmann, *Die Überwindung des "Eisernen Vorhangs": Die Abwanderung aus der DDR in die BRD und nach West-Berlin als innerdeutsches Migranten-Netzwerk* (Berlin, 2009).
29. In reverse, a disproportionately high number of skilled workers left the GDR (Roesler, "*Rübermachen,*" 29, 39).
30. Gerhard Neumeier, "'Rückkehrer' in die DDR: Das Beispiel des Bezirks Suhl 1961 bis 1972," *Vierteljahrshefte für Zeitgeschichte* 58, no. 1 (2010): 89.
31. Stöver, *Zuflucht*.
32. Schmelz, "Migration," 290.
33. Anna-Katharina Jung, "'Das bessere Deutschland': Motive westdeutscher Künstler zur Übersiedlung in die DDR," in *Klopfzeichen: Kunst und Kultur der 80er Jahre in Deutschland,* ed. Rainer Eckert and Bernd Lindner (Leipzig, 1999).
34. Tobias Wunschik, "Migrationspolitische Hypertrophien: Aufnahme und Überwachung von Zuwanderern aus der Bundesrepublik Deutschland in der DDR," *IMIS-Beiträge* 32 (2007): 39; Cornelia Röhlke, "Entscheidung für den Osten: Die West-Ost-Migration," in *Flucht im geteilten Deutschland: Erinnerungsstätte Notaufnahmelager Marienfelde,* ed. Bettina Effner and Helge Heidemeyer (Berlin, 2005), 103.
35. Andrea Schmelz, "West-Ost-Migranten im geteilten Deutschland der fünfziger und sechziger Jahre," in *50 Jahre Bundesrepublik—50 Jahre Einwanderung: Nachkriegsgeschichte als Migrationsgeschichte,* ed. Jan Motte, Rainer Ohliger, and Anne von Oswald, (Frankfurt, 1999), 91, 105.
36. Melanie List, "Ahnungslose Bürger? Die Ausreiseantragsteller aus den Bezirken Dresden und Rostock in den 1980er Jahren: Zwischenergebnisse eines Forschungsprojektes und ein Zeitzeugenaufruf," *Zeitgeschichte regional: Mitteilungen aus Mecklenburg-Vorpommern* 17, no. 1 (2013): 60.
37. Renate Hürtgen, *Ausreise per Antrag: Der lange Weg nach drüben; Eine Studie über Herrschaft und Alltag in der DDR-Provinz* (Göttingen, 2014).
38. Marion Detjen, "Permanente Existenzbedrohung: Abwanderung, Flucht, Ausreise," in *Revolution und Vereinigung 1989/90: Als in Deutschland die Realität die Phantasie überholte,* ed. Klaus-Dietmar Henke (Munich, 2009), 72.
39. Jan Philipp Wölbern, *Der Häftlingsfreikauf aus der DDR 1962/63–1989: Zwischen Menschenhandel und humanitären Aktionen* (Göttingen, 2014), 295, 302.
40. Detjen, "Existenzbedrohung," 73.
41. Bernd Eisenfeld, "Gründe und Motive von Flüchtlingen und Ausreiseantragstellern aus der DDR," *Deutschland Archiv* 1 (2004): 93.

42. Anja Hanisch, *Die DDR im KSZE-Prozess 1972–1985: Zwischen Ostabhängigkeit, Westabgrenzung und Ausreisebewegung* (Munich, 2012), 147f.
43. Helge Heidemeyer, "German Refugees and Immigrants from East Germany in West Germany," in Bade et al., *Encyclopedia of Migration*, 431.
44. Hanisch, *DDR*, 374.
45. Detjen, "Existenzbedrohung," 73.
46. List, "Ahnungslose Bürger?," 64.
47. GDR citizens could travel to Czechoslovakia without a visa and an invitation from 1967 (with a few lapses in between) and to Poland between 1972 and 1980.
48. Rüdiger Hachtmann, "Tourismusgeschichte—ein Mauerblümchen mit Zukunft! Ein Forschungsüberblick," *H-Soz-Kult*, 6 October 2011.
49. Rüdiger Hachtmann, *Tourismus-Geschichte* (Göttingen, 2007), 149.
50. Christopher Görlich, *Urlaub vom Staat: Tourismus in der DDR* (Vienna, 2012), 260; Axel Schildt, "'Die kostbarsten Wochen des Jahres': Urlaubstourismus der Westdeutschen (1945–1970)," in *Goldstrand und Teutonengrill: Kultur- und Sozialgeschichte des Tourismus in Deutschland 1945 bis 1989*, ed. Hasso Spode (Berlin, 1996), 69–85.
51. Gerlinde Irmscher, "Alltägliche Fremde: Auslandsreisen in der DDR," in Spode, *Goldstrand*, 57.
52. Brecht, "Integration," 93.
53. C. Michael Hall and Allan M. Williams, eds., *Tourism and Migration: New Relationships between Production and Consumption* (Dordrecht, 2002), 32.
54. Norbert Ropers, *Tourismus zwischen West und Ost: Ein Beitrag zum Frieden?* (Frankfurt, 1986), 80, table 2.5.
55. Sylvia Necker, "Die A 24 zwischen Hamburg und Berlin in den deutsch-deutschen Beziehungen der 1980er Jahre," in *Asymmetrisch verflochten?*, ed. Detlev Brunner, Udo Grashoff, and Andreas Kötzing (Berlin, 2013), 185, 189, 194.
56. Heike Wolter, *"Ich harre aus im Land und geh, ihm fremd": Die Geschichte des Tourismus in der DDR* (Frankfurt, 2009), 179.
57. Ropers, *Tourismus*, 196, table 4.1. The one million or so day trips that West Germans took to East Berlin each year are not included.
58. Ibid., 29, table 1.4.
59. René del Fabbro, *Transalpini: Italienische Arbeitswanderung nach Süddeutschland im Kaiserreich 1870–1918* (Osnabrück, 1996).
60. Ulrich Herbert, *Geschichte der Ausländerpolitik: Saisonarbeiter, Zwangsarbeiter, Gastarbeiter, Flüchtlinge* (Munich, 2001), 14–44.
61. Christoph Kleßmann, *Polnische Bergarbeiter im Ruhrgebiet 1870–1945: Soziale Integration und nationale Subkultur einer Minderheit in der deutschen Industriegesellschaft* (Göttingen, 1978).
62. Christoph Rass, *Institutionalisierungsprozesse auf einem internationalen Arbeitsmarkt: Bilaterale Wanderungsverträge in Europa zwischen 1919 und 1974* (Paderborn, 2010).

63. This treaty was modeled after the labor exchange agreement made between Nazi Germany and fascist Italy in 1938. See Roberto Sala, "Vom 'Fremdarbeiter' zum 'Gastarbeiter': Die Anwerbung italienischer Arbeitskräfte für die deutsche Wirtschaft (1938–1973)," *Vierteljahrshefte für Zeitgeschichte* 50 (2007): 93–120.
64. Herbert and Hunn, "Gastarbeiter," 283.
65. Mathilde Jamin, "Die deutsch-türkische Anwerbevereinbarung von 1961 und 1964," in *Fremde Heimat/Yaban, Silan olur: Eine Geschichte der Einwanderung aus der Türkei; Katalog zur Ausstellung, 15.2.–2.8.1998, im Ruhrlandmuseum Essen*, ed. Mathilde Jamin and Aytaç Eryılmaz (Essen, 1998), 75. At the urging of the Turkish government, Turkish labor migrants were given the same status as those from Greece and Spain in 1964.
66. Monika Mattes, "Migration und Geschlecht in der Bundesrepublik Deutschland: Ein historischer Rückblick auf die 'Gastarbeiterinnen' der 1960/70er Jahre," *Zeitgeschichte-Online*, January 2010, retrieved 23 May 2016, http://www.zeitgeschichte-online.de/thema/migration-und-geschlecht-der-bundesrepublik-deutschland.
67. Klaus J. Bade, *Migration in European History* (Malden, 2003), 231.
68. On the European dimensions of this debate, see Marcel Berlinghoff, "Der europäisierte Anwerbestopp," in *Das "Gastarbeiter"-System: Arbeitsmigration und ihre Folgen in der Bundesrepublik Deutschland und Westeuropa*, ed. Jochen Oltmer, Axel Kreienbrink, and Carlos S. Díaz (Munich, 2012), 149–64.
69. Konstantin Pritzel, "Gastarbeiter in der DDR," *Deutschland Archiv* 1, no. 1 (1970): 93.
70. Ibid., 92, 94.
71. Rita Röhr, *Hoffnung—Hilfe—Heuchelei: Geschichte des Einsatzes polnischer Arbeitskräfte in Betrieben des DDR-Grenzbezirks, Frankfurt/Oder 1966–1991* (Berlin, 2001).
72. Sandra Gruner-Domić, "Beschäftigung statt Ausbildung: Ausländische Arbeiter und Arbeiterinnen in der DDR (1961 bis 1989)," in Motte, Ohliger, and von Oswald, *50 Jahre Bundesrepublik*, 218.
73. The West German government spoke of job training as "development aid for Southern European countries" (Herbert and Hunn, "Gastarbeiter," 287).
74. Mirjam Schulz, "Migrationspolitik in der DDR: Bilaterale Anwerbungsverträge von Vertragsarbeitnehmern," in *Transit/Transfer. Politik und Praxis der Einwanderung in der DDR 1945–1990*, ed. Kim Christian Priemel (Berlin, 2011), 147.
75. In addition to entering into a treaty with the GDR, Vietnam also signed agreements at the beginning of the 1980s with the USSR, Bulgaria, and Czechoslovakia; as of 1988/89, approximately two hundred thousand Vietnamese were working in these countries. Cf. Klaus Fritsche, *Vietnamesische Gastarbeiter in den europäischen RGW-Ländern* (Berichte des Bundesinstituts für ostwissenschaftliche und internationale Studien, no. 6) (Cologne, 1991), 1f.
76. Gruner-Domić, *Beschäftigung*, 224.

77. Eva-Maria Elsner amd Lothar Elsner, *Ausländerpolitik und Ausländerfeindschaft in der DDR (1949–1990)* (Leipzig, 1994), 13. Soviet soldiers and diplomats are not counted in these figures.
78. In contrast to the FRG, the GDR was very much in favor of the wages earned by labor migrants being transferred to their home countries. This was supposed to reduce the purchasing power of these migrants in order to avoid a further escalation in the demand for rare consumer goods.
79. Herbert and Hunn, "Gastarbeiter," 301.
80. Dirk Jasper, "Ausländerbeschäftigung in der DDR," in *Anderssein gab es nicht: Ausländer und Minderheiten in der DDR*, ed. Marianne Krüger-Potratz (Münster, 1991), 152. Herbert and Hunn, "Gastarbeiter," 287.
81. This neologism tries to succinctly convey the mix of dictatorial paternalism and sociopolitical aid that could be found in the GDR; the GDR is often referred to as a "radicalized welfare state." Konrad H. Jarausch, "Realer Sozialismus als Fürsorgediktatur: Zur begrifflichen Einordnung der DDR," in *Aus Politik und Zeitgeschichte* 20 (1998), 33–46.
82. Christiane Mende, "Migration in die DDR: Über staatliche Pläne, migrantische Kämpfe und den real-existierenden Rassismus," in *Wer MACHT Demokratie? Kritische Beiträge zu Migration und Machtverhältnissen*, ed. Duygu Gürsel, Zülfukar Çetin, and Allmende e. V. (Münster, 2013), 157.
83. Cf. Manuela Bojadžijev, *Die windige Internationale: Rassismus und Kämpfe der Migration* (Münster, 2008).
84. Annegret Schüle, "'Proletarischer Internationalismus' oder 'ökonomischer Vorteil für die DDR'? Mosambikanische, angolanische und vietnamesische Arbeitskräfte im VEB Leipziger Baumwollspinnerei (1980–1989)," *Archiv für Sozialgeschichte* 42 (2002): 205; Maren Möhring, *Fremdes Essen: Die Geschichte der ausländischen Gastronomie in der Bundesrepublik Deutschland* (Munich, 2012), 80.
85. Annegret Schüle, "'Die ham se sozusagen aus dem Busch geholt': Die Wahrnehmung der Vertragsarbeitskräfte aus Schwarzafrika und Vietnam durch Deutsche im VEB Leipziger Baumwollspinnerei," in *Fremde und Fremd-Sein in der DDR: Zu den historischen Ursachen der Fremdenfeindlichkeit in Ostdeutschland*, ed. Jan Behrends, Thomas Lindenberger, and Patrice Poutrus (Berlin, 2003), 317.
86. Jessika Haack, "Ausländer in der DDR im Spiegel der überregionalen DDR-Tagespresse: Eine Analyse der Berichterstattung von den Anfängen der DDR bis zur Wiedervereinigung," in Priemel, *Transit/Transfer*, 247–71; Jan C. Behrends, Dennis Kuck, and Patrice G. Poutrus, "Thesenpapier: Historische Ursachen der Fremdenfeindlichkeit in den Neuen Bundesländern," in Behrends, Lindenberger, and Poutrus, *Fremde und Fremd-Sein*, 327–33.
87. Carlos Sanz Díaz, "Umstrittene Wege: Die irreguläre Migration spanischer Arbeitnehmer in die Bundesrepublik Deutschland," in Oltmer, Kreienbrink, and Díaz, *"Gastarbeiter"-System*, 119–32.

88. Michael Feige, *Vietnamesische Studenten und Arbeiter in der DDR und ihre Beobachtung durch das MfS* (Magdeburg, 1999). The Federal Republic also kept a close eye on the political activities of foreign workers because it feared Communist infiltration (Yvonne Rieker, "'Südländer,' 'Ostagenten' oder 'Westeuropäer'? Die Politik der Bundesregierung und das Bild italienischer 'Gastarbeiter,'" *Archiv für Sozialgeschichte* 40 (2000): 231–59). Likewise, the countries who sent workers, especially Spain under Franco and Greece during the military dictatorship, also tried to keep tabs on their labor migrants.
89. Almuth Berger, "Vertragsarbeiter: Arbeiter der Freundschaft? Die Verhandlungen in Maputo 1990," in *Wir haben Spuren hinterlassen! Die DDR in Mosambik. Erlebnisse, Erfahrungen und Erkenntnisse aus drei Jahrzehnten*, ed. Matthias Voß (Münster, 2005), 520.
90. Mende, "Migration," 156.
91. Alternatively, they were forced to have abortions: Berger, "Vertragsarbeiter," 520.
92. Rita Röhr, "Ideologie, Planwirtschaft und Akzeptanz: Die Beschäftigung polnischer Arbeitskräfte in Betreiben des Bezirkes Frankfurt/Oder," in Behrends, Lindenberger, and Poutrus, *Fremde und Fremd-Sein*, 305.
93. On the history behind this development, see Hans-Peter Schneider, "Das Asylrecht zwischen Generosität und Xenophobie: Zur Entstehung des Artikels 16 Absatz 2 Satz 2 Grundgesetz im Parlamentarischen Rat," *Jahrbuch für Antisemitismusforschung* 1 (1992): 219.
94. Patrice G. Poutrus, "Mit strengem Blick: Die sogenannten 'Polit. Emigranten,'" in Behrends, Lindenberger, and Poutrus, *Fremde und Fremd-Sein*, 238.
95. Patrice G. Poutrus, "Asylum in Postwar Germany: Refugee Admission Policies and Their Practical Implementation in the Federal Republic and the GDR between the Late 1940s and the Mid-1970s," *Journal of Contemporary History* 29, no. 1 (2014): 124.
96. Poutrus, "Asylum," 125.
97. FLN = Front de Libération Nationale (National Liberation Front), PLO = Palestine Liberation Organization, ANC = African National Congress, SWAPO = South-West Africa People's Organization. Poutrus, "Blick," 233.
98. Ackermann, "Flüchtling," 13.
99. Tobias Pieper, *Die Gegenwart der Lager: Zur Mikrophysik der Herrschaft in der deutschen Flüchtlingspolitik* (Münster, 2008), 43.
100. Bade, *Migration*, 267.
101. Ibid.
102. Georg J. Dufner. "Chile as a Litmus Test: East and West German Foreign Policy and Cold War Rivalry in Latin America," in *West Germany, the Global South and the Cold War*, ed. Agnes Bressensdorf, Christian Ostermann, and Elke Seefried (Oldenbourg 2017), 77–118.

103. Persecuted Christian Democrats from Chile, however, were not admitted. Cf. Jost Maurin, "Die DDR als Asylland: Flüchtlinge aus Chile 1973–1989," *Zeitschrift für Geschichtswissenschaft* 51, no. 9 (2003): 814, 818.
104. Bade, *Migration*, 270.
105. Poutrus, "Asylum," 123.
106. Poutrus, "Blick," 244.
107. Maurin, "DDR," 819.
108. Ibid., 824f.
109. Ibid., 815, 822.
110. Stefan Troebst, "'Grieche ohne Heimat': Hellenische Bürgerkriegsflüchtlinge in der DDR 1949–1989," *Totalitarismus und Demokratie* 2, no. 2 (2005): 245–71.
111. Patrice G. Poutrus, "Zuflucht im Nachkriegsdeutschland: Politik und Praxis der Flüchtlingsaufnahme in Bundesrepublik und DDR von den späten 1940er bis zu den 1970er Jahren," *Geschichte und Gesellschaft* 35 (2009): 160.
112. Poutrus, "Blick," 231.
113. Poutrus, "Asylum," 120.
114. Whereas the refugees came from thirty-nine different countries in 1966, there were already 101 different countries of origin among refugees in 1980; Serhat Karakayalı, *Gespenster der Migration: Zur Genealogie illegaler Einwanderung in der Bundesrepublik Deutschland* (Bielefeld, 2008), 169.
115. Pieper, *Lager*, 43.
116. Bade, *Migration*, 264, 268, 269.
117. Ibid., 235.
118. Karakayalı, *Gespenster*, 171.
119. Ibid.
120. Elias Steinhilper, "Die Norm Asyl und die politische Funktion der Ausnahme," *Powision: Neue Räume für Politik* 8, no. 16 (2014): 31.
121. Bade, *Migration*, 276.
122. Jochen Oltmer, *Globale Migration: Geschichte und Gegenwart* (Munich, 2012), 108.
123. See Veronika Heyde's presentation at the 2014 conference on 1989 as a global epoch-making year (quoted in Dan Prume, "Welt im Wandel: 1989 als globales Epochenjahr?," Conference Report, Akademie für Politische Bildung Tutzing, *H-Soz-Kult*, 10 October 2014, retrieved 23 March 2015, https://www.hsozkult.de/conferencereport/id/tagungsberichte-5598).
124. Hans-Hermann Hertle, *Chronik des Mauerfalls: Die dramatischen Ereignisse um den 9. November 1989*, 11th rev. ed. (Berlin, 2009).
125. Alon Confino, *Germany as a Culture of Remembrance: Promises and Limits of Writing History* (Chapel Hill, 2006), 223.
126. Heike Wolter, "DDR-Bürger auf Reisen: Zwischen Privatsache und Staatsangelegenheiten," in *Vergnügen in der DDR*, ed. Ulrike Häußler and Marcus Merkel (Berlin, 2009), 428.

127. Jürgen Dorbritz and Wulfram Speigner, "Die Deutsche Demokratische Republik—ein Ein- und Auswanderungsland?," *Zeitschrift für Bevölkerungswissenschaft* 16, no. 1 (1990): 67, 69, 72.
128. Hans-Ulrich Derlien, "Elitenzirkulation in Ostdeutschland 1989–1995," *Aus Politik und Zeitgeschichte* 5 (1998): 3.
129. Roesler, "'Abgehauen,'" 571.
130. Gehrmann, *Überwindung*, 232.
131. Claudia Schneider, "Als Deutsche unter Deutschen? 'Übersiedler aus der VR Polen' in der DDR ab 1964," in Priemel, *Transit/Transfer*, 54.
132. Nicole Hirschler-Horáková, "'Neue Arbeitskräfte aus dem Osten': 'Repatriierung' und Familienzusammenführung von Personen deutscher Herkunft aus der UdSSR in die DDR 1957," in *Migration steuern und verwalten: Deutschland vom späten 19. Jahrhundert bis zur Gegenwart*, ed. Jochen Oltmer (Göttingen, 2003), 378.
133. Silke Delfs, "Heimatvertriebene, Aussiedler, Spätaussiedler: Rechtliche und politische Aspekte der Aufnahme von Deutschstämmigen aus Osteuropa in der Bundesrepublik Deutschland," *Aus Politik und Zeitgeschichte* 48 (1993): 6.
134. Ibid., 7.
135. Klaus J. Bade and Jochen Oltmer, "Einführung: Aussiedlerwanderung und Aussiedlerintegration: Historische Entwicklung und aktuelle Probleme," in *Aussiedler: Deutsche Einwanderer aus Osteuropa*, ed. Klaus J. Bade and Jochen Oltmer (Osnabrück, 1999), 21.
136. Karen Schönwälder, "Invited but Unwanted? Migrants from the East in Germany, 1890–1990," in *The German Lands and Eastern Europe: Essays on the History of their Social, Cultural and Political Relations*, ed. Roger Bartlett and Karen Schönwälder (Basingstoke, 1999), 211.
137. Scott McCormack, "'Für mich sind das keine Deutschen,'" *Die Zeit*, 8 November 1996.
138. Delfs, "Heimatvertriebene," 8.
139. Amanda Klekowski von Koppenfels, "Willkommene Deutsche oder tolerierte Fremde? Aussiedlerpolitik und -verwaltung in der Bundesrepublik Deutschland seit den 1950er Jahren," in Oltmer, *Migration steuern*, 410f.
140. Ibid., 408f., 413f.
141. Franziska Becker, "Migration and Recognition: Russian Jews in Germany," *East European Jewish Affairs* 33, no. 2 (2008): 22.
142. Sonja Haug and Michael Wolf, "Jüdische Zuwanderung nach Deutschland," in *Neue Zuwanderergruppen in Deutschland* (Materialien zur Bevölkerungswissenschaft, no. 118), ed. Bundesinstitut für Bevölkerungsforschung (Wiesbaden, 2006), 66.
143. Ulrich Herbert, *Geschichte Deutschlands im 20. Jahrhundert* (Munich, 2014), 1174.
144. The talk was about "sprachlichen Brandsätzen," i.e., "fighting words"; cf. Siegfried Jäger, *BrandSätze. Rassismus im Alltag* (Duisburg, 1993).

145. Panikos Panayi, "Racial Violence in the New Germany 1990–93," *Contemporary European History* 3, no. 3 (1994): 280.
146. Pieper, *Lager*, 64.
147. Nora Räthzel, "Zur Bedeutung von Asylpolitik und neuen Rassismen bei der Reorganisation der nationalen Identität im vereinigten Deutschland," in *Rassismus in Europa*, ed. Christoph Butterwege and Siegfried Jäger (Cologne, 1992), 218. Translation by the translator of this volume.
148. Quoted according to Herbert, *Geschichte Deutschlands*, 1176.
149. Karakayalı, *Gespenster*, 176.
150. Bade, *Migration*, 280.
151. Rutvica Andrijašević et al., "Turbulente Ränder: Konturen eines neuen Migrationsregimes im Südosten Europas," *Prokla* 35, no. 140 (2005): 359.
152. Dirk Hoerder, Jan Lucassen, and Leo Lucassen, "Terminologies and Concepts in Migration Research," in Bade et al., *Encyclopedia of Migration*, xxxiii.
153. Nevim Çil, "Der andere und der fremde Außenseiter: Türkische Nachkommen im wiedervereinigten Deutschland," in *Insider—Outsider: Bilder, ethnisierte Räume und Partizipation im Migrationsprozess*, ed. IFADE (Bielefeld, 2005), 71.
154. *Duvarlar-Mauern-Walls* (dir. Can Candan, USA/TR, 2000).
155. Çil, "Außenseiter," 71, 69, 74.
156. Andrea Klimt, "Transnationale Zugehörigkeit: Portugiesen in Hamburg," in *"Wir sind auch da!" Über das Leben von und mit Migranten in europäischen Großstädten*, ed. Angelika Eder (Munich, 2003), 219.
157. Sabine Mannitz, "'West Side Stories': Warum Jugendliche aus Migrantenfamilien das wiedervereinigte Berlin als geteilte Stadt erleben," in *Migration und Integration in Berlin: Wissenschaftliche Analysen und politische Perspektiven*, ed. Frank Gesemann (Obladen, 2001), 286.
158. As Urmila Goel put it, "The West Germans are the undefined norm," whose privileges include, among others, the "natural continuity of their own history and the system in which they lived"; see Urmila Goel, "Westprivilegien im vereinten Deutschland," *Telegraph* 120/121 (2010).
159. Ina Dietzsch, "Deutsch-Sein in einem geteilten Land: Das Problem kultureller Zugehörigkeiten," in Behrends, Lindenberger, and Poutrus, *Fremde und Fremd-Sein*, 138.
160. Jenny B. White, "Turks in the New Germany," *American Anthropologist* 99, no. 4 (1997): 763.
161. Klimt, "Transnationale Zugehörigkeit," 221, note 23.
162. Çil, "Außenseiter," 57, 59.
163. Etienne Balibar, "Is There a 'Neo-Racism'?," in *Race, Nation, Class: Ambiguous Identities*, ed. Etienne Balibar and Immanuel Wallerstein (London, 1991), 17–28.
164. Schulz, "Migrationspolitik," 161; Gruner-Domić, "Beschäftigung," 215.
165. Christiane Mende, "Lebensrealitäten der DDR-ArbeitsmigrantInnen nach 1989 zwischen Hochkonjunktur des Rassismus und dem Kampf um Rechte,"

in *Kritische Migrationsforschung? Da kann ja jedeR kommen,* ed. Netzwerk MiRA, 104.
166. Berger, "Vertragsarbeiter," 522.
167. Mende, "Migration," 141.
168. Fritsche, *Vietnamesische Gastarbeiter,* 4.
169. Karin Weiss and Mike Dennis, eds., *Erfolg in der Nische? Die Vietnamesen in der DDR und in Ostdeutschland* (Münster, 2005).
170. Gertrud Hüwelmeier, *"Asiatown"—A Postsocialist Bazaar in the Eastern Part of Berlin,* MMG Working Paper 13-08 (Göttingen: Max Planck Institute for the Study of Religious and Ethnic Diversity, 2013), retrieved 12 March 2015, http://www.mmg.mpg.de/fileadmin/user_upload/documents/wp/WP_13-08_Huewelmeier_Asiatown.pdf .
171. Olaf Beuchling, "Vietnamese Refugees in Western, Central, and Northern Europe since the 1970s: The Example of France, Great Britain, and Germany," in Bade et al., *Encyclopedia of Migration,* 732.
172. Peter Widmann, "Gerettet und geduldet: Berliner Vietnamesen und die deutsche Flüchtlings- und Migrationspolitik," in *Umgang mit Flüchtlingen. Ein humanitäres Problem,* ed. Wolfgang Benz (Munich, 2006), 112.
173. Ibid., 113.
174. Mannitz, "'West Side Stories,'" 287.

BIBLIOGRAPHY

Ackermann, Volker. *Der "echte" Flüchtling: Deutsche Vertriebene und Flüchtlinge aus der DDR 1945–1961.* Osnabrück: Rasch, 1995.
Andrijašević, Rutvica, Manuela Bojadžijev, Sabine Hess, Serhat Karakayalı, Efthimia Panagiotidis, and Vassilis Tsianos. "Turbulente Ränder: Konturen eines neuen Migrationsregimes im Südosten Europas." *Prokla* 35, no. 140 (2005): 345–62.
Bade, Klaus J. *Migration in European History.* Malden: Blackwell, 2003.
Bade, Klaus J., and Jochen Oltmer. "Einführung: Aussiedlerwanderung und Aussiedlerintegration: Historische Entwicklung und aktuelle Probleme." In *Aussiedler. Deutsche Einwanderer aus Osteuropa,* edited by Klaus J. Bade and Jochen Oltmer, 9–53. Osnabrück: Rasch, 1999.
Bade, Klaus J., Pieter C. Emmer, Leo Lucassen, and Jochen Oltmer, eds. *The Encyclopedia of Migration and Minorities in Europe: From the 17th Century to the Present.* Cambridge: Cambridge University Press, 2011.
Balibar, Etienne. "Is There a 'Neo-Racism'?" In *Race, Nation, Class: Ambiguous Identities,* edited by E. Balibar and I. Wallerstein, 17–28. London: Verso, 1991.
Becker, Franziska. "Migration and Recognition: Russian Jews in Germany." *East European Jewish Affairs* 33, no. 2 (2008): 20–34.
Behrends, Jan C., Dennis Kuck, and Patrice G. Poutrus. "Thesenpapier: Historische Ursachen der Fremdenfeindlichkeit in den Neuen Bundesländern." In *Fremde und Fremd-Sein in der DDR: Zu den historischen Ursachen der*

Fremdenfeindlichkeit in Ostdeutschland, edited by Jan C. Behrends, Thomas Lindenberger, and Patrice Poutrus, 327–33. Berlin: Metropol, 2003.

Berger, Almuth. "Vertragsarbeiter: Arbeiter der Freundschaft? Die Verhandlungen in Maputo 1990." In *Wir haben Spuren hinterlassen! Die DDR in Mosambik: Erlebnisse, Erfahrungen und Erkenntnisse aus drei Jahrzehnten*, edited by Matthias Voß, 512–28. Münster: Lit, 2005.

Berlinghoff, Marcel. "Der europäisierte Anwerbestopp." In *Das "Gastarbeiter"-System: Arbeitsmigration und ihre Folgen in der Bundesrepublik Deutschland und Westeuropa*, edited by Jochen Oltmer, Axel Kreienbrink, and Carlos S. Díaz, 149–64. Munich: Oldenbourg, 2012.

Beuchling, Olaf. "Vietnamese Refugees in Western, Central, and Northern Europe since the 1970s: The Example of France, Great Britain, and Germany." In *The Encyclopedia of Migration and Minorities in Europe: From the 17th Century to the Present*, edited by Klaus J. Bade, Pieter C. Emmer, Leo Lucassen, and Jochen Oltmer, 730–33. Cambridge: Cambridge University Press, 2011.

Bispinck, Henrik. "'Republikflucht': Flucht und Ausreise als Problem für die DDR-Führung." In *Vor dem Mauerbau: Politik und Gesellschaft in der DDR der fünfziger Jahre*, edited by Dierk Hoffmann, Matthias Schwartz, and Hermann Wentker, 285–309. Munich: Oldenbourg, 2003.

Bojadžijev, Manuela. *Die windige Internationale: Rassismus und Kämpfe der Migration*. Münster: Westfälisches Dampfboot, 2008.

Bojadžijev, Manuela, and Serhat Karakayalı. "Autonomie der Migration: 10 Thesen zu einer Methode." In *Turbulente Ränder: Neue Perspektiven auf Migration an den Grenzen Europas*, 2nd ed., edited by Transit Migration Forschungsgruppe, 203–9. Bielefeld: Transcript, 2007.

Brecht, Christine. "Integration in der Bundesrepublik: Der schwierige Neuanfang." In *Flucht im geteilten Deutschland: Erinnerungsstätte Notaufnahmelager Marienfelde*, edited by Bettina Effner and Helge Heidemeyer, 83–95. Berlin: Be.Bra, 2005.

Brunner, Detlev, Udo Grashoff, and Andreas Kötzing. "Asymmetrisch verflochten? Einleitung." In *Asymmetrisch verflochten? Neue Forschungen zur gesamtdeutschen Nachkriegsgeschichte*, edited by Detlev Brunner, Udo Grashoff, and Andreas Kötzing, 11–17. Berlin: Links, 2013.

Çil, Nevim. "Der andere und der fremde Außenseiter: Türkische Nachkommen im wiedervereinigten Deutschland." In *Insider—Outsider: Bilder, ethnisierte Räume und Partizipation im Migrationsprozess*, edited by IFADE, 57–79. Bielefeld: Transcript, 2005.

Confino, Alon. *Germany as a Culture of Remembrance: Promises and Limits of Writing History*. Chapel Hill: University of North Carolina Press, 2006.

del Fabbro, René. *Transalpini: Italienische Arbeitswanderung nach Süddeutschland im Kaiserreich 1870–1918*. Osnabrück: Rasch, 1996.

Delfs, Silke. "Heimatvertriebene, Aussiedler, Spätaussiedler: Rechtliche und politische Aspekte der Aufnahme von Deutschstämmigen aus Osteuropa in der Bundesrepublik Deutschland." *Aus Politik und Zeitgeschichte* 48 (1993): 3–11.

Derlien, Hans-Ulrich. "Elitenzirkulation in Ostdeutschland 1989–1995." *Aus Politik und Zeitgeschichte* 5 (1998): 3–17.
Detjen, Marion. "Permanente Existenzbedrohung: Abwanderung, Flucht, Ausreise." In *Revolution und Vereinigung 1989/90: Als in Deutschland die Realität die Phantasie überholte*, edited by Klaus-Dietmar Henke, 67–80. Munich: DTV, 2009.
Díaz, Carlos Sanz. "Umstrittene Wege: Die irreguläre Migration spanischer Arbeitnehmer in die Bundesrepublik Deutschland." In *Das "Gastarbeiter"-System: Arbeitsmigration und ihre Folgen in der Bundesrepublik Deutschland und Westeuropa*, edited by Jochen Oltmer, Axel Kreienbrink, and Carlos S. Díaz, 119–32. Munich: Oldenbourg, 2012.
Dietzsch, Ina. "Deutsch-Sein in einem geteilten Land: Das Problem kultureller Zugehörigkeiten." In *Fremde und Fremd-Sein in der DDR: Zu den historischen Ursachen der Fremdenfeindlichkeit in Ostdeutschland*, edited by Jan C. Behrends, Thomas Lindenberger, and Patrice Poutrus, 127–39. Berlin: Metropol, 2003.
Dorbritz, Jürgen, and Wulfram Speigner. "Die Deutsche Demokratische Republik—ein Ein- und Auswanderungsland?" *Zeitschrift für Bevölkerungswissenschaft* 16, no. 1 (1990), 67–85.
Dufner, Georg J. "Chile as a Litmus Test: East and West German Foreign Policy and Cold War Rivalry in Latin America." In *West Germany, the Global South and the Cold War*, edited by Agnes Bressensdorf, Christian Ostermann, and Elke Seefried, 77–118. Oldenburg: de Gruyter, 2017.
Eisenfeld, Bernd. "Gründe und Motive von Flüchtlingen und Ausreiseantragstellern aus der DDR." *Deutschland Archiv* 93, no.1 (2004), 89–105.
Elsner, Eva-Maria, and Lothar Elsner. *Ausländerpolitik und Ausländerfeindschaft in der DDR (1949–1990)*. Leipzig: Rosa-Luxemburg-Verein, 1994.
Feige, Michael. *Vietnamesische Studenten und Arbeiter in der DDR und ihre Beobachtung durch das MfS*. Magdeburg: Landesbeauftragte für die Unterlagen des Staatssicherheitsdienstes der Ehemaligen DDR Sachsen-Anhalt, 1999.
Fritsche, Klaus. *Vietnamesische Gastarbeiter in den europäischen RGW-Ländern* (Berichte des Bundesinstituts für ostwissenschaftliche und internationale Studien, no. 6). Cologne: Bundesinstitut für ostwissenschaftliche und internationale Studien, 1991.
Gehrmann, Manfred. *Die Überwindung des "Eisernen Vorhangs": Die Abwanderung aus der DDR in die BRD und nach West-Berlin als innerdeutsches Migranten-Netzwerk*. Berlin: Links, 2009.
Glick-Schiller, Nina, Linda Basch, and Cristina Blanc-Szanton. "Transnationalism: A New Analytic Framework for Understanding Migration." *Annals of the New York Academy of Sciences* 645 (2009): 1–24.
Goel, Urmila. "Westprivilegien im vereinten Deutschland." *Telegraph* 120/121 (2010). Retrieved 12 March 2015, http://www.telegraph.ostbuero.de/120_121/goel.html.
Görlich, Christopher. *Urlaub vom Staat: Tourismus in der DDR*. Vienna: Böhlau, 2012.

Gruner-Domić, Sandra. "Beschäftigung statt Ausbildung: Ausländische Arbeiter und Arbeiterinnen in der DDR (1961 bis 1989)." In *50 Jahre Bundesrepublik—50 Jahre Einwanderung: Nachkriegsgeschichte als Migrationsgeschichte*, edited by Jan Motte, Rainer Ohliger, and Anne von Oswald, 215–40. Frankfurt: Campus, 1999.

Haack, Jessika. "Ausländer in der DDR im Spiegel der überregionalen DDR-Tagespresse: Eine Analyse der Berichterstattung von den Anfängen der DDR bis zur Wiedervereinigung." In *Transit/Transfer: Politik und Praxis der Einwanderung in der DDR 1945–1990*, edited by Kim Christian Priemel, 247–71. Berlin: Be.Bra, 2011.

Hachtmann, Rüdiger. *Tourismus-Geschichte*. Göttingen: Vandenhoeck & Ruprecht, 2007.

———. "Tourismusgeschichte—ein Mauerblümchen mit Zukunft! Ein Forschungsüberblick." *H-Soz-Kult* (2011). Retrieved 3 November 2014, http://www.hsozkult.de/literaturereview/id/forschungsberichte-1119.

Hahn, Sylvia. *Historische Migrationsforschung*. Frankfurt: Campus, 2012.

Hall, C. Michael, and Allan M. Williams, eds. *Tourism and Migration: New Relationships between Production and Consumption*. Dordrecht: Springer, 2002.

Hanisch, Anja. *Die DDR im KSZE-Prozess 1972–1985: Zwischen Ostabhängigkeit, Westabgrenzung und Ausreisebewegung*. Munich: Oldenbourg, 2012.

Harzig, Christiane, and Dirk Hoerder, eds. *What Is Migration History?* Cambridge, MA: Wiley, 2009.

Haug, Sonja, and Michael Wolf. "Jüdische Zuwanderung nach Deutschland." In *Neue Zuwanderergruppen in Deutschland* (Materialien zur Bevölkerungswissenschaft, no. 118), edited by Bundesinstitut für Bevölkerungsforschung, 65–82. Wiesbaden, 2006.

Heidemeyer, Helge. *Flüchtlingslager im Nachkriegsdeutschland*. Conference report. *H-Soz-Kult*. Retrieved 3 November 2014, http://hsozkult.geschichte.hu-berlin.de/tagungsberichte/id=4900.

———. *Flucht und Zuwanderung aus der SBZ/DDR 1945/1949–1961: Die Flüchtlingspolitik der Bundesrepublik Deutschland bis zum Bau der Berliner Mauer*. Düsseldorf: Droste, 1994.

———. "German Refugees and Immigrants from East Germany in West Germany." In *The Encyclopedia of Migration and Minorities in Europe: From the 17th Century to the Present*, edited by Klaus J. Bade, Pieter C. Emmer, Leo Lucassen, and Jochen Oltmer, 730–733. Cambridge: Cambridge University Press, 2011.

———. "Vertriebene als Sowjetflüchtlinge." In *Vertriebene in Deutschland: Interdisziplinäre Ergebnisse und Forschungsperspektiven*, edited by Dierk Hoffmann, Martita Krauss, and Michael Schwartz, 237–49. Munich: Oldenbourg, 2000.

Herbert, Ulrich. *Geschichte der Ausländerpolitik: Saisonarbeiter, Zwangsarbeiter, Gastarbeiter, Flüchtlinge*. Munich: Beck, 2001.

———. *Geschichte Deutschlands im 20. Jahrhundert*. Munich: Beck, 2014.

Herbert, Ulrich, and Karin Hunn. "Gastarbeiter und Gastarbeiterpolitik in der Bundesrepublik: Vom Beginn der offiziellen Anwerbung bis zum Anwerbestopp (1955–1973)." In *Dynamische Zeiten: Die 60er Jahre in den beiden deutschen Gesellschaften*, edited by Axel Schildt, Detlef Siegfried, and Karl Christian Lammers, 273–310. Hamburg: Hans Christian, 2000.

Hertle, Hans-Hermann. *Chronik des Mauerfalls: Die dramatischen Ereignisse um den 9. November 1989*, 11th rev. ed. Berlin: Links, 2009.

Hirschler-Horáková, Nicole. "'Neue Arbeitskräfte aus dem Osten': 'Repatriierung' und Familienzusammenführung von Personen deutscher Herkunft aus der UdSSR in die DDR 1957." In *Migration steuern und verwalten: Deutschland vom späten 19. Jahrhundert bis zur Gegenwart*, edited by Jochen Oltmer, 377–97. Göttingen: Vandenhoeck & Ruprecht, 2003.

Hoerder, Dirk, Jan Lucassen, and Leo Lucassen. "Terminologies and Concepts of Migration Research." In *The Encyclopedia of Migration and Minorities in Europe: From the 17th Century to the Present*, edited by Klaus J. Bade, Pieter C. Emmer, Leo Lucassen, and Jochen Oltmer, xxv–xxxix. Cambridge: Cambridge University Press, 2011.

Hürtgen, Renate. *Ausreise per Antrag: Der lange Weg nach drüben; Eine Studie über Herrschaft und Alltag in der DDR-Provinz*. Göttingen: Vandenhoeck & Ruprecht, 2014.

Hüwelmeier, Gertrud. *"Asiatown"—A Postsocialist Bazaar in the Eastern Part of Berlin*. MMG Working Paper 13-08. Göttingen: Max Planck Institute for the Study of Religious and Ethnic Diversity, 2013. Retrieved 12 March 2015, http://www.mmg.mpg.de/fileadmin/user_upload/documents/wp/WP_13-08_Huewelmeier_Asiatown.pdf.

Irmscher, Gerlinde. "Alltägliche Fremde: Auslandsreisen in der DDR." In *Goldstrand und Teutonengrill: Kultur- und Sozialgeschichte des Tourismus in Deutschland 1945 bis 1989*, edited by Hasso Spode, 51–67. Berlin: Moser, 1996.

Jäger, Siegfried. *BrandSätze: Rassismus im Alltag*. Duisburg: DISS, 1993.

Jamin, Mathilde. "Die deutsch-türkische Anwerbevereinbarung von 1961 und 1964." In *Fremde Heimat/Yaban, Silan olur: Eine Geschichte der Einwanderung aus der Türkei. Katalog zur Ausstellung, 15.2.–2.8.1998, im Ruhrlandmuseum Essen*, edited by Mathilde Jamin and Aytaç Eryılmaz, 69–83. Essen: Klartext, 1998.

Jarausch, Konrad H. "Realer Sozialismus als Fürsorgediktatur: Zur begrifflichen Einordnung der DDR." *Aus Politik und Zeitgeschichte* 20 (1998): 33–46.

Jasper, Dirk. "Ausländerbeschäftigung in der DDR." In *Anderssein gab es nicht: Ausländer und Minderheiten in der DDR*, edited by Marianne Krüger-Potratz, 151–89. Münster: Waxmann, 1991.

Jung, Anna-Katharina. "'Das bessere Deutschland': Motive westdeutscher Künstler zur Übersiedlung in die DDR." In *Klopfzeichen: Kunst und Kultur der 80er Jahre in Deutschland*, edited by Rainer Eckert and Bernd Lindner, 145–59. Leipzig: Faber & Faber, 1999.

Karakayalı, Serhat. *Gespenster der Migration: Zur Genealogie illegaler Einwanderung in der Bundesrepublik Deutschland.* Bielefeld: Transcript, 2008.

Karakayalı, Serhat, and Tsianos Vassilis. "Movements that Matter: Eine Einleitung." In *Turbulente Ränder: Neue Perspektiven auf Migration an den Grenzen Europas,* 2nd ed., edited by Transit Migration Forschungsgruppe, 7–17. Bielefeld: Transcript, 2007.

Klekowski von Koppenfels, Amanda. "Willkommene Deutsche oder tolerierte Fremde? Aussiedlerpolitik und -verwaltung in der Bundesrepublik Deutschland seit den 1950er Jahren." In *Migration steuern und verwalten: Deutschland vom späten 19. Jahrhundert bis zur Gegenwart,* edited by Jochen Oltmer, 399–419. Göttingen: Vandenhoeck & Ruprecht, 2003.

Kleßmann, Christoph. *Polnische Bergarbeiter im Ruhrgebiet 1870–1945: Soziale Integration und nationale Subkultur einer Minderheit in der deutschen Industriegesellschaft.* Göttingen: Vandenhoeck & Ruprecht, 1978.

Klimt, Andrea. "Transnationale Zugehörigkeit: Portugiesen in Hamburg." In *"Wir sind auch da!" Über das Leben von und mit Migranten in europäischen Großstädten,* edited by Angelike Eder, 211–32. Munich: Dölling & Galitz, 2003.

List, Melanie. "Ahnungslose Bürger? Die Ausreiseantragsteller aus den Bezirken Dresden und Rostock in den 1980er Jahren: Zwischenergebnisse eines Forschungsprojektes und ein Zeitzeugenaufruf." *Zeitgeschichte regional: Mitteilungen aus Mecklenburg-Vorpommern* 17, no. 1 (2013): 60–67.

Lüttinger, Paul. "Der Mythos der schnellen Integration: Eine empirische Untersuchung zur Integration der Vertriebenen und Flüchtlinge in der Bundesrepublik Deutschland bis 1971." *Zeitschrift für Soziologie* 15 (1986): 20–36.

Mannitz, Sabine. "'West Side Stories': Warum Jugendliche aus Migrantenfamilien das wiedervereinigte Berlin als geteilte Stadt erleben." In *Migration und Integration in Berlin: Wissenschaftliche Analysen und politische Perspektiven,* edited by Frank Gesemann, 273–91. Obladen: Leske + Budrich, 2001.

Mattes, Monika. "Migration und Geschlecht in der Bundesrepublik Deutschland: Ein historischer Rückblick auf die 'Gastarbeiterinnen' der 1960/70er Jahre." *Zeitgeschichte-Online,* January 2010. Retrieved 23 May 2016, http://www.zeitgeschichte-online.de/thema/migration-und-geschlecht-der-bundesrepublik-deutschland.

Maurin, Jost. "Die DDR als Asylland: Flüchtlinge aus Chile 1973–1989." *Zeitschrift für Geschichtswissenschaft* 51, no. 9 (2003): 814–31.

McCormack, Scott. "Für mich sind das keine Deutschen." In *Die Zeit,* 8 November 1996. Retrieved 8 March 2015 from http://www.zeit.de/1996/11/Fuer_mich_sind_das_keine_Deutschen.

Mende, Christiane. "Lebensrealitäten der DDR-ArbeitsmigrantInnen nach 1989 zwischen Hochkonjunktur des Rassismus und dem Kampf um Rechte." In *Kritische Migrationsforschung? Da kann ja jedeR kommen,* edited by Netzwerk MiRA, 103–22, 1 February 2012. Retrieved 1 June 2016 from http://edoc.hu-berlin.de/miscellanies/netzwerkmira-38541/all/PDF/mira.pdf.

———. "Migration in die DDR: Über staatliche Pläne, migrantische Kämpfe und den real-existierenden Rassismus." In *Wer MACHT Demo_kratie? Kritische Beiträge zu Migration und Machtverhältnissen*, edited by Duygu Gürsel, Zülfukar Çetin, and Allmende e. V., 151–64. Münster: Ed. Assemblage, 2013.

Möhring, Maren. *Fremdes Essen: Die Geschichte der ausländischen Gastronomie in der Bundesrepublik Deutschland*. Munich: Oldenbourg, 2012.

———. "Tourism and Migration: Interrelated Forms of Mobility" *Comparativ* 24, no. 2 (2014): 116–23.

Necker, Sylvia. "Die A 24 zwischen Hamburg und Berlin in den deutsch-deutschen Beziehungen der 1980er Jahre." In *Asymmetrisch verflochten? Neue Forschungen zur gesamtdeutschen Nachkriegsgeschichte*, edited by Detrlev Brunner, Udo Grashoff, and Andreas Kötzing, 183–94. Berlin: Links, 2013

Neumeier, Gerhard. "'Rückkehrer' in die DDR: Das Beispiel des Bezirks Suhl 1961 bis 1972." *Vierteljahrshefte für Zeitgeschichte* 58, no. 1 (2010): 69–91.

Ohliger, Rainer. "Menschenrechtsverletzung oder Migration? Zum historischen Ort von Flucht und Vertreibung der Deutschen nach 1945." *Zeithistorische Forschungen/Studies in Contemporary History* 2, no. 3 (2005). Retrieved 27 February 2012 from http://www.zeithistorische-forschungen.de/site/40208471/default.aspx.

Oltmer, Jochen. *Globale Migration: Geschichte und Gegenwart*. Munich: Beck, 2012.

Panayi, Panikos. "Racial Violence in the New Germany 1990–93." *Contemporary European History* 3, no. 3 (1994): 265–88.

Pieper, Tobias. *Die Gegenwart der Lager: Zur Mikrophysik der Herrschaft in der deutschen Flüchtlingspolitik*. Münster: Westfälisches Dampfboot, 2008.

Poutrus, Patrice G. "Asylum in Postwar Germany: Refugee Admission Policies and Their Practical Implementation in the Federal Republic and the GDR between the Late 1940s and the Mid-1970s." *Journal of Contemporary History* 49, no. 1 (2014): 115–33.

———. "Mit strengem Blick: Die sogenannten 'Polit. Emigranten.'" In *Fremde und Fremd-Sein in der DDR: Zu den historischen Ursachen der Fremdenfeindlichkeit in Ostdeutschland*, edited by Jan C. Behrends, Thomas Lindenberger, and Patrice Poutrus, 231–50. Berlin: Metropol, 2003.

———. "Zuflucht im Nachkriegsdeutschland: Politik und Praxis der Flüchtlingsaufnahme in Bundesrepublik und DDR von den späten 1940er bis zu den 1970er Jahren." *Geschichte und Gesellschaft* 35 (2009): 135–75.

Pritzel, Konstantin. "Gastarbeiter in der DDR." *Deutschland Archiv* 1, no. 1 (1970): 92–96.

Prume, Dan. "Welt im Wandel: 1989 als globales Epochenjahr?" Conference report, Akademie für Politische Bildung Tutzing. *H-Soz-Kult*, 10 October 2014. Retrieved 23 March 2015. https://www.hsozkult.de/conferencereport/id/tagungsberichte-5598.

Rass, Christoph. *Institutionalisierungsprozesse auf einem internationalen Arbeitsmarkt: Bilaterale Wanderungsverträge in Europa zwischen 1919 und 1974*. Paderborn: Schöningh, 2010.

Räthzel, Nora. "Zur Bedeutung von Asylpolitik und neuen Rassismen bei der Reorganisation der nationalen Identität im vereinigten Deutschland." In *Rassismus in Europa*, edited by Christoph Butterwege and Siegfried Jäger, 218. Cologne: Bund, 1992.

Rieker, Yvonne. "'Südländer,' 'Ostagenten' oder 'Westeuropäer'? Die Politik der Bundesregierung und das Bild italienischer 'Gastarbeiter.'" *Archiv für Sozialgeschichte* 40 (2000): 231–59.

Roesler, Jörg. "'Abgehauen': Innerdeutsche Wanderungen in den fünfziger und neunziger Jahren und deren Motive." *Deutschland Archiv* 4 (2003): 562–74.

———. "Rübermachen": Politische Zwänge, ökonomisches Kalkül und verwandtschaftliche Bindungen als häufigste Motive der deutsch-deutschen Wanderungen zwischen 1953 und 1961. Berlin: Helle Panke e.V., 2004.

Röhlke, Cornelia. "Entscheidung für den Osten: Die West-Ost-Migration." In *Flucht im geteilten Deutschland: Erinnerungsstätte Notaufnahmelager Marienfelde*, edited by Bettina Effner and Helge Heidemeyer, 97–113. Berlin: Be.Bra, 2005.

Röhr, Rita. *Hoffnung—Hilfe—Heuchelei: Geschichte des Einsatzes polnischer Arbeitskräfte in Betrieben des DDR-Grenzbezirks, Frankfurt/Oder 1966–1991*. Berlin: Wissenschafts Verlag, 2001.

———. "Ideologie, Planwirtschaft und Akzeptanz: Die Beschäftigung polnischer Arbeitskräfte in Betreiben des Bezirkes Frankfurt/Oder." In *Fremde und Fremd-Sein in der DDR: Zu den historischen Ursachen der Fremdenfeindlichkeit in Ostdeutschland*, edited by Jan C. Behrends, Thomas Lindenberger, and Patrice Poutrus, 283–307. Berlin: Metropol, 2003.

Ropers, Norbert. *Tourismus zwischen West und Ost: Ein Beitrag zum Frieden?* Frankfurt: Campus, 1986.

Sala, Roberto. "Vom 'Fremdarbeiter' zum 'Gastarbeiter': Die Anwerbung italienischer Arbeitskräfte für die deutsche Wirtschaft (1938–1973)." *Vierteljahrshefte für Zeitgeschichte* 50 (2007): 93–120.

Satjukow, Silke. *Besatzer. "Die Russen" in Deutschland 1945–1994*. Göttingen: Vandenhoeck & Ruprecht, 2008.

Schildt, Axel. "'Die kostbarsten Wochen des Jahres': Urlaubstourismus der Westdeutschen (1945–1970)." In *Goldstrand und Teutonengrill: Kultur- und Sozialgeschichte des Tourismus in Deutschland 1945 bis 1989*, edited by Hasso Spode, 69–85. Berlin: Moser, 1996.

Schmelz, Andrea. *Migration und Politik im geteilten Deutschland während des Kalten Krieges: Die West-Ost-Migration in die DDR in den 1950er und 1960er Jahren*. Opladen: Leske + Budrich, 2002.

———. "West-Ost-Migranten im geteilten Deutschland der fünfziger und sechziger Jahre." In *50 Jahre Bundesrepublik—50 Jahre Einwanderung: Nachkriegsgeschichte als Migrationsgeschichte*, edited by Jan Motte, Rainer Ohliger, and Anne von Oswald, 88–108. Frankfurt: Campus, 1999.

Schneider, Claudia. "Als Deutsche unter Deutschen? 'Übersiedler aus der VR Polen' in der DDR ab 1964." In *Transit/Transfer: Politik und Praxis der Einwande-*

rung in der DDR 1945–1990, edited by Kim Christian Priemel, 51–74. Berlin: Be.Bra, 2011.

Schneider, Hans-Peter. "Das Asylrecht zwischen Generosität und Xenophobie: Zur Entstehung des Artikels 16 Absatz 2 Satz 2 Grundgesetz im Parlamentarischen Rat." *Jahrbuch für Antisemitismusforschung* 1 (1992): 217–36.

Schönwälder, Karen. "Invited but Unwanted? Migrants from the East in Germany, 1890–1990." In *The German Lands and Eastern Europe: Essays on the History of their Social, Cultural and Political Relations*, edited by Roger Bartlett and Karen Schönwälder, 198–216. Basingstoke: Macmillan, 1999.

Schüle, Annegret. "'Die ham se sozusagen aus dem Busch geholt': Die Wahrnehmung der Vertragsarbeitskräfte aus Schwarzafrika und Vietnam durch Deutsche im VEB Leipziger Baumwollspinnerei." In *Fremde und Fremd-Sein in der DDR: Zu den historischen Ursachen der Fremdenfeindlichkeit in Ostdeutschland*, edited by Jan C. Behrends, Thomas Lindenberger, and Patrice Poutrus, 309–24. Berlin: Metropol, 2003.

———. "'Proletarischer Internationalismus' oder 'ökonomischer Vorteil für die DDR'? Mosambikanische, angolanische und vietnamesische Arbeitskräfte im VEB Leipziger Baumwollspinnerei (1980–1989)." *Archiv für Sozialgeschichte* 42 (2002): 191–210.

Schulz, Mirjam. "Migrationspolitik in der DDR: Bilaterale Anwerbungsverträge von Vertragsarbeitnehmern." In *Transit/Transfer: Politik und Praxis der Einwanderung in der DDR 1945–1990*, edited by Kim Christian Priemel, 143–68. Berlin: Be.Bra, 2011.

Schwartz, Michael. "Vertriebene im doppelten Deutschland: Integrations- und Erinnerungspolitik in der DDR und der Bundesrepublik." *Vierteljahrshefte für Zeitgeschichte* 56, no. 1 (2008): 101–51.

———. "Vertreibung und Vergangenheitspolitik: ein Versuch über geteilte deutsche Nachkriegsidentitäten." *Deutschland Archiv* 30 (1997): 177–95.

Steinert, Johannes-Dieter. "Drehscheibe Westdeutschland: Wanderungspolitik im Nachkriegsjahrzehnt." In *Deutsche im Ausland—Fremde in Deutschland: Migration in Geschichte und Gegenwart*, edited by Klaus J. Bade, 386–92. Munich: Beck, 1992.

Steinhilper, Elias. "Die Norm Asyl und die politische Funktion der Ausnahme." *Powision: Neue Räume für Politik* 8, no. 16 (2014): 31–33.

Sternberg, Jan Philipp. *Auswanderungsland Bundesrepublik: Denkmuster und Debatten in Politik und Medien 1945–2010*. Paderborn: Schöningh, 2012.

Stöver, Bernd. *Zuflucht DDR: Spione und andere Übersiedler*. Munich: Beck, 2009.

Troebst, Stefan. "'Grieche ohne Heimat': Hellenische Bürgerkriegsflüchtlinge in der DDR 1949–1989." *Totalitarismus und Demokratie* 2, no. 2 (2005): 245–71.

Urry, John. "Mobilities and Social Theory." In *The New Blackwell Companion to Social Theory*, edited by Bryan S. Turner, 477–95. Malden, MA: Wiley-Blackwell, 2009.

Weiss, Karin, and Mike Dennis, eds. *Erfolg in der Nische? Die Vietnamesen in der DDR und in Ostdeutschland*. Münster: Lit, 2005.

Widmann, Peter. "Gerettet und geduldet: Berliner Vietnamesen und die deutsche Flüchtlings- und Migrationspolitik." In *Umgang mit Flüchtlingen: Ein humanitäres Problem*, edited by Wolfgang Benz, 111–31. Munich: DTV, 2006.

White, Jenny B. "Turks in the New Germany." *American Anthropologist* 99, no. 4 (1997): 754–69.

Wölbern, Jan Philipp. *Der Häftlingsfreikauf aus der DDR 1962/63–1989: Zwischen Menschenhandel und humanitären Aktionen*. Göttingen: Vandenhoeck & Ruprecht, 2014.

Wolter, Heike. "DDR-Bürger auf Reisen. Zwischen Privatsache und Staatsangelegenheiten." In *Vergnügen in der DDR*, edited by Ulrike Häußler and Marcus Merkel, 425–43. Berlin: Panama, 2009.

———. *"Ich harre aus im Land und geh, ihm fremd": Die Geschichte des Tourismus in der DDR*, Frankfurt: Campus, 2009.

Wunschik, Tobias. "Migrationspolitische Hypertrophien: Aufnahme und Überwachung von Zuwanderern aus der Bundesrepublik Deutschland in der DDR." *IMIS-Beiträge* 32 (2007): 33–60.

CHAPTER 10

Sports and Society in the Rivalry between East and West

Jutta Braun

In a speech after the first free elections for the Volkskammer in the GDR on 18 March 1990, Wolfgang Schäuble, the West German minister of the interior, whose mandate included sports, declared that the successes achieved by East German sport had to be "rescued" for unified Germany.[1] Schäuble's sentiments echoed those of the West German sports organizations who hoped to get a glimpse into the secrets of the East German "sports miracle" (*Sportwunder*) after the fall of the Berlin Wall so that they could adopt some of its elements.[2] West German sports policy was focused in particular on the Olympic victories with which the GDR had been able to make a name for itself over decades. Politicians and sports associations did not realize until much later—and too late in the eyes of many experts—that the real "legacy" of GDR sport was an ailing recreational sport apparatus that was clearly in need of a complete overhaul.[3]

This history of sports in divided Germany was shaped by entanglements and differences that extended well beyond the Olympic Games. Especially in the world of soccer, there were significant differences, but also links and interactions between East and West that are quite relevant aspects of social history.[4] Similar fashions and trends also emerged in popular sports in East and West alike, but they took on different hues and forms of expression that were particular to each system.

Competing for Victory: Elite Sports in the 1970s and 1980s

The Olympics and the East German "Sportwunder"

During the Cold War, the Olympic Games, more so than any other major sporting event, were considered to be the ultimate venue for the rivalry between the systems. Initially, it had come as much of a surprise when the international socialist camp actually decided to take part in the Olympic movement after World War II. Prior to this point, the Soviet leadership had disdained the International Olympic Committee (IOC) as a clique of reactionary aristocrats, military men, and industrialists. It had set up its own competition, the Spartakiad, and celebrated socialist physical culture with impressive parades. In his last years in power, however, Stalin recognized the enormous draw of the spectacle of sports under the Olympic rings.[5] Thus, from the very beginning, the Soviet Union entered the Olympic arena with the intent to wage a proxy war in sports against "imperialism," and it very much intended to win—as did the GDR. Moreover, the socialist states gleaned an advantage from the amateur status of the Olympics, which formally excluded professional athletes from competing and could be used to political ends. For all intents and purposes, the elite East German athletes were professionals because they did devote most of their time and energy to competitive sport and their real jobs existed only on paper. Officially, however, these athletes competed as "amateurs" and were therefore able to perform exceptionally well. They were often jokingly referred to as "state amateurs" in the West.[6]

The competition with the "other Germany" created an additional incentive to strive for victory on both sides of the Wall, albeit with a very different level of political relevance. Usually, the GDR was the rather notorious loser in the battle between the systems with the FRG, and it actually had to keep its own people from trying to leave the country. But the realm of sports presented an exceptional opportunity to boost the country's image, not only in terms of the merits of the socialist system, but also on its own accord as an independent state: the relatively small GDR, with a population of just seventeen million, was able to win 755 Olympic medals, 768 world championships, and 747 European championships in forty years of sport history. After the Olympic Games of 1972 in Munich, the Cold War in sports between East and West Germany was definitely still alive and well.[7] The ramifications and the intensity of the rivalry had in fact only increased over time. The GDR achieved a striking victory just a bit later at the Olympic Games of 1976 in Montreal, when it not only won more medals than West Germany, but also more than the USA. The international sport scene was deeply impressed, particularly by the performance of the East German swim team. Despite the running jokes and rumors about the noticeably male appearance of the East German female athletes, East Germany was not stigmatized as a pariah because pharmaceutical assistance was still considered to be an appropriate means of improving performance in international sports at the time. The same held true for West Germany. In fact, in a now often cited and controversial statement made before the sports committee of the German Bundestag in 1977, the CDU representative Wolfgang Schäuble neither wanted to rule out nor condemn the use of such drugs in principle.[8]

Only isolated voices raised objections to this practice, such as Brigitte Berendonk, who had seen this doping firsthand on both sides as a former athlete in East and West Germany. She repeatedly made public statements, warning against the danger of creating "monsters."[9] References to international "equal opportunity" were often made as part of a reflexive, rather hollow argument made to defend doping research and the use of performance-enhancing drugs in one's own backyard on both sides.[10] Yet such seemingly similar patterns of legitimation cannot sweep away the differences in the way in which doping was used in the GDR and the FRG. The fact that the GDR was a dictatorship was very much a decisive factor even in sports because the state basically had total control over its athletes. Doping took place in West Germany with the informal approval of countless officials in the different sports associations, but it was mainly done within the interconnected circles of athletes, doctors, and coaches.[11] In East Germany, however, it was subject to centralized planning: since at least 1974, doping was organized and carried out systematically according to what was referred to as a *Staatsplanthema* (state planning schemes)—and it was sometimes achieved by the coercion and repression of the athletes themselves.[12] Although the details about this forced doping in the East had become known in West Germany through the sport refugees who had fled the GDR, it did not make nearly as much of a stir as other human rights violations taking place behind the Iron Curtain.[13] The West German sporting world in fact welcomed the doping expertise that East German sports medicine professionals brought with them when they defected to the West. Dr. Josef Nöcker, for example, was the man behind the infamous "Kolbe shot."[14] Likewise, Dr. Alois Mader made a name for himself as an influential expert in performance enhancement through the use of anabolic steroids after 1974, and Dr. Hartmut Riedel enjoyed a similar kind of fame at the end of the 1980s.[15]

Without a doubt, West German politicians and sport functionaries were most fascinated by the organizational aspects of the GDR's *Sportwunder*. Since the sports equivalent of the "Sputnik shock" in the summer of 1968, when the GDR beat out West Germany in the medal count for the first time, the question "do socialists run faster?"[16] symbolized the relentless search for functional elements that could be copied. But much of what contributed to the success of GDR athletes could not be replicated in West Germany simply because of the difference in the two systems. The completely disproportional amount of state funding that was pumped into elite sports in the GDR—the full extent of which was kept a secret until 1990—was only possible in a dictatorship. In a parliamentary democracy, elite sports always have to compete for funding with other areas of life subsidized by the state.[17] It was also hardly imaginable that West Germany would weigh and measure all schoolchildren in order to assess their potential talent for certain sport disciplines as it was done in the GDR. Likewise, all the many coercive efforts that the GDR state undertook to hinder or even prohibit sport disciplines in which only a few medals could be won would have been unthinkable. For instance, in order to promote the Olympic discipline of Judo, the GDR prohibited the practice of karate.[18]

West Germany was particularly curious about the competitive sports training facilities in the East, especially the children's and youth sport schools that were one important motor behind the GDR's sports machinery. The East Germans, however, did not let their Western competitors take a closer look, nor did they want to share much with their Soviet big brother.[19] Nonetheless, the West was able to get a better idea about the sports clubs in the GDR, which were not really Vereine (associations) anymore, despite the fact that most people still referred to them as such. For one, the kind of associational life typical of democratic civil societies no longer existed in the GDR. Moreover, these clubs actually functioned as highly specialized competitive sports complexes that invested an enormous amount of human resources to guarantee the best comprehensive coaching and training for their athletes.[20] After the disappointing medal performance of the West German team at the Sarajewo Olympic Games in 1984, the model of the GDR sports clubs seemed to be a viable option for a new training method in the eyes of the Federal Committee for Competitive Sports (Bundesausschuss Leistungssport, or BAL). Accordingly, the first Olympic training centers (Olympiastützpunkte, or OSP) that followed some principles of the GDR sports clubs were established in 1986. All the OSP were tasked with coaching and training cadres in several different Olympic disciplines at once, a practice that was an effort to emulate the centralized sports system of the GDR.[21] In spite of all of the efforts made by the West German sports associations, the GDR remained the more successful German team at the Olympic Games until its collapse.

Two Worlds of Competitive Sports

Until the end of the Cold War, international sports events were the stage for a direct struggle of power between East and West. Yet, the world of sports was still very much divided by the Iron Curtain because the socialist states refrained from participating in many professional sports for ideological reasons. The Eastern Bloc countries, for example, were missing at the most important spectator event in professional cycling, the

Tour de France. Instead, the East German cyclists pedaled for gold at the most important amateur race in the world, the Peace Race, which went through Warsaw, Berlin, and Prague.[22] The GDR enjoyed a surprisingly successful string of victories at this race, from the legendary performances of Täve Schur in the 1950s to the four-year string of gold medals won by Uwe Ampler in the 1980s. A rather strange German-German showdown occurred only once when, in honor of the 750th anniversary celebrations of the city of Berlin, the Senate of West Berlin made arrangements for the prologue of the Tour de France to run down the Kurfürstendamm in 1987; the furious GDR sports leadership then moved the start of the Peace Race to Karl-Marx-Allee in the East.[23] But the heyday of West German tennis in the 1980s remained unparalleled in the East. Not only did it spawn two exceptional world-class athletes, namely Boris Becker and Steffi Graf, but also it had a direct effect on recreational sports. The West German Wimbledon and Davis Cup victories inspired younger tennis athletes, and new tennis sections were created in sports associations all over the country. Within just a few years, the number of active members in these tennis clubs doubled.[24] The few tennis talents in the GDR could only watch wistfully from the other side of the Wall as they had to make do with the very limited amount of material support and coaching staff at their disposal; they also had to listen to people tell them that tennis was a "bourgeois" sport.[25] For the first time in 1988, when tennis officially became an Olympic sport, the prospects for tennis players improved in East Germany, but this was too late for the GDR.

In the mid-1980s, the separation of amateur and professional sports became much less rigid due to a change in the Olympic charter that was made by the IOC in Lausanne in 1986: in the future, the doors of the Olympic Games were to be opened for professional athletes. From then on, the Olympic villages were not only home to the spartan cadres of competitive athletes dependent on the meager funding that they received by the Stiftung Deutsche Sporthilfe, but also the glamorous stars of the sports business. When the tennis multimillionaire Steffi Graf moved into the Olympic village in Seoul in 1988 and Barcelona in 1992, she not only attracted envious glances from the East Germans, but also her West German colleagues and other nonprofessional athletes.[26]

One sport in particular had a different status on both sides of the Wall, namely Germany's favorite pastime, soccer. On this playing field, the combination of targeted support for grassroots soccer programs and a commercially successful professional league proved to be able to top the success of the state-managed soccer program in the GDR. Relatively late in the game in 1963, West Germany opted for a uniform system of leagues. It took until 1972 for professional soccer to become established through a series of incremental steps, such as the Statute on Contract Players. This marked the beginning of the success story of the German Bundesliga, which has also become a site of collective memory for the Germans.[27] The history of the different soccer clubs, such as Schalke 04 or Bayern München, is deeply entwined with the economic and social developments in the respective regions. As such, these clubs have contributed to the crystallization of local and regional identity.[28] The identities of the clubs themselves and their traditions date back to when they were founded, mostly around the turn of the nineteenth century. Soccer in the GDR took an entirely different path. After 1948, the SED pushed through a radical break with the bourgeois remnants of associational culture in East Germany, and the traditional club teams were either turned into socialist organizations with new names or entirely new clubs were founded.[29] For example, the army soccer team of the ASK Vorwärts and the Dynamo teams propped up by the "security forces" of the GDR (Stasi, police, and customs) implanted structures imported from the Soviet Union into East German soccer.

At the level of everyday life in the 1970s and 1980s, however, soccer was not very different in the GDR compared to West Germany. The regional teams in both German states were the bearers of the sports equivalent of hometown pride. Moreover, in contrast to the rest of the GDR sport system, soccer was able to develop a covert kind of capitalism: because of the immense popularity of the sport, club directors as well as regional SED officials had a great interest in "buying" the best players, which led to the establishment of a shadow system of illegal premiums and signing bonuses.[30] Internationally, however, the selection of players available in the GDR could never come close to achieving the level of performance offered by the West German international teams. The Deutscher Fußballbund (DFB) team had not only won three world championships and taken part in six of the final matches, but also had taken home two European championship victories by 1990. The GDR, on the other hand, had only taken part in a single final round of these championships in 1974. A great deal of speculation has surrounded the possible reasons for this difference in performance.[31] Yet it is clear that the focus of the SED sports leadership on medal-winning sports played a considerable role in this respect. In response to a question posed in 1986 by a West German reporter as to why there were so few tall players to be found on the GDR team, the soccer coach Lothar Kurbjuweit from Jena answered laconically, "The tall soccer players are rowers here!"[32] The East German team, however, did have its share of the limelight at the Olympic Games. As was so often the case in the GDR, the professional players from the GDR team competed as "amateurs" at the Olympic Games, and came up against the "proper" amateurs from the West. The GDR proudly won four Olympic medals in soccer, but no one really seemed to care.[33] Many soccer fans in the GDR began to look longingly over at the West. As a result of the immense popularity of the Bundesliga and the West German national team, many East German soccer fans started to follow more than one team: in addition to their GDR club, they often supported a West German club such as Bayern München or Hamburger Sport-Verien (HSV), or even the DFB national team. The SED and the Stasi, however, were not fans of this phenomenon, and they kept a close eye on the situation while imposing strict sanctions: if East German fans traveled to matches in the Eastern Bloc involving West German teams, their signs and slogans were highly censored. Even seemingly harmless slogans, such as "We welcome the FC Bayern München" aroused the ire of the GDR security apparatus. When the West German national team played a qualifying match for the European championships in Warsaw in 1971, the Stasi was on high alert as hundreds of fans traveled to the city from the GDR. Despite numerous targeted efforts to crack down on this, including widespread infiltration of the fan scene, the SED's apparatus never got this phenomenon under control.[34] It was particularly troubling to the GDR state that the insubordinate fans were almost all part of the so-called Wall generation, which meant—at least in the eyes of the SED—that they should not really have had any ties with the other Germany.[35] Whereas West Germany faced a mounting problem with violently aggressive right-wing radical fans in the 1970s and 1980s, the security forces in the GDR not only had a problem with such hooligans,[36] but also with another group of supposedly "criminal" soccer fans: the German-German away fans.[37]

The Cleft between Raison d'État and the Autonomy of Sports

According to the respective statutes, West German sports were committed to remaining "apolitical." For the most part, this meant that they sought to remain politically and religiously neutral as part of a conscious effort to break with the legacy of the Nazi period, as well as with the confessional and social divide that had occurred during the Weimar Republic. Yet in the system rivalry of the Cold War, the sports organizations, whether it be the German National Olympic Committee, the DSB (German Sport Federation), or the DFB—the latter of which was the most influential professional sports association—definitely took sides. For the most part, they did so by expressing their general agreement with the stance that the West German government took towards the GDR and the entire Eastern Bloc. Due to the tensions between the two superpower blocs in the 1980s, a number of fundamental conflicts emerged between the sports world and the political raison d'état of the West German government. Differences of opinion not only cropped up in terms of the notorious Olympic boycotts, but also in the run-up to the European soccer championships in 1988. In both cases, the West German sports associations found themselves being pressured by the West German government to conform to a political line. A similar cleft between bloc politics and the interests of the GDR's sports leadership also emerged in the late 1980s in the GDR, albeit under entirely different political circumstances.

The decision to boycott the Summer Olympic Games in Moscow in 1980, for example, is considered to be one of the greatest crises in West German sport. In response to the Soviet invasion of Afghanistan, U.S. President Jimmy Carter had issued an ultimatum on 20 January 1980 demanding that the Soviets withdraw their troops. His statement was coupled with the threat to either cancel or move the Olympic Games. The publicity attached to the Olympics was used to turn sports into a political symbol, even though the federal government refused to go along with the stronger economic boycott because it endangered the country's export interests. At this point in time, moreover, Olympic history was already rife with boycotts or the threat thereof,[38] and it was by no means the first time that Cold War power plays had been involved. But, it was the first time that the West German government played a key role in a boycott situation.[39]

The discussion that flared up in the following months and peaked in April and May 1980 had a broad international scope: in numerous states, especially in Western Europe, there was a tug-of-war between the governments and the respective national Olympic committees, only the latter of which were legally entitled to decide about their country's participation in the Games.[40] Despite considerable reservations, Federal Chancellor Helmut Schmidt finally declared himself in favor of a boycott in order to demonstrate his loyalty to the country's American ally. The recommendation of the federal government to refrain from participating in the Moscow Games was reinforced by a similar suggestion that was passed by an overwhelming majority in the German Bundestag on 23 April 1980. The head of the West German National Olympic Committee (NOC), Willi Daume, had opposed the boycott, but he ultimately capitulated in the face of this political front, about which he wrote, "What ultimately swayed the members of our committee was the vote of the German Bundestag, which pitted the weight (so to speak) of an entire grand coalition against our small committee."[41] In two face-to-face meetings in April 1980, Chancellor Helmut Schmidt had also tried to convince the representatives of the sports organizations to follow his lead. Schmidt left no doubt as to his expectations: as records of these conversations indicate, he stressed the importance of the fact "that sports in our country are not subject to the dictates of the federal government and the parliament, but rather are in charge of their own affairs and make their own decisions. . . . The federal government shall not exert pressure or threaten sanction, as is done in other countries. Yet it expects that sport will come to understand the existential demands of our people and the necessities of our alliance."[42] In a sibylline way, the Chancellor also explained that, if the NOC were to decide in favor of participating in the Games, the government "would not exercise any coercion, rescind any passports, or prevent anyone from using part of his vacation time for the Games."[43] In fact, however, the federal government had considered using such measures ultima ratio as a way to exert influence just prior to this point, but it came to the conclusion that it would not be legally possible to do so.[44]

In the end, the NOC voted on 15 May 1980 with fifty-nine to forty votes in favor of boycotting the Games. The fact that Germany—together with Norway—stood alone in Western Europe with this stance created trouble for both Willi Daume and Helmut Schmidt, but for different reasons: Daume's hopes of becoming IOC president were completely dashed, and Helmut Schmidt had to defend himself against accusations coming from the domestic side, and especially within his own party, that he was blindly loyal to the United States. Most proponents of the boycott came from the conservative milieu. This not only included the CDU/CSU, but also the national organizations for equestrian sports, fencing, and sailing, which were considered to be quite conservative as opposed to the handball and swimming associations.[45] The riders in many other states, including Britain, also stayed at home, as did many sailing competitors, even though their respective NOCs had not boycotted the Games. A demonstration that was held in Dortmund on 21 April 1980 under the motto *"Olympia lebt"* (The Olympics Are Alive) was intended to function as an athlete protest against the boycott. But it ultimately came to resemble a peace demonstration at the time in terms of style and audience, replete with the support of the German Communist Party. The Ministry of the Interior saw the planned demonstration as a sign of the "apolitical emotionality of a considerable number of our athletes."[46] The Olympic fencing champion and later the Deutscher Olympischer Sportbund (DOSB) and IOC President Thomas Bach spoke out decidedly in favor of participating in the Moscow Games in his role as speaker of the national team's athletes. He also later complained that the boycott "didn't accomplish anything."[47] At any rate, the boycott did force the government in Moscow to explain to its own people why one-third of the sports world had boycotted the Games.[48]

The deep cleft that had been forming between politics and sport since 1980 was clear to see in the attacks that Willi Daume launched at what he perceived to be the dishonest information policy of the federal government.⁴⁹ Sport journalists had also complained about a "spiral of silence" that seemed to be working in favor of the boycott.⁵⁰ In fact, silence reigned in many places—for instance, on television. West German television, which was still dominated by the monopoly of the public television stations, reduced its coverage of the Olympics to a minimum. As a result of a joint decision by the ARD and ZDF public television channels, only fifteen minutes of the Olympic Games in Moscow were broadcast on each channel daily instead of the usual ten to twelve hours of programming. Only six minutes of the three-hour-long opening ceremony were aired on German TV. Some smart entrepreneurs recorded the GDR coverage on video cassettes and then sold them on the domestic market in West Germany. Likewise, the DSB had the entirety of the GDR's television coverage of the Olympic Games archived on video cassettes in the Rhön region near the border.⁵¹

Similar to Willi Daume, albeit under the conditions of a completely different system, the East German sports director Manfred Ewald protested against a revenge boycott against the Games in Los Angeles that was being mandated by the Soviet Union, and which the GDR was expected to follow. As Ewald remembered it, he did have a disagreement with Erich Honecker about the decision, but he had no chance but to comply in the end because Honecker had pointed out the economic difficulties that the country would face if it marched out of tune with the boycott of the socialist front.⁵² At its session on 10 May 1984 in East Berlin, the NOC of the GDR reluctantly bowed to solidarity with its big brother and withdrew from the Olympics under the pretense that adequate security precautions had not been taken.⁵³ Just as four years earlier, the ones who suffered most from the boycott were the athletes themselves. Not surprisingly, some of their expressions of displeasure reached the ears of the Western media. The shot put athlete Udo Beyer, for example, spoke of a "hard decision," while the swimmer Roland Matthes stressed "how painful" it was not to be able to participate.⁵⁴

The trend toward using the participation or even the hosting of sports events to make a symbolic political statement that had emerged in the East as well as the West also reappeared as the 1988 Olympic Games approached. The Seoul Olympics had also been in danger of a boycott because South Korea did not maintain diplomatic relations with the socialist countries. This led to some strange bedfellows in the run-up to the Games because the "class enemies" Willi Daume and Manfred Ewald both had a vested interest in ensuring that the "Games would continue." At a confidential meeting of the two in East Berlin in June 1984, Ewald proposed that they should suggest to the IOC president Antonio Samaranch that the city of Munich could be an alternative host. Daume, who was flattered by this talk, was obviously amenable to the idea.[55] The main concern of the East German sports director was no longer the prestige that could be won by the rival West Germany, but that all the effort that had been put into his socialist sports apparatus would have been for nothing. The IOC and the GDR soon officially announced their Olympic reconciliation. At the 89th Session of the IOC that was held from 3 to 6 June 1985 in East Berlin, the GDR presented itself as the "prize pupil of the Olympic idea."[56] When Samaranch awarded the Olympic Order in gold to Erich Honecker at the Schauspielhaus on Gendarmenmarkt in Berlin, it was interpreted as an expression of gratitude in advance for the fact that the GDR would not join in another boycott. In fact, however, this act had already been planned since October 1983.[57] The pomp and circumstance surrounding this spectacle nonetheless indicated the great hope held by the SED leadership that its legitimacy could be boosted through the Olympics. The SED was not really aware of the crisis in the country, nor the serious nature of the oppositional movements, most of whom were not at all impressed by Olympic medals. The boos and whistles directed at the figure-skating icon Katarina Witt when she hosted a rock concert in Weißensee in 1988 and the parody of Witt in the popular underground song "Born in the GDR" from the punk band Sandow, which was critical of the GDR system, illustrate the great extent to which many younger East Germans saw the Olympic sports events as just a "gigantic piece of decoration for the government."[58]

West German soccer was also not immune to the effects of the East-West conflict in the 1980s. The system rivalry reared its head in a rather blatant way in 1985 when West Germany was named as the host for the UEFA (Union of European Football Associations) European Soccer Championships in 1988. West-Berlin was also in the running to be one of the cities that would host matches, but it was bumped out in the final plans. Under the leadership of Hermann Neuberger, the DFB was aware of the likely resistance to this plan among the three Eastern European members of the UEFA organization committee, which was why it had suggested West Berlin as a site for the opening match, but they had not made it a conditio sine qua non in their proposal to host the championships.[59] Politicians in West Berlin as well as portions of the press sharply criticized the DFB's willingness to concede,[60] resulting in a public reprimand of Neuberger by the federal government.[61]

The outrage that spread throughout West Berlin in early 1985 fed on the countless attempts that Moscow had made to cut off the city in a variety of ways as part of a strategy to practically and symbolically isolate West Berlin from West Germany. Here again, sports functioned as an instrument of political leverage. In 1971, the Soviet Union had already tried to prevent West Berlin from hosting matches of the World Championships in 1974. Hermann Neuberger, who was the head of the Fédération Internationale de Football Association (FIFA) organizing committee at the time, was only able to push through the city as a match location with a great deal of effort on his part.[62] Since the Eastern Bloc was more powerful in the European association than it was in FIFA, choosing West Berlin as a host city for the 1988 championships therefore presented an incalculable risk. In a board meeting on 27 February 1985 in Aachen, all the regional associations of the DFB, except for West Berlin, voted in favor of leaving West Berlin out of the lineup. The very same day, the minister of sports, Friedrich Zimmermann, composed a letter to Neuberger in which he voiced the opposition of the federal government, whose position was that "Berlin had to be included among the host cities when the European Soccer Championships take place in West Germany in 1988."[63] Bonn also decided to begin a diplomatic offensive: an aide memoire from the federal cabinet that was sent to the ministers of foreign affairs in UEFA countries that were friends of West Germany read, "The government of West Germany would find it very regrettable if the European Soccer Championships in 1988 were to take place in West Germany without Berlin (West) as a host city. If this were to be the case, then it would not consider it desirable for the DFB to be awarded the honor of hosting the 1988 European Soccer Championship."[64] In response, the DFB charged that the contents of the aide memoire marked a massive curtailment of the authority and autonomy of organized sport.[65] On 14 March 1985, West Germany was officially named the host for the European Championships by the UEFA in Bern, although several international sports representatives mocked what they considered to be an affront by Kohl's government.

The conflict in 1985 proved to be the most difficult balancing act between sports and politics since the boycott of the Moscow Olympics. Whereas the West German sports associations followed—albeit somewhat unwillingly—the priorities set by the federal government in 1980, the DFB and the DSB objected publicly and heftily against the intervention by the federal government in 1985. Ultimately, this controversy in 1985 had long-term consequences: in order to "compensate" for being left out of the European Championships in 1988, West Berlin was promised that it could be the permanent site of the final match of the DFB Cup, which has meant that Berlin still plays host to this sporting attraction even today.[66]

Commercial Transformations

The advent of a new Olympic age presented particular problems for the Communist side of the sports world. The Games in Los Angeles were in fact the first privately organized and financed Olympics in the history of the event. After the IOC named the city the host for the Summer Games in 1978, the residents of Los Angeles voted against using public funds to finance the Games in a referendum. Very likely, many of them had been discouraged from voting in favor by the financial disaster that had resulted in Montreal in 1976. The mayor of L.A., Tom Bradley, as well as the IOC, had no idea what to do, but then a few private companies came to the rescue as sponsors. The president of the organizational committee, businessman Peter Ueberroth, who was the son of German immigrants from Lübeck and head of a travel company, announced the beginnings of a "partnership between business and the Olympic Games."[67] With this new agenda, the IOC increased its own influence, especially in the Third World, thanks to millions in additional income. As a result, the Soviet Union was slowly pushed aside as a key player. Financially weak national Olympic committees, for example, now received additional money from a solidarity fund established by the IOC, making it possible for a record number of one hundred forty nations to participate in the Games. The IOC also generated a considerable amount of income by marketing its symbols, but more importantly, it made money through its shares of about a third[68] in the TV license fees for the Games, which had amounted to about thirty-four million dollars in 1984 alone. The growing power of capital reduced the influence of the Communist sporting world, which controlled only about 10 percent of the votes in the IOC.

When Mikhail Gorbachev took over the office of general secretary of the Soviet Communist Party in March 1985, the progressive split between the Soviet reformers and the East German hardliners also manifested itself in the world of sport. The GDR slowly began to feel itself left out in the cold by the Soviet Union in the fight against the most important demons in socialist sports propaganda, namely "commercialization" and "professionalism." Although Ewald originally banked on the idea that the Soviet Union would hold its stance, East Berlin found itself the "lone voice" as early as October 1986.[69] In November 1986 at the yearly conference of the socialist sports directors, the minister of sport, Marat Gramow, stated rather cautiously that the Soviet Union had nothing against professional elite sports, but rather that it only objected to the "professional abuse" of competitive sports.[70] The head of the NOC, Willi Daume, who—like the rest of the Olympic movement—had opposed permitting professional athletes to compete, quite bluntly admitted to the GDR sports director Manfred Ewald at a meeting in 1986 that he had now actually come to support the professionalization of the Games in order to make it more difficult for the socialist countries to win medals.[71]

Furthermore, it was difficult for the GDR to take advantage of certain facets of the progressive commercialization of sports from which numerous East European sports countries profited at the time, namely the temporary or permanent "lending" or "letting go" of socialist athletes to the West in exchange for hard cash in foreign currency; this had been done by Poland, Hungary, and the Czech Republic since the mid-1980s. In contrast, for the GDR it had always been a great risk to let athletes take part in competitions in the West because of the division of Germany, which made it rather tempting for many athletes to defect to the West. Katarina Witt, for example, was closely monitored by nine employees of the GDR sports apparatus when she took the first steps toward commercial figure skating performances. Her guards "could have been called into action in an emergency situation in order to make sure that nothing happened to her."[72] Despite the ideological considerations, however, it seemed that Ewald was impressed by some aspects of the boom in new marketing opportunities, for he noted, "What has been made possible by commercialism today is unbelievable. The Poles just got 1.4 million dollars for their soccer player Boniek. As our friends have told us, they estimate that about 600 athletes and trainers from Poland are involved in sports abroad in Western countries."[73]

At the same time, indignant GDR athletes began to ask more often whether they could keep the fees and prizes that they won instead of having to hand them over to the German Gymnastics and Sports Federation (Deutscher Turn- und Sportbund, or DTSB) as had been done in the past.[74] Yet the "class hate" directed at West German sports that had been cultivated by the GDR for decades now hindered a reform of sports policy. The star socialist athletes had always been treated as the property of the state. Since 1971—in the wake of several embarrassing defections of top-notch athletes to the West—the sports squads were subject to the meticulous scrutiny of the Stasi. Not only during training, but also in their private lives, agents kept tabs on them in order to prevent undesired contact with the West or attempts to defect. The legal transfer of GDR athletes to the West was therefore completely contrary to the principles of the entire ideological and organizational foundation of GDR sport as well as the SED dictatorship itself. Manfred Ewald involuntarily made it clear just how deeply ingrained this ideology of demarcation was in the run-up to the Olympic Games in Calgary in 1988. The West German news magazine *Der Spiegel* published a confidential directive addressed to sport functionaries and trainers in which the martial Cold War scenarios were redrawn and a call was made to "reaffirm and refresh the principle images of the enemy" in the minds of athletes.[75] When the text was made public, it created a political sports scandal, especially since the

SED had just promised to "dismantle the enemy images" in the wake of Honecker's visit to West Germany in September 1987.[76] As head of the NOC, Ewald valiantly tried to play down this text as a purely "provocative invention" at a press conference held to present the GDR Olympic team at the end of January in 1988.[77] The GDR sports leadership finally found itself caught up in a propaganda predicament of its own making: on the one hand, it had stuffed its athletes full of well-practiced inflammatory rhetoric and untruths, but then it found itself lying again as it tried to deny the whole thing with a red face after having been caught out by the West. Given the particularly hard line of ideological belligerency held by the GDR sports leadership,[78] as well as the fear that any permeability of the Wall would create an undesirable domino effect in terms of an exodus of athletes to the West, it seemed impossible that the kind of reforms that had taken place in other Eastern European states would come about in East Germany. Only in the closest circles of the polibüro could Erich Honecker concede with a wink in his eye in 1989 that "we also actually have professional sports. We don't really have to get upset about this. Soccer players are bought. The Oberliga players are indeed professional athletes."[79] Yet the SED could not, nor did it want to, take up with the suggestion made public by the Werder Bremen coach Otto Rehhagel in 1986, as well as other offers in kind, to set up an international exchange of players between East and West Germany—akin to what was already being done in other Eastern European states—which Rehhagel maintained would have advantages for both sides.[80] The SED and its sports leadership had seen elite sports throughout the decades as serving the primary purpose of state representation and, above all, drawing a line of demarcation between East and West Germany. As a result, they could not really get their heads around one of the basic principles of professional sports events. Manfred Ewald, for example, could not understand why "players such as Lendl in tennis and others compete against their own countrymen in sports contests." Indeed, he claimed "this doesn't really make any sense."[81]

In its last years, however, the GDR did come to terms with one aspect of this commercialization of sports—namely, advertising income. For the first time, an "advertising department" was created within the DTSB of the GDR that was responsible for coordinating the marketing of GDR sports in the West. According to the organ of the FDJ (Free German Youth), the *Junge Welt*, the GDR hoped to make a total of 130 million marks in 1988 through sports advertising.[82] Interestingly, however, this advertising was mostly for products that could not be bought in the GDR. The TV coverage of championships and international matches, for example, featured banner advertising for Agfa and Kodak, as well as Bauhaus and Erdgas. Likewise, the starting numbers for the GDR track and field athletes in 1988 bore the logo of the computer company Commodore. Additionally, at the Olympic Games in 1988, the GDR bobsled team wore BMW helmets because, as *Neues Deutschland* had recently assured, they were the "safest."[83] On the eve of its collapse, therefore, GDR sport had very cautiously adapted some of the mainstream reforms of the Eastern Bloc, at least in terms of brand advertising.

Popular Sports in the West, People's Sport in the GDR

Whereas the GDR mostly expanded only its competitive sports system, recreational sports gained in importance in West Germany in the 1970s. The birth of modern recreational sports is still considered to have come with the Zweiter Weg des Sports (The Second Path of Sports) campaign that was launched by the DSB in 1959. According to this concept, the focus would no longer be on competitive programs and high performance athletes only, but rather an effort would be made to offer a broad range of recreational sports programming in which performance enhancement was not the goal. This idea of "sports for all," which was deeply rooted in the specific German gymnastics tradition, quickly gained in popularity. By 1970, 16.7 percent of the population already belonged to a gymnastics or sports club, and these membership figures skyrocketed in the 1970s. Additionally, thanks to the initiative of the Golden Plan for the Creation of Recreational, Play, and Sports facilities, the necessary infrastructure of facilities, fields, pitches, etc. was put into place in order to satisfy the public need for leisure activities. In particular, the importance of the Trimm campaign in 1970 should not be underestimated. As Christian Wopp put it, "From a historical perspective, it made a decisive contribution to liberating sport activities from traditional norms and standards by propagating a more open understanding of sport."[84] Whereas the Second Path was primarily directed at the clubs and associations, the Trimm campaign, with its mascot "Trimmy" and slogans such as "get running again," targeted individual citizens. But it was not just the increase in the average body weight of West Germans that stood behind this initiative; rather, it was part of the multifaceted body policies that the state adopted as part of its efforts to protect the health of its citizens. This shift also included the campaigns against alcohol, smoking, and drugs, and for wearing seat belts in the car. Simultaneously, the general desire among West Germans to optimize their own bodies—not just through sport—increased. Diets, tanning, and individualized clothing styles also rose in prominence. The number of recreational athletes engaging in sport activities on their own grew, as did the membership figures for the sports clubs. As of 1980, 27.6 percent of the population participated in organized sports.[85]

Over the course of the 1980s, sporting activities also became more diversified. This mobilizing trend was not only reflected in the emergence of alternative kinds of movement and trend sports such as jogging, but also appeared in the form of a new commercial sector that was turning physical exercise in fitness studios into a form of self-optimization.[86] Especially in the 1980s, fashions in clothing, music, and sporting goods in areas such as bodybuilding or aerobics became all the more prevalent. Fitness was becoming a lifestyle as well as an indicator of youthfulness, attractiveness, and hipness all rolled into one. These developments were part of a process of "sportification" (*Versportlichung*) of culture,[87] which was perhaps best expressed by the triumph of the sneaker in the world of fashion.

In the GDR, popular sports, or "people's sports" as they were called in the East, were not only tied to the idea of improving personal fitness and quality of life; from the very beginning, sports were also linked to the collective welfare of society as a whole. Walter Ulbricht's saying "Everyone everywhere—sport once a week" was a reflection of the SED's goal to keep its labor force in shape, as well as guarantee the military preparedness of the population.[88] Although sports groups seemed to be omnipresent in residential communities and companies, "mass sport" in the GDR still remained the stepchild of the socialist planned economy throughout the decades.[89] This was further compounded by the focus of the GDR sports leadership on the Olympics. Indeed, the trendy kinds of sport that began to appear in East Germany in the 1970s harbored a real potential for conflict, as several hurdles stood in the way of their establishment. For one, the SED emphasized the need for sports organizations; individualists who jumped on their surf boards by themselves and without anyone else around did not fit the image of the East German sports apparatus. Similarly, the party often covered up the American or Western origins of these new sports by giving them a different name. Surfing, for example, became *Brettsegeln* (board sailing), while body building was called *Körperkulturistik* (physical culturism) and aerobics were offered as *Popgymnastik* (pop gymnastics). Moreover, in order to prevent any attempts to defect, *Brettsegeln* was permitted only on inland waters. Commercial surf schools were frowned upon, although some people—for example, the nephew of Karl Eduard von Schnitzler, the chief ideological propagandist in East German television—were given a license to operate some schools for a time.[90] The informal sporting scenes for climbers and skateboarders likewise ran into trouble due to official restrictions and the mistrust of state authorities.[91] Inspired by the jogging images coming from the United States and the "Trimm-Dich" movement in West Germany, many East Germans suddenly became more interested in running. The GDR channeled this trend into an official Eile mit Meile (Rush to the Mile) movement. At the same time, it also tolerated independently organized running events, such as the Rennsteiglauf, which were attracting more and more followers.[92] At the same time, however, these trends created new problems for the GDR. For example, as part of the "institutionalized culture of complaint" in the GDR, East Germans submitted all kinds of queries to the government about the lack of sporting goods. Most of these complaints were related to the supply of sports equipment and sports attire, especially running shoes. The state planned economy, however, was never able to keep up with the demand for these items in light of the boom in running that took place in the 1970s and 1980s.[93]

A further impediment against the development of popular sports in the GDR was the concentrated investment in competitive sports and the corresponding neglect of the sports facilities that were open to the broader public of the GDR. Existing sports centers fell victim to the residential housing program that was pushed through under Honecker, and then they were never replaced by new ones. For example, in Leipzig alone, this apparently affected twelve facilities over the years.[94] Not surprisingly, the press in the GDR was not permitted to report on any shortcomings. In 1986, however, an article appeared in an academic journal—presumably only for internal use—that criticized the state of sports facilities in the GDR.[95] The article was based on the assessment of the sports facilities in East Germany that had been carried out by the State Secretariat for Physical Culture and Sport and the Wissenschaftlich-Technische Zentrum Sportbauten (Scientific-Technical Center for Sport Buildings). The author of the article, who was also the head of this study, described the horrendous state of the indoor and outdoor public pools in very clear terms. According to his report, more than half of them could not be used without restrictions and limitations; he also provided a long list of the hygienic and structural problems in these pools.[96] The deficient state of people's sports in the GDR had become so blatantly apparent by the end of the 1980s that politicians at least paid lip service to attempts to turn the situation around. After becoming DTSB president in November 1988, Klaus Eichler propagated a series of reforms that clearly deviated from the previous course of sports policy that had focused almost entirely on competitive sports.[97] The official DTSB agenda also included a passage stating that "the growing need for gymnastics, strength training, cycling, mountain biking, bowling, swimming, water sports, hiking, tennis, table tennis, badminton, figure skating, and running . . . needs to be given more attention."[98] Yet this reform-minded sports agenda, as Hans Joachim Teichler has pointed out, made no mention of where the lacking bicycles, ice skates, and tennis rackets were to come from, nor what was to be done about the missing weight rooms, saunas, tennis courts, and so much more. In fact, this situation dramatically escalated because the production of high-end sports equipment, such as racing bikes and tennis rackets, had already been shut down or diverted to the export sector by mid-1989. The country's sports leadership had estimated that approximately two billion marks would be needed in the next five-year plan to finance the urgently necessary expansion of the country's sports infrastructure, but this plan was set aside in 1988 because of a lack of funds. Moreover, the funds that were provided to sports clubs continued to be divided clearly between Sport I ("medal intensive") and Sport II; the ratio between these two sport types was about 81.3 percent to 17.6 percent in 1989. Similarly, only 1.3 percent of the allotted Western currency was given to the seventeen sports associations for "non-medal-intensive sports."[99]

Transitions and Transformations since 1990

The Path to Unity in Sports

The fall of the Wall brought a whole new kind of freedom of movement for athletes in both Germanys, but for East Germans in particular. Up to this point, German-German sports had been constrained by the corset of the so-called sports protocol that had—in its guise as the "basic contract for sport"—ensured the implementation of *Ostpolitik* through athletic means from 1974 onward. Accordingly, a strict number of athletic engagements each year was supposed to guarantee regular contact between athletes at a personal level. In practice, the GDR used this "sport calendar" to reduce the scope of these meetings to a bare minimum and, given the long amount of time that they had to prepare for these interactions, to make them "secure," which meant that they were as frosty as possible.[100]

The collapse of the GDR brought an end to this practice. The official "permission for athletic travel" issued on 17 November 1989 was really only a formality because hundreds of sports meetings and matches had already taken place that very same year shortly after the Wall had fallen. Even before the Volkskammer elections on 18 March 1990 paved the way for reunification, the East German system began to adapt itself to the West German system. The so-called *Vereinigungsgesetz* (associational law) passed on 21 February 1990 permitted the free existence of civil society associations in East Germany for the first time ever. On the basis of this legislation, the world of GDR sport was radically reformed from a system of state-run organization and control to a sports system based on *Vereine*. This resulted in a blossoming of civil society in which the former factory sports groups and state-run clubs reformed themselves as associations, and many entirely new associations were established. At the same time, a major threat loomed over the heads of these new *Vereine* because they lost their financial foundation when their state funds were cut off in 1990 and many of the sponsoring factories and businesses disappeared. Even the darling of East German sport, namely the competitive sports organizations, had to switch from being the recipients of massive state subsidies to associations that were responsible for their own affairs and financing, which was not an easy task, to say the least. In some places, rather strange alliances were formed for a short time. Mercedes, for example, stepped in to keep the model athletic complex of the Stasi sports club Dynamo in Hohenschönhausen running for a few months.[101] On the other hand, the radical exodus of many top athletes and coaches to the West turned sports centers all over the place into "ghost facilities."[102] Some of the East German sports stars now followed the "call of money," which they could not have done during GDR times. Several of them were finally able to turn their dreams into reality as in the case of soccer players who could now play for a Bundesliga club.

Above all, however, many clubs in West Germany saw the chance to enhance their teams with top athletes from the GDR, such as the manager of the VfL Hameln who bought out several East German national handball players. Likewise, wrestlers, canoeists, fencers, and track and field athletes switched in droves to clubs in the old federal states.[103] Politicians, on the other hand, urged caution. Wolfgang Schäuble, for instance, called on the Bundesliga clubs to refrain from going on shopping sprees in the East while waving their money around. Helmut Kohl personally called upon Bayer AG to rein in Reiner Calmund's talent scouting among the East German soccer players, which the pharmaceutical company did reluctantly for only a very short time.[104] The transfer of the boxer Henry Maske from ASK Vorwärts Frankfurt/Oder to professional boxing represented a special case. This 1988 Olympic champion and former lieutenant colonel in the East German army sparked a boom in boxing in unified Germany with his victories. For many years prior to this point, boxing had not been very popular in West Germany, but, all of the sudden, it experienced a revival that was reminiscent of the era of Max Schmeling with jam-packed arenas. This wave of boxing fever was also supported by the new sports reporting coverage offered by private TV broadcasters. RTL, for example, made a major media event out of the matches of this world champion (1993–1996) as part of a profitable cooperative venture with the music industry.

The East German soccer clubs, however, found themselves faced with the challenge of adapting their structures to those of West Germany, which also meant jumping unprepared into the commercialization that had reigned in the Bundesliga since the end of the 1980s. In 1995, the "Bosman" judgment opened up the market for player transfers, which brought a huge increase in the percentage of foreigners playing in the Bundesliga, as well as skyrocketing salaries for soccer players. In the wake of this decision, East German soccer clubs found themselves confronted by a major "double change."[105] The adaption to the Western structures was accompanied by the need to respond to the ruptures that had been sparked by the "Bosman" case. Two paths of possible assimilation emerged: on the one hand, some of the East German clubs jumped on the bandwagon, so to speak. On 6 April 2001 in its match against VfL Wolfsburg, Energie Cottbus actually became the first Bundesliga club whose starting line-up was comprised entirely of players from other countries. On the other hand, the economically weak clubs in the East could hardly keep up with pressure of the transfer market, which led to a renaissance in the efforts of their own youth departments.[106] The integration of the East German clubs into the Bundesliga also coincided with a "changing of the tide in soccer reporting."[107] Private television not only fed into a further commercialization of the sport, but also spurred on a transition from classic sport reporting to sports entertainment shows and infotainment, which was what was offered as of 1992 with the SAT1 show "ran." Since the East German clubs had little experience with this commercialization or the media, it was difficult for them to capitalize on the increasing tabloidization of the sport to enhance their public images. Some of these clubs also faced a tough decision about which elements of their GDR traditions should be discarded, but also which aspects of this legacy should be kept in order to cater to the regional, or rather East German, longing for familiarity.[108]

Institutional Transfer and "Associational Growth"

Whereas a considerable portion of the East German sports elite headed to the West in 1990, institutional transfers ran in the opposite direction. New federal states were formed in the GDR, which then joined the Federal Republic in accordance with Article 23 of the *Grundgesetz*. Sports followed the same pattern. Regional associations for the different sports disciplines were created, and they joined together in newly founded state sports associations in the five new federal states. These new "corporative bodies"[109] then became part of the national Deutsche Sportbund. Over the course of 1990, several delegations of politicians and sports officials visited the former strongholds of the GDR elite sports apparatus.

These delegations were repeatedly bowled over by the "genius" innovations that had been made in the construction of the training facilities and sports centers.[110] They were also impressed by the vastness and the functional differentiation of the sport complexes, even though they already knew about these features in principle since the Olympic training centers that were set up in West Germany in the 1980s were rudimentary replicas of these East German centers. The reestablishment of Olympic training centers in the East shortly thereafter represented, in certain respects, the transfer of an old GDR structural concept to West Germany and then back to East Germany. Naturally, however, some aspects of this system had been altered to fit with the way in which West German competitive sports were organized. The Federal Republic also quickly showed a visible interest in two areas of GDR elite sports that had been kept strictly under wraps prior to this point: the creative innovations in sports equipment development and the "poison labs" (*Giftküchen*)[111] of the GDR doping system. The celebrated retainment of the doping laboratory in Kreischa and the Physical Training and Sports Research Institute (Forschungsinstitut für Körperkultur und Sport, or FKS) in Leipzig,[112] which were the centers of doping research and doping practice in the GDR, in the unification treaty met with staunch criticism, and not just among civil rights activists.[113]

At the level of the specific sport associations, each individual sports discipline had to go through its own process of reunification in 1990. They struggled with the integration of their different league systems in particular. In the GDR, for example, fourteen teams had played in the soccer Oberliga. Consequently, the question of how many of the favorite East German teams would be able to play in the First and Second Bundesliga was a key point of negotiation on the path to soccer unity. In order to retain as much as possible of the substance of GDR soccer, the Northeast German Soccer Association (Nordostdeutsche Fußballverband, or NOFV), which represented the East German clubs, initially proposed that all the GDR Oberliga teams should be admitted to the national professional leagues in united Germany. Four of the clubs were supposed to be admitted to the Bundesliga, and the other ten teams were supposed to be integrated in the Second Bundesliga. But this proposal met with stiff resistance in the DFB. In the end, a compromise was reached with what was called the "two-plus-six rule": the two best GDR clubs would become part of the First Bundesliga, while six other East German teams would join the Second Bundesliga. The rest of the East German teams had to make do with the amateur leagues, because there was not yet a third professional league at the time. Accordingly, the Oberliga season in 1990/91 was much like a "ghost league" representing the best of GDR soccer for one last time. But, more importantly, it was a contest to see which teams would qualify for the First Bundesliga, which turned out to be Hansa Rostock and Dynamo Dresden.

One rather sticky issue was still when the East German and West German soccer associations should be merged together into one national association. DFB president Hermann Neuberger appeared to be relatively immune to political pressure, just as he had been back in 1985. He wanted to let things take their time, and he did not see a merger occurring before 1992. This seemingly surprising reluctance stemmed from commercial considerations in the run-up to the European Championships in Sweden in 1992. Since West Germany and the GDR were supposed to be part of one qualifying group with Belgium and Scotland, a German-German national match was scheduled for the first time since the 1:0 victory of the GDR in Hamburg, creating a little sports sensation. The first match was supposed to take place in Leipzig, and the second match in Munich, and the lucrative contracts for TV rights and advertising had already been signed. In light of the path to unity, however, the DFB's plans started to seem a bit absurd. The first democratically elected president of the GDR soccer association, Hans-Georg Moldenhauer, maintained that it was irresponsible to delay the unification process in soccer so long. He appealed to the DFB leadership: "Didn't you see how the Wall has come down? Don't you know that an entire bloc has collapsed? Armies have been done away with! The Stasi, and everything else has collapsed and disappeared, and I am still supposed to head an independent soccer association bearing the name of the GDR until '92!"[114] In the end, Neuberger conceded and gave his approval for a faster unification of the two German soccer associations. The merger officially took place on 21 November 1990 in Leipzig, the place where the DFB had been founded originally. At this point, the West German national team had just won the World Championships for the third time in Rome in July 1990, and the win was already celebrated as a united German victory. In the wake of the championships in Rome in 1990, the German "soccer emperor" (*Fußballkaiser*) Franz Beckenbauer was nonetheless mistaken in a prediction that he euphorically and incautiously announced: "Once the GDR players join team," he claimed, "we will be unbeatable for years!"[115]

Beckenbauer was not the only sports official who was thinking about how unbeatable his team might be in the years to come. As early as March 1990, Wolfgang Schäuble, who was minister of the interior at the time, anticipated the creation of a joint team for the Olympic Games in Albertville and Barcelona in 1992.[116] Likewise, the first free-elected East German Minister-President Lothar de Maizière called for a unified team in his policy statement on 20 April 1990. Other countries in the West reacted rather skeptically to the prospect of joint German sports teams.

In March 1990, the daily sports newspaper *L'Equipe*, for example, fueled fears of a "German sports colossus," covering its front page with the image of a steely muscle man from the Nazi era. While other countries invoked the image of an invincible giant that was chomping at the bit to exercise its unified power on the sports field, many top East and West German athletes were anything but enthusiastic about the idea of a joint team. After all, a joint team meant that there would be fiercer competition for half as many places in the team line-ups.[117] The two national Olympic committees were unified in November 1990. Despite the reservations of many athletes, this represented the achievement of a sports dream for unified Germany: thanks in particular to the excellent performance of the East German athletes on the united Olympic team, the Federal Republic was able to celebrate the Winter Games of 1992 in Albertville as an amazing "unification victory." For the first time, the Federal Republic took first place in the medal count; eight out of ten German team's gold medals were won by athletes from the former GDR.

Learning from the Dictatorship?

Ultimately, however, the Federal Republic could not keep up this level of performance. In turn, this sparked a longer debate about the best way to ensure a new generation of stars. A key issue that repeatedly surfaced in these debates was therefore how to adapt the system of the youth sport schools (*Kinder- und Jugendsportschulen,* or *KJS*). As early as 1990, some voices began calling for a "de-ideologization"[118] of these schools that would then enable them to continue to operate. Between 1992 and 1996, attempts were made at five Berlin schools to "transform the former *KJS* into schools with an athletic emphasis." The goal was to test the possibilities for an optimal combination of sports and education.[119] In addition to the posited de-ideologization of these schools, they also had to follow a strict savings plan. Specific characteristics that used to define the *KJS* such as individual instruction, extended school time, or small classes could now only be financed in a very limited way. As the schools were then opened to pupils without ambitions in competitive sports, the athletic drills were also reduced. Despite these changes, the calls for a reform of the system of support for the athletic stars of the future continued, especially after the performance of the German team at the Atlanta Olympic Games in 1996 and the rather dour prognoses for the Sydney Olympics in 2000. Although officials initially considered following the French model, this proved to be untenable because of the difference in the mechanisms of elite recruitment in competitive sports in the two countries.[120] In France, elite sports have been seen as an opportunity for upward social mobility, especially for people at the bottom rungs of the social ladder. In Germany, however, many aspiring competitive athletes come from the middle or upper echelons of society. A career in professional sports, however, has been considered to be a potential "biographical trap"[121]—a conundrum that has yet to be resolved even today. According to a survey conducted by the Deutsche Sporthilfe athletic foundation in 2013, more than 90 percent of the A-cadres did not feel properly prepared for life after competitive sport. Recently, Chancellor Angela Merkel has become a patron for an internship program designed to secure aspiring athletes experience working in companies.

In the end, the *KJS* model experienced a renaissance in the second half of the 1990s. The former and new competitive sport stronghold in Potsdam was a pioneer in this process. At the sport school in Potsdam, specializations and the training of competitive athletes were once again more strongly anchored in the school's profile.[122] This new concept, which came to be known as the "Potsdam model," was poised to gain recognition nationwide. The new moniker, with its unmistakable links to the GDR system, was first the Composite School and Competitive Sports System (Schule-Leistungssport-Verbundsystem). In 1996, the Working Group "Sport and Economics," which was formed under the aegis of Helmut Kohl, then decided to use the label Elite Schools of Sport in the future. As early as 1998, there was already a network of twenty-nine schools with a sport emphasis, twenty-one of which were located in the new federal states; seventeen were distinguished as Elite Schools of Sport. Since this time, some elements have returned as common principles in these sport schools, such as morning training, flexible test and exam dates, extended school time, and the sorting out of students showing less talent. The return of some practices from the GDR era is quite apparent, but their reintroduction has continued to be controversial. Despite all of these efforts, the total package of care and long-term material security that had been provided to athletes by the athletic *Fürsorgediktatur*[123] of the GDR could not be offered in the federal German system. The question of whether new heights can be achieved by adopting GDR methods has reappeared time and time again within the context of sport policy.[124] Most recently, after the partially disappointing performance of the German team at the London Olympic Games in 2012, the notion of returning to the GDR approach to talent scouting was bandied about.[125]

"Doping for Germany"

In dealing with the doping past in German sport, a strong interactive dynamic evolved between the investigations of doping in the East and those in the West as early as 1990/91. As a result, over the course of the 1990s, the debates over doping took on a vehemence and thoroughness that were not to be found in any other Western state, and certainly not in any Eastern European state. The experience of the GDR dictatorship—whose doping system not only resulted in the usual sport fraud, but also led to major bodily injury—contributed to a kind of moral indignation that has ultimately fostered tougher criticism directed at current sport policy and its downsides.

In 1990, the attention of the sports world turned toward a comprehensive reappraisal of doping practices. After the end of the Cold War, many athletes, politicians, and sports fans hoped that it would be possible to systematically investigate the performance manipulation that had taken place in both the East and the West. The public discussion on doping took on an entirely new character after Manfred Höppner, the deputy director of the Sports Medicine Service of the GDR and the man responsible for the GDR doping system, sat down on the sofa of the Hamburg-based magazine *Stern* at the end of November in 1990. He sold his story about the detailed history of doping in the GDR to the magazine, complete with supporting documents.[126] Amid the wave of outrage over the apparent manipulation in the GDR, the land of the *Sportwunder*, an article in *Der Spiegel* made a huge splash just a few days later by revealing the massive doping violations in West German sport. It backed up its claims not only with eyewitness statements, but also written evidence.[127] Given the courage to come forward by the revelations about the doping system in the East, the West German athlete Claudia Lepping, one of the major instigators behind the *Der Spiegel* exposé, told what she knew about the machinations of the national coach of the track and field team, Jochen Spilker. Not only did the ugly sides of many East German medals in all their detail come to light within a very short time, but also these revelations stoked a controversy about the performance enhancement that had been going on in the Federal Republic. Headlines such as "Doping for Germany,"[128] left a stormy cloud over the first few months of a reunited country.

Over the years that followed, a series of different initiatives spurred further investigations into past doping. Two commissions of inquiry were set up within the context of organized sports. Interestingly, they were better able to shed light on the doping system in the former East because of the better paper trail. Despite what they found, however, there were virtually no consequences for those involved.[129] In contrast, the influence of a science-based pilot study conducted in 1991 can hardly be overestimated. Shortly after the Wall came down, the cancer researcher Prof. Dr. Werner Franke, from Heidelberg, and his wife, Brigitte Berendonk, published a volume titled *Doping-Dokumente: Von der Forschung zum Be-*

trug, in which they provided evidence of the state doping system in the GDR through numerous documents that they had found in their own research. This book also attested to the years of complicit involvement on the part of the East and West German doping doctors and professors.[130] In particular, the findings presented by Franke and Berendonk played an important role in the public debates about the continued employment of those who had been involved.

After all, not only the top East German athletes, but also successful trainers and sports doctors from the GDR were part of a much sought-after elite in unified German sport. This stood in stark contrast to other areas of society and the state in which East German personnel was often not welcomed at all because of the generally perceived lack of "formal qualifications, informal skills, and moral integrity."[131] West German sports organizations often turned a blind eye to the involvement of many former coaches and doctors from the GDR in doping, much of which was known and even documented. This led to ongoing controversies in the sports world. A short phase began at the end of the 1990s in which swimmers as well as track and field athletes hoped to invalidate any suspicions through "formal declarations of honor." The *Frankfurter Allgemeine Zeitung*, on the other hand, hinted at one possible effect of this practice: whoever wanted to be able to compete in the future should never admit that they had doped.[132] The German Swimming Association (DSV) followed a similar principle in dealing with the past. After signing a statement under oath, East German coaches and doctors were allowed to accompany the national team that competed at the World Championships in January 1991 in Perth, Australia. It should be noted, however, that they did not have to fear any legal consequences for giving falsified testimony because these statements were not made before a court.[133] This made it possible, for example, for a sports doctor who was later proven to be legally guilty of underage doping to become one of the official team doctors for the DSV at the championships in Perth.[134] The ski association, which faced similar personnel issues, argued relatively openly that it did not want to have to make do without these coaches who had been involved in doping in the past because other countries were waiting in the wings to snap them up.[135] As of October 1991, four former head coaches from the GDR who were tainted by their involvement in doping were working in Austria, including the swim coach Rolf Gläser, who was later sentenced.[136]

The public debates and internal sport controversy came to a head in the case of the former GDR head coach Bernd Schubert, who had been a head coach for the German Track and Field Association (DLV) since January 1991. He celebrated a stellar performance with the GDR national team at the European Championships in Split in 1990, which made him much sought after in the West. But his past came to haunt him as the research done by Brigitte Berendonk in particular cast a shadow on his reputation; the third civil chamber of the state court in Heidelberg determined that he could be identified as a "proven doping specialist" and an "active participant in doping with anabolic drugs," but the DLV nevertheless kept him on as a coach.[137] At the beginning of December in 1991, moreover, twenty East German coaches confirmed in a statement that doping had taken place in GDR swim teams. They also declared that they would strictly refrain from using such methods in the future. Since the contracts of these coaches were scheduled to expire on 31 December 1991, this statement was more than likely prompted by their desire to maintain a "positive social prognosis."[138] The initiator behind this "collective self-accusation" was Harm Beyer, a member of the swimming presidium, whose stated goal was to retain the skilled specialized knowledge that they could offer.[139] This statement was countered by a signature petition in which West German colleagues spoke out against the continued employment of these coaches from the East who were compromised by their involvement in doping.[140] The press, however, surmised that these West German coaches were not necessarily motivated by just their disgust with the GDR doping system, but also by the fact that they would soon be competing for a reduced number of coaching jobs after the Barcelona Olympics in 1992.[141]

The conflict brewing over these personnel issues was not resolved until several years later after Professor Werner Franke filed a criminal law suit against different GDR coaches and doctors in 1996. This move ultimately led to the Moabit doping trials as well as numerous other subsequent trials at the state level. Even Manfred Ewald and Manfred Höppner received suspended sentences. The details about the brutal methods and irreparable long-term consequences of these doping practices that came to light over the course of the trials not only enraged the lawyers involved, but also the general public.[142] As a form of "history on trial,"[143] the doping trials became a central part of the legal process of dealing with SED injustices.[144]

In addition, sports were part of another aspect of dealing with the GDR legacy. This process of working through the transgressions of the SED dictatorship also called the values of organized sport into question in unified Germany. The different sports organizations and the DOSB, for example, were highly unsettled by the position of two GDR sprint runners who held world records. Ines Geipel and Gesine Tettenborn[145] insisted on having their records erased from the annals of the track and field association after the turn of the millennium because their record times had been achieved with the help of doping drugs. Ines Geipel argued in favor of giving up-and-coming athletes a fair chance, rather than setting the bar unrealistically high; her "doping-tainted" record from 1984 still stands as the world record time even today.[146] In calling for the removal of their times from the records, both athletes effectively questioned the fundamental principle of "higher, faster, further," as well as the primary emphasis that had been put on winning medals, not only in the East, but also in the old West. Not surprisingly, the association reacted rather unenthusiastically to their requests. In the end, the names of the two athletes were replaced with a star, but the record times remained unchallenged on the books. This handling stemmed from the fact that Geipel's and Tettenborn's relay colleagues had not chosen to distance themselves from the record time that the team had achieved together.

The Transformation of Recreational Sports

The dire situation of popular sports in the GDR first became the subject of public debate after the collapse of the SED regime. A DTSB conference in Kleinmachnow that was held on 7 November 1989, for example, devolved into a back and forth among the functionaries who were worried about the future of competitive sports in the country.[147] The question of who was responsible for the miserable state of the East German sports facilities arose for the first time.[148] In light of the apparent resentment of much of the population against the enormous cost of the competitive sports system, DTSB vice president Thomas Köhler stated that ordinary "people" would now have to "be let in and allowed to take part in sports activities" at the centers that had been reserved for top athletes.[149] Accordingly, training centers that were once closed off in many places opened their doors to the general population for the first time at the end of 1989. Yet the disappearance of countless factory sports facilities, which were dismantled for financial reasons after 1989, and the miserable state of the buildings that forced many sports centers to shut down (such as the central stadium in Leipzig or the Friesen pool in Berlin) only further exacerbated the unsatisfactory situation in the eyes of East Germans. Thanks to the investment support law that took effect in 1992 and the Golden Plan East for the Construction of Sports Facilities that was put into place in 1998—which was modeled in name and concept after the West German Golden Plan of the 1960s—a number of new sports centers and facilities were built in the new federal states. Nevertheless, according to the German sports facility census that was released on 1 July 2000, 57.8 percent (1993: 82.5 percent) of the indoor pools and 63 percent (1993: 91.4 percent) of the outdoor pools were still in need of renovation.[150]

In addition to the state of sports facilities, sports participation in the new federal states has been a major point of ongoing discussion. Given the degree of organization in sport in the former GDR, scholars now agree that the official statistics on the recreational side of the DTSB are not a realistic reflection of the actual involvement of the broader population in organized sport activities. This has to do with the high number of obligatory members who were counted in the statistics but did not actually take part in sport, as well as the constant political pressure that was put on the association to report steadily increasing membership figures.[151] In a comparative study, the Ministry for Education, Youth and Sport (MBJS) of the state of Brandenburg determined that participation in organized associational sports in Brandenburg had increased significantly since the end of the GDR. The study was based in part on corrected GDR statistics for Potsdam, Cottbus, and Frankfurt/Oder, which counted about two hundred thousand recreational athletes, accounting for about 7 to 8 percent of the population. The statistics for 2002, on the other hand, indicated that participation had climbed to 10.8 percent, and the figures for 2012 show that 12.7 percent of the population was involved in organized sport.[152] Despite this generally positive development, there is still a shortfall. Recreational sports in Germany are still strikingly divided along a clear East-West split.[153] Whereas between 28 and 40 percent of the population in the old federal states belonged to sports associations in 2012, only between 13 and 17 percent of the population in the former East did the same—less than half compared to the West.

Scholars have still not come to an agreement about the underlying causes for this asymmetry between East and West. Some have rightly pointed to the social turbulence experienced within East German society that was unleashed by the reunification process. When the large factories disappeared, for example, the social attachment to their sports clubs and organizations went with them. According to a sports science analysis conducted by Jürgen Baur and Sebastian Braun, almost a fifth of the active members of sports clubs in the GDR were no longer involved in organized sports after 1989. Many of them continued their athletic activity within a more informal context (44.7 percent) or ended their athletic commitment altogether (34.7 percent).[154] That said, the "turbulence in organized sport over the course of the transformation process"[155] that was pointed out by scholars around the turn of the twenty-first century can no longer fully account for the continued "difference in unity" on its own.[156] Rather, long-term cultural influences, such as the fundamental differences in present-day associational culture in East and West, also need to be taken into account. For example, some scholars have posited that widespread "passive membership" in the West, whereby many family members belong to the same local sports club although not all of them actively participate in sports, was not a common practice in the

East. But, the validity of such conclusions is still doubted by some. The recreational sports commissioner of the Brandenburg Ministry of Sport, Manfred Kruczek, for example, has argued that the participation of children and teenagers in sports in the old federal states is double as high as in the new federal states, but that there would be no reason to assume a high number of passive members in these age cohorts.[157] Likewise, the lack of attachment to recreational sports clubs may be something that is being passed down within families.

Despite the end of the state sport system in the GDR, the expectations of the state vis-à-vis sports organizations, as well as the demands of these sports organizations on the state, have increased significantly compared to the old West Germany today, more than twenty-five years after reunification. Since the 1990s, for example, the interest in the health benefits of sports has increased significantly: efforts to strengthen physical resources, as well as the influence of health-related behaviors, have fed into the inclusion of an overarching concept within the mission of the DSB in 1998, namely "health programs in sports associations." This idea was also written into the mission statements of the public health insurance companies in 2000, and the close cooperation between municipal governments, sports associations, and insurance companies in this sector has become a permanent part of the political agenda.[158]

Whereas the state has sought to decrease costs in the health care system through the physical mobilization of the population in recreational sports, elite competitive sports continue to be an expensive and controversial line on government budgets. Alongside providing financial support for competitive sports in the narrow sense of subsidizing the associations of the different sports disciplines, the state has had to invest a considerable amount of money of late to finance anti-doping measures. Since the collapse of the Communist bloc, which had stood in the way of an internationalization of anti-doping policies,[159] the pressure on sports organizations to crack down on doping has increased significantly. The IOC's global conference on doping in Lausanne at the beginning of February in 1990 proved to be a turning point in this regard, functioning as a "key factor in the establishment of an international political anti-doping regime."[160] This ultimately resulted in the establishment of the World Anti-Doping Agency (WADA) in November 1999, which represented a "public-private partnership" between organized sport and national governments. As a result, the German state has now also become partly responsible for the fight against doping in the country. The capital needed to establish the National Anti-Doping Agency in 2002, for example, came almost entirely from public funds, with the exception of a small percentage that was contributed by sports organizations. Moreover, the anti-doping legislation that was passed in 2015 made the federal German justice system responsible for the prosecution of doping violations on a large scale for the first time.

Despite some criticism about the way in which the state promotes competitive sports, the role of the state in supporting top-level athletes remains unquestioned. Not even the conflict of values between *Sieg-Code*—the imperative to win—and the proclaimed goal of a more humane competitive sports system has changed the fact that "medals are the real currency in the sports system."[161] Even unified Germany has continued to follow the same common international patterns of thought that a successful competitive sports program represents and reflects the competitive potential of the country as a whole, despite the fact that the East German experience has taught quite a different historical lesson in this respect.

The history of sport in East and West Germany has definitely been part of a "geteilte Geschichte" in a shared, yet divided sense. In many respects, the two countries followed different trajectories, but the permanent competition between the two states in the 1970s and 1980s wove a thick web of entanglements and reference points on both sides of the Wall. Since the West Germans kept a close eye on the success and methods used by the East German teams, the relationship between the two German states was less asymmetric in this respect than it was in many others. The GDR turned into the "land of wonder" in competitive sports, but really only in select Olympic disciplines as it could not keep up with the top-level athletes in international soccer or tennis. In fact, East German fans tended to rally behind the teams and athletes from West Germany in those sports in which the East could not compete with the best. At the same time, the approaches to sport in East and West differed considerably. Whereas the GDR put its money on a centralized system of support for elite sports and tended to neglect the recreational level, grassroots sports began to blossom in the West in the 1970s. The case of recreational sports in unified Germany, moreover, has shown just how persistent these differences can be. Likewise, the "doubled transformation" can also be traced very clearly in sport after 1990. The debates over the socialist promotion of sport have led to debates and changes in the sports system of the FRG, whether it be in terms of doping or talent scouting. Even today, the former *Sportwunder* of the GDR, which stood for both the dangers and horrors of a dictatorship as well as a supposed lost paradise of optimal athletic performance, is still a legend within the world of international sport.

Jutta Braun is a research associate at the Center for Contemporary History (ZZF) in Potsdam and head of the Center for German Sports History in Berlin. She has widely published on the history of divided Germany and German sports history. She directed a research project on the history of the East German national team and she is currently working on a project on East German health policy in the Cold War. Her most recent book is *Im Riss zweier Epochen: Potsdam in den 1980er und 1990er Jahren.*

NOTES

1. "Schäuble will Erfolg des DDR-Sports retten," *Frankfurter Allgemeine Zeitung,* 22 March 1990.
2. "Hauptausschuss des DSB diskutiert Einigungsprozess," *Frankfurter Rundschau,* 25 June 1990.
3. Hans Joachim Teichler, "Sportentwicklung in Ostdeutschland nach der Wende," *Horch und Guck* 14 (2005): 40–43.
4. Jutta Braun and René Wiese, "DDR-Fußball und gesamtdeutsche Identität im Kalten Krieg," *Historical Social Research/Historische Sozialforschung* 30 (2005): 191–210.
5. Jenifer Parks, "Verbal Gymnastics: Sports, Bureaucracy and the Soviet Union's Entrance into the Olympic Games, 1946–1952," in *East Plays West: Sport and the Cold War,* ed. Stephen Wagg and David L. Andrews (New York, 2007), 27–44; Mike O'Mahony, *Sport in the USSR: Physical Culture—Visual Culture* (London, 2006), 151ff.
6. Allen Guttmann, *The Olympics: A History of the Modern Games* (Illinois, 2002); Arnd Krüger, *Sport und Politik. Von Turnvater Jahn zum Staatsamateur* (Hannover, 1975).
7. Research so far has mainly focused on the period until 1972. See Uta Andrea Balbier, *Kalter Krieg auf der Aschenbahn. Der deutsch-deutsche Sport 1950–1972* (Paderborn, 2006); Tobias Blasius, *Olympische Bewegung, Kalter Krieg und Deutschlandpolitik 1949–1972* (Frankfurt a. M., 2001).
8. Peter Danckert and Holger Schück, *Kraftmaschine Parlament. Der Sportausschuss und die Sportpolitik des Bundes* (Aachen, 2009).
9. "Züchten wir Monstren?," *Die Zeit,* 5 December 1969; "Der Sport geht über den Rubikon," *Süddeutsche Zeitung,* 26/27 February 1977. Brigitte Berendonk was the East German Vierkampf champion in 1958, the West German junior pentathlon champion in 1959, and the German discus champion in 1971; she participated in the 1968 and 1972 Olympics on the West German team.
10. See Giselher Spitzer, *Sieg um jeden Preis. Doping in Deutschland: Geschichte, Recht, Ethik 1972–1990* (Göttingen, 2013), 50f.
11. This also included doping research conducted by the Federal Institute for Sport Sciences. See Erik Eggers and Giselher Spitzer, "Das BISp-Forschungsprojekt 'Regeneration und Testosteron' 1985–1993," in *Sieg um jeden Preis.*

Doping in Deutschland: Geschichte, Recht, Ethik 1972–1990, ed. Erik Eggers and Giselher Spitzer (Göttingen, 2014), 155–258.

12. Giselher Spitzer, *Doping in der DDR—ein historischer Überblick zu einer konspirativen Praxis. Genese, Verantwortung, Gefahren* (Cologne, 2013).
13. "Schluck Pillen oder kehr Fabriken aus," *Der Spiegel*, 19 March 1979.
14. The West German rower Peter Michael Kolbe collapsed just before the finish line in the single scull finals in Montreal due to the side effects of a performance-enhancing shot of cocarboxylase.
15. See Spitzer, *Doping in der DDR*.
16. Willi Knecht, "Laufen Sozialisten schneller?" *Deutschland Archiv* 1 (1969): 1–9.
17. Hans Joachim Teichler and Klaus Reinartz, eds. *Das Leistungssportsystem der DDR in den 1980er Jahren und im Prozess der Wende* (Schorndorf, 1999).
18. Klaus Reinartz, "Die Zweiteilung des DDR-Sports auf Beschluss der SED," in *Das Leistungssportsystem der DDR in den 1980er Jahren und im Prozess der Wende*, ed. Hans Joachim Teichler and Klaus Reinartz (Schorndorf, 1999), 55–85.
19. René Wiese, "Staatsgeheimnis Sport—Die Abschottung des Leistungssportsystems der DDR," *Historical Social Research* 32 (2007): 154–71.
20. See Hans Joachim Teichler, "Die Sportclubs," in Teichler and Reinartz, *Das Leistungssportsystem*, 187–269.
21. Eike Emrich and Ronald Wadsack, *Zur Evaluation der Olympiastützpunkte. Betreuungsqualität und Kostenstruktur* (Cologne, 2005), 7; Eike Emrich, *Zur Soziologie der Olympiastützpunkte. Eine Untersuchung zur Entstehung, Struktur und Leistungsfähigkeit einer Sportförderorganisation* (Niedernhausen, 2006).
22. Ralf Schröder and Hubert Dalkamp, *Nicht alle Helden tragen Gelb. Die Geschichte der Tour de France*, 4th ed. (Göttingen, 2011); for the Peace Race in the early phase, see Molly Wilkinson-Johnson, *Training Socialist Citizens: Sports and the State in East Germany* (Leiden, 2008), 165f.
23. Ronald Huster, "Duell an der Spree. Radsport im geteilten Berlin," in *Sportstadt Berlin im Kalten Krieg. Prestigekämpfe und Systemwettstreit*, ed. Jutta Braun and Hans Joachim Teichler (Berlin, 2006), 285–314.
24. Ulrich Kaiser, *Tennis in Deutschland. Von den Anfängen bis 2002* (Berlin, 2002).
25. Dorota Winiarska, *Bürgerlicher Sport in der DDR und Polen 1945–1989* (Hamburg, 2005); "Der verpönte Sport—Wie SED und Stasi das Tennis in der DDR drangsalierten," *Die Welt*, 14 November 2002.
26. "Das geht mir auf den Geist," *Der Spiegel*, 19 September 1988; "Interessiert die unser Elend?," *Der Spiegel*, 3 August 1992.
27. See Gunter Gebauer, "Die Bundesliga," in *Deutsche Erinnerungsorte: eine Auswahl*, ed. Étienne François and Hagen Schulze (Munich, 2005), 463–76.
28. Nils Havemann, *Samstags um halb vier. Die Geschichte der Fußball-Bundesliga* (Munich, 2013), 68–69.

29. Hans Joachim Teichler, "Die schwierigen Anfänge des Fußballsports in der SBZ/DDR," in *Fußball in Geschichte und Gesellschaft. Tagung der dvs-Sektionen Sportgeschichte und Sportsoziologie vom 29.9.–1.10.2004 in Münster*, ed. Michael Krüger and Bernd Schulze (Hamburg, 2006), 75–81.
30. For case studies on Thuringia, see Michael Kummer, *Die ungleichen Bedingungen von FC Rot Weiß Erfurt und FC Carl Zeiss Jena in der DDR* (Eisenach, 2012).
31. Jutta Braun, "Abseits der Bundesliga. Zur Aufarbeitung des DDR-Fußballs," *Aus Politik und Zeitgeschichte* 27/28 (2013): 41–46. A joint project of the Center for German Sports History (Zentrum deutsche Sportgeschichte) and the Center for Contemporary History (Zentrum für Zeithistorische Forschung), commissioned by the German Soccer Federation (DFB), is currently conducting systematic research on the history of soccer in East Germany.
32. "Der Fußball-Trainer aus Jena leistet sich Träume, weil er Realist ist." *Frankfurter Allgemeine Zeitung*, 18 September 1986.
33. 1964 Bronze, 1972 Bronze, 1976 Gold, and 1980 Silver.
34. Jutta Braun, "Sportfreunde oder Staatsfeinde?," *Deutschland Archiv* 37 (2004): 440–47; Jutta Braun and Hans Joachim Teichler, "Fußballfans im Visier der Staatsmacht," in *Sport in der DDR. Eigensinn, Konflikte, Trends*, ed. Hans Joachim Teichler (Cologne: 2003), 561–86.
35. Mary Fulbrook, "Generationen und Kohorten in der DDR. Protagonisten und Widersacher des DDR-Systems aus der Perspektive biographischer Daten," in *Die DDR aus generationengeschichtlicher Perspektive. Eine Inventur*, ed. Annegret Schüle, Thomas Ahbe, and Rainer Gries (Leipzig, 2006), 113–30
36. Christoph Lorke, "'Ungehindert abreagieren.' Hooliganismus in der späten DDR im Spannungsfeld von Anstandsnormen, Sozialdisziplinierung und gesellschaftlichen Randlagen," *Deutschland Archiv* 45 (2012): 240–249.
37. In the divided city of Berlin, the friendship between the fans of the Hertha BSC and Union clubs was particularly virulent and politically controversial. See René Wiese, "Wie der Fußball Löcher in die Mauer schoss," in *Sportstadt Berlin im Kalten Krieg. Prestigekämpfe und Systemwettstreit*, ed. Jutta Braun and Hans Joachim Teichler (Berlin, 2006), 239–84.
38. Karl Lennartz, "Olympische Boykotte," in *Sportgeschichte erforschen und vermitteln. Jahrestagung der dvs-Sektion Sportgeschichte vom 19.–21. Juni 2008 in Göttingen*, ed. Andrea Bruns, and Wolfgang Buss (Hamburg, 2009), 179–200.
39. All told, forty-two states, most of whom where predominantly Islamic, withdrew from the Olympics. The key role played by West Germany was seen by Daume and the IOC primarily in terms of its role-model effect for the West European National Olympic Committees. Letter from IOC-President Lord Michael Killanin to Daume, dated 9 May 1980, Willi-Daume-Archiv/DOA.
40. See Jim Riordan, "Great Britain and the 1980 Olympics: Victory for Olympism," in *Sport and International Understanding*, ed. Maaret Ilmarinen (Berlin, 1984), 138–44.

41. The recommendation of the parliament was passed with 476 votes in favor, eight against, and nine abstains. Letter Daume to Bahr, dated 28 May 1980, Willi-Daume-Archiv/DOA.
42. Vermerk über das Gespräch der Bundesregierung mit Vertretern der Sportorganisationen über die Teilnahme an den Olympischen Sommerspielen 1980 in Moskau am 29. April 1980 im Bundeskanzleramt (5 May 1980) [Note on the conversation of the Federal Government with representatives of the sports organizations about the participation in the Summer Olympics in 1980 in Moscow on 29 April 1980 in the Federal Chancellery (5 May 1980)], Bundesarchiv Koblenz (BAK) 139/1995.
43. Ibid.
44. Referat S4, Bonn 15 April 1980, Herrn Minister über Staatssekretär Dr. Fröhlich. Betr. Olympiaboykott. Unterrichtung des Herrn Ministers für die Kabinettssitzung am 16.4.1980. Anlage 4: Einwirkungsmöglichkeiten der Bundesregierung [Department S4, Bonn, 15 April 1980, Minister of State Dr. Fröhlich. Subject. Olympic boycott. Information from the ministers for the cabinet meeting on 16 April 1980. Appendix 4: Impact options of the Federal Government], BAK 139/1995.
45. "Mit Bitternis und Sand im Mund," *Der Spiegel*, 19 May 1980.
46. BMI, Abteilungsleiter 3, Staatssekretär Dr. Konow, Bonn, 16.4.1980 über Herrn Chef BK, Herrn Bundeskanzler Betr: Olympische Sommerspiele 1980 in Moskau [BMI, Head of Department 3, State Secretary Dr. Konow, Bonn, 16 April 1980 on Mr. Chef BK, Chancellor re: Olympic Summer Games 1980 in Moscow], BAK B 139/1995.
47. "Olympia Boykott von 1980 hat nichts gebracht. Interview mit Eberhard Gienger," *Die Welt*, 26 March 1980.
48. Evelyn Mertin, "The Soviet Union and the Olympic Games of 1980 and 1984: Explaining the Boycotts to Their Own People," in *East Plays West: Sport and the Cold War*, ed. Stephen Wagg and David L. Andrews (New York, 2007), 235–52.
49. Letter Daume to the national sports associations, 31 March 1980, Willi-Daume-Archiv/DOA.
50. Hans-Dieter Krebs, "Die Zeit der Boykottbewegungen," in *Deutschland in der olympischen Bewegung. Eine Zwischenbilanz*, ed. Nationales Olympisches Komitee für Deutschland (Frankfurt a. M., 1999), 309.
51. "'Sturm der Entrüstung ist ausgeblieben.' Interview mit TV-Sportkoordinator Hans Heinrich Isenbarth," *Der Spiegel*, 28 July 1980.
52. Manfred Ewald and Reinhold Andert, *Ich war der Sport: Wahrheiten und Legenden aus dem Wunderland der Sieger* (Berlin, 1994), 184.
53. *Deutsches Sportecho*, 11/12 May 1984.
54. Krebs, "Die Zeit der Boykottbewegungen," 313.
55. DTSB der DDR, Präsident, 7 June 1984. Aktennotiz. Persönliches Gespräch zwischen Manfred Ewald und Willi Daume [DTSB of the GDR, President, 7 June 1984. File note. Personal conversation between Manfred Ewald and Willi Daume], Archiv NOK/Frankfurt a. M.

56. The GDR media deliberately turned a blind eye to the boycott of the Games in Los Angeles. Lists of the Olympic medal winners stopped after the Games in Moscow in 1980; see "Von Boykott keine Rede," *Sonntag Aktuell,* 2 June 1985.
57. This can be gleaned from a report of the NOC Secretary and IM "Victor" Wolfgang Gitter. Treffbericht [Meeting report], 15 October 1983, Archiv des Bundesbeauftragten für die Unterlagen des Staatssicherheitsdienstes der ehemaligen DDR (BStU), MfS-HA XX 69254/92.
58. As expressed by the Neue Forum Leipzig/Arbeitsgruppe Sport, Zur Ethik und Moral des Sports, 4 December 1989, printed in Giselher Spitzer, Hans Joachim Teichler, and Klaus Reinartz, eds., *Schlüsseldokumente im DDR-Sport. Ein sporthistorischer* Überblick *in Originalquellen* (Aachen, 1998), 328–31.
59. Cf. DFB, controversy around the European championship in 1988, BAK 136/24413.
60. "Fußball-Notopfer," *Bonner Rundschau,* 20 February 1985.
61. "Zimmermann kritisiert DFB," *Süddeutsche Zeitung,* 21 February 1985.
62. "Die WM 74 und Berlin: FIFA musste Statuten ändern," *Stuttgarter Zeitung,* 13 March 1985.
63. Telex from Dr. Zimmermann to Präsident DFB, Neuberger, 27 February 1985, BAK B 136/24413.
64. AA, Witte, 26 February 1985, encoded Plurez to Paris, Den Haag, Rome, Lisbon, Reykjavik, Edinburgh, Vienna, Bern, London, BAK 136/29699.
65. Notes by Gieseler, 14 March 1985, on the session of the Sports Committee of the German Bundestag on the European Soccer Championships 1988 with special attention to the position of the DSB on 13 March 1985 in Bonn, Bundeshaus, BAK 136/24413.
66. Jutta Braun, "Inselstadt im Abseits?" in *Sportstadt Berlin im Kalten Krieg. Prestigekämpfe und Systemwettstreit,* ed. Jutta Braun and Hans Joachim Teichler (Berlin, 2006), 150–83
67. Guttmann, *Olympics,* 160ff.; "Unglaublich missbraucht. Kaltblütig missbraucht," *Der Spiegel,* 8 August 1983.
68. The other two-thirds went to the solidarity funds of the National Olympic Committees and the international associations.
69. As put by the general secretary of the NOC Wolfgang Gitter. IM Victor. Meeting Report, 28 October 1986, BStU, MfS-HA XX 69254/92.
70. Meeting Report, 29 November 1986, BStU, MfS-HA XX 69254/92.
71. IM "Victor." Report on a Trip of the NOC Delegation to the 50th Bobsled World Championships in 1986 in Berchtesgaden/FRG, 25 February 1986, BStU, MfS-HA XX 69254/92.
72. Niederschrift der ZAIG 2 über die wesentlichsten Inhalte eines Gespräches des Genossen Minister mit dem Präsidenten des DTSB, Genossen Ewald, und dem Leiter der Abteilung Sport, Genossen Hellmann [Transcript of ZAIG 2 on the essential contents of a conversation of the comrade minister with the president of the DTSB, Comrade Ewald, and the head of the Sports Depart-

ment, Comrade Hellmann], 31 March 1986, in Der Bundesbeauftragte für die Unterlagen des Staatssicherheitsdienstes der ehemaligen Deutschen Demokratischen Republik (BStU), ed., *MfS und Leistungssport: Ein Recherchebericht. Reihe A: Dokumente; 1/1994* (Berlin, 1994), 112.
73. Ibid.
74. Ibid.
75. Siegfried Müller and Heinz Schwidtmann, "Ausgewählte Schwerpunkte der politisch-ideologischen Vorbereitung von Leistungssportlern auf die Olympischen Winterspiele 1988," *Theorie und Praxis des Leistungssports* 25 (1987): 9–22.
76. Grundwertekommission der SPD and Akademie für Gesellschaftswissenschaften beim ZK der SED, ed., *Der Streit der Ideologien und die gemeinsame Sicherheit* (Berlin, 1987).
77. "Festigung prinzipieller Feindbilder," *Der Spiegel*, 25 January 1988; "Rückspiegel," *Der Spiegel*, 1 February 1988.
78. Rüdiger Bergien, "Erstarrter Bellizismus. Die SED-Funktionäre und ihr Weg in den Herbst '89," in *1989 und die Rolle der Gewalt*, ed. Martin Sabrow (Göttingen, 2013), 32–55.
79. Minutes of the politburo session on 14 February 1989, Stiftung Archiv der Parteien und Massenorganisationen der DDR im Bundesarchiv (SAPMO) DY 30/IV/2/2.039/70.
80. "Otto Rehhagel will DDR-Kicker in die Bundesliga holen," *Bonner Rundschau*, 27 February 1987. See Jutta Braun, "Klassenkampf im Flutlicht," in *Sport in der DDR. Eigensinn, Konflikte, Trends*, ed. Hans Joachim Teichler (Cologne, 2004), 123f.
81. BStU, *MfS und Leistungssport*, 112.
82. *Junge Welt*, 17 July 1988. Up to this point, Adidas was the only company that had managed to gain a strong foothold in the GDR. See Barbara Smit, *Die Dasslers—Drei Streifen gegen Puma* (Bergisch Gladbach, 2007).
83. "Neues Weltbild," *Der Spiegel*, 8 August 1988.
84. Christian Wopp, *Entwicklung und Perspektiven des Freizeitsports* (Aachen, 1995), 55.
85. Jürgen Dieckert, "Freizeitsport in Deutschland," in *Handbuch Freizeitsport*, ed. Jürgen Dieckert and Christian Wopp (Schorndorf, 2002), 25–32.
86. Arnd Krüger and Bernd Wedemeyer, eds., *Kraftkörper—Körperkraft: Zum Verständnis von Körperkultur und Fitness gestern und heute* (Göttingen, 1995).
87. See Helmut Digel, *Sportentwicklung in der Moderne* (Schorndorf, 2013), 259.
88. Jochen Hinsching, ed., *Breitensport in Ostdeutschland—Reflexion und Transformation* (Hamburg, 2000).
89. Hajo Bernett, *Körperkultur und Sport in der DDR* (Schorndorf, 1994), 11.
90. René Wiese and Ronald Huster, "Entstehung und Entwicklung des Brettsegelns in der DDR," in Teichler, *Sport in der DDR*, 425–500.
91. Kai Reinhart, *"Wir wollten einfach unser Ding machen." DDR-Sportler zwischen Fremdbestimmung und Selbstverwirklichung* (Frankfurt a. M., 2010).

92. Kai Reinhart and Michael Krüger, "Massensport in der Grauzone," *Horch und Guck* 21 (2012): 16–18.
93. See the analysis of these submissions by Hans Joachim Teichler, "Konfliktlinien des Sportalltags. Eingaben zum Thema Sport," in Teichler, *Sport in der DDR*, 535–60.
94. Taken from a speech at the first free discussion of the DTSB in Kleinmachnow, 7 November 1989; see Teichler and Reinartz, *Leistungssportsystem*, 529.
95. H.-J. Götze, "Grundlagen und neue Tendenzen für die Planung von Sporteinrichtungen im Zeitraum nach 1986," *Theorie und Praxis der Körperkultur* 35 (1986): 339–45.
96. Götze, "Grundlagen," 342f. Quoted in Sebastian Klawohn, *Die Sportstätteninfrastruktur der DDR—die besondere Situation der Hallen- und Schwimmbäder* (Potsdam, 2010), 62.
97. Teichler and Reinartz, *Leistungssportsystem*, 421ff.
98. See Entwurf "Entschließung des VIII. Turn- und Sporttages des DTSB der DDR" [Draft "Resolution of the 8th gymnastics and sport day of the DTSB of the GDR"], Berlin, 19 October 1989, SAPMO DY 12/Sekr. 89 (2). As quoted in Teichler and Reinartz, *Leistungssportsystem*, 425.
99. Ibid., 426.
100. Jutta Braun, "Klassenkampf nach Kalenderplan. 30 Jahre deutsch-deutsches Sportprotokoll," *Deutschland Archiv* 37 (2004): 405–14.
101. Ferdinand Kösters, *Verschenkter Lorbeer. Sportpolitik in Deutschland zur Zeit der Wende 1989/1990* (Münster, 2009), 113.
102. Ibid., 124.
103. Jutta Braun, "Go West! Trainer und Spitzensportler wechseln in den 'goldenen Westen,'" in *Chronik der Sporteinheit. Vom Mauerfall bis zur Aufnahme der fünf neuen Landessportbünde am 15. Dezember 1990 in den Deutschen Sportbund*, ed. Michael Barsuhn, Jutta Braun, and Hans Joachim Teichler (Frankfurt a. M., 2006), 28.
104. Rainer Calmund, *fußballbekloppt. Autobiographie* (Munich, 2008), 121.
105. Raj Kollmorgen, "Zwischen 'nachholender Modernisierung' und 'doppeltem Umbruch.' Ostdeutschland und deutsche Einheit im Diskurs der Sozialwissenschaften," in *Diskurse der deutschen Einheit: Kritik und Alternativen*, ed. Frank Thomas Koch and Hans-Liudger Dienel (Wiesbaden, 2011), 27–67.
106. Christian Hinzpeter, "Die positive Seite der Medaille: Der Fall 'Bosman' hat nicht bloß Schattenseiten für den Fußball," in *Quo Vadis, Fußball? Vom Spielprozess zum Marktprodukt*, ed. Walter Ludwig Tegelbeckers and Dietrich Milles (Göttingen, 2000), 78.
107. Walter Ludwig Tegelbeckers, "Spiegel der 'Erlebnisgesellschaft'? Der Fußball im Wandel vom Spielprozess zum Marktprodukt," in Tegelbeckers and Milles, *Quo Vadis, Fußball?*, 14.
108. Even before the last GDR Oberliga season in 1990/91, BFC Dynamo changed its name to FC Berlin. In May 1999, the great majority of those present at

the members' assembly voted in favor of changing the name back. "BFC Dynamo wiedergeboren," *Berliner Zeitung*, 4 May 1999.
109. Raj Kollmorgen, *Das ungewollte Experiment. Die deutsche Vereinigung als "Beitritt": Gründe, Prozesslogik, Langzeitfolgen*, thesis, Otto-von-Guericke Universität, Magdeburg, 2013, 10.
110. Ferdinand Kösters, *Verschenkter Lorbeer. Sportpolitik in Deutschland zur Zeit der Wende 1989/1990* (Münster, 2009), 118ff.
111. Ibid., 51.
112. "Bisher war hier kein Fremder," *Der Spiegel*, 22 January 1990.
113. Article 39 in the unification treaty reads as follows: "Within this framework, the Physical Training and Sport Research Institute (FKS) in Leipzig, the doping control laboratory recognized by the International Olympic Committee (IOC) in Kreischa (near Dresden) and the Sports Equipment Research and Development Centre (FES) in Berlin (East) shall—each in an appropriate legal form and to the extent necessary—be continued as institutions in the united Germany or attached to existing institutions."
114. As cited in Michael Barsuhn, "Die Wende und Vereinigung im Fußball 1989/90," in Braun and Teichler, *Sportstadt Berlin*, 404. The quote comes from an eyewitness interview that Michael Barsuhn had conducted with Hans-Georg Moldenhauer on 19 November 2004 in Magdeburg.
115. On the significance of the World Championship victories in 1954, 1974, and 1990 for German national identity, see Jutta Braun and Ulrich Hagemann, eds., *Deutschland—einig Fußballland? Deutsche Geschichte nach 1949 im Zeichen des Fußballs. Fachdidaktische Handreichung zur politisch-historischen Urteilsbildung* (Baltmannsweiler, 2008).
116. "Schäuble: Eine Mannschaft '92," *Frankfurter Allgemeine Zeitung*, 13 March 1990.
117. This came from a survey conducted by the Sport Information Service; "Wider Vereinigung," *Süddeutsche Zeitung*, 6 June 1990.
118. The first and last GDR Minister of Sport, Cordula Schubert, had already called for this. See Ferdinand Kösters, *Verschenkter Lorbeer*, 42.
119. Wolf-Dietrich Brettschneider and Guido Klimek, *Sportbetonte Schulen. Ein Königsweg zur Förderung sportlicher Talente?* (Paderborn, 1998), 9–15.
120. Sebastian Braun, "Spitzensportler als nationale Eliten im internationalen Vergleich," *Sportwissenschaft* 28 (1998): 54–72.
121. This personal biography dilemma has been analyzed in detail; see Karl Heinrich Bette and Uwe Schimank, *Doping im Hochleistungssport. Anpassung durch Abweichung* (Frankfurt a. M., 1995).
122. Joachim Boelcke, *Damit Talente Sieger werden. Geschichte der Sportschule Friedrich-Ludwig-Jahn Brandenburg a. d. H./Potsdam* (Wilhelmshorst, 2002).
123. Jutta Braun and René Wiese, "Eine sportliche 'Fürsorgediktatur'? Planung, Förderung und Repression im Sport der DDR," *Horch und Guck* 21 (2012): 4–9.

124. The journalist Willi Knecht claimed that the widespread wave of GDR nostalgia in the sports world stemmed from this intended adoption of GDR methods: Willi Knecht, "Mit DDR-Methodik vom Tiefpunkt Sydney zu neuen Höhen in Salt Lake City?" *Deutschland Archiv* 34 (2001): 450–56.
125. "Birgit Fischer will Sichtungssystem der DDR reanimieren," *Süddeutsche Zeitung*, 12 September 2012.
126. "Wie die DDR Sieger machte," *Stern*, 29 November 1990; "Ich stehe heute noch dazu," *Stern*, 29 November 1990.
127. "Extrem viel reingepumpt," *Der Spiegel*, 3 December 1990. See in this case Andreas Singler and Gerhard Treutlein, *Doping im Spitzensport. Sportwissenschaftliche Analysen zur nationalen und internationalen Leistungsentwicklung* (Aachen, 2000), 257ff.
128. "Dopen für Deutschland," *Frankfurter Allgemeine Zeitung*, 11 December 1990.
129. Jutta Braun, "Dopen für Deutschland—die Diskussion im vereinten Sport 1990–1992," in *Hormone und Hochleistung. Doping zwischen Ost und West*, ed. Klaus Latzel and Lutz Niethammer (Cologne, 2008), 151–70.
130. Brigitte Berendonk, *Doping-Dokumente. Von der Forschung zum Betrug* (Berlin, 1991).
131. Kollmorgen, *Das ungewollte Experiment*, 12
132. "Kindermann unterzieht Mediziner einem Dopingtest," *Frankfurter Allgemeine Zeitung*, 19 December 1990.
133. "Eidesstattliche Versicherung gegen Doping," *Frankfurter Allgemeine Zeitung*, 26 June 1991.
134. "Delikate Frage," *Der Spiegel*, 4 February 1991.
135. "Es werden Wunder geschehen," *Der Spiegel*, 7 October 1991.
136. Ibid.
137. "Auch Schubert und Klümper unterliegen. Einstweilige Verfügungen gegen das Berendonk-Buch weitestgehend abgelehnt," *Süddeutsche Zeitung*, 5 December 1991.
138. "Ost-Schwimmtrainer bestätigen DDR-Doping," *Frankfurter Allgemeine Zeitung*, 3 December 1991.
139. "Kollektive Selbstbezichtigung," *Süddeutsche Zeitung*, 3 December 1991.
140. "Doping-Folgen," *Berliner Morgenpost*, 9 December 1991.
141. "Trainer in Konfrontation," *Berliner Zeitung*, 10 December 1991.
142. On the course that these trials took, see Steven Ungerleider, *Faust's Gold: Inside the East German Doping Machine* (New York, 2001); Hans-Joachim Seppelt and Holger Schück, *Anklage: Kinderdoping. Das Erbe des DDR-Sports* (Berlin, 1999).
143. Norbert Frei, Dirk van Laak, and Michael Stolleis, eds., *Geschichte vor Gericht. Historiker, Richter und die Suche nach Gerechtigkeit* (Munich, 2000).
144. On the statistics related to the doping processes, see Klaus Marxen, Gerhard Werle, and Petra Schäfter, eds., *Die Strafverfolgung von DDR-Unrecht. Fak-

ten und Zahlen (Berlin, 2007). According to these statistics, charges were made in a total of thirty-eight trials on systematic doping and one petition for a penalty order was submitted. Of the forty-seven sentences that were handed down, thirty carried fines and seventeen were prison sentences on probation; ibid., 28 and 43.

145. On the biographies of the two athletes caught between success and the dictates of the system in the GDR see Jutta Braun, "Thüringer Sportler in der Diktatur," in *Zwischen Erfolgs- und Diktaturgeschichte. Perspektiven der Aufarbeitung des DDR-Sports in Thüringen*, ed. Jutta Braun and Michael Barsuhn (Göttingen, 2007), 12–85.

146. "In der biografischen Falle. Die Rekordprüfung konfrontiert den DLV auch mit der Duldung der westdeutschen Dopingpraxis," *Berliner Zeitung*, 24 December 2005.

147. Cf. Dok. 4: Kleinmachnow 7 November 1989: Die erste offene Diskussion im DTSB [Doc. 4: Kleinmachnow 7 November 1989: The first open discussion in the DTSB]. Teichler and Reinartz, *Leistungssportsystem*, 490.

148. Ibid., 532; [Discussion report Edelfried Buggel], in: Doc. 4: Kleinmachnow 7 November 1989: The first open discussion in the DTSB.

149. Ibid., 504.

150. Ständige Sportministerkonferenz der Bundesländer, *Sportstättenstatistik der Länder* (Berlin, 2007), 35–36.

151. Walter Ludwig Tegelbeckers, "SG-Sport im Spiegel von Planung und 'Erfüllung.' Eine regionale Studie zu Proportionen und Disproportionen im DTSB-organisierten Basissport," in Teichler, *Sport in der DDR*, 135–235. See Hans Joachim Teichler, "Sportentwicklung in Ostdeutschland," *dvs-Informationen* 18 (2003): 17–20.

152. According to Manfred Kruczek (MBJS) at the "Ersten Breitensportkonferenz" [First grassroots sports conference] of the Landeshauptstadt Potsdam held at the University of Potsdam, 11 December 2012.

153. Teichler "Sportentwicklung in Ostdeutschland," 20.

154. Jürgen Baur and Sebastian Braun, eds., *Der vereinsorganisierte Sport in Ostdeutschland* (Cologne, 2001), 138.

155. Ibid., 141.

156. Lothar Probst, *Differenz in der Einheit. Über die kulturellen Unterschiede der Deutschen in Ost und West. 20 Essays, Reden und Gespräche* (Berlin, 1999).

157. According to Manfred Kruczek (MBJS) at the "Ersten Breitensportkonferenz" of the Landeshauptstadt Potsdam held at the University of Potsdam, 11 December 2012.

158. See Walter Brehm, "Gesundheitssport," in *Sportwissenschaftliches Lexikon*, ed. Peter Röthig and Robert Prohl (Schorndorf, 2003), 224–26; Klaus Bös et al. *Gesundheitsorientierte Sportprogramme im Verein: Analysen und Hilfen zum Qualitätsmanagement; Expertise im Auftrag des Deutschen Sportbundes* (Frankfurt a. M., 1998); Walter Brehm, Iris Pahmeier, and Sabine Brinkmann, *Gesundheitsförderung durch sportliche Aktivierung als gemeinsame*

Aufgabe von Ärzten, Krankenkassen und Sportvereinen. Entwicklung, Erprobung und Evaluation einer gemeindebezogenen Modellmaßnahme (Bielefeld, 1992).
159. Michael Krüger and Stefan Nielsen, "Die Entstehung der Nationalen Anti-Doping Agentur in Deutschland (NADA) im Kontext der Gründung der Welt Anti-Doping Agentur (WADA)," *Sport und Gesellschaft* 10 (2013): 59.
160. Ibid., 61. The Council of Europe's Convention on Doping in 1989 also played a role in this development because it also required the states that signed it to comply with certain guidelines; ibid., 63.
161. Eike Emrich, Christian Pierdzioch, and Christian Rullang, "Zwischen Regelgebundenheit und diskretionären Spielräumen: Die Finanzierung des bundesdeutschen Spitzensports," *Sport und Gesellschaft* 10 (2013): 5.

BIBLIOGRAPHY

Archival Materials
Archiv NOK/Frankfurt a. M.
BAK 136 24413.
BAK 136 29699.
BAK 139/1995.
BAK B 136 24413.
BStU, MfS-HA XX 69254/92.
SAPMO DY 30/IV/2/2.039/70.
Willi-Daume-Archiv/DOA.

"Auch Schubert und Klümper unterliegen. Einstweilige Verfügungen gegen das Berendonk-Buch weitestgehend abgelehnt." *Süddeutsche Zeitung*, 5 December 1991.
Balbier, Uta Andrea. *Kalter Krieg auf der Aschenbahn. Der deutsch-deutsche Sport 1950–1972*. Paderborn: Schöningh, 2006.
Barsuhn, Michael. "Die Wende und Vereinigung im Fußball 1989/90." In *Sportstadt Berlin im Kalten Krieg. Prestigekämpfe und Systemwettstreit*, edited by Jutta Braun and Hans Joachim Teichler, 376–416. Berlin: Links, 2006.
Baur, Jürgen, and Sebastian Braun. *Freiwilliges Engagement und Partizipation in ostdeutschen Sportvereinen. Eine empirische Analyse zum Institutionentransfer*. Cologne: Sport und Buch Strauß, 2000.
———, eds. *Der vereinsorganisierte Sport in Ostdeutschland*. Cologne: Sport und Buch Strauß, 2001.
Berendonk, Brigitte. *Doping-Dokumente. Von der Forschung zum Betrug*. Berlin: Springer, 1991.
Bergien, Rüdiger. "Erstarrter Bellizismus. Die SED-Funktionäre und ihr Weg in den Herbst '89." In *1989 und die Rolle der Gewalt*, edited by Martin Sabrow, 32–55. Göttingen: Wallstein, 2012.

Bernett, Hajo. *Körperkultur und Sport in der DDR*. Schorndorf: Hofmann, 1994.
Bette, Karl Heinrich, and Uwe Schimank. *Doping im Hochleistungssport. Anpassung durch Abweichung*. Frankfurt a. M.: Suhrkamp, 1995.
"Birgit Fischer will Sichtungssystem der DDR reanimieren." *Süddeutsche Zeitung*, 12 September 2012.
"Bisher war hier kein Fremder." *Der Spiegel*, 22 January 1990.
Blasius, Tobias. *Olympische Bewegung, Kalter Krieg und Deutschlandpolitik 1949–1972*. Frankfurt a. M.: Lang, 2001.
Boelcke, Joachim, Hugdietrich Schulze, Mathias Iffert, and Klaus R. Ziemer. *Damit Talente Sieger werden. Geschichte der Sportschule Friedrich-Ludwig-Jahn Brandenburg a. d. H./Potsdam*. Wilhelmshorst: Märkischer Verl., 2002.
Bös, Klaus, Walter Brehm, Elke Opper, and Joachim Saam. *Gesundheitsorientierte Sportprogramme im Verein: Analysen und Hilfen zum Qualitätsmanagement; Expertise im Auftrag des Deutschen Sportbundes*. Frankfurt a. M.: Deutscher Sportbund, 1998.
Braun, Jutta. "Abseits der Bundesliga. Zur Aufarbeitung des DDR-Fußballs." *Aus Politik und Zeitgeschichte* 27/28 (2013): 41–46.
———. "Gutachten zum Themenfeld Sport für die Enquetekommission 5/1 des Brandenburger Landtags zur Aufarbeitung der Geschichte und Bewältigung von Folgen der SED-Diktatur und des Übergangs in einen demokratischen Rechtsstaat im Land Brandenburg." Potsdam, 12 January 2013. Retrieved 29 June 2018, https://www.landtag.brandenburg.de/media_fast/5701/Gutachten%20Dr.%20Braun_Sport_11%2002%202013.pdf.
———. "Dopen für Deutschland—die Diskussion im vereinten Sport 1990–1992." In *Hormone und Hochleistung. Doping zwischen Ost und West*, edited by Klaus Latzel and Lutz Niethammer, 151–70. Cologne: Böhlau, 2008.
———. "Go West! Trainer und Spitzensportler wechseln in den 'goldenen Westen.'" In *Chronik der Sporteinheit. Vom Mauerfall bis zur Aufnahme der fünf neuen Landessportbünde am 15. Dezember 1990 in den Deutschen Sportbund*, edited by Michael Barsuhn, Jutta Braun, and Hans Joachim Teichler. Frankfurt a. M.: Deutscher Sportbund, 2006.
———. "Inselstadt im Abseits?" In *Sportstadt Berlin im Kalten Krieg. Prestigekämpfe und Systemwettstreit*, edited by Jutta Braun and Hans Joachim Teichler, 150–83. Berlin: Links, 2006.
———. "Klassenkampf im Flutlicht." In *Sport in der DDR. Eigensinn, Konflikte, Trends*, edited by Hans Joachim Teichler, 61–132. Cologne: Sport und Buch Strauß, 2004.
———. "Klassenkampf nach Kalenderplan. 30 Jahre deutsch-deutsches Sportprotokoll." *Deutschland Archiv* 37 (2004): 405–14.
———. "Sportfreunde oder Staatsfeinde?" *Deutschland Archiv* 37 (2013): 440–47.
———. "Thüringer Sportler in der Diktatur." In *Zwischen Erfolgs- und Diktaturgeschichte. Perspektiven der Aufarbeitung des DDR-Sports in Thüringen*, edited by Jutta Braun and Michael Barsuhn, 12–85. Göttingen: Verl. Die Werkstatt, 2015.

Braun, Jutta, and Hans Joachim Teichler. "Fußballfans im Visier der Staatsmacht." In *Sport in der DDR. Eigensinn, Konflikte, Trends*, edited by Hans Joachim Teichler, 561–86. Cologne: Sport und Buch Strauß, 2003.
Braun, Jutta, and René Wiese. "DDR-Fußball und gesamtdeutsche Identität im Kalten Krieg." *Historical Social Research/Historische Sozialforschung* 30 (2005): 191–210.
———. "Eine sportliche 'Fürsorgediktatur'? Planung, Förderung und Repression im Sport der DDR." *Horch und Guck* 21, no. 1 (2012): 4–9.
Braun, Jutta, and Ulrich Hagemann, eds. *Deutschland—einig Fußballland? Deutsche Geschichte nach 1949 im Zeichen des Fußballs. Fachdidaktische Handreichung zur politisch-historischen Urteilsbildung*. Baltmannsweiler: Schneider Hohengehren, 2008.
Braun, Sebastian. "Spitzensportler als nationale Eliten im internationalen Vergleich." *Sportwissenschaft* 28 (1998): 54–72.
Brehm, Walter. "Gesundheitssport." In *Sportwissenschaftliches Lexikon*, edited by Peter Röthig and Robert Prohl, 224–26. Schorndorf: Hofmann, 2003.
Brehm, Walter, Iris Pahmeier, and Sabine Brinkmann. *Gesundheitsförderung durch sportliche Aktivierung als gemeinsame Aufgabe von Ärzten, Krankenkassen und Sportvereinen. Entwicklung, Erprobung und Evaluation einer gemeindebezogenen Modellmaßnahme*. Bielefeld: Institut für Dokumentation und Information, Sozialmedizin und öffentliches Gesundheitswesen (IDIS), 1992.
Brettschneider, Wolf-Dietrich, and Guido Klimek. *Sportbetonte Schulen. Ein Königsweg zur Förderung sportlicher Talente?* Paderborn: Meyer & Meyer, 1998.
Calmund, Reiner. *fußballbekloppt. Autobiographie*. Munich: Goldmann, 2008.
Danckert, Peter, and Holger Schück. *Kraftmaschine Parlament. Der Sportausschuss und die Sportpolitik des Bundes*. Aachen: Meyer & Meyer, 2009.
"Das geht mir auf den Geist." *Der Spiegel*, 19 September 1988.
"DDR: Schluck Pillen oder kehr Fabriken aus." *Der Spiegel*, 19 March 1979.
"Delikate Frage." *Der Spiegel*, 4 February 1991.
Der Bundesbeauftragte für die Unterlagen des Staatssicherheitsdienstes der ehemaligen Deutschen Demokratischen Republik (BStU), ed. *MfS und Leistungssport: Ein Recherchebericht. Reihe A: Dokumente; 1/1994*. Berlin: Der Bundesbeauftragte für die Unterlagen des Staatssicherheitsdienstes der ehemaligen Deutschen Demokratischen Republik, 1994.
"Der Fußball-Trainer aus Jena leistet sich Träume, weil er Realist ist." *Frankfurter Allgemeine Zeitung*, 18 September 1986.
"Der Sport geht über den Rubikon." *Süddeutsche Zeitung*, 26/27 February 1977.
"Der verpönte Sport—Wie SED und Stasi das Tennis in der DDR drangsalierten." *Die Welt*, 14 November 2002.
Deutsches Sportecho, 11/12 May 1984.
"Die WM 74 und Berlin: FIFA musste Statuten ändern." *Stuttgarter Zeitung*, 13 March 1985.

Dieckert, Jürgen. "Freizeitsport in Deutschland." In *Handbuch Freizeitsport*, edited by Jürgen Dieckert and Christian Wopp, 25–32. Schorndorf: Verlag Hofmann, 2002.
Digel, Helmut. *Sportentwicklung in der Moderne*. Schorndorf: Hofmann, 2013.
"Dopen für Deutschland." *Frankfurter Allgemeine Zeitung*, 11 December 1990.
"Doping-Folgen." *Berliner Morgenpost*, 9 December 1991.
"Eidesstattliche Versicherung gegen Doping." *Frankfurter Allgemeine Zeitung*, 26 June 1991.
Emrich, Eike. *Zur Soziologie der Olympiastützpunkte. Eine Untersuchung zur Entstehung, Struktur und Leistungsfähigkeit einer Sportförderorganisation*. Niedernhausen: Schors-Verlag, 1996.
Emrich, Eike, Christian Pierdzioch, and Christian Rullang. "Zwischen Regelgebundenheit und diskretionären Spielräumen: Die Finanzierung des bundesdeutschen Spitzensports." *Sport und Gesellschaft* 10 (2013): 3–26.
Emrich, Eike, and Ronald Wadsack. *Zur Evaluation der Olympiastützpunkte. Betreuungsqualität und Kostenstruktur*. Cologne: Sport und Buch Strauß, 2005.
"Es werden Wunder geschehen." *Der Spiegel*, 7 October 1991.
Ewald, Manfred, and Reinhold Andert. *Ich war der Sport: Wahrheiten und Legenden aus dem Wunderland der Sieger*. Berlin: Elefanten Press, 1994.
"Extrem viel reingepumpt." *Der Spiegel*, 3 December 1990.
"Festigung prinzipieller Feindbilder," *Der Spiegel*, 25 January 1988.
"Fußball-Notopfer." *Bonner Rundschau*, 20 February 1985.
Frei, Norbert, Dirk van Laak, and Michael Stolleis, eds. *Geschichte vor Gericht. Historiker, Richter und die Suche nach Gerechtigkeit*. Munich: Beck, 2000.
Fulbrook, Mary. "Generationen und Kohorten in der DDR. Protagonisten und Widersacher des DDR-Systems aus der Perspektive biographischer Daten." In *Die DDR aus generationengeschichtlicher Perspektive. Eine Inventur*, edited by Annegret Schüle, Thomas Ahbe, and Rainer Gries, 113–30. Leipzig: Leipziger Universitätsverlag, 2006.
Gebauer, Gunter. "Die Bundesliga." In *Deutsche Erinnerungsorte: eine Auswahl*, edited by Étienne François and Hagen Schulze, 463–76. Munich: Beck, 2005.
Götze, H. J. "Grundlagen und neue Tendenzen für die Planung von Sporteinrichtungen im Zeitraum nach 1986." *Theorie und Praxis der Körperkultur* 35 (1986): 339–45.
Guttmann, Allen. *The Olympics: A History of the Modern Games*. Champaign: Univ. of Illinois Press, 2002.
"Hauptausschuss des DSB diskutiert Einigungsprozess." *Frankfurter Rundschau*, 25 June 1990.
Havemann, Nils. *Samstags um halb vier. Die Geschichte der Fußball-Bundesliga*. Munich: Siedler, 2013.
Hinsching, Jochen, ed. *Breitensport in Ostdeutschland—Reflexion und Transformation*. Hamburg: Czwalina, 2000.
Hinzpeter, Christian. "Die positive Seite der Medaille: Der Fall 'Bosman' hat nicht

bloß Schattenseiten für den Fußball." In *Quo Vadis, Fußball? Vom Spielprozess zum Marktprodukt,* edited by Walter Ludwig Tegelbeckers and Dietrich Milles, 76–79. Göttingen: Verl. Die Werkstatt, 2000.

Huster, Ronald. "Duell an der Spree. Radsport im geteilten Berlin." In *Sportstadt Berlin im Kalten Krieg. Prestigekämpfe und Systemwettstreit,* edited by Jutta Braun and Hans Joachim Teichler, 285–314. Berlin: Links, 2006.

"Ich stehe heute noch dazu." *Stern,* 29 November 1990.

"In der biografischen Falle. Die Rekordprüfung konfrontiert den DLV auch mit der Duldung der westdeutschen Dopingpraxis," *Berliner Zeitung,* 24 December 2005.

"Interessiert die unser Elend?" *Der Spiegel,* 3 August 1992.

Junge Welt, 17 July 1988.

Kaiser, Ulrich. *Tennis in Deutschland. Von den Anfängen bis 2002.* Berlin: Duncker und Humblot, 2002.

Klawohn, Sebastian. *Die Sportstätteninfrastruktur der DDR—die besondere Situation der Hallen- und Schwimmbäder.* Report. Potsdam: Universität Potsdam, 2010.

"Kollektive Selbstbezichtigung." *Süddeutsche Zeitung,* 3 December 1991.

Kollmorgen, Raj. *Das ungewollte Experiment. Die deutsche Vereinigung als "Beitritt": Gründe, Prozesslogik, Langzeitfolgen.* Thesis, Otto-von-Guericke Universität, Magdeburg, 2013.

———. "Zwischen 'nachholender Modernisierung' und 'doppeltem Umbruch.' Ostdeutschland und deutsche Einheit im Diskurs der Sozialwissenschaften." In *Diskurse der deutschen Einheit: Kritik und Alternativen,* edited by Frank Thomas Koch and Hans-Liudger Dienel, 27–67. Wiesbaden: VS Verl. für Sozialwissenschaften, 2011.

Kösters, Ferdinand. *Verschenkter Lorbeer. Sportpolitik in Deutschland zur Zeit der Wende 1989/1990.* Münster: Verlagshaus Mosenstein und Vannerdat, 2009.

Knecht, Willi. "Laufen Sozialisten schneller?" *Deutschland Archiv* 1 (1969): 1–9.

———. "Mit DDR-Methodik vom Tiefpunkt Sydney zu neuen Höhen in Salt Lake City?" *Deutschland Archiv* 34 (2001): 450–56.

Krebs, Hans-Dieter. "Die Zeit der Boykottbewegungen." In *Deutschland in der olympischen Bewegung. Eine Zwischenbilanz,* edited by Nationales Olympisches Komitee für Deutschland, 307–15, Frankfurt a. M.: NOK für Deutschland, 1999.

Kruczek, Manfred. *Erste Breitensportkonferenz der Landeshauptstadt Potsdam an der Universität Potsdam, Potsdam, 11 December 2012.* Potsdam: Universität Potsdam, 2012.

Krüger, Arnd. *Sport und Politik. Von Turnvater Jahn zum Staatsamateur.* Hannover: Fackelträger-Verlag, 1975.

Krüger, Arnd, and Bernd Wedemeyer, eds. *Kraftkörper—Körperkraft: Zum Verständnis von Körperkultur und Fitness gestern und heute.* Göttingen: Univ.-Verl. Göttingen, 1995.

Krüger, Michael, and Stefan Nielsen. "Die Entstehung der Nationalen Anti-Doping Agentur in Deutschland (NADA) im Kontext der Gründung der Welt Anti-Doping Agentur (WADA)." *Sport und Gesellschaft* 10 (2013): 55–59.

Kummer, Michael. *Die ungleichen Bedingungen von FC Rot Weiß Erfurt und FC Carl Zeiss Jena in der DDR.* Eisenach: Tulpe Verlag, 2012.

Lennartz, Karl. "Olympische Boykotte." In *Sportgeschichte erforschen und vermitteln. Jahrestagung der dvs-Sektion Sportgeschichte vom 19.–21. Juni 2008 in Göttingen,* edited by Andrea Bruns and Wolfgang Buss, 179–200, Hamburg: Czwalina, 2009.

Lorke, Christoph. "'Ungehindert abreagieren.' Hooliganismus in der späten DDR im Spannungsfeld von Anstandsnormen, Sozialdisziplinierung und gesellschaftlichen Randlagen." *Deutschland Archiv* 45 (2012): 240–249.

Marxen, Klaus, Gerhard Werle, and Petra Schäfter, eds. *Die Strafverfolgung von DDR-Unrecht. Fakten und Zahlen.* Berlin: Stiftung zur Aufarbeitung der SED-Diktatur, 2007.

Mertin, Evelyn. "The Soviet Union and the Olympic Games of 1980 and 1984: Explaining the Boycotts to Their Own People." In *East Plays West: Sport and the Cold War,* edited by Stephen Wagg and David L. Andrews, 235–52. New York: Routledge, 2007.

"Mit Bitternis und Sand im Mund." *Der Spiegel,* 19 May 1980.

Müller, Siegfried, and Heinz Schwidtmann. "Ausgewählte Schwerpunkte der politisch-ideologischen Vorbereitung von Leistungssportlern auf die Olympischen Winterspiele 1988." *Theorie und Praxis des Leistungssports* 25 (1987): 9–22.

"Neues Weltbild." *Der Spiegel,* 8 August 1988.

"Olympia Boykott von 1980 hat nichts gebracht. Interview mit Eberhard Gienger." *Die Welt,* 26 March 1980.

O'Mahony, Mike. *Sport in the USSR: Physical Culture—Visual Culture.* London: Reaktion Books, 2006.

"Ost-Schwimmtrainer bestätigen DDR-Doping." *Frankfurter Allgemeine Zeitung,* 3 December 1991.

"Otto Rehhagel will DDR-Kicker in die Bundesliga holen." *Bonner Rundschau,* 27 February 1987.

Parks, Jenifer. "Verbal Gymnastics: Sports, Bureaucracy and the Soviet Union's Entrance into the Olympic Games, 1946–1952." In *East Plays West: Sport and the Cold War,* edited by Stephen Wagg and David L. Andrews, 27–44. New York: Routledge, 2007.

Probst, Lothar. *Differenz in der Einheit. Über die kulturellen Unterschiede der Deutschen in Ost und West. 20 Essays, Reden und Gespräche.* Berlin: Links, 1999.

Reinartz, Klaus. "Die Zweiteilung des DDR-Sports auf Beschluss der SED." In *Das Leistungssportsystem der DDR in den 1980er Jahren und im Prozess der Wende,* edited by Hans Joachim Teichler and Klaus Reinartz, 55–85. Schorndorf: Hofmann, 1999.

Reinhart, Kai. *"Wir wollten einfach unser Ding machen." DDR-Sportler zwischen Fremdbestimmung und Selbstverwirklichung.* Frankfurt a. M.: Campus, 2010.

Reinhart, Kai, and Michael Krüger. "Massensport in der Grauzone." *Horch und Guck* 21 (2012): 16–18.

Riordan, Jim. "Great Britain and the 1980 Olympics: Victory for Olympism." *Sport and International Understanding*, edited by Maaret Ilmarinen, 138–44. Berlin: Springer, 1984.

"Rückspiegel." *Der Spiegel*, 1 February 1988.

"Schäuble will Erfolg des DDR-Sports retten." *Frankfurter Allgemeine Zeitung*, 22 March 1990.

"Schäuble: Eine Mannschaft '92." *Frankfurter Allgemeine Zeitung*, 13 March 1990.

Schröder, Ralf, and Hubert Dalkamp. *Nicht alle Helden tragen Gelb. Die Geschichte der Tour de France*, 4th ed. Göttingen: Verl. Die Werkstatt, 2011.

Seppelt, Hans-Joachim, and Holger Schück. *Anklage: Kinderdoping. Das Erbe des DDR-Sports*. Berlin: Tenea Verl. für Medien, 1999.

Singler, Andreas, and Gerhard Treutlein. *Doping im Spitzensport. Sportwissenschaftliche Analysen zur nationalen und internationalen Leistungsentwicklung*. Aachen: Meyer & Meyer, 2000.

Smit, Barbara. *Die Dasslers—Drei Streifen gegen Puma*. Bergisch Gladbach: Bastei Lübbe, 2007.

Spitzer, Giselher. *Doping in der DDR—ein historischer Überblick zu einer konspirativen Praxis. Genese, Verantwortung, Gefahren*. Cologne: Sportverlag Strauß, 1998.

———. *Sieg um jeden Preis. Doping in Deutschland: Geschichte, Recht, Ethik 1972–1990*. Göttingen: Sportverlag Strauß, 2013.

Spitzer, Giselher, Hans Joachim Teichler, and Klaus Reinartz, eds. *Schlüsseldokumente im DDR-Sport. Ein sporthistorischer Überblick in Originalquellen*. Aachen: Meyer & Meyer, 1998.

Spitzer, Giselher. *Sieg um jeden Preis. Doping in Deutschland: Geschichte, Recht, Ethik 1972–1990*. Göttingen: Sportverlag Strauß, 2013.

Sportministerkonferenz. *Sportstättenstatistik der Länder*. Berlin: Ständige Konferenz der Sportminister der Länder in der Bundesrepublik Deutschland, 2003.

"'Sturm der Entrüstung ist ausgeblieben.' Interview mit TV-Sportkoordinator Hans Heinrich Isenbarth." *Der Spiegel*, 28 July 1980.

Tegelbeckers, Walter Ludwig. "SG-Sport im Spiegel von Planung und 'Erfüllung.' Eine regionale Studie zu Proportionen und Disproportionen im DTSB-organisierten Basissport." In *Sport in der DDR. Eigensinn, Konflikte, Trends*, edited by Hans Joachim Teichler, 135–235. Cologne: Sport und Buch Strauß, 2003.

———. "Spiegel der 'Erlebnisgesellschaft'? Der Fußball im Wandel vom Spielprozess zum Marktprodukt." In *Quo Vadis, Fußball? Vom Spielprozess zum Marktprodukt*, edited by Walter Ludwig Tegelbeckers and Dietrich Milles, 9–15. Göttingen: Verl. Die Werkstatt, 2000.

Teichler, Hans Joachim. "Die schwierigen Anfänge des Fußballsports in der SBZ/DDR" In *Fußball in Geschichte und Gesellschaft. Tagung der dvs-Sektionen Sportgeschichte und Sportsoziologie vom 29.9.–1.10.2004 in Münster*, edited by Michael Krüger and Bernd Schulze, 75–81. Hamburg: Czwalina, 2006.

———. "Die Sportclubs." In *Das Leistungssportsystem der DDR in den 1980er Jahren und im Prozess der Wende*, edited by Hans Joachim Teichler and Klaus Reinartz, 187–269. Schorndorf: Hofmann, 1999.

———. "Konfliktlinien des Sportalltags. Eingaben zum Thema Sport." In *Sport in der DDR. Eigensinn, Konflikte, Trends*, edited by Hans Joachim Teichler, 535–60. Cologne: Sport und Buch Strauß, 2003.

———. "Sportentwicklung in Ostdeutschland." In *dvs-Informationen* 18 (2003): 17–20.

———. "Sportentwicklung in Ostdeutschland nach der Wende." *Horch und Guck* 14 (2005): 40–43.

Teichler, Hans Joachim, and Klaus Reinartz, eds. *Das Leistungssportsystem der DDR in den 1980er Jahren und im Prozess der Wende*. Schorndorf: Hofmann, 1999.

"Trainer in Konfrontation." *Berliner Zeitung*, 10 December 1991.

Ungerleider, Steven. *Faust's Gold: Inside the East German Doping Machine*. New York: St. Martin's Press, 2001.

"Unglaublich missbraucht. Kaltblütig missbraucht." *Der Spiegel*, 8 August 1983.

"Von Boykott keine Rede." *Sonntag Aktuell*, 2 June 1985.

"Wider Vereinigung." *Süddeutsche Zeitung*, 6 June 1990.

"Wie die DDR Sieger machte." *Stern*, 29 November 1990.

Wiese, René, and Ronald Huster. "Entstehung und Entwicklung des Brettsegelns in der DDR." In *Sport in der DDR. Eigensinn, Konflikte, Trends*, ed. by Hans Joachim Teichler, 425–500. Cologne: Sport und Buch Strauß, 2003.

Wiese, René. "Staatsgeheimnis Sport—Die Abschottung des Leistungssportsystems der DDR." *Historical Social Research* 32 (2007): 154–71.

———. "Wie der Fußball Löcher in die Mauer schoss." In *Sportstadt Berlin im Kalten Krieg. Prestigekämpfe und Systemwettstreit*, edited by Jutta Braun and Hans Joachim Teichler, 239–84. Berlin: Links, 2006.

Wilkinson-Johnson, Molly. *Training Socialist Citizens: Sports and the State in East Germany*. Leiden: Brill, 2008.

Winiarska, Dorota. *Bürgerlicher Sport in der DDR und Polen 1945–1989*. Hamburg: Kovač, 2005.

Wopp, Christian. *Entwicklung und Perspektiven des Freizeitsports*. Aachen: Meyer & Meyer, 1995.

"Zimmermann kritisiert DFB." *Süddeutsche Zeitung*, 21 February 1985.

"Züchten wir Monstren?" *Die Zeit*, 5 December 1969.

CHAPTER 11

Bridge over Troubled Water?
Mass Media in Divided Germany

Frank Bösch and Christoph Classen

The history of the media in divided Germany is full of contradictions and interconnections. At first glance, it seems as if there was hardly any other area in which the differences between the two countries before 1989 were as monumental as they were in terms of media. While the GDR had a centralized media system that was subject to strong political control, the contours of the media landscape in West Germany were shaped by the freedom of the press and a colorful array of different outlets, which included everything from American soaps to Communist papers. Simultaneously, the media formed an important bridge across the divide between East and West, allowing mutual observation and interrelations even at the height of the Cold War. Since most GDR citizens regularly watched Western TV and listened to Western radio, commentators noted early that East Germans "left the country every night." Likewise, there was talk of an "electronic reunification"[1] or "two states, but one radio and TV nation."[2] Moreover, the role of the media after reunification was no less dynamic than before the Wall came down. On the one hand, the West German media system moved part and parcel into the East. West German publishers took over most of the newspapers in the GDR as well as the newly created private stations, which seemed to create a tight bond between the two media worlds after 1990. On the other hand, the media markets and media use in West and East Germany are still quite different even today.

This chapter looks at the interplay of these structural differences and new entanglements. From this perspective, the 1970s mark a period in which media interaction between East and West intensified exponentially: whereas only radio broadcasts had crossed the border prior to this point, the full supply of televisions in East German households established an audiovisual link between the GDR and the FRG. The silent tolerance of the presence of West German radio and television in the GDR, which were now no longer blocked by jamming, abetted this media transfer.[3] Furthermore, media content in the GDR began to draw more heavily on West German productions. It increased its trade in Western television programs and films while also boosting its own production of programming that was modeled after Western entertainment formats. Likewise, a new kind of journalistic exchange evolved after the GDR accredited West German correspondents for the first time in 1973 because it allowed for regular reports from within East Germany to reach a Western audience. However, the West German press was still banned in the GDR, and West Germans ignored the East German papers. Nonetheless, the print media in the two countries still engaged in an ongoing dialog of response. That said, it has to be borne in mind that most of these interactions were strongly one-sided because there was very little media reception of content from the GDR in West Germany.

Although the media systems quite clearly differed in their political natures, there were similarities in media use in both German states. According to surveys, a good two-thirds of East as well as West Germans named watching television as their favorite leisure activity at the end of the 1960s, followed by reading the papers. The popularity of watching films in movie theaters, in contrast, sunk to an all-time low in both Germanys in the 1960s.[4] Additionally, as in most other industrialized countries, the proportion of entertainment within the media landscape grew on both sides of the Wall. Both countries experienced a concentration of the press market and increased media differentiation according to specific target audiences, especially in terms of newspapers. Even in the GDR, where the SED controlled and subsidized the media, it still became a consumer good, and it became impossible for the party to ignore its citizens' desire for entertainment. After 1990, the East German media landscape in particular underwent a radical transformation in which it adopted Western structures.

Scholars still disagree about how to assess the media in the GDR, as well as the media communication between the two Germanys. For a long time, the GDR media was simply seen as part of a uniform and centrally controlled propaganda apparatus that ignored the desires of the population in order to follow the dictates of the SED in the boring style so characteristic of the party. Correspondingly, scholarship focused primarily on the way the SED controlled the media.[5] Rather than attributing a powerful influence to this propaganda as was done for other dictatorships, and especially National Socialism, scholars stressed the lacking influence of the media in the GDR, especially in light of the competition coming from the West.[6] Nowadays, however, researchers have come to appreciate the increasing media response to the wishes of the public and Western influence, which allowed more entertainment and service programming offered by GDR television in particular to enjoy a stronger resonance.[7] Additionally, some studies have argued that the GDR developed a certain kind of national identity that coalesced around its television programming from the 1970s onward.[8] Such debates about the social impact of media, and especially its growing significance as an everyday consumer good, have helped to develop an effective lens for comparing the history of the media in East and West.

Separate Worlds? East and West German Print Media in the 1970s and 1980s

Great differences existed between the print media in the two Germanys, and the exchange between the two appears to have been rather limited at first glance. Whereas the newspaper landscape blossomed in Western Europe from the 1950s onward, featuring everything from small local papers to tabloids full of pictures and a critical highbrow press, standard newspapers in the East consisted of thin party papers with tightly printed pages full of success stories coming from the socialist world and slurs directed against the West. Perhaps the most glaring differences were to be found in the freedom of the press. In the wake of the *Spiegel* affair, state press laws were passed in West Germany in the mid-1960s that protected the investigative work of journalists by granting them special rights. The constitution of the GDR upheld the freedom of opinion in Article 27 ("The freedom of the press, the radio, and television is guaranteed"), but this was undermined by the SED's claim to leadership. The SED controlled the press through its license requirements and control over the distribution of paper, its selection and training of journalists, its censorship of the media, its interference in careers, and central regulations. Whereas the press was primarily privately owned in the West, and the Kartellamt (the West German antitrust authority) sought to prevent monopolies, the daily papers in the East were put out only by the SED, the bloc parties, and mass organizations, with the notable exception of the church press. In particular, the agitation department of the Central Committee of the SED and the press office of the chairman of the Council of Ministers controlled the news in the country through written directives and regular meetings with the editors-in-chief of the SED papers in Berlin.[9] The news agency ADN and the newspaper *Neues Deutschland* also disseminated central directives. As head of state, Erich Honecker often signed off on the content that was to appear in *Neues Deutschland* before publication or on the main television news show, the *Aktuelle Kamera*, before it was broadcasted. In West Germany, in contrast, even just attempts by politicians to control the media could easily turn into full-fledged scandals. Press reports often relied on the major news agency, the dpa, but it was financed by the media companies themselves and subject to competition from other agencies.

The journalist profession also differed markedly between the two countries, even in terms of the education and training required. In the Federal Republic, there was no formal vocational training paths for journalists, nor was journalism ever a separate university major. In the GDR, however, anyone who wanted to go into journalism was basically required to earn a degree from the School of Journalism in Leipzig or from the journalism department at the university there.[10] This meant, of course, that aspiring journalists were preselected on the basis of their ideological commitment, and they underwent a further process of indoctrination. Likewise, the image of the profession in West Germany—at least in the last thirty years of the twentieth century—was primarily investigative in nature, whereas it was seen as a particularly partisan profession in the East that was committed to strengthening socialism. Accordingly, about 85 percent of the journalists in 1975 belonged to the SED and still others were members of the bloc parties; on the eve of the GDR's collapse, about 90 percent of them belonged to the association of professional journalists in the GDR (the VDJ).[11] A systematic analysis of the number of unofficial employees (*Inoffizielle Mitarbeiter*, or *IM*) of the secret police—the Stasi— involved in journalism is still lacking. However, case studies related to individual papers have shown that there was probably a high percentage of *IM*s employed by the papers. Despite the close alignment of the print media with the SED, journalists had an ear to the ground in their conversations with the general population that could be useful for the security apparatus. In 1987, for example, ten of the fourteen local chief editors of the regional daily *Freie Erde* were active *IM*s.[12]

These kinds of differences were indeed manifold in divided Germany, creating a rather static contrasting image between East and West. Yet it is still very worthwhile to trace some of the similar, overarching developments that took place in both countries. For example, further explanation is needed to account for the striking fact that newspaper circulation spiked in the 1960s and 1970s in the GDR and the FRG, despite the fact that many had expected the popularity of the press to decline in the face of mounting competition coming from television. In the West, the number of papers sold daily climbed from about 15 million to over 20 million, and it remained at this high level until the fall of the Wall.[13] Between 1963 and 1988, the number of daily newspapers printed jumped from 5.8 million to 9.5 million, rising most rapidly in the 1970s.[14] On average, this meant 1.5 newspapers per household, which was twice as much as in West Germany. Parallel to this increase in circulation, a larger variety of newspapers and magazines appeared in both states. The number of popular magazine copies almost doubled in West Germany from 56 million in 1968 to 105 million in 1988.[15] In the GDR, too, this figure climbed in the 1970s and 1980s by about 25 to 50 percent, and in some cases (such as *Guter Rat*) by even 100 percent.[16] The demand for some titles was even much higher in the GDR, but a lack of paper as well as political directives generated a gap between supply and demand. On the days on which these sought-after magazines appeared, lines usually formed at the newsstands in the mornings, especially since it was sometimes impossible to get a subscription for them.

This parallel press boom cannot be put down just to cheaper prices, which had been made possible by state subsidies in the GDR and the sharply rising income from advertising in the West.[17] Rather, the shared historical heritage of the two Germanys factored into this development: both countries drew on a German newspaper and reading tradition that can be traced back to the late eighteenth century. As early as around 1900, as part of the first mass press boom, the reading of periodicals became a permanent part of leisure and everyday life in Germany. This corresponded to the predominantly Protestant culture of writing, as well as early reading ages that were generally prevalent in northern Europe. In southern Europe, on the other hand, daily newspapers never enjoyed the same popularity, even after 1945, and radio and television dominated the media landscape.[18] As a result, newspaper use was much more similar between the two German states than it was compared to respective political allies, such as Italy or Romania.

Furthermore, the press boom was connected to a politicization of the societies in East and West, but also to the development of an increasingly differentiated culture of leisure, entertainment, and consumption that ultimately had a depoliticizing effect. In particular, the politicization of society at the beginning of the 1970s corresponded to the expansion of the daily press and the weekly political magazines. The need for political information grew on both sides of the Wall just as the press became even more politically active. The rapid growth in the number of government decisions that affected the personal lives of Germans also surely played a role, as did the promise that citizens were supposed to be able to participate more in these decision-making processes. In West Germany, the growth of the daily press was followed by a rise in party and trade union membership, as well as a larger public involvement in civil society in the 1970s. Likewise, the circulation of the party papers grew alongside the membership figures for the SED and other mass organizations; the SED press ensured that new members were made aware of the official interpretations of the day's events, making it easier for people to toe the party line in official situations.[19] But, just like the growth of the SED, the increased circulation of the newspapers was part of a process controlled by the party itself. That said, the newspaper boom was also tied to a growing need for more local and regional information. In the East as well as the West, surveys showed that most people were looking for more domestic and local news that would help them navigate through daily life better.[20] Since the 1970s, a new interest in local life had accompanied the erosion of the great Utopian visions of modern society in both German states. This awarded the regional newspapers a key position because radio or television coverage of local news was spotty at best, especially when GDR residents tuned into Western stations. The local sections of the district papers in the East, which were usually only about one page in an eight-page newspaper, at least had a little room to maneuver. In some areas, the bloc party newspapers even came to play a central role because of their local reporting. Moreover, it was the non-editorial part of the papers that was often important in terms of everyday life: surveys indicated that the obituaries and the classified sections were the most read parts of the newspapers on either side of the Wall. The immense popularity of the local classifieds with their apartment ads and for sale sections, as well as the municipal affairs sections, underpinned the fast-paced boom in free papers full of ads. In 1960, the weekly circulation of these publications was about two million, but this figure had multiplied six times over by 1980.[21] Although people often made fun of their articles on local associations and dignitaries, these papers were nonetheless an expression of an increased interest and involvement in local affairs.

The press became more strongly consolidated in both Germanys, although at different points in time, which lent the regional papers with several local sections more weight. More importantly, the reasons behind this development differed; in the West, economic competition propelled this shift, while it was political directives that changed the constellation of the press landscape in the East. At the same time, both media systems responded to readers' desire for more local and regional information in addition to the primary political coverage. In 1989, for example, thirty-seven separate papers were published in the GDR, but there were 291 different local editions that included the same national coverage. From a political perspective, this consolidation was desirable because it offered a way to secure the SED's power over the interpretation of the news, to rein in differences of opinion, and to save money. Additionally, this tapped into the tradition of the Social Democratic Party (SPD) and the Communist Party of Germany (KPD) before 1933, both of which strove to establish a centralized party press. In the West, the consolidation of the press achieved a very similar level when compared to the respective population data. The number of independent papers continued to drop dramatically in the 1970s, slipping from 225 in 1953 to 124 in 1981 with 1,258 local editions; the number of newspaper publishing houses also sank by a third. On average, each editorial board published about eleven editions in the West, compared to eight in the East.[22] As a result, the number of counties in which the local paper enjoyed a monopoly increased in the West; this was already the case in a third of the local counties in the mid-1970s, but it had occurred in half of them by the time the Wall came down. The variety of the press in the West, however, was not too large concerning tabloids. Among the papers sold on the streets, the tabloid *BILD* accounted for over 80 percent of the market, and its publisher, Axel Springer, became the strongest newspaper publisher by far.

In terms of popular magazines, both the circulation figures and the number of titles doubled. Whereas the readership for city magazines and specialist magazines for different hobbies, sports, or lifestyles grew, the classic illustrated magazines lost readers. The circulation of the Hamburg-based magazine *Stern*, for example, began to decline in 1980, but some once-successful illustrated magazines such as *Bunte*, *Neue Revue*, and *Quick* had already begun to lose readers in the 1970s; some of them even disappeared entirely (including *Kristall* in 1966, and *twen* in 1971). Here, too, the growing strength of individual publishing houses, such as Burda, Bauer, or Gruner + Jahr, led to a concentration of ownership in the magazine world. Contrary to what was often assumed, it was not television that pushed many smaller publishers out of business, but rather a general process of economic consolidation, as well as the pressure created by advertising customers who preferred to invest their money in media with higher circulations. Indeed, if it had not been for tighter legal restrictions, especially the act governing press mergers from 1976, and the regular media reports of the West German government, the consolidation of the press in the Federal Republic would most likely have been even stronger.[23] At the end of the 1970s, however, a phase of stabilization set in, just as it did in the GDR. The 1980s stood for consistency in the press world, although a far-reaching restructuring process engulfed the airwaves.

Since the Kaiserreich, the German daily newspapers had been linked traditionally to individual parties or political movements. Since the Nazis destroyed most of the party papers or had assimilated them into their regime, the GDR made a radical effort to recouple the press and the party. The daily newspapers in the GDR were tightly linked to the SED, the few permitted politically independent bloc parties, and mass organizations. The SED published seventeen newspapers, while the GDR bloc parties CDU (Christian Democratic Union) and LDPD (Liberal Democratic Party of Germany) put out five, and the NDPD (National-Democratic Party of Germany) put out six smaller papers, but the content was very similar across the board. All of these papers appeared in numerous local editions. They were not present in all counties, but they were quite strong in some.[24] The content of these papers was largely determined by the respective leading journalists and political constellations.[25] But, above all, it was the news agency ADN that played a key role in the distribution of news throughout the country. Even the two papers with the highest circulation, *Neues Deutschland* and *Freie Erde,* cited the news agency as the source of almost half of their articles.[26] Characteristically, the structure of the daily press in the GDR remained extremely static in the 1970s and 1980s.

In West Germany, on the other hand, the end of the 1960s brought a politicization and polarization of the press that was part of a more fundamental transformation in the meantime. The large party papers and the press outlets that were close to specific parties collapsed in the 1960s, marking the end of a dominant German tradition that had existed since the nineteenth century. The SPD was hit particularly hard by this transition. Even in major cities such as Berlin, it either had to shut down its once popular party papers (such as *Telegraf* and *Nachtdepesche* in 1972), sell them (like the *Hamburger Morgenpost* in 1981), or, as in the case of the *Neue Hannoversche Presse,* merge with the bourgeois competition. One alternative for the SPD was to sell some of its shares in publications. This was more lucrative economically, but it also meant giving up some political influence.[27] Likewise, the 1960s also saw the decline of the confessional papers that were close to the CDU, such as *Christ und Welt* and *Rheinischer Merkur.*

At the same time, the Western press was caught up in a process of political polarization in which previously independent newspapers and magazines began to cater more closely to a particular party line.[28] While the weeklies *Die ZEIT, Der Spiegel,* and *Stern* moved closer to the SPD, the newspapers *BILD* and *FAZ,* as well as some illustrated magazines, more clearly threw their support behind the Christian Democrats. In contrast to the British (tabloid) press, they refrained from openly and directly campaigning for the parties during election, but they did lean more heavily toward political education in their reporting.[29] The tone of articles became sharper, and campaigns directed at political "opponents"—for example, against the SPD chairman and federal chancellor Willy Brandt, or the CSU chairman and minister-president of Bavaria Franz Josef Strauß—became part of the daily agenda. Correspondingly, the number of journalists who were party members also increased in the West as part of this polarization process in the 1970s. In particular, however, conservative politicians and political advisors, such as Elisabeth Noelle-Neumann, charged that since the 1970s the majority of journalists had been leaning to the left, which seemed to have influenced their reporting.[30] Others complained of the dominance of conservatives, first and foremost in the guise of the Springer publishing house.[31]

Accordingly, the neutrality and objectivity of the media was not only discussed in the GDR, but also was critically assessed in West Germany, especially in regard to the *BILD* newspaper. Books such as *Die verlorene Ehre der Katharina Blum* (*The Lost Honor of Katharina Blum*), written by the prominent author Heinrich Böll in 1974, or the undercover report *Der Aufmacher* (*Lead Story*) put together by the investigative journalist Günter Wallraff about the reckless and made-up reports written by tabloid journalists, only further fueled the emotional flames of these debates. That said, neither the readers of *BILD* nor those of *Neues Deutschland* should be underestimated. As scholars of British cultural studies have already shown in terms of the tabloid press, readers did not believe everything that was printed in these papers, but rather they filtered this information on their own, sometimes even with cynical jokes.[32]

This polarization of the media and a new kind of attachment to the political parties also appeared on the political margins in West Germany. Right-wing extremist papers, for example, were becoming more popular again in the 1970s. For instance, the radical right-wing *Deutsche National-Zeitung*, which appeared weekly, achieved six-figure sales in copies sold. It developed into a central forum and source of funding for the right-wing extremist parties such as the DVU (German People's Union) that flourished in the 1980s; the paper's publisher, Gerhard Frey, was in fact the chairman of the DVU.[33] The rise of the left-wing press was even more pronounced. *unsere zeit* which began as a Communist daily paper in 1969, achieved a circulation of about sixty thousand copies in the 1970s with the help of the SED. The *taz*, a leftist-alternative West German paper first printed in 1979, emerged from the same milieu as the Green Party, which got started around this time as well. The era of party-affiliated press outlets had not come to an end in West Germany around 1970; rather, it had developed new contours.

One of the major changes within the West German press market in the 1970s and 1980s was the sudden burst of the alternative press onto the scene. By 1980, there were already 390 leftist-alternative newspapers that sold a total of about 1.6 million copies, and the number of titles had doubled by the end of the 1980s.[34] In a certain sense, this came to resemble the formation of a social-moral milieu akin to what had taken place among the Social Democrats and the Catholics in the early Kaiserreich. Special bookstores, bars, and shops catered to these groups, as did new press outlets that created communication networks within their respective milieus. The emergence of these alternative newspapers corresponded to the growing significance attached to local politics. These papers differed fundamentally from the mainstream West German press at first, and they were definitely different than those in the GDR. Most of them were organized in a grassroots democratic way, and those involved either volunteered their time or were paid meager salaries. These papers did not really have any commercial aspirations because their goal was to promote the spread of "authentic" reports and to discuss issues from the world of their readers.[35] Accordingly, most of these papers only had a circulation of a few thousand. Nevertheless, the alternative city magazines in the major cities soon achieved five-figure readership numbers, such as *tip* and *Zitty* in Berlin, *Pflasterstrand* in Frankfurt, and *Oxmox* in Hamburg.[36] As it quickly became apparent, the readers of these papers were usually less interested in the political content than they were in the information about local events. Combined with the commercialized city magazines, however, the alternative press still reached a circulation of over seven million copies.

Meanwhile, in socialist Eastern Europe, especially in Poland, an underground press without state licenses also flourished in the 1970s. It was largely responsible for the dissemination of alternative viewpoints throughout the country.[37] Referred to as samizdat publications, these papers reached millions of readers as part of the Solidarność (Solidarity) movement. In the GDR, however, the oppositional press was not nearly as prominent as the samizdat in Poland. Over the course of the 1980s, at least a few alternative papers appeared that dealt with peace, human rights, or environmental issues, but only a few hundred copies were printed of each edition. The few smaller oppositional papers often appeared under the aegis of the church, such as the *Umweltblätter* from the Zionskirche. The only widely distributed press that remained independent from the SED was that of the church. The church had over thirty-four different papers, with a circulation of about four hundred thousand copies, but it mostly had to refrain from addressing political issues.[38] The small circulation of the oppositional papers in the GDR stemmed in part from the tight surveillance of the Stasi. The spirit of resistance also seemed to be stronger in Poland, which meant that more people wrote and read these kinds of publications. Moreover, the West German media provided a flow of information into the GDR, which ensured there was at least a partial network through which the opposition in the GDR could communicate.

This politicization of the press was also accompanied by a simultaneous process of depoliticization, indicated at first by the boom in magazines. Although these publications were still grounded in the ideology of the GDR, they nonetheless reflected the trend toward a more differentiated consumer society even within the confines of socialism. They drew lines within society, separating groups according to generation or gender, but also in terms of hobbies, interests, or lifestyles, thereby shaping preferences, norms, or certain behaviors. In general, a much smaller variety of magazines was available in the GDR, especially since this kind of differentiation was not desired and the GDR did not have a comparable consumer industry that fostered such a process. Additionally, the rising price of paper on the world market in the 1970s also put further limitations on such magazines. Nonetheless, millions of the often similar entertainment, service, and advice magazines were read in both German states. The magazines with the highest circulations in East and West Germany were television guides (such as *Hörzu* and *FF-dabei*), women's magazines (such as *Brigitte* and *Für Dich*), or illustrated entertainment news weeklies (such as *Bunte* and *Neue Berliner Illustrierte*).[39] They presented nonpolitical stars from the entertainment world, touted travel destinations, or gave advice about everyday things. In doing so, however, they could also greatly influence desires and social behaviors.[40] The illustrated weeklies and women's magazines in the GDR, for example, established role models similar to those in the West. Although they may have shown women working in technical professions, these women were usually depicted in a service setting, doing schematic work, or in a caring role. They also provided tips for fashion, the home, or handicrafts.[41] The simultaneous success of these really rather conservative women's magazines in East and West indicates just how firmly embedded traditional gender roles were at the time; they also help to explain their persistence, despite the high level of female employment in the GDR and the feminist campaigns in the West. Even magazines that were new to the scene, such as *Bild der Frau*, quickly achieved an impressive circulation of 2.5 million, but only a fraction of this number of copies were sold of the often-cited feminist magazine *Emma*. *Courage*, another feminist magazine, folded not long after it was launched.

In addition, an increased number of children's and youth magazines appeared on the market in both Germanys. Although comics had initially been dismissed in both states as American brainwashing that dulled the mind, they soon became a legitimate form of entertainment on both sides of the Wall. Corresponding magazines even appeared in the GDR, such as *Mosaik, Bummi,* and *Atze,* the latter of which had more of an ideological bent. Generally speaking, the children's and youth press in East Germany was much more political in its outlook than in West Germany. Interestingly the *Junge Welt* put out by the FDJ (Free German Youth) was the subscription magazine with the highest circulation in all of Germany in the 1980s.[42] To a certain extent, the SED permitted East German adaptations of popular cultural magazines directed at a young audience, such as the West German *Bravo*, which promoted stars, music records, and brand name items while offering advice and sex education, but without providing much political content in a strict sense. Even the highly popular monthly FDJ magazine *Neues Leben* moved beyond its political education mission to become more like *Bravo*, complete with photo stories on puberty questions and a section called "Professor Bormann explains," which was modeled after the "Dr. Sommer" Q & A section in *Bravo*; it also began to include posters, personal ads, readers' forums, and some seminude photos.[43] With a circulation of over five hundred thousand copies, *Neues Leben* was even more widespread (per capita), and it was in much higher demand. These magazines helped to bring the sexual revolution to the youth in both countries, breaking down the taboos that had surrounded homosexuality or contraception. At the same time, they introduced teenagers in the West especially, but also in the East, to a generation-specific consumer and music culture, although the political subtext never disappeared in the GDR.

The "do-it-yourself" trend also made its way into the magazine market in the two German states in the 1970s. Garden work, cooking, and handicrafts became more significant again in this era of automation. Their revival accompanied a process of individualization within daily life as well as the formation of new shared lifestyles. In the West, these advice-giving publications were linked to new sales techniques developed by the consumer industry (including home and garden stores, fashion chains, and supermarkets) and the production of nondurable, modular products (such as IKEA furniture).[44] Although the GDR lacked such a huge selection of products, the magazines still gave ideas about how to make something creative and new out of the resources that were available, and they also praised the value of goods made in the GDR. Simultaneously, these magazines bridged classic social divides on both sides of the Wall, in part through "special interest" formats. Such special interest groups were addressed in the GDR, for example, in the guise of magazines such as *Der Modelleisenbahner* for model train hobbyists, *Wohnen im Grünen* for gardeners, and *Der Hund* for dog lovers. In West Germany, free magazines and those put out by associations grew to be the most popular in terms of circulation; magazines such as the *Apotheken Rundschau*, which was handed out in pharmacies, or the *ADAC-Motorwelt*, which went to all the members of the ADAC automobile club (akin to AAA in the United States) also became influential lobby publications within "consumer democracy." The power of these rather apolitical magazines in East and West rested on their ability to shape social norms and desires.

Journalists as Intermediaries between East and West

Fundamental changes also occurred in the realm of communication between the two German states at the beginning of the 1970s. Until 1973, there were no permanent West German correspondents in the GDR, although GDR journalists were allowed to report from West Germany. Western reports on the GDR mostly came from official sources, but also sometimes from statements made by GDR citizens that had been smuggled out of the country. Direct journalistic reporting by Western journalists about the GDR, such as the famous "Reise in ein fernes Land" (A Trip to a Faraway Country), published by three journalists from *Die ZEIT* in 1964, was still an exception rather than the rule.[45] The GDR feared critique and espionage attempts if it formally accredited West German journalists, while West Germany was worried that such a move might boost the image of the GDR and work in favor of official diplomatic recognition for the GDR. As media coverage expanded around the globe, gaining new momentum through satellite-supported live television, the refusal of the GDR to admit Western journalists did in fact prove to be detrimental to the country's efforts to achieve international recognition.

The multifaceted control of the media by the SED was never limited to only the domestic side of things because the party always kept a close eye on the image of the GDR abroad.[46] It was continually plagued by the fear that countries in the West would snap up any inconsistent reports or even critique coming from inside the GDR. Moreover, in contrast to West Germany, the GDR sent hardly any correspondents abroad, with the exception of the news agency ADN and *Neues Deutschland*, which only served to further isolate the GDR in the eyes of the world.

Around 1970, the GDR became increasingly aware of the fact that it was cutting itself off from the West German public as well as the rest of the globe. As part of the Basic Treaty that was signed in 1972, both sides agreed to give journalists the right of freedom of information and reporting. Furthermore, the establishment of the Department for Journalistic Relations at the beginning of the 1970s and an International Press Center in 1977 were part of a concerted effort on behalf of the GDR to increase its presence abroad.[47] As part of this move, almost twenty West German journalists were accredited in East Berlin; as of 1973, only four GDR journalists were working in West Germany: two from the ADN, one from the radio and one from *Neues Deutschland* (which further underscores the lesser status of the other newspapers).[48] There were also West German travel correspondents who applied for permission to enter the country to report on specific events. The GDR required the correspondents from the West to pay dearly for their East German offices and to establish a permanent residence in the GDR—without a doubt so that they could keep better tabs on them while also underscoring the status of the GDR as a separate state. When these reporters had questions, they were initially only allowed to contact the Department for Journalistic Relations at the Ministry of Foreign Affairs, but as of 1976, they were also permitted to contact the individual press offices. They could not move freely within the country. Travel outside of East Berlin had to be cleared ahead of time, and most of the time someone was assigned to accompany them on these officially registered trips. In 1979, these restrictions were tightened even further after a series of reports appeared about protests. The Stasi, of course, had kept a close eye on the West German correspondents in the country from the very beginning.[49]

In terms of daily life, however, these journalists usually just went about normal business. Many of the West German correspondents emphasized in interviews as well as in their memoirs that they had not faced many difficulties living in the GDR.[50] It was easier and less obvious for print journalists to move among the public than for television journalists, whose cameras attracted attention. As an analysis of the content of the reports on the GDR in two West German newspapers in 1987/88 revealed, their articles often covered topics such as the church and opposition movements, as well as attempts to flee across the border or emigrate.[51] The correspondents saw themselves as intermediaries between East and West because they established a joint public space. Rather early on, for example, they were also referred to as "diplomats in shirtsleeves," because they acted as political and cultural mediators between the two German states.[52] At the same time, many of the West German journalists tested the boundaries of their journalistic freedom by publishing articles that the SED deemed to be too critical—for example, a report about the forced adoptions of *Republikflüchtlingen* (political refugees) that appeared in *Der Spiegel* in 1975. The GDR did in fact expel five correspondents in the first decade, and the office of *Der Spiegel* in East Berlin remained closed from 1978 to 1985. It was not until the run-up to Erich Honecker's official visit to West Germany in 1987 that the situation became less tense for reporters in the East.

The West German correspondents played a key role for the opposition movements in the GDR in the 1970s and 1980s. Their information and their reports often referred back to the churches and dissidents, and the journalists tested the reaction of the SED to what they were saying. Moreover, these journalists sought to strengthen dissident groups by acting as a protective shield, but sometimes these efforts backfired.[53] The correspondents smuggled texts and documents, as well as photos and films, from dissidents back to the West, where they were then published with a GDR audience in mind. For example, the East German photographer Ludwig Rauch, who had been banned from publishing since 1986, secretly sold his images in West Germany, and they then appeared without his knowledge in magazines such as *Stern*. The Stasi was aware of these practices, but generally tolerated them at times in the 1980s.

For the most part, the West German correspondents wrote about political affairs related to German-German relations that therefore affected the FRG. They tended to ignore aspects of everyday life in the GDR, perhaps because it seemed to be rather static, which made it anything but newsworthy in the West.[54] Despite conversations with the churches and dissidents, their main sources of information remained the GDR media and official SED statements. Furthermore, the West German correspondents did not have a monopoly on the reporting on the GDR because their reports were often augmented with information coming from foreign news agencies.

In reverse, West Germany became less significant for the GDR press. Most of their articles were primarily designed to sing the praises of their own society and that of their socialist brothers. The percentage of articles covering the West in general in the two most important SED papers, *Neues Deutschland* and *Junge Welt*, sank to just 20 percent, whereas the FRG accounted for only about 5 percent of the news reports. In terms of content, most of these reports on the West were critical in tone. Nevertheless, the critique of West Germany in *Neues Deutschland* and *Junge Welt* actually declined in the mid-1980s.[55] Quite apparently, Honecker's planned state visit as well as the tighter socioeconomic entanglements between the two Germanys had begun to have an effect on the media coverage.

Television and Radio before 1989

Although it was strictly prohibited to import newspapers and magazines from the West into the GDR, which minimized the influence of these print media outlets, it was much more difficult for the GDR to keep radio and television programming out of the country by virtue of the fact that radio waves pay no respect to national borders. For this reason, there were probably not many areas in which the asymmetrical entanglements between the two German states were as strong as in the case of radio and television. Of course, this "spillover"—which referred to the ability to receive radio and television programs from neighboring countries—was not specific to the case of divided Germany. But, it had a particular significance within the context of the German-German rivalry because there were no language or cultural barriers that had to be overcome. Both sides therefore made a huge effort to reach the population on the other side of the Wall, and both feared that the propaganda coming from the other side might prove to be too successful.[56] In the 1960s, West Germany sought to dampen the harmful influence of GDR television, for example, by extending its television coverage into the morning hours and broadcasting this television programming along the border with the GDR via special facilities designed for this purpose. Given that many West Germans could not even receive this programming on their televisions, the primary goal was to reach the shift workers in the GDR; a separate morning program was first set up for the West in 1981.[57] Until the early 1970s, the GDR had also broadcasted radio channels that targeted the West German population, including its *Deutschlandsender, Deutscher Soldatensender,* and *Freiheitssender 904*.[58] At the same time, it did not quit jamming the popular American RIAS radio station until the fall of 1978. It apparently did so because this stood in the way of the efforts of the GDR to achieve international recognition, but also because the effort to keep this up heavily outweighed the effects.[59]

What could be offered on cross-border radio and how it was used differed between East and West. The way in which the country was divided worked in favor of the West: the FRG had a broadcasting location right in the middle of the GDR—in West Berlin—which made it easier to supply the northern portion of the GDR in particular with Western television and radio programming. Moreover, thanks to the long length of the border in the south, it was basically possible to receive West German signals almost everywhere in the GDR. It was only difficult to pick up Western terrestrial signals in some smaller areas in the northeast and around Dresden (or the signal was weak, which meant the picture quality was poor), which lent this region the nickname "valley of the unaware."

On the other side of the Wall, it was really only possible to receive GDR television in West Germany relatively close to the border; even the GDR radio stations had difficulty penetrating the farther away regions in the south and west of the Federal Republic. Nonetheless, East German radio signals could be received across about half of West Germany and in the major metropolitan areas such as Hamburg or the Ruhr Valley.

This imbalance between East and West was also evident in technical infrastructure, the number of programs offered, and broadcasting times.[60]

Figure 11.1. Technical Coverage of Radio DDR I in West Germany, Medium Wave, Daytime, 1975 (BArch DM 3/14391)

Consequently, all the efforts made by the SED leadership to convince the population to turn off the whisperings of the class enemy, even with repressive means, were not very successful in the end. Although it was taboo to track the TV ratings for West German programs in the GDR, their immense popularity can still be determined indirectly. For example, the GDR's own statistics indicated that only one-third of the GDR population still watched the main East German evening television programming in 1982,[61] which indirectly implies that an average of approximately 20 to 25 percent tuned into West German prime time television.[62] Accordingly, by the 1970s and 1980s at the latest, it appears to have become quite natural for large portions of the GDR population to complement their East German media intake with West German media content. The situation in the West was different, though. Although about half of West Germans could listen to at least one East German radio station if they wanted to even in the 1950s and 1960s, only a small majority occasionally tuned in to these channels. East German talk radio also had a very negative image in West Germany.[63] Indeed, the Germans seemed to belong to a "common radio and TV nation" from an East German perspective more so than from a West German one, although West German programming was in fact the common denominator between the two.[64]

Over the course of the 1970s and 1980s, the attempts to influence the population on the other side of the Wall decreased in both Germanys. There were only a few West German radio and television programs, such as the highly conservative show *ZDF Magazine* with Gerhard Löwenthal (1969–1987), that dealt offensively with the GDR. For the most part, their programming was directed exclusively at the West German population. Over the course of the 1970s, the GDR discontinued its radio propaganda aimed at the West, it quit jamming the West German stations, and it mostly stopped using repressive measures to crack down on receiving signals from the West. As the new head of the GDR, Erich Honecker even issued a public statement to the effect that everyone could "tune into or turn off West German television as they wished."[65] Yet, the attempts to establish a political line of demarcation between the two countries and to immunize the population against external propaganda never disappeared entirely in the GDR. This was reflected, for example, in the continued production of the program *Der Schwarze Kanal* with Karl-Eduard von Schnitzler until the fall of 1989. This show was designed to immunize East Germans against the influence of West German TV by commenting on snippets taken from West German programming.

In the 1980s, the GDR even tolerated satellite receivers that had been built secretly by local groups in order to be able to receive private West German television channels.[66] Although the overarching organs of the state and the party initially tried to crack down on this practice and to remove receivers that had been set up without permission, the Politburo caved in during the summer of 1988 and liberalized the process for getting a license for satellite receivers. It feared the potential for major conflict in light of the increased number of prominent cases. From this point on, there were no longer any legal provisions that stood in the way of East Germans watching television from the FRG, not even in the areas in which terrestrial signals could not be picked up.[67] The failure of the GDR's efforts to achieve demarcation in terms of the media certainly had to do with detente politics, but it was also very much the result of media innovations, as well as technical and, not least, social dynamics.

The rise of television as the new main media form contributed significantly to these processes. By the mid-1970s, almost every household in West Germany owned a television set (95 percent); in East Germany, 80 percent of households had a television at this point as well.[68] As a result, radio became more like background noise that ran throughout the day, and movie theaters suffered under a massive lack of visitors, especially from among the older population groups.[69] For more and more Germans, watching television became a permanent part of the evening ritual. Not without reason, then, political interest in television increased in both German states, but this manifested itself in very different ways. In the GDR, the political character of mass media was taken for granted, but as of the 1960s, the influence of the SED on television grew considerably.[70] This could be seen, for example, in the creation of a central television supervisory body (Staatliches Komitee für Fernsehen) in 1968, although this kind of centralized, tight direction and control by the SED did not differ fundamentally from that of other media.[71]

The public radio stations in West Germany had also functioned as a stage for partisan political power plays after the Allies withdrew from the country. The political intervention directed at television in West Germany also increased in the 1960s, and it primarily targeted the new journalistic formats that took a critical stance on politics, such as *Panorama*.[72] In the 1970s, this interference took on a new dimension as the public radio and television stations were systematically drawn into the fight between the political camps to control television reporting in the country. These battles were not limited to creating scandals over individual people or programs, but rather developed a structural character. In light of the wave of RAF terrorism, the new *Ostpolitik*, and the economic crisis, political polarization generally increased in West Germany after the grand coalition dissolved in 1969. Moreover, a growing number of conflicts began to erupt over personnel decisions in the supervisory boards of the different stations.[73] Political "equilibrium"[74] became the phrase of the day, and especially the conservative side began to demand more equity in what were sometimes denunciating campaigns.⁷⁵ The fee for radio and television that was set by the government proved to be a key way to exercise political pressure on the stations, especially because the expansion of television programming, and color TV in particular, was very expensive, which meant that it could not be financed through the limited advertising income of the stations alone. The conservative camp's attempt to smash the large public broadcasting station in the north, the NDR, failed in 1980 merely for formal legal reasons.

Ultimately, this contest for political influence over radio and television in West Germany led to structural changes with far-reaching consequences after the government changed hands in 1982, namely the opening of the field to private radio and television companies. When the private television channels PKS (which was later renamed as SAT.1) and RTL-plus started in January 1984 (initially as part of a regional and temporary "pilot cable project"), it put an end to the monopoly of non-commercial radio and television programming. Despite the resistance of the Social Democrats and the churches, who warned of the dangers of private channels to the bitter end, there was no turning back.⁷⁶ In addition to the Christian Democrats, it was primarily the publishing and advertising sectors that had campaigned for commercial programming, which was a source of potential profit for these branches. But it was actually more the availability of new distribution technology such as broadband cable and satellite television offering additional transmission options that made it seem necessary to expand the number of channels in the country.⁷⁷

The political influence on radio broadcasting, and in particular on television as the then leading medium, was articulated in the plural and federal political system of the Federal Republic in a proportional manner via negotiation between the political camps. It differed according to the concrete political constellations in each federal state. In particular, personnel management functioned as a kind of preemptive form of programming policy. Furthermore, there was an important corrective in place to counteract such practices, namely the judgments on radio and television cases that had been passed down by the Federal Constitutional Court since 1961. Consequently, the type and scope of political influence over these media differed fundamentally from the situation in the centralized GDR, where it was virtually set in stone that the media was supposed to function as an instrument for securing the SED's monopoly on power. Despite the consistency of this point, however, the system through which the party controlled these media did adapt to changing circumstances that came about in the GDR. Yet, there was no liberalization involved in this process. Rather, the state's control of the media only seemed to increase in the 1970s and 1980s.[78]

However, both systems did share in the assumption that the media had a very strong influence on the population, which could affect political opinions and voting behavior. Accordingly, media content was seen as a guarantee or danger for the respective claims to power, which made it seem worthwhile, if not downright necessary, to have as much control as possible over this input. Both systems therefore still rested on the traditional assumption that the "masses" could be manipulated, which had first emerged at the end of the nineteenth century as a critical reaction against the societalization (*Vergesellschaftung*) of politics.[79]

Additionally, a major change also occurred in radio and television across the system divide in the 1970s and 1980s at the level of production and programming. It can best be described as an adaptation to the primary desires of audiences for entertainment and light consumer programming. In television, the trend toward more programming options and longer on-air times continued. A second television channel appeared in the GDR in 1969, for instance, although it only aired for a rather meager four hours a day at first, and mostly offered reruns or educational programming. After the launch of color television in West Germany in the summer of 1967, color TV also came to the GDR with the introduction of the second TV station, but not without a clear element of demarcation: rather than adopting the Western PAL technical norm, the GDR opted for the French SECAM system that was also used in the Soviet Union, which meant that West German television could only be watched in black and white in East Germany without an extra decoder. The dire financial situation in the GDR, however, made it impossible to provide the funds for the second channel to offer a full array of programming.[80]

A second channel had already been introduced in the FRG in 1961, followed by a number of regional public television channels over the course of the 1960s that had also developed into full-coverage channels. A separate morning television program was introduced in 1981 in the West, and the daily on-air time for the main two public television stations as well as the GDR station was about fourteen hours in the 1980s. This programming expansion made it more difficult for the stations to fill the time with their own productions. Consequently, channels soon developed into distribution outlets that often chose the less expensive option of buying the rights for movies or foreign television shows rather than going to the expense of developing their own productions.

The resulting dependence on the international acquisitions market fostered the commercialization and internationalization of television programming. In particular, series from the United States and England often aired on West German television, and a similar development—although more latent—also took place in the GDR. As early as the 1970s, the percentage of imported television series from Western Europe and America broadcast on East German television was about 40 percent. By the end of the 1980s, there were more U.S. productions being aired in the GDR than television films from the Soviet Union.[81] In the 1970s, the direct contacts and program trading between the GDR and West Germany also began to increase. In particular, film rights were sold across the border in both directions, especially since the GDR moved into the synchronization market on a massive scale at the end of the 1980s in order to draw more foreign currency into the country.[82] The exchange of news images, however, went only one way: the socialist states consistently drew much of their image material from the Western Eurovision network, but the (carefully selected) images offered by the Eastern Intervision did not attract much interest in the West.[83]

The preferences of viewers, in contrast, did not differ all that much between East and West. On both sides of the Wall, mysteries, sports, films, and entertainment shows were very popular, just as they were in other European industrialized states. Accordingly, media use was more heavily influenced by the need for relaxation and balance in both countries than by the respective political systems. Moreover, East and West Germans shared an interest in "as little news and information as seemed to be necessary,"[84] as well as a desire for counseling and orientation, which was also offered by the similarly popular service shows. Interestingly, the GDR public turned its back even more on "hard" political content in the 1980s than ever before: the viewer quotas for the main news show *Aktuelle Kamera* sank from around 15 percent in the 1970s to not more than 10 percent in the decade that followed, and far fewer tuned into *Der Schwarze Kanal*.[85] Young people in particular seemed to be distancing themselves from GDR television coverage. As indicated by GDR research surveys in the 1980s, they clearly showed a preference for media from the West, even for political information, while the credibility of the GDR media continued to drop.[86]

The increasing popularity of entertainment shows was also reflected in the growth in the number of series and genre productions in both Germanys. The public competitors ARD and ZDF, for example, added more mysteries, westerns, and science fiction series, as well as movies, to their evening line-ups from the 1970s onward. Faced with the prospect of the competition that was going to come from private television, they tried to preempt potential losses in ratings by airing American series such as *Dallas* (which ARD began broadcasting in 1982) and *Dynasty* (which had been shown on ZDF from 1983). The silent competition of ARD and ZDF led to extensive programming reforms in the GDR in 1971/72, as well as in 1982/83, which included a noticeable increase in entertainment shows that were clearly modeled after Western formats. In particular, the programming schedules were aligned with those of West German television. The airing times for journalistic shows, for example, were shifted so that they would not have to compete with entertainment programming on the Western airwaves.[87]

The East German leaders were well aware of the threat that this convergence with Western television posed for the country. They sought to avoid these dangers by keeping "hard politics" in the form of news programs such as *Aktuelle Kamera* firmly on a course of demarcation directed against West Germany. At the same time, they also experimented with new formats in the 1970s that tried to use Western lifestyles as a cover for politically correct messages, such as on the FDJ program *RUND*.[88]

Similar trends can also be detected in radio programming. The advent of television forced radio to become an easily consumable companion to daily life that offered smaller programming bits, such as short news updates, journalistic pieces, or "service coverage" with weather and traffic information. Simultaneously, radio formats appeared that catered to the popular culture and music interests of different target groups, such as teenagers; these included the GDR's *DT 64* that hit the air in 1964 and the West German *RIAS Treffpunkt* that got going in 1968, as well as *Pop Shop* (SWF, from 1970).[89] Although it has always been cheaper to produce radio programs than television, commercialization nonetheless came to radio due to the growing demand for catchy pop music programming. Stations could not produce enough music on their own to keep these programs running over the long term, which meant that they had to pay considerable sums in licensing fees. There were also attempts to limit the amount of pop music being aired in both German states. In the West, for example, the so-called "record wars" erupted in 1965 in which the ARD radio stations boycotted current albums, and pop music was only played every now and then on these stations in the following years.[90] The GDR, on the other hand, had already introduced the infamous "60/40 rule" in 1958 that dictated that 60 percent of the songs played on the radio had to come from the Eastern Bloc. Cultural and political resentments mixed with economic considerations in both cases. For example, this was a way for the GDR to limit expenditures in foreign currency. In the 1970s and 1980s, however, the radio formats that catered to youth culture (as well as the service stations) could no longer avoid playing British and American pop music. Over the long term, it was impossible for radio in both West and East Germany to avoid playing by the rules of the game in the increasingly international music industry.[91]

Even before commercial radio and television got started in both German states, entertainment and listener preferences had already become more important. This trend had appeared across different countries relatively early in radio before reaching television as well. As a result, both countries had to rely on foreign productions. The practical constraints associated with this led to tighter webs of German-German entanglements in the form of programming exchanges—despite the fundamental opposition between the two systems.

In West Germany, this development fit right in within the liberal consumer society that had emerged, and it was even forced through commercial radio. The GDR, in contrast, went on the defensive. For all intents and purposes, it had opened itself up to the capitalist consumer culture of the West, and it was being measured according to it. But this consumerism contradicted the core of its political agenda, despite the fact that it could not even keep up with the West. Radio and television developed across the system divide—at least from the perspective of the recipients—into consumer goods as well as powerful agents of consumer society. Consequently, they ultimately undermined the political ideal of real socialism.

In 1984, the first private television channels started airing in West Germany, but this year hardly represented much of a break with the past for most contemporaries. At first, these channels appeared only within the framework of temporary pilot projects with a limited spatial scope. Furthermore, the installation of the necessary cable wires that were needed as the technical foundation to support private cable television did not go according to plan. The interest of the population in getting cable connections lagged far behind initial expectations.[92] Accordingly—and not least because of the extremely high level of investment required—the financial situations of the private channels remained difficult for a long time. RTL-plus was the first to make a profit in 1992, followed by Pro 7 in the mid-1990s. They had been saved only by the fact that they had been given terrestrial frequencies, which was not intended originally.[93] The high losses suffered by private television at the beginning fostered a consolidation process, ultimately leaving only two private television conglomerates to compete with the public TV channels. Both of these private groups had their roots in print media: in addition to RTL/Bertelsmann, there was the SAT.1 Group that was primarily owned by Springer-Verlag and the film rights agent Leo Kirch. They offered scheduled television that was financed through commercials so that little, in fact, remained of the vision of interactive communication that had played such a considerable role in the debates over private TV (with the notable exception of the not so popular "open channels"). Attempts to establish a profitable form of pay TV as in other European countries failed at first in the face of the strong competition from free TV. Indeed, this pointed to the limits of commercialization, as well as the still strong position of public radio and television.

The Transformation of the Media since 1989

The media contributed to the collapse of Communism and the fall of the Berlin Wall. Its most important function over the long term had been to build the bridges of communication across the Wall, connecting Eastern Europe with the West in a way that trumped propaganda while fostering other social expectations. The reforms propagated by Gorbachev under the name Glasnost also affected the media as of 1987; media outlets were supposed to become more transparent and more truthful, which might have served to improve the government's control over society. The veil that was drawn over the nuclear accident at Chernobyl was an important catalyst behind this move. Not only were many residents within the Communist realm outraged at the way in which the media downplayed the situation, but also Gorbachev himself.[94]

The way in which the freedom of the press was introduced shortly thereafter, however, did not follow the same pattern throughout Eastern Europe. In Hungary, for example, the press was already given more freedom in 1986, and the license requirement was lifted in the summer of 1989. Likewise, the Polish dissent paper *Gazeta Wyborcza* became legal in May of 1989. Especially in Hungary and Estonia, journalists sought a critical dialog with the state; meanwhile, it seemed as if a "tele-revolution" had taken place in Romania because the first Hungarian TV reports and the then live images of Ceaușescu broadcast in Romania expedited the protests against the government.[95] The media in Czechoslovakia meanwhile remained loyal to the state for quite a while. The East German media was also not a main instigator in the events of 1989, although the often-cited youth network DT 64 had reported earlier about the protests, and it had broadcasted cassettes made by East German bands that played unconventional music.[96] Even as late as the beginning of October 1989, the GDR press still referred to the demonstrators on the streets as "Rowdies" from the West who had infiltrated the country. The East German papers did not print critical letters to the editor or even critical reporting until masses of people were protesting in the streets and Honecker resigned.

West German television, however, played a key role in the collapse of the GDR.[97] It kept the first German protesters informed about similar actions taking place, thereby further promoting the demonstrations.

Simultaneously, the West German cameras served as a shield against a "Chinese solution" with a violent crackdown. In particular on 9 November, the West German news fueled the flames of the announcement of the freedom to travel that pushed East Germans to the border, tearing down the Wall earlier than had been planned.

As the Berlin Wall collapsed, a transformation also set in within the East German media. In order to regain credibility, it began to report more openly about protests and grievances within the country. On 4 November 1989, GDR television broadcasted live coverage of a four-hour demonstration at Alexanderplatz, and the number of viewers who tuned into *Aktuelle Kamera* skyrocketed. Beginning at the end of October, programs such as *Prisma* or *Elf 99* also fostered the collapse of the SED with investigative reports about scandals, such as the luxurious lives of the Politburo members living in a forest community near Wandlitz.[98] The viewers of these programs were intensely involved in this transformation of the media: some television discussions prompted almost fifty thousand people to call in,[99] and the larger daily newspapers received about six hundred letters to the editor each day as part of a dialog about the reforms.[100]

In addition, structural reforms were made after the Wall came down. Beginning in mid-November, the SED newspapers dismissed their editors-in-chief, and the editorial boards promoted either the deputy editors or section editors to these highest posts. The papers gradually loosened themselves from the SED, and then later the PDS (Party of Democratic Socialism), from January 1990 onward, which led them to seek partners in the West to make up for the missing state subsidies. They sought to build up the trust of the population by offering the newly established opposition parties space on their pages to introduce themselves. Likewise, the papers started to change their names to better relate to their cities or regions: *Freie Erde* (Free Earth), for example, became *Nordkurier* (Northern Courier), while *Das Volk* (The People) turned into *Thüringer Allgemeine* (Thuringian General). This was symptomatic of the shifting outlook in the East that focused strongly on the construction of regional identities.

Since the early 1990s, West German publishing houses had tried to gain a foothold in the East German media market. This was not something specific to East Germany; rather, it was characteristic of all of Central Europe. It also corresponded with the general trend toward internationalized media companies that had set in at the end of the 1980s in the West. The WAZ Group, for example, had already acquired almost half of the Austrian newspaper with the highest circulation, *Neue Kronen Zeitung*, in 1987, while Springer-Verlag became involved in Austria's *Standard* newspaper. After 1990, the governments in the postsocialist states sought to steer this process to their own ends. The conservative government that came to power in Hungary, for example, gave preference to conservative companies in the privatization process, which made it easier for Axel Springer to buy up a number of media outlets in the country.[101]

At the beginning of the 1990s, even the circulation figures for the most popular GDR papers plummeted. Sales of daily newspapers had already fallen in 1990 by a third, to under six million copies. While the highest circulation dailies, *Neues Deutschland* and *Junge Welt*, were able to keep their heads above water due to their association with the PDS, the number of copies sold sank rapidly. Not surprisingly, two-thirds of the country's newspapers also disappeared in the first three years.[102] What did come as a shock, however, was that larger publications such as *Neue Berliner Illustrierte* and *Für Dich* were not able to stay afloat. Other successful popular publications, such as the TV magazine *FF dabei*, the entertainment weekly *Wochenpost*, and the women's magazine *Sybille*, also caved in the mid-1990s, although the employees of the latter did make a last-ditch effort to save it by taking it over.

The rapid collapse of these publications can be explained in part by the hike in their sales prices, especially after the currency union took place and the state subsidies fell away. Even the West German Communist newspaper *Die Wahrheit*, which was financed with SED support, closed down at the end of 1989, and the DKP daily *unsere zeit* from Neuss only survived without subsidies from the SED in the form of a small weekly paper. The East German press also had difficulties adjusting to the West German distribution system. But the main reason behind the collapse of the East German press was the influx of long-desired newspapers and magazines from the West into the East as of 1990. For a short time around 1990, a colorful mix of old SED publications, newly created press outlets of the East German opposition and West German publishers, and established West German media circulated throughout the former GDR. The high number of copies of West German publications sold at first expressed the great desire of East Germans to catch up with the West, whether it be in terms of politics and entertainment or erotic magazines such as *Playboy* because pornography had been prohibited in the GDR.

The great variety of media offerings in the East peaked in early 1991 before it began to decrease dramatically. A rapid process of media consolidation occurred as the transformation of socialist society gained momentum. Many of the media outlets were bought out by West German publishing houses, but journalism and media use remained particularly East German. Four major West German publishers—Bauer, Burda, Gruner + Jahr, and Springer—were especially successful in buying out

East German media through the Treuhand (trust agency) and establishing new publications; the WAZ Group was also quite successful on the daily newspaper market. The fifteen SED district newspapers with the highest circulation were particularly sought-after by West German publishers. The Kartellamt determined, however, that each publishing house could take over only one SED district paper, but these newspapers nonetheless usually achieved a much stronger dominance over the regional markets compared to the West. The bloc parties' press outlets were also quickly bought out: the FAZ Group purchased many of the bloc-CDU papers, while Springer snapped up the NDPD outlets. The news agency ADN was sold to the Deutscher Depeschendienst (ddp), which was renamed ddp/ADN in the 1990s, and the ADN image service Zentralbild went to the Deutsche Presse Agentur (dpa). The media landscape in reunified Germany thus fell almost entirely into the hands of West German publishers.

That said, however, the media landscapes in East and West since the 1990s have still differed from one another over the long term. With the continued dominance of the ex-SED regional press, fundamental structures of the GDR media system have remained in place. This has often been criticized as "privatization by oligopolies," which has preserved the GDR districts as spaces of communication, leaving hardly any room for national or local papers.[103] Indeed, as of the mid-1990s, the former district newspapers still accounted for over 90 percent of the newspapers sold in the former GDR.[104] Their subscriber bases and regional anchoring, as well as their publishing and printing facilities, gave them a decided advantage over the few newly established papers and the smaller publications put out by the bloc parties. Furthermore, their content was also a better fit for their readership than that of many of the new papers or those imported from the West.

The number of separate editorial offices with a full staff therefore sank rapidly in East Germany as early as 1992, even dropping below the GDR level. But, it was not only East German papers that failed after 1990; many newly established West German papers never really got their feet on the ground in the East. Even in Berlin, where many Western publishers optimistically started new papers with lofty goals of taking advantage of the high population density within the city, several of these foundling papers soon died off. The Burda/Murdoch venture with a new tabloid paper *Super!* failed after just a year, despite the fact that they had hired journalists from *BILD* and fed into East German resentments against the West. On its second day, in a much-cited lead story, the paper proclaimed, "Poser Wessi beat to death with a beer bottle. . . . All of Bernau is happy that he is dead."[105] In contrast, the ex-SED paper that the conglomerate bought, *Berliner Zeitung*, was able to hold its own. But they were never able to turn it into a real national paper for the capital, and even today it is still most successful in East Berlin. The journalistic gap was particularly prominent in Berlin. *BILD*, for example, began printing two additions, one for Berlin-West and one for Berlin-East/Brandenburg, both of which catered to the different views and demands of their respective readers in the years that followed.[106] Even financial papers such as *Capital* and *Wirtschaftswoche* produced separate editions for the East. Among the newly established publications, it was primarily the city magazines that survived thanks to the upswing in regional identity formation.

Not only the media landscape and media content, but also the use of media differed between East and West in the 1990s and differs even still today. News magazines such as *Der Spiegel* hardly sold in the East, and the same held true for upper-middle-class lifestyle magazines such as *Geo* or *Cosmopolitan*.[107] East Germans also tuned in to the critical political journalism shows on public television less frequently, preferring the tabloid programs on private television or the regional East German channel MDR. This pointed not only to a specific East German identity-building process, but also to a media-based demarcation directed against the old FRG.

Advice and counseling formats held their ground in the magazine sector, which also reflected a traditional, crisis-related use of media. For example, the magazine *Guter Rat* (Good Advice), which first appeared as a women's magazine in East Germany in 1945 and then continued as an advice magazine, still exists; after 1990, it survived in the form of a consumer magazine in East Germany published by West German companies. Humor also continued to differ between East and West: the satire magazine *Eulenspiegel* has continued to be the East German counterpart to the West German *Titanic*, just as the East German *Mosaik* has held its own against the Disney comics of the West. The illustrated magazine *Superillu* in particular has reflected the ongoing differences in taste between East and West. This weekly, put out by the Burda Verlag, has advertised that it is read by a fifth of East Germans, which is more than *Der Spiegel, Fokus, Stern,* and *Bunte* all together. It succeeded with a mix of specifically East German celebrity news, advice columns, and entertainment, thereby contributing to the solidification of a special East German consciousness. In turn, it also fostered the success of the PDS.

Several studies from the 1990s show that the East German daily papers strengthened a specific East German identity. The press often wrote from an East German perspective, including attempts to point blame at "the West." Especially the former SED newspapers commented frequently on the problems that had resulted from reunification in the eyes of East Germans, such as unemployment; they drew a clear line of demarcation vis-à-vis the West, but they neglected to point out the links between these issues and the troubles that had plagued the GDR economy. Articles in these press outlets also tended to divide East and West Germany more often into the old and the new federal states, but these distinctions were not made as often in the press in the former West,[108] mostly because they tended to ignore the East altogether.

There were also differences in international news coverage in East and West. The East German media did not offer as much international reporting as its counterpart in the West in the mid-1990s. It focused more often on Eastern Europe, whereas West German newspapers continued to offer more coverage of topics related to the West and what was then termed the Third World.[109] Likewise, the media in East and West also adopted different tones in their respective judgments. The newspapers in the East more frequently just repeated statements without adding much critical commentary of their own. This can be interpreted as part of a style left over from GDR times, but it also reflects a conscious effort to exercise political restraint in light of the political transformations taking place. In exchange, the East German press tended to offer more practical advice for life, especially the former SED outlets.[110]

This not only had to do with readers' expectations and the traditions of the respective papers, but also the social structure of the journalist community. In light of the new constellations of ownership, accusations that the newspapers were hiring only West German journalists quickly spread in East Germany. Yet, in actuality, there was a high level of continuity in personnel, despite the fact that most of the East German journalists prior to 1989 had been members of the SED and had served as a mouthpiece for the party for a long time. Personnel changes were made primarily at the highest levels, but these firings hardly affected editorial staff. The editors-in-chief of the SED district papers were switched out at the end of 1989, but they were almost entirely replaced by successors who came from within their own editorial ranks. According to statistics from the time, about half of these new editors-in-chief remained in charge in the years that followed.[111] Around 70 percent of the employees in the main former GDR papers stayed on, while only about 30 percent of the journalists who went to work for a few newly established publications were from the GDR. As surveys indicated, about 60 percent of journalists who were working in East Germany before the fall of the Wall were still employed as journalists in 1992, and only a fifth came from the West. Similarly, only about a fourth of the editors-in-chief were West Germans.[112] Among these journalists, there was not much self-critical reflection on the past, and the differences between them and their colleagues from the West were often still considerable. It should be noted, however, that the West

German publishers were also not very interested in working through the GDR past.[113]

Studies on journalists in East and West have detected numerous similarities in self-identification between the two groups based on surveys from the 1990s, but they have also identified noticeable differences. East German journalists, for example, saw themselves more idealistically as advisors and educators, and they were more sensitive in dealing with the upheavals in the East in their work.[114] West German journalists—who had been strongly affected by the ghost of the *Spiegel* affair—were more likely to break rules in order to get information; the East Germans saw themselves more as advocates for the disadvantaged.[115] These differences between East and West also appeared in local journalism. The local sections of the newspapers in the East were smaller, but the service sections were more extensive; in the former district papers, moreover, criticism was mostly voiced only through quotes from third parties.[116] Content analyses have criticized that these papers made local affairs less transparent and that they concentrated on political officials. The lack of willingness to participate in politics in East Germany may in part explain this development.[117] Comparative studies of postsocialist countries in Central Europe have come to the conclusion that the media in these countries also tended to rely more heavily on official sources after 1990 as well.[118]

Additionally, the lack of variety within the press landscape in East Germany has been discussed critically since the beginning of the 1990s. Based on surveys, the argument has been made that the East Germans had an authoritarian understanding of democracy and placed less value on a free choice of newspapers or the freedom to demonstrate as compared to security in the event of illness.[119] Others have countered this thesis, pointing out that the East Germans hardly had a chance to familiarize themselves with a free selection of print media and understand its value because the press landscape had only blossomed for such a short time in 1990.[120] East Germans were also more mistrustful of journalistic work: according to surveys conducted at the end of 1992, for example, 75 percent of East Germans did not trust the papers, whereas this figure was only 50 percent in the West.[121] They were also much less trustful of regional subscription magazines and television than West Germans.[122] The East German experience with propaganda and the country's annexation to the Federal Republic definitely seems to have left its mark on the credibility of the media.

This list of deficits appears in a different light when it is examined within the context of later developments in West Germany. Many trends appeared quickly in East Germany after 1990 that later appeared not only in numerous postsocialist countries, but also in the West. These included the (further) consolidation and erosion of the press, the tight hold of regional monopolies within the newspaper landscape, and the persistence of a special regional consciousness that propped up the corresponding print media. Financially weak, newly founded local newspapers, for example, hardly had a chance anywhere—not just in East Germany. In the West, too, almost all attempts to establish new daily newspapers or news magazines had failed since the 1950s. Furthermore, many entirely different lifestyle publications folded in the 1990s in the old Federal Republic as well, ranging from the entertainment magazine *Quick* (1992) to the Protestant *Deutsches Allgemeines Sonntagsblatt* (2000) and the satire magazine *Mad* (1995). The decided preference for service and advice magazines in the East also proved to be a harbinger of what was to become a general trend. Even one of the successful new magazines on the West German market, *Focus*, increasingly offered a mix of politics and service content. Likewise, akin to what had taken place in East Germany in the early 1990s, classifieds and marketing catalogs proved to be one of the most successful print media. They were able to sustain a large readership even in the Internet Age, although the free dailies never managed to take hold in Germany.

The negative assessments of the East German media landscape also look different when the case in East Germany is compared to other postsocialist countries. After 1990, it was hoped everywhere that the freedom of the press would foster the democratization process. In actuality, however, democracy only came slowly to the former Eastern Bloc, and it still appears to be in danger in some countries.[123] In contrast to the other postsocialist contexts, such as southeastern Europe, Slovakia, and especially Russia, the role of state paternalism in the transformation of the media in East Germany was less pronounced. The involvement of foreign Western publishers in media takeovers in the other socialist countries was also stronger, although it was the German Springer-Verlag that played a major role in this process. In Czechoslovakia, for example, about half of the periodicals landed in Western hands. Many of the publications of the opposition, such as *Gazeta Wyborcza* in Poland and *Lidove noviny* in Czechoslovakia, lost some of their readers. The widespread popularity of strong tabloid media and private stations that were often politicized can at least partially account for the rapid success of populist parties in Central Europe.[124]

Furthermore, the radio and television landscape in East Germany was largely shaped by the importation of structures from the Federal Republic. The remarkably quick transition from propaganda to independent journalism that took place beginning in 1989 and the short boom in critical formats did not help GDR television in the long run. Doubts as to the potential for reform, a lack of trust in existing personnel, and an interest in keeping a tight check on the competition coming from private television contributed to the rapid dismantling of the GDR television system under the leadership of Rudolf Mühlfenzl, the radio and television commissioner for the new federal states. The rights and property of GDR television were turned over to the states at the end of 1991 or transferred to the federal state media authorities that were still in the process of being put into place.[125] A bit later, two multistate systems were set up with the stations MDR (Saxony, Saxony-Anhalt, and Thuringia) and the fusion of SFB and ORB to rbb (Berlin and Brandenburg), while Mecklenburg-Western Pomerania joined up with NDR. In the West, this model was also replicated in the fusion of SDR and SWF. Only a few cases deviated from this course, such as the privatization of the regional GDR radio station Berliner Rundfunk or the merger of the former GDR channel Deutschlandsender Kultur with RIAS and Deutschlandfunk to form the national radio station DeutschlandRadio.[126]

Due to the sudden disappearance of old familiar stations, formats, and programs in East Germany, as well as the recruitment of the majority of the executive personnel from the West, the media was given a chance to guide and absorb some of the impact of the change in everyday life in East Germany. Yet the "shock therapy" (as the head of NDR at the time, Jobst Plog, referred to it) that actually took place ensured a further loss of trust in the media.[127] Indeed, citizens of the former GDR often felt as if they were witnessing a "colonization" or "invasion" of sorts. Accordingly, the regional public channels were later quite successful in the new federal states with their "ostalgic" return to programs and symbols from the East German past.[128]

In place of the trusted, rather staid GDR television world, the East was confronted with the overwhelming new dynamics of a "dual system" consisting of commercial and public service providers. They now had a much larger selection of programs and broadcasting times to choose from. As of 1986, for example, Berlin had sixteen television channels, offering a total of 145 hours of programming a day; by 1992, city residents could tune into thirty-four channels that aired a total of 493 hours of programming per day, with more on the way.[129] The greater variety of programming available through special-interest channels that popped up beside the established broadcasters had an effect on both public and private television. While the latter still had to make do with a very modest share of the market in the second half of the 1980s (in 1987, RTL was at 1.3 percent, and SAT.1 came in at 1.5 percent), about the same number of viewers tuned into each of the full-coverage channels ARD, ZDF, RTL, and SAT.1 with a market share of about 15 percent in the 1990s.[130] The growth in programming, as well as a series of smaller units such as commercials, trailers, weather, or stock market updates, also changed perceptions of time: they awakened a general impression of fragmentation and acceleration. Initially, private channels made a name for themselves by offering niche programming dealing with sex and violence or action adventure. Then, in order to protect their images, they transitioned into more innovative talk formats ("confrontainment") in the 1990s, satisfying the human desire for voyeurism with relationship shows or reality TV. This "explosion of intimacy" was countered by the public television broadcasters who strengthened their profiles as providers of information, although they did make some concessions to the style of the new competition. Notwithstanding these changes, however, the public channels were much less successful in East Germany than the private broadcasters. Without a doubt, the commercialization of the media and the transformation of radio and television into consumer goods took on a new dimension with the growing success of the private stations and their focus on younger target audiences, who were more relevant from an advertising perspective.

Furthermore, although the average amount of television consumption remained fairly constant at around two hours a day until the mid-1980s, this amount soon climbed rather quickly to over three hours.[131] In East Germany, the average was about a half an hour more in all age groups.[132] East Germans also watched commercial television much more frequently, and they were more interested in entertainment than information when compared to people living in the old federal states.[133] Not only the different social circumstances in East and West after reunification contributed to this divergence, but also the greater distance vis-à-vis political content that resulted from the experience of dictatorship in the East. This was also further reinforced by what was seen as the "West German" perspective on East Germany propagated in the national media outlets.[134] Accordingly, the gap was also reflected in the still much lower following for national newspapers and news magazines in the former East. However, the differences that still persist today rest primarily on the social and economic divide between East and West that has by no means disappeared over time, not just on regional background alone.[135]

The combination of liberalization, pluralization, and individualization that took place in the 1990s was a truly German phenomenon, but it hit the East Germans with a much greater force. The transformation of radio and television was also in and of itself part of this development. Yet, at the same time, media content helped German society to deal with this insecurity at both an individual and collective level, be it in the form of residual elements of life in the GDR in East German regional programming, ritualized television news programs, or serial entertainment.[136]

Conclusion

Without a doubt, the media created an essential bridge between East and West. Whereas radio had already taken on this function in the 1950s, stronger and wider bridges were built in the 1970s through the West German television that was watched on both sides of the Wall and the reports of correspondents on either side. Not only the public television stations in the West, but also the state broadcasters in the GDR eventually had to cater to viewers' wishes for more entertainment. Television and radio therefore fostered the emergence of a consumer society in both German states, generating a desire for consumer goods that could hardly be stilled in the East. In doing so, they contributed to the replacement of traditional norms of collectivity and duty in the GDR with the promise of individual development and expression as part of what became a "trap of modernity" for the East German state. Print media in both states remained separate, but the borders were at times permeable. East German newspapers adopted Western formats, styles, and trends, for example, which promoted pluralization and consumption within the GDR. Even the development of the most different newspapers imaginable in terms of politics on both sides of the Wall did exhibit some structural commonalities: the high circulation of these dailies in East and West reflected their growing importance in providing social orientation in both a democracy and a dictatorship. This also manifested itself in the shared interest of East and West Germans in local and regional news, classifieds, and advice/service formats. At the same time, the limits and asymmetry of this media entanglement was readily apparent. West Germans paid very little attention to GDR television and radio, but the increasing commercialization and entertainment focus of the media spread clearly from West to East and not the other way around.

In 1990, when the West German media system was mapped on to East Germany and West German media conglomerates came to dominate the East German market, it initially seemed as if a true process of reunification was in full swing. Yet a myriad of differences soon appeared despite shared elements and even direct structural ties. The differences in preferences between East and West Germans in their choice of television programming, magazines, and newspapers, as well as the strongly regional contours of the East German media market, have pointed to the persistence of cultural and social borders, which the media itself has also fostered. Arrogant views of the East coming from within the West have not been few and far between. Not only was the seeming monopoly of the regional press mocked, but also the success of private television and local commercial stations. From a long-term perspective, however, media developments in East Germany in the 1990s foreshadowed trends that soon emerged even more strongly in the West. Nonetheless, media use is still very much divided along the lines of the old Wall between East and West.

Frank Bösch is professor of European history at the University of Potsdam and Director of the Center for Contemporary History in Potsdam. He is the author of several books on modern German and European history, including *Die Adenauer-CDU* (2001), *Das konservative Milieu* (2002), and *Öffentliche Geheimnisse* (2009). His most recent book is *Mass Media and Historical Change: Germany in International Perspective, 1400–2000* (Berghahn Books, 2015).

Christoph Classen is a senior research associate at the Centre for Contemporary History (ZZF) in Potsdam. His research interests are focused on contemporary and media history, and his most recent publication is "History of Private and Commercial Television in Europe," in *VIEW Journal of European Television History and Culture* 6, no. 11 (ed., with Luca Barra and Sonja De Leeuw, 2017).

NOTES

1. Kurt R. Hesse, *Westmedien in der DDR. Nutzung, Image und Auswirkungen bundesrepublikanischen Hörfunks und Fernsehens* (Cologne, 1988), 9.
2. Axel Schildt, "Zwei Staaten—eine Hörfunk- und Fernsehnation. Überlegungen zur Bedeutung der elektronischen Massenmedien in der Geschichte der Kommunikation zwischen der Bundesrepublik und der DDR," in *Doppelte Zeitgeschichte. Deutsch-deutsche Beziehungen 1945–1990*, ed. Arnd Bauerkämper, Martin Sabrow, and Bernd Stöver (Bonn, 1998), 58–71.
3. Christoph Classen, "'Um die Empfangsmöglichkeiten . . . des Senders RIAS völlig auszuschalten.' Störsender in der DDR 1952 bis 1988," *Rundfunk und Geschichte* 40, no. 3–4 (2014): 25–40.
4. Michael Meyen, *Denver Clan und Neues Deutschland. Mediennutzung in der DDR* (Berlin, 2003), 42; this comparative data up to 1975 was taken from Elizabeth Prommer, *Kinobesuch im Lebenslauf. Eine historische und medienbiographische Studie* (Konstanz, 1999), 350–51.
5. Gunter Holzweißig, *Die schärfste Waffe der Partei. Eine Mediengeschichte der DDR* (Cologne, 2002). In a similar vein, see the sections on the GDR in Heinz Pürer and Johannes Raabe, eds., *Presse in Deutschland*, 3rd ed. (Konstanz, 2007), 173–211. For an approach that differs from that of Holzweißig, but nonetheless emphasizes the tight control of the media, see Anke Fiedler, *Medienlenkung in der DDR* (Cologne, 2014).

6. Christoph Classen, "Two Types of Propaganda? Thoughts on the Significance of Mass-Media Communications in the Third Reich and the GDR," *Totalitarian Movements and Political Religions* 8, no. 3–4 (2007): 537–53.
7. Michael Meyen and Anke Fiedler, *Die Grenze im Kopf. Journalisten in der DDR* (Berlin, 2011); Richard Oehmig, "Besorgt mal Filme." *Der internationale Programmhandel des DDR-Fernsehens* (Göttingen, 2016).
8. Jan Palmowski, *Inventing a Socialist Nation: Heimat and the Politics of Everyday Life in the GDR, 1945–90* (Cambridge, 2009), 81–89, 120–28.
9. Katrin Bobsin, *Das Presseamt der DDR. Staatliche Öffentlichkeitsarbeit für die SED* (Cologne, 2013); Jürgen Wilke, *Presseanweisungen im zwanzigsten Jahrhundert. Erster Weltkrieg—Drittes Reich—DDR* (Cologne, 2007), 290–304.
10. Daniel Siemens and Christian Schemmert, "Die Leipziger Journalistenausbildung in der Ära Ulbricht," *Vierteljahrshefte für Zeitgeschichte* 61, no. 2 (2013): 201–37. See also the memories of GDR journalists in Meyen and Fiedler, *Die Grenze im Kopf*.
11. Julia Martin, "Der Berufsverband der Journalisten in der DDR (VDJ)," in *Journalisten und Journalismus in der DDR. Berufsorganisation—Westkorrespondenten—Der Schwarze Kanal*, ed. Jürgen Wilke (Cologne, 2007), 7–78, here 65.
12. Christiane Baumann et al., "*Vertrauen ist gut—Kontrolle ist besser.*" *Schlaglichter auf 38 Jahre SED-Bezirkszeitung Freie Erde* (Bremen, 2013), 65–66.
13. These figures are drawn from Heinz Pürer and Johannes Raabe, *Presse in Deutschland* (Konstanz, 2007), 124.
14. Stefan Matysiak, "Die Entwicklung der DDR-Presse. Zur ostdeutschen historischen Pressestatistik," *Deutschland Archiv* 42, no. 1 (2009): 59–73, here 60.
15. IVW-Data, cited from Sabine Hilgenstock, *Die Geschichte der BUNTEN (1949–1988). Die Entwicklung einer illustrierten Wochenzeitschrift mit einer Chronik dieser Zeitschriftengattung* (Frankfurt a. M., 1993), 9.
16. Data in D. Löffler, "Publikumszeitschriften und ihre Leser. Zum Beispiel: Wochenpost, Freie Welt, Für Dich, Sybille," in *Zwischen "Mosaik" und "Einheit." Zeitschriften in der DDR*, ed. Simone Barck, Martina Langermann, and Siegfried Lokatis (Berlin, 1999), 48–60, here 49.
17. Whereas two-thirds of the sales income came from advertising in the West, nine-figure subsidies proved to be necessary to keep the papers afloat in the East. In 1989, the SED paper alone received 332 million marks in subsidies; cf. Pürer and Raabe, *Presse*, 379.
18. On this long-term international perspective, see Frank Bösch, *Mediengeschichte. Vom asiatischen Buchdruck bis zum Fernsehen* (Frankfurt a. M., 2011).
19. Dorothee Harbers, *Die Bezirkspresse der DDR (unter besonderer Berücksichtigung der SED-Bezirkszeitungen). Lokalzeitungen im Spannungsfeld zwischen Parteiauftrag und Leserinteresse* (Marburg, 2003), 241–42.
20. Compare the surveys conducted by the SED in 1967 in Michael Meyen, *Denver Clan*, 107–108.

21. Marco Haas, *Die geschenkte Zeitung. Bestandsaufnahme und Studien zu einem neuen Pressetyp in Europa* (Münster, 2005), 72.
22. Beate Schneider and Dieter Stürzebecher, *Wenn das Blatt sich wendet. Die Tagespresse in den neuen Bundesländern* (Baden-Baden, 1999), 102.
23. See also Jürgen Wilke, "Die Tagespresse der achtziger Jahre," in *Die Kultur der 80er Jahre*, ed. Werner Faulstich (Munich, 2005), 69–90, here 72.
24. Matysiak, *Entwicklung der DDR-Presse*, 62.
25. Jürgen Schlimper, "Thesen zur Geschichte der Leipziger Volkszeitung seit 1946," in *"Natürlich—die Tauchaer Straße!" Beiträge zur Geschichte der "Leipziger Volkszeitung,"* ed. Jürgen Schlimper (Leipzig, 1997), 469–506.
26. Michael Meyen and Wolfgang Schweiger, "'Sattsam bekannte Uniformität'? Eine Inhaltsanalyse der DDR-Tageszeitungen 'Neues Deutschland' und 'Junge Welt' (1960–1989)," *Medien & Kommunikationswissenschaft* 56, no. 1 (2008): 82–100.
27. On press involvement from the perspective of the SPD, see Friedhelm Boll, *Die deutsche Sozialdemokratie und ihre Medien. Wirtschaftliche Dynamik und rechtliche Formen* (Bonn, 2002); Uwe Danker, Markus Oddey, and Daniel Roth, *Am Anfang standen Arbeitergroschen. 140 Jahre Medienunternehmen der SPD* (Bonn, 2003). For a CDU/CSU perspective, see Andreas Feser, *Der Genossen-Konzern. Parteivermögen und Pressebeteiligungen der SPD* (Munich, 2002).
28. Christina von Hodenberg, *Konsens und Krise. Eine Geschichte der westdeutschen Medienöffentlichkeit 1945–1973* (Göttingen, 2006), 362.
29. Frank Esser, *Die Kräfte hinter den Schlagzeilen. Englischer und deutscher Journalismus im Vergleich* (Freiburg i. Br., 1998).
30. Elisabeth Noelle-Neumann, *Die Schweigespirale: Öffentliche Meinung—unsere soziale Haut* (Munich, 1980).
31. More details in Frank Bösch, "Zwischen Technikzwang und politischen Zielen: Wege zur Einführung des privaten Rundfunks in den 1970/80er Jahren," *Archiv für Sozialgeschichte* 52 (2012): 191–210.
32. Meyen, *Denver Clan*, 55–56; John Fiske, "Popularity and the Politics of Information," in *Journalism and Popular Culture*, ed. Peter Dahlgren and Colin Sparks (London, 1992), 45–63.
33. Peter Dudek and Hans-Gerd Jaschke, *Die Deutsche National-Zeitung. Inhalte, Geschichte, Aktionen* (Munich, 1981).
34. Sven Reichardt, *Authentizität und Gemeinschaft. Linksalternatives Leben in den siebziger und frühen achtziger Jahren* (Berlin, 2014), 223–318, especially 241–42.
35. Nadja Büteführ, *Zwischen Anspruch und Kommerz: Lokale Alternativpresse 1970–1993* (Münster, 1995), 471–72.
36. Early editions in Otfried Jarren, *Kommunale Kommunikation* (Munich, 1984), 254.
37. For a comparison, see Friederike Kind-Kovács and Jessie Labov, eds., *Samizdat, Tamizdat, and Beyond: Transnational Media During and After Socialism*

(New York, 2013); Jan C. Behrends and Thomas Lindenberger, eds., *Underground Publishing and the Public Sphere. Transnational Perspectives* (Münster, 2014).
38. Jens Bulisch, *Evangelische Presse in der DDR. "Die Zeichen der Zeit" (1947–1990)* (Göttingen, 2006), 403.
39. Cf. Simone Barck, Martina Langermann, and Siegfried Lokatis, eds., *Zwischen "Mosaik" und "Einheit." Zeitschriften in der DDR* (Berlin, 1999).
40. Not much research has been done on this so far; on the early period, see Lu Seegers, *Hör zu! Eduard Rhein und die Rundfunkprogrammzeitschriften (1931–1965)* (Potsdam, 2001).
41. For an analysis of the images from *Für Dich* and the *Neue Berliner Illustrierten* in the 1970s and 1980s, see Irene Dölling, *Der Mensch und sein Weib. Frauen- und Männerbilder. Geschichtliche Ursprünge und Perspektiven* (Berlin, 1991), 166–231.
42. Michael Meyen and Anke Fiedler, *Wer jung ist, liest die Junge Welt. Die Geschichte der auflagenstärksten DDR-Zeitung* (Berlin, 2013).
43. Michael Rauhhut, "Erinnerungen an 38 Jahre Jugendmagazin neues leben," in Simone Barck, Martina Langermann, and Siegfried Lokatis, *Zwischen "Mosaik" und "Einheit."*
44. Petra Eisele, "Do-it-yourself-Design: Die IKEA-Regale IVAR und BILLY," *Zeithistorische Forschungen/Studies in Contemporary History* 3, no. 3 (2006), 439–448.
45. Marion Gräfin Dönhoff, Rudolf Walter Leonhardt, and Theo Sommer, *Reise in ein fernes Land. Bericht über Kultur, Wirtschaft und Politik in der DDR* (Hamburg, 1964).
46. Cf. Fiedler, *Medienlenkung*, 419.
47. Denis Fengler, "Westdeutsche Korrespondenten in der DDR," in Wilke, *Journalisten und Journalismus in der DDR*, 79–216, here 90, 119–20.
48. Beatrice Dernbach, *DDR-Berichterstattung in bundesdeutschen Qualitätszeitungen* (Berlin, 2008), 39.
49. Fengler, "Westdeutsche Korrespondenten," 176–95.
50. Dernbach, *DDR-Berichterstattung*, 38–42, 57, 176.
51. In 1987/88, 13 and 11 percent in *Süddeutsche Zeitung* and *Frankfurter Allgemeine Zeitung*; Dernbach, *DDR-Berichterstattung*, 126, 144.
52. Jürgen Döschner, "Zehn Jahre bundesdeutsche Korrespondenten in der DDR. Eine Zwischenbilanz," *Deutschland Archiv* 17, no. 8 (1984): 859–69.
53. Fengler, "Westdeutsche Korrespondenten," 161, 196–97.
54. Petra S. Hartmann-Laugs and Anthony Goss, *Deutschlandbilder im Fernsehen*, vol. 2 (Cologne, 1988); Dernbach, *DDR-Berichterstattung*, 176–77.
55. Meyen, "'Sattsam bekannte Uniformität'?," 97.
56. Jens Ruchatz, "Einleitung," in *Mediendiskurse deutsch/deutsch*, ed. Jens Ruchatz (Weimar, 2005), 7–22.
57. Claudia Dittmar, *Feindliches Fernsehen: Das DDR-Fernsehen und seine Strategien im Umgang mit dem westdeutschen Fernsehen* (Bielefeld, 2010), 141.

58. The latter two have been conspiratorially run; see Klaus Arnold, *Kalter Krieg im Äther. Der Deutschlandsender und die Westpropaganda der SED* (Münster, 2002); Jürgen Wilke, "Radio im Geheimauftrag. Der Deutsche Freiheitssender 904 und der Deutsche Soldatensender 935 als Instrumente des Kalten Krieges," in *Zwischen Pop und Propaganda. Radio in der DDR*, ed. Klaus Arnold and Christoph Classen (Berlin, 2004), 249–66. A concept for a television program (*Deutschland Fernsehen*) that was targeted at West Germany had already been thrown out a decade earlier; see Claudia Dittmar, *Feindliches Fernsehen*, 153–55.
59. Christoph Classen, "Jamming the RIAS: Technical Measures against Western Broadcasting in East Germany (GDR) 1945–1989," in *Airy Curtains in the European Ether*, ed. Alexander W. Badenoch, Andreas Fickers, and Christian Henrich-Franke (Baden-Baden, 2013), 321–46.
60. Konrad Dussel, "Rundfunk in der DDR und in der Bundesrepublik. Überlegungen zum systematischen Vergleich," in Arnold and Classen, *Zwischen Pop und Propaganda*, 301–21.
61. Christa Braumann, "Fernsehnutzung zwischen Parteilichkeit und Objektivität. Zur Zuschauerforschung in der ehemaligen DDR," *Rundfunk und Fernsehen* 42, no. 4 (1994): 524–41, here 531.
62. Meyen, *Denver Clan*, 75.
63. Michael Meyen, "'Geistige Grenzgänger.' Medien und die deutsche Teilung," *Jahrbuch für Kommunikationsgeschichte* 1 (1999): 192–231; Axel Schildt, *Zwei Staaten*, 60.
64. See Franziska Kuschel, *Schwarzhörer, Schwarzseher und heimliche Leser. Die DDR und die Westmedien* (Göttingen, 2016).
65. Rüdiger Steinmetz and Reinhold Viehoff. eds., *Deutsches Fernsehen Ost* (Berlin, 2008), 297.
66. Franziska Kuschel, "Between Hostility and Concession: The Conflict about Western Commercial Broadcasting in the GDR, 1985–1989," *Transnational Broadcasting in Europe 1945–1990*, ed. Christoph Classen, special edition of *SPIEL, Neue Folge. Eine Zeitschrift zur Medienkultur* 2, no. 1 (2016): 107–22.
67. Ibid.; Gunter Holzweißig, *Zensur ohne Zensor. Die SED-Informationsdiktatur* (Bonn, 1997), 171.
68. Rudolf Stöber, *Mediengeschichte. Die Evolution "Neuer" Medien von Gutenberg bis Gates*, vol. 2: *Film—Rundfunk—Multimedia* (Wiesbaden, 2003), 87.
69. Knut Hickethier, ed., *Institution, Technik und Rahmenaspekte der Programmgeschichte des Fernsehens* (Munich, 1993), 417; for detailed information on demographic changes of the cinema audience, see Joseph Garncarz, *Hollywood in Deutschland. Zur Internationalisierung der Kinokultur 1925–1990* (Frankfurt a. M., 2013), 145–46.
70. See Henning Wrage, *Die Zeit der Kunst. Literatur, Film und Fernsehen in der DDR der 1960er Jahre. Eine Kulturgeschichte in Beispielen* (Heidelberg, 2008).
71. Fiedler, *Medienlenkung*.

72. Gerhard Lampe and Heidemarie Schumacher, *Das "Panorama" der 60er Jahre. Zur Geschichte des ersten politischen Fernsehmagazins der BRD* (Berlin, 1991).
73. Norbert Schneider, "Parteieneinfluß im Rundfunk," in *Fernsehen und Hörfunk für die Demokratie. Ein Handbuch über den Rundfunk in der Bundesrepublik Deutschland*, 2nd ed., ed. Jörg Aufermann, Wilfried Scharf, and Otto Schlie (Opladen, 1981), 116–26.
74. On the origins of this, see Martin Stock, "'Ausgewogenheit.' Ein Begriff macht Karriere," *Unsere Medien, unsere Republik: Mediengeschichte als Geschichte der Bundesrepublik Deutschland* 4 (1990): 30–31.
75. On the so-called "Rotfunk" campaign, see Josef Schmidt, "Klaus von Bismarck und die Kampagne gegen den WDR," *Archiv für Sozialgeschichte* 41 (2001): 349–82.
76. Frank Bösch, "Zwischen Technikzwang," 191–210.
77. Peter M. Spangenberg, "Der unaufhaltsame Aufstieg zum 'Dualen System.' Diskursbeiträge zu Technikinnovationen und Rundfunkorganisation," in *Medienkultur der 70er Jahre. Diskursgeschichte der Medien nach 1945*, ed. Irmela Schneider, Christina Bartz, and Isabell Otto (Wiesbaden, 2004), 21–39.
78. Fiedler, *Medienlenkung*, 339–41.
79. See Helmuth Berking, *Masse und Geist. Studien zur Soziologie in der Weimarer Republik* (Berlin, 1982).
80. Steinmetz and Viehoff, *Deutsches Fernsehen Ost*, 395.
81. Knut Hickethier, *Geschichte des Deutschen Fernsehens* (Stuttgart, 1998), 329; Steinmetz and Viehoff, *Deutsches Fernsehen Ost*, 398.
82. Thomas Beutelschmidt and Richard Oehmig, "Connected Enemies? Programming Transfer between East and West during the Cold War and the Example of East German Television," in *VIEW Journal of European Television History and Culture* 3, no. 5 (2014): 60–67.
83. Christian Henrich-Franke and Regina Immel, "Making Holes in the Iron Curtain?: The Television Programme Exchange across the Iron Curtain in the 1960s and 1970s," in Alexander Badenoch, Andreas Fickers, and Christian Henrich-Franke, *Airy Curtains*, 177–213, here 184.
84. For radio cf. Axel Schildt, *Moderne Zeiten. Freizeit, Massenmedien und Zeitgeist in der Bundesrepublik der 50er Jahre* (Hamburg, 1995), 235.
85. Michael Meyen, *Denver Clan*, 73–101.
86. Peter Förster, "Die deutsche Frage im Bewußtsein der Bevölkerung in beiden Teilen Deutschlands. Das Zusammengehörigkeitsgefühl der Deutschen. Einstellungen junger Menschen in der DDR," in *Materialien der Enquete-Kommission "Aufarbeitung von Geschichte und Folgen der SED-Diktatur in Deutschland,"* ed. Deutscher Bundestag (Baden-Baden, 1995), 2:1212–380, especially 1236–37.
87. Steinmetz and Viehoff, *Deutsches Fernsehen Ost*, 293.
88. Ibid., 302.

89. Konrad Dussel, *Deutsche Rundfunkgeschichte*, 3rd ed. (Konstanz, 2010), 213–15; Heiner Stahl, *Jugendradio im kalten Ätherkrieg. Berlin als eine Klanglandschaft des Pop 1962–1973* (Berlin, 2010).
90. Wolfgang Rumpf, "Popgefühle im Äther. Popmusik—Ein Tabu im ARD-Rundfunk der 1960er," Online Publication of the Arbeitskreis Studium Populärer Musik, 16 November 2006, retrieved 17 June 2016, http://www.aspm-samples.de/Samples5/rumpf.pdf.
91. Edward Larkey, *Rotes Rockradio. Populäre Musik und die Kommerzialisierung des DDR-Rundfunks* (Münster, 2007); Edward Larkey, "Radio Reform in the 1980s: RIAS and DT-64 Respond to Private Radio," in *Cold War Cultures: Perspectives on Eastern and Western European Societies*, ed. Annette Vowinckel, Marcus M. Payk, and Thomas Lindenberger (New York, 2012), 76–93; Klaus Nathaus, "Turning Values into Revenue: The Markets and the Field of Popular Music in the US, the UK and West Germany (1940s to 1980s)," *Historical Social Research* 36, no. 3 (2011): 136–63; Alexander W. Badenoch, "'In What Language Do You Like to Sing Best?' Placing Popular Music in Broadcasting in Post-war Europe," *European Review of History* 20, no. 5 (2013): 837–57.
92. Even sixteen years after cable TV had been introduced (1996), only two-thirds of all households had cable connections instead of the 90 percent that had been planned originally; Hickethier, *Geschichte des Deutschen Fernsehens*, 419.
93. Bösch, "Zwischen Technikzwang," 201.
94. Melanie Arndt, *Tschernobyl. Auswirkungen des Reaktorunfalls auf die Bundesrepublik und die DDR* (Erfurt, 2011).
95. Barbara Thomaß and Michaela Tzankoff, eds., *Medien und Transformation in Osteuropa*, (Wiesbaden, 2001), 249.
96. Susanne Binas, "Die 'anderen Bands' und ihre Kassettenproduktionen—Zwischen organisiertem Kulturbetrieb und selbstorganisierten Kulturformen," in *Rockmusik und Politik. Analysen, Interviews und Dokumente*, ed. Peter Wicke and Lothar Müller (Berlin, 1996), 48–60, here 50.
97. See Thomas Großmann, *Fernsehen, Revolution und das Ende der DDR* (Göttingen, 2015); Frank Bösch, "Medien als Katalysatoren der Wende? Die DDR, Polen und der Westen 1989," *Zeitschrift für Ostmitteleuropa-Forschung* 59 (2010): 459–71.
98. Thomas Schuhbauer, *Umbruch im Fernsehen, Fernsehen im Umbruch. Die Rolle des DDR-Fernsehens in der Revolution und im Prozess der deutschen Vereinigung 1989–1990 am Beispiel des Jugendmagazins "Elf 99"* (Berlin, 2001), 224–25.
99. For example, calls flooded in after the show *Donnerstagsgespräch: Zuschauer fragen—Politiker antworten* aired on GDR television beginning in mid-October 1989, in which high-level SED functionaries answered viewers' questions: Franca Wolff, *Glasnost erst kurz vor Sendeschluss. Die letzten Jahre des DDR-Fernsehens (1985–1989/90)* (Cologne, 2002), 278.

100. Ellen Bos, *Leserbriefe in Tageszeitungen der DDR. Zur "Massenverbundenheit" der Presse 1949–1989* (Opladen, 1993), 232.
101. András Lánczi and Patrick O'Neil, "Pluralization and the Politics of Media Change in Hungary," in *Post-Communism and the Media in Eastern Europe*, ed. Patrick O'Neil and Frank Cass (London, 1997), 82–101.
102. Michael Haller, Barbara Held, and Hartmut Weßler, "Wendeversuche in der Sackgasse: Umbau, Untergang, Neuanfang der Zeitschriften in den neuen Bundesländern," in *Presse Ost—Presse West. Journalismus im vereinten Deutschland*, ed. Michael Haller, Klaus Puder, and Jochen Schlevoigt (Berlin, 1995), 121–35.
103. Schneider and Stürzebecher, *Wenn das Blatt*, 210. Schneider had already voiced this critique in 1991: Beate Schneider, "Pressemarkt Ost. Ein Refugium des 'Demokratischen Zentralismus,'" in *Medien im vereinten Deutschland: nationale und internationale Perspektiven*, ed. Walter A. Mahle (Bonn, 1991), 71–80.
104. Beate Schneider, "Nach allen Regeln der Zunft. Zeitungswettbewerb in Deutschland," in Haller, Puder, and Schlevoigt, *Presse Ost—Presse West*, 55.
105. N.n., "Angeber-Wessi mit Bierflasche erschlagen," *Super!*, 3 May 1991, 1; Barbara Held and Thomas Simeon, *Die zweite Stunde Null. Berliner Tageszeitungen nach der Wende (1989–1994)* (Berlin, 1994), 64–70.
106. Held and Simeon, *Die zweite Stunde Null*, 268.
107. Haller, Held, and Weßler, *Wendeversuche*, 131.
108. Horst Pöttker, "Fortschreibung alter Identitäten. Fremd- und Selbstbilder in der Presse des vereinten Deutschlands," in Haller, Puder, and Schlevoigt, *Presse Ost—Presse West*, 235–44, especially 240.
109. Helmut Scherer, "Die Darstellung von Politik in ost- und westdeutschen Tageszeitungen. Ein inhaltsanalytischer Vergleich," *Publizistik* 42, no. 4 (1997): 413–38; on the basis of front pages: Pöttker, "Fortschreibung," 237.
110. On the national press, see Scherer, *Darstellung*, 416–17; Wiebke Möhring, *Die Lokalberichterstattung in den neuen Bundesländern. Orientierung im gesellschaftlichen Wandel* (Munich, 2001), 68.
111. Schneider and Stürzebecher, *Wenn das Blatt*, 65.
112. Dieter Stürzebecher, "Woher kommen sie, wie denken sie, was wollen sie?," in Haller, Puder, and Schlevoigt, *Presse Ost—Presse West*, 207–25, here 215; Beate Schneider, Klaus Schönbach, and Dieter Stürzebecher, "Journalisten im vereinigten Deutschland. Strukturen, Arbeitsweisen und Einstellungen im Ost-West-Vergleich," *Publizistik* 38, no. 3 (1993): 353–82, here 358–59.
113. Angelika Holterman, *Das Geteilte Leben. Journalistenbiographien und Medienstrukturen zu DDR-Zeiten und danach* (Opladen, 1999).
114. Möhring, *Die Lokalberichterstattung*, 47–48.
115. Stürzebecher, *Woher kommen sie*, 223–24.

116. Möhring, *Die Lokalberichterstattung,* 65, 137, 173; Beate Schneider, Wiebke Möhring, and Dieter Stürzebecher, *Ortsbestimmung. Lokaljournalismus in den neuen Ländern* (Konstanz, 2000),174–84.
117. Schneider and Stürzebecher, *Wenn das Blatt,* 212.
118. Andrew Milton, "'News Media Reform in Eastern Europe': A Cross-National Comparison," in *Post-Communism and the Media in Eastern Europe,* ed. Patrick O'Neil (Portland, 1997), 7–23.
119. Hans Halter, "Der Geschmack der Freiheit," *Der Spiegel* 45 (1996): 64–70, here 69.
120. Schneider and Stürzebecher, *Wenn das Blatt,* 208.
121. Schneider, "Nach allen Regeln der Zunft, " 63.
122. Hans Dieter Gärtner and Stefan Dahlem, "Informationsverhalten der Zeitungsleser 'hüben und drüben,'" in Haller, Puder, and Schlevoigt, *Presse Ost—Presse West,* 75–94, here 85. These East-West differences are pointed out emphatically in Sophie Burkhardt, "Information versus Unterhaltung," in *Deutsche Kontraste 1990–2010, Politik—Wirtschaft—Gesellschaft—Kultur,* ed. Manuela Glaab, Werner Weidenfeld, and Michael Weigl (Frankfurt a. M., 2010), 585–618.
123. Owen V. Johnson, "The Media and Democracy in Eastern Europe," in *Communicating Democracy: The Media and Political Transitions,* ed. Patrick O'Neil (Boulder, 1998), 103–24, here 112.
124. Katarina Bader, *Medialisierung der Parteien, Politisierung der Medien: Interdependenzen zwischen Medien und Politik im postsozialistischen Polen* (Wiesbaden, 2013), 425.
125. Hickethier, *Geschichte des Deutschen Fernsehens,* 502–04; Ernst Dohlus, "In der Grauzone—Wie der Staatsrundfunk der DDR aufgelöst wurde, Menschen, Material und Programmvermögen," *Deutschland Archiv,* 22 September 2014, retrieved 17 June 2016, http://www.bpb.de/191086.
126. Ernst Elitz, "Der nationale Hörfunk als Produkt der Einheit. Das Beispiel DeutschlandRadio," in Arnold and Classen, *Zwischen Pop und Propaganda,* 183–87.
127. As cited in Hickethier, *Geschichte des Deutschen Fernsehens,* 514.
128. Christoph Classen, "Das Sandmännchen," in *Erinnerungsorte der DDR,* ed. Martin Sabrow (Munich, 2009), 342–50.
129. Hickethier, *Geschichte des Deutschen Fernsehens,* 432.
130. Ibid., 485.
131. Ibid., 490.
132. Wolfgang Mühl-Benninghaus, *Unterhaltung als Eigensinn. Eine ostdeutsche Mediengeschichte* (Frankfurt a. M., 2012), 334–35.
133. Ibid., 336.
134. Thomas Ahbe, Rainer Gris, and Wolfgang Schmale, eds., *Die Ostdeutschen in den Medien. Das Bild von den Anderen nach 1990* (Leipzig, 2009).
135. Olaf Jandura and Michael Meyen, "Warum sieht der Osten anders fern? Eine repräsentative Studie zum Zusammenhang zwischen sozialer Position

und Mediennutzung," *Medien & Kommunikationswissenschaft* 58 (2010): 208–26; Hans-Jörg Stiehler, "Mediennutzung 1995 bis 2005 in West- und Ostdeutschland: ein Test der These von der Populationsheterogenität am Beispiel von Fernsehen und Tageszeitungen," in *Mediatisierung der Gesellschaft?*, ed. Jörg Hagenah and Heiner Meulemann (Münster, 2012), 119–39.
136. Hickethier, *Geschichte des Deutschen Fernsehens*, 536–38.

BIBLIOGRAPHY

Ahbe, Thomas, Rainer Gris, and Wolfgang Schmale, eds. *Die Ostdeutschen in den Medien. Das Bild von den Anderen nach 1990*. Leipzig: Leipziger Universitätsverlag, 2009.

Arndt, Melanie. *Tschernobyl. Auswirkungen des Reaktorunfalls auf die Bundesrepublik Deutschland und die DDR*. Erfurt: Landeszentrale für politische Bildung Thüringen, 2011.

Arnold, Klaus. *Kalter Krieg im Äther. Der Deutschlandsender und die Westpropaganda der SED*. Münster: LIT, 2002.

Badenoch, Alexander W. "'In What Language Do You Like to Sing Best?' Placing Popular Music in Broadcasting in Post-war Europe." *European Review of History* 20, no.5 (2013): 837–57.

Baumann, Christiane et al. *"Vertrauen ist gut—Kontrolle ist besser." Schlaglichter auf 38 Jahre SED-Bezirkszeitung Freie Erde*. Bremen: Kurierverlag, 2013.

Bader, Katarina. *Medialisierung der Parteien, Politisierung der Medien: Interdependenzen zwischen Medien und Politik im postsozialistischen Polen*. Wiesbaden: Springer, 2013.

Behrends, Jan Claas, and Thomas Lindenberger, eds. *Underground Publishing and the Public Sphere. Transnational Perspectives*. Münster: LIT, 2014.

Berking, Helmuth. *Masse und Geist. Studien zur Soziologie in der Weimarer Republik*. Berlin: WAV, 1982.

Beutelschmidt, Thomas and Richard Oehmig. "Connected Enemies? Programming Transfer between East and West during the Cold War and the Example of East German Television." *VIEW Journal of European Television History and Culture* 3, no. 5 (2014): 60–67.

Binas, Susanne. "Die 'anderen Bands' und ihre Kassettenproduktionen—Zwischen organisiertem Kulturbetrieb und selbstorganisierten Kulturformen." In *Rockmusik und Politik. Analysen, Interviews und Dokumente*, edited by Peter Wicke and Lothar Müller, 48–60. Berlin: Christoph Links, 1996.

Bobsin, Katrin. *Das Presseamt der DDR. Staatliche Öffentlichkeitsarbeit für die SED*. Cologne: Böhlau, 2013.

Boll, Friedhelm. *Die deutsche Sozialdemokratie und ihre Medien. Wirtschaftliche Dynamik und rechtliche Formen*. Bonn: Dietz, 2002.

Bos, Ellen. *Leserbriefe in Tageszeitungen der DDR. Zur "Massenverbundenheit" der Presse 1949–1989*. Opladen: VS Verlag für Sozialwissenschaften, 1993.

Bösch, Frank. "Medien als Katalysatoren der Wende? Die DDR, Polen und der Westen 1989." *Zeitschrift für Ostmitteleuropa-Forschung* 59 (2010): 459–71.

———. *Mediengeschichte. Vom asiatischen Buchdruck bis zum Fernsehen*. Frankfurt a. M.: Campus, 2011.

———. "Zwischen Technikzwang und politischen Zielen: Wege zur Einführung des privaten Rundfunks in den 1970/80er Jahren." *Archiv für Sozialgeschichte* 52 (2012): 191–210.

Braumann, Christa. "Fernsehnutzung zwischen Parteilichkeit und Objektivität. Zur Zuschauerforschung in der ehemaligen DDR." *Rundfunk und Fernsehen* 42, no. 4 (1994): 524–41.

Bulisch, Jens. *Evangelische Presse in der DDR. "Die Zeichen der Zeit" (1947–1990)*. Göttingen: Vandenhoeck & Ruprecht, 2006.

Burkhardt, Sophie. "Information versus Unterhaltung." In *Deutsche Kontraste 1990–2010, Politik—Wirtschaft—Gesellschaft—Kultur*, edited by Manuela Glaab, Werner Weidenfeld, and Michael Weigl, 585–618. Frankfurt a. M.: Campus, 2010.

Büteführ, Nadja. *Zwischen Anspruch und Kommerz: Lokale Alternativpresse 1970–1993*. Münster: Waxmann, 1995.

Classen, Christoph. "Das Sandmännchen." In *Erinnerungsorte der DDR*, edited by Martin Sabrow, 342–50. Munich: C. H. Beck, 2009.

———. "Jamming the RIAS: Technical Measures against Western Broadcasting in East Germany (GDR) 1945–1989." In *Airy Curtains in the European Ether*, edited by Alexander W. Badenoch, Andreas Fickers, and Christian Henrich-Franke, 321–46. Baden-Baden: Nomos, 2013.

———. "Two Types of Propaganda? Thoughts on the Significance of Mass-Media Communications in the Third Reich and the GDR." *Totalitarian Movements and Political Religions* 8 (2007): 537–53.

———. "'Um die Empfangsmöglichkeiten ... des Senders RIAS völlig auszuschalten.' Störsender in der DDR 1952 bis 1988." *Rundfunk und Geschichte* 40, no. 3–4 (2014): 25–40.

Danker, Uwe, Markus Oddey, and Daniel Roth. *Am Anfang standen Arbeitergroschen. 140 Jahre Medienunternehmen der SPD*. Bonn: Dietz, 2003.

Dernbach, Beatrice. *DDR-Berichterstattung in bundesdeutschen Qualitätszeitungen*. Berlin: LIT, 2008.

Dittmar, Claudia. *Feindliches Fernsehen: Das DDR-Fernsehen und seine Strategien im Umgang mit dem westdeutschen Fernsehen*. Bielefeld: Transcript, 2010.

Dohlus, Ernst. "In der Grauzone—Wie der Staatsrundfunk der DDR aufgelöst wurde. Menschen, Material und Programmvermögen." *Deutschland Archiv*, 22 September 2014. Retrieved 17 June 2016, http://www.bpb.de/191086.

Dölling, Irene. *Der Mensch und sein Weib. Frauen- und Männerbilder. Geschichtliche Ursprünge und Perspektiven*. Berlin: Dietz, 1991.

Döschner, Jürgen. "Zehn Jahre bundesdeutsche Korrespondenten in der DDR. Eine Zwischenbilanz." *Deutschland Archiv* 17, no. 8 (1984): 859–69.

Dudek, Peter, and Hans-Gerd Jaschke. *Die Deutsche National-Zeitung. Inhalte, Geschichte, Aktionen.* Munich: PDI, 1981.

Dussel, Konrad. *Deutsche Rundfunkgeschichte.* 3rd ed. Konstanz: UVK, 2010.

———. "Rundfunk in der DDR und in der Bundesrepublik. Überlegungen zum systematischen Vergleich." In *Zwischen Pop und Propaganda. Radio in der DDR,* edited by Klaus Arnold and Christoph Classen, 301–21. Berlin: Christoph Links, 2004.

Eisele, Petra. "Do-it-yourself-Design: Die IKEA-Regale IVAR und BILLY." *Zeithistorische Forschungen/Studies in Contemporary History* 3, no. 3 (2006): 439–48. Retrieved 17 June 2016, http://www.zeithistorische-forschungen.de/3-2006/id=4458.

Elitz, Ernst. "Der nationale Hörfunk als Produkt der Einheit. Das Beispiel DeutschlandRadio." In *Zwischen Pop und Propaganda. Radio in der DDR,* edited by Klaus Arnold and Christoph Classen, 183–87. Berlin: Christoph Links, 2004.

Esser, Frank. *Die Kräfte hinter den Schlagzeilen. Englischer und deutscher Journalismus im Vergleich.* Freiburg i. Br.: Karl Alber, 1998.

Fengler, Denis. "Westdeutsche Korrespondenten in der DDR." In *Journalisten und Journalismus in der DDR. Berufsorganisation—Westkorrespondenten—Der Schwarze Kanal,* edited by Jürgen Wilke, 79–216. Cologne: Böhlau, 2007.

Feser, Andreas. *Der Genossen-Konzern. Parteivermögen und Pressebeteiligungen der SPD.* Munich: Bonn Aktuell, 2002.

Fiedler, Anke. *Medienlenkung in der DDR.* Cologne: Böhlau, 2014.

Fiske, John. "Popularity and the Politics of Information." In *Journalism and Popular Culture,* edited by Peter Dahlgren and Colin Sparks, 45–63. London: Sage, 1992.

Förster, Peter. "Die deutsche Frage im Bewußtsein der Bevölkerung in beiden Teilen Deutschlands. Das Zusammengehörigkeitsgefühl der Deutschen. Einstellungen junger Menschen in der DDR." In *Materialien der Enquete-Kommission "Aufarbeitung von Geschichte und Folgen der SED-Diktatur in Deutschland,"* edited by Deutscher Bundestag, 2:1212–380. Baden-Baden: Nomos, 1995.

Garncarz, Joseph. *Hollywood in Deutschland. Zur Internationalisierung der Kinokultur 1925–1990.* Frankfurt a. M.: Stroemfeld, 2013.

Gärtner, Hans Dieter, and Stefan Dahlem. "Informationsverhalten der Zeitungsleser 'hüben und drüben.'" In *Presse Ost—Presse West. Journalismus im vereinten Deutschland,* edited by Michael Haller, Klaus Puder, and Jochen Schlevoigt, 75–94. Berlin: Vistas, 1995.

Gräfin Dönhoff, Marion, Rudolf Walter Leonhardt, and Theo Sommer. *Reise in ein fernes Land. Bericht über Kultur, Wirtschaft und Politik in der DDR.* Hamburg: Nannen, 1964.

Großmann, Thomas. *Fernsehen, Revolution und das Ende der DDR.* Göttingen: Wallstein, 2015.

Gumbert, Heather L. *Envisioning Socialism: Television and the Cold War in the German Democratic Republic.* Ann Arbor: University of Michigan Press, 2014.

Haas, Marco. *Die geschenkte Zeitung. Bestandsaufnahme und Studien zu einem neuen Pressetyp in Europa*. Münster: LIT, 2005.

Haller, Michael, Barbara Held, and Hartmut Weßler. "Wendeversuche in der Sackgasse: Umbau, Untergang, Neuanfang der Zeitschriften in den neuen Bundesländern." In *Presse Ost—Presse West. Journalismus im vereinten Deutschland*, edited by M. Haller, K. Puder, and J. Schlevoigt, 121–35. Berlin: Vistas, 1995.

Halter, Hans. "Der Geschmack der Freiheit," *Der Spiegel* 45 (1996): 64–70.

Harbers, Dorothee. *Die Bezirkspresse der DDR (unter besonderer Berücksichtigung der SED-Bezirkszeitungen). Lokalzeitungen im Spannungsfeld zwischen Parteiauftrag und Leserinteresse*. Marburg: Tectum, 2003.

Hartmann-Laugs, Petra S., and Anthony John Goss. *Deutschlandbilder im Fernsehen*. Vol. 2. Cologne: Wissenschaft und Politik, 1988.

Held, Barbara, and Thomas Simeon. *Die zweite Stunde Null. Berliner Tageszeitungen nach der Wende (1989–1994)*. Berlin: Spiess, 1994.

Henrich-Franke, Christian, and Regina Immel. "Making Holes in the Iron Curtain?: The Television Programme Exchange across the Iron Curtain in the 1960s and 1970s." In *Airy Curtains in the European Ether*, edited by A. W. Badenoch, A. Fickers, and C. Henrich-Franke, 177–213. Baden-Baden: Nomos, 2013.

Hesse, Kurt R. *Westmedien in der DDR. Nutzung, Image und Auswirkungen bundesrepublikanischen Hörfunks und Fernsehens*. Cologne: Wissenschaft und Politik, 1988.

Hickethier, Knut. *Geschichte des Deutschen Fernsehens*. Stuttgart: J.B. Metzler, 1998.

———, ed. *Geschichte des Fernsehens in der Bundesrepublik Deutschland*. Vol. 1: *Institution, Technik und Rahmenaspekte der Programmgeschichte des Fernsehens*. Munich: Fink, 1993.

Hilgenstock, Sabine. *Die Geschichte der BUNTEN (1949–1988). Die Entwicklung einer illustrierten Wochenzeitschrift mit einer Chronik dieser Zeitschriftengattung*. Frankfurt a. M.: Peter Lang, 1993.

Hodenberg, Christina von. *Konsens und Krise. Eine Geschichte der westdeutschen Medienöffentlichkeit 1945–1973*. Göttingen: Wallstein 2006.

Holterman, Angelika. *Das Geteilte Leben. Journalistenbiographien und Medienstrukturen zu DDR-Zeiten und danach*. Opladen: Leske + Budrich, 1999.

Holzweißig, Gunter. *Die schärfste Waffe der Partei. Eine Mediengeschichte der DDR*. Cologne: Böhlau Verlag, 2002.

———. *Zensur ohne Zensor. Die SED-Informationsdiktatur*. Bonn: Bouvier, 1997.

Jandura, Olaf, and Michael Meyen. "Warum sieht der Osten anders fern? Eine repräsentative Studie zum Zusammenhang zwischen sozialer Position und Mediennutzung." *Medien & Kommunikationswissenschaft* 58 (2010): 208–26.

Jarren, Otfried. *Kommunale Kommunikation. Eine theoretische und empirische Untersuchung kommunaler Kommunikationsstrukturen unter besonderer Berücksichtigung lokaler und sublokaler Medien*. Munich: Minerva, 1984.

Johnson, Owen V. "The Media and Democracy in Eastern Europe." In *Communicating Democracy: The Media and Political Transitions*, edited by Patrick O'Neil, 103–24. Boulder: Lynne Rienner Pub, 1998.

Kind-Kovács, Friederike, and Jessie Labov, eds. *Samizdat, Tamizdat, and Beyond: Transnational Media During and After Socialism.* New York: Berghahn, 2013.

Kuschel, Franziska. "Between Hostility and Concession: The Conflict about Western Commercial Broadcasting in the GDR, 1985–1989." *Transnational Broadcasting in Europe 1945–1990*, edited by Christoph Classen, special edition of *SPIEL, Neue Folge. Eine Zeitschrift zur Medienkultur* 2, no. 1 (2016): 107–22.

———. *Schwarzhörer, Schwarzseher und heimliche Leser. Die DDR und die Westmedien.* Göttingen: Wallstein, 2016.

Lampe, Gerhard et al. *Das "Panorama" der 60er Jahre. Zur Geschichte des ersten politischen Fernsehmagazins der BRD.* Berlin: Spiess, 1991.

Lánczi, András, and Patrick O'Neil. "Pluralization and the Politics of Media Change in Hungary." In *Post-Communism and the Media in Eastern Europe*, edited by Patrick O'Neil, 82–101. London: Frank Cass, 1997.

Larkey, Edward. "Radio Reform in the 1980s: RIAS and DT-64 Respond to Private Radio." In *Cold War Cultures: Perspectives on Eastern and Western European Societies*, edited by Annette Vowinckel, Marcus M. Payk, and Thomas Lindenberger, 76–93. New York: Berghahn, 2012.

———. *Rotes Rockradio. Populäre Musik und die Kommerzialisierung des DDR-Rundfunks.* Münster: LIT, 2007.

Löffler, Dietrich. "Publikumszeitschriften und ihre Leser. Zum Beispiel: Wochenpost, Freie Welt, Für Dich, Sybille." In *Zwischen "Mosaik" und "Einheit." Zeitschriften in der DDR*, edited by Simone Barck, Martina Langermann, and Siegfried Lokatis, 48–60. Berlin: Christoph Links, 1999.

Martin, Julia. "Der Berufsverband der Journalisten in der DDR (VDJ)." In *Journalisten und Journalismus in der DDR. Berufsorganisation—Westkorrespondenten—Der Schwarze Kanal*, edited by Jürgen Wilke, 7–78. Cologne: Böhlau, 2007.

Matysiak, Stefan. "Die Entwicklung der DDR-Presse. Zur ostdeutschen historischen Pressestatistik." *Deutschland Archiv* 42, no.1 (2009): 59–73.

Meyen, Michael. *Denver Clan und Neues Deutschland. Mediennutzung in der DDR.* Berlin: Christoph Links Verlag, 2003.

———. "'Geistige Grenzgänger.' Medien und die deutsche Teilung." *Jahrbuch für Kommunikationsgeschichte* 1 (1999): 192–231.

Meyen, Michael, and Anke Fiedler. *Die Grenze im Kopf. Journalisten in der DDR.* Berlin: Panama, 2011.

———. *Wer jung ist, liest die Junge Welt. Die Geschichte der auflagenstärksten DDR-Zeitung.* Berlin: Christoph Links, 2013.

Meyen, Michael, and Wolfgang Schweiger. "'Sattsam bekannte Uniformität'? Eine Inhaltsanalyse der DDR-Tageszeitungen 'Neues Deutschland' und 'Junge Welt' (1960–1989)." *Medien & Kommunikationswissenschaft* 56, no. 1 (2008): 82–100.

Milton, Andrew. "News Media Reform in Eastern Europe: A Cross-National Comparison." In *Post-Communism and the Media in Eastern Europe*, edited by Patrick O'Neil. 7–23, Portland: Frank Cass Publisher, 1997.

Möhring, Wiebke. *Die Lokalberichterstattung in den neuen Bundesländern. Orientierung im gesellschaftlichen Wandel.* Munich: Fischer, 2001.

Mühl-Benninghaus, Wolfgang. *Unterhaltung als Eigensinn. Eine ostdeutsche Mediengeschichte.* Frankfurt a. M.: Campus, 2012.

Nathaus, Klaus. "Turning Values into Revenue: The Markets and the Field of Popular Music in the US, the UK and West Germany (1940s to 1980s)." *Historical Social Research* 36, no.3 (2011): 136–63.

Noelle-Neumann, Elisabeth. *Die Schweigespirale: Öffentliche Meinung—unsere soziale Haut.* Munich: Piper, 1980.

Oehmig, Richard. *"Besorgt mal Filme." Der internationale Programmhandel des DDR-Fernsehens.* Göttingen: Wallstein, 2017.

Palmowski, Jan. *Inventing a Socialist Nation: Heimat and the Politics of Everyday Life in the GDR, 1945–90.* Cambridge: Cambridge University Press, 2009.

Prommer, Elizabeth: *Kinobesuch im Lebenslauf. Eine historische und medienbiographische Studie.* Konstanz: UVK Medien, 1999.

Pöttker, Horst. "Fortschreibung alter Identitäten. Fremd- und Selbstbilder in der Presse des vereinten Deutschlands." In *Presse Ost—Presse West. Journalismus im vereinten Deutschland,* edited by Michael Haller, Klaus Puder, and Jochen Schlevoigt, 235–44. Berlin: Vistas, 1995.

Pürer, Heinz, and Johannes Raabe, eds. *Presse in Deutschland.* 3rd ed. Konstanz: UTB Medien, 2007.

Rauhut, Michael. "Erinnerungen an 38 Jahre Jugendmagazin neues leben." In *Zwischen "Mosaik" und "Einheit." Zeitschriften in der DDR,* edited by Simone Barck, Martina Langermann, and Siegfried Lokatis. Berlin: Ch. Links Verlag, 1999.

Reichardt, Sven. *Authentizität und Gemeinschaft. Linksalternatives Leben in den siebziger und frühen achtziger Jahren.* Berlin: Suhrkamp, 2014.

Ruchatz, Jens. "Einleitung." In *Mediendiskurse deutsch/deutsch,* edited by Jens Ruchatz, 7–22. Weimar: VDG, 2005.

Rumpf, Wolfgang. "Popgefühle im Äther. Popmusik—Ein Tabu im ARD-Rundfunk der 1960er." *Online-Publikationen des Arbeitskreis Studium Populärer Musik,* 16 November 2006. Retrieved 17 June 2016, http://www.aspm-samples.de/Samples5/rumpf.pdf.

Scherer, Helmut. "Die Darstellung von Politik in ost- und westdeutschen Tageszeitungen. Ein inhaltsanalytischer Vergleich." *Publizistik* 42, no. 4 (1997): 413–38.

Schildt, Axel. *Moderne Zeiten. Freizeit, Massenmedien und Zeitgeist in der Bundesrepublik der 50er Jahre.* Hamburg: Hans Christian Verlag, 1995.

———. "Zwei Staaten—eine Hörfunk- und Fernsehnation. Überlegungen zur Bedeutung der elektronischen Massenmedien in der Geschichte der Kommunikation zwischen der Bundesrepublik und der DDR." In *Doppelte Zeitge-*

schichte. Deutsch-deutsche Beziehungen 1945–1990, edited by Arnd Bauerkämper, Martin Sabrow, and Bernd Stöver, 58–71. Bonn: J. H. W. Dietz, 1998.

Schlimper, Jürgen. "Thesen zur Geschichte der Leipziger Volkszeitung seit 1946." In "Natürlich—die Tauchaer Straße!" Beiträge zur Geschichte der "Leipziger Volkszeitung," edited by Jürgen Schlimper, 469–506. Leipzig: Gesellschaft für Nachrichtenerfassung und Nachrichtenverbreitung, Verlagsgesellschaft für Sachsen/Berlin mbH, 1997.

Schmidt, Josef. "Klaus von Bismarck und die Kampagne gegen den WDR." Archiv für Sozialgeschichte 41 (2001): 349–82.

Schneider, Beate. "Nach allen Regeln der Zunft. Zeitungswettbewerb in Deutschland." In Presse Ost—Presse West. Journalismus im vereinten Deutschland, edited by Michael Haller, Klaus Puder, and Jochen Schlevoigt, 53–64. Berlin: Vistas, 1995.

———. "Pressemarkt Ost. Ein Refugium des 'Demokratischen Zentralismus.'" In Medien im vereinten Deutschland: nationale und internationale Perspektiven, edited by Walter A. Mahle, 71–80. Bonn: UVK, 1991.

Schneider, Beate, Wiebke Möhring, and Dieter Stürzebecher. Ortsbestimmung. Lokaljournalismus in den neuen Ländern. Konstanz: UVK, 2000.

Schneider, Beate, Klaus Schönbach, and Dieter Stürzebecher. "Journalisten im vereinigten Deutschland. Strukturen, Arbeitsweisen und Einstellungen im Ost-West-Vergleich." Publizistik 38, no. 3 (1993): 353–82.

Schneider, Beate, and Dieter Stürzebecher. Wenn das Blatt sich wendet. Die Tagespresse in den neuen Bundesländern. Baden-Baden: Nomos, 1999.

Schneider, Norbert. "Parteieneinfluß im Rundfunk." In Fernsehen und Hörfunk für die Demokratie. Ein Handbuch über den Rundfunk in der Bundesrepublik Deutschland, 2nd ed., edited by Jörg Aufermann, Wilfried Scharf, and Otto Schlie, 116–26. Opladen: VS Verlag für Sozialwissenschaften, 1981.

Schuhbauer, Thomas. Umbruch im Fernsehen, Fernsehen im Umbruch. Die Rolle des DDR-Fernsehens in der Revolution und im Prozess der deutschen Vereinigung 1989–1990 am Beispiel des Jugendmagazins "Elf 99." Berlin: Logos, 2001.

Seegers, Lu. Hör zu! Eduard Rhein und die Rundfunkprogrammzeitschriften (1931–1965). Potsdam: Verlag für Berlin-Brandenburg, 2001.

Siemens, Daniel, and Christian Schemmert. "Die Leipziger Journalistenausbildung in der Ära Ulbricht." Vierteljahrshefte für Zeitgeschichte 61, no. 2 (2013): 201–37.

Spangenberg, Peter M. "Der unaufhaltsame Aufstieg zum 'Dualen System.' Diskursbeiträge zu Technikinnovationen und Rundfunkorganisation." In Medienkultur der 70er Jahre. Diskursgeschichte der Medien nach 1945, edited by Irmela Schneider, Christina Bartz, and Isabell Otto, 21–39. Wiesbaden: VS Verlag für Sozialwissenschaften, 2004.

Stahl, Heiner. Jugendradio im kalten Ätherkrieg. Berlin als eine Klanglandschaft des Pop 1962–1973. Berlin: Landbeck, 2010.

Steinmetz Rüdiger, and Reinhold Viehoff, eds. *Deutsches Fernsehen Ost. Eine Programmgeschichte des DDR-Fernsehens*. Berlin: Verlag für Berlin-Brandenburg, 2008.

Stiehler, Hans-Jörg. "Mediennutzung 1995 bis 2005 in West- und Ostdeutschland: ein Test der These von der Populationsheterogenität am Beispiel von Fernsehen und Tageszeitungen." In *Mediatisierung der Gesellschaft?*, edited by Jörg Hagenah and Heiner Meulemann, 119–39. Münster: LIT, 2012.

Stöber, Rudolf. *Mediengeschichte. Die Evolution "Neuer" Medien von Gutenberg bis Gates*. Vol. 2: *Film—Rundfunk—Multimedia*. Wiesbaden: Westdeutscher Verlag, 2003.

Stock, Martin. "'Ausgewogenheit.' Ein Begriff macht Karriere." *Unsere Medien, unsere Republik: Mediengeschichte als Geschichte der Bundesrepublik* 4 (1990): 30–31.

Stürzebecher, Dieter. "Woher kommen sie, wie denken sie, was wollen sie?" In *Presse Ost—Presse West. Journalismus im vereinten Deutschland*, edited by Michael Haller, Klaus Puder, and Jochen Schlevoigt, 207–25. Berlin: Vistas, 1995.

Thomaß, Barbara, and Michaela Tzankoff, eds. *Medien und Transformation in Osteuropa*. Wiesbaden: VS Verlag für Sozialwissenschaften, 2001.

Wilke, Jürgen. "Die Tagespresse der achtziger Jahre." In *Die Kultur der 80er Jahre*, edited by Werner Faulstich, 69–90. Munich: Wilhelm Fink, 2005.

———. *Presseanweisungen im zwanzigsten Jahrhundert. Erster Weltkrieg—Drittes Reich—DDR*. Cologne: Böhlau, 2007.

———. "Radio im Geheimauftrag. Der Deutsche Freiheitssender 904 und der Deutsche Soldatensender 935 als Instrumente des Kalten Krieges." In *Zwischen Pop und Propaganda. Radio in der DDR*, edited by Klaus Arnold and Chistoph Classen, 249–66. Berlin: Christoph Links, 2004.

Wolff, Franca. *Glasnost erst kurz vor Sendeschluss. Die letzten Jahre des DDR-Fernsehens (1985–1989/90)*. Cologne: Böhlau, 2002.

Wrage, Henning. *Die Zeit der Kunst. Literatur, Film und Fernsehen in der DDR der 1960er Jahre. Eine Kulturgeschichte in Beispielen*. Heidelberg: Universitätsverlag Winter, 2008.

INDEX

A
Adenauer, Konrad, 74
Afghanistan, Soviet march into, 48, 74, 349, 508
arms race, 51, 65–66, 124, 359, 380
automatization, Chapter 5, 366, 368–69

B
Bach, Thomas, 509
Bahro, Rudolf, 64
Balibar, Etienne, 477
Baur, Jürgen, 530
Beck, Ulrich, 150, 293
Beckenbauer, Franz, 523
Beck-Gernsheim, Elisabeth, 293
Becker, Boris, 505
Bell, Daniel, 293, 351
Benneter, Klaus Uwe, 56
Berendonk, Brigitte, 503, 526–28
Berlin Wall, 6, 11, 24–25, 69, 74, 104, 149, 454, 469, 475, 476, 507, 515, 575–76
Bernal, John Desmond, 356–57
Beyer, Harm, 528
Beyer, Udo, 510
Biermann, Wolf, 1, 14, 64, 251, 454
BKA (Federal Criminal Police Office), 373–74
Bohley, Bärbel, 50, 64, 74
Böll, Heinrich, 559
Bradley, Tom, 513
Brandt, Willy, 1, 14, 20, 47, 48, 51, 53, 56, 62, 68, 559. See also *Ostpolitik*
Braun, Sebastian, 530

BSE, 173, 175
Bundesbank (the German central bank), 107–108, 120. *See also* monetary policies

C
Calmund, Reiner, 520
Carter, Jimmy, 508
Castell, Manuel, 351
CDU (Christian Democratic Union of Germany), 56–57, 70, 77, 79–82, 109, 175, 196, 203, 317, 401, 467, 472, 473, 558
Chernobyl, 21, 66, 150, 157, 166, 171, 362, 575. *See also* nuclear energy
Chile, 464–66
China, 49, 69, 73, 357, 471, 576
churches, 60–61, 67, 71, 77, 164, 560, 565
Club of Rome, 299, 309
coffee crisis (1977), 16, 53, 305
COMECON (Council for Mutual Economic Assistance), 117–18, 122–25, 252, 259, 296–98, 349–50, 362, 380, 396, 458–61
computer, 21–22, 258–264, 267–70, 278, Chapter 7
  computer games, 354–55, 370–71
  hacker, 360, 375
Confino, Alon, 469
consumption, 105, 114, Chapter 6
  cars, 309–312, 355
  clothing, 305–09
  critique of, 70, 169–70, 299

food and goods, 305–09
housing, 16, 55, 206–07, 213, 252, 461, 465, 301–304
marketing, 22, 295, 298–300, 310–12, 350, 513–16, 555–57, 570, 582
supermarket, 19, 169, 268, 271, 298
CSU (Christian Social Union in Bavaria), 57, 77, 175, 467, 472–73
Czechoslovak Socialist Republic (ČSSR), 118, 164, 259, 298, 459, 467–68, 575, 582

D
Dahrendorf, Ralf, 255
Daume, Willi, 508–10, 513
Deutsch, Karl W., 351
DFB (Deutscher Fußballbund, German Football Association), 506–07, 511–12, 522–23
DGB (Deutscher Gewerkschaftsbund, German Trade Union Federation), 56, 245, 254
digital revolution. *See* computer
discrimination
of foreigners, 166, 454, 461–62, 471–77 (*see also* right-wing extremism)
See also women
dissidents, 55, 157, 168, 453–54, 565. *See also* social movements
DSB (Deutscher Sportbund, German Sport Federation), 507, 510, 512, 516, 531
DTSB (Deutscher Turn- und Sportbund, German Gymnastics and Sports Federation), 514–15, 518, 529–30
Dutschke, Rudi, 163

E
economic crisis, 18, 71, 73, *Chapter 2*, 162, 206, 210, 248, 250, 369

job crisis, 366–67, 398 (*see also* unemployment)
education, 8, 16, 22, 27–28, 45–46, 52–54, 72, 199–201, 203, 212, 221–22, 242, 244, 313, 318, 321–22, 324, 363, 371–72, *Chapter 8*, 554, 558, 562, 571
employment sectors, transformation of, 111–114, 116–117, 197–203, *Chapter 5*. *See also* unemployment
environmental policy, *Chapter 3*
European Economic Community (EEC), 49, 119–121, 459
European Union (EU), 160, 165, 217, 421–22
Ewald, Manfred, 510, 513–15, 528

F
family, 21, 47, 54, 60, 195, 199, 203–06, 212, 214, 217, 220, 224–27, 294, 301–02, 313–326, 400, 405–08, 448, 455–65, 471, 530
FDGB (Free German Trade Union Federation), 58, 62, 242, 245–46
FDJ (Free German Youth), 415–16, 515, 562
federalism, 28, 108, 127, 158, 204, 395–96, 417, 420–26
financial crisis, 217, 222, 256
in GDR, 107, 469, 511
Fordism, 19, 114, 247–256, 261–63, 267, 269, 271, 274, 277–79
Franke, Werner, 526–28
Frankfurt am Main, 367, 374, 475
Frankfurt Oder, 520, 530
FDP (Free Democratic Party), 58, 77, 155, 175, 472

G
Gastarbeiter (guestworkers). *See* migration: labor
Geipel, Ines, 528–29
Gläser, Rolf, 527

globalization, 8, 15, 125–126, 205, 209, 217, 240–41, 260–61, 270, 353
Gorbachev, Mikhail, 54, 71, 75, 77 455, 513, 575
Graf, Steffi, 505
Gramow, Marat, 513
Great Britain, 15, 70, 108, 162, 175, 195, 218–19, 211, 297, 448–49, 558–59
Green Party, 50, 70–71, 75–76, 77, 81, 155, 161–162, 165, 167–169, 1974–75. *See also* social movements: environmental movements
Gueffroy, Chris, 469

H
Havel, Vaclav, 64
Havemann, Robert, 64
Helsinki. *See* OSCE
Herold, Horst, 374
Hitler, Adolf, 79
Honecker, Erich, 16, 18, 47, 48, 51, 53, 54, 58, 62, 71, 73, 105, 115, 123, 156, 157, 206, 207, 209, 240, 252, 267, 296, 297, 301, 363, 399, 409, 510, 511, 515, 518, 554, 564, 565, 568, 575
Honecker, Margot, 395, 399
Höppner, Manfred, 526, 528
Hübner, Peter, 17, 254, 257
Huff, Tobias, 157
Hungary, 164, 459, 464, 467, 469, 514, 575, 577

I
IBM (International Business Machines Corporation), 11, 268, 359–62, 367
industrial revolution, third, 21, 114, 208, 255, 357, 365. *See also* STR
information privacy, 373–375

Ingelhart, Ronald, 293
internet, 27, 80, 174, 268, 270, 277, *Chapter 7*, 582
Intershop, 53, 124, 307, 364
Iran, 49, 466

J
Japan, 71, 121, 249, 255, 258–59, 351, 355–58, 362, 380

K
Kahn, Herman, 356
Kelly, Petra, 50, 51, 64, 71, 161, 162, 167, 171
Keynesianism, 18, 108–09, 204, 216–17
Kohl, Helmut, 48, 56, 74, 75, 80, 81, 109, 191, 474, 512, 520, 525
Köhler, Thomas, 529
KPD (Communist Party of Germany), 246, 557
Krelle, Wilhelm, 200
Krömke, Claus, 251
Kruczek, Manfred, 531

L
leisure time, 249, 370, 562. *See also* consumption
Lepping, Claudia, 526
Löwenthal, Gerhard, 568
Lübbe, Hermann, 414

M
Mader, Alois, 503
de Maizière, Lothar, 523
Marshall Plan, 103
Marxism, 64, 72, 104, 163, 201, 250, 351, 356–57
Maske, Henry, 520
Matthes, Roland, 510
Media, *Chapter 11*
  print media, 27, 468, 553–563
  See also television; computer
Mensch, Gerhard, 110

Merkel, Angela, 82, 174–75, 525
Microsoft, 263, 360
migration, 22–23, 25, 79, 104, 224, Chapter 9
    asylum, 25, 78–80, 449, 463–481
    Aussiedler (German resettlers from East Europe), 449–51, 468
    between East and West Germany, 451–456, 468–472, 477
    education, 403–04, 410
    Jewish migrants, 472
    labor, 198, 448–49, 451, 457–463, 466–67, 471, 480
    Turkish migrants, 166, 461, 474, 476–77
    Vietnamese migrants, 460, 462, 472, 478–79
militarization. See arms race
Moldenhauer, Hans-Georg, 523
monetary policies, 107–108
Mühlfenzl, Rudolf, 583

N
neoliberalism, 7, 13, 26, 108–09, 126–27, 162, 166, 226, 273–276
Neuberger, Hermann, 511–12, 523
newspaper. See media: print media
Nipperdey, Thomas, 414
Noelle-Neumann, Elisabeth, 519
Nöcker, Josef, 503
nuclear energy, 13, 20, 61, 64–69, 361–62, 70, 147, 149, 151–52, 155, 158, 160–66, 174–75, 361, 374, 575, 362

O
oil crisis (1973 and 1979), 15, 162, 352, 459
Olympic Games, 3, 22, 27, 49, 501–516, 522–24, 525, 528, 532
    boycott of (1980), 22, 508–12
OSCE (Organization for Security and Cooperation in Europe), 49, 469

Helsinki Accords (1975), 14, 16, 49–50, 455
Ostprodukte, 309
Ostpolitik (approach), 14, 48, 49, 519, 569

P
Parsons, Talcott, 203
PDS (Party of Democratic Socialism), 27, 63, 77–78, 576–77, 597
peaceful revolution (1989), 12, 50–51, 59–63, 69, 72–76, 122, 125, 191, 240, 294, 296, 353, 378, 380, 416, 425, 467–70, 519, 575–76
Plog, Jobst, 583
Poland, 63, 72, 74, 105, 123, 164, 172, 307, 457, 459, 464, 471, 475, 514, 560, 582
political culture, Chapter 1
political participation, 76–77, 79
political parties
    in general, 395
    party membership, 56–59
    See also CDU; FDP; Green Party; PDS; SED; SPD
Poverty. See unemployment
Prague Spring (1968/69), 55, 351, 378, 381
public opinion, 53–54, 61–63
privatization (Treuhand), 126–129, 578. See also neoliberalism

R
radioactive waste, 158–159
RAF (Red Army Faction), 65, 374, 569
Rationalization, 18, 208, Chapter 5, 299, 350–52, 354, 356, 358–59, 362, 365–68, 379
Rauch, Ludwig, 565
Reichelt, Hans, 157
reunification. See peaceful revolution
Riedel, Hartmut, 503
Riesenhuber, Heinz, 371

right-wing extremism, 78–79, 462, 473–74, 507, 559. *See also* discrimination
right-wing populism, 25, 81, 356, 473, 559
Rosendahl, Heide, 3

S
Samaranch, Antonio, 510–11
Schabowski, Günter, 469
Schäuble, Wolfgang, 501, 503, 520, 523
Schelsky, Helmut, 198
Schily, Otto, 75, 170
Schmidt, Helmut, 47, 56, 68, 158, 508–09
Schmidt, Rainer, 373
Schnitzler, Karl Eduard von, 517, 568
Schubert, Bernd, 527
scientification (*Verwissenschaftlichung*), 15, 357, 397, 408–414
SED (Socialist Unity Party of Germany), 6, 9–10, 14, 16–17, 19–21, 27, 47–48, 51, 54–55, 58–64, 66, 68–69, 72–75, 78, 79–80, 103–106, 111, 114, 116, 125, 128, 157, 159, 164, 196, 200–03, 206–09, 212, 213–14, 240–46, 251, 253–54, 257–61, 272, 297, 306, 309, 311, 350, 362, 365, 377–79, 395, 400, 404, 408–09, 411–13, 416, 454, 456, 469, 471, 506–07
   Central Committee (ZK, Zentralkommittee), 156–57, 356, 399, 413, 463, 553
   Eighth Party Congress (1971), 156, 297, 415
   Ninth Party Congress (1976), 53
   politburo of (Politbüro), 48, 62, 251, 356, 413, 415, 463, 569, 576
   media and, *Chapter 11*
social movements, 52, 63–72. *See also* youth culture
   environmental movements, 69, 160–169, 412–13
   peace movement, 60, 65–67
   women's rights movement, 68
social policy agenda (Agenda 2010, Hartz Reforms), 26, 217–220, 226, 275
Solga, Heike, 202
Solidarność (solidarity), 50, 72, 560
Soviet Union. *See* USSR
SPD (Social Democratic Party of Germany), 48, 56–57, 75, 77–78, 81–82, 196, 203, 205, 217, 317, 414, 423, 472, 474
Spilker, Jochen, 526
sport, 3, 27, *Chapter 10*
   doping, 3, 27, 503, 522, 525–29, 531–32
Springer, Axel, 557, 559, 574, 576–78, 582
Sputnik shock, 22, 356, 422, 503
Stalinism
   Stalinist industrialization policies, 104, 116, 241, 297
   in sports, 502
Stasi, 22, 47–48, 51, 53, 62, 66, 68, 73, 79, 164, 353, 362–63, 375, 381, 418, 462, 465, 507, 514, 520, 523, 554, 560, 564–65
Stecher, Renate, 3
Steinbuch, Karl, 356
STR (Scientific-technical revolution, Wissenschaftlich-technische Revolution), 351, 357, 359, 367, 409. *See also* industrial revolution, third
Strauß, Franz Josef, 47, 51, 123, 559

T
Taylorism, 248, 251, 253, 254, 262, 269–73, 278. *See also* Fordism
Teichler, Hans Joachim, 518–19
Teichler, Klaus, 518

telephone, 12, 269, 302, 308, 361, 377
television, 6, 12, 19–20, 24, 27, 47, 61–63, 114, 165, 170, 240, 302, 361, 364, *Chapter 11*
    in FRG, 52, 165, 240, 260, 521, *Chapter 11*
    in GDR, 63, 308, 364, 517, 552, 566, *Chapter 11*
    sport in, 510, 513, 515, 517, 520–23
terrorism, 65, 68–69, 352, 374, 569
Tettenborn, Gesine, 528–29
Third World, 211, 464, 513, 580
Touraine, Alain, 351
tourism. *See* travel
Toyotism, 249–50, 256. *See also* Japan
Trabant, 252, 310. *See also* consumption: cars
trade, 117–123
trade unions. *See* DGB; FDGB
travel, 18, 47–48, 54, 259, 270, 350, *Chapter 9*, 507, 519, 564, 576. *See also* leisure time

U

Ueberroth, Peter, 513
UEFA (Union of European Football Associations), 511–12
Ulbricht, Walter, 105, 357, 399, 517
unemployment, 13–14, 17, 21, 26, 78, 80–81, 107–08, 113–16, 127, 129, 131, 162, 192, 196, 198, 205, 210–11, 216–19, 223–25, *Chapter 5*, 352, 401, 460, 579
uprising of 1953 in East Germany (17 June), 104, 246, 253
USA (United States of America), 5, 11, 15, 21, 49, 52, 64, 71, 108, 119, 154–55, 162, 168, 170, 175, 240, 254, 268, 273–75, 302, 349, 351, 362, 372, 376, 448–49, 508–09, 517–18, 561, 566, 571–74

USSR (Union of Soviet Socialist Republics; Soviet Union), 17, 49–50, 64, 75, 104, 122, 164, 349, 356, 362, 455, 459, 472, 502, 511–13, 571–72

V

Volkswagen (VW), 255, 311, 355, 368

W

Wartburg, 252, 310
Weizenbaum, Joseph, 373
welfare state, *Chapter 4*
Wende (turning point, 1989/90). *See* peaceful revolution
Wertewandel (change in values), 15, 51–52, 154, 278, 300, 323
Wilms, Dorothee, 371
Witt, Katarina, 511, 514
women
    abortion, 23, 319–20
    childcare, 206, 215, 220, 302, 313–327 (*see also* family)
    clothing, 306–07 (*see also* consumption)
    discrimination and inequality, 23–24, 68, 193, 199–201, 206, 210–11, 225–226, 244, 250, 268, 271–73, 278, 317–20
    education, 407–8, 425
    feminist groups, 68, 561
    migration, 449, 458, 461–62, 480
    voting, 52–53
    women' magazines, 313–14, 561, 577

Y

youth culture, 25, 27, 53, 56, 62, 70–72, 306–07, 370–71, 375, 415–16, 517, 561–62, 573

Z

Zimmermann, Friedrich, 512

www.ingramcontent.com/pod-product-compliance
Lightning Source LLC
Chambersburg PA
CBHW072042110526
44590CB00018B/3006